NARCOSTATES

NARCOSTATES

Civil War, Crime, and
the War on Drugs in
Mexico and
Central America

William L. Marcy

LYNNE
RIENNER
PUBLISHERS

BOULDER
LONDON

Paperback edition published in the United States of America in 2025 by
Lynne Rienner Publishers, Inc.
1800 30th Street, Suite 314, Boulder, Colorado 80301
www.rienner.com

© 2023 by Lynne Rienner Publishers, Inc. All rights reserved

ISBN: 978-1-962551-66-3 (pb: alk. paper)

The Library of Congress cataloged the hardcover edition of this book as follows:
A Cataloging-in-Publication record for the hardcover edition of
this book is available from the Library of Congress.

British Cataloguing in Publication Data
A Cataloguing in Publication record for the hardcover edition of
this book is available from the British Library.

Printed and bound in the United States of America

The paper used in this publication meets the requirements
of the American National Standard for Permanence of
Paper for Printed Library Materials Z39.48-1992.

5 4 3 2 1

Contents

	Foreword, *De Leon Petta Gomes da Costa*	vii
1	The Opening of a Narcotrafficking Corridor	1
2	Early US Counternarcotics Efforts in Mexico	15
3	"Cocaine Guns" and Civil War in Central America	35
4	The Emergence of the Mexican Cartel Networks	65
5	Mexico in Crisis	85
6	The Colombian Cartels Expand Their Reach	101
7	The War on Drugs Spills into Central America	141
8	Mexico's Cartel Wars	179
9	The Militarization of the US-Mexican War on Drugs	203
10	The Mexican Cartels and Youth Gangs in Central America	225
11	Narcotrafficking and the Immigration Crisis	263
12	Closing the Corridor?	303
	Narcotraffickers by Name and by Cartel Affiliation	309
	List of Acronyms	315
	Bibliography	323
	Index	345
	About the Book	359

Foreword

As St. Augustine once said, "For what are states but large bandit bands, and what are bandit bands but small states?" The same statement still holds true after several centuries, particularly when it comes to the interactions between national governments, organized crime, and drug trafficking on the American continent.

As drug trafficking now forms an integral part of Central American states' GDP, the main question becomes, "Why haven't state leaders been able to prevent this issue from getting so ingrained in their geopolitical systems?" William L. Marcy answers this question in this thorough examination of the history and evolution of Mexico's and Central America's drug wars.

Drawing on a multitude of primary sources, archival materials, and previous works, Marcy delineates the "narcotrafficking corridor," explaining how Mexico became a major narcotics producer and transit country, how Central America came to be the regional pivot for narcotics moving northward, and how the Mexican cartels deepened their presence in Central America with the help of gangs and contraband networks.

Beginning with the evolution of US counternarcotics policy in Mexico during the Nixon administration—including the implementation of Operation Intercept and its transformation into the Mexican government's permanent antinarcotics campaign—Marcy provides a broad survey of Central America's conflicts and the rise of narcotrafficking during the civil war era. He also demonstrates how traffickers exploited Central America's fragile peace to turn the region into a transnational pipeline for moving illegal goods, money, weapons, and people.

Narcostates delves into the numerous factors that have contributed to the evolution of the region's drug wars, along with the effects of narcoviolence, the steps taken to combat it, and the impact of US policy throughout

viii   *Foreword*

the region. It provides an in-depth analysis of how Colombian traffickers expanded into Mexico and Central America in the 1980s and 1990s, how Mexican cartels eventually took over the region's distribution networks and routes, and the challenges confronting Mexican and Central American authorities in their efforts to stem the spread of narcotrafficking. The US government's solution has been to militarize the drug war. However, militarization has raised as many questions as it has answered. It is fascinating to read how Marcy draws parallels between the militarization of the drug war and the Colombianization of Mexico.

The United States' aggressive posture and increased military aid to Mexico were critical components of US efforts to secure its southern border while fighting both the drug war and the war on terror. Marcy clearly identifies the link between drug trafficking and terrorism and how proceeds from drug sales might be used to fund terrorist acts. The drug war should not be viewed as a secondary national security concern for the United States. The rise in violence and instability in this region poses a serious threat to the United States. In addition, given the growing power of the Mexican cartels, it is not unreasonable to believe that the drug war will eventually lead to a political meltdown in Mexico. The economic and political consequences of this meltdown could exacerbate the already acute refugee and immigration crisis or invite hostile foreign actors to intervene along the US border, potentially destabilizing the United States from within.

Marcy's book also serves as a warning for my country, Brazil, as it comes at a critical and dramatic juncture. Following several years of progress against money laundering, drug trafficking, and organized crime, several political figures linked to narcotrafficking have returned to politics. Brazil's progress seems to have stalled, which will have an impact on the region's political and economic climate. This is something that historians will have to investigate in the future. For the time being, Marcy's book offers an excellent and in-depth exposé of what happens to states when drug trafficking, criminal organizations, and civil war collide.

—*Prof. Dr. De Leon Petta Gomes da Costa,*
International Relations Research Center at
the University of São Paulo

1

The Opening of a Narcotrafficking Corridor

In October 1997, members of the Mara Salvatrucha (MS-13) gang stopped the Chiapas-Mayab train at Mexico's Tapachula railroad station near the Chiapas-Guatemala border. As immigrants clamoring to get to the United States attempted to board the northbound train, a member of the gang walked to the platform and told the immigrants, "We have a pact with the devil and we have to shoot three people. Three days ago, we shot one and they did not die. We have to draw blood, and one of you has to die today."[1]

This act symbolized the nearly endless continuation of armed conflict in Central America after decades of civil war. However, the violence was not isolated to Central America. To the north, Mexico had become a major narcotics-producing and transit country, with powerful cartels that possessed the ability to challenge the authority of the government. Earlier, between 1970 and 1980, narcotraffickers had corrupted Mexico from within, nearly causing a total breakdown of society and government control.

This book examines the relationship between Mexico and Central America and how narcotrafficking and counternarcotics in both of these regions and the United States have contributed to the current miasma. The rise of the Mexican drug trafficking organizations (DTOs), how they supplanted the Colombians in the drug trade, and the crucial role that Central America played in facilitating the Mexican takeover are all topics covered in this study. Within that framework, there are numerous operational components presented here. Central America and its civil war era were pivotal to the shift in narcopower from the Colombians to the Mexicans. US and Mexican counternarcotics policies escalated the drug war conflict in Mexico, causing the Mexican DTOs to move deeper into Central America, which had only begun to recover from its civil wars. It was there that the Mexicans expanded their criminal activities in association with the regional

1

2   Narcostates

gang networks that had become involved in the drug trade during the post–civil war era. Finally, to gain control of the situation, the United States launched policy initiatives in Mexico and Central America—known as the Mérida Initiative and the Central American Regional Security Initiative—which were criticized for militarizing the conflict. The results of these policies are in the process of being assessed.

Mexican Cartel Evolution

By the mid-1990s, the Mexican cartels had wrested control of the drug trade from the Colombians and were fighting among themselves and against the government to dominate it. Emerging from decades of civil war, Central America found itself drawn into the US and Mexican governments' war on drugs as Mexico became the regional pivot for narcotics moving northward. By the mid-2000s, after the Mexican government adopted a more militaristic counternarcotics policy, the cartels vigorously resisted the country's efforts to rein them in. Simultaneously, the Mexican cartels modified their operations by deepening their presence in Central America with the help of gangs and contraband networks. Still recovering from the civil war era, Central America did not have the resources to control the flow of narcotics or the increasing lawlessness within its own borders. By 2010, pervasive Mexican narcotrafficking networks operated throughout all Central American countries, forcing governments there to conduct their own costly and deadly war against narcotraffickers.

Three generations of Mexican cartels have evolved from small networks into heavily armed, pseudomilitary organizations that rivaled each other for control over narcotics moving from the Andean region through Central America into Mexico. The first generation existed during the 1970s and consisted of competing contraband smugglers, such as Alberto Sicilia Falcón, Pedro Avilés Pérez, and Pablo Acosta Villarreal. They taught their trade to the second-generation cartel leaders, especially Miguel Ángel Félix Gallardo, Rafael Caro Quintero, and Ernesto Fonseca Carrillo, the fathers of the Guadalajara cartel. After the arrest of Félix Gallardo in 1989, the cartel was divided among his lieutenants—the Arellano Félix brothers, Joaquín Guzmán Loera ("El Chapo"), and Amado Carrillo Fuentes—who would go on to form the rival Tijuana, Sinaloa, and Juárez cartels, respectively.

Initially, the first- and second-generation Mexican cartels had no desire to take on the Mexican government's police and military. Instead, they sought to corrupt politicians and officials in the military and police to control them from within. Throughout the 1990s, the second-generation cartels incrementally stepped up their resistance to the Mexican state while they warred among each other for territorial control with increasing savagery. By 2010, external and internal pressures created fractures within the Gulf,

Sinaloa, Tijuana, and Juárez cartels that led to the formation of Mexico's third-generation cartels, such as Los Zetas, La Familia Michoacana, and the Cártel de Jalisco Nuevo Generación (CJNG).

By 2014, many of the second-generation cartel leaders were either dead or imprisoned. The third-generation capos reorganized the old cartels or formed new splinter cartels that turned on their parent organizations while carving out territory of their own using unprecedented levels of violence and sadism.

As the cartels evolved, Mexico experienced three waves of criminal violence and lawlessness due to the Mexican government's aggressive stance against narcotrafficking and power struggles among the cartels. The first wave occurred between the 1985 death of Drug Enforcement Administration (DEA) agent Kiki Camarena, the 1993 arrest of Gulf cartel kingpin Juan García Ábrego, and the 1994 corruption scandal surrounding the assassination of political leader José Ruiz Massieu. The second wave followed Gallardo's decision to divide territorial control among his lieutenants. After his arrest in 1989, Gallardo tried to run the cartel from jail, but by the mid-1990s he was no longer in control. His lieutenants went to war for control over the Guadalajara cartel's trafficking networks. The first prison escape by El Chapo Guzmán in 2001 intensified the bloody contest for control over Mexico's narcotrafficking corridors or *plazas* until 2007. A shift in cartel alliances and the implementation of President Felipe Calderón's Mérida Initiative in 2008 triggered the third wave, prompting ferocious confrontations with Mexico's military and security forces despite the cartels' ceaseless efforts to corrupt them. Mexican government pressure, combined with the ongoing cartel war, spawned a convulsive shift in cartel allegiances and an unprecedented wave of violence. The third wave lasted roughly until 2014 when El Chapo was arrested a second time. The cartel war subsided following his arrest. However, the arrest did not mean that the Mexican cartels' territorial disputes were permanently settled. Mexico's third-generation upstarts wanted the plazas of distribution entirely for themselves. Low-intensity conflicts would continue.

From Political Violence to Criminal Violence

In the second half of the twentieth century, the people of Mexico and Central America experienced a marked shift from political to criminal violence. During the 1960s and 1970s, the Partido Revolucionario Institucional (PRI) dominated Mexico, which existed as a single-party authoritarian state. Following the Tlatelolco Massacre in October 1968, Mexican guerrilla movements challenged the PRI's legitimacy. The guerrillas aligned themselves with Mexico's rural peasantry (campesinos). As the guerrillas and campesinos forged alliances, the US government pressured Mexico to control its border

4 Narcostates

and narcotics production. Mexico's acceptance of US counternarcotics policies exacerbated political opposition to the Mexican government, as Mexico's security services conducted counternarcotics operations in the remote countryside while simultaneously waging a "dirty war" against leftist guerrillas who sympathized with the campesinos that lived and produced narcotics in those remote regions. Although the guerrilla insurgencies subsided in the late 1970s, Mexico's drug war did not. The Mexican effort evolved into the Permanent Campaign against narcotrafficking—a campaign the government undertook reluctantly.

While these events unfolded in Mexico, Central America convulsed with civil war as revolutionary insurgencies developed in Nicaragua, El Salvador, Guatemala, and, to a lesser extent, Honduras. The near feudal relations in the countryside and the lack of political and agrarian reform led to extreme poverty, unemployment, and social dislocation during the 1970s and 1980s. As the Cold War heightened regional tensions, the United States and USSR both vied for regional influence by providing military assistance to revolutionary and counterrevolutionary forces. By the end of the 1980s, guns, drugs, and revolution had become synonymous. Within the chaos, the foundation was laid for turning Mexico and Central America into a hotbed for narcotrafficking. The proceeds from drug smuggling fueled the conflict and, in turn, further expanded Central American narcotrafficking.[2] Within the chaos, narcotrafficking not only survived, it thrived.

In Nicaragua, allegations of drug smuggling were levied against all participants in the conflict. This included the Alianza Revolucionaria Democrática (ARDE) and the Fuerza Democrática Nicaragüense (FDN), which worked in conjunction with the US Central Intelligence Agency (CIA). Sandinista and Cuban involvement was also alleged by the US State Department. Greater evidence was levied against Panamanian dictator Manuel Noriega, who played both sides of the Central American conflict, ultimately leading to the US invasion of Panama in 1989. Significantly, all of these actors were alleged to have developed narcotrafficking ties with Colombia's Medellín cartel and the Guadalajara organization in Mexico.[3]

In the aftermath of civil war, narcotrafficking and production remained omnipresent. The cultivation of marijuana and opium continued in both Mexico and Guatemala. With civil war winding down, narcotrafficking through Central America expanded during the early 1990s. By this point, the Mexican cartels' affiliation with the Colombian cartels was well-established. After the defeat of the Medellín and Cali cartels and the closing of the Caribbean corridor, Andean drug traffickers shifted their operations to the Pacific corridor and Central America.[4]

Despite the need to confront this problem, Central American nations were in the process of military demobilization. The question before them was how to implement counternarcotics enforcement programs without

The Opening of a Narcotrafficking Corridor   5

making the programs appear as military repression in the form of new counterinsurgency operations.

By the mid-1990s, the Mexicans replaced the Colombian DTOs as Latin America's dominant narcotics traffickers. With the expansion of their power, they extended their influence throughout the Central American isthmus. While the Mexican cartels expanded their reach into Central America, the Colombian cartels decentralized their operations. The Colombians handed over the responsibility for the transportation and sale of narcotics in the United States to the Mexican cartels. As the transfer occurred, the Mexican cartels were under increasing pressure at home for a series of high-profile assassinations, such as the murder of Cardinal Posadas Ocampo in 1993 and the assassination of PRI presidential candidate Colosio Murrieta in 1994. To avoid further detection, the Mexican cartels took advantage of Central America's post–civil war power vacuum to extend their reach throughout the region.

To deal with the cartels, the Mexican government militarized the war on drugs, stirring up a hornets' nest in both Mexico and Central America. Pressured by the United States, in 2004 President Vicente Fox incorporated the Mexican military into the government's counternarcotics strategy, which altered Mexican society. What was once business as usual, with minimal but sometimes high-profile casualties, turned into a low-intensity conflict. Mexico and Central America watched their homicide rates rise exponentially. Barely a decade since their civil wars had ended, Central American violence swelled once again. As the narcotrafficking industry shifted in response, Central American governments did not have enough time to develop effective counternarcotics programs. The demobilization of Central American military and guerrilla forces converted many who participated in the civil wars into hired hands for the Mexican DTOs.[5] The deportation of former refugees from the United States back to Central America during the mid-1990s added fuel to the fire. Among the deportees were members of Central American street gangs, such as MS-13 and Calle 18 (18th Street) with criminal records. While imprisoned in the United States, these gang members had become subordinates of the Mafia Mexicana (La eMe), which was tied to the Mexican cartels. Upon their return to Central America, the gang members organized and created a network that ran from Central America to the United States. As that network expanded, the gangs became auxiliaries of the Mexican cartels who now controlled the narcocorridor from South America to Mexico.[6]

Central America never recovered from its civil wars. High unemployment among its youth, accompanied by military demobilization and the Mexican drug war, led to a confluence of former revolutionaries, counterrevolutionaries, gangs, and Central American crime syndicates operating in coordination with the various Mexican cartels. By 2008, two-thirds of all cocaine entering the United States passed through Central America into Mexico, with Panama, El Salvador, Honduras, and Guatemala being designated by the United States as major transitory countries for narcotics (see Figure 1.1).[7]

Because of a lack of resources and political will, as well as corruption within Mexican and Central American security forces, crime networks took advantage of Mexico's permeable border and Central America's weak political institutions to smuggle narcotics, precursor chemicals, and impoverished migrants into Mexico and the United States. The Mexican and Central American governments were simply incapable of controlling this multibillion-dollar industry headed by criminal organizations that maintained sophisticated technological and military capabilities. As the traffickers fought among themselves and against government forces, a new security crisis erupted in Mexico and Central America bringing unprecedented levels of brutality and violence that resembled the revolutionary political violence of previous generations.

During the first decade of the twenty-first century, headlines in Mexico and Central America reported drug-related crimes that often reached barbaric proportions:

Figure 1.1 Major Trafficking Routes Through Central America to Mexico

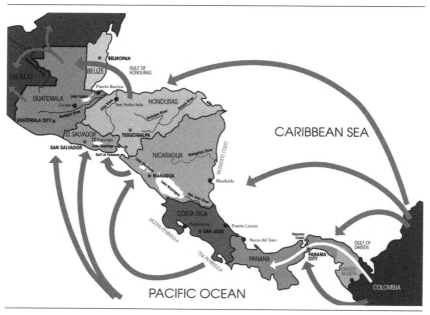

On February 27, 2000, Tijuana police chief Alfredo de la Torre was murdered on a Tijuana highway. The attackers peppered his vehicle with 102 bullets from automatic weapons. De la Torre was murdered on the same highway where Tijuana police chief Federico Benítez López was ambushed and assassinated in April 1994.[8]

In February 2002, thirty Honduran antinarcotics officers raided a safehouse near El Salvador's border. A shootout erupted between the police and the Villanueva gang. After the raid, an arsenal of grenades, antitank guns, and AK-47s were found in the house. The gang was considered responsible for 210 kidnappings, several bank robberies, and the movement of Colombian cocaine through Central America's Caribbean ports. Evidence confiscated in the raid linked the gang to the Arellano Félix cartel.[9]

In September 2006, Father Ricardo Antonio Romero, a Catholic priest and a critic of the culture of violence and drugs that rampaged throughout El Salvador, was beaten to death. Romero was organizing a protest against the wave of violence in Sonsonate, El Salvador, where the homicide rate stood at 77 murders per 100,000 residents.[10]

In December 2008 within Tegucigalpa, two *asesinos de moto* (motorcycle killers) opened fire on the vehicle carrying General Julián González, the Honduran director of the Office for Combating Drug Trafficking. Five days prior to his assassination, González had accused Hugo Chávez and the Colombian guerrillas, the Fuerzas Armadas Revolucionarias de Colombia (FARC), of trafficking in cocaine. He also alleged that Manuel Zelaya, the president of Honduras, was under investigation for moving cocaine through Honduras.[11]

On January 8, 2010, the body of Hugo Hernández, a thirty-six-year-old man affiliated with the Ciudad Juárez cartel, was dumped on the streets of Los Mochis, a town located in the state of Sinaloa. His body was cut into seven pieces. Hernández's face was peeled off, stitched onto a soccer ball, and left in a bag near the city hall. A note from the Sinaloa cartel accompanied the ball. It read, "Happy New Year, because this will be your last."[12]

On May 15, 2011, thirty to forty Los Zetas killed twenty-seven peasants by decapitation on a farm in the northern Petén region of Guatemala as an act of retribution for the theft of 2,000 kilos of cocaine. The owner of the farm reportedly stole the cocaine from Los Zetas.[13]

These and similar stories were almost endless. By the end of the decade, reports of victims found dismembered or with their hearts cut out or hung from bridges with *narcomantas* (banners) displayed around their bodies became daily occurrences. Necklacing—placing a tire full of gasoline around a person's neck and setting it on fire—or the *el guiso* (the stew)—dousing victims with gasoline and burning them alive in oil barrels—were just a few of the many ways the DTOs disposed of their enemies. Kidnapping, extortion,

8   *Narcostates*

and murder for hire to grease the wheels of narcotics and arms trafficking became the norm.

The US War on Drugs

The bloodletting shocked the world. The United States wanted its border controlled, but to do so meant that the Mexican and Central American governments had to pick a fight with forces they were reluctant to engage. The US solution to the drug problem remained the same as the one they employed in the Andean region—the militarization of the war on drugs, which came in the form of the 2008 Mérida Initiative. Initially applied to both Mexico and Central America, with the majority of funding going to Mexico, the Mérida Initiative increased the Mexican military's role against narcotrafficking. Mexico was required to confront heavily armed criminal organizations that operated not only on the outside but within the state itself. In Central America, the fragile post–civil war peace was placed under enormous strain. To confront the DTO-gang network, the Northern Triangle countries—Guatemala, El Salvador, and Honduras— had to implement *mano dura* (heavy-handed) policies that resembled the counterinsurgency strategies they had employed during the 1980s. Ultimately, Central American nations realized that a regional solution was necessary to deal with the drug war problem, much like the regional framework that had been necessary to end Central America's civil conflicts.[14] With US financial assistance, the 2010 Central American Regional Security Initiative (CARSI) was the outgrowth of Central American cooperation to confront narcotrafficking. These governments criticized the conditions for US aid because it relied too much on a military solution like the Mérida Initiative in Mexico. Nonetheless, by 2014, many of the major drug capos were arrested or killed and the violence diminished slightly. The bigger problem was that Mexican traffickers were now firmly established in Central America; the reduction of narcoviolence would only be temporary.

The Ongoing Cartel War, 2014–Present

The victor at the end of Mexico's third wave of criminal violence was Ismael Zambada García ("El Mayo"), a Sinaloa cartel leader who kept a low profile and had assisted the Mexican and US governments to confront the more violent cartels that were also, conveniently, his enemies. El Mayo's maneuvering bought a temporary truce in Mexico as he became boss. However, other third-generation cartels, such as Los Zetas and the CJNG, remained in the wings. Despite a temporary reduction in drug-related violence in Mexico, Mexican cartel rivalries triggered a crime wave in Central America. Thousands of people were driven from their homes and migrated toward the United States, leading the US government to declare that its border was overwhelmed by Central American refugees, especially from 2015 to 2022.

The situation remained complex, with multiple concurrent themes: (1) the evolution of the Mexican DTOs and their methods of transporting narcotics through the Central American and Mexican narcocorridor; (2) the ongoing difficulties faced by Mexican and Central American authorities in their attempts to halt the proliferation of narcotrafficking; and (3) the destabilizing impact of feckless US policies.

About the Book

Fully understanding the dynamics of the war on drugs in Central America is impossible without considering the conditions in Mexico and vice versa. Rather than looking at Mexico and Central America as separate stories, the book examines the region as a whole. Covering the period from 1972 to 2020, the questions that will be asked include the following: How did the region devolve into the lawless narcotrafficking corridor and distribution hub that exists today? What effect did Central America's civil wars have on the proliferation of narcotrafficking through the Central American isthmus and Mexico? Why did the war on drugs in Mexico become so murderous? How and why did the drug war in Mexico spill over into Central America after its civil wars ended? What were the methods and major events that Mexican narcotraffickers and their Central American affiliates used to challenge the legitimacy of state power in Mexico and Central America? To what extent was the narco industry institutionalized in both Mexico and Central America? Why did Central American police and military reorganizations in the post–civil war period and the implementation of the Mérida Initiative and CARSI fail to rein in the cartels? Finally, did US policy "Colombianize" the drug wars in Mexico and Central America?[15]

This book is based extensively on primary sources, including US embassy reports to the State Department, Agency for International Development (USAID) analyses, DEA administrative reports, CIA country studies, presidential papers, UN and World Bank economic studies, Organization of American States (OAS) studies, congressional reports, Government Accountability Office[16] (GAO) reports, newspapers, and personal interviews. Important documents were also found in the National Archives and the National Security Archives at George Washington University. Much of the core material in this book was made available through a declassification process with the US State Department and the Department of Justice.

10   *Narcostates*

The documents employed in this book give a unique perspective of how US government policies toward narcotrafficking developed. It is important to note that these sources hold their own inherent biases and are limited because of national security interests surrounding the war on drugs. In general, US government sources provide accounts that favor the US administrations that have been in charge. As a consequence, the reliability of these documents varies. To correct this imbalance, I have attempted to provide documents and secondary sources that offer a range of perspectives. Other primary materials, such as newspapers, contain their own biases—they only provide accounts of events as seen through the eyes of a reporter and the biases of the editorial staff.

While efforts have been made to present primary and secondary sources from multiple perspectives, the nature of and secrecy surrounding narcotrafficking make it impossible to ever present a complete documentation of the drug war. Any information regarding the narcotics industry, including the production and transportation of narcotics, is just an estimate. There is no way to know how much money was generated, nor is there any way to know for certain the motivations of all actors involved. On all sides of the war on drugs, secrecy, disinformation, corruption, and murder have been omnipresent.

Examining the history of how the social dynamics of revolution in Central America and Mexico transformed into the struggle between the DTOs and regional governments merits attention because the subject is relatively new and few have approached both subjects from this perspective. This book is an attempt to investigate the comprehensive mix of ideas about revolution, narcotics trafficking, the rise of the cartels, and governmental counternarcotics policies in relation to the war on drugs, militarization, and security.

Chapter 2 examines the Nixon administration's implementation of Operation Intercept and how it evolved into the Mexican government's permanent campaign against narcotics. The permanent campaign became part of Mexico's "dirty war" against subversives and brought institutional corruption, which negatively affected Mexico's security services and relations with the United States.[17] By the end of the 1970s, the permanent campaign had solved nothing. Mexico evolved into a major transit hub for moving narcotics northward.

Chapter 3 provides a broad overview of Central America's conflicts and the development of narcotrafficking during the civil war era, including the role of the Contras and Sandinistas, as well as the regime of Manuel Noriega in Panama. Investigations of drug trafficking during the civil war era have looked at either the role of CIA-Contra-Panamanian drug trafficking or Nicaraguan-Cuban drug trafficking. The goal of this chapter is not to revise or revisit that debate, but rather to provide context in which the drug war can be viewed as an extension of Central America's civil wars.

Chapter 4 focuses on Mexico and the evolution of Mexico's first- and second-generation cartels during the 1980s and 1990s. It outlines the rivalries and alliances and explains how divisions among the cartels turned into a full-blown cartel war. By covering the second-generation cartels, the chapter will also show how these DTOs became dominant forces within Mexico through their ability to corrupt the country's political, judicial, and domestic security institutions.

Chapter 5 reviews Mexico's growing political instability in the early 1990s as a result of the cartel wars. An important development at this time was the implementation of NAFTA and Mexico's subsequent economic collapse in 1994, which gave impetus to the narcotrafficking economy at the same moment the Mexican government was forced to face down the cartels. The chapter then focuses on the effect of the drug war on the Zapatista rebellion and the assassinations of presidential candidate Luis Donaldo Colosio Murrieta and the PRI's general secretary, José Ruiz Massieu, during the presidency of Carlos Salinas de Gortari (1988–1994).

Chapter 6 examines a neglected area of the drug war, namely the growing relationship between Mexican and Colombian DTOs. It first investigates the establishment of Colombian narcotics distribution networks in Mexico, then describes how the Mexican cartels seized control of the drug trade following the collapse of the Medellín and Cali cartels. The chapter also depicts how traffickers embedded themselves throughout Central America at a time when the region was thought to be relatively free from narcotrafficking.

Chapter 7 is concerned with the dilemma of creating effective counternarcotics forces in post–civil war Central America and the proliferation of criminal gangs there. A regional counternarcotics program was outlined by the Central American governments, but the financial and political will to implement a coordinated program did not emerge.

Chapter 8 returns to Mexico and the emergence of the cartel wars from 2000 to 2014. In 2000, four major cartels were fighting over territory; by the end of the decade, they would all splinter. Ultimately, the third-generation cartels defied and then rivaled their parent cartels for control over Mexico's plazas of distribution.

Chapter 9 looks at the Mexican government's response to the burgeoning power of the cartels. The chapter makes the case that the increasing participation of the Mexican military and implementation of the Mérida Initiative against the cartels exacerbated the cartel wars. The militarization of Mexico's drug war also had the effect of increasing corruption within the armed forces and driving the cartels deeper into Central America.

Chapter 10 returns to Central America and the regional security threat presented by narcotrafficking in the new millennium. The chapter covers

12   *Narcostates*

the deepening crisis presented by the confluence of gangs and Mexican DTOs and how this led to the implementation of CARSI.

Chapter 11 discusses the evolution of the drug war in Mexico and Central America from 2014 to the present and how it became an inseparable conflict that permeated both Mexico and Central America.

Chapter 12 concludes the book with an analysis of what has been discussed and draws comparisons between Mexico and Colombia while considering whether it will ever be possible to close the narcocorridor.

Notes

1. Jorge Fernández Menéndez and Víctor Ronquillo, *De los Maras a los Zetas: Los secretos del narcotráfico, de Colombia a Chicago* (Mexico City: Debolsillo, 2007), 37.

2. United Nations Office on Drugs and Crime, *Crime and Development in Central America: Caught in the Crossfire* (New York: UN, May 2007), 26.

3. William L. Marcy, *The Politics of Cocaine* (Chicago: Lawrence Hill Books, 2010), 83–133.

4. James Sutton, "U.S. Counternarcotics Strategy in Latin America: Good Intentions and Poor Results," *The Americas* 4, no. 1 (October–November 1991): 6; Nancy Nusser and Charles Holmes, "Colombian Drug Cartels Moving into Central America," *Atlanta Journal and Constitution*, April 28, 1991, sec. A, p. 10; and Francisco E. Thoumi, *Illegal Drugs, Economy, and Society* (Baltimore: Johns Hopkins University Press, 2003), 101.

5. US Congress, House of Representatives, Subcommittee on Western Hemisphere Affairs of the Committee on International Relations, *The Illicit Drug Transit Zone in Central America*, 109th Cong., 1st sess., November 9, 2005, 4.

6. Thelma Mejía, "Central America: Soaring Violent Crime Threatens Democracy," Inter Press Service (Tegucigalpa), September 22, 2008, 2.

7. Ibid.

8. Molly Moore, "Mexicans Stunned by Killing of Police Chief; Attack in Tijuana Follows Tough Talk by President," *Washington Post*, February 29, 2000, sec. A, p. 15.

9. Freddy Cuevas, "Honduran Police Break Up Drug Ring," Associated Press, February 9, 2002.

10. Hector Tobar, "El Salvador Violence Hits Record Levels," *Miami Sun Sentinel*, April 28, 2007; Hector Tobar, "Salvadoran Gangs Push Violence to Record Levels," *Los Angeles Times*, April 1, 2007.

11. Mariano Castillo, "Anti-Drug Chief Killed in Honduras," CNN, December 8, 2009; Ioan Grillo, "Behind the Murder of Honduran Drug Czar," *Time*, December 17, 2009.

12. "Mexican Drug Gang Sinks to New Level of Brutality, Stitches Rival on Football," *Guelph Mercury* (Canada), January 8, 2010, sec. A, p. 1.

13. Ken Ellingwood and Alex Renderos, "Massacre Leaves 27 Dead in Northern Guatemala," *Los Angeles Times*, May 15, 2011; Elyssa Pachico, "With Guatemala Massacre, Mexico Drug Gang Rules by Terror," InSight Crime, May 19, 2011, www.insightcrime.org; Hannah Strange, "Profile: Brutal Cartel Boss Who Took Sadistic Killing to New Level," *Telegraph*, July 16, 2013, www.telegraph.co.uk; US Congress, House of Representatives, Committee on Foreign Affairs, Western

Hemisphere Subcommittee of the House Foreign Affairs Committee, *Hearing on Violence in Central America*, 110th Cong., 1st sess., June 26, 2007, 8.

14. Colleen McGuiness and Patricia M. Russotto, *U.S. Foreign Policy: The Reagan Imprint* (Washington, DC: Congressional Quarterly Inc., 1986), 74. The peace plans were called Esquipulas I and II. See Chapter 2.

15. "Colombianization" is best defined as using narcotics profits and terroristic violence to subvert the institutions of a specific country from within while government counternarcotics programs become militarized and increasingly violent in their implementation.

16. In 2004, GAO's legal name changed from the General Accounting Office to the Government Accountability Office, per GAO.gov.

17. Peter Watt and Roberto Zepeda, *Drug War Mexico: Politics, Neoliberalism, and Violence in the New Narcoeconomy* (London: Zed Books, 2012), 31.

2

Early US Counternarcotics Efforts in Mexico

When President Richard Nixon entered the White House in 1969, his administration increased pressure on the Mexican government to halt the flow of narcotics into the United States. Mexico's acceptance of the 1961 UN Single Convention on Narcotic Drugs established an international regime for Mexico to reduce the production and transportation of narcotics. In 1969, the Nixon administration pressured Mexico to implement a joint US-Mexico border control program called Operation Intercept, which evolved into a permanent border control program called Operation Cooperation. Using a carrot-and-stick approach to gain Mexican cooperation, the United States supplied equipment to conduct crop eradication programs. Crop eradication experienced some success, but it also alienated campesinos in regions such as Sinaloa and Guerrero because the crop substitution programs were poorly executed. The substitution programs soon built solidarity with Mexican guerrillas who were rebelling against the Mexican government following the October 1968 Tlatelolco Massacre. Mexico's counternarcotics programs were further complicated by corruption. The Policía Judicial Federal de México (PJFM), which administered narcotics control programs in the 1970s, were poorly paid and susceptible to bribery. Concerned with police corruption, the United States took matters into its own hands and violated Mexico's sovereignty to entrap traffickers. Political tensions between the United States and Mexico combined with corruption, regional instability, and geography turned Mexico into a narcotics transshipment point by the end of the 1970s. As a result, Mexico found itself reluctantly drawn into a permanent campaign against narcotrafficking.

16 *Narcostates*

Nixon and Mexico

During the Nixon administration, the United States made Mexico the centerpiece of its international counternarcotics policy. In 1969, Nixon postulated that he had a national responsibility to stop the United States from being destroyed by drugs. The problem was not limited to any region of the country or to any segment of society.[1] Turkish heroin processed in France was smuggled through Europe, Latin America, or Mexico.[2] According to the US Department of State, of the approximately three tons of heroin entering the United States annually, 80 percent came from France using opiates originating in Turkey, 15 percent was of Mexican origin, and another 5 percent came from Asia.[3] By the early 1970s, US-French efforts had dismantled a large portion of the French Connection, while US diplomatic pressure significantly reduced the production of Turkish poppies. The closing off of Turkish and French sources redirected opium production to other parts of the world, especially Mexico.

The change in transportation routes led to an increase in Mexican opium and marijuana production.[4] The United States responded by tightening border controls, increasing the presence of the US Bureau of Narcotics and Dangerous Drugs (BNDD) in Mexico, and implementing interdiction and eradication programs using the Mexican military. US policy toward Mexico gradually moved from mutual cooperation to intensified US diplomatic pressure on Mexico to maintain stringent counternarcotics programs.

A long history of counternarcotics cooperation between the two governments dated back to 1948, when Mexico launched La Gran Campaña to stamp out drugs. Joint efforts increased during the 1960s. According to Otis Mulliken, the deputy director of international economic and social affairs at the Department of State, following Mexico's ratification of the UN Single Convention on Narcotic Drugs in 1961, "numerous acts of cooperation between enforcement officials" in the two countries "resulted in many arrests and the elimination of narcotics laboratories in Mexico."[5] In 1961, the United States had provided approximately $500,000 for Mexico to purchase equipment to control the production and distribution of narcotics.[6] Despite US assistance, the flow of narcotics continued across the entire length of the US-Mexico border; US officials considered it virtually impossible to patrol to apprehend smugglers.[7]

Mexican officials responsible for the suppression of narcotics did not uniformly or enthusiastically support US efforts. However, as the Mexican government became aware of the domestic dangers posed by narcotrafficking, Mexico backed the 1963 Joint United States–Mexico Narcotic Commission. As a result, US and Mexican authorities initiated a program of consultation and cooperation to eradicate narcotics at its source. The Nixon administration continued the policy of cooperation developed by the

Kennedy and Johnson administrations, with the exception that Nixon imposed a much more rigorous policy on Mexico.[8]

In September 1969, Nixon initiated a stringent counternarcotics program along the US-Mexican border called Operation Intercept. The main objective was to stop traffickers from smuggling narcotics through US ports of entry. The operation called for the inspection of all people and vehicles crossing the border from Mexico into the United States.[9] It also involved the mobilization of federal agencies and the use of aircraft, patrol boats, radar, esoteric instruments such as dog sniffers, and above all, the full weight of the government's publicity apparatus.[10]

To induce Mexican government acquiescence, Operation Intercept placed economic pressure upon Mexico, which strained relations. The operation depressed border commerce by 50 to 90 percent and caused the United States–Mexican Border Cities Association to mobilize congressmen, governors, and mayors to protest the policy. The speaker of the Mexican Cámara de Diputados (Chamber of Deputies) stated that the program brought "ill will" and created a "problem between the two countries."[11] The Mexican government conveyed to the United States that the "intensive surveillance along the border of pedestrians and vehicles had gone a long way toward destroying the feeling of friendship" between the two countries. In response, Richard Kleindienst, the US deputy attorney general, proposed to the Mexican government that they change the name of Operation Intercept to Operation Cooperation. A press release from the US Justice Department noted that Operation Cooperation was designed to substantially increase efforts to "stop smuggling, to destroy the sources of drugs in Mexico, and to crack down on the distribution system."[12] In changing the name, Kleindienst argued for the implementation of new border procedures, including the free flow of pedestrian traffic, more flexible vehicular inspection at peak hours, and the elimination of individual car inspections.[13] The name was changed in October 1969, but differences over border control continued.

Mexican resistance to Operation Cooperation initiated a series of bilateral talks from October 27–29, 1969. The talks ended with the issuance of the Joint Declaration of the United States and Mexican Delegations that announced the creation of a joint working group whose goal was to identify the possible bases for agreement between the two governments. The group also agreed to submit a progress report that would make recommendations to the respective governments.[14] The group's proposal recommended increased detection, interdiction, eradication, and other counternarcotics activities. Notwithstanding these bilateral efforts, Mexico's ratification of the recommendations was not forthcoming. According to the US embassy in Mexico, the Mexican government refused to sign the recommendations because of "smoldering bitterness about Operation Intercept," and its "absolute unwillingness to do anything under pressure, real or imagined,

18   *Narcostates*

from the United States."[15] Although it felt that it was doing so under duress, the Mexican government eventually signed the document. By mid-1970, both President Nixon and President Díaz Ordaz reaffirmed Mexico's support and determination to suppress the international trafficking of narcotics.[16] The creation of the joint working group established a permanent framework for counternarcotics cooperation.

Because of the group's recommendations and the various methods by which smugglers brought drugs into the United States via Mexico, the Nixon administration emphasized interdiction to counter the flow. In addition to legal border crossings, smugglers moved narcotics across the border using airplanes from clandestine airfields or by rendezvousing with ships at sea. They also utilized shrimp boats and other vessels that were not subject to customs inspection.[17] To deal with the ingenious ways drugs entered the United States, the joint working group recommended that officials on both sides of the border exchange intelligence information and evidence regarding transit smuggling and that they strengthen inspection techniques and procedures, especially with regard to ships, planes, luggage, and passengers coming from known source areas.[18]

Prior to 1973, fifteen agents worked for the BNDD in Mexico City, covering both Mexico and Central America. The agents collected intelligence on traffickers and informed the US Customs Bureau on possible smuggling operations. Customs maintained responsibility for interdiction efforts along the border. Their agents carried out surveillance activity against the clandestine arrivals of boats and aircraft, increased examinations of commercial air and sea cargo, and examined mail packages for contraband.[19] The bureau also implemented the use of electronic sensors to detect illicit border traffic. Because the system required hundreds or perhaps thousands of Customs officials stationed all along the border, US officials considered the program to be an inefficient use of manpower.[20]

By 1973, cooperation between US and Mexican authorities and the exchange of intelligence led to the creation of a customs-to-customs program that included US funds for a detector dog program and aircraft radio equipment to improve communication between the two agencies.[21] Increased customs measures, high-tech equipment, and intelligence sharing became the rudimentary formula for US-Mexican interdiction efforts. However, US efforts also began to emphasize the issue of crop eradication—a policy that would fuel unrest in Mexico's rural areas.

Eradication, Rural Instability, and Student Unrest

In 1969, the Nixon administration increased pressure on Mexico to end illicit drug processing, especially opium production.[22] Opium poppy and marijuana

Early US Counternarcotics Efforts in Mexico **19**

eradication programs began with Operation Cooperation, which made crop eradication a crucial component of US-Mexican counternarcotics operations. To comply with US demands to curtail marijuana and opium cultivation, the Mexican government changed its Agrarian Code in 1971 to make the growing of opium an offense punishable by fine, imprisonment, and/or the confiscation of the land involved in its production.[23] Under the Echeverría presidency, the Mexican government formulated an eradication program known as Operación Combate Contra el Narcotráfico (CANADOR).[24]

At the time, opium and marijuana cultivators concealed their illicit crops among legitimate harvests while planting smaller narcotics crops in even more remote regions.[25] The rough and inaccessible terrain hamstrung Mexico's eradication efforts.[26] To gain access to these areas, the United States offered Mexico $1 million in material assistance to purchase helicopters and light aircraft during Operation Cooperation. By 1972, the United States agreed to provide another $51.3 million in training assistance to utilize helicopters, communications equipment, and weapons.[27] Between 1969 and 1971, nearly 12,000 members of the Mexican army destroyed 10,356 poppy fields and burned 2,468 marijuana fields. This number substantially increased to 6,540 plots of poppies and 8,112 marijuana plots destroyed in 1973 alone.[28] Although the US and Mexican governments were committed to narcotics eradication, US officials warned that crop eradication provided substantial incentive among sectors of Mexico's population to conduct large-scale resistance.[29]

The eradication programs heightened tensions between the Mexican government and its campesino population, which began receiving increasing support from antigovernment student and guerrilla organizations. Richard B. Craig, one of the few scholars to study Mexican drug problems during the 1970s, wrote in 1978 that it was "no mere accident that the principal marijuana and opium producing states are also the centers of rural poverty and have long been the scenes of guerrilla movements, land seizures, caciquismo (boss politics or bossism), and rural unrest." Craig added that those states "lie outside the mainstream of Mexican life" and are inhabited by an "economically desperate" population. He concluded that "such is the plight of these campesinos, because they have little to lose and much to gain by cultivating or trafficking in illicit drugs."[30] The incentive to grow narcotics was enormous because the value of a marijuana crop was forty times the value of any alternative crop.[31]

With crops destroyed and land confiscated, nationalist, antigovernment, and anti-US sentiments forged bonds between Mexico's student radicals and campesinos. The campesinos' hostility was fueled by confrontations with the Mexican army in the poor, remote areas such as Guerrero, Sonora, Jalisco, and Sinaloa (see Figure 2.1). Student opposition to the Mexican government, based on the students' rights movement, Marxist

Figure 2.1   Map of Mexico

ideology, and sympathy for the campesino cause, grew in conjunction with campesino resistance.[32]

In July 1968, a series of student riots and protests occurred in Mexico City. The unrest focused on bad conditions at the university, anger at the state governor, and the unpopularity of a particular teacher or rector who did not condone student radicals and their challenge to the PRI's dominance over the Mexican political system. With the approaching 1968 Mexico City Summer Olympics, the radicals increased public disruptions. The government responded by charging that the Mexican Communist Party, under the influence of the Soviet Union, was behind the student protests.[33] The Ordaz government feared its international image would be damaged if the unrest continued during the Olympics. Sixteen days before the opening of the games, student riots culminated with the Tlatelolco Massacre on October 2, 1968. The police killed anywhere from 30 to possibly 300 people and arrested another 1,300. The police justified their action by alleging that student protesters opened fire upon them. Students and witnesses levied counter charges against the government, claiming that Mexican authorities fired first. The massacre marked a turning point. For the remainder of the decade, increasing student radicalism and violent confrontations characterized student relations with the government.

After the massacre, a crackdown on the universities by the military and police temporarily quelled student unrest. When President Echeverría replaced

President Ordaz on December 1, 1971, students became restless once again, blaming Echeverría for the Tlatelolco Massacre because he had been Mexican minister of the interior at the time of the incident. Although Echeverría labored to overcome his former image, tensions between the government and the students continued over the fate of the one to two thousand political prisoners being held as a result of the 1968 riots.[34] Echeverría sought to divert student animosity by releasing several prisoners, but conservative elements in the PRI, who opposed Echeverría's willingness to compromise by kowtowing to student demands, forced him to confront the students.

The situation became worse when a conservative organization known as the Halcones mounted attacks on student leftists. The Halcones were university-age students who were the sons of people friendly with the PRI that had been trained by army personnel and supplied with $200,000 worth of weapons and equipment.[35] Backed by conservative elements in the PRI, the actions of the Halcones initiated a *guerra sucia* ("dirty war") that widened the breach between students and the government. Inspired by the Cuban Revolution, student-based guerrilla *focos* ("cadres") formed in the cities and in the remote rural interior. It was at this point that the student and campesino movements united.

As the dirty war spread, several student revolutionary movements championed nationalistic, antigovernment, pro-campesino positions. In Jalisco, the Frente de Estudiantes Revolucionarios (FER), typified this orientation. The FER advocated the overthrow of the Mexican state by a coalition of students, workers, and campesinos. They presented themselves as an exploited class whose interests lay with the underprivileged, whose role was to serve as the vanguard for the eventual overthrow of the establishment. They argued that students were being manipulated to promote the political fortunes of leaders who owed their loyalty to "Yankee imperialism."[36] In a State Department telegram, the US embassy in Mexico noted that the participation of students in the campesino movement was quite significant, because the students moved off campus to express their solidarity with the campesinos and to encourage campesino protests. Students at the Universidad de Sinaloa called for student unity with campesino and worker movements. Several marches and demonstrations against the Echeverría government occurred as a result of the unity effort.[37] In Juárez, students marched against the government, condemning the PRI for building its progress on the ruins of the poor. In a public statement, they declared that unless the youth of Mexico united, "the present dictatorial regime" would "continue to kill the hopes and ignore the rights of the people."[38]

The emergent solidarity between students and campesinos created a situation in which student unrest and opposition to Mexican counternarcotics programs became inseparable. In Guerrero, counternarcotics efforts

22 Narcostates

encountered violent opposition from the student-campesino movement. Several guerrilla organizations operated there, including the Asociación Cívica Nacional Revolucionaria (ACNR), the Movimiento de Acción Revolucionaria (MAR) (trained in North Korea and aligned with the FER), and a peasant movement led by Lucio Cabañas Barrientos that was associated with as many as ten other groups located throughout Mexico. Another revolutionary group implicated in drug trafficking was the Federación de Estudiantes de Guadalajara in the state of Jalisco. Most guerrillas were students or dropouts who were occasionally joined by teachers and professors.[39] All groups were Marxist-oriented.

Because of the revolutionary activity, the US State Department considered Guerrero a lawless area. According to Richard B. Craig, for "the military and the police, it was simply a matter of being outgunned by growers and traffickers who were equipped with the most recent types of automatic weapons acquired under a barter system of guns for dope."[40] As early as 1970, reports of Mexican narcotics agents being ambushed in Guerrero surfaced.[41] In 1972, two attacks on army convoys by guerrillas under the command of Cabañas Barrientos killed at least twenty-six soldiers and captured fifty weapons. Not only were hit-and-run attacks a part of the guerrillas' modus operandi, but they also used kidnappings and extortion to pay for revolution.[42] Although the student guerrillas never posed a serious threat to the PRI's hold on power, their activities in narcotics-producing regions hindered ongoing counternarcotics efforts.[43]

The PRI used the war on drugs to clamp down on political dissent. The government directed the military to fight insurgent focos and suppress the campesino populace, while the intelligence agency, Dirección Federal de Seguridad (DFS), exploited the dirty war against subversives to increase its participation in counternarcotics operations. García Paniagua, chief of the DFS from 1976 to 1978, actively supported the new role for his department.[44] Because of raids against rebels, its paramilitary wing, the Brigada Blanca, discovered rural narcotics warehouses, some of which received no protection from the guerrillas and others that were protected by the guerrillas.[45] Despite some successes, the simultaneous use of the Mexican military and police against subversives and narcotraffickers produced systemic corruption within Mexico's security forces. And because the United States was more concerned about the growth of Marxist subversion in Mexico, corruption was not on their list of priorities.[46]

Corruption and Drug Trafficking

According to Mexican historian Luis Astorga, "drug trafficking was just another profitable business that could be achieved by powerful members" of the PRI because the "political positions occupied by some of them" enabled the PRI to "control, tolerate, or regulate" drug trafficking. Drug trafficking became a business that developed from within the power structure, and drug traffickers were a new class of outlaws who depended on political and police protection but were banned from political activity.[47] Along the US-Mexico border there were towns whose entire existence was primarily based upon smuggling contraband into and out of Mexico. As a consequence, there was a vast amount of corruption along the border in Mexico.[48] Known as the mordida system, under-the-counter payments bought protection from official scrutiny. It was also the traditional means that trafficking groups used to run operations and to eliminate their competition.[49] Relations between traffickers and the police were so familiar that in 1973 the BNDD reported witnessing a PJFM official drinking with three known traffickers.[50]

Narcocorruption further strained US-Mexico relations. Mexican officials denied that it was as widespread as US officials contended.[51] Even when the local Mexican officials were honest, they had little control over what happened along the border. In one case, US personnel knew of a marijuana storage and outlet facility with its own landing strip thirty miles from the border, but they were unable to get the Mexicans to take any action. US authorities accused Mexican authorities of "dragging their heels" and withholding drug-related information.[52] BNDD officers felt that their efforts were limited by Mexico's refusal to extradite known traffickers and by Mexican laws that prevented US agents from making arrests or performing undercover work in Mexico.[53] Mexico was a country whose public, police, and legal system resented US intrusions and viewed narcotics control as a question of sovereignty.

Tougher border controls and intensified interdiction and crop eradication programs constituted the essential framework of Operation Cooperation. Yet, the majority of the counternarcotics efforts were carried out on Mexican territory, which in turn placed a strain on Mexico's political system. Although Mexico received substantial aid from the United States, it was Mexico alone that faced the problem of how to interdict and eradicate narcotics. Counternarcotics caused friction between the two nations along the legal points of entry into the United States, heightened the internal conflict between the Mexican government and its campesino-student populations, and fostered general resentment between the two nations over Mexico's level of effort to stop the flow of drugs. Regardless, Mexico was a signatory to the UN Single Convention of 1961. As long as homegrown cartels produced and trafficked narcotics in and through its sovereign territory, the Mexican government was obligated to make narcotics control an integral part of its domestic agenda. Narcotics control became a permanent part of bilateral relations or what the Mexican people referred to as La Campaña Permanente.

Narcotics Take Hold in Mexico, 1974–1978

By 1974, Mexico surpassed the rest of the world as the major producer and trafficker of narcotics for the US market, replacing Turkey as the dominant producer of heroin. It also became the principal source of marijuana for the US market until Colombia replaced Mexico in 1977.[54] The majority of Mexico's marijuana and opium was grown in the Sierra Madre Occidental mountains and the Mexican states of Sinaloa, Durango, and Chihuahua. This region became known as the Triángulo Dorado. Mexico stepped up its counternarcotics operations there, but old and new difficulties with the United States persisted. Disagreements arose over jurisdiction, cooperation, and the decision to use herbicides to conduct eradication programs. Simultaneously, corruption and socioeconomic turmoil made joint programs difficult to execute.

It was not until 1974 that Mexico acknowledged that it was a major source for raw opium and marijuana and a major transshipment point for South American cocaine.[55] Between 1974 and 1976, Mexico supplanted Europe and Asia as the primary source of heroin (classified as Mexican brown heroin) in the United States, producing nearly 70 percent of the heroin and 90 percent of the marijuana entering the United States.[56] By 1976, the estimate for opium rose to 89 percent.[57] Although increased arrests and seizures occurred along the US-Mexico border, the flow of narcotics did not stop. In 1976, the cumulative average of DEA, Customs, and INS (Immigration and Naturalization Service) seizures on the Mexican border totaled only 6 percent of the heroin, 3 percent of the cocaine, and 13 percent of the marijuana entering the United States.[58] The tonnage seized or destroyed continued to increase annually, while Mexico's drug-related violence became more common, leading to the killing of two DEA agents, four Mexican police officers, and thirty civilians in 1976.[59] Mexico had joined the front lines in the war on drugs.

Eradication and Interdiction

In 1974, crop eradication efforts remained limited. The Mexican government could not effectively cover all the areas where narcotics production occurred, especially in Mexico's remote, inaccessible areas. Although the DEA believed that the Mexican government was earnest in its effort, 15 to 20 percent of the opium and 60 percent of the marijuana was harvested before enforcement officials could reach or destroy the plants.[60] The hospitable climate for growing these plants and the ability of the campesinos to replant fields within a few weeks of their destruction made it virtually impossible to halt production. The Mexican government reached the conclusion that its traditional interdiction and manual eradication programs were ineffective and requested US technical assistance. In January 1974, the United States helped Mexico implement Operation SEA/M (Special Enforcement Activity in Mexico) to counter the flow of opium and heroin out of Sinaloa. One month later, a second joint task force, Operation End-Run, began operations in Guerrero, concentrating on marijuana and heroin interdiction.[61]

The use of aerial herbicides, aerial photographic detection, and forward military bases became a part of Mexico's revised approach toward eradication. In early 1974, the United States and Mexico planned to use herbicides to eliminate opium and marijuana fields, but political sensitivities and the need for experiments and demonstrations concerning the use of herbicides delayed the program until 1975. It was not until 1976 that the herbicide-spraying program became fully operational.[62] The deployment of the PJFM and the Mexican army to construct forward bases enabled herbicide-spraying helicopters to reach remote targets. The forward bases were necessary because they cut down on helicopter turnaround time, thereby achieving greater man-hour and flying-hour cost efficiency.[63]

The next step in the eradication program was the development of an aerial photographic detection system that officials expected would improve the planning of future poppy eradication operations. To aid the Mexican government, the United States contributed $700,000 in 1975 to build five forward bases in the poppy-growing areas of Sinaloa, Durango, and Chihuahua and, in the following year, several million for specialized aircraft. The DEA reported a fourfold increase in the number of poppy fields destroyed using herbicides between 1975 and 1976. These numbers were significant. In 1975, only 4,733 fields were destroyed. By 1976, that number grew to 20,115.[64] The DEA reported that in 1978, Mexico's share of the heroin market decreased to 65 percent, down from 89 percent in 1976. In 1976, incoming president López Portillo pledged his full support for Mexico's joint narcotics control program, placing an emphasis on poppy eradication. Taking his support into account, the US State Department noted that while the program achieved "some success in reducing the supply of Mexican heroin available in the United States," López Portillo's promise to "wage war" against narcotics would likely be "a well-nigh impossible task." In the opinion of the State Department, as long as there was US demand, Mexico would remain a major source of heroin for the US market.[65]

In addition to crop eradication programs, the DEA recognized that it had to improve its interdiction efforts. In 1974, the DEA initiated Operation Trident, which focused on the trafficking of narcotics produced in Mexico.[66] At the same time, the DEA, Customs, the BNDD, the FBI, and the Federal Aviation Administration (FAA) all collected information on narcotics trafficking, but it was not coordinated. To rectify this, the DEA created the El Paso

Intelligence Center (EPIC) in September 1974. EPIC was designed to be an intelligence clearinghouse by providing a communications database to support ground, sea, and air enforcement operations for the appropriate federal, state, and local enforcement agencies located along the border and for key regional offices including Mexico City and the DEA headquarters in Washington.[67] As US counternarcotics measures matured, EPIC expanded into a national drug intelligence center that supported US law enforcement entities focused on worldwide drug smuggling.[68]

Crop Substitution

While eradication and interdiction became tools in Mexico's war on drugs, President Echeverría noted that the best method to stop narcotics cultivation was the development of crop substitution programs. It was hoped that crop substitution would make campesinos less reliant on narcotics production for their incomes.[69] Between 1960 and 1970, Mexican unemployment rose by 487 percent while economic growth in Mexico's rural areas stagnated at 2 percent, although 58 percent of Mexico's population lived in those regions. Poverty forced campesinos to migrate to the big cities or turn toward marijuana and opium poppy production, particularly in the northern states of Sonora, Sinaloa, Chihuahua, and Durango.[70] According to the Mexican Secretaría de la Defensa Nacional (SEDENA), there were few alternative sources of income for the campesinos. The eradication programs threatened to increase campesino "recruitment to Mexican insurgents" or "at the least" risked the increase of campesinos illegally entering the United States "to seek employment."[71] Realizing that eradication programs were a growing problem, Echeverría argued that it was necessary to create "new employment opportunities" by creating "income replacement programs" that accompanied "crop replacement efforts." In addition, members of a US delegation to Mexico argued that a program such as this helped the Mexican government in "dealing with the problem of public apathy as well as the lucrative temptations proffered by the traffickers to campesinos to grow narcotics."[72]

Regardless of the recommendations, crop substitution made little headway at this point in the drug war. In 1976, the United States and Mexico were only beginning to explore possibilities for income substitution in producing areas.[73] But because opium poppy and marijuana production was illegal, the Mexican government could not provide assistance to replace illicit crops. The Mexican government feared that providing crop substitution assistance would be tantamount to condoning narcotics production. Furthermore, the government believed that crop substitution programs inadvertently encouraged narcotics cultivation because they incentivized farmers to grow narcotics in order to receive assistance.[74] Crop substitution was, therefore, ignored as a long-term program for reducing the economic motivation to cultivate narcotics. Instead, short-term law enforcement programs such as eradication and interdiction were favored.[75] The possibility of starting an effective crop substitution program came too late. Drugs had become an integral part of Mexico's society and economy.

Persistent Corruption and Bilateral Disputes

Corruption and the DEA's reluctance to cooperate with the PJFM reduced the effectiveness of counternarcotics operations. According to the DEA, the PJFM was susceptible to corruption because of poor working benefits and pay—PJFM officers received roughly $150–$200 a month. They did not have job security, hospital insurance, or retirement benefits. As a result, narcotics became a way to earn additional funds. To address corruption, the Mexican government restructured the police force, establishing a career police service in 1975.[76] During this transition, the Federal Judicial Police Academy was established in July 1974. The DEA provided assistance in the first training cycle, although the main burden of teaching counternarcotics procedures remained with the Mexican government. Because of looming corruption within the PJFM, the DEA never fully committed to this program. Up until 1977, the DEA showed a marked disinterest in building local antinarcotics leadership, establishing more effective organizations, and transferring appropriate management skills to their Mexican counterparts.[77] The US embassy in Mexico, rather than the DEA, provided the majority of US managerial expertise for the Mexican government's police restructuring program.[78] Ironically enough, the DEA's limited involvement in Mexico's police restructuring left the PJFM more prone to corruption and deficient in its capacity to make structural changes. A sense of disconnectedness emerged between the DEA and PJFM. Even though the two agencies continued to cooperate on narcotics matters, their differences fomented mistrust over the next decade.

The lack of full cooperation created a dispute about the DEA's jurisdictional powers within Mexico. In 1974, seventy-nine DEA agents operated out of Mexico City. With the exception of Panama, the agents covered all of Mexico and Central America.[79] Because of nationalist sentiment and opposition to foreign agents operating on Mexican soil, the Mexican government prevented DEA agents from making arrests or performing undercover work. Mexico also established laws that blocked the extradition of traffickers to the United States. In 1976, Mexico accused the DEA of violating its sovereignty by entrapping drug dealers on Mexican soil, conducting unreported reconnaissance flights over Mexico, and making illegal apprehensions of suspects who were rendered to the United States. These activities infuriated the Mexican government. According to a source within

28   Narcostates

the Mexican attorney general's office, it was an affront to Mexico to have US "agents act as police" on Mexican soil by granting themselves the power to "arrest Mexicans," or "to carry arms when they should not, to make reconnaissance flights on their own, and to do undercover work behind our backs." The source also added that "there was a lot of pride and rivalry on both sides of the border."[80] Indeed, pride and rivalry prevented both governments from achieving their mutual goal of curtailing narcotics production and trafficking.

Because of the disputes over sovereignty, the US Congress revised the US Foreign Relations and Intercourse Act in 1976. The law prohibited the DEA from participating directly in any foreign police arrests. It also required DEA agents to be authorized by the host country to operate technical equipment, to operate in an undercover capacity, or to assist in the training of officers.[81] The amendment was enacted in order to reduce tensions over US violations of national sovereignty and to encourage countries like Mexico to participate in US counternarcotics initiatives.[82] Despite US assurances, friction continued into the late 1970s due to Mexico's insistence on maintaining its independence. Seeking to avoid being perceived as a US puppet, the Mexican government curtailed US involvement in enforcement activities, which led to disputes over Mexico's counternarcotics commitment.[83] The DEA acted aggressively because they believed that Mexican authorities were not doing enough. Yet, by violating Mexico's sovereignty, US actions undermined cooperation. The belief that the Mexican government was "not doing enough" remained a recurrent theme.

Gunrunning and money laundering became another source of bilateral friction. From the Mexican perspective, US agents exhibited a lack of concern regarding the flow of firearms across the border, which were traded for narcotics and delivered to Mexican revolutionary organizations.[84] Allegations arose that Mexican bank employees were exchanging millions of dollars for drug dealers as large surpluses of US currency began accumulating in Mexico.[85] In a 1977 hearing on the proceeds of narcotics trafficking in Chicago, the governor of Illinois estimated that there was "at least $100 million flowing through the banking institutions" in Chicago to Mexico alone.[86] In addition, Mexican banks shipped millions of dollars to affiliate banks in the United States where it could be laundered and moved offshore. The weaknesses of the Mexican banking system became a detriment to enforcement and added to the complications of cooperation between the two nations.

Responding to US complaints, the Mexican government issued a white paper titled "On the Campaign Against Drug Traffic" stating that narcotics crimes "are generated in the United States" and not Mexico, because Mexico and other Latin American countries only "acted in the intermediate process of the crime being committed." The white paper added that "there must be some actions done in the market of consumption to abate demand,"

Early US Counternarcotics Efforts in Mexico 29

because the "problem does not lie in the plant" but in the person who has the "need for its product and requires its consumption."[87] The disputes over jurisdiction and the persistent recriminations over Mexico's laxity created smoldering feelings of animosity between the two governments that continued into the next century.

Notes

1. US President, *The Public Papers of the Presidents of the United States* (Washington, DC: Office of the *Federal Register* National Archives and Records Service, 1971), 986–987; Richard M. Nixon, "Remarks at Opening Session of the Governors' Conference at the Department of State" (December 3, 1969).

2. Harvey R. Wellman, "Address by Harvey R. Wellman: The International Aspects of Drug Abuse Control," *State Department Bulletin*, May 17, 1971, 640 (Washington, DC: National Security Archives, Narcotics: Drug Documents, box 54).

3. US Department of State, "Memorandum for the President: Request for a Recommendation on the Heroin Problem," October 20, 1969, 3 (Washington, DC: National Archives, Nixon Presidential Materials Project, Nixon Presidential Materials Staff, National Security Council Files, 1969–1973, box 357).

4. US Department of State, Office of the Inspector General of Foreign Assistance, "International Narcotics Control Program—Mexico," June 17, 1977, 4 (Washington, DC: National Security Archives, Narcotics: Carter FOIA, box 39). See also Richard B. Craig, "La Campaña Permanente: Mexico's Antidrug Campaign," *Journal of Interamerican Studies and World Affairs* 20, no. 2 (May 1978): 107–131.

5. Otis E. Mulliken to Phil Robertson, "Letter to the Chico Enterprise Record," April 20, 1961, 1 (Washington, DC: National Archives, General Records of the Department of State, Bureau of Inter-American Affairs, Records Relating to Mexico).

6. Robert M. Sayre to Mr. Vallon, "Program with Mexico for Narcotics Enforcement," June 6, 1961, 1 (Washington, DC: National Archives, General Records of the Department of State, Bureau of Inter-American Affairs, Records Relating to Mexico, box 49).

7. Thomas J. Dodd, Chairman of the Senate Subcommittee to Investigate Juvenile Delinquency, "Press Release on the Joint United States–Mexico Narcotic Commission," March 28, 1963, 1 (Washington, DC: National Security Archives, Narcotics: Drug Documents, Presidential Libraries, box 54).

8. Ibid., 2–9.

9. Felix Belair, "Operation Intercept," *New York Times*, October 2, 1969, 49, cited from Lawrence A. Gooberman, *Operation Intercept: The Multiple Consequences of Public Policy* (New York: Pergamon Press, 1974), 2. See also Cabinet Committee on International Narcotics Control, *World Opium Survey 1972* (Washington, DC: Department of State, August 17, 1972), 58 (National Archives, Nixon Presidential Materials Project, Nixon Presidential Materials Staff, National Security Council Files, 1969–1973, box 359).

10. Gooberman, *Operation Intercept*, 2.

11. US President, *The Public Papers of the Presidents of the United States*, "Remarks at a Bipartisan Leadership Meeting on Narcotics and Dangerous Drugs," October 23, 1969, 838.

12. Statement of Deputy Attorney General Richard Kleindienst and Assistant Secretary of the Treasury Eugene Rossides, October 23, 1969, 1, cited in Gooberman, *Operation Intercept*, 3–4.

30   *Narcostates*

13. Bud Krogh to John Ehrlichman, "Status Report on Negotiations with Mexico Re: Operation Intercept," October 8, 1969, 1 (Washington, DC: National Archives, Nixon Presidential Materials Project, White House Special Files, Staff Member and Office Files, Egil Krogh, 1969–1973, box 30).

14. Richard Kleindienst, "Joint Declaration of the United States and Mexican Delegations," October 30, 1969, 1–2 (Washington, DC: National Archives, Nixon Presidential Materials Project, White House Special Files, Staff Member and Office Files, Egil Krogh, 1969–1973, box 30); US Department of State, "Current Media Reaction Report for October 27, 1969," October 27, 1979, 2 (Washington, DC: National Archives, Nixon Presidential Materials Project, White House Special Files, Staff Member and Office Files, Egil Krogh, 1969–1973, box 31).

15. American Embassy Mexico to Secretary of State William Rogers, "Narcotics, Marihuana, and Dangerous Drugs: Working Group Report No. 10," December 11, 1969, 1 (Washington, DC: National Archives, Nixon Presidential Materials Project, White House Special Files, Staff Member and Office Files, Egil Krogh, 1969–1973, box 30).

16. US President, *The Public Papers of the Presidents of the United States*, "Joint Statement Following Discussions with President Díaz Ordaz of Mexico," August 21, 1970, 687.

17. US Congress, House of Representatives, Committee on Foreign Affairs, *The World Narcotics Problem: The Latin American Perspective: Report of Special Study Mission to Latin America and the Federal Republic of Germany*, 93rd Cong., 1st sess., March 21, 1973, 20.

18. United States–Mexico Joint Working Group, "Narcotics, Marihuana, and Dangerous Drugs: Report of the United States–Mexico Joint Working Group," December 12, 1969, 5 (Washington, DC: National Archives, Nixon Presidential Materials Project, White House Special Files, Staff Member and Office Files, Egil Krogh, 1969–1973, box 31).

19. Bud Krogh to John Ehrlichman, "Intensified Anti-Smuggling Efforts by the Bureau of Customs," June 9, 1970, 2 (Washington, DC: National Archives, Nixon Presidential Materials Project, White House Special Files, Staff Member and Office Files, Egil Krogh, 1969–1973, box 30).

20. House of Representatives, *World Narcotics Problem*, 21.

21. US Department of State, "Narcotics Country Paper on Mexico," March 1, 1974, 2–3 (Washington, DC: National Security Archives, Narcotics: Drug Documents, Presidential Libraries, box 54).

22. US Congress, Senate, Committee on Foreign Relations, *International Traffic in Narcotics: Hearing Before the Committee on Foreign Relations*, 92nd Cong., 1st sess., July 1, 1971, 130, Statement of Harvey R. Wellman, Assistant to the Secretary of State for Narcotics Matters.

23. Senate, *International Traffic*, 130.

24. Peter Watt and Roberto Zepeda, *Drug War Mexico: Politics, Neoliberalism, and Violence in the New Narcoeconomy* (London: Zed Books, 2012), 48. CANADOR was referred to as Operation Condor after 1974 but should not be confused with the counterterrorist operation in the Southern Cone.

25. Craig, "La Campaña Permanente," 108.

26. US Department of State, "International Narcotics Control: Foreign Assistance Appropriations Act, Fiscal Year 1976 Budget," n.d., 32 (Washington, DC: National Security Archives, Narcotics: Drug Documents, Presidential Libraries, box 46).

27. US Congress, Senate, Committee on the Judiciary of the United States Senate, *Impact on U.S. Security, Hearings Before the Subcommittee to Investigate*

the Administration of the Internal Security Act and Other Internal Security Laws, 92nd Cong., 2nd sess., August 14, 1972, 257; and US Department of State Press, "Report of William P. Rogers Entitled International Narcotics Control Summary," 10.

28. Craig, "La Campaña Permanente," 116.

29. Tom Whitehead to Bud Krogh, "Attachment: Proposed Major Program Issue on Marihuana Policy," September 29, 1969, 1 (Washington, DC: National Archives, Nixon Presidential Materials Project, White House Special Files, Staff Member and Office Files, Egil Krogh, 1969–1973, box 30).

30. Craig, "La Campaña Permanente," 118–119.

31. Whitehead to Krogh, "Attachment: Proposed Major Program Issue on Marihuana Policy," 1.

32. American Embassy Mexico to Secretary of State, "Confidential Telegram," July 1968, 2 (Washington, DC: National Archives, General Records of the Department of State, Political and Defense, Records Relating to Mexico 1967–1969, box 2340).

33. Ibid.; American Embassy Mexico to Secretary of State, "Analysis of Student Disturbances," August 1968, 1–2 (Washington, DC: National Archives, General Records of the Department of State, Political and Defense, Records Relating to Mexico 1967–1969, box 2343).

34. US Department of State, Bureau of Intelligence and Research, "Mexico: Government Repression of Students Causes Crisis," June 18, 1971, 1 (Washington, DC: National Archives, General Records of the Department of State, Political and Defense, Records Relating to Mexico 1967–1969, box 2476). See Larry Rohter, "20 Years After Massacre, Mexico Still Seeking Healing for Its Wounds," New York Times, October 2, 1988, www.nytimes.com.

35. Bureau of Intelligence and Research, "Mexico," 4.

36. American Consul Guadalajara to Department of State, "Reaction to the Movimiento de Acción Revolucionaria in Jalisco—a Crackdown on the Frente de Estudiantes Revolucionarios," March 29, 1971, 3–5 (Washington, DC: National Archives, General Records of the Department of State, Subject and Numeric Files, Political and Defense, Records Relating to Mexico 1970–1973, box 2476).

37. American Embassy Mexico City to Secretary of State, "Meeting of Solidarity with Sinaloa at UNAM and Campesino March on Capital," April 1972, 1–3 (Washington, DC: National Archives, General Records of the Department of State, Subject and Numeric Files, Political and Defense, Records Relating to Mexico 1970–1973, box 2476).

38. American Consulate Ciudad Juárez to Department of State, "Student Demonstrations in Observance of Fourth Anniversary of Tlatelolco Massacre," October 12, 1972, 3 (Washington, DC: National Archives, General Records of the Department of State, Subject and Numeric Files, Political and Defense, Records Relating to Mexico 1970–1973, box 2474).

39. US Department of State, Bureau of Intelligence and Research, "Mexico: Terrorism Still on the Rise," November 29, 1972, 2–3 (Washington, DC: National Archives, General Records of the Department of State, Subject and Numeric Files, Political and Defense, Records Relating to Mexico 1970–1973, box 2476). See also American Consul, Guadalajara to Department of State, "Reaction to the Movimiento de Acción Revolucionaria in Jalisco," 6–7.

40. US Department of State, Bureau of Intelligence and Research, "Mexico: An Emerging Internal Security Problem?," September 23, 1971, 2 (Washington, DC: National Archives, General Records of the Department of State, Subject and Numeric Files, Political and Defense, Records Relating to Mexico 1970–1973, box 2475).

32   Narcostates

41. American Embassy Mexico to Secretary of State, "Telegram," October 1970, 1 (Washington, DC: National Archives, General Records of the Department of State, Subject and Numeric Files, Political and Defense, Records Relating to Mexico 1970–1973, box 2476).

42. US Department of State, Bureau of Intelligence and Research, "Mexico: Terrorism Still on the Rise," 2–4.

43. American Consul Guadalajara to Department of State, "Student Politics in Guadalajara," March 6, 1973, 2 (Washington, DC: National Archives, General Records of the Department of State, Subject and Numeric Files, Political and Defense, Records Relating to Mexico 1970–1973, box 2475).

44. Watt and Zepeda, *Drug War Mexico*, 44; Sam Dillon, "Javier García Paniagua, 61, Mexican Ruling Party Loyalist," *New York Times*, November 28, 1998. García Paniagua was the Mexican secretary of defense (1964–1970) and a senator from the state of Jalisco (1970–1976). After serving as the chief of the DFS, he later became subsecretary of the interior (1978–1980).

45. Dillon, "Javier García Paniagua"; Samuel Dillon and Julia Preston, *Opening Mexico: The Making of a Democracy* (New York: Farrar, Strauss and Giroux, 2004), 45.

46. Peter Dale Scott and Jonathan Marshall, *Cocaine Politics: Drugs, Armies, and the CIA in Central America* (Berkeley: University of California Press, 1991), 40.

47. Luis Astorga, "Drug Trafficking in Mexico: A First General Assessment," Discussion Paper No. 36, Management of Social Transition Project: United Nations Educational, Scientific, and Cultural Organization (n.d.), www.unesco.org/most /astorga.htm.

48. House of Representatives, *World Narcotics Problem*, 21.

49. US Congress, House of Representatives, Committee on International Relations, *The Shifting Pattern of Narcotics Trafficking: Report of a Study Mission to Mexico, Costa Rica, Panama, and Colombia*, 94th Cong., 2nd sess., January 6–18, 1976, 12. The PJFM was a national police force run by Mexico's attorney general.

50. House of Representatives, *World Narcotics Problem*, 15.

51. Craig, "La Campaña Permanente," 119.

52. House of Representatives, *World Narcotics Problem*, 21–23; Craig, "La Campaña Permanente," 119–120.

53. US General Accounting Office, *Report to the Congress: Difficulties in Immobilizing Major Narcotics Traffickers*, GAO-B175424, December 21, 1973, 24–25 (Washington, DC: National Security Archives, Narcotics: Drug Documents, GAO Reports, box 54).

54. House of Representatives, *Shifting Pattern of Narcotics Trafficking*, 1–5.

55. Ibid., 8.

56. US Congress, Senate, Committee on Government Operations, *Federal Drug Enforcement Part 5: Hearings Before the Permanent Subcommittees on Investigations*, 94th Cong., 2nd sess., August 23–26, 1976, 1060; US General Accounting Office, *Efforts to Stop Narcotics and Dangerous Drugs Coming from and Through Mexico and Central America*, GAO B-175425, December 31, 1974, 2.

57. General Accounting Office, *Opium Eradication Efforts in Mexico: Cautious Optimism Advised*, GAO 77-6, February 18, 1977, 1.

58. US Congress, Senate, Committee on the Judiciary, *Federal Efforts to Stem the Flow of Drugs Across the U.S.-Mexican Border*, 95th Cong., 1st sess., April 18, 1978, 5, Statement of William J. Anderson, Deputy Director General Government Division. The INS is now known as ICE (Immigration and Customs Enforcement).

Early US Counternarcotics Efforts in Mexico   33

59. Senate, Committee on Government Operations, *Federal Drug Enforcement Part 5*, 1061.

60. General Accounting Office, *Efforts to Stop Narcotics and Dangerous Drugs*, 14.

61. Ibid.; US Drug Enforcement Agency, *The DEA Years: DEA History Book 1970–1975*, Drug Enforcement Agency, 37, https://www.dea.gov/sites/default/files /2018-07/1970-1975%20p%2030-39.pdf.

62. House of Representatives, *Shifting Pattern of Narcotics Trafficking*, 9–10. The herbicide gramaxone was sprayed from helicopters.

63. US Department of State, "International Narcotics Control Foreign Assistance Appropriation Act, Fiscal Year 1976 Budget," 32 (Washington, DC: National Security Archives, Narcotics: Drug Documents, Presidential Libraries, box 54).

64. Senate, Committee on Government Operations, *Federal Drug Enforcement Part 5*, 1064.

65. US General Accounting Office, *Gains Made in Controlling Illegal Drugs, yet the Drug Trade Flourishes*, GAO 80-4, October 25, 1979, 39.

66. US Drug Enforcement Agency, *DEA History Book 1970–1975*, 37.

67. US Congress, House of Representatives, Committee on Government Operations, *Law Enforcement on the Southwest Border: Hearings Before the Subcommittee of the Committee on Government Operations*, 93rd Cong., 2nd sess., August 10–14, 1974, 148, Statement of John Bartels, Administrator of the Drug Enforcement Agency.

68. US Drug Enforcement Agency, *DEA History Book 1970–1975*, 37.

69. House of Representatives, *Shifting Pattern of Narcotics Trafficking*, appendix 5, Joint Statement Released at Press Conference upon Completion of Study Mission, January 20, 1976, 36.

70. Watt and Zepeda, *Drug War Mexico*, 46.

71. Inspector General of Foreign Assistance, "International Narcotics Control Program—Mexico," General Accounting Office, June 17, 1977, 18 (Washington, DC: National Security Archives, Narcotics, FOIA Releases, box 39).

72. House of Representatives, *Shifting Pattern of Narcotics Trafficking*, 11.

73. Ibid., 36.

74. General Accounting Office, *Efforts to Stop Narcotics and Dangerous Drugs*, 14.

75. General Accounting Office, *Gains Made in Controlling Illegal Drugs*, 44.

76. General Accounting Office, *Efforts to Stop Narcotics and Dangerous Drugs*, 18–19.

77. Inspector General of Foreign Assistance, "International Narcotics Control Program—Mexico," 17. See also US Department of State, "International Narcotics Control Foreign Assistance Appropriation Act, Fiscal Year 1976 Budget," 33.

78. US Department of State, "International Narcotics Control Foreign Assistance Appropriation Act, Fiscal Year 1976 Budget," 17.

79. House of Representatives, Committee on Government Operations, *Law Enforcement on the Southwest Border*, 148.

80. Senate, *Federal Drug Enforcement Part 5*, 1061, Letter of Charles M. Percy of the Committee on Government Operations to Peter Bensinger, DEA administrator.

81. Ibid., 1066; 22 U.S. Code, 2291 (c), Foreign Relations and Intercourse Act, Amended as Public Law 94–329, title V, §504(b), June 30, 1976, 90 Statute, 764, Drug Enforcement Administration—Functions and Guidelines Relating to Operations in Foreign Countries, June 30, 1976.

34   *Narcostates*

82. US General Accounting Office, "Drug Control in South America, Having Limited Success—Some Progress but Problems Are Formidable," GAO 78-45, March 28, 1978, 21.

83. American Embassy Mexico to Secretary of State, "GOM Requests Elimination of DEA Spotters," January 1978, 1 (Washington, DC: National Security Archives, Narcotics, Carter, box 39).

84. Senate, *Federal Drug Enforcement Part 4*, 859–860, Statement by Eugene T. Rossides, Assistant Secretary of the Treasury for Enforcement, Tariff, and Trade Affairs.

85. Senate, *Federal Drug Enforcement Part 5*, 1263.

86. US Congress, House of Representatives, Select Committee on Narcotics Abuse and Control, *Investigation of Narcotics and Money Laundering in Chicago: Report of the Select Committee on Narcotics Abuse and Control*, 95th Cong., 1st sess., February 1978, 11.

87. House of Representatives, *Shifting Pattern of Narcotics Trafficking*, 56. The white paper was delivered on February 15, 1976.

3

"Cocaine Guns" and Civil War in Central America

Marxist-inspired guerrilla insurgencies took up arms in several Central American countries during the late 1970s. Although Guatemala had been in the throes of civil war since 1954, the Sandinista overthrow of dictator Anastasio Somoza in 1979 focused the region's attention on Nicaragua, fueling revolutionary and counterrevolutionary activities across Central America.

The enormous imbalance in political and economic power made the region ripe for revolution. Nicaragua, Guatemala, Honduras, El Salvador, and Costa Rica all became susceptible to the destabilizing effects of revolution. A large percentage of Central America's population experienced political disenfranchisement and abject poverty. They backed revolutionary movements because the oligarchic elites continuously hindered reform. With the Cold War looming over Central America, the United States provided military assistance to prop up the oligarchies, which safeguarded US economic and political interests. Using US-backed counterinsurgency methods, Central American military forces brutally suppressed guerrilla movements and marginalized sectors of society to prevent insurrection and revolt. As an extension of the campaigns against the guerrillas, paramilitary death squads became an important counterrevolutionary tool to crush the insurgents. By the mid-1980s, civil wars were drowning the region in blood.

As the regional conflicts peaked, Central America became a transit zone for cocaine traveling northward through Mexico into the United States. The civil wars discouraged excessive levels of trafficking, but opportunities remained. The corrupting influence of narcodollars extended into governments and guerrilla movements alike. Allegations of drug trafficking were leveled against Nicaragua's Sandinista regime and the Cuban government. Simultaneously, the CIA-backed Contras were accused of

36   *Narcostates*

participating in drug trafficking as well. A further twist to the story was Panamanian dictator Manuel Noriega, who played both sides of the Central American conflict and profited from drug trafficking and money laundering operations. Although the CIA considered Noriega their asset, he never served a single master. Instead, Noriega served himself. During his 1983–1989 dictatorship, Noriega enriched himself by assisting the Medellín cartel to conduct business with the Contras and the Sandinistas.

Due to the two concurrent themes—revolution and drug trafficking—this chapter is divided into two parts. In order to provide a general overview for those who are not familiar with the region's turbulent history, the first part provides a brief summary of Central America's conflicts. The names, organizations, and places that appear in this chapter need to be put into context because they reappear again in future chapters. The second part deals with the question of Contra, Sandinista, and Panamanian drug trafficking during the Contra War. This subject has been covered by other scholars and by this author in *The Politics of Cocaine*; consequently, it is not necessary to go into extensive detail on the subject here.[1] However, a general summary of drug trafficking during the Contra War is important, because it establishes the framework to explain the development of Colombian narcotrafficking through Central America and how the Mexican cartels eventually took over the drug trade.

The Central American Conflicts

The Guatemalan Nightmare

In 1954, following the CIA-backed overthrow of Guatemalan President Jacobo Árbenz Guzmán, Guatemala entered into a civil war that lasted until 1996. Successive military juntas ruled the country until 1983.[2] Opposition to the military governments grew, and by the late 1970s, four Marxist-inspired guerrilla organizations were formed to challenge the military's hold on power. Guided by Fidel Castro, the Guatemalan revolutionaries met in Managua during 1980 to form the Unidad Revolucionaria Nacional Guatemalteca (URNG).[3] The rebels claimed that they were fighting for a "national revolution" leading to "a change of structures."[4] A wave of terrorism spread across Guatemala as the guerrillas carried out assassinations and kidnappings. In 1982, the URNG launched an offensive that put the Mexican army on a state of alert along its southern borders. According to one Mexican official, Mexico "implemented the state of alert to defend the country's southern border and lucrative oil fields against a possible spillover from Central America's turbulent wars."[5]

An estimated 140,000 to 200,000 Guatemalans died during the forty-two years of conflict. With the nation's institutions in the hands of the military, bitter struggles for power ensued. US support for the 1954 coup, and later US support for the military governments, fed the civil war and propped up Guatemala's oligarchy. With the exception of the Carter years, varying levels of US aid created a situation in which the Guatemalan military did not see the necessity of coming to the bargaining table. Instead, it carried out scorched earth policies that decimated villages throughout the country.[6] Because US aid stiffened the resolve of the military, it committed enormous human rights abuses that fanned the flames of war and the resolve of Guatemala's guerrillas.

It was not until the mid-1990s, when Guatemala's population was simply exhausted by war, that both sides negotiated a peace resolution. The election of Marco Cerezo Arévalo (1986–1991), a nonmilitary politician from the Democracia Cristiana Guatemalteca (DCG), as Guatemala's first democratically elected president since 1966, started the peace process. Because the combatants were incapable of reaching a compromise, the negotiations stalled. Consequently, during the ongoing negotiations, Arévalo turned to his military intelligence outfit, the D-2, to conduct counterinsurgency operations despite the fact that the D-2 had a reputation for committing human rights abuses and corruption.[7] Ultimately, he did reach an agreement with the URNG to hold peaceful elections in 1990.

Jorge Antonio Serrano Elías served as president from 1991 to 1993, until he attempted an *auto-golpe* (self-coup) with the purpose of suspending the constitution to fight corruption. Despite his "coup" attempt, Serrano Elías supported continued peace talks with the URNG that led to political accommodation and peace terms under his successor, Ramiro de León Carpio (1993–1996).

The civil war caused widespread corruption. As will be seen later, allegations of narcotrafficking were leveled against the army and the military's intelligence unit, the D-2.[8] Concentrated in Guatemala's highlands, the civil war was fought exactly where opium poppies and marijuana were grown. Allegations of drug trafficking were also levied against the Guatemalan guerrillas. Fighting in the northern highlands opened Guatemala's porous border with Mexico to the movement of weapons and drugs. As the civil war came to an end in the 1990s, Guatemala became a major transshipment point for narcotics. Meanwhile, in 1993, the United States began deporting Guatemalan refugees with criminal records. These refugees formed a criminal network that extended from Guatemala through Mexico to the United States. By the end of the 1990s, Guatemala faced another state of emergency due to organized crime. Ill-prepared for this new fight, Guatemala would once again resort to military measures to control the lawlessness now associated with narcotrafficking.

38 *Narcostates*

El Salvador's Blood Bath

During the twentieth century, El Salvador endured periods of bloodshed and dictatorship that ultimately erupted into civil war. In December 1980, José Napoleón Duarte Fuentes became the head of a reformist military junta called the Junta Revolucionaria de Gobierno (JRG), which overthrew the previous military government. Up to this point, the military ruled El Salvador on behalf of the Fourteen Families—the historic oligarchic elite that controlled the land and the economy. Duarte began a series of land and banking reforms, but they failed to improve the economic imbalances.[9] The campesinos did not benefit from his land reforms because, in order to take possession of the land, the campesinos were required to have owned their parcel for thirty years, which they did not. Moreover, because the campesinos had no land to put up as collateral, they could not obtain credit and were displaced.[10]

Following the JRG's seizure of power in 1979, Salvadoran Marxists came to believe that revolution was their only alternative. Immediately following the appointment of Duarte as head of the junta, the Salvadoran revolutionaries, united under the banner of the Frente Farabundo Martí para la Liberación Nacional (FMLN), launched a nationwide attack against the government on January 10, 1981. With Cuban and Nicaraguan help, external support for the Salvadoran guerrillas intensified. By 1982, the FMLN maintained 4,000–6,000 full-time guerrillas with a logistical support network of 10,000 sympathizers.[11]

When the FMLN launched its offensive in January 1981, its goal was to defeat the Salvadoran military before the inauguration of Ronald Reagan as president of the United States. The guerrillas hoped that a popular insurrection would follow and collapse the Salvadoran government, which in turn would force the Reagan administration to recognize a fait accompli in El Salvador. Despite the FMLN's efforts, the army remained intact and the people did not rally en masse to their cause. According to FMLN Comandante Alejandro Montenegro, "There was no popular backing for an insurrection."[12] In the wake of the FMLN's uprising, El Salvador's oligarchy considered the JRG to be too soft on communist radicalism. They withdrew their support for the JRG and backed Major Roberto D'Aubuisson Arrieta's Alianza Republicana Nacionalista (ARENA) party, which controlled the National Assembly from 1982 to 1985. D'Aubuisson assembled death squads to eliminate the FMLN revolutionaries and was alleged to have had a hand in the March 24, 1980, assassination of Archbishop Óscar Romero.[13] From 1982 onward, El Salvador settled into a protracted civil war characterized by repression, disappearances, and assassinations.

When the civil war ended in 1992, El Salvador was in a state of disarray. Within a decade, it would succumb to the influence of drug trafficking. Reagan believed that El Salvador, guided by reformists within the Salvadoran military, would deter both the communists and the far right from continuing the violence. Preventing the existing government in El Salvador from collapsing was the goal, although it came at a high cost and through questionable means. The civil war killed an estimated 70,000 to 80,000 people and led to the disappearance of another 8,000. More than a half million Salvadorans became displaced refugees, many fleeing to the United States. Some of their children formed Salvadoran street gangs in the United States, and many were deported back to El Salvador after the war. These gangs would come to dominate El Salvador's criminal underworld during the 1990s. In the postwar era, institutional corruption made the creation of a national force capable of resisting the influence of narcotrafficking nearly impossible. Arms trafficking routes established during the civil war became narcotrafficking routes. At the conclusion of El Salvador's civil war, narcotics replaced the ideological conflict with crime, perpetuating a new cycle of violence from which there seemed to be no escape.

The Secret War in Honduras

Prior to the 1980s, the political situation in Honduras was much different from other Central American nations. In comparison, it had a relatively small population and was one of the poorest nations in Latin America. It never developed an oligarchy that was as powerful as those in other Central American countries because its traditional landowners did not participate in the nineteenth-century agro-export boom. Two large US agro-exporting firms, Vaccaro and the United Fruit Company, owned much of the land and dominated Honduran political life throughout the twentieth century. Because of their economic and political influence, Honduras was characterized as the quintessential banana republic.[14]

By 1982, a variety of economic and social problems in conjunction with Nicaragua's Sandinista revolution led the Honduran government to support anti-Sandinista counterrevolutionaries known as the Contras.[15] Honduras became strategically important because it served as a supply route from Nicaragua to the Salvadoran and Guatemalan guerrillas. In order to stop the flow of arms, Ronald Reagan stepped up US aid to the Honduran military. From 1981 to 1985, the United States provided Honduras with $169 million.[16] During this same period, USAID handed $572 million over to the Honduran government in what was known as the *lluvia de dolares* (the rain of dollars) to help Honduras pay its external debts.[17] In exchange for this aid and with power securely in the hands of the Honduran military, Honduras backed Reagan's policy of supporting Contra forces stationed along the Nicaragua-Honduras border.[18]

40   *Narcostates*

The 570-mile border between Nicaragua and Honduras became a hotbed of subversion. Border incidents broke out as the Sandinistas attempted to disrupt the Contras in Honduras.[19] As part of that effort, the Sandinistas activated dormant guerrilla cells affiliated with the Honduran Communist Party, such as the Movimiento Popular de Liberación (MLP), also known as the Cinchoneros.[20] The Honduran military responded by launching a counterinsurgency program against the radicals that included a death squad known as Battalion 3-16. The conflict intensified between 1986 and 1987 when Sandinista ground troops launched several incursions into Honduras against Contra forces. The Reagan administration cited these attacks as proof that the Sandinistas planned to overthrow the Honduran government.[21] Although the incursions convinced the US Congress to provide the Contras with an extra $100 million in 1986, the subsequent Iran-Contra scandal led to a de-escalation of the border conflict. Fed up with the Reagan administration, the US Congress cut off aid to the Contras, effectively putting an end to the conflict.

The problem for Honduras was that it emerged from the civil war era with weak democratic institutions because of the Honduran military's reliance on US aid. The military governments that had dominated Honduran politics were rife with corruption, and this opened the door to narcotrafficking. The presence of Contra forces also exposed Honduras to narcotrafficking because the Contras were alleged to have used narcotics as a means to finance their counterrevolution after the US Congress imposed aid restrictions in 1984. Furthermore, Honduras lingered in poverty, making it one of the poorest countries in the Western Hemisphere. The mixture of weak institutions, economic malaise, and the illicit drug trade would turn Honduras into a narcotrafficking hub in the post–civil war era.

The Nicaraguan Revolution: A Revolution Betrayed?

The January 1978 assassination of *La Prensa* newspaper owner Joaquín Chamorro commenced a wave of opposition that led to the overthrow of Nicaragua's dictator, Anastasio Somoza Debayle Jr. ("Tachito") in 1979. Chamorro used his paper to criticize the fact that Somoza owned one-third of Nicaragua's registered property and had built up a $300 million fortune by running a large network of national industries.[22] Opposition to Somoza grew following the military's mismanagement of a 6.2 magnitude earthquake that devastated the center of Managua in December 1972. Then, in 1974, a group of thirteen guerrillas from the Frente Sandinista de Liberación Nacional (FSLN) raided a party of a wealthy businessman and took the foreign minister hostage. The FSLN, known as the Sandinistas, were a

"Cocaine Guns" and Civil War in Central America   41

Marxist-Leninist guerrilla group formed in 1961.[23] They received international support from Cuba and stated in their Historic Program that they would govern through a "revolutionary structure."[24] As a result of the military crackdown following the raid, the Sandinistas gathered momentum, reaching a crescendo in 1979.[25]

The Somoza regime imploded as the Sandinistas prepared for their final offensive.[26] A Sandinista raid on the Congressional National Palace in August 1978 led by Comandante Edén Pastora ("Comandante Cero") that took nearly 1,500 prisoners won the popular imagination of the Nicaraguan people opposed to Somoza. The National Guard's reprisals on civilians following the September Insurrection of 1978 completely discredited the regime.[27] Constant criticism and military pressure demoralized the National Guard, paving the way for the Sandinistas to launch their final offensive in June 1979.[28] Within weeks, the Sandinistas held the countryside, the majority of the cities, and half of Managua. On July 19, 1979, Somoza resigned. Within twenty-four hours, the National Guard disintegrated and the Sandinistas seized power.[29]

Nationwide celebrations swept Nicaragua following the defeat of Somoza, but fulfilling the promises of the revolution was a separate matter. Despite Sandinista promises to the Organization of American States (OAS) to hold free elections and to pursue a nonaligned foreign policy, questions about their intentions arose. The FSLN excluded the middle-class business sector from the governing process even though it had been crucial to the Sandinista victory. By excluding the Social Christian and the Conservative parties, the FSLN filled the most important cabinet positions with party members.[30] In their *72-Hour Document*, the Sandinistas stated that they only worked with other anti-Somoza forces as a tactical maneuver "until they were able to consolidate their dominance over Nicaragua." They also stated that their true enemy was the United States, that they supported revolution throughout Latin America, and that they must build an army to assure the "revolutionary loyalty" of the Nicaraguan people.[31]

The Sandinista revolution elevated Central America to the center of US foreign policy. Secure in their success, the Sandinistas overtly and covertly promoted revolution among neighboring Central American nations. The Sandinistas also began a rapid military buildup and deepened their ties to Cuba and the Soviet Union. In 1984, they received Soviet military aid in the form of Mi-24 assault helicopters, radar-controlled air defense weaponry, and T-55 tanks, which gave Nicaragua a military advantage over its neighbors.[32] Nicaraguan military assistance to guerrillas in El Salvador, Guatemala, and Honduras turned the region's internal conflicts into an international issue. Perceiving that the Sandinista victory was part of a larger Soviet effort to expand their influence worldwide, the Reagan administration developed

42   Narcostates

the Reagan Doctrine, which backed anticommunist counterrevolutionaries throughout the world. In Nicaragua, they were known as the Contras.

The Contra War

In opposition to the Sandinista government, the United States began openly—and then covertly—supporting the Contras, who were mobilizing in Honduras and Costa Rica. Internal Nicaraguan support for the Contras came from cattle ranchers and agricultural producers, the Catholic Church hierarchy, and the Miskito Indians living along the Atlantic Coast who objected to various Sandinista policies. The initial support the Sandinistas received from the workers and campesinos eroded and shifted over to the Contras. The Contras were split into two camps—one operating out of Honduras, the other out of Costa Rica. The Costa Rican organization called themselves the Alianza Revolucionaria Democrática (ARDE), while the Honduran organization was initially known as the Fuerza Democrática Nicaragüense (FDN).[33] In 1985, the FDN was reorganized into the Unión Nicaragüense Opositora (UNO), as further defections to the Contras occurred following the 1984 national elections, which were considered fraudulent by the anti-Sandinista opposition.[34]

The US Congress provided aid to the Contras but limited their funding solely for the purpose of stopping Nicaraguan weapons from reaching Central American guerrillas, particularly the insurgency in El Salvador.[35] Secretly, though, the Reagan administration hoped that the aid would be used to make "the Contras strong enough to the point where the Sandinistas will come to the bargaining table, but not so strong so that they would be able to overthrow the Nicaraguan government."[36] Concerned that the Reagan administration might escalate the conflict along the lines of the Vietnam War, Democrats in Congress passed the Boland Amendments in 1983 and 1985 to put limits on the administration's Contra policy.[37] However, those restrictions did not deter the administration's efforts to subvert the Sandinista government. To get around congressional restrictions, the administration employed the CIA to covertly supply the Contras. When the Sandinistas shot down a C-123 plane carrying contraband for the Contras, the CIA's Contra operations went public. This event led to the 1986 Iran-Contra affair and the indictments of Reagan's National Security Council (NSC) chiefs Robert McFarlane and John Poindexter, Secretary of Defense Caspar Weinberger, and, most importantly, NSC staff member Lieutenant Colonel Oliver North.[38] Iran-Contra irreparably damaged the administration's ability to carry out its Central American policy. Moreover, it was from this scandal that the general public also caught a glimpse of Contra cocaine smuggling used to finance their operations.

With the Reagan administration mired in the Iran-Contra affair, the military phase of the Contra War ended. The de-escalation of hostilities led

"Cocaine Guns" and Civil War in Central America   43

to a renewal of the Contadora peace process, which had stalled in 1984.[39] On February 14, 1989, five Central American nations decided to enforce a peace plan proposed by Costa Rican President Óscar Arias. Known as Esquipulas I and II, the plan required all Central American governments to stop aiding guerrillas in other countries, to negotiate ceasefires with rebels along international borders, and to hold free elections.[40] Accordingly, Nicaraguan President Ortega agreed to hold elections in February 1990. Because intermittent fighting still occurred, a UN peacekeeping force was sent to Nicaragua to ensure that all sides honored their political and military commitments. With US backing, Violeta Chamorro, the wife of assassinated newspaper publisher Joaquín Chamorro, won the presidency. Daniel Ortega gave up his position as president in a peaceful transition of power, but the Sandinistas retained control over many parts of the Nicaraguan government, including the defense and interior ministries, the military, and the police. In the days ahead, Chamorro faced a difficult power struggle with the FSLN.

Costa Rica's Democracy Tested

As the oldest and most stable government in Central America, Costa Rica's economic and social structure was unlike any other in the region. Because its economy did not depend on mining or a large agro-export economy, Costa Rica never developed a landed oligarchy. However, a coffee export boom during the late nineteenth century altered the nation's political landscape in favor of coffee growers who acquired government connections. Fraudulent elections and periods of civil unrest became more frequent until coffee grower José Figueres Ferrer reversed this trend and established a stable democracy during the Revolution of 1948.[41] Figueres's revolution brought about a revision of Costa Rica's constitution and established mechanisms to hold fair elections, as well as the abolition of the army, though the decision to abolish the army was not without consequence. Costa Rica became reliant on outside powers such as the United States to guarantee its sovereignty, while at the same time, Nicaraguan guerrillas and later drug traffickers would use it as a base of operations and a transit zone without much interference.

During the 1980s, Costa Rica suffered from an economic crisis. Costa Rica had borrowed heavily from foreign governments to finance its growth, bureaucracy, and welfare system.[42] Due to world price fluctuations for its major exports (coffee and bananas), and increased prices for imported oil, Costa Rica encountered a balance of payments crisis.[43] As a remedy, the government implemented higher taxes and austerity measures, but the consequences of this decision meant higher costs for government services as unemployment surged. President Monge Álvarez (1982–1986) cut off aid to the Ministry of Agriculture, resulting in an increase in landless

44 Narcostates

campesinos who clashed with the government after squatting on idle land. It had become apparent that Costa Rica's prosperity was based on an economic shell game that relied on borrowed money.

The escalation of Nicaragua's civil war and Sandinista-sponsored subversion also tested the resiliency of Costa Rica's democratic institutions. During Nicaragua's revolution, Costa Rica gave tacit approval for the Sandinistas to receive arms shipments from Panama, Venezuela, and Cuba.[44] After the revolution, protecting weapons caches stored in Costa Rica became important to the Sandinistas because they could be sold on the black market or transferred to the FMLN in El Salvador.[45] Inspired by the Nicaraguan revolution and with Cuban and Nicaraguan encouragement, Costa Rican radicals such as the Movimiento Revolucionario del Pueblo (MRP) and the Partido Revolucionario de los Trabajadores Centroamericanos (PRTC) conducted a series of subversive activities to undermine the Costa Rican government.[46] The government viewed workers' demands for better social conditions as communist provocations.[47] With the presence of the ARDE on Costa Rica's Nicaraguan border, the Sandinistas facilitated a bomb plot to kill Edén Pastora and Alfonso Robelo.[48] In 1982, Costa Rica established the Organización de Emergencia Nacional (OEN), a 10,000-man quasi-military unit, to deal with threats of subversion.[49] The Nicaraguan conflict had become a danger to Costa Rica's democracy because many viewed the need to form the OEN as a step toward eroding the country's constitution.

Costa Rica's democratic stability is a fable of history. After its 1948 revolution, Costa Rica lived on borrowed time. By 1980, inherent problems appeared in its model of growth. An economic meltdown aggravated by the Central American civil wars exposed the fragility of its democracy. As conditions deteriorated, Costa Rican subversives dabbled in armed conflict. With no standing military and a weak economy, Costa Rica was nearly paralyzed. It played the role of an active, willing sanctuary for the Sandinistas to launch their revolution. After the Sandinista revolution, Costa Rica's weak military apparatus tolerated the Contras on its soil. When the Contra War ended, the weakness of its security services left it vulnerable to narcotraffickers.

Narcotrafficking and the Central American Conflicts

Noriega: Whose Man in Panama?

The story of Manuel Noriega begins with his 1969 appointment as the chief of the Guardia Nacional de Panamá's intelligence branch (G2) by military

"Cocaine Guns" and Civil War in Central America 45

strongman Omar Torrijos (1968–1981). In this position, Noriega acted as a go-between for the US and Cuban intelligence services and as a representative of the Medellín cartel. Through their Floridian accountant Milian Rodríguez, the Medellín cartel employed Noriega to launder money for them. Rodríguez testified during his trial that the Medellín cartel initially used National Guard officers to launder money for them between 1976 and 1979. In 1979, Noriega, representing the National Guard, negotiated an agreement with the cartel to provide services for their money laundering operations, taking a percentage off the top for himself.[50]

In 1980, he provided weapons and an active sanctuary in Panama for the Cuban-backed Movimiento Abril 19 (M-19) guerrillas. In 1981, the M-19 kidnapped the daughter of Medellín cartel kingpin Fabio Ochoa to extort money for their cause, precipitating a war between the cartel and the M-19. The guerrillas were overwhelmed by the cartel's paramilitary force, Muerte a Secuestradores (MAS), and sued for peace.[51] Because Noriega maintained contact with Cuba and the cartel, both parties asked for his mediation. As a result, he arranged for the Cuban ambassador to Colombia, Fernando Ravelo-Renedo, to serve as a liaison between the cartel and the M-19.[52]

Noriega became the de facto leader of Panama after being promoted to general and given command of the National Guard in August 1983. In that position, he allowed the Medellín cartel to move into Panama. Carlos Lehder, a cofounder of the Medellín cartel, claimed that Noriega sent a lawyer to the cartel with a message stating that "if they wished to do business in Panama, the general was ready to listen."[53] By 1983, Noriega was laundering billions of dollars for the Medellín cartel, often meeting its money-laden planes at Tocumen International Airport. Floyd Carlton, Manuel Noriega's personal pilot, testified that Pablo Escobar and the Medellín cartel's accountant, Gustavo Gaviria Rivero (Escobar's cousin), paid Noriega $200,000 to $300,000 per load flown by Carlton from Colombia to Panama. Noriega laundered his proceeds using the Bank of Commerce and Credit International (BCCI).[54] The BCCI laundered money for anyone regardless of their political affiliation, serving clients such as the CIA, British MI-6, Israeli Mossad, Pakistani Inter-Services Intelligence, Colombian drug cartels, and Middle Eastern "terrorists" such as Abu Nidal.[55]

Through the BCCI, Noriega facilitated the Harari Network, a secret Contra operation established by the Reagan administration and the Israeli government in 1982. The Harari Network integrated the movement of Contra supplies with the movement of cocaine for Colombia's Medellín and Cali cartels. The BCCI also played a large role in the Iran-Contra affair. Initially, Israel was used as a middleman with the Iranians, but Oliver North cut them out and proposed that the net profits from the sale of antitank missiles to Iran could be diverted to the Contras.[56] As part of the Iran-Contra operation, the CIA used the BCCI to provide short-term credit for the sale

46   Narcostates

of roughly 1,000 missiles to Iran. The transaction ran through the BCCI, which diverted the net profit to a Credit Suisse account used by North to finance the Contras.[57]

With Noriega's permission, the Medellín cartel set up a cocaine processing plant at La Palma on the Panamanian border with Colombia. To get this facility underway, the cartel gave a $4 million payoff to Noriega. On May 29, 1984, the Fuerzas de Defensa de Panamá (PDF) shut down the facility. Although Noriega received an estimated $4 to $7 million to provide a safe haven for the cartel's operations, the PDF conducted this raid because the Colombian government pressured Noriega to act against the Medellín cartel after it assassinated Colombian minister of justice Rodrigo Lara Bonilla in April 1984. Noriega constantly fended off charges by Panamanian opposition groups who accused him of being involved in the drug trade. The raid on La Palma was intended to divert attention away from his narcotics-related activities.[58]

Because Noriega had deceived them, the Medellín cartel threatened to have him killed. Under duress, Noriega traveled to England to put some distance between himself and the Medellín cartel. According to his intelligence aide, José Blandón, on Noriega's return trip to Panama, he stopped in Cuba to ask for Fidel Castro's mediation. Castro helped him because he feared that if Noriega was removed from power, his own dealings in Panama, Colombia, and Central America would come to an end.[59] José Blandón reported that Castro acted as a mediator between the Medellín cartel and Noriega because Castro believed that he needed "to have an influence over Colombia's drug trafficking world" if he was going "to have influence over Colombia's political world."[60] Castro and Noriega agreed that Noriega would return the cartel's La Palma protection money along with the plant's confiscated equipment. At the conclusion of this meeting, Noriega told Blandón "that everything had been arranged and they were going to proceed according to Castro's approval." Nevertheless, Noriega still felt threatened. To guarantee Noriega's safety, Castro dispatched a twenty-five-man unit to accompany Noriega back to Panama.[61]

Tensions between Noriega and the Medellín cartel also grew over the First Interamericas Bank. Noriega had enriched himself by allowing the Medellín and Cali cartels to use the bank for money laundering operations. The First Interamericas Bank was owned by Jorge Ochoa Vásquez, a Medellín cartel leader, and Gilberto Rodríguez Orejuela, a Cali cartel founding member. They had known each other since childhood, and at that time, both cartels were not interfering in each other's markets. In 1985, the United States pressured Noriega to close the First Interamericas Bank for being a money laundering front that violated Panamanian banking laws. Its closure further weakened his relationship with the Medellín cartel and forced the cartel to branch out into Nicaragua and Honduras.[62]

Noriega's manipulation of the warring factions in Central America and his profiteering from the cocaine trade created too much opposition for him to remain in power. Because Noriega became less cooperative with the CIA at a critical time when the CIA's efforts to support the Contras were running into severe logistical and political difficulties within the US Congress, and because Noriega provided ideological and material support to the Sandinistas and the FMLN, he fell out with the US government.[63] Noriega's relationship with the CIA deteriorated in 1986, when details regarding his ties with the Medellín cartel became public in articles written by CIA mouthpiece Seymour Hersh.[64]

On February 4, 1988, a federal grand jury in Miami indicted Noriega and Medellín cartel members Pablo Escobar, Fabio Ochoa, and Jorge Ochoa on multiple narcotics trafficking charges. Consequently, Noriega moved closer to Cuba and Nicaragua. Taking advantage of the situation, Cuba and Nicaragua funneled weapons into Panama and helped Noriega form civilian paramilitary forces called Dignity Battalions.[65] With the war in Nicaragua winding down and an intolerable state of affairs existing in Panama, the United States looked for a pretext to remove him. On the night of December 16, 1989, four US officers were fired upon at a PDF checkpoint outside the Canal Zone. Three days later, the US military launched Operation Just Cause. On January 3, 1990, Noriega surrendered himself to US forces after taking sanctuary for ten days in the apostolic nunciature of the Catholic Church in Panama City.[66]

Like Icarus, Noriega flew too close to the sun. The CIA overlooked his drug trafficking as long as he facilitated their Contra operations. His ties to Cuba and his break with the CIA turned him into a security risk for the United States and its management of the canal. The indictments against him for drug-related activities were simply a means to remove the CIA's man in Panama who had become a liability. By this point, he had solidified Panama as a center of narcotics trafficking and money laundering, with the Medellín cartel clearly extending its influence from Panama into the Central American–Mexican narcocorridor.

Allegations of Sandinista-Cuban Drug Trafficking

In 1985, a study by the US Joint Chiefs of Staff (JCS) recommended that US armed forces interdict narcotrafficking operations in Central America, listing the existence of a narco-guerrilla nexus as a "national security problem."[67] According to Antonio Farach, a former minister to the Nicaraguan embassies in Venezuela and Honduras who defected to the United States in 1983, the Sandinistas became involved in the drug trade because they needed money "for their revolution."[68] A US State Department cable also noted that "Nicaragua's need for hard currency and its desire to foment

48 Narcostates

instability by providing arms to Latin American guerrilla groups are sufficient motivations to prompt its regime's involvement in illegal international drug trafficking" that it did "for particularly mercenary reasons."[69] The State Department cable alleged that money from narcotics helped Nicaragua pay for its revolution and buy weapons for subversives in Latin America and the Middle East.[70]

The Medellín cartel expanded into Nicaragua when Pablo Escobar sent Floyd Carlton, a pilot for both Noriega and the cartel, to locate airstrips that could accommodate drug-laden aircraft. In the process of doing so, the Medellín cartel developed ties with an aide to Sandinista interior minister Tomás Borge. The aide, Federico Vaughan, gave the cartel permission to keep their own hangar at Los Brasiles Airport, a military airfield northwest of Managua.[71] The existence of the hangar became public in 1986 when Reagan, in an attempt to win congressional funding for the Contras, alleged that the Sandinistas were involved in drug trafficking. In a national television address, Reagan showed pictures taken in 1984 by DEA informant Barry Seal at the Los Brasiles Airport.[72] In those pictures, Vaughan was filmed loading cocaine onto a plane with Pablo Escobar.[73] After Reagan went public, the DEA refused to implicate the "Minister of the Interior or other Nicaraguan officials," but did confirm that a "junior aide to Interior Minister [Vaughan] was indicted in 1984 for drug trafficking."[74] Although the United States could not link any Sandinista official directly to Pablo Escobar or Jorge Ochoa, a State Department cable noted that Vaughan worked for Borge's import and export firm, the H&M Corporation.[75]

Those who doubted the administration's story believed that Los Brasiles might have been a black propaganda operation to defame the Sandinista government just when the Reagan administration was seeking more Contra aid.[76] Using Barry Seal to provide evidence against the Sandinista government added further skepticism surrounding the Reagan administration's assertions. At one time, Seal worked for both the CIA and the Medellín cartel. Because disinformation is a CIA trademark, the Los Brasiles operation was placed under heavy scrutiny and partially discredited owing to Seal's shadowy past.[77]

Although doubts surrounding the Vaughan-Escobar sting remained, the Robert Vesco case added to the allegations that linked Federico Vaughan and the Sandinista government to narcotrafficking. Robert Vesco was a notorious money launderer and narcotics trafficker who fled the United States under duress in 1972.[78] In 1981, while residing in Nassau, Vesco worked with Carlos Lehder to smuggle narcotics from Lehder's Bahamian lair in Norman's Cay. Following the breakup of Lehder's operation in 1982, Vesco fled the Bahamas and received protection from the Sandinista government. In Nicaragua, Vesco became involved in drug smuggling once again. According to the congressional testimony of James Herring, a narcotics trafficker who "voluntarily" became a US government informant in 1983, Vesco helped the Nicaraguan government build a cocaine processing laboratory near Managua.[79] Herring disclosed that an unidentified Colombian rebel group utilized Vaughan's diplomatic immunity to smuggle money and drugs into Nicaragua. Herring claimed that as the operation progressed, Vesco procured the money for the cocaine, and the Sandinistas provided the security. From their sales, Vesco and Vaughan divided the proceeds. Herring quoted Vaughan as saying that the money that the "Nicaraguans were getting out of this sale" would "go back into their economy." Herring also met Tomás Borge, who told him, "We appreciate your help." To give legitimacy to his testimony, Herring passed a polygraph test. Despite his background and questionable motivations, Herring's testimony was cited as evidence that the Sandinistas permitted traffickers to use Nicaragua as a base to transport cocaine.[80]

The Sandinistas responded to the charges against them by saying that they considered "it one more try of the Reagan administration to discredit the government of Nicaragua."[81] In January 1985, a Sandinista communiqué announced that the "false allegations against it" originated with Medellín cartel member Jorge Luis Ochoa and Cali cartel member Gilberto Rodríguez Orejuela. The Sandinistas stated that the two men made the claim so as to prevent their extradition to the United States from Spain after they were arrested while attempting to establish a cocaine network in Europe.[82]

The 1982 Guillot Lara case raised allegations that the Cuban government also facilitated drug trafficking. Juan Lazaro Pérez, also known as "Johnny Crump," a convicted Colombian drug dealer and associate of Guillot Lara, a Colombian marijuana smuggler, provided much of the evidence in this case. In 1979, Crump and Guillot Lara met with Ravelo-Renedo, the Cuban ambassador to Colombia, and requested permission to use Cuba as a layover for their loads. Crump testified that around 1980, René Rodríguez Cruz, a member of the Central Committee of the Communist Party of Cuba, authorized the plan and instructed Gonzalo Bassols-Suárez, Cuba's first secretary to Colombia, to act as an intermediary between Lara and the Cuban government.[83] Crump, Lara, and the Cubans struck a deal in which Cuba agreed to provide safe passage for the narcotics-laden vessels in exchange for $500,000 per shipment.[84]

Because of several mishaps, Crump and Lara's venture with the Cubans failed. Crump and Lara barely broke even, but the Cubans still expected payment. Seeing an opportunity, the Cuban Dirección General de Inteligencia (DGI), took advantage of Crump and Lara's compromised position. The DGI proposed that in order for Crump and Lara to pay their debt, they should smuggle weapons to the M-19 guerrillas in Colombia.

50   Narcostates

The DGI also believed that since Lara and Jaime Bateman (the leader of the M-19) were old schoolmates, their former association would facilitate the operation.[85]

The M-19 operation was as unsuccessful as their previous operation. One ship sank and another was seized. Lara was forced to go into hiding. In 1982, Lara's associate, Johnny Crump, was arrested in Miami for narcotics trafficking. In exchange for his testimony, he received a twenty-five-year suspended sentence with six years of probation. Crump's other accomplices verified his testimony after their arrest by US authorities. From their combined testimony the United States tried René Rodríguez Cruz, Vice Admiral Aldo Santamaría Cuadrado, Ambassador Fernando Ravelo-Renedo, and Cuban First Secretary Gonzalo Bassols-Suárez in absentia.[86] According to DEA Special Agent in Charge Peter Gruden, "We are not saying this is the policy of the Cuban government. . . . We don't know and we have not suggested there is a conspiracy by the Cuban government in general."[87]

Another case that implicated the Cuban government came from the testimony of Mario Estévez González. Estévez González was a former sergeant in the Cuban Ministry of the Interior (MININT). In 1981, he was arrested by the United States while transporting 2,500 pounds of marijuana off the Florida coast. Facing many years in prison, in 1983 he supplied evidence against the Cuban government in exchange for immunity. Under oath before Congress, Estévez González testified that the DGI undertook a top-secret operation to grow and smuggle high-grade marijuana into the United States. He also claimed that Aldo Santamaría, a vice admiral in the Cuban navy, told him, "We are finally going to have a drug store in the U.S."[88]

After his arrest in 1987 and in exchange for a sentence reduction, Carlos Lehder made further claims about Cuban and Nicaraguan drug trafficking during the trial of Manuel Noriega. In November 1991, Lehder testified that he had met with Nicaraguan officials in 1984 to discuss moving cocaine through Nicaragua. He stated that the Medellín cartel chose Nicaragua as an alternative to Panama because Noriega had become increasingly greedy. He also alleged that the Cubans were behind Nicaragua's drug smuggling. According to Lehder, "the Cubans were in charge of that cocaine conspiracy in Nicaragua." He added that after "several meetings in Managua" while acting on behalf of the Medellín cartel's transportation operations, "it was the Cubans" who took charge of organizing the cocaine network from Nicaragua to the United States. He added that the "Nicaraguans wouldn't move a finger" without the approval of the Cuban government and the head of the DGI's Americas Department, Manuel Piñeiro Losada. Lehder also claimed that he twice met with Raúl Castro, Cuba's minister of defense, and the chief of Cuba's special forces Colonel Antonio de la Guardia, to obtain permission to fly cocaine shipments over Cuban airspace.[89]

The arrest of Reinaldo Ruiz in 1989 provided evidence that led to Cuba's greatest scandal. Ruiz ran a cocaine smuggling ring that shipped 1,000-pound loads of cocaine into the United States. Ruiz testified that cocaine was transported to Florida using the Cuban base at Varadero with the full cooperation of Colonel Pardo, the commander of naval operations at the base. Ruiz claimed that his son, Ruben, would fly cocaine from Colombia to Varadero, where it would be transferred to Ruiz's boat by members of the Cuban military and MININT. According to Fidel Castro, the testimony of Reinaldo Ruiz and information from Colombian sources would lead to the Arnaldo Ochoa and Antonio de la Guardia cases.[90]

On June 15, 1989, Colonel Antonio de la Guardia, General Arnaldo Ochoa Sánchez, and twelve subordinates were denounced by Raúl Castro and jailed on corruption and drug trafficking charges. Ochoa and de la Guardia's alleged crimes were not connected, but both men were charged with treason. De la Guardia was charged with the crime of smuggling six tons of Colombian cocaine, worth $3.4 million between 1987 and 1988. Ochoa, a military hero from the Cuban revolution who also fought in Angola and Ethiopia, was brought up on three charges. The most important charge was that he conspired with Pablo Escobar to build coca refineries in Cuba in order to send cocaine shipments to the United States.[91] On July 13, 1989, a firing squad executed both Ochoa and de la Guardia. Their executions showed that Cuba was willing to prosecute traffickers, but at the same time, they showed that Cuba could no longer maintain that it had an unimpeachable record on drugs. Other observers alleged that Castro ordered their executions because both men were Castro's political rivals.[92]

The US-Contra Connection and Drug Trafficking

When the 1984 Boland Amendment blocked Contra funding, the Contras allegedly began to participate in the narcotics trade in order to garner revenue. As the Reagan administration leveled charges against the Sandinista government, the Sandinistas countered by accusing the CIA-backed Contras. The US State Department responded by claiming that they had "no evidence to support charges that the Nicaraguan armed resistance" was "involved in drug trafficking."[93] Despite this denial, evidence existed that pointed to the contrary.

Senator John Kerry's 1986 report launched the inquiry into Contra narcotics trafficking. Kerry initially investigated the Honduran-based FDN Contras for their involvement in gunrunning, drug trafficking, and terrorist activity.[94] He found no substantial evidence against them, but during the investigation, Costa Rican security forces arrested Adolfo "Popo" Chamorro,

52   Narcostates

the second in command of the ARDE in Costa Rica.[95] At the time, the CIA alleged that it had cut off all direct assistance to the ARDE because it knew that ARDE personnel trafficked in narcotics, although it continued to use trusted intermediaries (cutouts) to covertly supply the ARDE.[96] This covert supply operation turned into a drugs-for-guns enterprise running out of Costa Rica.

When the ARDE was formed in 1983, Costa Rica was ill-equipped to deal with the threat posed by the Colombian cartels. During their insurrection, the Sandinistas maintained air bases in Costa Rica to import Panamanian, Cuban, and Venezuelan weapons. After the Sandinistas overthrew the Somoza regime, those air bases were used for drug trafficking.[97] According to former CIA contract pilot Tosh Plumlee, drug smugglers used the Santa Elena airstrip in northern Costa Rica "for years, even before Lieutenant Colonel Oliver North came looking for a staging area for arms flights into Nicaragua's Southern Front."[98] Following the formation of the ARDE, the Costa Rican airfields became conduits for the movement of guns and drugs. According to Karl Prado, an officer within the ARDE, "drug traffickers approached political groups like the ARDE" to make "deals in order to camouflage their activities."[99]

Evidence also emerged from the Kerry investigation that the Costa Rican ranch of US citizen John Hull had become a staging point for the Contras to run guns and drugs. According to a CIA cable, traffickers used the ranch for "smuggling in the paste and that some of the people who live in the area have been associated with contraband/drug smuggling." At the ranch, traffickers exchanged cocaine brought in from Panama or Colombia for weapons carried in from Ilopango Air Force Base in El Salvador. Between 1983 and 1986, the pilots carried the cocaine from Hull's ranch back to Ilopango or flew directly on to Miami.[100] A Costa Rican investigation of Hull and his ranch alleged that Manuel Noriega provided the pilots used by Lieutenant Colonel Oliver North to resupply the Contras. Prior to his falling out with the US government, Noriega's pilots flew weapons from Panama to Costa Rica to the Contras, where the weapons were offloaded. The planes then continued to the United States loaded with cocaine.[101]

Jack Terrell, a contractor for a private Contra supply organization, Civilian Military Assistance, substantiated Kerry's allegations. Terrell claimed he participated in both the Honduran and Costa Rican supply operations. He alleged that Hull was a narcotrafficker and moved cocaine to the United States.[102] Costa Rica indicted Hull in January 1989 but released him pending his trial. In July 1989, while awaiting trial, Hull, with the assistance of the DEA, fled to Haiti and then to the United States. The Costa Rican government demanded his extradition, but the United States refused. In the end, Costa Rica abandoned its effort to prosecute Hull.

An important figure in the Contra drugs-for-arms efforts was Juan Matta-Ballesteros, who owned SETCO airline. SETCO was contracted by the CIA to deliver weapons to the Contras. Matta-Ballesteros was a well-known trafficker who maintained close ties to the Honduran government and military after he helped Policarpo Paz García seize power in 1978. Matta-Ballesteros also played an important role in bringing the Medellín and Guadalajara cartels together.[103] According to SETCO pilot Tosh Plumlee, SETCO transported drugs and weapons between Costa Rica, Honduras, and Mexico on behalf of the Medellín-Guadalajara network established by Matta-Ballesteros. Plumlee alleged that the cartels, assisted by the CIA and with the protection of the Mexican DFS, used a ranch in Veracruz owned by Caro Quintero to supply the Contras and transport cocaine into Mexico.[104] Due to public revelations surrounding Matta-Ballesteros's involvement in narcotics trafficking, the CIA replaced SETCO as a Contra supply source in 1985. US Customs officials became suspicious of SETCO after they seized 5,000 kilos of cocaine in containers shipped by SETCO from Honduras to Florida.[105] Further investigations into the Contras and SETCO revealed other drug smuggling networks associated with the airline. Senator Kerry's investigation reported that "one of the pilots selected to fly Contra missions for SETCO was Frank Moss, who had been under investigation as an alleged drug trafficker since 1979."[106] In 1985, Moss formed his own air transport company to supply the Contras, called Hondu-Carib. In 1987, the DEA seized a plane owned by Hondu-Carib that linked the company to a drugs-for-guns operation with the Contras. Following the seizure, the DEA confiscated its business papers and discovered the names and telephone numbers of two CIA officers, making it nearly impossible for the CIA to deny their involvement with Hondu-Carib.[107]

Oliver North's diary provided further evidence of a Contra-CIA drug link using Hondu-Carib. North speculated that Mario Calero, the FDN's supply officer and brother to FDN leader Adolfo Calero, worked with Frank Moss to smuggle narcotics on a DC-6 supply plane that operated out of Honduras and New Orleans. North also wrote in his diary that General Secord told him that $14 million worth of weapons stored in a Honduran warehouse for Contra use "came from drugs."[108] The Sandinistas alleged that much of the money for humanitarian aid ended up in the personal bank accounts of Contra leaders and was used to finance illegal activities such as drug smuggling.[109]

Another operation associated with Oliver North that also involved Noriega and the FDN Contras was DIACSA, a Miami-based airplane parts and supply company that operated in Costa Rica. Floyd Carlton, Noriega's personal pilot, used DIACSA to plan smuggling ventures, to assemble large cash proceeds from narcotics transactions, and to place telephone calls for narcotics ventures. Carlton also coordinated landing strips in

Panama and Costa Rica to refuel and move cocaine northward. Even though the president of DIACSA, Alfredo Caballero, was under investigation for cocaine trafficking and money laundering, he received a contract from the State Department's Nicaraguan Humanitarian Assistance Office (NHAO) to provide supplies for the Contras. On April 1, 1985, North wrote in his diary that NHAO contractor Robert Owen warned him about FDN Comandante José Robelo's "potential involvement with drug-running" and FDN Comandante Sebastián González's involvement with "drug-running out of Panama."[110] Between 1984 and 1985, the FDN employed DIACSA to deposit money into Contra coffers through interaccount transfers. In other words, DIACSA served as a means for North to launder money for the Contras in order to circumvent congressional prohibitions on aid. Despite the indictments against Caballero and Carlton in 1985, the State Department continued to use DIACSA to deliver humanitarian aid to the Contras.[111]

Published by the *San Jose Mercury News*, Gary Webb's 1996 "Dark Alliance" series reignited the controversy surrounding the CIA and the FDN. Webb's investigation centered on information that the FBI had arrested a high-ranking FDN leader named Oscar Danilo Blandón Reyes for narcotics trafficking. According to Webb, Blandón Reyes told the US Department of Justice that he was under the protection of the CIA and that the profits were for "the Contra revolution." Blandón Reyes also claimed that he received orders from Juan Norwin Meneses Cantarero, a convicted drug dealer and known associate of FDN leader Adolfo Calero.[112] A 1984 DEA report confirmed Webb's allegation that the DEA suspected as far back as 1976 that Meneses Cantarero was a major cocaine trafficker.[113] In 2014, Coral Baca, the person who put Webb on to the original story, gave an interview in which she alleged she had counted the cash that Adolfo Calero "picked up [in] duffel bags full of drug money" multiple times at Contra fundraisers in the San Francisco Bay Area during the 1980s.[114]

Despite Webb's evidence, US authorities blocked his attempt to delve deeper into the case. Federal prosecutors obtained a court order blocking Webb's access to documents that tied Blandón Reyes to the CIA. In the *Washington Post* and the *Los Angeles Times*, Webb's story faced a great deal of scrutiny from reporters who discredited it for failing to provide any substantial proof of a CIA-Contra link.[115] The discrediting of Webb's reporting damaged his career. Webb stated that the reason for the distortion of his work was that "the press had gone from being a watchdog to being a guard dog." Webb also blamed the failure to substantiate his allegations on his editors, who omitted parts of his story. Webb left the *San Jose Mercury News* in 1997. In 1998, despite twenty-six rejections, Webb published his book, *The Dark Alliance*.[116] The book was generally ignored; what Webb uncovered still has yet to see the full light of day.

The Legacy of Drugs and Civil War

Central America's civil wars demoralized a generation or two. In Guatemala, there were 150,000–200,000 dead, roughly 1,000,000 internal refugees, and 400,000 displaced refugees.[117] In El Salvador, 70,000–80,000 had been killed and 500,000 had been displaced as refugees. In Nicaragua, revolution, violence, and conflict took the lives of more than 10,000 people between 1978 and 1979 and an estimated 10,000–43,000 more between 1981 and 1989. While the numbers for Costa Rica and Honduras were negligible in comparison, they also suffered from the effects of war with the erosion of their democratic principles and liberties. The Sandinista revolution, the subsequent Contra War, and the conflicts in Guatemala and El Salvador turned the 1980s into a decade of repression in Central America. By the 1990s, neither the guerrillas nor the counterrevolutionaries could achieve victory as exhaustion set in. The problem facing Central America was how to establish a new order in the post–civil war era.

During the civil wars, lawlessness and the need to finance revolution and counterrevolution opened the door to narcotrafficking, deeply impacting Guatemala, El Salvador, Nicaragua, and Honduras. To varying degrees and with different aims, many actors—Contras, Panamanians, Colombians, Cubans, Sandinistas, and agents of the US government—facilitated narcotrafficking through Central America. Ian Fleming's quote, "Once is happenstance. Twice is coincidence. The third time it's enemy action," rings true when all of the evidence is analyzed.[118] A great deal of circumstantial evidence pointed to some type of Contra, Sandinista, and Cuban involvement in drugs-for-guns operations. Likewise, Panama under Noriega could not escape the scourge. In every instance, the Colombian Medellín cartel is conspicuously present. Although the evidence against Manuel Noriega was suppressed until it was politically convenient, the US indictment of Noriega on drug trafficking charges became the justification for the 1989 US invasion of Panama. In the case of Cuba and Nicaragua, much of the evidence depended on the testimony of convicted drug dealers and intelligence agents, who may have told their interrogators anything they wanted to hear in order to escape harsh sentencing. The only real evidence of Cuban involvement in narcotrafficking came from the de la Guardia and Ochoa cases. With regard to the Contras, much of the evidence comes from Senator Kerry's report, which also relied on circumstantial evidence. While Kerry provided evidence that members of the ARDE trafficked in narcotics, there is enough plausible deniability to prevent the establishment of any direct link to the CIA or other Contra organizations. As Gary Webb found out, any further investigation into CIA or Contra drug smuggling would entail access to classified documents that will never be made public. The same point can be made about the Cuban and Nicaraguan governments, where access to

56 Narcostates

government archives is even more restricted. Nevertheless, continued US government cover-ups for illegal covert activities only serve to undermine public faith in US government institutions.[119]

By the mid-1990s, restoring the peace—not the movement of drugs— was the main priority. Balancing the peace against new security arrangements became an obstacle to establishing postwar stability in each country. New counternarcotics programs that increased police power, combined with the potential for that power to be abused, became a major impediment to the development of Central American counternarcotics programs. Seeing an opening, the Colombian and Mexican drug trafficking organizations (DTOs) took advantage of the weak authority vested in Central America's military, judicial, and police institutions during the post–civil war era.

Recent narcotrafficking and gang security crises in Central America are inextricably linked to the events of the 1980s. The civil wars in Central America weakened the entire region and transformed it into a stepping-stone for the Colombian cartels. By 1990, the Colombian and Mexican DTOs were moving tons of cocaine through Central America into Mexico. As the Colombian cartels faded, the Mexican DTOs filled the void by dominating narcotrafficking activities from South America to Central America, Mexico, and the United States. While insurgency and cocaine production became the center of attention in Colombia, narcopower shifted to the Mexican DTOs. The development of those DTOs, their hold over Mexico, and their takeover of the drug trade during the 1980s–1990s will be examined next.

Notes

1. Alexander Cockburn and Jeffery St. Clair, *Whiteout: The CIA, Drugs, and the Press* (New York: Verso Books, 1998), 1–418; Peter Dale Scott and Jonathan Marshall, *Cocaine Politics: Drugs, Armies, and the CIA in Central America* (Berkeley: University of California Press, 1991), 1–279; Gary Webb, *Dark Alliance: The CIA, Contras, and the Crack Cocaine Explosion* (Toronto: Hudson House, 1998), 1–592; Rachel Ehrenfeld, *Narco-Terrorism* (New York: Basic Books, 1990), 1–14; Joseph D. Douglas, *Red Cocaine: The Drugging of America and the West*, 2nd ed. (London: Edward Harle, 1999), 1–182; Alan Cunningham, "Trafficking for a Cause: Cuban Drug Trafficking Operations as Foreign Policy," MA Thesis (Norwich University, 2021) 19–50.

2. J. C. King, Chief Western Hemisphere Division, "Jacobo Árbenz, Ex-President of Guatemala—Operations Against," Memorandum for CI/ICD PP/OPS, Central Intelligence Agency, May 15, 1957, 1; David F. Schmitz, *Thank God They're on Our Side: The United States and Right Wing Dictatorships 1921–1965* (Chapel Hill: University of North Carolina Press, 1999), 1.

3. James Robert Whelan and Franklin A. Jaeckle, *The Soviet Assault on America's Southern Flank* (Washington, DC: Regnery Gateway, 1988), 171. Other guerrilla *focos* included the Ejército Guerrillero de los Pobres—a Leninist movement founded in 1972 by Rolando Morán. In 1979, the Organización Revolucionario del Pueblo en Armas emerged in the southern highlands supported by indigenous Indians.

"Cocaine Guns" and Civil War in Central America 57

4. "The Guerrillas on the Volcano," *The Economist*, September 21, 1985, 41.

5. Whelan and Jaeckle, *Soviet Assault*, 173.

6. Thomas L. Hughes to Secretary of State, "Guatemala: A Counter-Insurgency Running Wild?," Secret Intelligence Note 43, US Department of State, October 23, 1967, 1; US Embassy Guatemala to Secretary of State, Washington, DC, "Subject: Analysis of Rios Montt Government After Eleven Months," Guatemala 01353 181952Z, February 1983, 2.

7. Morton I. Abramowitz to Dave Durenberger, Chairman of the Senate Select Committee on Intelligence, "Secret Letter," US Department of State, July 1986, 2–3. Information collected by Kate Doyle and Carlos Osorio, *US Policy in Guatemala: 1966–1996*, National Security Archive Electronic Briefing Book, No. 11, http://nsarchive.gwu.edu/NSAEBB/NSAEBB11/docs; "The D-2 Conducts Human Rights Investigations," Central Intelligence Agency, November 1989, 1–2. During his presidency, Cerezo Arévalo folded the presidential intelligence service, the Archivos, into the D-2. In 1983, Guatemala's military intelligence changed its name from the G-2 to the D-2.

8. Carlos Osorio, "National Security Archive Briefing Book No. 32: Units and Officers of the Guatemalan Military," National Security Archive, n.d., https://nsarchive2.gwu.edu/NSAEBB/NSAEBB32/vol1.html.

9. Office of African and Latin American Analysis, "El Salvador Significant Political Actors and Their Interaction [redacted]" (Washington, DC: Central Intelligence Agency, April 1984), 1–3. The JRG attempted to implement reforms but suppressed all political opposition. Between 1979 and 1982, the JRG went through three incarnations. Duarte was the last junta leader.

10. Whelan and Jaeckle, *Soviet Assault*, 147–154.

11. Constantine Menges, "Background Paper: Central America" (Washington, DC: Central Intelligence Agency, July 1983), 6–7.

12. Bernard Weinraub, "Cuba Directs Salvadoran Insurgency, Former Guerrilla Lieutenant Says," *New York Times*, July 28, 1983, sec. A, p. 10.

13. US Department of State, *El Salvador: The Search for Peace* (Washington, DC: US Department of State, September 1981), 5; and American Embassy Caracas to RUEHC/Secretary of State Washington, DC, "Subject: Ambassador Kilpatrick's Lunch Conversation with D'Aubuisson and ARENA Leaders," Caracas 01249 141345Z, February 1983, 3. The ARENA Party ruled in a coalition with the Partido de Concertación Nacional.

14. Tom Barry and Deb Preusch, *The Central America Fact Book* (New York: Grove Press, 1986), 251.

15. Menges, "Background Paper: Central America," 10–12; Timothy Ashby, *The Bear in the Back Yard* (New York: Prentice Hall, 1987), 134.

16. US Department of State, *Background Paper: Nicaragua's Military Build-up and Support for Central American Subversion* (Washington, DC: US Department of State, July 18, 1984), 20–28. In 1985, US aid represented 76 percent of Honduras's military budget.

17. Barry and Preusch, *Central America Fact Book*, 258.

18. Steve C. Ropp and James A. Morris, eds., *Central America: Crisis and Adaptation* (Albuquerque: University of New Mexico Press, 1983), 203.

19. US Department of State, *Revolution*, 15. The first incident was July 22, 1979. Twelve more followed.

20. US Department of State, *Background Paper: Central America* (Washington, DC: US Department of State, May 27, 1983), 11–12; Movimiento Popular de Liberación, "Comunicado: Llamamiento al Pueblo Hondureño Para Oponerse a la

58 *Narcostates*

Agresión Imperialista a Centroamérica," Centro de Documentación de los Movimientos Armados, November 20, 1984, www.cedema.org/ver.php?id=2531. The MLP gained notoriety in 1981 when they hijacked a Honduran National Airlines flight, and in 1982 when they seized the Chamber of Commerce in San Pedro Sula. The MLP merged into the Directorio Nacional Unificado–Movimiento de Unidad Revolucionario (DNU-MRH) in 1983 along with the Castroite Movimiento Revolucionario Francisco Morazán (MRFM) and the Partido Revolucionario de los Trabajadores Centroamericanistas de Honduras (PRTC) led by Dr. Antonio María Reyes Mata, who had been with Che Guevara in Bolivia in 1966.

21. Tim Merrill, ed., *Honduras: A Country Study* (Washington: GPO for the Library of Congress, 1995), http://countrystudies.us/honduras. Battalion 3-16 allegedly "disappeared" 140 people.

22. John Tierney, *Somozas and Sandinistas: The U.S. and Nicaragua in the Twentieth Century* (Washington, DC: Council of Interamerican Security, 1982), 53. Somoza owned the airlines, the shipping line, and the cement, textile, coffee, beef, and sugar industries. Tachito succeeded his brother, Luis Somoza Debayle, the effective dictator from 1956 to 1967, and his father, Anastasio Somoza García, dictator from 1933 until his 1956 assassination.

23. Ashby, *Bear in the Back Yard*, 105.

24. Shirley Christian, *Nicaragua: Revolution in the Family* (New York: Vintage Books, 1986), 34.

25. US Department of State, *Revolution Beyond Our Borders* (Washington, DC: US Department of State, September 1985), 3.

26. Morris H. Morley, *Washington, Somoza and the Sandinistas* (Cambridge: Cambridge University Press, 1994), 140.

27. Claribel Alegría and D. J. Flakoll, *Nicaragua: La revolución Sandinista* (Mexico City: Ediciones, 1982), 321–346.

28. William LeoGrande, "The Revolution in Nicaragua: Another Cuba," *Foreign Affairs* 58, no. 1 (Fall 1979): 41.

29. Tierney, *Somozas and Sandinistas*, 65. Somoza left Nicaragua for Guatemala on July 13, 1979. He went into exile in Paraguay, where he was assassinated on September 17, 1980.

30. Christian, *Nicaragua: Revolution*, 130.

31. Frente Sandinista de Liberación Nacional, *The 72-Hour Document: The Sandinista Blueprint for Constructing Communism in Central America* (Washington, DC: Department of State, Coordinator of Public Diplomacy for Latin America and Caribbean, 1986), 1–15.

32. US Department of State, *The Soviet-Cuban Connection in Central America and the Caribbean* (Washington, DC: US Department of State, 1985), 19; US Department of State, "Review of Nicaragua's Commitments to the OAS," *US Department of State Bulletin* 84 (September 1984): 69.

33. Max Singer, "Nicaragua: The Stolen Revolution," US Information Agency, 1983, 1–23. ARDE was composed of members from Pastora's faction and former Sandinistas, such as Alfonso Robelo, a Sandinista junta member and leader of the business-oriented Movimiento Democrático Nicaragüense (MDN), Edmundo Chamorro's Fuerzas Armadas Revolucionarias Nicaragüenses (FARN), the Consejo Superior de la Empresa Privada (COSEP), and Miskito Indians led by Brooklyn Rivera. The FDN was formed in 1981 and was composed of two groups: the Legión 15 de Septiembre, made up of students and members of Somoza's National Guard led by Enrique Bermúdez Varela (Somoza's military attaché to Washington), and the Unión Democrática Nicaragüense (UDN), led by José

"Cocaine Guns" and Civil War in Central America   59

Francisco Cardenal, the president of the Nicaraguan Chamber of Construction. As Sandinista problems with northern peasants and Miskito Indians grew, the Alanzia por el Progreso del Miskitos and Sumos (ALPROMISU) led by Steadman Fagoth joined the FDN.

34. Edward Cody, "Nicaraguan Vote Unlikely to Appease Critics," *Washington Post*, February 25, 1984, sec. A, p. 22. The elections were marred by allegations of voter intimidation and restrictions on political activity due to an ongoing state of emergency. Arturo Cruz Porras, the director of Nicaragua's Central Bank and leader of the Coordinadora Democrática Nicaragüense (CDN), went into exile and joined Adolfo Calero, a leader within the Partido Conservador Demócrata (PCD), and Alfonso Robelo, who broke with the ARDE in 1984 to join the FDN.

35. US Department of State, "Economic Sanctions Against Nicaragua," *US Department of State Bulletin* 85, July 1985, 77.

36. US Congress, Senate, Committee on Foreign Relations, *U.S. Policy Options with Respect to Nicaragua and Aid to the Contras: Hearing Before the Committee on Foreign Relations*, 100th Cong., 1st sess., January 28, 1987, 123.

37. James M. Scott, "Interbranch Rivalry and the Reagan Doctrine in Nicaragua," *Political Science Quarterly* 112, no. 2 (Summer 1997): 244; Karl Grossman, *Nicaragua: America's New Vietnam?* (Sag Harbor, NY: Permanent Press, 1984), 179; Cynthia Arnson, *Crossroads: Congress, the President, and Central America 1976–1993* (University Park: Pennsylvania State University Press, 1993), 125.

38. Lawrence E. Walsh, *Final Report of the Independent Counsel for Iran/Contra Matters* (Washington, DC: US Court of Appeals for the District of Columbia Circuit, August 1983), xv–xviii. Ex–US Marine Eugene Hasenfus was the sole survivor of the C-123 that was shot down. He survived by parachuting out of the plane after it was damaged. Hasenfus was in charge of parachuting items out of the plane down to the Contras.

39. Colleen McGuiness and Patricia M. Russotto, *U.S. Foreign Policy: The Reagan Imprint* (Washington, DC: Congressional Quarterly Inc., 1986), 74.

40. Lindsey Gruson, "Latin American Presidents Announce Accord on Contra Bases," *New York Times*, February 15, 1989, sec. A, p. 1.

41. Whelan and Jaeckle, *Soviet Assault*, 185. The revised constitution also outlawed the Communist Party and nationalized the banks. Figueres Ferrer held the presidency twice, in 1953–1958 and in 1970–1974.

42. Barry and Preusch, *Central American Fact Book*, 190–192.

43. Ropp and Morris, *Central America: Crisis and Adaptation*, 177.

44. US Department of State, *Revolution*, 16.

45. US Congress, Senate, Subcommittee on Terrorism, Narcotics, and International Operations of the Committee on Foreign Relations, *Drugs, Law Enforcement, and Foreign Policy*, 100th Cong., 2nd sess., December 1988, 40–41.

46. American Embassy San Jose to Secretary of State Washington, DC, "Subject: Sandinistas and Terrorists in Costa Rica," San Jose 00882 081855Z, February 1982, 1–2; Ronny Rojas, "La profunda huella de Fidel Castro en Costa Rica," *Al Día* (Costa Rica), March 9, 2008, www.aldia.cr. Subversive activities included kidnappings of foreign businessmen and attacks against US and Costa Rican authorities.

47. Barry and Preusch, *Central American Fact Book*, 188–189.

48. "Bomb Kills Nicaraguan in Costa Rica," *Washington Post*, June 30, 1983, sec. A, p. 35.

49. Jean Hopfensperger, "Army-less Costa Rica Builds 10,000-Man Civil Force," *Christian Science Monitor*, January 26, 1983, www.csmonitor.com.

60   Narcostates

50. US Congress, Senate, Subcommittee on Terrorism, *Drugs, Law Enforcement*, 81. Noriega was appointed head of the G-2 by Torrijos after Noriega helped Torrijos to put down a coup attempt in December 1969.

51. American Embassy Bogotá to Secretary of State Washington, DC, "Extradition: Carlos Lehder Speaks Out," January 1984, 2 (Washington, DC: National Security Archive, Narcotics Collection, Colombia: Cartels, US Operations, Corruption, box 8).

52. US Congress, Senate, Subcommittee on Terrorism, *Drugs, Law Enforcement*, 106; and John Dinges, *Our Man in Panama* (New York: Random House, 1990), 131.

53. Dr. Ricardo Lasso Guevara, *U.S.A. vs. Noriega: Enemigos o Amigos* (Panamá City: Litho Impresora Panamá, 1994), 91. Noriega rose to power a chief of staff for the National Guard after he participated in a March 1982 power sharing coup alongside General Rubén Darío Paredes, and Colonel Roberto Díaz Herrera.

54. US Congress, Senate, Subcommittee on Terrorism, *Drugs, Law Enforcement*, 81–86.

55. Rodney Stich, *Defrauding America: Encyclopedia of Secret Operations by the CIA, DEA, and Other Government Offices*, 4th ed. (Alamo, CA: Silverpeak Enterprises, 2008), 355–381. For further reading, see James Adams, *A Full Service Bank* (London: Gallery Books, 1993); and Jonathan Beaty, *The Outlaw Bank* (New York: Random House, 1993).

56. Walsh, *Final Report of the Independent Counsel*, xv–xvii. SAVAK stands for Sāzemān-e Ettelā'āt va Amniyat-e Keshvar. The missiles sold to Iran were tube launched, optically tracked, wire guided (TOW) antitank missiles.

57. US Congress, House of Representatives and Senate, House Select Committee to Investigate Covert Arms Transactions with Iran and Senate Select Committee to Investigate Military Assistance to Iran and the Nicaraguan Opposition, Daniel Inouye and Lee H. Hamilton, Report of the Congressional Committees Investigating the Iran Contra Affair, S. Rept. no. 100-216 and H. Rept. no. 100-433., 100th Cong., 1st sess., November 17, 1987, 31–34. Deposition of Emanuel Floor, Congressional Iran/Contra Committees, June 8, 1987. Manucher Ghorbanifar, an arms dealer and former member of Shah Reza Pahlavi's SAVAK, played a large role in the Iran-Contra operation. Ghorbanifar approached the CIA to arrange an arms-for-hostages deal with Iran in order to release CIA operatives Frank Reed, Joseph Cicippio, Edward Tracy, and David Jacobsen, who were being held by the Lebanese Hezbollah.

58. US Congress, Senate, Subcommittee on Terrorism, *Drugs, Law Enforcement*, 101–102. Noriega created the PDF by merging the National Guard's military and police forces.

59. Ehrenfeld, *Narco-Terrorism*, 43.

60. US Congress, Senate, Subcommittee on Terrorism, *Drugs, Law Enforcement*, 65.

61. Ibid., 66.

62. Valerie Rush and Gretchen Small, "The Crimes of the Medellín Cartel," *Executive Intelligence Review* 14, no. 8 (February 20, 1987): 40–42.

63. US Congress, Senate, Subcommittee on Terrorism, *Drugs, Law Enforcement*, 73–88.

64. Seymour M. Hersh, "Panama Strongman Said to Trade in Drugs, Arms, and Illicit Money," *New York Times*, June 12, 1986, sec. A, p. 1.

65. Ronald H. Cole, "Joint Staff Special Historical Study, Operation Just Cause: Planning and Executions of Joint Operations in Panama February 1988–January 1990" (Washington, DC: Department of Defense: Joint Chiefs of Staff, December 1990), 3. The report cites the following report: "National Military Intelligence Support Team (NMIST), Panama Intelligence Task Force (ITF) to USSOUTHCOM J-

"Cocaine Guns" and Civil War in Central America 61

2, 280150Z," December 1989, S Pan Binder J-5/DDPMA/WHEM, Msg USCINSCO to JCS140325Z, April 1988, TS, Pan. Fact Bk. J-3/JOD/WHEM.

66. Andrew Rosenthal and Elaine Sciolino, "Noriega's Surrender Chronology; Vatican Issues an Ultimatum, and a General Takes a Walk," *New York Times*, January 5, 1990, sec. A, p. 1. Noriega took refuge in the nunciature four days after the invasion. Noriega remained imprisoned in the United States until his death on May 29, 2017.

67. George C. Wilson, "The Military Urges Wider Drug War, Training Central American Teams, Blocking Transport Envisioned," *Washington Post*, June 20, 1985, sec. A, p. 22.

68. US Congress, Senate, Subcommittee on Alcoholism and Drug Abuse of the Committee on Labor and Human Resources, *Drugs and Terrorism, 1984*, 98th Cong., 2nd sess., August 2, 1984, 79, Testimony of Antonio Farach. Farach also claimed the Sandinista government wanted to use drugs as a "political weapon" to "destroy the youth of their enemies," particularly the United States.

69. US Mission United Nations to American Embassy Bogotá, "Security Council Meeting on Nicaraguan Complaint," USUN 02109 080059Z, September 1984, 3.

70. US Mission USUN New York to Secretary of State Washington, DC, "Security Council Meeting on Nicaraguan Complaint," USUN 02109 080101Z, September 1984, 3.

71. Senate, Subcommittee on Terrorism, *Drugs, Law Enforcement*, 67, Testimony of Floyd Carlton. See Joel Brinkley, "U.S. Accuses Managua of Role in Cocaine Traffic," *New York Times*, July 19, 1984, sec. A, p. 6.

72. Robert Parry, "Reagan Lashes Sandinistas for Alleged Drug Trafficking," Associated Press, March 17, 1986, https://apnews.com/article/0fe1520154f06 e2f877ee5033b35e009.

73. US Congress, Senate, Subcommittee on Alcoholism and Drug Abuse of the Committee on Labor and Human Resources, *Role of Nicaragua in Drug Trafficking*, 99th Cong., 1st sess., April 19, 1985, 17; US Embassy San Jose to USIA Washington, DC, "Senator Hawkins Visit to Costa Rica," San Jose 08195 181907Z, October 1984, 1–2. The plane was flown by Barry Seal, who was working for the DEA.

74. David L. Westrate, interview by author [tape recording], November 10, 2006, Buffalo. David L. Westrate was the deputy administrator for the DEA. Joel Brinkley, "Drug Agency Rebuts Reagan Charge," *New York Times*, March 19, 1986, sec. A, p. 3.

75. American Embassy Managua to Secretary of State Washington, DC, "Drug Trafficker Federico Vaughn," Managua 01535 122306Z, March 1985, 1.

76. Robert Parry and Peter Kornbluh, "Iran Contra's Untold Story," *Foreign Policy*, no. 72 (Autumn 1988): 3–30. Robert Parry and Peter Kornbluh argued that Barry Seal's operation was part of a covert propaganda operation run by the Reagan administration to influence the media and public to support the administration's policies. Alexander Cockburn claimed that Jorge Ochoa and Seal planned "the operation against the Sandinistas," to keep "Seal out of prison and Ochoa in the good graces of the intelligence community." Cockburn, *Whiteout*, 318–322.

77. US Congress, House of Representatives, Committee on Foreign Affairs, *Developments in Latin American Narcotics Control, November 1985*, 99th Cong., 1st sess., November 12, 1985, 25; Robert L. Jackson, "Vesco Linked to Cuban Drug Smuggling," *Los Angeles Times*, April 30, 1985, http://articles.latimes.com/1985 -04-20/news/mn-21749_1_recent-drug-smuggling.

78. Michael Gillard, "U.S. News: Robert Vesco," *Guardian*, May 20, 2008, www.theguardian.com. In 1972, the US government indicted Vesco for making a secret $200,000 donation to President Nixon's Committee to Re-Elect the President

62   Narcostates

(CREEP). Vesco fled the United States for Costa Rica, where he donated money to the Nixon administration to halt an investigation into Vesco's embezzlement scheme using Investors Overseas Services, an offshore, Geneva-based mutual fund. In 1980, he persuaded the Libyan government to pay Jimmy Carter's brother Billy $220,000 for a failed oil deal. After the Nicaraguan operation ended, Cuba permitted his entry. In 1995, the Cuban government jailed him for trying to defraud investors, including Raúl Castro, over the alleged success of a cancer and AIDS drug known as Trixolan.

79. Senate, Subcommittee on Alcoholism and Drug Abuse, *Role of Nicaragua in Drug Trafficking*, 27, Testimony of James Herring. See also "Cuba and Cocaine," *Frontline*, episode 910, WGBH Educational Foundation of the Public Broadcasting Service, February 5, 1991, www.pbs.org/wgbh/pages/frontline/shows/drugs/archive /cubaandcocaine.html. Herring met Vesco through Jitze Kooistra, a fugitive drug dealer. Herring's Everything Goes, Inc., procured hard-to-find items for Kooistra.

80. Senate, Subcommittee on Alcoholism and Drug Abuse, *Role of Nicaragua in Drug Trafficking*, 31–40.

81. American Embassy Managua to Secretary of State Washington, DC, "Borge Speaks on U.S. Policy, FSLN Unity, Contras and Elections," Managua 40805 301503Z, August 1984, 2; Jackson, "Vesco Linked to Cuban Drug Smuggling."

82. American Embassy Managua to Secretary of State Washington, DC, "Government of Nicaragua Denies Involvement in Drug Trafficking," Managua 00697 011513Z, January 1985, 1; "Capturados en España y absueltos en Colombia," *El Espectador* (Madrid), July 18, 2012, www.elespectador.com.

83. Senate, Subcommittee on Terrorism, *Drugs, Law Enforcement*, 46–58; US Congress, House of Representatives and Senate, Subcommittee on Security and Terrorism of the Committee on the Judiciary, the Subcommittee on Western Hemisphere Affairs of the Foreign Relations Committee, and the Senate Drug Enforcement Caucus, *The Cuban Government's Involvement in Facilitating International Drug Traffic*, 98th Cong., 1st sess., April 30, 1983, 81–82.

84. House of Representatives and Senate, *Cuban Government's Involvement*, 115–122, Testimony of Crump in Hearings Before Congress, April 30, 1983.

85. Ibid., 19–20.

86. US Congress, Senate, Subcommittee on Terrorism, Narcotics, and International Communications, *Drugs, Law Enforcement, and Foreign Policy: Panama*, 100th Cong., 2nd sess., February 8–11, 1988, 106; Ehrenfeld, *Narco-Terrorism*, 44; *United States v. Jaime Guillot Lara, Fernando Ravelo Renedo, Gonzalo Bassols Suárez, Aldo Santamaría Cuadrado*, United States District Court Southern District of Florida No. 82-643 Cr-Je, November 6, 1982, www .latinamericanstudies.org/drugs/indictment-82.htm.

87. "U.S. Indicts Four Castro Officials on Drug-Trafficking Conspiracy," *Miami Herald*, November 6, 1982, www.latinamericanstudies.org/drugs/indicted.htm.

88. Jim McGee, "Castro Backs Drug Traffic, U.S. Claims," *Miami Herald*, May 1, 1983, sec. A, p. 1; Selwyn Raab, "A Defector Tells of Drug Dealing by Cuban Agents," *New York Times*, April 4, 1983, sec. B, p. 1.

89. Robert L. Jackson, "Ex-Drug Kingpin Testifies Against Noriega: Carlos Lehder Tells of Former Panamanian Leader's Links to Medellín Cartel," *Los Angeles Times*, November 20, 1991, www.latimes.com. Larry Rother, "Former Smuggler Ties Top Officials of Cuba and Nicaragua to Drug Ring," *New York Times*, November 21, 1991, sec. A, p. 1.

90. Richard Cole, "Prosecutors: Traffickers Implicate More Top Cuban Officials," Associated Press, August 21, 1989, https://apnews.com; "Cuba and Cocaine," *Frontline*.

"*Cocaine Guns*" and *Civil War in Central America*   **63**

91. US Congress, House of Representatives, Committee on Foreign Affairs, *Cuban Involvement in International Narcotics Trafficking*, 100th Cong., 1st sess., July 25–27, 1989, 5–10; Julia Preston, "The Trial That Shook Cuba," *New York Review of Books*, December 7, 1989, 23.

92. Bretton G. Sciaroni, "Castro Deeply Involved in Drug Running," *Human Events*, July 29, 1989, 10; Arturo Cruz, "Anatomy of an Execution," *Commentary*, November 1989, 55.

93. Secretary of State Washington, DC to American Embassy, Bonn, "Charges of Drug Trafficking by Nicaraguan Armed Resistance," State 057354 261115Z, February 1986, 1.

94. Senate, *Drugs, Law Enforcement, and Foreign Policy*, 1–42. Adolfo Calero, the head of the FDN, denied these allegations.

95. Warren Richey, "Justice Officials Find No Crime Link to Contra Leaders," *Christian Science Monitor*, May 9, 1986, 3; Mark Tran, "Drugs and Arrest of Contra Leader Upsets Aid Plan/U.S. Senate to Investigate Cocaine Charges Against Nicaraguan Rebels," *Guardian*, April 25, 1986, 1.

96. Senate, *Drugs, Law Enforcement, and Foreign Policy*, 52.

97. Ibid., 40–41.

98. John McPhaul, "27 Years Later, CIA Pilot Tells of Using Secret Costa Rican Airstrip to Traffic Guns and Cocaine," *Tico Times* (Costa Rica), December 9, 2013, www.ticotimes.net.

99. Senate, *Drugs, Law Enforcement, and Foreign Policy*, 41.

100. Central Intelligence Agency, "Other Individuals Involved in Trafficking: John Floyd Hull," CIA Library: General Reports, Cocaine, The Contra Story, n.d., https://www.cia.gov/library/reports/general-reports-1/cocaine/contra-story/other.html. Colonel James Steele, the chief of the US MAAG in El Salvador, directed the Contra supply operation. The United States maintained another resupply base in Aguacate, Honduras.

101. Central Intelligence Agency, "Pilots, Companies, and Other Individuals Working for Companies," CIA Library: General Reports, Cocaine, The Contra Story, n.d., https://www.cia.gov/library/reports/general-reports-1/cocaine/contra-story/pilots.html.

102. Central Intelligence Agency, "Appendices: The Contra Story—Jack Terrell," CIA Library: General Reports, Cocaine, The Contra Story, n.d., https://www.cia.gov/library/reports/general-reports-1/cocaine/contra-story/append.html. Terrell claimed to have contacts within the CIA and revealed to the FBI the names of CIA and Department of Defense personnel involved in anti-Sandinista activity.

103. *United States v. Juan Ramon Matta Ballesteros*, "Order Denying Motion to Dismiss Indictment," No. PCR 86-00511-RV. 700 F. Supp 528, United States District Court, N.D. Florida, Pensacola Division, August 4, 1988. "Matta Ballesteros residió hasta 1985 en Madrid, donde organizó numerosos envíos de cocaína a EE UU," *El País* (Madrid), December 4, 1990, http://elpais.com. In 1970, US authorities arrested Matta. Not enough evidence existed to convict him for trafficking, but he received a five-year prison sentence for visa violations. He bribed his way out of the Eglin Air Force Base prison in 1971 and fled to Mexico. In 1974, Mexican police arrested him for drug smuggling. He was released in 1975, and after the death of Sicilia Falcón that year, he joined the Guadalajara cartel. In 1977, Matta-Ballesteros was arrested in Colombia and imprisoned in Bogotá's La Picota prison, where he awaited extradition to the United States. The Medellín cartel made two attempts to free him using *plata o plomo* (bribery or bullets). When their first offer was rejected, the cartel murdered the warden,

64   Narcostates

Alcides Armendi. In the second attempt, the cartel freed Matta-Ballesteros after bribing the guards with $2 million.

104. Wayne Schmidt, "Report of Investigation" (Washington, DC: Drug Enforcement Agency, February 13, 1990), 1–3, https://web.archive.org/web/20120217172856/http://toshplumlee.info/pdf/DEAfiles.pdf.

105. Senate, *Drugs, Law Enforcement, and Foreign Policy*, 77.

106. Ibid., 44–45.

107. Central Intelligence Agency Inspector General, "Report of Investigation: Allegations of Connections Between CIA and the Contras in Cocaine Trafficking to the United States, Line 896" (Washington, DC: *Central Intelligence Agency*, October 8, 1998), http://ciadrugs.homestead.com/files/index-cia-ig-rpt.html.

108. Oliver North, "Entry, 9 August 1985," Oliver North File: His Diaries, E-Mail, and Memos on the Kerry Report, Contras, and Drugs, Washington, DC: National Security Archive Electronic Briefing Book No. 113, www.gwu.edu/~nsarchiv/NSAEBB/NSAEBB113/index.htm.

109. American Embassy Managua to Secretary of State Washington, DC, "Official GON News Agency Repeats Charges of Contra Involvement in Drug Trafficking," Managua 02456 152307Z, April 1986, 1.

110. The Courier to the Hammer, "The Southern Front," Oliver North Diaries, April 1, 1985, 2–4 (Washington, DC: National Security Archive, The Contras, Cocaine, and Covert Operations Part II, http://nsarchive.gwu.edu/NSAEBB/NSAEBB2/index.html).

111. Senate Subcommittee on Terrorism, *Drugs, Law Enforcement,* 48–49.

112. Gary Webb, "Crack Plague's Roots Are in Nicaragua War; Colombia-Bay Area Drug Pipeline Helped Finance CIA-Backed Contras 80s Efforts to Assist Guerrillas; Left Legacy of Drugs and Gangs in Black L.A.," *San Jose Mercury News*, August 18, 1996, sec. A, p. 1.

113. Sandlaino Gonzalez, "Meneses-Cantero, Norwin: File Opening Report—Debriefing of STF-78-0006," San Jose Costa Rica: DEA Report of Investigation, February 6, 1986, 1 (National Security Archive, The Contras, Cocaine, and Covert Operations, http://nsarchive.gwu.edu/NSAEBB/NSAEBB2/index.html).

114. Ryan Grim, Matt Sledge, and Matt Ferner, "Key Figures in CIA-Crack Cocaine Scandal Begin to Come Forward," *Huffington Post*, October 10, 2010, www.huffingtonpost.com.

115. Tim Weiner, "CIA Says That It Has Found No Link Between Itself and the Crack Trade," *New York Times*, December 19, 1997, sec. A, p. 23.

116. Susan Paterno, "The Sad Saga of Gary Webb," *American Journalism Review* (June/July 2005), http://ajrarchive.org/Article.asp?id=3874. Webb worked for the California State Legislature until his suicide in 2004.

117. James Smith, "Economic Migrants Replace Political Refugees," Migration Institute, April 1, 2006, http://www.migrationpolicy.org/article/guatemala-economic-migrants-replace-political-refugees.

118. Ian Fleming, *Goldfinger* (London: Jonathan Cope, 1959), 211.

119. CIA aid to al-Qaeda in Syria is a case in point. [Redacted] to RHEFDIA/DIA Washington, DC, "Subject: [Redacted] Former Libya Military Weapons Shipped to Syria via Port of Benghazi Libya," Department of Defense Information Report 051443Z (October 12, 2012), 1–3; and [Redacted] to RHEFDIA/DIA Washington, DC, [Subject Redacted], Department of Defense Information Report Iraq 050839Z (August 12, 2012), 287–293.

4

The Emergence of the Mexican Cartel Networks

In the 1980s, Mexico's cartel networks matured while civil unrest and conflict spread to nearly every Central American nation. Out of Mexico's long-standing first-generation cartels, which consisted of competing marijuana, opium, and auto theft syndicates, its second-generation cartels emerged. The second generation unified under the leadership of Miguel Félix Gallardo, who forged the Guadalajara cartel during the late 1970s. During his reign, Félix Gallardo and the Guadalajara cartel would almost single-handedly dominate the flow of cocaine through Mexico. Following the death of DEA agent Kiki Camarena Salazar in 1985, the United States pressured the Mexican government to take action against the Guadalajara cartel, causing its collapse in 1989. The cartel then divided into the Tijuana, Sinaloa, and Juárez cartels, which began to dispute territorial control over Mexico's drug trafficking plazas. Staking out its own territory in Matamoros, the Gulf cartel led by Juan García Ábrego was the only major Mexican cartel to rival the Guadalajara cartel, employing corruption as its primary means to avoid detection.

As the flow of drugs through Mexico surged, Mexican drug traffickers demonstrated a capacity to corrupt Mexican officials with near impunity. Widespread and well-documented accusations of corruption were levied against the Mexican attorney general's office, the Procuraduría General de la República (PGR), the Policía Judicial Federal (PJFM), and the intelligence service known as the Centro de Investigación y Seguridad Nacional (CISEN). The most astonishing claim was that García Ábrego had gained access to the presidency of Carlos Salinas de Gortari (1988–1994). The cartels knew that the key to success was from within.

66 *Narcostates*

First-Generation Mexican Traffickers

Three *narcotraficantes*—Alberto Sicilia Falcón, Pedro Avilés Pérez, and Pablo Acosta Villarreal—were the fathers of Mexico's modern cartel network. Each played an important role in the development of the Guadalajara and Juárez cartels.[1] The success of drug trafficking in Mexico is largely due to their early efforts and their ability to corrupt the police and military.

Alberto Sicilia Falcón was a Cuban American and an occasional CIA asset who maintained ties to the intelligence agencies of Mexico and Cuba. He participated in the CIA's assassination program, called Operation Mongoose, that targeted Fidel Castro. Falcón told the author James Mills that his role in the operation was to pick up and deliver arms and agents to Cuba. Operating out of Tijuana and Baja California, Falcón ran drugs north into the United States and weapons south into Mexico and Central America.[2] Falcón's involvement in the drug trade was facilitated by Gastón Santos, the political boss of San Luis Potosí and the son of Gonzalo Santos, a general of noteworthy fame from the Mexican Revolution. Gastón Santos moved marijuana grown by guerrillas in Guerrero to safe houses owned by Falcón in Mexicali. Using his contacts in arms dealing, Falcón established a guns-for-drugs operation between the United States and Mexico, from which it was alleged that members of the PRI, potentially even President Echeverría, profited.[3] Falcón's marijuana operation brought him into competition with future members of the Guadalajara cartel, because the only other major source of marijuana was in Sinaloa. Following Falcón's 1975 arrest, his underworld contacts, especially those with Matta-Ballesteros, were absorbed into Félix Gallardo's Guadalajara cartel.

Pedro Avilés Pérez, known as El Leon del Norte (Lion of the North), was a doctor from Sinaloa and one of Mexico's first-generation narcotraffickers. His power extended from Sinaloa to Durango and Sonora. He pioneered the use of airplanes to traffic marijuana and heroin into the United States during the 1960s and was the first Mexican to import cocaine from South America.[4] He was also the uncle of Joaquín Guzmán Loera ("El Chapo"). Avilés Pérez met Félix Gallardo while both men worked as bodyguards for the governor of Sinaloa.[5] In addition to establishing ties with Félix Gallardo, Avilés Pérez mentored Rafael Caro Quintero and Ernesto Fonseca Carrillo in marijuana cultivation and smuggling. Together they moved tons of marijuana worth millions of dollars into the United States using tractor trailers.[6] During Operation CANADOR, Mexican authorities put an end to Avilés Pérez's reign as a capo. In September 1978, the PJFM ambushed and killed him in a shootout while he was conducting smuggling operations using an estimated three hundred clandestine airfields in northern Mexico.[7]

The third first-generation capo, Pablo Acosta Villarreal, took control over the drug trade in Chihuahua between 1968 and 1978. In 1968, he was arrested in Presidio, Texas, and charged with possession of an ounce of heroin. At Fort Leavenworth prison, he developed contacts with Anglo and Chicano smugglers.[8] After his release from prison in 1973, he returned to Mexico in 1976 and took over Chihuahua. During this time, Acosta Villarreal employed Fonseca Carrillo as his treasurer while mentoring Carrillo's nephew, Amado Carrillo Fuentes, the future don of the Juárez cartel. With Fonseca Carrillo's help, Acosta Villarreal moved cocaine through Chihuahua.[9] Acosta Villarreal's ability to corrupt high-ranking PJFM and Mexican army officials ensured his success as he transported cocaine from Colombia to Chihuahua.[10] By the mid-1980s, Acosta Villarreal was one of the most important traffickers in Mexico.

The Guadalajara Cartel

Miguel Ángel Félix Gallardo, Rafael Caro Quintero, and Ernesto Fonseca Carrillo are the fathers of Mexico's modern drug trafficking organizations (DTOs). They founded the Guadalajara cartel, which controlled drug trafficking in the Mexican states of Sinaloa, Sonora, Durango, and Jalisco during the 1980s.[11] With hundreds of millions of US dollars at their disposal, the Guadalajara cartel corrupted officials within the Mexican government, police, military, and intelligence services in order to dominate the drug trade.

By developing connections with Colombian cartels, Gallardo became "El Padrino," the Guadalajara cartel's godfather.[12] In 1963, at the age of seventeen, Gallardo served as an officer in the Sinaloa judicial police. He was chosen to work as a bodyguard and a chauffeur for the governor of Sinaloa, Leopoldo Sánchez Celis, who introduced him to President López Portillo's (1976–1982) attorney general, Oscar Flores Sánchez.[13] As a bodyguard, Gallardo met fellow bodyguard Avilés Pérez, who brought him into the marijuana and heroin trade. Around 1975, Gallardo met Matta-Ballesteros, who introduced Gallardo to Medellín cartel representative Gonzalo Rodríguez Gacha ("El Mejicano") in 1977. As Gallardo began moving cocaine for the Medellín cartel, he developed networks that ran throughout Mexico toward Sinaloa and Baja. With Sicilia Falcón in jail, Gallardo used his political connections, especially those with Jalisco governor Flavio Romero de Velasco, to become a real estate investor and financier in Jalisco. By 1980, Gallardo had turned Jalisco into a money laundering haven. Simultaneously, Gallardo began efforts to corrupt officials, developing ties to Antonio Toledo Corro, the governor of Sinaloa, between 1981 and 1986.[14] Another politically connected associate of Gallardo was Arcadio Valenzuela, the president of the Mexican Banks Association and owner of Banpacifico until 1982. Through his contacts, Gallardo laundered his enormous profits through Jalisco's real

68   Narcostates

estate market, including Guadalajara's Plaza Mexico Commercial Center and properties in Puerto Vallarta.[15]

Following the PJFM's 1978 assassination of Avilés Pérez, the Guadalajara cartel coalesced under Gallardo's control. Despite allegations that Fonseca Carrillo arranged for Avilés Pérez's assassination, his death changed everything. With CANADOR in full swing, Caro Quintero and Fonseca Carrillo needed a new base of operations. Gallardo's influence in Jalisco offered them all of the protection they needed. Together, they moved their operations from Culiacán to Guadalajara, where Félix Gallardo arranged introductions to powerful politicians and law enforcement personnel in the state of Jalisco. And it was from Guadalajara that they initiated trafficking operations with the Colombian Medellín and Cali cartels. By 1980, Jalisco was flourishing as a safe haven for narcotraffickers.[16]

The Murder of DEA Agent Kiki Camarena and Its Aftermath

Described as "a wild guy," Caro Quintero traveled in well-armed convoys and carried an AK-47 at all times.[17] The US government alleged that his operation smuggled more than 10,000 tons of marijuana into the United States. His marijuana operation cultivated 10,000 hectares in Sonora. He accumulated personal wealth of more than $500 million, owned more than thirty properties, and invested in more than 300 businesses.[18] Although allegations existed that he had kidnapped campesinos, it was widely believed that he was a "generous *patrón*, loved and respected," by those who worked for him.[19] To launder his cash, he invested in legitimate businesses: auto distributors, hotels in Sinaloa and Sonora, a gas station company, a beauty products store, a shoe company, and a resort spa.[20]

Caro Quintero paid millions to commanders of the DFS intelligence agency for protection. For example, he paid $5 million to the DFS comandante in Tijuana for each load of marijuana sent to the United States. He paid another $5 million to the PJFM comandante of Sonora to protect his marijuana growing operations. He also paid 10 million pesos every week to a PJFM comandante in Chihuahua to protect his largest growing operation—rancho El Búfalo.[21] At one point, Caro Quintero offered to pay Mexico's external debt if the government would let him grow marijuana without interference.[22]

On the night of November 6, 1984, the PJFM raided El Búfalo with 170 federal agents and 270 soldiers from the 35th Battalion of the Mexican army using fifteen helicopters and three Cessna planes. The police confiscated 500 tons of marijuana stored in warehouses and another 400 tons still growing in the fields. Caro Quintero blamed the raid on the DEA, especially upon agent Kiki Camarena, and vowed to get revenge. Two years before, Camarena had directed the confiscation of 220 hectares of mari-

The Emergence of the Mexican Cartel Networks   69

juana from another ranch owned by Caro Quintero. The raid on El Búfalo threw Caro Quintero into a fit of rage and initiated a series of events that brought down the Guadalajara cartel.

In February 1985, Caro Quintero's men kidnapped Camarena outside the US consulate in Guadalajara, taking him to a house only ten minutes away. Upon his arrival, Caro Quintero embraced him and said, "I told you I was going to have you in my hands, you son of a bitch."[23] Soon thereafter, Fonseca Carrillo visited the house. Fonseca Carrillo shouted at Caro Quintero, "You imbecile, . . . don't you realize what a tough spot you've put us in? This isn't just any idiot. This is a U.S. government employee."[24] For thirty-six hours, Caro Quintero's men beat, tortured, and interrogated Camarena. Parts of the interrogation were recorded. On those tapes were the voices of Caro Quintero and a Mexican police official interrogating Camarena. They asked Camarena to provide information on DEA agents in Mexico, but he revealed little.[25] After two days of interrogation, Camarena died from a blunt force trauma to his head. Present at the scene were Caro Quintero, a bodyguard, and an officer of the DFS.[26] On March 5, 1985, Camarena's body was found along with the body of his Mexican pilot wrapped in plastic alongside a road sixty miles from Guadalajara.[27]

In the decades since, allegations have surfaced that the CIA participated in Camarena's abduction and murder. According to a Fox News report, CIA assets were present during the torture of Camarena. The CIA assets were allegedly members of the Mexican DFS.[28] According to the Mexican magazine *Proceso*, director of EPIC Phil Jordan, DEA agent Hector Berrellez, and Tosh Plumlee, a contract pilot for the CIA, claimed that the CIA ordered the murder of Camarena.

According to the story, the CIA took a portion of the profits from Matta-Ballesteros's Mexican-Colombian operation and delivered the money to the Contras.[29] Camarena came across this operation through interviews with Tosh Plumlee and Manuel Buendía, a journalist with Mexico City's *Excélsior* newspaper.[30] Through his informants, Camarena learned that the CIA, under the protection of the DFS, used a ranch in Veracruz owned by Caro Quintero to supply the Contras.[31] The DEA suspected that the ranch was used as a makeshift runway for planes loaded with weapons for the Contras. After dropping off the weapons in Honduras and Nicaragua, the planes continued to Colombia and then returned to the ranch in Veracruz laden with Medellín cocaine.[32] Buendía reported that, in cooperation with the CIA's Contra resupply operation, the DFS looked the other way in regard to the smuggling operation running out of Caro Quintero's ranch. According to journalist Anabel Hernández, the CIA used the DFS to set up clandestine landing strips in Mexico to be used as refueling points for their Contra resupply operations, which were also used to smuggle cocaine into the United States from Colombia.[33] In May 1984, Buendía was assassinated

70   *Narcostates*

by his former source within the DFS, chief José Antonio Zorrilla Pérez. Zorrilla Pérez allegedly killed Buendía because Buendía was going to reveal information linking Zorrilla Pérez to the Guadalajara cartel.[34]

Regardless of the theories surrounding the assassination of Camarena, the United States pressured Mexico to arrest Camarena's killers. As the Mexican government ramped up its police effort, the Guadalajara cartel became ultraparanoid, going so far as to murder two Jehovah's Witnesses in June 1985 because the cartel thought they were DEA agents canvassing Guadalajara. At the time of the murders, four other Jehovah's Witnesses went missing in Guadalajara as well, but their bodies were never found.[35] Mexican pressure forced Caro Quintero to flee Mexico. As he was departing, the PJFM cornered him at the Guadalajara airport on March 17, 1985. With the DEA watching, PJFM Comandante Pavón Reyes walked out to a private plane on the tarmac and spoke to an armed man standing by the plane. During this discussion, Caro Quintero told Pavón Reyes that they "had to find a way to fix this" or the shooting would start.[36] Returning to the DEA agents, Pavón Reyes falsely informed them that the man he was speaking to was a DFS agent and that he had given the plane permission to depart. As the plane was taxiing down the runway, Caro Quintero waved an AK-47 from the door of the plane and shouted, "Next time, my children, bring better weapons, not toys!" He then waved a champagne bottle, took a swig, and closed the jet door.[37] The former director of the DEA, Francis Mullen, accused the PJFM of intentionally allowing Caro Quintero to escape to Costa Rica.[38] Comandante Pavón Reyes was accused of taking a $250,000 bribe to facilitate the escape.[39]

Mexican prosecutors brought indictments against nine men for the killing of Camarena, including two former police officers. The other defendants were charged as accessories to the murder, including PJFM Comandante Pavón Reyes. Both Caro Quintero and Fonseca Carrillo were arrested within a month of Camarena's murder. After receiving a tip about his whereabouts, the DEA, with the help of Costa Rican police, captured Caro Quintero in Costa Rica on April 4, 1985.[40] A forty-man Costa Rican SWAT team captured Caro Quintero and his men while they slept.[41] Three days later, Fonseca Carrillo was captured in Puerto Vallarta.

In the aftermath of the arrests, both Caro Quintero and Fonseca Carrillo confessed. Both men later claimed that their confessions were forced through torture and denied responsibility for any crime.[42] While awaiting trial, both men lived like kings at Mexico City's Reclusorio Norte jail. The prisoners turned their two-story cellblock, which normally held 250 prisoners, into a virtual mansion. Their cells were outfitted with air conditioning, a pool table, an aquarium, Turkish baths, video equipment, a television set, fruit trees, gardens, telephone and radio equipment, and even fighting roost-

The Emergence of the Mexican Cartel Networks   71

ers. In cellblock 10, where Caro Quintero lived, reporters found a fully equipped kitchen with two large refrigerators, living and dining rooms, an office furnished with a large desk, marble bathrooms, and several bedrooms, including a master bedroom with wall-to-wall carpeting, a king-size bed, and satin sheets. Up to twenty other people who were not inmates, including friends, relatives, and "assistants," lived in the block. Their extravagant imprisonment became public after Caro Quintero and Fonseca Carrillo publicly accused the prison director of trying to extort $1 million in exchange for preventing their transfer to maximum-security cells. Learning of this, the director of Mexico City prisons transferred both men to maximum security jails.[43]

Shortly after the discovery of their lavish lifestyle at Reclusorio Norte, the Mexican government tried and convicted both men for murdering Camarena and his pilot. Caro Quintero received forty years for murder and received another seventy-six years for kidnapping and drug trafficking.[44] Although the DEA and CISEN claimed Caro Quintero remained in full control of the Sonora cartel from prison, his brother, Miguel Ángel Caro Quintero, directed the cartel's marijuana and cocaine business on the outside. In 1992, Miguel was briefly detained for tax evasion but used threats and bribes to evade jail. In 2001, he was arrested on weapons charges, and in 2009, he was extradited to the United States. During that time, the Sinaloa and Arellano Félix cartels absorbed what remained of the Sonora cartel.[45] Fonseca Carrillo received a 40-year sentence for murder and another 104 years for kidnapping, drug trafficking, and arms smuggling.[46]

Caro Quintero's boss, Félix Gallardo, remained on the run for several years until his capture on April 8, 1989. He had been wanted on drug and weapons trafficking charges, and Camarena's murder was the last straw. PJFM officers drove up to his residence in the Jardines del Bosque neighborhood of Guadalajara, surrounded the house, cut off the electricity, and stormed inside. Surprising the household, they easily captured Gallardo and his men without a shot being fired. The capture was possible because Gallardo's wife refused to cook for his bodyguards, so instead they ate breakfast in town, enabling the police to pinpoint Gallardo's residence.[47] The head of the DEA in Mexico, Ed Heath, praised the Mexican government's courage, because Gallardo operated for more than fifteen years "with impunity . . . because of the protection he received."[48] The US government wanted to extradite Gallardo, but the Mexican government refused, insisting that his trial and sentence be served in Mexico before they would consider extradition to the United States.

Because the DEA believed that the Mexican government was not totally forthcoming in the Camarena case, it pursued the arrest and conviction of others involved in the abduction, torture, and murder of Camarena.

72   Narcostates

This included Honduran drug kingpin Matta-Ballesteros, whom the United States sentenced to life without parole for his involvement, and Verdugo-Urquidez, a cartel lieutenant, who received a 360-year prison sentence with the possibility of parole after 60 years.[49] On the same day that Gallardo was arrested, the Mexican army arrested 600 members of the Culiacán municipal police and the Sinaloa PJFM for protecting the Guadalajara cartel. Noteworthy arrests included Moreno Espinosa, the head of the PJFM in Sinaloa, and Lizárraga Coronel, the director of public safety in Culiacán. Gallardo had paid Espinosa $10,000 and Coronel $5,000 in bribes monthly. Also arrested was the regional commander of the Tamaulipas state police.[50]

Devastated by the widespread corruption, the Mexican government restructured its security services and dismissed corrupt officers. In 1985, out of an estimated 2,200 agents in the DFS, more than 400 were dismissed.[51] The DFS was merged into the Centro de Investigación y Seguridad Nacional (CISEN), which acted as the Mexican equivalent of the CIA. In addition, between 1988 and 1989, the attorney general's office (PGR) fired another 243 people for incompetence and/or negligence.[52]

Meanwhile, Félix Gallardo could not be stopped from running his empire out of Reclusorio Sur prison in Mexico City. He bribed prison officials to give him a free hand to work out of his jail cell and equipped his office with cellular telephones and a fax machine. His bodyguards performed clerical work. Trying to maintain control from prison, he assigned drug trafficking plazas to his former lieutenants.[53]

El Güero, El Chapo, and the Sinaloa Cartel

Born in Sinaloa, Héctor Palma Salazar ("El Güero") started his criminal career as a car thief and then became a gunman for Félix Gallardo. A psychological report on El Güero described him as egocentric and highly dangerous.[54] Arrested in Arizona on drug trafficking charges in 1978, El Güero served eight years in a US prison. Upon his release in 1986, he returned to Mexico and helped Félix Gallardo establish connections with the Cali cartel. Following Félix Gallardo's incarceration, El Güero was given command over San Luis Río Colorado, as well as nominal control over the cartel. After the loss of a major cocaine shipment, El Güero fell out of favor with Félix Gallardo. Feeling threatened, El Güero turned against Félix Gallardo and proposed a partnership with Joaquín Guzmán Loera ("El Chapo"), a soon-to-be infamous *narcotrafficante* who had been given control over Tecate by Félix Gallardo.[55]

El Chapo was born in La Tuna, a small village in the Sierra Madre Occidental Mountains located in Sinaloa. His father was a *gomero* (opium farmer), but he learned the drug business from his uncle, Avilés Pérez.[56]

The Emergence of the Mexican Cartel Networks   73

After joining the Guadalajara cartel, El Chapo started out as a foreman on Caro Quintero's El Búfalo ranch. Over time, El Chapo and El Güero's power within the Guadalajara cartel grew. El Güero became responsible for the security of narcotics once they entered Mexico, while El Chapo was responsible for moving drugs to the border and smuggling them into the United States. Colombian traffickers nicknamed El Chapo "El Rapido" because he moved narcotics across the US border in less than forty-eight hours.[57]

El Chapo was a ruthless taskmaster. He executed employees for delayed deliveries. Even if heavy rains washed away the roads and prevented delivery, he still enforced retribution. When he became the head of the Sinaloa cartel, he became even more heartless. He kidnapped unsuspecting campesinos and migrants and forced them to work in his drug laboratories and plantations. When the forced laborers outlived their usefulness, he had them murdered and thrown into mass graves. El Chapo also used his "slaves" to dig border tunnels into the United States. In May 1990, the US Customs Service discovered a massive tunnel underneath a warehouse in Douglas, Arizona. Wide enough to accommodate a small truck, the tunnel ran the distance of sixty miles south to the home of El Chapo's lawyer across the border in Agua Prieta, Sonora. Following that discovery, El Chapo built another tunnel in Tijuana without the permission of the Arellano Félix brothers, who had been given control over Tijuana by Félix Gallardo. El Chapo and El Güero's incursion into Tijuana triggered a decades-long feud with the Arellano Félix cartel.[58]

The Arellano Félix Family

The Arellano Félix family became involved in drug trafficking through Sicilia Falcón, whose contraband operations were absorbed by Félix Gallardo in 1975. Benjamín was the first family member to traffic in narcotics during the early 1980s. With the help of his uncle, Jesús Labra Avilés ("El Chuy"), Benjamín consolidated control over Tijuana. El Chuy was a financial mastermind who served as the organization's treasurer and had extensive business contacts, especially in the entertainment and sports industries. Although Benjamín was the heart of the organization, El Chuy was the brain despite the fact that it was not until 1998 that he was identified as a prominent member within the cartel. El Chuy remained a figure within the cartel until his arrest by the Mexican army during his son's soccer match on March 11, 2000.[59]

Other important members of the cartel included brothers Ramón, Francisco Rafael, Francisco Javier, and Eduardo. Ramón was in charge of security, using brutal methods to torture and kill anyone who got in the way. His methods included suffocating rivals with a clear plastic bag while his obese henchman bounced up and down on their chests. He also employed the

74   Narcostates

"Colombian necktie"—he sliced the informant's throat below the chin and pulled their tongue out through the cut. Another technique was called carne asada—burning his foes alive on a bed of flaming tires.[60] Francisco Javier, the family's youngest brother, was third in command. In a 1994 shootout, the Baja California State Police helped him evade capture by the DFS.[61] However, on December 4, 1993, he was apprehended by Mexican authorities for the murder of Cardinal Juan Posadas Ocampo. The eldest brother, Francisco Rafael, ran the cartel after his other brothers had been captured and/or killed. Initially he did not play a large role in the cartel, but as the owner of the Franky'O discothèque in Mazatlán, he formed alliances with the local police that the cartel later exploited. Eduardo was a surgeon. He did not join the cartel until after the year 2000, when he began coordinating drug shipments to the United States.[62]

With Félix Gallardo's blessing, the Arellano Félix brothers ran Tijuana. With their rivals for Tijuana eliminated, the Arellano Félix brothers and El Chuy rose to prominence, amassing a fortune and forging relationships with Tijuana's most powerful citizens.[63] For his part, Ramón recruited the rich, idle sons of prominent Tijuana families at the city's discothèques. Known as the narcojuniors, they became auxiliaries of the cartel. The narcojuniors became hooked on the easy money, women, and drugs that the cartel offered.[64] During the cartel war of the 1990s, the mortality rate for narcojuniors increased precipitously.

Carrillo Fuentes and the Juárez Cartel

Fathered by Pablo Acosta Villarreal, the Juárez cartel emerged as a major DTO after Gallardo's arrest in 1989. Acosta Villarreal mentored Amado Carrillo Fuentes, who would become the leader of the cartel and one of Mexico's most infamous traffickers.[65] Carrillo Fuentes's fame would earn him the name El Señor de los Cielos, translated as the "lord of the skies." He entered the drug trade when his uncle, Ernesto Fonseca Carrillo, sent him to oversee the cross-border operations of Acosta Villarreal in Ciudad Juárez. Monthly, Acosta Villarreal and Carrillo Fuentes flew five tons of cocaine from Colombia to Ojinaga, which sits on the Rio Grande across the border from Presidio, Texas.

Following the murder of Kiki Camarena, US pressure on the Mexican police to do more led to the death of Acosta Villarreal in April 1987. Led by PJFM Comandante González Calderóni and with assistance from the FBI, the PJFM raided Acosta Villarreal's hideout in Chihuahua. When Calderóni ordered him to surrender, Acosta Villarreal shouted, "Go away . . . fuck your mother, Calderóni . . . you will never take me from here alive." The police opened fire on the house, which caught on fire and killed Acosta Villarreal.[66] Rumors of betrayal surrounded his death. DEA

The Emergence of the Mexican Cartel Networks   75

sources later alleged that Carrillo Fuentes paid a PJFM comandante $1 million to have Acosta assassinated.[67]

In the wake of Acosta Villarreal's death, Rafael Aguilar Guajardo, a former Mexican DFS commander, assumed control over Juárez. While serving in the DFS, Aguilar Guajardo extorted money from Juárez-based traffickers. In 1985 he quit the DFS and, together with Acosta Villarreal, Carrillo Fuentes, and businessman Muñoz Talavera, formed the Juárez cartel in conjunction with the Guadalajara cartel. At one point, Aguilar Guajardo's estimated net worth was $100 million. During his reign, Carrillo Fuentes and Carvajal Paternina (a Colombian businessman and naturalized Mexican citizen) purchased an airline called Aviación Cóndor. From their office in Acapulco, they purchased cocaine in Cartagena, Colombia, flew it to Ciudad Juárez, and then smuggled it into the United States.[68] Government pressure against Aguilar Guajardo and Carvajal Paternina led Carrillo Fuentes to assume control over the Juárez cartel in 1993. In 1989, the DEA confiscated twenty-one tons of cocaine belonging to Carvajal Paternina in a Los Angeles warehouse. During the investigation into the warehouse, Mexican authorities discovered that Carvajal Paternina owned a house that once belonged to the former Mexican president Luis Echeverría Álvarez (1970–1976). Carvajal Paternina realized that he was a wanted man and feared for his life. He fled to France and then to Italy, where he evaded extradition until his death from a heart attack in 1995.[69] While Carvajal Paternina fought extradition, Aguilar Guajardo was mysteriously gunned down outside a Cancún restaurant on April 12, 1993. There were rumors that Carrillo Fuentes ordered the assassination, and with the death of Aguilar Guajardo, it became clear that Carrillo Fuentes had absolute control over the Juárez cartel.[70]

Carrillo Fuentes's success relied upon his ability to bribe and co-opt the Mexican law enforcement system. In 1989, prior to becoming the leader of the Juárez cartel, he was arrested at a wedding ceremony. Carrillo Fuentes was sent to the Reclusorio Sur prison in Mexico City, where he negotiated his release with Mexico's drug czar, Javier Coello Trejo, for an unspecified sum of money estimated in the millions of dollars.[71] In March 1989, Senator Jessie Helms, reacting to Carrillo Fuentes's release, publicly accused Coello Trejo of collaborating with Mexican drug traffickers.[72] Six months later, Coello Trejo was fired from his job as the deputy attorney general in charge of overseeing the PJFM's counternarcotics police. According to the official record, instead of indicting him for taking bribes from the cartels, Mexico dismissed him for human rights abuses and the mistreatment of prisoners.[73]

Carrillo Fuentes developed a vast money laundering network that penetrated Mexico's banking system by placing his agents inside the banks. In many instances, the bank employees were his family members or family

76   *Narcostates*

members of his lieutenants. Through banking agents, Carrillo Fuentes patronized small money exchanges and major banks, such as the Banco Internacional that was bought in 2002 by HSBC—a bank well-known for money laundering. In 1992, a Mexican banking commission revealed that an aerodrome in Cancún similar to one used by the Juárez cartel in Ciudad Juárez was built using drug money laundered through Banco Internacional.[74]

With his enormous wealth and familial ties, Carrillo Fuentes also corrupted the judicial system. His most important source of protection came from General Gutiérrez Rebollo, the head of the PGR's counternarcotics agency, Instituto Nacional para el Combate a las Drogas (INCD) from 1996 to 1997. Created in 1993, the INCD was the Mexican version of the DEA. The general was chosen as the head of the INCD to show the world Mexico's willingness to fight the war on drugs. With access to the government's operations against the cartels, Gutiérrez Rebollo pursued rival cartels while protecting the interests of Carrillo Fuentes and the Juárez cartel. His tie to Carrillo Fuentes was found out when it was discovered that the lavish apartment he lived in was owned by a lieutenant for Carrillo Fuentes.[75] Only two months after taking over the INCD, Gutiérrez Rebollo was arrested in February 1997 for facilitating cocaine shipments and for accepting millions of dollars in bribes from Carrillo Fuentes.[76]

Around 1991, the Sinaloa cartel formed a strategic alliance with the Juárez cartel to control the Pacific coast corridor.[77] El Chapo and El Güero had already challenged Félix Gallardo's distribution of power when they encroached upon Arellano Félix territory in Tijuana. From jail, Félix Gallardo sought to retaliate against El Güero for abandoning the Arellano Félix family. Félix Gallardo targeted members of El Güero's family.[78] To protect himself, El Güero developed a plan to join up with Carrillo Fuentes. His plan was to replace the Arellano Félix organization and take control over Mexico's Pacific narcotrafficking corridor by coordinating with the Juárez cartel. According to DEA chief of intelligence in Mexico Larry Villalobos, "Very shortly they joined up with Amado Carrillo Fuentes, who really loved them. And they also loved Amado. They were known as the Sinaloa cartel, but Amado Carrillo controlled it from Juárez to Veracruz."[79] Carrillo Fuentes brokered deals for the cartel by pooling large drug shipments and assigning different smuggling tasks to his partners. Together with El Chapo and El Güero, Amado Carrillo Fuentes created an unrivaled narcotransport enterprise.[80]

The Gulf Cartel

The Gulf cartel, also known as the Matamoros cartel, was founded by Juan Nepomuceno Guerra (1915–2001) and his brothers Arturo and Roberto, who smuggled whiskey into the United States during the 1920s era of Prohibition. After Prohibition ended, he became involved in the trafficking of cocaine and heroin. By the late 1980s, his connections were so vast that he became a real estate investor in the state of Tabasco with the father of future Mexican president Carlos Salinas de Gortari.[81] Except for a brief detention on tax evasion charges in 1991, Nepomuceno Guerra's political connections prevented him from being charged as a smuggler.

Juan García Ábrego became the head of the Gulf cartel during the 1980s. He was a US citizen from Las Palomas, Texas, who also held Mexican citizenship.[82] He started his criminal career as a car thief for his uncle, Nepomuceno Guerra. During the 1970s, he began trafficking marijuana. As he learned the drug trade, he transformed the Gulf cartel into a cocaine smuggling operation.[83] In 1984, García Ábrego took control of the cartel following a stroke that left Nepomuceno Guerra partially paralyzed. However, his coronation as the head of the Gulf cartel did not go uncontested. A rival in the cartel nicknamed El Cacho challenged his authority. In response, García Ábrego sent assassins to kill El Cacho, but they only wounded him. García Ábrego ordered another attempt and sent assassins to a clinic where El Cacho was recuperating from his wounds. The assassins fired 300 bullets into the clinic, killing eight bystanders including El Cacho's sister. El Cacho survived the attack but succumbed to his initial wounds. In 1987, García Ábrego cemented his control over the Gulf cartel when he assassinated Tomas Morlet, a DFS agent representing the Guadalajara cartel who tried to force García Ábrego out of Matamoros.[84]

As the 1980s cocaine boom exploded, García Ábrego diversified his operations into legitimate businesses that served as money laundering and trafficking fronts. To launder his money, he employed Carlos Reséndez Bertolucci, a businessman from Nuevo León and the financial brain of the organization, to create an iron-working business front. By 1987, Ábrego's associates had created several front companies for the Gulf cartel, each capable of laundering millions of dollars. To protect the cartel's operations, García Ábrego established an armed commando unit. Working within that structure were members of the DFS and PJFM.[85]

Complex schemes were employed to launder Gulf cartel money. In one instance, the Gulf cartel deposited money into the First City Texas Bank, which then transferred the money to the Bankers' Trust of New York. From there, money was delivered to shell corporations in the Cayman Islands that then lent the money back to the Gulf cartel to acquire legitimate businesses.[86] US prosecutors estimated that by the late 1990s, the Gulf cartel earned between \$10–\$20 billion annually.[87] At the time of his arrest in 1996, García Ábrego possessed \$500 million in investments, including a steel factory, a meat-packing plant, a car transport company, and cattle ranches, such as the El Tejano ranch that covered 24,000 hectares.

The Gulf cartel operated all along the US-Mexico border. By 1989, the cartel was running operations in the cities of Matamoros and Monterrey,

78   *Narcostates*

located in Tamaulipas and Nuevo León, respectively.[88] At this point, the cartel was transporting more than 100 metric tons of cocaine into the United States annually.[89] Cocaine brought to Matamoros was smuggled across the border, stockpiled in Brownsville, and then sent to Houston. From Houston, it was distributed nationally, principally to New York and Los Angeles.[90]

García Ábrego was able to smuggle, store, and distribute huge amounts of drugs by bribing Mexican officials at all levels of government. As governors of Tamaulipas, Américo Villarreal Guerra (1987–1993) and Manuel Cavazos Lerma (1993–1999) opened the door for García Ábrego.[91] With the state's permission, García Ábrego built a municipal market in Matamoros, which served as the city's commercial center. In return, Ábrego received protection from the Tamaulipas state police.[92] He also received protection from PJFM Comandante González Calderóni, the killer of Juárez cartel founder Acosta Villarreal. Ábrego allegedly paid González Calderóni $7 million for each shipment of cocaine that passed into the United States. Other bribed officials included López Parra, the head of the PJFM antinarcotics police in Nueva León, and García Villalón, the director of the PGR's Dirección General de Investigación de Narcóticos.[93] García Ábrego allegedly paid López Parra, García Villalón, and Coello Trejo (the deputy attorney general for the PGR) $1.5 million per month in bribes. His ability to corrupt the government went so far as to include the assertion that President Salinas attended parties at his home with the full knowledge that he was a drug trafficker.[94] Other allegations existed that Salinas's brother Raúl was an accomplice who used his position to advance García Ábrego's interests.[95]

By the mid-1990s, Mexico's drug trafficking network was controlled by four principal cartels: Sinaloa, Tijuana, Juárez, and Gulf cartels. The arrest of Félix Gallardo splintered the Guadalajara cartel. Rivalries among former associates combined with the rising power of the Gulf cartel became an all-out war for Mexico's drug trafficking plazas. Nevertheless, despite the cartels' territorial disputes, their combined operations brought tons of cocaine, marijuana, and heroin into the United States on an annual basis. They could not have shipped this amount and escaped arrest without their ability to corrupt leaders within the police, the army, the intelligence agencies, and the PRI. As expressed by one observer of the conflict, "Command of the shadow economy guaranteed riches and political influence."[96]

Notes

1. Geraldo Galarza, "1985 el año que se deseató el narco," *Excélsior* (Mexico), October 8, 2013, www.excelsior.com.

2. James Mills, *The Underground Empire: Where Crime and Governments Embrace* (New York: Dell, 1986), 74–75, 520–523; US Congress, Senate, Committee

The Emergence of the Mexican Cartel Networks 79

on Government Operations, *Illicit Traffic in Weapons and Drugs Across the United States Mexican Border,* 95th Cong., 1st sess., January 12, 1977 (Washington, DC: GPO, 1977). Falcón operated out of Baja California.

3. Senate, Committee on Government Operations, *Illicit Traffic in Weapons and Drugs*; US Congress, House of Representatives, House Report 105-780, *Intelligence Authorization Act for Fiscal Year 1999, Comments by Reps. Millender-McDonald, A Tangled Web: A History of CIA Complicity in Drug International Trafficking*, 105th Cong., 2nd sess., May 7, 1998, p. H2944, http://www.pinknoiz.com/covert/MOU.html.

4. José Alfredo Andrade Borges, *La Historia Secreta del Narco: Desde Navolato Vengo* (Mexico City: Editorial Oceano de Mexico, 1999), 57–63; "Pedro Avilés Pérez," *Todo Sobre Narcotráfico en Mexico* (blog), January 15, 2010, http://todosobrenarcotraficoenmexico.blogspot.com/2010/01/pedro-aviles-perez.html.

5. John Lee Brook, *Blood and Death: The Secret History of Santa Muerte and the Mexican Drug Cartels* (London: Headpress Publishing, 2016), 3. The Sinaloa governor was Leopoldo Sánchez Celis.

6. E. C. Pérez, "The Guadalajara Cartel Part II: Business and Prosperity," *Kique's Corner* (blog), September 17, 2009, http://ecperez.blogspot.com/2009/09/guadalajara-cartel-part-ii-business-and.html.

7. Patricia B. McRae, "Reconceptualizing the Illegal Narcotics Trade: Its Effect on the Colombian and Mexican State" (paper presented at the Southeastern Conference on Latin American Studies, Savannah, GA, April 12, 1998).

8. Terence E. Poppa, *Drug Lord: The Life and Death of a Mexican Kingpin*, 3rd ed. (El Paso, TX: Cinco Puntos Press, 2010), 30–32.

9. Ibid.

10. Ibid., 64–73.

11. Gareth A. Jones, "Drugs, Violence, and Insecurity in Mexico," in *South America, Central America, and the Caribbean 2012*, 20th ed. (London: Europa Editions, 2011).

12. "The Rise of Mexico's Narco State," *Borderland Beat*, August 13, 2012, www.borderlandbeat.com.

13. American Embassy Mexico to DEAHQS Washington, DC, "Subject: TB 88-0001-[Redacted]-GFAN 86-8003-[Redacted]-Operation Columbus PRTB-85-0032, Operation Leyenda, Mexico 09040 102240Z, April 1989, 1–2; Héctor Aguilar Camín, "Narcos Historias Extraordinarias," *Nexos*, May 2007, www.nexos.com.

14. Executive Intelligence Review, "Medellín Cartel Loses Top Agent in Mexico," *Executive Intelligence Review* 16, no. 19 (May 15, 1989), 46; Larry Rother, "In Mexico, Drug Roots Run Deep," *New York Times*, April 16, 1989, sec. A, p. 14, www.nytimes.com.

15. Executive Intelligence Review, "Medellín Cartel Loses," 46.

16. American Embassy Mexico, "Subject: TB 88-0001-[Redacted]," 3–4. Flavio Romero de Velasco was the governor of Jalisco from 1976 until 1982.

17. Richard J. Meislin, "Drugs Change Face of Mexican Tourist Mecca," *New York Times*, March 20, 1985, sec. A, p. 3.

18. US Department of State, "Narcotics Rewards Program: Rafael Caro Quintero," www.state.gov/narcotics-rewards-program-target-information-wanted/caro-quintero-rafael, accessed March 5, 2022.

19. Linaloe R. Flores, "Los negocios de Caro desde prisión eran el secreto más conocido," *Sin Embargo* (Mexico), July 10, 2016, www.borderlandbeat.com.

20. US Department of the Treasury, "Treasury Sanctions the Network of Drug Lord Rafael Caro Quintero," June 12, 2013, www.treasury.gov/press-center/press-releases/Pages/jl1981.aspx.

80 Narcostates

21. Aguilar Camín, "Narco Historias extraordinarias," www.nexos.com.mx/?p =12886.

22. Flores, "Los negocios de Caro."

23. Jim Newton, "Camarena's Abduction and Torture Described," *Los Angeles Times*, December 10, 1992, http://articles.latimes.com/1992-12-10/local/me-2364_1 _ranking-mexican.

24. Robert J. McCartney, "Mexican Antidrug Drive Focuses on Cocaine, DEA Official Calls 44 Arrests in 10 Days Spectacular," *Washington Post*, April 15, 1985, sec. A, p. 16.

25. Kim Murphy, "Tape of Drug Agent's Torture Is Made Public," *Los Angeles Times*, June 7, 1988. The police official was Sérgio Espino Verdín. The DFS agent was Tomas Morlet.

26. P. Coster, "The Cocaine Connection," *Courier Mail* (Australia), March 9, 1985.

27. William F. Weld to Lawrence Lippe, "Memorandum: Recommendation for the Prosecution of Rene Verdugo and Mario Martínez for Their Participation in the Kidnap/Murder of DEA Special Agent Enrique Camarena," US Department of Justice, March 11, 1987, 4 (Washington, DC: The National Security Archive, Mexico-United States Counternarcotics Policy 1969–2013). Weld was assistant attorney general of the Criminal Division, and Lippe was chief of the General Litigation and Legal Advice Section.

28. John McPhaul, "Reports: CIA Present During U.S. Drug Agent's Torture-Murder," *Tico Times* (Costa Rica), October 14, 2013, www.ticotimes.net.

29. Luis Chaparro and J. Jesús Esquivel, "A Camarena lo ejecutó la CIA, no Caro Quintero," *Proceso* (Mexico), December 12, 2013, www.proceso.com. The agents stated that Camarena's assassin was Félix Ismael Rodríguez, a CIA operative who participated in the Bay of Pigs operation, the killing of Che Guevara in Bolivia, the Phoenix program in Vietnam, and the Iran-Contra operation. Because Honduran trafficker Matta-Ballesteros ran the SETCO airline that serviced the Contras, Rodríguez associated with Caro Quintero. Many shadowy but unprovable events have been attributed to Rodríguez.

30. Marjorie Miller, "Journalist's Death Unravels Network: Killing in Mexico Reveals Trail of Police Corruption," *Los Angeles Times*, July 7, 1989, http://articles .latimes.com/1989-07-07/news/mn-3216_1_police-corruption.

31. Wayne Schmidt, "Report of Investigation," Drug Enforcement Agency, February 13, 1990, 1, https://web.archive.org/web/20120217172856/http://toshplumlee .info/pdf/DEAfiles.pdf; Henry Weinstein, "Informant Puts CIA at Ranch of Agent's Killer," *Los Angeles Times*, July 5, 1990, www.latimes.com.

32. Schmidt, "Report of Investigation," 3; Bill Conroy, "Assassinated DEA Agent Kiki Camarena Fell in CIA Operation Gone Awry," *The Narcosphere*, October 27, 2013, www.narconews.com.

33. Anabel Hernández, *Narcoland: The Mexican Drug Lords and Their Godfathers*, trans. Ian Bruce (New York: Verso Books, 2013), 52–53.

34. Miller, "Journalist's Death."

35. American Embassy Mexico to Secretary of State, Washington, DC, "Possible Threat to Religious Groups," Mexico 09307 171816Z, October 2000, 1–2; Richard J. Meislin, "Bodies in Mexico Believed Americans," *New York Times*, June 18, 1985, sec. A, p. 3; Ronald L. Soble, "Mexican Cartel May Have Killed 4: Investigation: The Four Jehovah's Witnesses Disappeared in Guadalajara in 1984. Authorities Believe They Were Mistaken for U.S. Drug Agents," *Los Angeles Times*, October 20, 1989, www.latimes.com.

The Emergence of the Mexican Cartel Networks   81

36. Ronald J. Ostrow and Paul Huston, "Camarena Case Suspect Caught in Costa Rica," *Los Angeles Times*, April 5, 2008, http://articles.latimes.com/1985-04 -05/news/mn-27158_1_Caro Quintero.

37. Pérez, "The Guadalajara Cartel Part III."

38. Richard J. Meislin, "Body of U.S. Drug Agent Found in Mexico," *New York Times*, March 7, 1985, sec. A, p. 1. The plane taken by Caro Quintero was registered to la Compañía Proveedora de Servicios de Guadalajara, whose owners, Eduardo and Javier Cordero Staufert, were later charged with laundering 500 million Mexican pesos for Caro Quintero. Mullen was DEA director from November 10, 1983, to March 1, 1985.

39. American Embassy Mexico to Secretary of State, Washington, DC, "Newspaper Article—Drug Murder Investigation," Mexico 08232 181742Z, April 1985, 4.

40. Aguilar Camín, "Narcos Historias extraordinarias." The farm was owned by two Mexicans: Inés Calderón and Jesús Félix Gutiérrez.

41. Ostrow and Huston, "Camarena Case."

42. Richard J. Meislin, "Mexicans Arrest Second Top Drug Suspect: Second in a Week," *New York Times*, April 11, 1985, sec. A, p. 1.

43. William Branigin, "2 Drug Lords Lived Lavishly in Mexico City Cellblocks; Pair Wanted in 1985 Slaying of U.S. Agent," *Washington Post*, July 20, 1989, sec. A, p. 1.

44. Aguilar Camín, "Narcos Historias extraordinarias." Quintero was released in August 2013. That same month, the FBI requested the Mexican government to rearrest and extradite Quintero, who then disappeared. The FBI placed Quintero back on its most wanted list in April 2018.

45. *United States of America v. Rafael Caro Quintero*, T.18,U.S.C.,§§ 924(c)(l)(A)(i),924(c)(l)(A)(ii),924(c)(l)(A)(iii), (United States District Court Eastern District of New York, January 20, 2017), 1–14; US Attorney's Office, "Miguel Angel Caro Quintero Sentenced to Prison for Trafficking Massive Amounts of Marijuana from Mexico to the United States," February 5, 2010, www.justice.gov /archive/usao/co/news/2010/February10/2_5_10.html. Miguel received a seventeen-year prison term in 2010.

46. Larry Rother, "Mexican Drug Leaders Guilty in the Killing of a U.S. Agent," *New York Times*, December 13, 1989, sec. B, p. 10.

47. William Branigin, "Bodyguards' Eating Habits Eased Capture of Drug Kingpin," *Washington Post*, April 13, 1989, sec. A, p. 41.

48. William Branigin, "Mexicans Arrest Prime Drug Suspect: Félix Gallardo Led DEA's Wanted List," *Washington Post*, April 11, 1989, sec. A, p. 1.

49. Henry Weinstein, "Man Gets Life Term for Running Drug Syndicate," *Los Angeles Times,* January 17, 1990, http://articles.latimes.com/1990-01-17/news/mn -86_1_los-angeles-history; "900 Year Prison Terms Recommended for Two in Camarena Case," *Los Angeles Times*, October 20, 1988, http://articles.latimes.com /1988-10-20/news/mn-5349_1_prison-terms.

50. American Embassy Mexico, "Mexican Authorities Arrest Major Trafficker," Mexico 08993101942Z, 1; Aguilar Camín, "Narcos Historias extraordinarias."

51. Robert J. McCartney, "Mexico Removes Police Suspected of Corruption; Two Forces Reportedly Oust Hundreds," *Washington Post*, May 17, 1985, sec. A, p. 25.

52. American Embassy Mexico to Secretary of State Washington, DC, "Subject: Status of Mexican Drug Enforcement Efforts," Mexico 31651 221921Z, December 1989, 2. The DFS and the Dirección General de Investigaciones Políticas y Sociales (DGIPS) merged into the Dirección General de Investigación y Seguridad Nacional

82   Narcostates

(DGISN), which then became the CISEN. The CISEN was founded by Jorge Carrillo Olea (director from 1989 to 1990 and governor of Morelos from 1994 to 1998), later identified as an associate of the Juárez and Gulf cartels.

53. Tim Golden, "Violently, Drug Trafficking Rebounds in Mexico," *New York Times*, March 8, 1993, sec. A, p. 3; Jesús Blancornelas, *El Cartel: Los Arellanos Félix: La mafia más poderosa en la historia de América Latina* (México City: Random House Mondadori, 2002), 54.

54. American Embassy, Mexico to RHLBAAA/USCINCSO, "Summary of Significant News Releases/Mexico," Mexico 000368 142013Z, January 1997, 0051 (National Security Digital Archive, Mexico-U.S. Counternarcotics Policy 1969–2013).

55. American Embassy Mexico to Secretary of State Washington, DC, "Who Is El Güero Palma," Mexico 13575 040949Z, June 1995, 2; American Embassy Mexico to DEA Headquarters Washington, DC, "Summary of Significant News Releases," Mexico 14370 111611Z, July 1995, 3–4; "Tijuana Cartel," *African Narco News* (blog), January 3, 2013, http://african-business.blogspot.com/2013/01/tijuana-cartel.html#!/2013/01/tijuana-cartel.html.

56. Malcolm Beith, "On the Trail of El Chapo," *Australian Magazine*, 1st ed., September 11, 2010, 12; Chivis, "During First Incarceration, El Chapo Summoned DEA to Turn in Arellano Félix," *Borderland Beat*, March 10, 2014, www.borderlandbeat.com.

57. Chivis, "During First Incarceration."

58. Beith, "On the Trail of El Chapo," 12.

59. *Narcos Famosos* (Mexico City: Aimee SBP, 2009), 21–28. El Chuy was tied to the Arellano Félix family through his marriage to Agustina Félix Zazueta, the Arellano Félixes' aunt on their mother's side.

60. "Tijuana Cartel," *African Narco News*.

61. "Members of the Arellano Félix Organization," *Frontline*, n.d., http://web.archive.org/web/20121113141137/http://www.pbs.org/wgbh/pages/frontline/shows/drugs/business/afo/afomembers.html; "Los Arellano Félix habrían vendido la plaza de Tijuana a una nueva bana," *La Jornada* (Mexico), February 21, 2001, http://web.archive.org/web/20090422183637/http://www.jornada.unam.mx/2000/02/21/el.html.

62. "Alleged Drug Kingpin Being Held in Killing of Cardinal," *The Gazette* (Canada), December 7, 1993, sec. A, p. 7.

63. "La Nueva Generación de Narcotraficantes," *Dossier Politico* (Mexico), June 12, 2005, www.dossierpolitico.com.

64. Christopher Reed, "Cocaine Kings Score in Needle Match," *Guardian*, April 16, 1996, 9. Narcojuniors of note include Fabian Martínez ("El Tiburon"), Federico Sánchez Valdez ("G-1"), and Merardo León Hinojosa ("El Abulon").

65. Poppa, *Drug Lord*, 186.

66. Borges, *La Historia Secreta*, 74–75; Héctor González, "Los Prófugos deal Salinato," *Agencia Mexicana de Información*, no. 781, February 21, 2007, www.red-ami.com/cgi-bin/ed_seccion.cgi?dt=21/02/2007&ref=20070221/090/20070220-132332.txt.

67. "Confidential DEA Summary: Guillermo González Calderóni," *Frontline*, n.d., www.pbs.org/wgbh/pages/frontline/shows/mexico/family/secretdea.html.

68. Borges, *La Historia Secreta*, 80.

69. "Salinas Acusado de Narcotrafico," *Hoy* (Ecuador), July 30, 1995, www.hoy.com. In June 1993, the Mexican police confiscated Carvajal Paternina's $3 million house in Ciudad Juárez, which was once owned by President Echeverría.

The Emergence of the Mexican Cartel Networks   83

70. Marjorie Miller, "Suspected Drug Lord Shot to Death at Mexican Resort," *Los Angeles Times*, April 15, 1993, http://articles.latimes.com/1993-04-15/news /mn-23097_1_cancun-attack; Borges, *La Historia Secreta del Narco*, 100.

71. Borges, *La Historia Secreta del Narco*, 81–86. The marriage was between Heriberto Leyva and Angélica Chaparro. The prison is in Xochimilco.

72. William Branigan, "Allegations of Corruption Rile Mexicans, Helms Accuses Leaders of Drug Related Activity," *Washington Post*, March 18, 1989, sec. A, p. 29. Following the arrest of Gulf cartel leader García Ábrego in January 1996, Coello Trejo's former aide, González Calderóni, revealed that Coello Trejo took millions of dollars in bribes from cartels.

73. Marjorie Miller, "Mexico's Tough Drug Czar Loses His Job," *Los Angeles Times*, October 16, 1990, http://articles.latimes.com/1990-10-16/news/mn-2539_1 _human-rights.

74. American Embassy Mexico to DEA Headquarters Washington, DC, "Subject: Summary of Significant News Releases/Mexico," Mexico 09026 032338Z, April 1992, 2.

75. Julia Preston, "A General in Mexico's Drug War Is Dismissed on Narcotics Charges," *New York Times*, February 19, 1997, sec. A, p. 1. The lieutenant was Eduardo González Quirate.

76. Tracy Wilkinson, "José de Jesus Gutiérrez Rebollo Dies at 79; Disgraced Mexican General," *Los Angeles Times*, December 20, 2013, http://articles.latimes .com/2013/dec/20/local/la-me-José-Gutiérrez-rebollo-20131221.

77. Borderland Beat Reporter Buggs, "Sinaloa Cartel," *Borderland Beat*, August 30, 2010, www.borderlandbeat.com.

78. Mexico Institute, "The Félix Gallardo Organization," Woodrow Wilson Institute, January 14, 2000, www.wilsoncenter.org.

79. Chivis, "During First Incarceration."

80. Tim Golden, "Mexican Connection Grows as Supplier to the U.S.," *New York Times*, July 30, 1995, sec. A, p. 1.

81. Sam Dillon, "Matamoros Journal; Canaries Sing in Mexico, but Uncle Juan Will Not," *New York Times*, February 9, 1996; "Cartel del Golfo: Juan Nepomuceno Guerra," *Cero Miedo* (Mexico), December 18, 2010, http://ceromiedo .wordpress.com.

82. Tim Golden, "A Drug Figure Is Said to Offer to Surrender to Mexicans," *New York Times*, August 23, 1995, sec. A, p. 5.

83. Borderland Beat Reporter Buggs, "Gulf Cartel," *Borderland Beat*, May 11, 2009, www.borderlandbeat.com.

84. Yolanda Figueroa, *El Capo del Golfo: Vida y Captura de Juan García Ábrego* (Mexico City: Editorial Grijalbo, 1996), 41; Sam Dillon, "Mexican Drug Gang's Reign of Blood," *New York Times*, February 4, 1996, sec. A, p. 10. El Cacho's full name was Casmiro Espinosa Campos. Among the eight killed were also a husband and a son visiting their ailing wife and mother, and a bedridden thirty-five-year-old woman.

85. Figueroa, *El Capo del Golfo*, 146–148; José Luis Trueba Lara, *García Ábrego* (Mexico City: Editorial Posada, 1996), 47–48. Chief of security was José Pérez de la Rosa ("El Amable"). On the payroll were Indalecio Ríos (DFS) and Eloy Treviño García (PJFM).

86. Luis Astorga, *El Siglo de las Drogas*, 2nd ed. (Mexico City: Random House, 2016), 197.

87. Paul B. Carroll, "García Is the Enemy in the War on Drugs," *Wall Street Journal*, December 13, 1994, sec. A, p. 15.

84 *Narcostates*

88. US Department of Justice, "Mexican Drug Fugitive Named to FBI's Most Wanted List," March 9, 1995, www.justice.gov/opa/pr/Pre_96/March95/133c.txt.html.

89. US Department of State Mexican Affairs to State Department/ARA/Mexico City, "Background Paper: Juan García Ábrego," January 15, 1996, 1 (National Security Archive Electronic Collection, México-U.S. Counternarcotics Policy 1969–2013).

90. US Congress, Senate Foreign Relations Committee, Subcommittee on the Western Hemisphere, "International Drug Trafficking Organizations in Mexico," 104th Cong., 1st sess., August 8, 1995, www.justice.gov/dea/pubs/cngrtest/ct950808 .htm, Statement of DEA Administrator Thomas A. Constantine. Cocaine was sold in Houston for $17,000 to $23,000 per kilogram. In Los Angeles and New York, it was valued between $23,000 and $25,000 per kilogram.

91. "La Historia Narcopolitica," *El Universal* (Mexico), June 17, 2012, www .eluniversal.com.

92. Trueba Lara, *García Ábrego*, 57.

93. Astorga, *El Siglo*, 208–211; Beatriz Johnston Hernández, "Plática de narcos grabada por el FBI, revela nexos de González Calderóni," *Proceso* (Mexico), February 5, 2003, www.proceso.com; "González Calderóni, hilo de la maraña narcopolítica," *Proceso* (Mexico), February 5, 1993, www.proceso.com.

94. *United States of America v. Juan García Ábrego*, http://caselaw.findlaw.com /us-5th-circuit/1396381.html; Ciero Miedo, "Cartel del Golfo: Juan García Ábrego," n.d., https://ceromiedo.wordpress.com, accessed March 5, 2022.

95. Tim Golden, "Salinas's Brother Charged in Mexican Assassination," *New York Times*, March 1, 1995, sec. A, p. 1.

96. John P. Sullivan and Adam Ekus, "State of Siege: Mexico's Criminal Insurgency," in *Mexico's Criminal Insurgency*, ed. John P. Sullivan and Robert J. Bunker (Bloomington, IN: IUniverse, Inc., 2012), 8.

5

Mexico in Crisis

The conflict between the Sinaloa and the Arellano Félix cartels put an end to all that remained of Félix Gallardo's empire. Their war began in 1989 when El Chapo moved Sinaloa operations into Tijuana, angering the Arellano Félix brothers whose control of Tijuana had been assured by Félix Gallardo. Multiple assassination attempts against cartel leaders accompanied by the brutal—and often sadistic—murders of their lieutenants and soldiers followed. Caught in the crossfire were innocent civilians, a Catholic cardinal, and at least two political leaders. In the midst of growing economic and political instability, Mexico's internecine cartel conflicts continued well into the 1990s.

Cartel violence, internal insurrection, and corruption brought Mexico to its knees. Allegations linking the cartels and the PRI to the 1994 assassination of presidential candidate Donaldo Colosio undermined Mexico's political system. Concurrently, Mexico experienced serious economic and political disruptions. The 1994 implementation of the North American Free Trade Agreement (NAFTA) and the tightening of international interest rates brought the Mexican economy to the brink of collapse. In Chiapas, the Ejército Zapatista de Liberación Nacional (EZLN) led a rebellion of campesinos against the PRI government, resulting in the disintegration of Mexico's border with Guatemala. Although the EZLN did not condone narcotrafficking, the ensuing lawlessness turned Chiapas into a drug trafficking corridor. In addition to all else, the 1994 investigation into the assassination of José Ruiz Massieu, the PRI's general secretary, revealed the Salinas administration's ties to narcotraffickers. By the mid-1990s, Mexico appeared to be on the verge of becoming a narcostate.

86 *Narcostates*

The Cartel War and the Murder of
Cardinal Posadas Ocampo

The cartel war erupted on January 30, 1989, when a Sinaloa trafficker and pilot named Armando López ("El Rayo") was killed while attempting to mediate the territorial dispute between Benjamín Arellano Félix and El Chapo over Tijuana.[1] Revenge drove El Chapo and El Güero to assassinate associates close to Félix Gallardo and the Arellano Félix family.[2] In January 1990, the Arellano Félix cartel escalated the war by beheading El Güero's first wife and his five-year-old son.[3] Bent on revenge, El Güero formed a death squad that committed a series of murders including the assassination of Rodolfo Sánchez Duarte, Félix Gallardo's godson who was also the son of Leopoldo Sánchez Celis, the governor of Sinaloa from 1963 to 1968.[4] The assassinations resumed in 1992 when four relatives and five friends of Félix Gallardo were abducted, murdered, and dumped into a ravine in Guerrero. These killings were followed by a massive raid to kill the Arellano Félix brothers at the Christine Discothèque in Puerto Vallarta on November 8, 1992. Although the attempt failed, the brazen attack in the center of Puerto Vallarta created international headlines.[5]

The assassination of Cardinal Posadas Ocampo brought to light the chaos of the cartel war as well as the Mexican people's growing mistrust of their leaders and institutions. On May 24, 1993, El Chapo traveled to Guadalajara to hunt down the Arellano Félix brothers, but they were ready for him. According to the official story, both gangs converged on the Guadalajara airport in search of each other. An informant told Ramón Arellano Félix that El Chapo was flying out of Guadalajara and would be arriving at the airport in a white Mercury Grand Marquis. When Ramón and a squad of twenty armed men arrived at the airport parking lot in three trucks, they saw their target and opened fire.[6] The hitmen riddled the Grand Marquis with twenty-six bullet holes. But, unbeknownst to Ramón, El Chapo sped away in a green Cutlass. When the shooting stopped, the body of Cardinal Juan Posadas Ocampo was found inside the Grand Marquis. Visiting the airport to greet the papal nuncio, the cardinal was hit by fourteen bullets and died instantly. Also killed were the driver and four other bystanders.

The Arellano Félix gang apparently blundered by mistaking the cardinal's car for El Chapo's car.[7] Or did they? The official police story was that Cardinal Posadas Ocampo was not the intended target. The unofficial story claimed that he was the target all along. As the story went, he had publicly criticized Mexico's drug trafficking epidemic and was killed because he was too outspoken. Members of the Mexican Catholic Church hierarchy speculated that he was assassinated to frame the Arellano Félix brothers and to direct attention away from Mexican government officials. Cardinal Sandoval

Íñiguez criticized the government's subsequent investigation of the murder. He maintained that the evidence, which pointed to a different conclusion, was swept under the rug to protect high-ranking officials from prosecution. He further alleged that the cardinal was killed on the direct orders of government officials to prevent the cardinal from revealing what he knew.[8] Sandoval Íñiguez himself was also accused of having ties to drug traffickers. In his defense, he maintained that the Mexican attorney general, Jorge Carpizo McGregor, was trying to frame him for refusing to accept the results of the government's investigation. Although he was cleared of any wrongdoing, the suspicion of a cover-up did not end there.[9] Benjamín Arellano Félix issued a statement asserting that the Tijuana and Sinaloa cartels were being framed and that the Mexican government was to blame for the murder.[10]

The Mexican Government Response

The killing of the cardinal was big news, and the cartel war exploded into Mexico's public consciousness. To repair his credibility with the public and the Catholic Church, President Carlos Salinas de Gortari (1988–1994) launched an unprecedented effort against narcotrafficking.[11] He declared drug trafficking an international problem and a threat to Mexico's national security.[12] Early in his administration, Mexico endorsed the 1988 UN Convention Against Drug Traffic and Dependency on Psychotropic Substances. Salinas also backed bilateral antinarcotics agreements with multiple governments and greatly expanded Mexican eradication and interdiction efforts.[13] Figures 5.1, 5.2, and 5.3 show the success of Salinas's eradication efforts and drug seizures.

Salinas's professed commitment to Mexico's counternarcotics program spurred the Mexican government to reform and strengthen the program from within. In June 1993, Salinas cleaned house within the PGR with a one-day dismissal of sixty-seven narcotics agents tied to the cartels. He also instituted financial incentives to fight corruption.[14] On the day that he dismissed the PGR personnel, Salinas created the Instituto Nacional para el Combate a las Drogas (INCD), styled after the DEA, and promised closer ties between Mexico and the United States in the areas of intelligence sharing and the apprehension of suspects.[15]

Following Posadas Ocampo's murder, the Mexican police intensified the manhunt for members of the Sinaloa and Tijuana cartels. The Arellano Félix brothers, along with El Chapo and El Güero, became Mexico's most wanted. The Mexican government issued a $5 million dollar reward for their arrest. Radio and TV stations repeatedly displayed their pictures and broadcast announcements offering a reward for their apprehension.[16]

After being spotted in El Salvador, El Chapo fled to Guatemala, but he failed to bribe his way out of trouble and was extradited to Mexico on June

Figure 5.1 Marijuana Eradication and Cultivation in Hectares, 1989–1995

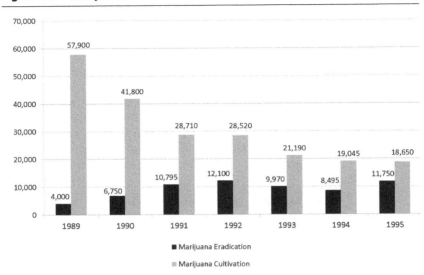

Source: US Department of State, Bureau of International Narcotics and Law Enforcement Affairs, *1996 International Narcotics Control Strategy Report Vol. I*, 149.

Figure 5.2 Marijuana Seizures in Metric Tons, 1989–1995

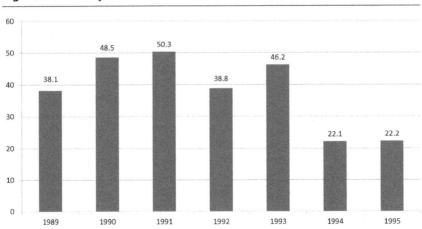

Source: US Department of State, Bureau of International Narcotics and Law Enforcement Affairs, *1996 International Narcotics Control Strategy Report Vol. I*, 149.

Figure 5.3 Cocaine Seizures in Metric Tons, 1989–1995

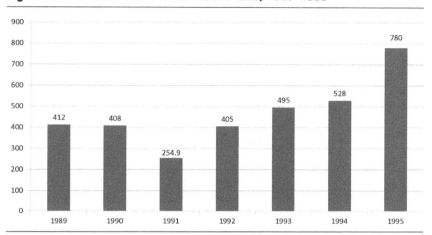

Source: US Department of State, Bureau of International Narcotics and Law Enforcement Affairs, *1996 International Narcotics Control Strategy Report Vol. I*, 149.

9, 1993. Incarcerated at Puente Grande maximum security prison in Jalisco, El Chapo lived in complete luxury. He took over the prison by corrupting the guards, including the warden. Alcohol, drugs, and prostitutes were readily available. Family members could come and go.[17] El Chapo handed external control of the cartel over to his brother while he managed his empire from prison. He remained imprisoned until January 19, 2001, when he escaped in order to avoid extradition to the United States.

The war with the Arellano Félix cartel expanded to include Amado Carrillo Fuentes's Juárez cartel after he partnered with the Sinaloa cartel. On November 24, 1993, the Arellano Félixes attempted to assassinate Carrillo Fuentes at the Ochoa Bali Hai restaurant in Mexico City. The narcojuniors killed three of his bodyguards, but he and his family managed to escape. The Arellano Félixes knew that they would never get past his armed guards, but they were sending a message—any attempt to move in on Tijuana would be blocked.[18]

After El Chapo's incarceration in 1993, police pressure on El Güero Palma grew. He lived in Sonora with his second wife, protected by the police. He consistently co-opted the Sonora police with monthly payments totaling more than $8 million and sent payments to the Guadalajara police totaling $40 million a month. Many of the police were employed as bodyguards, assassins, and convoy guards for El Güero. According to US embassy analysts, because of El Güero's ability to hide in plain sight, the

90 *Narcostates*

government of Mexico had to assume that "entire police bodies" were completely compromised. However, a failure to maintain security following the crash of his Lear jet led to the arrest of El Güero and thirty-five PJFM officers. On June 22, 1995, the PGR and army had noticed the plane's erratic flight activity just before it crashed near the Tepic airport in the state of Nayarit. Although the crash site was deserted when the authorities arrived, Mexico's military intelligence recorded suspicious vehicles traveling to Guadalajara from Tepic, which led to the surprise capture of El Güero.[19]

Mexican Instability

In the midst of the Tijuana-Sinaloa cartel war, Mexico suffered another setback equal to, if not greater than, the death of Cardinal Posadas Ocampo. On March 24, 1994, Donaldo Colosio Murrieta, the presidential candidate for the PRI, was assassinated while campaigning in Tijuana. Allegations, rumors, and conspiracy theories proliferated following the assassination. The indictments of three Tijuana judicial policemen, followed by the indictment of a CISEN officer, fueled suspicions about the assassination.[20] The Mexican people could not understand the inadequate security around Colosio that allowed a gunman to get close enough to shoot him execution style. Many Mexicans believed that his political rivals or Mexican drug lords were involved. The subsequent assassination of Tijuana Police Chief Federico Benítez raised the public's skepticism to an all-time high as the investigation ran into a dead end.[21] An investigation ordered by President Ernesto Zedillo (1994–2000) muddied the waters when it led to the arrests of Othón Cortés Vázquez, a PRI operative who was identified as a second assassin, and Fernando de la Sota, the head of Colosio's bodyguard detail.[22] De la Sota's arrest further discredited the Mexican government's story when it was learned that he was a former DFS agent who became a CIA asset in Mexico City from 1990 to 1992, and then a PJFM officer until he was forced out in 1992 for protecting the Juárez cartel.[23] Because the government's narrative left so many questions unanswered, the Mexican people's faith in their political institutions was significantly diminished.

Following Colosio's death, Mexico descended deeper into economic and political uncertainty. Prior to his death, Mexico pegged the peso to the US dollar, but an influx of foreign capital caused an overvaluation of the peso. With the changes in trade relationships accompanying the 1994 NAFTA agreement, Mexican products could no longer compete with cheaper imports. Added to this, the US Federal Reserve Bank raised interest rates in 1994. Foreign capital fled Mexico in search of higher returns in the United States. A wave of divestment befell the Mexican economy. To maintain market stability, the Mexican government asked the US Securities and Exchange Commission to delay trading in American Depository Receipts (foreign stocks traded on the US stock exchange).[24] President Salinas then devalued the peso by 15 percent while the Mexican Central Bank raised interest rates to prevent further capital flight. To prevent interest rates from going higher, the Mexican government also bought Mexican treasuries known as Tesbonos with its foreign reserves. With few investors purchasing Mexican debt and a steady decline in Mexico's US dollar reserves, Mexico became illiquid. Having no other alternatives, the Mexican government floated the peso on the open market, ending its policy of pegging the peso to the dollar. This decision led to another 40 percent devaluation of the peso.

The Mexican economic meltdown became known as the Tequila Crisis and spread throughout Latin America. Since Mexico's default in 1982, this was the second time that the Mexican economy was near collapse. To prevent a collapse, Mexico received international loans totaling almost $50 billion. The Clinton administration secured $20 billion in loans, the International Monetary Fund offered credit of $17.7 billion, and the Bank for International Settlements offered another $10 billion in credit. Mexico's economy slipped to a negative 5.8 percent in 1995 but rebounded in 1996 with an annual growth rate of 5.9 percent. Unemployment remained elevated throughout 1995 with Mexico's unemployment rate reaching 6.9 percent in early 1996, 5.2 percent by the end of the year, and 4.1 percent in 1997.[25]

The economic downturn damaged the Mexican people's political support for the country's neoliberal programs, including NAFTA, which was already viewed as a gateway for drug smuggling into the United States. Mexican cartels sought to use NAFTA as a means to increase their cross-border shipments. They used *maquiladora* plants (free trade warehousing areas) and land purchases along the border to facilitate the flow of drugs northward.[26] According to one analyst at the US Army's Southern Command, new "opportunities for trafficking" would be explored if the "net effect of NAFTA is more trade." The analyst added, "If traffickers can use more secure smuggling methods under the cover of legitimate trade, fewer illegal/clandestine means might be used." In an era of reduced government spending, US border control agents were hard-pressed to keep up with inspections as Mexican imports increased.[27] According to a task force from the US Customs Bureau called Operation Alliance, "opportunities for traffickers" were "significantly greater with NAFTA."[28]

The US State Department rejected any idea that NAFTA increased the opportunity for smuggling. US ambassador to Mexico, John Negroponte, claimed the argument was unfounded and argued that the logic was wrong. If more Mexican imports meant more opportunities for drug smuggling, then the same was true in the other direction; there would be more precursor

92 Narcostates

chemicals shipped into Mexico from the United States.[29] The Salinas government, which had negotiated NAFTA, also countered the critics by arguing that NAFTA increased US-Mexican collaboration and ensured greater access to the resources necessary to fight drug traffickers because of the hefty revenues that Mexico would earn from the cross-border trade. To underscore his commitment to reduce cross-border drug trafficking, President Salinas ordered his deputy treasury secretary to clean up the customs service, especially their widespread tolerance for *mordidas* (bribes).[30]

Coupled with the economic crisis and the assassination of Colosio, an indigenous revolt in Chiapas further crippled Mexico. The EZLN—the Zapatistas—began their rebellion in January 1994, two months before Colosio's murder. With the influence of Catholic liberation theology, the loss of land following the 1970s oil boom, and the debt crisis of the 1980s, the indigenous campesinos of southern Mexico began to view rebellion as a means to improve their conditions. The implementation of NAFTA ignited the rebellion. By forcing Mexico to phase out subsidies on corn, sugar, and coffee, NAFTA undermined the traditional economy of the Indian campesinos.[31] The Salinas government also turned a blind eye to ranchers and loggers who forced Indians off their lands. The Zapatistas viewed the loss of land as a violation of the *ejido* system—a system that dated back to the Mexican Revolution and gave Indian squatters the right to occupy unused land. As Salinas's secretary of social development, Donaldo Colosio led a populist antipoverty campaign to alleviate the effects of Salinas's neoliberalization programs on Mexico's poor. A large amount of the campaign's aid to buy land and build schools and hospitals went to Chiapas's campesinos. The EZLN viewed the campaign as a PRI ploy to placate the population while keeping them impoverished and dependent.[32] In protest, the Zapatistas hoped to initiate a nationwide movement calling for "jobs, land, housing, food, health, independence, freedom, democracy, justice, and peace."[33] The stated goal of the EZLN was not to overthrow the government but rather to challenge the PRI's hold on power in order to force reforms that guaranteed representation for all Mexicans.[34]

A large swath of Chiapas was held by the Zapatistas until peace talks brought about a negotiated settlement. The Zapatistas captured several villages and the towns of Altamirano and Las Margaritas in southern Chiapas but had limited resources to wage a protracted military campaign. The Mexican government swiftly deployed 70,000 soldiers to Chiapas in order to stop the Zapatistas from making any further gains. The Zapatistas' strategy, however, was to attract worldwide attention in order to pressure the government into discussions while avoiding armed conflict as much as possible. At the beginning of 1994, a fragile peace was struck, which was then followed by negotiations. The government offered to initiate public works programs in Chiapas such as the building of roads, housing, health clinics, and schools. It also promised to implement electoral reform and to develop a land reform program within six months.[35]

More than a year later, in November 1995, the Mexican government and the Zapatistas finalized the peace process that guaranteed "the exercise of [Indigenous] forms of socio-cultural and political organization [and] access to the use and enjoyment of natural resources, except those whose management corresponds to the nation." This meant that the Indigenous people of Mexico could assert their political autonomy while allowing the Mexican government to retain control over Chiapas, which held vast oil reserves for the state oil monopoly, Petróleos Mexicanos (PEMEX).[36]

In relation to drug trafficking, the Zapatistas created a lawless situation along the Guatemalan border with Chiapas where the EZLN, the Mexican government, and drug traffickers competed for power. When the rebellion started, the Salinas administration claimed it was an attempt by external influences, in this case Guatemalan guerrillas and drug cartels, to destabilize Mexico.[37] The chief threat to national security, according to General García Magana, was drug smuggling, which was "more serious than the armed conflict in Chiapas."[38] Despite the EZLN's prohibition on drug use and trafficking, the Zapatistas denounced any Mexican military effort to secure the Chiapas border as a covert pretext to abrogate the peace. In February 1996, the US Department of State reported that Mexican traffickers were taking advantage of the lack of border controls to transport cocaine through Chiapas, noting that it was impossible to stop due to local circumstances.[39]

The Massieu Assassination

The murder of José Ruiz Massieu, the general secretary of the PRI, exposed the deep links between the government and the Gulf cartel. Ruiz Massieu was shot and killed on September 28, 1994, by gunman Aguilar Treviño, who received $17,000 for the assassination.[40] Massieu's brother Mario led the investigation into the assassination.[41] Officially, he concluded that his brother's murder was the result of a conspiracy devised inside the PRI by Congressman Manuel Muñoz Rocha, who disappeared and was never seen again after this revelation.[42] Mario Massieu also accused President Salinas and PRI officials of obstructing justice.[43]

When Ernesto Zedillo became president of Mexico, he reopened the investigation. In March 1995, Zedillo's attorney general ordered the arrest of Raúl Salinas, the brother of former President Carlos Salinas, on the charge of planning Massieu's murder. The PGR had determined that when Muñoz Rocha initially disappeared, he took refuge in Raúl's home. They also provided evidence that he used Raúl's credit cards during his escape and received an $80,000 payment that could be traced back to Raúl.[44]

94   Narcostates

Raúl Salinas's ties to the Gulf cartel and money laundering operations were unequivocally exposed by the Massieu investigation. Implicated in the laundering of tens of millions of narcodollars were his wife, her brother, Massieu's brother Mario, Citibank, and the Basic Commodities Distribution Corporation (CONASUPO), led by Raúl Salinas. Guillermo Pallomari, an accountant for the Cali cartel (Ábrego's principal source of cocaine), testified that the Cali cartel paid $80 million to Mexican politicians between 1990 and 1993 and that half of the money went directly to Raúl Salinas.[45] Others placed under investigation included Raúl's chief of staff, his private secretary, and Mexico's secretary of the navy.[46] As a result of the scandal, Raúl Salinas lost all political protection. In 1999, he received a fifty-year jail sentence for the murder of Massieu. In 2005, his conviction was overturned, and he was released from prison. The charges of money laundering were dropped as well.

In 1995, the US Justice Department arrested Massieu's brother in New Jersey while he was in the process of transporting $46,000 through the United States en route to Spain. The Justice Department alleged that he took $9.9 million in bribes from traffickers and granted them immunity from prosecution in exchange for the money. In September 1999, he committed suicide while awaiting trial in the United States. In his suicide note, he denied having a hand in his brother's murder and accused Zedillo of covering up his brother's murder for political reasons on behalf of the PRI.[47]

According to Bernard Aronson, the US assistant secretary of state for Western Hemisphere affairs (1989–1993), Carlos Salinas was unaware of the corruption within his government. Aronson added that it would have been counterproductive to criticize the Salinas administration for corruption, as it would have jeopardized US-Mexican cooperation at a time when the Mexican government was ramping up its counternarcotics efforts.[48] Regardless of Carlos Salinas's culpability, the revelations about Raúl Salinas embittered the Mexican people and caused President Salinas to go into a self-imposed exile in Ireland.[49]

The Mexican State in Danger of
Becoming a Narcostate

Mexico showed signs of degenerating into a failed state. The ruling PRI was discredited for being thoroughly corrupt. The Tequila Crisis of 1994–1995 raised alarm bells in banks and governments throughout the world. Narcotraffickers were operating with impunity. Upon assuming the presidency in 1995, Zedillo tried to reverse course. However, in 1996, the US Congress refused to certify Mexico as a fully cooperative country in its efforts to control narcotics. Twice before, in 1987 and 1988, the US Congress introduced bills to decertify Mexico, but those threats were met with passive resistance. For example, José Ruiz Massieu once commented that he was "not worried so much about decertification as he was about the innovations of narcotraffickers." Chihuahua's governor, Fernando Baeza Meléndez, commented that international cooperation, not US certification, was important. Attorney General Coello Trejo stated that he too was not concerned about decertification but rather the "well-being of his people, which required better salaries, arms, vehicles, and radar systems."[50]

In 1996, the situation in Mexico was much different than it had been in 1988. Even though the Zedillo government eradicated 40 percent more crops in 1995 than in 1994, reduced marijuana cultivation from 5.4 metric tons in 1994 to 3.6 metric tons in 1996, and extradited Juan García Ábrego, the United States still decertified Mexico. The opinion of the US government and Congress was that "Mexico needed to do more."[51] In July 1996, both the House and the Senate placed restrictions on Mexico in the Foreign Operations Appropriations Act for fiscal year 1997. The final version of the bill provided that not less than $2.5 million would be withheld from Mexico until President Clinton reported that Mexico reduced the flow of illegal drugs to the United States and took action to prosecute drug traffickers and money launderers. Following the arrest of General Gutiérrez Rebollo in 1997, the United States recertified Mexico. However, several members of Congress opposed the decision and introduced resolutions to disapprove recertification. The Coverdell-Feinstein Amendment, which passed on March 20, 1997, required the US government to report about improvements in ten areas of drug control, including action against drug cartels, extradition, eradication, and money laundering activities.[52]

The Mexican people and government were trapped between US drug law requirements and the power of narcotraffickers. According to Sandalío González, former special agent in charge of the DEA's El Paso office, "The war on drugs does not exist; it is a myth because, in reality, the authorities do not use the appropriate resources in the manner that they need to. They spend much money on counternarcotics operations, but they do not use a necessary and sufficient amount to reduce demand in the United States."[53] Pressuring Mexico to do more looked good on paper, but executing those efforts was another story. Pursuing a "kingpin strategy" proved to be problematic. The dismantling of the Guadalajara cartel only served to create new drug trafficking organizations (DTOs). As the Mexican government continued to bear down on cartel leadership, new leaders would emerge.

Corruption within the political system limited Mexico's success in the drug war. Since its founding in 1929, the PRI's single-party, corporatist system turned a blind eye when it came to contraband smuggling.[54] Mexican drug traffickers were businessmen fulfilling a demand in the United States. With mountains of cash, they gained access to the government,

96   Narcostates

which permitted them to bribe officials in the PRI as well as Mexico's police, military, and intelligence agencies. The cartels gained political leverage, which empowered them to expand their operations at the expense of their competitors. While elements within the government sought to eliminate the individual cartels, the cartels bought off enough officials to prevent their destruction. Local authorities across Mexico tried to curb the corruption and violence generated by narcotrafficking, but more often than not they were compelled to make deals with the cartels, whose members were already protected by other law enforcement officials.[55] This method of corruption was perfected by Carrillo Fuentes's Juárez cartel and García Ábrego's Gulf cartel.

Mexico's institutions were gravely threatened by the narcotrade. The assassinations of Donaldo Colosio and José Massieu were shrouded in a conspiracy involving drug traffickers and the PRI. The inept investigation of Colosio's murder, followed by a string of murders that implicated the Arellano Félix cartel, engendered a sense of disillusionment. Following the killing of Massieu, the people's faith in Salinas's government was shaken because of Mexico's economic crash and a growing revulsion for PRI corruption. The arrest and suicide of Massieu's brother Mario confounded any effort to get to the bottom of Massieu's death and the extent of government corruption in Mexico.[56] For the Mexican people, the Massieu investigation verified what they already knew: narcotraffickers dominated the Mexican government.

If conjecture failed to show that Mexico was becoming a failed narcostate, then political reality demonstrated the truth. NAFTA, the 1994 peso crisis, and the Zapatista rebellion in Chiapas all contributed to the expansion of the drug trade. Despite assertions to the contrary, NAFTA increased the flow of narcotics across the US-Mexico border. The peso crisis that accompanied NAFTA nearly broke the Mexican economy. The depth of the meltdown and the conditions of the US bailout made the recovery for Mexico long and hard. The lack of employment opportunities and the expansion of the maquiladora industry along the US-Mexico border turned narcotrafficking into an alternate form of employment. Meanwhile, the Zapatista rebellion transformed Mexico's southern border into a sieve through which narcotraffickers imported South American cocaine into Mexico. Although the Zapatistas had nothing to do with narcotrafficking, their uprising inadvertently helped the Mexican cartels.

By the mid-1990s, the Mexican cartels were growing in power as events in South America and the Caribbean compelled Colombian traffickers to rely on the Mexican cartels to move their drugs. As the major Colombian cartels collapsed, the Mexican cartels expanded their operations. The winding down of Central America's civil wars and the changing business relationship between the Mexican and Colombian cartels provided an opportune moment for the Mexican cartels to take over the drug trade.

Notes

1. "Los Arellano Félix habrían vendido la plaza de Tijuana a una nueva bana," *La Jornada* (Mexico), February 21, 2001, http://web.archive.org/web/20090422183637 /http://www.jornada.unam.mx/2000/02/21/el.html.

2. Froylan Enciso, *Drogas, narcotráfico y política en México protocolo de hipocresía 1969–2000* (México City: Editorial Oceano, 2004), 237–238. A significant assassination was that of Carlos Morales García ("El Pelacuas"), an attorney for Félix Gallardo and the Arellano Félix brothers.

3. American Embassy Mexico to DEA Headquarters Washington, DC, "Summary of Significant News Releases," Mexico 14370 111611Z, July 1995, 3–4. El Güero's first wife was Guadalupe Leija de Palma. Her assassin was Rafael Clavel Moreno, a Venezuelan trafficker who seduced her before killing her.

4. American Embassy Mexico to Secretary of State Washington, DC, "Who Is El Güero Palma," Mexico 13575 040949Z, June 1995, 3; Enciso, *Drogas,* 238.

5. Tijuano, "The War for Tijuana: A 20+ Year Conflict Part I," *Borderland Beat,* May 22, 2013, www.borderlandbeat.com. Fifty assassins went disguised as members of the PJFM. The bodyguard, David Barron, noticed something wrong and helped Ramón escape. Francisco Javier was captured and told the war wasn't against the family, but against Ramón for killing El Rayo.

6. Tim Golden, "Mexican Cardinal Killed During Airport Shooting," *The Age* (Australia), May 26, 1993, International Section, p. 11.

7. American Embassy Mexico to DEA Headquarters Washington, DC, "Summary of Significant News Releases," Mexico 14370 111611Z, July 1995, 3–4.

8. "Conspiracy Cardinal Resigns; Served as Archbishop of Guadalajara for 17 Years," *Mexico Gulf Reporter,* December 7, 2011, www.mexicogulfreporter.com.

9. Kevin G. Hall, "Mexican Cardinal's Finances, Ties to Racetrack Owner Probed," *Philadelphia Inquirer,* October 27, 2003, http://articles.philly.com.

10. Tijuano, "The War for Tijuana: Part I."

11. DIA Washington, DC, to DIA CURINTEL, "Mexico: Ongoing Drug Trafficker Turf War," Item Number 00398119 Serial DIR 387-93 (June 29, 1993), 2.

12. American Embassy Mexico, "Subject: Status of Mexican Drug Enforcement Efforts," 4.

13. US Department of State, Bureau of International Narcotics and Law Enforcement Affairs, *1996 International Narcotics Control Strategy Report Vol. I* (Washington, DC: US Department of State, March 1997), 149.

14. Reuters, "Mexican Drug Inquiry Leads to Dismissal of 67 Officers," *New York Times,* June 16, 1993, sec. A, p. 13.

15. George W. Grayson, "NAFTA and the War on Drugs," *Journal of Commerce,* July 7, 1993, sec. A, p. 8.

16. DIA Washington, DC, "Mexico: Ongoing Drug Trafficker Turf War," 2.

17. Morris Thompson, "Kingpin Came-Went at Prison Escape Renews Calls to Clean Up Mexico's Corrupt Prison System," *San Jose Mercury News,* January 24, 2001, sec. A, p. 8.

18. Borges, *La Historia Secreta,* 111–112; Jose Guaderrama, "Una familia ligada al narcotráfico, la cárcel, y la tragedia," *El Universal* (Mexico), October 10, 2014, http://archivo.eluniversal.com.mx/nacion-mexico/2014/impreso/una-familia -ligada-al-narcotrafico-la-carcel-y-la-tragedia-219244.html.

19. American Embassy Mexico to DEA Headquarters Washington, DC, "Summary of Significant News Releases," Mexico 14370 111611Z, July 1995, 9. Tepic is located in Nayarit. As the jet approached Tepic, it ran out of fuel and

98   *Narcostates*

crash-landed on a ranch in the Ahuacatlan municipality. El Güero's safe house was in the Jardines de la Patria neighborhood. His second wife, Claudia Meza, seven bodyguards, and Guadalajara PJFM Comandante Pinto Aguillera were also arrested.

20. Tracey Eaton, "Mexican Assassination Part of an Elaborate Plot," *Ottawa Citizen* (Canada), April 5, 1994, sec. A, p. 1. Aburto Martínez was the assassin. Later, a security guard, Tranquilino Sánchez Venegas, was charged as an accomplice for pushing Colosio's security chief away.

21. Tim Golden, "Mexico Arrests State Prosecutor as Accomplice to Drug Ring," *New York Times*, May 5, 1994, sec. A, p. 7. Tijuana's deputy state attorney, Sergio Ortiz Lara, was alleged to have been behind the killing on the Tijuana cartel's behalf.

22. "Mexico Detains More Suspects: Cover-Up Theory in Colosio Killing," *Globe and Mail* (Canada), February 27, 1995.

23. Tim Weiner, "Former CIA Man Linked to Murder," *Globe and Mail* (Canada), August 3, 1995. De la Sota worked for the DFS from 1973 to 1985. He was accused of protecting Juárez cartel cofounder Rafael Aguilar Guajardo.

24. "Mexico, Inflation Fears Hit Stocks," *St. Louis Post-Dispatch*, March 25, 1994, sec. F, p. 1.

25. "Mexican Financial Markets, Politicians Cheered by Clinton Initiative," *Washington Post*, February 1, 1995, sec. A, p. 6; World Bank, *World Economic Development Indicators*, Mexican Unemployment, Washington, DC: World Bank, 2020, http://databank.worldbank.org/data/reports.aspx?source=2&country=MEX&series=&period=.

26. Joint Staff Washington, DC to AIG 7883 RUEHME USDAO, "Narcotics: Possible Intentions of Mexican Drug Organizations," Item Number 00608297 220130Z, January 1992, 0447.

27. USCINCSO Quarry Heights to RUEHBO/American Embassy Bogotá, "Free Trade Agreements and Drug Trafficking," Item Number 520305 301506Z, July 1993, 2.

28. Tracey Eaton, "NAFTA Brings Dirty Money with the Clean; Drug Traffic and Corruption Spell Violence Along the Border," *San Jose Mercury News*, August 31, 1998, sec. A, p. 11.

29. American Embassy Mexico to RUEHC Secretary of State Washington, DC, "Free Trade Agreements and Drug Trafficking: NAFTA," Mexico 20267 172120Z, August 1993, 18.

30. George W. Grayson, "NAFTA and the War on Drugs," *Journal of Commerce*, July 7, 1993, sec. A, p. 8. Between 1990 and 1992, Salinas had already discharged 269 federal agents.

31. Tod Robberson, "How Mexico Brewed a Rebellion: Economic Progress Trampled Indian Farms, State Quashed Protests," *Washington Post*, January 9, 1994, sec. A, p. 31.

32. Andres Oppenheimer, "Uprising Jolts Mexico's Political Climate," *San Jose Mercury News*, January 4, 1994, sec. A, p. 8.

33. Stephen J. Wagner and Donald Schulz, *The Awakening: The Zapatista Revolt and Its Implications for Civil-Military Relations and the Future of Mexico* (Carlisle Barracks: Strategic Studies Institute, US Army War College, December 30, 2004), 1.

34. Ibid., 1.

35. Ted Bardacke, "Mexico and Rebel Leaders Agree on Reforms," *Washington Post*, March 3, 1994, sec. A, p. 1.

36. "Mexico, Rebels Agree on Autonomy Pact," *Washington Post*, November 20, 1995, sec. A, p. 16.

37. Wagner and Schulz, *The Awakening*, 8.

38. American Embassy Mexico to DEA Field Division Los Angeles, "Subject: Summary of Significant News Releases/Mexico," Mexico 12953 201605Z, June 1995, 3.

39. American Embassy Mexico to DEA Field Division Houston, "Subject: Summary of Significant News Releases/Mexico," Mexico 0026778 221735Z, February 1996, 2.

40. Nancy Nusser, "Conspiracy in Mexican Politician's Death? Drugs, Money Laundering Surround Killing, Reports Say," *Atlanta Journal-Constitution*, October 2, 1994, sec. A, p. 14.

41. *Mario Ruiz Massieu v. Janet Reno*, US Court of Appeals for the Third Circuit, US District Court for the District of New Jersey, 915 F. Supp. 681, February 28, 1996, https://law.justia.com/cases/federal/district-courts/FSupp/915/681/1618129/. Mario Ruiz Massieu was ambassador to Denmark from 1990 to 1993. For part of 1993, he served as the deputy attorney general; in 1994, he was the Undersecretary for the Department of Government, and from May to November of 1994 he again held the position of deputy attorney general.

42. Mark Fineman, "Ex-President's Brother Held in Mexico Slaying: Assassination: Raúl Salinas de Gortari Is Accused of Masterminding the Killing of Ruling Party's No. 2 Official," *Los Angeles Times*, March 1, 1995. Muñoz Rocha came from Tamaulipas.

43. *Mario Ruiz Massieu v. Janet Reno*, https://law.justia.com/cases/federal/district-courts/FSupp/915/681/1618129.

44. John Ward Anderson, "Hard Times Find the Salinas Brothers," *Washington Post*, March 13, 1996, sec. A, p. 15.

45. Laura Hays, "Raúl Salinas Linked to Colombian Drug Lords," *Globe and Mail* (Canada), March 14, 1998, sec. A, p. 1.

46. John Ward Anderson, Molly Moore, and Douglas Farah, "Officials Probe Gulf Cartel, U.S. Bank Ties; Government Agency in Mexico May Be Criminal Cash Cow," *Washington Post*, May 11, 1997, sec. A, p. 1; US Congress, Senate Foreign Relations Committee, "International Drug Trafficking Organizations in Mexico," www.researchgate.net/publication/292148076_Political_corruption_and_drug _trafficking_in_Mexico_Opening_Statement. Salinas's chief of staff was José Cordoba Montoya. His private secretary was Justo Ceja Martínez. The secretary of the navy was Admiral Mauricio Scheleske Sánchez, who resigned but was not charged with a crime.

47. Damian Whitworth, "Cocaine Killers," *The Times* (England), December 8, 1999, Features sec.; Tim Golden, "Mexican in U.S. Suicide Note, Blames Zedillo for His Death," *New York Times*, September 17, 1999, www.nytimes.com.

48. Bernard W. Aronson (assistant secretary of state for Western Hemisphere affairs 1989–1993), telephone interview with author, October 10, 2011.

49. Carlos Puig, "Ruiz Massieu, el crimen perfecto," *Nexos* (Mexico), September 1, 2014, www.nexos.com.

50. American Embassy Mexico to DEAHQS Washington, DC, "Summary of Significant News Releases in the Republic of Mexico (February 24–March 2, 1989)," Mexico 06398 110154Z, March 1989, 3–4; American Embassy Washington, DC, to DEA Headquarters Washington, DC, "Subject: Summary of Significant News Releases in the Excelsior," Mexico 07948 301559Z, March 1989, 2.

51. "Narcotics Control Fact Sheet #2," 1.

52. K. Larry Storrs, *Mexican Drug Certification Issues: U.S. Congressional Action 1986–2002* (Washington, DC: Congressional Research Service, October 22, 2002), 2.

100 Narcostates

53. J. Jesús Esquivel, *La DEA en Mexico: Una Historia Oculta del Narcotráfico Contada por los Agentes* (Mexico City: Random House Mondadori, 2013), 171.

54. Watt and Zepeda, *Drug War in Mexico*, 1–35.

55. American Embassy Mexico to RUEHC/Secretary of State Washington, DC, "Mexico Monthly Narcotics Report April 1994," Mexico 12999 312229Z, May 1994, 2.

56. Carlos Puig, "Ruiz Massieu."

6

The Colombian Cartels Expand Their Reach

During the 1980s, the US-led multinational counternarcotics program—Operation Bahamas, Turks, and Caicos (OPBAT)—effectively closed the Caribbean corridor to narcotraffickers. Responding to the dragnet, Colombian DTOs expanded into Central America and appealed to the Guadalajara and Gulf cartels to reroute their operations through Mexico. Rampant corruption within Mexico's military and security agencies and the porous nature of the US southwestern border facilitated the Colombian-Mexican connection.[1] Despite the disintegration of the Guadalajara cartel, Colombian traffickers continued to rely on Mexico's second-generation cartels to transport their product. By 1989, 70 percent of Colombia's cocaine was passing through Mexico, often transiting through Central America first.[2] Colombian trafficking through Mexico went from minimal to conspicuous, as evidenced by the 950 Colombian nationals who were detained in Mexico City's prison system on drug charges in March 1989.[3]

When Colombian enforcement efforts brought down the Medellín and Cali cartels, their successors fractured into multiple minicartels. Colombian drug lords devised a new business model that eliminated the need for them to supervise the entire distribution process. Instead, they developed a decentralized model that prevented the Colombian government from completely disrupting operations. The Colombians concentrated their efforts on production and distribution into Mexico, while allowing the Mexican cartels to serve as middlemen who trafficked Colombian cocaine into the United States from Mexico. The chief of the Mexican narcotics investigation unit, Javier Coello Trejo, who would later come under scrutiny for being an accomplice to the Mexican cartels, succinctly described the situation: Mexico was a "trampoline for Colombian cocaine."[4] During this transition, the Mexican cartels took over the Colombian distribution networks

102   Narcostates

in the United States. Led by Juárez cartel capo Amado Carrillo Fuentes, the Mexicans presented the Colombians with a de facto situation—the Mexican cartels would become the primary distributors in the United States, and the Colombians would become the primary suppliers of cocaine, moving it north through Central America into Mexico. By the late 1990s, the Mexican cartels had evolved into the supercartels that the Medellín and Cali cartels once were.

As Central America's conflicts came to an end, the Colombian and Mexican DTOs began to view the region as an important stepping-stone for their operations. Mexican government interdiction efforts forced Colombian and Mexican traffickers to switch to Guatemala, and later the rest of Central America, as an alternative route for cocaine shipments.[5] Although traffickers had previously avoided Central America, they started to develop multiple techniques and routes to move their product through Central America into Mexico. Corruption and the use of force to intimidate government officials and businessmen were key factors in the region's drug trade. Weak government institutions and nonexistent counternarcotics programs in Central America further facilitated Colombian and Mexican DTO operations. The adaptability and perspicacity of the DTOs gave them a permanent foothold in both Mexico and Central America well before effective countermeasures could be developed.

The Medellín Cartel in Mexico

In the late 1980s, with their Caribbean routes closing down, the Medellín cartel began looking for new distribution routes. In *Drug Lord*, Terrence Poppa writes that because doing business through Florida had become too costly, the Medellín cartel turned toward the Mexicans, with whom they ran small-scale operations. Previously, the Medellín cartel had been unable to establish an independent presence in Mexico and only began to prosper with the assistance of the Guadalajara cartel.[6] The initial point of contact between the Guadalajara cartel and the Medellín cartel was established by Honduran trafficker Matta-Ballesteros who brought Félix Gallardo and Rodríguez Gacha together. Conjointly, both cartels moved thousands of pounds of Medellín cocaine through Mexico to a remote airstrip in Arizona.[7] Matta-Ballesteros would then transport the cocaine to southern California, where it was distributed throughout the United States.[8]

The first efforts between the Medellín cartel and Mexican traffickers concentrated on developing existing marijuana smuggling routes along the US-Mexico border to transport cocaine into the United States. The cartel worked actively with the Mexican DTOs to develop clandestine airfields to carry cocaine into Mexico, where they transferred it to US-registered airplanes for delivery across the border.[9] As early as 1986, the State Department warned that the Medellín cartel was collaborating with Mexican traffickers such as Pablo Acosta to establish an aviation route from Colombia into the northern state of Chihuahua. They also purchased farms and ranches to establish airfields on both sides of the US-Mexico border, including properties in Ojinaga, just across from Big Bend National Park in Texas. In 1989, the DEA reported that the Medellín cartel had established landing strips in Hermosillo in the state of Sonora.[10] Often, the Medellín cartel would fly cocaine into northern Mexico and turn it over to Mexican nationals, who transported it across the border where the Colombian distributors picked it back up.[11]

Other unique methods of smuggling cocaine and marijuana across the border included the use of surfboards, gas trucks, oil drums, tacos, and the false bottoms of cars.[12] Working with the Guadalajara cartel, the Medellín cartel also used tractor trailers to move cocaine from Colombia to Guadalajara, then on to Tijuana and across the border into the United States.[13] The Colombians paid $1,000 for each kilo of cocaine that the Mexican smugglers delivered to them in the United States.[14]

As the Medellín cartel stepped up its war against the Colombian government, the US State Department reported that the PJFM was seizing weapons bound for the cartel in Colombia. In February 1988, the PJFM seized 100 AK-47 rifles and 65,000 rounds of ammunition from an Agua Prieta concrete block factory owned by Félix Gallardo. At the scene, the PJFM arrested six members of the Medellín cartel who were in the process of preparing those weapons and other military equipment, such as night scopes, for shipment to Colombia.[15] Following the raid, US and Mexican authorities raised concerns over an increase in the use of sophisticated weapons by traffickers.[16] The arrest of Mexican drug trafficker Ramón Chávez confirmed this fact. Chávez was arrested in 1987 while delivering weapons to the Medellín cartel as part of a drugs-for-guns transaction. In this deal, the Medellín cartel traded 600 kilograms of cocaine in exchange for 800 AK-47 rifles in order to reinforce their "little war" against the Colombian government's extradition policies.[17]

The 1989 arrest of Giuseppe Ponsiglione in Ciudad Juárez and the simultaneous seizure of 1,385 kilos of cocaine in Chihuahua and Oaxaca was a major event for Mexico and the cartels. Ponsiglione came from Palermo, Italy, and was a member of the French Connection. He was also one of the main representatives of the Medellín cartel in Mexico, coordinating operations with the Guadalajara cartel. His arrest showed that a wide international narcotrafficking network functioned in Mexico that included the French Connection, the Colombian cartels, and the Mexican cartels. When speaking of the French Connection's ties to the Colombian and Mexican cartels, James Mills, author of *The Underground Empire,* pointed out that "there was formed between Latin Americans, Asians, Europeans, and

104   *Narcostates*

Americans an international conduit connecting criminal organizations on four continents . . . [and] through this conduit [they] moved drugs, weapons, and money with relative ease and security."[18] By 1989, the DEA was reporting that Colombian and other South American traffickers had moved their operations into Mexico working in conjunction with Mexican DTOs.[19] That same year the State Department noted that authorities in the state of Guadalajara were losing the fight against drugs and that the Medellín cartel was using Guadalajara as a shipping point for the US market.[20]

As the Medellín cartel began to disintegrate during the early 1990s, the Mexican government forced the cartel to change its methods of operation in Mexico. Rather than paying the Mexican DTOs cash to move cocaine across the border, the Medellín cartel paid them in narcotics and allowed them to establish their own distribution networks in the United States.[21] In the Los Angeles area, Mexicans or Mexican-Americans picked up cocaine from planes landing in the desert east of Los Angeles and transported it into the city.[22] The Mexican government's arrest of Javier Pardo Cardona and the Muñoz Talavera brothers in 1992 signaled the end of the Medellín cartel's operations in Mexico. Pardo Cardona established a radio communications and air route system for the Medellín cartel that ran through Panama, Honduras, Guatemala, and Mexico. His network smuggled tons of cocaine into the United States and laundered money through real estate purchases, banking operations, and investments on the Mexican stock exchange.[23] The Muñoz Talavera brothers appeared to be honest businessmen from Juárez, but in reality they covertly transported nearly 400 tons of cocaine and laundered millions of dollars on behalf of the Juárez and Medellín cartels between 1988 and 1992.[24] Their arrests created a vacuum in Mexico that the Medellín cartel could not fill.

The Cali Cartel Moves In

The Cali cartel, a longtime rival of the Medellín cartel, quickly assumed control of Mexican trafficking routes following the Medellín cartel's collapse in 1993. Their presence had been observed as early as 1989, when the DEA reported that the Cali cartel had developed a communications command center in Mexico City to coordinate operations throughout Mexico, Central and South America, the United States, and Europe. In March 1990, Mexican police arrested several Cali cartel operatives in Guadalajara. They were in Mexico to fill the void left by the decline of both the Medellín and Guadalajara cartels. The Cali cartel's goal was to establish a drug ring working out of Guadalajara while simultaneously preparing clandestine airstrips in places like Guanajuato for cocaine coming from Cali.[25] According to the Mexican PGR, in the first three months of 1990 alone, the Cali cartel smuggled 6,023 kilos or almost six tons of cocaine through Guadalajara.[26] By November 1990, the State Department reported that because the "government of Colombia focused on the Medellín cartel with success, the Cali cartel became responsible for most of the trafficking through Mexico."[27] Mexican police reports illustrated the Cali cartel's vast air-trafficking network: near Todos Santos on the Baja Peninsula (an uncontested territory between the Mexican cartels at this time), a Cessna 441 with a Mexican registry crashed when it ran out of fuel. The plane started in Colombia's Valle del Cauca and was bound for California when it crashed. Mexican authorities seized 685 kilos of cocaine and arrested three Colombians, all members of the Cali cartel.[28]

The Cali cartel worked closely with the Gulf cartel to move cocaine through Mexico toward the United States. Instead of the more flamboyant operations of the Medellín cartel, the Cali cartel preferred to associate with Mexican traffickers who effectively "greased the palms" of officials within the Mexican system. As the United States stepped up efforts to close down the Caribbean corridor in the 1980s, the Cali cartel developed close ties with García Ábrego, the leader of the Gulf cartel, who offered to handle all of the Cali cartel's cocaine shipments into the United States in exchange for 50 percent of the profits.[29] In 1993, the State Department reported that the Cali cartel in association with García Ábrego was investing heavily in Cancún and had set up a money laundering scheme using front companies in Quintana Roo.[30] By 1994, the Gulf cartel handled as much as "one-third of all cocaine shipments" into the United States from Cali cartel suppliers.[31]

The Cali cartel shared mutual interests with the Arellano Félixes. In 1991, they collaborated in the execution of Juan Salcido Uzeta ("El Cochiloco"). Salcido Uzeta was a former lieutenant for Caro Quintero and a cofounder of the Sinaloa cartel operating in Mazatlán who ran cocaine for the Medellín cartel out of Jalisco, Sinaloa, and Colima. Salcido Uzeta signed his own death warrant when he stole four tons of Cali cartel cocaine bound for the Arellano Félixes. The Cali cartel blamed the Arellano Félixes, and in order to rectify the situation, a deal was reached between the two cartels. If the Cali cartel killed Salcido, Ramón Arellano Félix would pay the Cali cartel for the lost shipment and assume control over Salcido's plaza of distribution. The arrangement was a win-win situation for both parties because it eliminated a rival associated with the Sinaloa and Medellín cartels. On October 9, 1991, Cali assassins fired more than seventy bullets into Uzeta's SUV as he drove through Zapopan, Jalisco, instantly killing Uzeta and a Mexican army lieutenant accompanying him in the SUV.[32]

Despite cartel disputes, business came first for the Cali cartel. In order to promote its interests, the cartel approached the Juárez cartel.[33] In January 1992, Carrillo Fuentes, the emerging capo of the Juárez cartel, made an agreement with the Cali cartel to fly cocaine-laden Boeing 727 jets directly from Colombia to Mexico. This air-trafficking operation made Carrillo

106 *Narcostates*

Fuentes the most powerful trafficker in Mexico and earned him the nickname "Lord of the Skies."[34] In 1991, the State Department noted that Colombian traffickers associated with the Cali cartel were "using increasingly faster and more sophisticated aircraft to smuggle cocaine to Mexico." They also reported that the traffickers adapted their tactics to law enforcement efforts by "unloading their smuggling aircraft much faster" and "dispersing sooner."[35] Carrillo Fuentes's smuggling innovations marked these changes. It soon became apparent that Mexico needed interceptor-chase aircraft rather than helicopters, but by this point it was too late.

The Deluge

The Cali and Juárez cartels laundered enormous sums of money through Mexico's financial sector. The DEA estimated that Carrillo Fuentes's smuggling operations generated tens of millions of dollars per week for both cartels, reportedly forwarding $20–$30 million to Colombia for each operation.[36] Inevitably, these narcodollars entered Mexico's banking system. For example, Operation Cadence, a PGR anti–money laundering operation, seized $35 million in laundered money, resulting in the arrest of several Cali cartel and Juárez cartel associates, along with officials from twenty-six Mexican banks. Operation Cadence also revealed that the Cali-Juárez operatives laundered their proceeds by depositing them in Mexican banks, such as Banca Confia, Bancomer, and Banca Serfin using US wire transfers. After receiving the deposits, the banks issued bank drafts that could be deposited into other accounts, from which the funds could be transferred to untraceable offshore accounts.[37]

In coordination with its Mexican allies, the Cali cartel relied heavily on corruption to advance its interests in Mexico. They preferred to work with García Ábrego and Carrillo Fuentes because they worked within the Mexican political system, taking advantage of the PRI's single-party rule. Initially, the Cali cartel established contacts among Mexican government officials and private sector businessmen from Jalisco and Ciudad Juárez through former Dirección Federal de Seguridad (DFS) member and Juárez cartel founder Rafael Aguilar Guajardo.[38] After Aguilar Guajardo was assassinated on April 12, 1993, the Cali cartel joined forces with Carrillo Fuentes because he maintained tight security and compartmentalized his organization. Like García Ábrego, who put Raúl Salinas, the brother of Mexico's President Carlos Salinas, in his back pocket, Carrillo Fuentes paid off many Mexican officials to look the other way.[39]

Corruption now ran rampant through the Mexican political system. According to one convicted trafficker, the "Gulf cartel grew" with the "support of the corrupt political system" in Mexico. The Mexican police—the

PJFM—"controlled 90 percent of the drug trafficking" in Mexico because the cartels "control the PJFM."[40] For example, in Queretaro state, the PGR arrested seven PJFM policemen for selling 282 kilos of cocaine that they took from a wrecked Colombian Aero Commander jet that crashed 100 miles outside Mexico City.[41] In the case of the Juárez cartel, the US embassy reported in 1997 that five Mexican army generals were in the pay of Carrillo Fuentes.[42] His great wealth enabled him to broker security for Colombian drug shipments as well as Mexican marijuana and heroin shipments. According to the DEA director of intelligence, Phil Jordan, the Carrillo Fuentes organization operated with the "complete assurance" that "drugs will move through Mexico virtually untouched." For example, Carrillo Fuentes used his proceeds to buy protection for warehouses where the Colombians stored cocaine. One US law enforcement official stated, "We've pinpointed those warehouses for the Mexican authorities time and again, but nothing gets done. They're never raided."[43]

The Cali cartel now ran multiple operations across Mexico. Aided by Carrillo Fuentes, the Cali cartel moved cocaine into Mexico using clandestine airstrips in Monterrey, Tamaulipas, and Ocampo.[44] Using front companies as cover, the cartel also delivered cocaine in shipments of lumber, chocolate, coffee, and tropical fruits, such as bananas.[45] They wrapped shipments in different colors to indicate ownership of the shipment. They also marked shipments with names like "soccer" or "lider" for identification when distributing cocaine at its destination.[46] In Campeche, the fishing and fish packing industries collaborated with the Cali cartel to distribute cocaine to locations in Mexico using refrigerated trucks. Tuna boats departed Buenaventura, Colombia, en route to the Gulf of Mexico, where they anchored 500 miles offshore and offloaded fifteen to twenty metric tons of cocaine onto smaller vessels that proceeded to Mexican ports.[47]

Mexican politicians complained about the 600 percent increase in the movement of cocaine that occurred between 1991 and 1993 as trafficking routes from South America to North America changed.[48] The Mexican government seized 33.9 metric tons in 1989 and a "record" 46.5 metric tons in 1990. Between January and March 1990, the PJFM seized an estimated 6,023 kilos of cocaine.[49] In response, Colombian and Mexican traffickers began varying their methods of operation. Traffickers sometimes used daytime hours for air transit, attempted maritime smuggling, and utilized land-air transshipments from Guatemala.[50] Reports also noted that traffickers were unloading their aircraft much faster, making arrests and seizures more difficult.[51] Through the establishment of transshipment points for airdrops, storage facilities, and landing sites, the Cali cartel and its affiliates developed a major presence along the border states of the Yucatán Peninsula (Yucatán, Quintana Roo, and Campeche) and the nearby states of Chiapas,

108   *Narcostates*

Veracruz, Tabasco, and Oaxaca.[52] Despite Mexican efforts, the availability and price of cocaine bound for the United States remained constant.[53] In 1995, the State Department reported that in Baja California traffickers were becoming so "sophisticated in drug smuggling techniques" that they were able to move cocaine through Mexico with impunity.[54] These were the halcyon days for the Mexican DTOs.

The Rise of the Mexican DTOs

The Cali cartel did not show a preference in deciding to work with one Mexican DTO over another. Because 70 percent of the cocaine consumed in the United States came from Colombia, the Mexican traffickers tolerated the presence of the Colombians.[55] The Cali cartel moved its product into Mexico but allowed the Mexican DTOs to take the risk of trafficking narcotics across the border. In exchange, the Colombians gave a share of their profits to the Mexican DTOs. As long as the Mexicans promised not to operate in the traditional Colombian strongholds, particularly New York, Miami, and the rest of the Eastern Seaboard, the Mexicans and Colombians were able to work cooperatively.[56] As the relationship progressed, the Mexican DTOs came to dominate trafficking from Colombia into the United States, using Central America as their springboard.[57]

The collapse of the Cali cartel in 1995 was the turning point for Mexico's DTOs. Because the Juárez cartel moved Cali cartel cocaine into the United States, the collapse of the Cali organization enabled the Juárez traffickers to take over their US markets. Since the Cali cartel relied on the Juárez cartel's transportation network and used Juárez as staging area for its shipments, Carrillo Fuentes demanded that the Cali cartel pay for his services with cocaine rather than cash.[58] Over time, the Juárez cartel gained access to the Cali cartel's exclusive New York City market.[59] In 1995, with the Cali cartel on the run, the Juárez cartel muscled it out of business. Carrillo Fuentes told its leaders that he planned to bypass their refining and shipping operations and purchase cocaine paste directly from Peruvian and Bolivian coca growers.[60]

In 1996, Carrillo Fuentes called for meetings in Central America with the Colombian DTOs that had emerged in the wake of the collapse of the Medellín and Cali cartels. In those meetings, Fuentes told the Colombians that they must give up their US markets. The Mexicans would allow the Colombians to transport cocaine from the Andes, but they could only carry it as far as Mexico, where they would be paid in cash. From Mexico, Carrillo Fuentes would direct the transportation and distribution of cocaine into and throughout the United States.[61] As a result, the Juárez cartel assumed control over US markets, and with assistance from former Cali and Medellín middlemen, it moved cocaine through Central America and

Mexico to the United States. According to an unnamed Colombian intelligence officer, at the time of Carrillo Fuentes's death, Colombian organizations depended on the Mexicans to get 60 to 70 percent of their cocaine into the United States. Melvyn Levitsky, the US assistant secretary of state for narcotics matters between 1989 and 1993, underscored that point, stating that the "Colombians had no choice" but to accept the Mexican offer.[62] Because of Carrillo Fuentes's bold moves, the Juárez cartel now eclipsed the Medellín and Cali cartels in their heyday. Under Carrillo Fuentes, the Mexicans metamorphosed from being simple intermediaries to being the owners of the trade.[63]

With the demise of the Medellín and Cali cartels, smaller, more dangerous, and more violent minicartels emerged in Colombia.[64] The minicartels "democratized" in reaction to Colombia's "kingpin strategy," which focused on capturing or killing leaders of criminal organizations.[65] The Colombian cartels no longer maintained an integrated structure. Instead, they organized into small, decentralized groups that worked together.[66] To add layers of protection to their operations, the cartels employed technology, such as encryption techniques, cellular phone cloning, and firewall-protected chat rooms that could not be penetrated by intelligence agencies. Making detection even more difficult, traffickers subcontracted jobs to specialists, who worked on a job-to-job basis rather than as part of a permanent structure that might be easily detected.[67] Instead of shipping tons of cocaine at one time, they included only 100 or 200 kilos in a shipment.[68]

After the demise of the Cali cartel, the Norte de Valle cartel became the most important of the minicartels in Colombia.[69] Between 1990 and 2008, the Norte del Valle cartel exported more than 1.2 million pounds (500 metric tons) of cocaine worth in excess of $10 billion from Colombia to the United States. The vast majority of those shipments moved through Mexico.[70] Working with the various Mexican DTOs, the Norte de Valle cartel shipped cocaine loads to Mexico via speedboats, fishing vessels, and other maritime conveyances for delivery to the United States.[71] Known as a high-tech cartel, they utilized a fleet of minisubmarines, employed military intelligence hardware to map out the radar position of US spy planes, and developed cell phone detection and jamming techniques. Their enforcement measures were ruthless, as they routinely killed their enemies with chainsaws and dumped their body parts into Colombia's Río Magdalena.[72] This new cartel represented the decentralization of trafficking in Colombia. Their members worked as independent traffickers who cooperated by franchising their heroin and cocaine operations. The Norte de Valle cartel sometimes worked with Colombian paramilitary and guerrilla groups to move cocaine. These groups included the Autodefensas Unidas de Colombia (AUC), a right-wing paramilitary group, and the Fuerzas Armadas Revolucionarias de Colombia (FARC), a left-wing guerrilla group.

110 *Narcostates*

The Mexican cartels also worked with Colombia's BACRIM (Bandas Criminales). The BACRIM appeared as a "new" organized crime syndicate consisting of former paramilitary members from the AUC (which demobilized in 2004) and traffickers from the Medellín and Cali cartels.[73] The BACRIM operated as individual armed groups who held territorial control over narcotrafficking corridors. Like an onion, they organized themselves into layers: in the center was the leader, while regional lieutenants controlled turf in the second layer, who in turn subcontracted labor and production to Los Invisibles (the Invisibles), which formed the third layer. The Invisibles did not belong to the BACRIM; they produced and refined coca but did not move it. Because the BACRIM's leadership stemmed from Colombia's paramilitary organizations, they provided their own security for the transfer of cocaine to the Mexicans.[74] The BACRIM acted more like a criminal organization than a paramilitary force, and it was no match for the better organized FARC, which became increasingly involved in narcotrafficking.[75]

Turning Point for Mexico and Central America

The Mexican cartel capos of the 1980s and 1990s, like the capos in the Medellín and Cali cartels, were businessmen in a high-stakes enterprise. Having learned from the Medellín and Cali cartels, the Mexicans assumed control over the drug trade in the mid-1990s. Following the disintegration of the Guadalajara, Medellín, and Cali cartels, Mexico's second-generation cartels began to engage in a bitter fight for territorial control. As this transition occurred, the Mexican government (like the Colombian government of the 1980s) stood on the precipice of launching its own war against narcotrafficking. However, the Mexican DTOs had been proactive and were already expanding into Central America with their Colombian counterparts.

The major turning point for Mexico occurred on October 13, 1990. On that date, the Mexican government implemented a policy of intercepting Colombian aircraft in Mexican airspace. In the operation, the Mexican government seized ten metric tons of cocaine using Cessna planes. At the time, the magnitude of the seizure was unprecedented. Assessing the situation, a US State Department cable noted that the air train to Mexico seemed to have been halted and that the Colombians were relocating their air operations to Central America.[76] To further limit Colombian use of Mexican airspace and to show its willingness to cooperate with the United States, the Mexican government allowed US surveillance aircraft to fly over its sovereign territory.[77] As Central America's civil wars faded, the Colombian and Mexican DTOs started to view Central America as an important steppingstone for their operations. In early 1991, the State Department reported that major seizures of Colombian cocaine by Mexican authorities had forced Colombian traffickers to use Guatemala as an alternative route for US-bound cocaine shipments.[78] By the mid-1990s, narcotraffickers were operating in every country in Central America. How and why this happened is the next subject of focus.

The Colombian and Mexican Cartels
Move into Central America

Before the mid-1980s, drug trafficking through Central America was viewed by most governments as a nuisance. Countering the revolutionary insurgencies was a greater concern. However, as early as 1986, the situation began to change—a CIA internal memorandum commented that the drug trade in Central America was flourishing and that law enforcement agencies in Costa Rica, El Salvador, Guatemala, and Honduras were making small, but significant marijuana and cocaine seizures as well as confiscating processing materials.[79] In 1988, US Assistant Secretary of State of International Narcotics Matters (INM) Ann B. Wrobleski testified to the House Foreign Affairs Committee that "drug trafficking and, in some instances, narcotics production," were breaching "the boundaries of Guatemala, Honduras, and Costa Rica." Wrobleski added that these countries "lie on the path between the coca fields of the Andes and the cocaine markets of the U.S." and suggested that "official involvement in several Central American countries" also existed. Behind it all were "the well-armed and well-financed Medellín and Cali cartels" using "sophisticated aircraft, communications, and other technological aids" that put the police forces of Central America at a disadvantage.[80]

Beginning in April 1990, US government agencies observed that Colombian and Mexican traffickers were varying their operational methods. Following the Mexican government's crackdown on direct air shipments between Mexico and Colombia, the traffickers adjusted their routes and moved their transshipment staging areas to Central America.[81] Guatemala became an important location because of its porous border with Mexico. According to intelligence gathered by the State Department, the Cali cartel put a moratorium on multi-aircraft drug convoys to Mexico and shifted its aviation operations southward into Guatemala and perhaps El Salvador after Mexico began its air interdiction program in 1990. Once their cocaine arrived in Central America, the cartel moved it into Mexico by land, sea, and air.[82] In 1992, the State Department reported that since 1989, the most heavily used cocaine shipment routes ran from Colombia through Central America to Mexico.[83] By 1993, 165 to 275 tons of cocaine and heroin, out of an estimated 1,100 tons produced in all of South America, moved through Central America annually.[84]

The end of Central America's civil wars opened the region to narcotrafficking precisely at the same moment US authorities forced the closure of

112 Narcostates

the Caribbean trafficking corridor.[85] Traffickers who had avoided Central America because of armed insurgencies now looked to Central America as a way to supplement routes through Mexico and the Caribbean. According to political scientist Stephen S. Dudley, the conflicts in Guatemala, Honduras, and El Salvador laid the foundation for "weapons trafficking, money laundering, and contraband traffic."[86] Peace accompanied by the implementation of NAFTA in January 1994 opened the spigot. A relaxation of controls along the US-Mexico border made it easier for cocaine from the Andes to move through Central America into Mexico and then on to the United States.[87] Narcotraffickers smuggled drugs in multiple ways, including the use of overland routes along the Pan-American Highway, low-flying aerial operations, maritime routes using speedboats, or through a combination of all three.[88] According to the DEA, "the entire Central American isthmus" "became a trampoline" with a lot of "cooperation among traffickers from different countries."[89]

Guatemala:
The Big Step

With no air-search radar capability, unmonitored airfields, and an uncontrolled border with Mexico, Guatemala became a primary transshipment point for the Colombian cartels during the early 1990s.[90] Because the Mexican government made it difficult for traffickers at the Inter-American Highway border crossing, they developed routes through the sparsely populated, mountainous, and tropical regions of southern Mexico bordering Guatemala.[91] In 1992, US ambassador to Guatemala Thomas Stroock warned that the United States faced a dire situation of "trying to prevent the takeover of Central American countries by drug traffickers." Stroock added that "originally Mexico had been the bridge for drug traffickers," but because of "antidrug activities in Mexico," Guatemala had become a "warehouse for international drug traffickers" with "hundreds of clandestine airfields."[92]

Traffickers shifted their operations from Mexico to Guatemala using maritime, land, and air transshipment methods.[93] As an air-bridge transit zone, Guatemala presented an attractive opportunity for traffickers because it contained hundreds of unmonitored landing strips and no radar capability.[94] From the landing strips, cocaine was transferred to conveyances bound for the United States while precursor chemicals were transshipped to other parts of Central and South America.[95] According to Guatemala's military police chief, Colonel Ortega Menaldo, the Colombians offloaded drugs on Guatemala's southern coast by sea and then transited them by air through Mexican airspace to the United States.[96] Traffickers bought property and invested large sums of money for the construction of runways and warehouses to store narcotics.[97] Menaldo added that the Colombians maintained a low profile and employed Guatemalans whenever possible for financial transactions or the ownership of farms.

In certain stretches, the Guatemala-Mexico border was considered non-existent. It was dangerous and poorly patrolled by the authorities of both countries.[98] The US embassy in Guatemala considered the border a "sieve" because of the "high concentration of weapons, guerrillas, and narcotics" crossing the frontier.[99] The main guerrilla organization—Unidad Revolucionaria Nacional Guatemalteca (URNG)—operated along the Mexican border in northern Quiche, western San Marcos, and Petén. Their presence undermined border security, because they relied on Mexico as a location for weapons, rest, relaxation, and training. URNG collusion with lower-level Mexican officials facilitated the arrangement because the Mexican officials seemed more "interested in extorting bribes from those crossing [the border] than halting the flow of illegal commodities or travelers." The State Department also expressed concern that the guerrilla and drug activity along Mexico's border "supplemented the Nicaraguan pipeline to the Farabundo Marti National Liberation (FMLN) in El Salvador."[100] The border became increasingly dangerous, and intelligence indicated that the main guerrilla function along the border was to provide protection to either the growers of opium or to the transporters of drugs.[101]

Guatemala's guerrillas became linked to traffickers because they shared areas of operation. According to Colonel Mario Mérida, the head of Guatemala's Directorio Inteligencia Militar (Military Intelligence Directorate), two of the four organizations that comprised the URNG maintained a link to the drug trade. The Fuerzas Armadas de Rebeldes (FAR) protected drug flights, while another rebel group, the Ejército Guerrillero de los Pobres (EGP), guarded opium poppy fields. Most of the guerrilla narcoactivity was carried out by local commanders as opposed to being coordinated by URNG's four Mexico-based comandantes.[102] The FAR was strong in Petén where numerous clandestine airfields existed, while the EGP was strongest in Huehuetenango and Quiche where opium poppies were cultivated.[103] Although there were 1,000 active guerrillas with an estimated 8,000 auxiliaries along the Guatemala-Mexico border, the guerrillas did not pose a serious threat to the Colombian traffickers. In the Guatemalan countryside, the military's scorched-earth policy preoccupied both the military and the URNG to the point where neither side could seriously disrupt trafficker operations.[104]

Along Guatemala's border, it became difficult to separate guerrilla activity from narcotrafficker activity. With the exception of legal border crossings, there was no central authority along the border. The government of Mexico denied that it allowed the URNG and the FMLN to run their wars out of Mexico and also refuted the claim that the guerrillas kept "themselves supplied from Mexico," or used "refugee camps as staging grounds."[105]

114   *Narcostates*

At the time, the Mexican military did not have the capability to mount antiguerrilla, antinarcotics, or antiweapons smuggling operations and showed little interest in doing so; it wanted to avoid being drawn into a conflict along its border.[106] From the Guatemalan government's perspective, while the Mexican government did not provide covert support for the URNG, Mexican corruption, collusion, and ineptness allowed guerrillas, coyotes, and drug traffickers to have access to Mexico.[107] Despite these differences, the US ambassador to Guatemala and the governments of Mexico and Guatemala recognized that they needed to address the proliferation of guns, drugs, and guerrillas along the border. In 1990, both governments agreed to focus resources and reporting on the border area and on Central American political activities in Mexico, including the FMLN and Guatemalan guerrilla groups. The United States also expected the Mexican government to share relevant drug trafficking information derived from its radar net.[108]

As Mexico stepped up its air-interdiction program, DTOs altered their operations by incorporating land and sea routes through Guatemala. As a result, Guatemala turned into a staging area for overland shipments from Panama and seaborne shipments originating in Colombia, Panama, and elsewhere.[109] Traffickers concentrated their activities in three regions: the coastal Pacific plains of southwestern Guatemala, the river valleys and isolated jungle flatlands of the northern Petén region, and the area around Lake Izabal in eastern Guatemala.[110]

Despite the limited role of the military in counternarcotics operations, narcotics-driven corruption spread within Guatemala's law enforcement institutions. Because appointments were not attained through merit but through favoritism and a willingness to "play the game," corruption plagued Guatemala's treasury police and customs service. Customs officials took bribes, and contraband moved freely without inspection.[111] Corruption was endemic because the salaries of officials and officers were insufficient to maintain even a modest standard of living and support a family. It became common for incomes to be supplemented by taking bribes, sharing in the proceeds of an illicit deal, or skimming and reselling confiscated drugs.[112]

Evidence of military corruption mounted in the 1990s. The most famous case occurred in December 1990 with the arrest of Lieutenant Colonel Ochoa Ruiz, who worked for the D-2 (Directorate of Military Intelligence) monitoring the movement of narcotics in Guatemala. Smuggling cocaine for the Cali cartel, Ruiz used his rank to pass checkpoints without his vehicle being inspected.[113] In 1990, Guatemalan authorities, assisted by the DEA, arrested him for smuggling a half-ton of cocaine into Tampa, Florida.[114] Because he was a military officer, the Guatemalan military initially dismissed all charges against him. US pressure forced Guatemala to retry him in its highest civilian court, the Constitutional Court. On March 23, 1994, the court ordered his extradition to the United States. One week later, assassins killed Judge Eduardo González Dubón, the chief justice who had ruled in favor of extradition. Shamelessly, on April 12, the court reversed its decision.[115] Other cases emerged; Colonel González Salan used military assets from his headquarters to assist traffickers by providing security for air and ground transshipments, intelligence support, and the co-option of local law enforcement.[116]

The problem of corruption also manifested itself deep within Guatemala's political institutions. In 1990, the Policía Nacional arrested Mayor Arnoldo Vargas Estrada of Zacapa for drugs and weapons smuggling, seizing 287 kilos of cocaine at the time of his arrest. His operation reportedly moved 4,000 pounds of cocaine by small planes through his private ranch in Zacapa.[117] In another case, Eduardo Tagus Matus, the Guatemalan congressional alternate deputy for the Partido Alianza Popular 5 (AP-5), was accused of having ties to the Cali cartel when a cartel operative was arrested carrying an ID card that Tagus Matus had provided. According to the US embassy, since there was "little oversight of the drug policy" in Guatemala, there was a "greater temptation" for Guatemalan politicians to "take drug money to help pay the bills."[118]

While US and Guatemalan counternarcotics efforts eliminated opium and marijuana production (see Chapter 7), they did not stop the movement of narcotraffickers in and out of Guatemala. The continuation of the civil war until 1996 prevented the Guatemalan government from securing its borders. However, narcotrafficking never became a part of guerrilla operations in Guatemala as it had been in Colombia and Peru. According to US Assistant Secretary of State for Narcotics Matters Melvyn Levitsky, "Opium never became a popular issue for the insurgency because the opium growers were mostly connected to Mexican syndicates and were not a part of the base that supported the insurgency."[119] Narcotics was not an ideological issue used to perpetuate revolution because a tradition of narcotics crop production, such as coca in the Andes, never existed in Guatemala.[120] Nevertheless, evidence exists that the guerrillas did profit from narcotrafficking, but they were not alone in doing so. Elements within the military also profited. As the war wound down, cocaine became a commodity that Guatemalan military and police officials could enrich themselves from because they controlled the contraband routes along the border. Because of its proximity to Mexico, Guatemala bore the brunt of narcotrafficking during the 1990s. With a preestablished presence in Honduras, Nicaragua, Costa Rica, and Panama, narcotrafficking swept over Central America like a virus.

El Salvador:
Engulfed by the Cocaine Octopus

The Chapultepec Peace Accord between the Salvadoran government and the FMLN-led insurgency went into effect on February 1, 1992. Nine thousand

116   *Narcostates*

FMLN guerrillas and another 63,000 government soldiers laid down their arms. As the opposing forces demobilized, a wave of crime and general lawlessness flared up.[121] US State Department sources predicted that, of the "thousands of unskilled demobilized FMLN combatants and Salvadoran soldiers," some would "retain their arms and resort to banditry."[122] The State Department also expressed dissatisfaction regarding the FMLN's decommissioning of weapons. Rather than turning in their weapons, the State Department feared that the FMLN planned to sell their weapons to criminals and Guatemalan guerrillas, and use the proceeds to fund political activities and covert actions. By 1993, crime in El Salvador had become such a problem that even the FMLN recognized it as a national problem. That same year, Óscar Santamaría, the architect of the peace accord, declared that the crime wave had started with the "large-scale demobilization of the military and the FMLN" and "the reduction in police manpower as a result of the accords."[123]

While the main source of crime came in the form of banditry along El Salvador's roads, traffickers used every means possible to move cocaine through El Salvador.[124] Using the Inter-American Highway to move cocaine and heroin through El Salvador, smugglers showed great ingenuity. In one instance, traffickers hollowed out pallets of drywall sheets by cutting out the middle of the pallets and filling them with cocaine. Salvadoran authorities claimed that traffickers took advantage of the lack of radar to land aircraft at remote airstrips that once serviced cotton plantations along the Pacific coast. Another smuggling method was to use El Salvador as a third-party transit route. At the port of Acajutla, traffickers unloaded Colombian and Peruvian cocaine in order to change its point of origin. The traffickers thought that by doing so, their cargo would face less scrutiny when it arrived in the United States than it would if it had been shipped straight from Andean drug-producing countries.[125]

During the later stages of the civil war, members of El Salvador's military were accused of involvement in the drug trade. As early as 1987, the DEA reported that cocaine was being smuggled through El Salvador's Comalapa and Ilopango airports by Salvadorans, joined by Colombians and Mexicans.[126] By 1989, the DEA received increasing but unconfirmed reports that the Salvadoran army and air force were smuggling narcotics through Ilopango.[127] Many officers allegedly involved in drug smuggling also belonged to death squads accused of abusing human rights and plotting coups. The 1989 case of Major Salvador Figueroa Mendoza became one of the first narcotics trafficking cases brought against a Salvadoran military officer.[128] In 1992, another prosecution brought charges against three ESAF officers for attempting to sell thirty kilos of cocaine to a DEA agent working undercover in El Salvador.[129] Finally, a lieutenant colonel was accused of dealing with narcotraffickers when he was arrested in 1992 by the Salvadoran Unidad Ejecutiva Antinarcóticos (UEA) for trying to sell four 500-pound bombs to narcotraffickers.[130]

Allegations that El Salvador's political elite profited from the drug trade existed as early as 1985 when US Customs arrested a Salvadoran national named Francisco "Chico" Guirola with $5,975,850 in unmarked $20 and $100 bills. Guirola was a political fundraiser and a personal friend of Roberto D'Aubuisson of the Alianza Republicana Nacionalista (ARENA) party. Guirola's arrest revealed that El Salvador's political right wing and drug dealers knew each other and were possibly using drug money to finance ARENA.[131] In 1997, eight retired military officers accused the Salvadoran government of being a corrupt narcostate when they issued the Santa Elena Report, calling for a military coup to reset the political situation because only the military could reestablish law and order. The Santa Elena Report came in the wake of money laundering allegations associated with a national banking scandal that defrauded $147 million from the banking system.[132] The retired officers claimed in the report that the government and ARENA protected a "corrupt political and economic elite involved in narcotics trafficking and money laundering" whose origins could be traced back to the CIA's drugs-for-arms operations conducted in El Salvador on behalf of the Nicaraguan Contras. The report proclaimed that the new drug elite had displaced the traditional land-based oligarchy, deriving its power from financial speculation and their continued support for Salvadoran death squads.[133]

Narcotrafficking replaced leftist insurgency as the new subversive force in El Salvador. According to Captain Óscar Pena, the head of El Salvador's Executive Antinarcotics Unit, narcotrafficking "will be our next war, because the terrain is so fertile here. . . . If we do not take corrective measures, we will have a much more serious problem than we have now."[134] The end of the civil war enabled narcocorruption because drug trafficking had existed in El Salvador prior to the creation of its counternarcotics program. El Salvador's initial program would suffer from political divisions within the new government, which now incorporated the FMLN. As a new security framework was worked out with the FMLN, the Salvadoran government relied on a demobilized and demoralized National Guard to deter crime.[135] In many respects, El Salvador's counternarcotics program faced an uphill struggle before it even began.

El Salvadoran President Alfredo Cristiani (1989–1994) expressed deep concern over the expansion of the drug trade in El Salvador.[136] El Salvador's first major bust occurred in 1992, when six Cali cartel associates were arrested attempting to transport three metric tons of cocaine through El Salvador. The smugglers used a front company owned by the Cali cartel to import large loads of agricultural products into the Salvadoran port of Acajutla. Salvadoran authorities believed that the smugglers then used the Mexican airline Transportes Aeromar to move the cocaine from El Salvador to Mexico.[137] In June 1993, Salvadoran police seized six metric tons of cocaine with a street value

118   *Narcostates*

of $205 million. It was the largest bust in Salvadoran history to that date. Salvadoran police reported that they had arrested four Mexican traffickers from the Sinaloa cartel and one Colombian during the bust.[138] By 1993, El Salvador was starting to rival Guatemala as a narcotrafficking hub.[139]

Honduras:
An Unimpaired Haven

Although Honduras did not suffer from the impact of civil war during the 1980s, it became a significant transit route for cocaine destined for the United States and Europe.[140] Honduras had not prioritized narcotics control since its domestic narcotics consumption was limited, and its government considered there to be more pressing national security concerns. However, unconfirmed reports about Honduran guerrillas and the narcotics trade began to surface. After several large seizures, including a $500 million seizure of Colombian cocaine in 1986, the State Department claimed that intelligence sources indicated a link between drug trafficking, the cultivation of large amounts of marijuana, and the activities of armed insurgents such as the Honduran Cinchoneros. Although no confirmed links to the insurgents were made, the Honduran government's position on narcotics control changed as drug usage in its northern regions increased, the conventional security threat declined, and the United States heightened its emphasis on narcotics control.[141]

In the late 1970s and early 1980s, Matta-Ballesteros exerted considerable influence over Honduras's drug trade and government. The 1978 discovery of the bodies of Mary and Mario Ferrari set off a military coup backed by Matta-Ballesteros. Using a Honduran beer factory as a front, the Ferraris, in association with Matta-Ballesteros, trafficked in cocaine, weapons, and emeralds. Members of the Honduran military profited from the relationship and looked the other way. As the investigation into their deaths unfolded, it revealed a connection between the Ferraris, Matta-Ballesteros, and the Honduran military. Colonel Leónidas Torres Arias (the chief of military intelligence), Colonel Ramón Reyes Sánchez (the director of Central Penitentiary), Lieutenant Colonel Juan Ángel Barahona (the Honduran Interpol Chief), and Colonel Armando Calidonio were accused of being a part of Matta-Ballesteros's drug network. As judicial pressure mounted, Interpol Chief Barahona accused General Policarpo Paz García of doing nothing about military officers involved in drug trafficking. Because the investigation threatened to bring down the Honduran military, General Paz García, supported by Matta-Ballesteros, launched a coup on August 7, 1978, to overthrow Honduran President General Juan Alberto Melgar Castro.[142]

US pressure on Honduras led to the 1982 election of Roberto Suazo Córdova as president. However, Colonel Torres Arias remained the head of

The Honduran Directorio de Investigaciones Nacionales (DIN) and served as the liaison between the Honduran government and the CIA-backed Contra training camps. Torres Arias coordinated with the CIA's Duane "Dewey" Clarridge, as well as Honduran general Álvarez Martínez and the president, Paz García, both of whom were viewed by the United States as being in Matta-Ballesteros's pay. In 1982, Torres Arias was told by the US ambassador to Honduras, John Negroponte, that he had been under a year-long investigation for alleged involvement in narcotics trafficking.[143]

Matta-Ballesteros, in conjunction with the Medellín and Cali cartels, smuggled large quantities of cocaine through Honduras. Following a temporary self-imposed exile in Spain in the aftermath of the Ferrari murders, Matta-Ballesteros ran SETCO airlines for CIA Contra supply operations while also putting together the Guadalajara-Medellín network. Moreover, as early as 1982, Matta-Ballesteros began smuggling hundreds of kilos of cocaine through Honduras in association with the Cali cartel, with San Pedro Sula serving as the main transit point.[144] Following the DEA's 1988 rendition of Matta-Ballesteros from Honduras to the United States via the Dominican Republic, the Colombians attempted to fill the void, only to be superseded by Mexican DTOs.[145] When Mexico implemented its air-interdiction program in 1991, the US embassy in Honduras believed that it "would force traffickers towards Honduras and other northern tier countries."[146] By the mid-1990s, Colombian DTOs operating in Honduras included the FARC, ELN, AUC, and the Norte de Valle cartel.[147] A State Department cable in 2002 noted that both the FARC, and to a lesser extent the AUC, "had been active in Honduras" and were attempting to "exchange cocaine for weapons."[148] Nonetheless, by this time, Mexican DTOs, especially the Sinaloa cartel, had solidified their hold over trafficking routes through Honduras. After pushing out Honduran competitors, the Mexican DTOs worked in combination with the Colombian BACRIM to move narcotics through Honduras.[149]

Throughout the 1990s, weak customs controls and a large amount of vehicular traffic enabled the free flow of cocaine through Honduras via land routes.[150] However, the principal route utilized by traffickers to move narcotics through Honduras was the country's coastline, with its countless inlets and mangrove coves and a large fishing fleet to provide cover.[151] Because of close familial ties and a minimal government presence, the Bay Islands acted as the primary transit route.[152] Using ships and small boats, Honduran traffickers transported narcotics to the Caribbean islands, such as the Cayman Islands, where they divided it into smaller loads bound for Florida.[153] In 1995, the State Department reported that transit by sea was on the rise and relatively risk-free for traffickers because the Honduran navy had limited resources and inadequate training.[154] In one incident, Honduran authorities seized 3,900 pounds of cocaine when smugglers

120 *Narcostates*

threw their shipment overboard after being spotted by a helicopter. No arrests occurred because the traffickers' speedboat escaped into the safety of the Honduran coast.[155]

The Honduran government considered counternarcotics efforts to be a drain on the country's limited resources.[156] Military officials with little or no police training received senior positions within the National Police. The lack of financial resources further complicated the Honduran military's ability to deal with drug trafficking.[157] Law enforcement personnel in Honduras received as little as $60 per month, and corruption was rife.[158] Few proactive measures were initiated to address the threat posed by narcotraffickers.[159] Although the Honduran government did pass laws in 1993 to seize all assets used in the illicit traffic of drugs, no money laundering laws existed to strengthen these laws.[160] Honduras did not propose a comprehensive counternarcotics plan until 1999, but by that point, it was too late.

Nicaragua:
Peace Brings Traffickers

Because of its remote, scarcely populated coastlines, access to the Inter-American Highway, and limited government resources, Nicaragua became favored territory for narcotraffickers.[161] The 1987 Esquipulas Peace Agreement ended the country's civil war, but peace and stability did not ensue. The Sandinista government lost the 1990 national elections while working people suffered 50 percent unemployment. A weak central government replaced the Sandinistas and could not cope with the expanding drug trade along its coastlines. According to Fernando Caldera, a Nicaraguan police chief, drug traffickers stayed away from Nicaragua's coasts during the Contra war because they ran into a "well-trained [Sandinista] army backed by widespread radar and counterespionage in the interior."[162]

As the Contra War wound down, Nicaragua became a conduit for Colombian and Mexican traffickers moving their product through Central America.[163] As early as 1986, the Sandinistas discovered drug trafficking networks tied to foreign nationals from France and Italy. These drug rings operated on the Atlantic and Pacific coasts.[164] Traffickers also took advantage of the many small, rural airstrips that remained from the civil war.[155] In 1988, Colombian officials claimed that drug traffickers were increasingly using Nicaragua's airstrips as waypoints for Colombian cocaine shipments bound for the United States. Officials described Nicaragua's coastal interior as "a black hole" because drug shipments could not be tracked after small airplanes landed and discharged their cargo.[166]

As early as 1990, Nicaraguan officials were reporting incidents of drug trafficking along both coasts. Limited maritime assets left Nicaragua's Atlantic Miskito Coast wide open to Colombian traffickers. In May 1990, the

DEA reported a systematic increase of drug trafficking in Puerto Cabezas and the Bluefields.[167] According to the DEA, smugglers frequently used this coastline because of its numerous hidden inlets and estuaries. Traffickers air-dropped drug loads from low-lying aircraft to waiting speedboats that carried contraband into inlets and estuaries.[168] Seaborne arms-for-drugs transactions were carried out in the vicinity of Colombia's San Andrés Island and Corn Island, forty miles off Nicaragua's Atlantic coast, where drugs acted as a substitute for cash. Boats left Nicaragua with weapons and returned with cocaine that subsequently moved north.[169] In 1990, the State Department received intelligence that members of the Sandinista army were involved arms-for-drugs transactions. The rogue military members carried out their transactions at sea, leaving the coastal ports in boats loaded with weapons and returning with drugs to be transported to Managua. The State Department's report also noted that some of the weapons from the deal went to the FMLN in El Salvador to prepare for an end-of-year offensive in 1991.[170]

Despite the evidence, the Sandinista government denied that it had a narcotrafficking problem. The government stated that "drug production, trafficking, and related activities are insignificant in Nicaragua."[171] Even though the Sandinistas denied the existence of drug traffickers using their sovereign territory, they signed an agreement with Costa Rica to exchange narcotics information. The State Department viewed this pact as an "acknowledgement that trafficking may be a problem in Nicaragua."[172] The Sandinista chief of police, René Vivas Lugo, alleged that the militaries of Honduras, El Salvador, and Guatemala controlled the drug trade and were turning Nicaragua and Central America into a springboard for narcotics moving between South America, Mexico, and the United States. Vivas Lugo ended by asserting that the Sandinistas were doing their best to combat the growing traffic with no foreign assistance of any kind.[173] After the Sandinistas lost power in 1991, the Nicaraguan vice minister of the interior, Dr. José Pallais, freely acknowledged that "narcotrafficking was becoming a problem for all Nicaraguans."[174]

Costa Rica:
The Unguarded Neutral

Limited government resources turned Costa Rica into a transitory zone during the early 1990s. Because Costa Rica banned the existence of a standing military after its 1948 revolution, it had no professional national police force or ships or aircraft to curtail traffickers. Costa Rica's limited defense and security capabilities opened it up to criminal groups, narcotics traffickers from the Andean ridge, and potentially international terrorists, who sought to take advantage of Costa Rica's pluralistic society.[175] As a result, Costa Rica's lightly armed police force found itself matched against well-armed and technologically sophisticated smuggling networks.[176] In the ports of Puntarenas

122   Narcostates

and Limón, Costa Rican security forces increasingly encountered criminals armed with AK-47s and M-16s purchased from narcotraffickers.[177]

Like its neighbors, Costa Rica did little to restrain narcotrafficking even as its expansion became more conspicuous during Nicaragua's Contra War. Costa Rican President Luis Alberto Monge Álvarez (1982–1986) referred to Pablo Escobar's presence in Nicaragua and his alleged ties to the Sandinistas as "a diabolical combination of drugs and arms."[178] Simultaneously, Costa Rica also raised allegations of Contra drug smuggling. Despite its claims, Costa Rica desired neutrality during Nicaragua's conflict, so it did not provoke any of the conflict's participants. As a result, traffickers were able to operate along the Costa Rican border with near impunity. The Medellín cartel was reported to be well-entrenched, and in 1986 the police raided a cocaine refinement laboratory in the town of Santa Maria de Ujarrás.[179]

Although drug production in Costa Rica remained limited to scattered marijuana cultivation, by 1991, the country was gaining importance as a transshipment point for cocaine from South America.[180] Traffickers transported narcotics along both coasts by boat or plane. Like Nicaragua, the majority of Costa Rica's maritime transshipments entered via San Andrés Island.[181] Much of the maritime cocaine entered Costa Rica as legitimate seaborne cargo.[182] Large ships also unloaded their cargo onto smaller speedboats, which ferried the narcotics to the shores of the Pacific and Atlantic coasts. Following a similar pattern seen along the coasts of other Central American nations, Costa Rican fishermen regularly found plastic bundles dropped by planes. In one incident, fishermen found a barrel equipped with a radio transmitter floating offshore with 3,000 kilos of cocaine.[183] In another incident, a helicopter with concealed compartments was found abandoned floating in the ocean near the Costa Rica–Panama border.[184] Traffickers also transported smaller cocaine shipments via private aircraft, and in some instances commercial aircraft as well.[185] The 1991 proliferation of crack cocaine in Limón was directly linked to the expansion of trafficking and corruption within the port city and was followed by a spike in Colombian heroin transiting through Costa Rica in 1993.[186] Costa Rican Interior Minister Luis Fishman Zonzinski declared Costa Rica to be "wide open to cocaine smugglers" and added that "we have no army, no radar, no planes, no boats. . . . There's very little we can do to stop the growing flow."[187]

The growing seriousness of Costa Rica's trafficking problem went public in 1993, when five gunmen calling themselves the Death Command kidnapped eighteen Supreme Court justices. The kidnappers demanded $8 million and safe passage out of the country. Although the Costa Rican government denied the kidnappers were connected to narcotraffickers, pundits compared the kidnapping to the M-19 assault on the Colombian Palace of Justice in 1986. Unofficial reports alleged that the kidnappers really wanted to free Alzate Urquijo ("El Arete"), the treasurer for the Medellín cartel. Costa Rican authorities had arrested El Arete in San José during Operation Green Ice, which netted 1,100 pounds of cocaine.[188] The standoff ended when authorities rescued the justices and arrested the kidnappers at the Juan Santamaría Airport as they boarded a jet bound for Guatemala. It turned out that the kidnappers were not members of the Medellín cartel but former members of the Costa Rican judicial police. A former narcotics agent trained by the DEA led the gang.[189] While not directly related to the drug trade, the cloud of narcotrafficking surrounding the kidnapping portended potential dangers ahead.

In the late 1980s and early 1990s, Costa Rica's political and economic systems were beset by narcocorruption. In 1985, a Costa Rican investigative body discovered that a US drug trafficker named James Lionel Casey had donated $2,000 to former president Daniel Oduber Quirós (1974–1978). Oduber Quirós denied knowing anything about Casey's history but was suspended from the Partido Liberación Nacional (PLN).[190] In 1992, Costa Rican authorities charged Antonio López Callejas, the director of the maritime section of Public Security, with drug-related corruption. Even though there was insufficient evidence to convict López Callejas, as the director of maritime security his case showed Costa Rica's growing vulnerability to drug trafficking.[191] Because the Costa Rican economy had suffered a near meltdown in the early 1980s, it implemented a policy of economic liberalization to promote growth. The resulting reduction in exchange and market controls increased Costa Rica's susceptibility to narcocorruption. In 1993, the Costa Rican government indicted fourteen companies for money laundering on behalf of the Colombian cartels.[192] The economic disruption also generated a pool of unskilled labor that joined the narcoeconomy.[193]

The most serious case of corruption was that of Ricardo Alem León. His story as a narcotrafficker began in the mid-1980s when he held a high rank within the PLN. During Óscar Arias's 1986 presidential run, Alem became his close advisor. As a reward for Alem's efforts, Arias appointed him as the head of the Banco Centroamericano de Integración Economía (BCIE) in 1987. Alem took advantage of his position and laundered over $50 million for the Colombian cartels. Using the Juan Santamaría Airport, he employed "mules" to carry cash into Costa Rica. Once in Costa Rica, they deposited the money into the Banco Nacional de Costa Rica. Alem then transferred it over to Colombian accounts in Panama. Because of irregularities in his bank accounts, Óscar Arias forced Alem to resign from his post in the PLN. Then, in June 1988, police stopped an Alem mule named Mario Valverde Zamora at the Juan Santamaría Airport carrying $749,000 in his briefcase. Costa Rican authorities linked the mule to Alem and conducted three trials between 1990 and 1993, all of which ended in his dismissal. Facing a fourth trial, Alem fled to the United States in April 1995. Shortly thereafter, the

124   *Narcostates*

DEA arrested him at the Miami Holiday Inn with 15 kilos of cocaine in his possession. That year, a Miami court sentenced him to nine years in prison for drug trafficking. In order to curry favor with the authorities, Alem accused two Costa Rican legislative assembly deputies of engaging in corrupt activities.[194] Alem also accused Costa Rican Supreme Court magistrate Rodolfo Emilio Piza Escalante of taking drug money from notorious money launderer Robert Vesco between 1974 and 1978 in order to become a PLN deputy legislator. All three publicly denied the allegations.[195] Alem was not finished there, though. In 1997, Alem helped Costa Rican authorities entrap Leónel Villalobos Salazar, a former congressman and PLN secretary. Together with Alem, Villalobos Salazar was charged with organizing a drug trafficking ring between Colombia, Panama, and Costa Rica that exported 3,000 kilos of cocaine to the United States. At the time of his arrest, he was in possession of 1.5 kilos of cocaine and was purportedly intending to ship another 30 kilos to the United States.[196]

Midway through the 1990s, it became manifest that Costa Rica's security forces were ill-prepared to deal with the proliferation of Colombian and Mexican DTOs. Narcotraffickers took advantage of Costa Rica's minimal police presence and increasingly used the country as a transit point. As a result, Costa Rica's political institutions became vulnerable to corruption. During the next decade, Costa Rica faced an uphill battle against narcotics-related crime.

Panama:
Post-Noriega Disequilibrium

Even after the US military's Operation Just Cause (December 1989–January 1990) removed Noriega from power, Panama remained an important money laundering and drug trafficking hub.[197] According to Melvyn Levitsky, "After Noriega, the U.S. did not pay close enough attention to what was going on."[198] The DEA flatly stated that Operation Just Cause only temporarily disrupted money laundering.[199] In Noriega's absence, Panama became a free-for-all for traffickers. Adding to the free-for-all atmosphere, Panama's new leadership decided to limit the strength of its defense and police forces.[200] With $6 billion in foreign debt, a 14 to 16 percent unemployment rate, and inadequate security to hinder crime, the situation in Panama appeared worse than it was under Noriega.[201] The US State Department believed that Panama's narcotics problems were caused by its proximity to the Andean region, its weak law enforcement capabilities, the dollar economy of the Colón Free Trade Zone (CFTZ), poor control over its ports and airports, and its significant role in the international financial sector as a result of its banking secrecy laws.[202]

With 135 miles of dense rain forest along its border with Colombia, 1,700 miles of coastline marked with coves suited for smuggling, and more than 1,500 offshore islands, Panama is a smuggler's dream.[203] Narcotics smuggled into Panama were often transferred to unregistered ships waiting in Panamanian waters or moved out of the country using authorized seaport and airport facilities.[204] According to the DEA, Panama seized 3,959 kilos of cocaine in 1990 compared to 1,728 kilos a year earlier.[205] Traffickers often paid Panamanian employees with cocaine paste (*bazuco*), which they sold to Kuna Indians and urban youth.[206] Cocaine seizures accelerated throughout the decade. The question for Panama was whether Noriega's ouster resulted in an increase in Panamanian seizures or whether traffickers took advantage of the political situation in Panama to expand their operations there.

In 1993, small-scale coca plant production appeared on plots of around ninety hectares in the Darién region bordering Colombia. Panamanian security forces found several maceration pits where traffickers broke coca leaves down into paste by mixing coca with lime and kerosene.[207] US authorities suspected that Colombian paramilitaries and FARC guerrillas were conducting small-scale coca harvesting and building drug labs in Darién.[208] However, Panama's law enforcement agencies could do little to disrupt this activity; they lacked the manpower to patrol all transshipment points, especially in the inaccessible Darién region.[209]

The democratically elected government of Guillermo Endara Galimany (1989–1993) worked closely with the United States, but his administration was plagued by allegations that it associated with narcotraffickers and money launderers. He espoused a broad moral opposition against narcotrafficking and money laundering, but high-level corruption made this claim insincere.[210] In 1990, the Panamanian newspaper *El Siglo* reported that Endara worked as a lawyer and director for Interbanco, which laundered money for the Medellín and Cali cartels.[211] Endara was also accused of establishing offshore bank accounts for traffickers affiliated with Griselda Blanco, a top-ranking member of the Medellín cartel.[212] The imprisonment of the reporter who revealed this information did not strengthen Endara's credentials.[213] In another scandal, Endara's association with wealthy businessman Eleta Almarán significantly tainted Endara's reputation. Almarán acted as the CIA's conduit of cash for Endara's 1989 campaign. In April 1989, the DEA arrested Eleta Almarán along with Panama's former ambassador to Belize in Macon, Georgia. Charges were brought against Almarán for importing 600 kilos of cocaine into the United States and conspiring to launder an estimated $300 million in profits. Endara's selection of Ricardo Arias Calderón as vice president did not improve his reputation either. Ricardo's brother was Jaime Arias Calderón, who had been the president of the First Interamericas Bank while the Cali cartel controlled its operations. Jaime was also the co-owner of the Banco Continental, which allegedly laundered $40 million in drug money for the Partido Demócrata Cristiano to finance its opposition to Noriega, as well as the political ambitions of Ricardo.[214]

126 *Narcostates*

According to the DEA, the biggest problem for law enforcement in Panama emanated from the use of Panama as a money laundering center and Panama's "inability or unwillingness" to curb those operations.[215] By the end of Noriega's regime, drug traffickers and money launderers considered him bad for business. After his removal by the US military, the situation in Panama soon changed. In 1990, as money laundering increased, Panama provided the US government with information concerning 300 frozen bank accounts suspected of being linked to drug trafficking. Compared to only $8.5 billion in 1989, bank deposits fueled by drug money reached $21 billion in 1991. The number of shell companies set up in Panama climbed to more than 1,300 a month in 1991 from an estimated 800 a month in 1989.[216]

The CFTZ added to the money laundering problem. Located on the Atlantic side of the Panama Canal, the CFTZ is a 740-acre site in the city of Colón. Within the zone there are 2,300 legitimate and illegitimate companies conducting $30 billion worth of customs-, excise-, and duty-free business annually.[217] Because of the high volume of cargo and the limited number of agents, Panamanian customs authorities could only inspect 5 percent of the containers passing through the CFTZ. Within the CFTZ, traffickers disguised illegal transactions among the high volume of legitimate transactions.[218] Part of the difficulty in monitoring the movement of drugs in and out of the zone came from the disassembly and transfer of legitimate commercial goods to other shipping containers, which made it easy to disguise drug shipments.[219] Almost all business within the zone directly or indirectly helped launder drug money through a process called dollar discounting—traffickers sold their dollars at a loss (often 25 percent) to businesses within the zone that needed US dollars. In exchange for the US dollars, Colombian pesos were deposited into trafficker accounts in Colombia or Panama. False bills of lading for legitimate business transactions, such as the purchase of overvalued or undervalued goods owned by the trafficker, helped disguise dollar discounting.[220]

In 1994, at the end of Endara's presidency, the United States threatened to decertify Panama's antidrug program on the grounds that it failed to curb money laundering in any meaningful way, but the United States ultimately certified Panama on the basis of national security interests.[221] By mid-decade, Panama looked more and more like a narcostate. Notwithstanding the Panamanian government's stated support for US counternarcotics objectives, limiting the growth of narcotrafficking would remain a formidable obstacle.

Central America:
A Trafficker's Paradise

At the start of the 1990s, Central America appeared vulnerable to organized crime and narcotrafficking. Colombian and Mexican traffickers boosted

The Colombian Cartels Expand Their Reach   127

their presence in Guatemala as Mexico attempted to close its southern border. With Guatemala still mired in its forty-year conflict, traffickers used the lack of government authority and the Guatemalan guerrillas' need for money to assert their presence along the northern border with Mexico. As trafficking operations in Guatemala grew, narcocorruption infiltrated Guatemala's institutions. Although it was not yet apparent to the Guatemalan people when their civil war ended, narcotrafficking would become the next security crisis, draining more life from the exhausted nation.

Guatemala was not alone. Central America as a whole was confronted with the problem of narcotrafficking. In *Bribes, Bullets, and Intimidation*, Bunck and Fowler identify Central America as "bridge countries" for narcotics moving north.[222] Their geographic proximity to the major drug producing countries in the Andes and the presence of weak or nonexistent governmental institutions were easily exploited by drug cartels. Narcotics were transported across the region by land, sea, and air. The use of speedboats and the mixing of narcotics with legitimate container shipments were just two methods employed by smugglers. With the exception of Honduras (because of the arrest and extradition of Matta-Ballesteros), drug seizure rates increased in every Central American nation throughout the decade.

Corruption existed in every Central American country. It would become the bane of each nation's counternarcotics effort. Drug trafficking spawned a new form of clandestine subversion. Weak infrastructure and military demobilizations in Nicaragua and El Salvador resulted in alternative employment opportunities for former soldiers as narcotraffickers. Corruption in El Salvador prompted many former generals to call for a military coup against an administration they believed was profiting from narcotrafficking. In Honduras, the apprehension of Matta-Ballesteros temporarily reduced the influence of traffickers, but the Honduran government's anemic counternarcotics program allowed corruption to infiltrate the Honduran police and military. In Costa Rica and Panama, corruption appeared at the highest levels of government. Corruption within the PLN, an emergent narcoeconomy, and the kidnapping of eighteen Supreme Court justices by members of the Costa Rican judicial police were signs of difficult challenges ahead. Of all nations, Panama faced some of the greatest threats. Because of its geographic position and the Colón Free Trade Zone, Panama was the country most vulnerable to corruption and money laundering. Following Noriega's removal, the evidence against high-ranking members of the Endara government, including President Endara himself, offered little optimism for Panama.

Mexico's narcoinsurgency and the proliferation of narcotrafficking throughout Central America replaced civil war as the new regional security threat. As will be seen next, the creation of effective counternarcotics programs was hindered by political roadblocks. As a result, Central America's

128 *Narcostates*

enforcement efforts would seem inept, dilatory, and tainted by corruption. By the end of the 1990s, the upsurge in narcotrafficking combined with deficiencies within Central America's counternarcotics police forces resulted in a resurgence of violence reminiscent of the civil war era. The war on drugs became the new conflict, involving ex-guerrillas, ex-military, and ex-refugees. Entering the new millennium, Central America could not find the peace it needed and deserved.

Notes

1. Mary Layne, Scott Decker, Meg Townsend, and Caben Chester, "Measuring the Deterrent Effect of Enforcement Operations on Drug Smuggling 1991–1999," *Trends in Organized Crime,* no. 7, Office of National Drug Control Policy (March 2002): 66–87, https://doi.org/10.1007/s12117-002-1013-2.

2. William Branigin, "Cocaine Flow Goes On; Cartel War, Seizures Have Little Effect," *Washington Post,* November 21, 1989, sec. A, p. 1.

3. American Embassy Mexico to DEA Headquarters Washington, DC, "Subject: Post Reporting Plan—Drug Trafficking in Mexico—the Colombian Presence [Redacted]," Mexico 08122 312045Z, March 1989, 3; American Embassy Mexico to DEA Headquarters Washington, DC, "Subject: Post Reporting Plan—Drug Trafficking in Mexico—the Colombian Presence [Redacted]," Mexico 12050 091950Z, May 1990, 2.

4. Brook Larmer, "Colombians Take Over Coke Trade in Mexico," *Christian Science Monitor*, January 9, 1989, 1. Coello Trejo resigned from his position due to allegations of corruption.

5. American Embassy Mexico to DEA Headquarters Washington, DC, "Subject: Post Reporting Plan—Drug Trafficking in Mexico—the Current Cocaine Situation in Mexico," Mexico 10460 032111Z, May 1991, 2.

6. Terrence Poppa, *Drug Lord: The Life and Death of a Mexican Kingpin*, 3rd ed. (El Paso, TX: Cinco Puntos Press, 2010), 177.

7. Malcolm Beith, "On the Trail of El Chapo," *Australian Magazine*, September 11, 2010, 12; June S. Beittel, *Mexico's Drug Trafficking Organizations: Source and Scope of the Rising Violence*, Report R-41576 (Washington, DC: Congressional Research Service, April 15, 2013), 7–9; Douglas Farah and Molly Moore, "Mexican Drug Traffickers Eclipse Colombian Cartels; Onetime Underlings Extend Reach into U.S.," *Washington Post*, March 30, 1997, sec. A, p. 1.

8. Secretary of State Washington, DC, to American Embassy Tegucigalpa, "Subject: Judicial Assistance: Letters Rogoatory: U.S. v. Juan Ramon Matta Ballesteros," State 032842 022125Z, February 1989, 3.

9. American Embassy Mexico to Secretary of State Washington, DC, "Prominent Mexicans Charged in Sweep Against Medellín Drug Ring," Mexico 18327 222346Z, July 1988, 1; American Consul Guadalajara to Secretary of State Washington, DC, "Guadalajara April 12 Press Coverage of Miguel Félix Gallardo," Guadalajara 01796 131940Z, April 1989, 1.

10. American Embassy Washington, DC, "Subject: Post Reporting Plan," 08122 312045Z, 1–3; Poppa, *Drug Lord*, 177.

11. US Congress, Senate, Committee on Governmental Affairs, Permanent Subcommittee on Investigations, *Structure of International Trafficking Organizations*, 101st Cong., 1st sess., September 12–13, 1989, 136.

The Colombian Cartels Expand Their Reach **129**

12. American Embassy Washington, DC, to DEA Headquarters Washington, DC, "Subject: [Redacted] Summary of Significant News Releases in the Republic of Mexico," Mexico 01205 172052Z, January 1990, 3.

13. American Embassy Mexico to Secretary of State Washington, DC, "PJFM Arrests Medellín Cartel Member in Guadalajara," Mexico 22072 292344Z, August 1989, 1.

14. Farah and Moore, "Mexican Drug Traffickers Eclipse," sec. A, p. 1.

15. American Consul Guadalajara to Secretary of State Washington, DC, "Government of Mexico Anti-Narcotics Report Blow Against Medellín Cocaine Cartel," Guadalajara 00488 021909Z, February 1988, 1.

16. US Congress, *Structure of International Trafficking Organizations*, 121.

17. Secretary of State Washington DC to U.S. Mission Vienna, "Subject: Mexican Police Confiscate Arms Destined for the Medellín Cartel," State 043784 120209Z, February 1988, 2.

18. James Mills, *The Underground Empire: Where Crime and Governments Embrace* (New York: Doubleday and Company, 1986), 553–556. Ponsiglione posed as a businessman named José Casteñada Gutiérrez who ran a chain of haberdasheries that specialized in men's clothing in Mexico City and along the US-Mexico border.

19. American Embassy Washington, DC, "Subject: Post Reporting Plan," 08122 3 12045Z, 1.

20. American Embassy Mexico to Secretary of State Washington, DC, "Post Reporting Plan: Narcotics Coverage in the Mexican Media," Mexico 00785 111944Z, January 1989, 1–2.

21. Douglas Farah, "Drug Lords' Influence Pervading Mexico; Neighbor, Last Line of Defense for U.S., Now Likened to Colombia," *Washington Post*, April 4, 1995, sec. A, p. 1. Instead of $1,000 a kilo, the Mexicans sold cocaine for up to $15,000 per kilo.

22. US Congress, *Structure of International Trafficking Organizations*, 136.

23. American Embassy Mexico to Secretary of State Washington, DC, "Subject: Narcotics Monthly Program Report, May 1992," Mexico 16102 262354Z, June 1992, 1–2, Names: Rafael and Eduardo Muñoz Talavera.

24. American Embassy Mexico to Secretary of State Washington, DC, "Subject: Narcotics Roundup September 9–October 8, 1992," Mexico 25205 151705Z, October 1992, 3–5; American Consul Ciudad Juárez to Secretary of State Washington, DC, "Subject: Chihuahua Police Continue Prosecution of Cocaine Traffickers," Ciudad 01642 031735Z, November 1989, 1–3. Released in 1995, Rafael Muñoz Talavera was killed in 1998 while trying to consolidate control over the Juárez cartel after the death of Carrillo Fuentes in 1997.

25. American Embassy Mexico to Secretary of State Washington, DC, "Subject: MFJP Seizes Major Shipment of Cali Cocaine and Arrest Two Colombian Traffickers," Mexico 07061 201550Z, March 1990, 1.

26. American Embassy Mexico to Secretary of State Washington, DC, "Subject: Weekly Narcotics Roundup: March 12–16," Mexico 06757 162025Z, March 1990, 2.

27. Secretary of State Washington, DC, to American Embassy Mexico, "Subject: Levitsky Meeting with Cordoba," State 395391 220627Z, November 1990, 4.

28. American Embassy Mexico to Secretary of State Washington, DC, "Weekly Narcotics Roundup October 1–15," Mexico 27381 052329Z, October 1990, 2.

29. Beittel, *Mexico's Drug Trafficking*, 14.

130   Narcostates

30. American Embassy Mexico to Secretary of State Washington, DC, "Subject: Drug Trafficking Through Southeastern Mexico," Mexico 13075 032150Z, June 1993, 2–3.

31. Barry Bosworth, Susan M. Collins, and Nora Claudia Lustig, eds., *Coming Together? Mexico-U.S. Relations* (Washington, DC: Brookings Institution Press, 1997), 210.

32. "The War for Tijuana," *Before It's News*, May 22, 2013, http://beforeitsnews .com; Froylan Enciso, *Drogas, narcotráfico y política en México protocolo de hipocresía 1969–2000* (Mexico: Editorial Oceano, 2004), 237–238.

33. Tim Golden, "The Mexican Connection Grows as the Supplier to the U.S.," *New York Times*, July 30, 1995, sec. A, p. 1. Amado Carrillo Fuentes's uncle was Ernesto Fonseca Carrillo.

34. Farah and Moore, "Mexican Drug Traffickers Eclipse," sec. A, p. 1.

35. American Embassy Mexico to Secretary of State Washington, DC, "Subject: Weekly Narcotics Roundup, April 8–12, 1991," Mexico 08028 081924Z, April 1991, 3–4.

36. "Confidential DEA Summary: Guillermo González Calderóni," *Frontline*, April 8, 1997, www.pbs.org/wgbh/pages/frontline/shows/mexico/family/secretdea .html.

37. Jerry Seper, "Bust Hits at Cartels' Bankers: 112 Arrested; Drugs, $35 Million Seized," *Washington Times*, May 19, 1998, sec. A, p. 1.

38. American Embassy Mexico to DEA Headquarters Washington, DC, "Subject: Summary of Significant News Releases/Mexico [Redacted]," Mexico 08818 162204Z, April 1993, 3.

39. "The Mexican Connection Drugs: President Ernesto Zedillo Needs to Act Swiftly if Mexico Is to Avoid Becoming a Narco-Democracy Like Colombia," *Globe and Mail* (Canada), December 18, 1995, Economic section.

40. American Embassy Mexico to DEA Field Division, Los Angeles, "Subject: Summary of Significant News Releases Mexico," Mexico 12953 201605Z, June 1995, 3–4.

41. American Embassy Mexico, "Subject: Weekly Narcotics Roundup October 1–15," 3.

42. American Embassy Mexico to Secretary of State Washington DC, "Subject: Monthly Counternarcotics Strategy Report—March 1997," Mexico 03918 011901Z, April 1997, 5–7. The three generals listed in the report were Mario Arturo Acosta Chaparra, Francisco Quiroz Hermosillo, and Jorge Maldonado Vega.

43. Mike Gallagher, "King of the Kingpins," *Albuquerque Journal*, March 3, 1997, sec. A, p. 1.

44. American Embassy Mexico to DEA Headquarters Washington, DC, "Subject: Monthly Narrative Report January 1990," Mexico 03560 141815Z, February 1990, 2–5; American Embassy Mexico, "Subject: Post Reporting Plan— Drug Trafficking," 12050 091950Z, 1–4. Nuevo Leon and Ocampo are in the state of Coahuila and were considered Gulf cartel territory.

45. American Embassy Mexico, "Subject: Subject: Post Reporting Plan—Drug Trafficking," 12050 091950Z, 3; James Brooke, "Cali the Quiet Cartel Profits by Accommodation," *New York Times*, July 14, 1991, sec. A, p. 3.

46. American Embassy Mexico to DEA Headquarters Washington, DC, "Current Cocaine Situation in Mexico," Mexico 10460 032110Z, May 1991, 1–2.

47. American Embassy Mexico to DEA Headquarters Washington, DC, "Subject: Drug Trafficking Through Southeastern Mexico," Mexico 13075 032142Z, June 1993, 2–4.

The Colombian Cartels Expand Their Reach 131

48. Ibid., 1.

49. American Embassy Mexico "Subject: PJFM Seizes Major Shipment of Cali Cocaine," 2; American Embassy Mexico to Secretary of State Washington, DC, "Weekly Narcotics Roundup: March 12–16," Mexico 06757 162028Z, March 1990, 4.

50. American Embassy Mexico, "Subject: Current Cocaine Situation," 2.

51. American Embassy Mexico to Secretary of State Washington, DC, "Subject: Weekly Narcotics Roundup April 8–12, 1991," Mexico 08358 122228Z, April 1991, 2–3.

52. American Embassy Mexico, "Subject: Drug Trafficking Through Southeastern Mexico," 1–2.

53. American Embassy Mexico, "Subject: Current Cocaine Situation," 2.

54. American Embassy Mexico, "Subject: Summary of Significant News Releases Mexico," June 1995, 3.

55. American Embassy Mexico to Secretary of State, Washington, DC, "Subject: The Mexican Illicit Drug Threat: A Community Assessment," Mexico 09286 100038Z, April 1990, 2–3.

56. Farah and Moore, "Mexican Drug Traffickers Eclipse," sec. A, p. 1.

57. American Embassy Mexico to DEA Headquarters Washington, DC, "Summary of Significant News Releases Mexico," Mexico 03146 082002Z, February 1994, 3.

58. Ibid.

59. Douglas Farah, "Mexican Control of the U.S. Cocaine Market Grows," *Washington Post*, August 5, 1997, sec. A, p. 11.

60. Farah and Moore, "Mexican Drug Traffickers Eclipse," sec. A, p. 1.

61. Ibid.

62. Melvyn Levitsky, US assistant secretary of state for narcotics matters 1989–1993, interview with the author, June 20, 2014.

63. Mark Fineman, "Battle over Drug Cartel Follows Death of Its Lord," *Los Angeles Times*, July 29, 1997, http://articles.latimes.com.

64. Ann W. O'Neill, "Colombia Drug Kingpins Face Trial in Miami," *South Florida Sun Sentinel*, November 24, 2004, www.cocaine.org/colombia/cali.html. At the time, there were an estimated 300 minicartels.

65. José Rosso Serrano Cadena, general of the Colombian National Police 1994–2000, internet correspondence with author, January 19, 2007.

66. Linda Diebel, "Cocaine Trade Goes Low-Key: Narco-Kings Eschew Flashy Hollywood-Style of Predecessors, but Are Just as Dangerous," *Toronto Star* (Canada), June 6, 1998, sec. A, p. 9.

67. Douglas Farah, "Colombian Drug Cartels Exploit Tech Advantage," *Washington Post*, November 19, 1999, sec. A, p. 17.

68. Diebel, "Cocaine Trade," sec. A, p. 9.

69. Andrés López López, *El Cártel de los Sapos* (Bogotá: Editorial Planeta Colombiana, 2008), 33.

70. US Attorney's Office, Eastern District of New York, "Colombian Trafficker with Links to Mexican and Colombian Cartels Extradited from Mexico to the U.S." (Washington, DC: US Department of Justice, June 10, 2010), www.justice.gov/usao /nye/pr/2010/2010jun17.html.

71. US Department of Justice, "United States Announces RICO Charges Against Leadership of Colombia's Most Powerful Cocaine Cartel" (Washington, DC: US Department of Justice, May 6, 2004), 1.

72. David Robbins, *Heavy Traffic: 30 Years of Headlines and Major Ops from the Case Files of the DEA* (New York: Chamberlain Brothers, 2005), 185.

132   Narcostates

73. American Embassy Bogotá to RUEHBU/Embassy Buenos Aires, "Subject: [Redacted] SFIP Summary Intelligence on the Oficina de Envigado and BACRIM–Los Paisas Drug Trafficking Organization v. Members and Activities," Bogotá 2350 241400Z, July 24, 2009, 3–4.

74. Jeremy McDermott, "The BACRIM and Their Position in Colombia's Underworld," InSight Crime, May 2, 2014, www.insightcrime.org.

75. James Bosworth, "Honduras: Organized Crime Gaining amid Political Crisis: Working Paper Series on Crime in Central America" (Washington, DC: Woodrow Wilson International Center for Scholars, Latin American Program, December 2010): 11. The Arellano Félix organization formed a three-way drug trafficking ring with the Russian Mafia and the FARC. The Sinaloa cartel cooperated with the FARC in Honduras.

76. American Embassy Mexico to Secretary of State Washington, DC, "Weekly Narcotics Roundup: November 19–23, 1990," Mexico 31672 240020Z, November 1990, 3–4.

77. American Embassy Mexico to DEA Headquarters Washington, DC, "Subject: [Redacted] Summary of Significant News Releases in the Republic of Mexico, January 25–31, 1991," Mexico 03667 142318Z, February 1991, 2.

78. American Embassy Mexico to DEA Headquarters Washington, DC, "Subject: Post Reporting Plan—Drug Trafficking in Mexico—the Current Cocaine Situation in Mexico," Mexico 10460 032111Z, May 1991, 2.

79. Central Intelligence Agency, "Memorandum for Deputy Director of Central Intelligence, "Subject: PFIAB" (Washington, DC: Central Intelligence Agency, CIA-RDP88G01117R001003990002-7, September 9, 1986), 5.

80. Secretary of State Washington, DC, to American Embassy Belize, "Subject: House Foreign Affairs Testimony RE:INSCR," State 090720 240432Z, March 1988, 2–3.

81. Stephen Meiners, "Central America: An Emerging Role in the Drug Trade" (Austin, TX: Stratfor Global Intelligence, March 25, 2009), www.stratfor.com; US General Accounting Office, *Drug Control: Interdiction Efforts in Central America Have Had Little Impact on the Flow of Drugs*, Report to the Chairman, Subcommittee on Information, Justice, Transportation, and Agriculture, Committee on Government Operations, House of Representatives (Washington, DC, August 2, 1994), 1–2.

82. American Embassy Mexico to Secretary of State Washington, DC, "Subject: Weekly Narcotics Roundup: November 5–9, 1990," Mexico 30664 100003Z, November 1990, 2.

83. American Embassy Mexico, "Subject: Drug Trafficking Through Southeastern Mexico," 13075 032150Z, 3.

84. Douglas Farah and Tod Robberson, "Drug Traffickers Build a New Central American Route to the U.S.," *Washington Post*, March 28, 1993, sec. A, p. 1.

85. US General Accounting Office, *Drug Control: Interdiction*, 5–6.

86. Stephen Dudley, "Drug Trafficking Organizations in Central America: Transportistas, Mexican Cartels, and Maras," in *Organized Crime in Central America: The Northern Triangle*, ed. Cynthia Aronson and Eric L. Olson, Woodrow Wilson Institute Reports on the Americas no. 29 (Washington, DC: Woodrow Wilson Institute, November 2011), 18–62.

87. Douglas Farah and Tod Robberson, "U.S. Style Gangs Build Free Trade in Crime," *Washington Post*, August 28, 1995, sec. A, p. 1.

88. Meiners, "Central America."

89. David R. Dye, "Nicaraguan Cocaine Bust Reveals New Cartel Route," *Christian Science Monitor*, January 26, 1994, World sec., p. 1.

The Colombian Cartels Expand Their Reach   **133**

90. American Embassy Guatemala to Secretary of State Washington, DC, "Subject: Embassy Counternarcotics Strategy: Guatemala," Guatemala 07558 131643Z, October 1995, 2.

91. American Embassy Mexico, "Subject: Drug Trafficking Through Southeastern Mexico," 13075 032150Z, 2.

92. American Embassy Mexico to DEA Headquarters Washington, DC, "Subject: Summary of Significant News Releases/Mexico," Mexico 09026 032338Z, April 1992, 2.

93. Farah, "Drug Traffickers," sec. A, p. 1.

94. General Accounting Office, *Drug Control: Interdiction*, 14.

95. US Department of State, International Narcotics Matters, "Narcotics Country Profile: Guatemala," State WPPJFG29, December 20, 1990, 2.

96. Joint Chiefs of Staff Washington, DC to AIG 11888, "Subject: IRR [Redacted] Comments by Senior Army Officer Concerning Drugs," R 090104Z, June 1990, 0004 (National Security Archive, Guatemala Project).

97. Frank Smyth, "A New Kingdom of Cocaine; for Colombia's Powerful Cali Cartel, the Crucial Connection Is Guatemala," *Washington Post*, December 26, 1993, sec. C, p. 4.

98. American Embassy Guatemala to Secretary of State Washington, DC, "Subject: The Guatemala-Mexican Border and Support for Guerrillas and Drug Traffickers," Guatemala 08886 191715Z, July 1990, 2.

99. American Embassy Guatemala to Secretary of State Washington, DC, "Subject: Across the Mexican Border: Guns, Drugs, and Guerrillas," Guatemala 02162 212358Z, February 1990, 1.

100. Ibid., 2; American Embassy Guatemala, "Subject: The Guatemala-Mexican Border," 2.

101. American Embassy Guatemala, "Subject: Across the Mexican Border," 02162 220000Z, 3.

102. American Embassy Guatemala to Secretary of State Washington, DC, "Subject: The De León Administration and Drugs: Some Guatemalan Perspectives and Attitudes," Guatemala 13761 201642Z, December 1993, 4.

103. Ibid., 3.

104. Smyth, "A New Kingdom of Cocaine," sec. C, p. 4; American Embassy Guatemala, "Subject: Across the Mexican Border," 02162 220001Z, 4.

105. American Embassy Guatemala, "Subject: The Guatemala-Mexican Border," 1.

106. American Embassy Guatemala, "Subject: Across the Mexican Border," 02162 220000Z, 3–4.

107. American Embassy Guatemala, "Subject: The Guatemala-Mexican Border," 1–2. The URNG's headquarters and press service operated out of Mexico City.

108. Ibid.; American Embassy Mexico to Secretary of State Washington, DC, "Subject: Mexico-Guatemalan Border Action Plan," Mexico 12190 101857Z, May 1990, 1.

109. American Embassy Guatemala, "Subject: Embassy Counternarcotics Strategy: Guatemala," 3.

110. General Accounting Office, *Drug Control: Interdiction*, 14.

111. Defense Intelligence Agency, "Guatemala: Counterdrug Intelligence Summary," DIR-55-92, October 1992, 13 (National Security Archive, Guatemala Project).

112. American Embassy Guatemala, "Subject: Embassy Counternarcotics Strategy: Guatemala," 4.

134 Narcostates

113. American Embassy Guatemala to Secretary of State Washington, DC, "Subject: Denial of Ochoa Extradition," Guatemala 09207 071549Z, October 1994, 1–2.

114. Smyth, "A New Kingdom of Cocaine," sec. C, p. 4; Frank Smyth, "Has Guatemala Become the Cali Cartel's Bodega?," *Wall Street Journal*, March 10, 1995, sec. A, p. 5.

115. Frank Smyth, "Even Court Approved Extraditions Have a Troubled Bloody History in Guatemala," InSight Crime, July 19, 2012, www.insightcrime.org.

116. [Redacted], "Subject: [Redacted] Military Involvement in Drug Trafficking," Department of Defense, November 5, 1993, 0063–0064 (National Security Archive, Guatemala Project).

117. American Embassy Guatemala to Secretary of State Washington, DC, "Subject: Mayor of Zacapa Arrested for Drug Trafficking on U.S. Request Pending Extradition," Guatemala 15523 282046Z, December 1990, 1 (National Security Archive, Guatemala Project). Zacapa was located in Military Zone 7.

118. American Embassy Guatemala to Secretary of State Washington, DC, "Subject: The de León Administration and Drugs: Some Guatemalan Perspectives and Attitudes," Guatemala 13761 201642Z, December 1993, 4. AP-5 was an offshoot party allied to Guatemala's Partido Social Democrático (PSD) from 1990 to 1999. The cartel operative was there as part of a real estate transaction in Petén.

119. Melvyn Levitsky, interview, June 20, 2014.

120. American Embassy Guatemala to Secretary of State Washington, DC, "Subject: Revised Post Operating Plan for Guatemala—FY 93—Second Revision," Guatemala 00164 071918Z, January 1993, 1.

121. American Embassy San Salvador to Secretary of State Washington, DC, "Monthly Status Report—February 1992," San Salvador 02475 042010Z, March 1992, 1.

122. American Embassy San Salvador, "Monthly Status Report—February 1992," 2.

123. American Embassy San Salvador to Secretary of State Washington, DC, "Subject: GOES Launches National Plan to Combat Crime," San Salvador 01942 250044Z, February 1993, 2. Santamaría negotiated the 1992 Chapultepec Peace Accord with the FMLN.

124. General Accounting Office, *Drug Control: Interdiction*, 22.

125. Alfredo Cristiani, "El Salvador: Cristiani on Cooperation Against Drug Trafficking, Use of Army Against Crime," Radio YSKL, San Salvador–BBC Summary of World Broadcasts, February 11, 1993.

126. American Embassy San Salvador to Secretary of State Washington, DC, "Subject: Annual Narcotics Status Report (ANSR) for 1986," San Salvador 04089 302239Z, March 1987, 2.

127. American Embassy San Salvador to American Embassy Guatemala, "Subject: General Bustillo Requests Additional Information and Assistance to Deal with Air Force Narcotics Problem," San Salvador 00008 031918Z, January 1989, 1.

128. Secretary of State Washington, DC, to American Embassy San Salvador, "Subject: Information on ESAF Officers for Ad Hoc Commission," State 256728 101822Z, August 1992, 6.

129. Ibid.; American Embassy San Salvador to Secretary of State Washington, DC, "Subject: Official Informal," San Salvador 08040 051400Z, August 1992, 2. The leader was Lieutenant Colonel Tomás Calvo Alfaro.

130. American Embassy San Salvador to Secretary of State Washington, DC, "Subject: Official Informal," San Salvador 08089 080017Z, August 1992, 2.

131. American Secretary of State to All American Republic Diplomatic Posts, "Subject: ARA New Items of February 19, 1985," State 049861 190908Z, February

1985, 10–11; Craig Pyes and Laurie Becklund, "Inside Dope in El Salvador," *New Republic*, April 15, 1985, 15–19. Napoleón Duarte's PDC (Christian Democratic Party) claimed that drug money would be used by ARENA to corrupt the political process.

132. American Embassy San Salvador to Secretary of State Washington, DC, "Subject: Group Argues Military Should Act to End Narco-Corruption; Finding No Resonance, Leader Recants," San Salvador 04328 220305Z (October 1997), 3; and Manuel R. Párraga, "El fraude del siglo y la complicidad del Estado: Caso INSEPRO/FINSEPRO," *Revista Probidad* (January–February 2001): 53–55, https://silo.tips/download/revista-probidad. The lieutenant colonel was Roberto Leiva Jacobo.

133. American Embassy San Salvador "Subject: Group Argues," 3. Retired Colonel Roberto Antonio Rodríguez Murcia gave the report credibility but later disavowed it. The new oligarchy included the following families: Cristiani, Baldochi, Suster, Domenech, Siman, Kriete, Barrera, Poma, Orellana, and González Giner.

134. Farah, "Drug Traffickers," sec. A, p. 1.

135. American Embassy San Salvador, "Subject: GOES Launches National Plan," 4.

136. Alfredo Cristiani, "El Salvador: Cristiani on Cooperation Against Drug Trafficking, Use of Army Against Crime," Radio YSKL, San Salvador–BBC Summary of World Broadcasts, February 11, 1993.

137. American Embassy San Salvador to Secretary of State Washington, DC, "Subject: Senior COAN Officials Protest Supreme Court Plans to Release Suspect in 3 Ton Cocaine Case," San Salvador 01481 101750Z, February 1992, 2–4; Kenneth Freed, "Salvadoran Government Shows Signs of Losing Interest in Bank Looting Scandal," *Los Angeles Times*, July 26, 1991, http://articles.latimes.com.

138. "Salvador Bust," *USA Today*, June 11, 1993, sec. A, p. 4.

139. General Accounting Office, *Drug Control: Interdiction*, 22.

140. Ibid., 17.

141. American Embassy Tegucigalpa to Secretary of State Washington, DC, "Request for FY 92 International Narcotics Training for Honduras," Tegucigalpa 05897 010029Z, May 1991, 3.

142. Thelma Mejía, "Unfinished Business: The Military and Drugs in Honduras," *The Transnational Institute: Drugs and Democracy Program*, December 1, 1997, https://www.tni.org/en/article/unfinished-business-the-military-and-drugs-in-honduras. The Ferraris were found dead in an artesian well on June 15, 1978, at the San Jorge farm in what is now the Cerro Grande neighborhood of Tegucigalpa. Barahona was accused of allowing Matta-Ballesteros to leave the country when the murder was committed so as to remove any suspicion of his involvement.

143. American Embassy Tegucigalpa to Secretary of State Washington, DC, "Telegram: Meeting with General Álvarez," Tegucigalpa 09345 (October 25, 1982), 1. National Security Archive: Negroponte File, http://nsarchive.gwu.edu/NSAEBB /NSAEBB151/.

144. Marie Bunck and Michael Ross Fowler, *Bribes, Bullets, and Intimidation* (University Park: Pennsylvania State University, 2012), 274.

145. James Bosworth, "Honduras: Organized Crime Gaining amid Political Crisis," Working Paper Series on Crime in Central America," Woodrow Wilson International Center for Scholars, December 2010, 3. Honduran extradition law prevented the Honduran government from extraditing Matta-Ballesteros directly to the United States. As a result, he was put on a plane to the Dominican Republic, where he was then picked up by the DEA at Santo Domingo Las Américas Airport and flown to New York, where he was charged for participating in the murder of Kiki Camarena.

136 Narcostates

146. American Embassy Tegucigalpa, "Request for FY 92 International," 2.

147. Bosworth, "Honduras: Organized Crime," 3.

148. American Embassy Tegucigalpa to Secretary of State Washington, DC, "Subject: Foreign Terrorist Organizations—Post Has None to Recommend for Inclusion in FTO List," Tegucigalpa 02760 011444Z, October 2002, 2.

149. Bosworth, "Honduras: Organized Crime Gaining amid Political Crisis," 11–12.

150. General Accounting Office, *Drug Control: U.S. Counterdrug Activities in Central America*, GAO/T-NSIAD-94-251 (Washington, DC, General Accounting Office, August 2, 1994), 2–4. Benjamin F. Nelson was the associate director for International Affairs Issues, National Security and International Affairs Division in the GAO.

151. American Embassy Tegucigalpa to American Embassy, Rome, "1996 Narcotics Workplan for Honduras," Tegucigalpa 02009 262228Z, April 1996, 1.

152. General Accounting Office, *Drug Control: Interdiction*, 17.

153. David Adams, "Drug Running Pirates Tarnish Caribbean Paradise," *London Times*, February 5, 1994, Overseas section.

154. American Embassy Tegucigalpa to Secretary of State Washington, DC, International Narcotics Control Strategy Report: Honduras," Tegucigalpa 07330 152300Z, December 1995, 1.

155. "Cocaine from a Showdown Near Honduras," *New York Times*, May 16, 1997, sec. A, p. 16.

156. American Embassy Tegucigalpa to Secretary of State Washington, DC, "Subject: FY 93 Military Assistance for Honduras," Tegucigalpa 12791 222202Z, September 1992, 3.

157. General Accounting Office, *Drug Control: Interdiction Efforts*, 17–20.

158. US Department of State, Bureau for International Narcotics and Law Enforcement Affairs, *1997 International Narcotics Control Strategy Report Vol. I.* (Washington, DC: US Department of State, March 1998), 138–140.

159. American Embassy Tegucigalpa to Secretary of State Washington, DC, "International Narcotics Control Strategy Report: Honduras," Tegucigalpa 07330 152300Z, December 1995, 1.

160. American Embassy Tegucigalpa to Secretary of State Washington, DC, "Subject: Honduran Congress Passes Law on Drug Asset Seizure," Tegucigalpa 04867 202342Z, May 1993, 1.

161. General Accounting Office, *Drug Control: Interdiction*, 23.

162. Dye, "Nicaraguan," 1.

163. American Embassy Managua to Secretary of State Washington, DC, "Subject: Narcotics Trafficking Developments," Managua 01411 191342Z, February 1991, 3.

164. American Embassy Managua to Secretary of State Washington, DC, "Sandinista Police Break-Up of Large Drug Ring," Managua 07498 200033Z, November 1986, 1.

165. US Department of State, Bureau for International Narcotics Matters, *1993 International Narcotics Control Strategy Report Vol. I* (Washington, DC: US Department of State, April 1993), 171–172.

166. Farah and Robberson, "Drug Traffickers," sec. A, p. 1.

167. American Embassy Panama to Secretary of State Washington, DC, "Subject: [Redacted] On Arms and Drug Trafficking in Nicaragua," Panama 10035 252203Z, October 1991, 1.

168. General Accounting Office, *Drug Control: Interdiction*, 23.

The Colombian Cartels Expand Their Reach   137

169. American Embassy Panama to Secretary of State Washington, DC, "Subject: [Redacted] On Arms and Drug Trafficking in Nicaragua," Panama 10035 252203Z, October 1991," 1; John Otis, "Island Off of Nicaragua Serves as Hub for Refugees, Drugs; Officials Ignore Smugglers Den," *Washington Times*, December 28, 1992, sec. A, p. 1.

170. American Embassy Panama, "Subject: [Redacted] On Arms," 2–3.

171. American Embassy Managua to Secretary of State Washington, DC, "International Narcotics Control Strategy Report—Nicaragua," Managua 08571 112332Z, December 1987, 1–2.

172. American Embassy Managua to Secretary of State Washington, DC, "1989 International Narcotics Control Strategy Report—Nicaragua," Managua 00078 051710Z, January 1989, 2.

173. American Embassy Managua to Secretary of State Washington DC, "Subject: Police Chief Accuses U.S. of Protecting Military Drug Traffickers," Managua 07414 270033Z, October 1990, 2. Lugo was a brigade comandante during the revolution and the director general of the National Police from 1979 to 1982 and 1989 to 1992.

174. American Embassy Managua to Secretary of State Washington, DC, "Subject: Details Regarding Nicaraguan Seizure of Large Cocaine Shipment," Managua 03492 072324Z, June 1990, 1.

175. American Embassy San José to Secretary of State Washington, DC, "Subject: FY 1996 Request for Promoting Peace (Regional Peace and Security)—Costa Rica," San José 05136 292224Z, July 1994, 2–3.

176. American Embassy San José to Secretary of State Washington, DC, "Subject: FY 1993 Security Assistance Reporting Requirements," San José 05437 212120Z, May 1991, 3.

177. American Embassy San José to Secretary of State Washington, DC, "Subject: FY 1995 Security Assistance Reporting Requirements (Part 1): FMF ESF and Narcotics AIASA," San José 05427 192344Z, July 1993, 3.

178. American Embassy San José to USIA Washington, DC, "Senator Hawkins' Visit to Costa Rica," San José 08195 181907Z, October 1984, 3.

179. Bunck and Fowler, *Bribes,* 145–148.

180. American Embassy San José to Secretary of State Washington, DC, "Subject: Costa Rican National Security and Security Assistance (Mission Reporting Plan Submission)," San José 06589 130459Z, June 1987, 3.

181. US Department of State, Bureau of Narcotics and Law Enforcement Matters, *1998 International Narcotics Control Strategy Report Vol. I* (Washington, DC: US Department of State, March 1999), 127; General Accounting Office, *Drug Control: Interdiction,* 21.

182. American Embassy San José, "Subject: FY1993," 4.

183. Scott, "With Few Weapons," 11.

184. Shirley Christian, "Central America: A New Drug Focus," *New York Times*, December 16, 1991, sec. A, p. 10.

185. General Accounting Office, *Drug Control: Interdiction,* 20.

186. American Embassy San José, "Subject: FY 1995," 2–3.

187. Scott, "With Few Weapons," 11.

188. Douglas Farah, "Gang in Costa Rica Kidnaps 18 Judges and Vows to Blow Up the Supreme Court," *Washington Post*, April 28, 1993, sec. A, p. 13.

189. "Costa Rican Police Free Kidnapped Judge," *St. Petersburg Times*, April 30, 1993, sec. A, p. 9.

190. "The Struggle for Peace," *Tico Times*, May 19, 2006, https://ticotimes.net; Bunck and Fowler, *Bribes*, 135.

191. US Department of State, *1992 International Narcotics Control Strategy Report*, Bureau for International Narcotics and Law Enforcement Affairs, US Department of State, February 1993, http://dosfan.lib.uic.edu/ERC/law/INC/1993/03.html.

192. US Department of State, *1998 International Narcotics Control Strategy Report Vol. I*, 129. In January 1997, authorities arrested two Public Security Ministry officers for accepting bribes and allowing cocaine to enter Costa Rica.

193. Bunck and Fowler, *Bribes*, 140.

194. US Department of State, *1998 International Narcotics Control Strategy Report Vol. I*, 129; Carlos Agaton, "Reportaje Especial: Investigaciones vinculan a Óscar Arias con el Dictador Manuel Antonio Noriega y con redes del narcotráfico," *Agaton* (Nicaragua), August 30, 2016, https://carlosagaton.blogspot.com; Eillyn Jíminez and Carlos Arguedas, "Ricardo Alem en la mira de la justicia desde 1988, regresa al ojo público," *La Nación* (Costa Rica), January 8, 2021, 10, www.pressreader.com. While he was being tried in the United States, Costa Rican courts sentenced him to thirteen years in absentia. The two deputies were Víctor Julio Brenes and Edelberto Castilblanco. In 2005, Alem was released from jail and returned to Costa Rica. In 2008, he was arrested for storing 35 kilos of cocaine in a warehouse he owned in San José. Police alleged that Alem was moving cocaine from Costa Rica to Guatemala, where it was then exported to Germany. In 2010, Alem was sentenced to twenty years in prison.

195. Universidad de Costa Rica, "Narcotráfico, Democracia y Soberanía Nacional en Costa Rica," *Anuario de Estudios Centroamericanos* 25, no. 2 (1999): 33–47; Loría Quirós, *De Caro Quintero a Ricardo Alem*, 129–159; Giannina Segnini and Ronald Moya, "Alem dice que financió a dos diputados del PLN," *La Nación* (Costa Rica), March 8, 1997, vvw.nacion.com.

196. "Costa Rica: Conmoción política por detención de ex diputado socialdemócrata," *La Prensa* (Honduras), March 1, 1997, www1.udel.edu/leipzig/texts2/pra01037.htm; US Department of State, *1997 International Narcotics Control Strategy Report Vol. I*, 57.

197. US General Accounting Office, *The War on Drugs: Narcotics Control in Panama* GAO/NSIAD-91-233 (Washington, DC: General Accounting Office, July 1991), 1.

198. Levitsky, interview, June 20, 2014.

199. General Accounting Office, *Drug Control: Interdiction*, 24.

200. Joseph B. Treaster, "Cocaine Is Again Surging out of Panama," *New York Times*, August 13, 1991, sec. A, p. 1.

201. American Embassy Panama to Secretary of State Washington, DC, "Subject: Panama One Year After," Panama 10665 271539Z, November 1990, 2; World Bank, *Indicators: Panama Unemployment Total Percentage of the Labor Force* (Washington, DC: World Bank), http://data.worldbank.org/indicator/SL.UEM.TOTL.ZS?page=4.

202. American Embassy Panama to Secretary of State Washington, DC, "Subject: FY 95 Panama Budget Submission," Panama 03448 232305Z, April 1993, 2.

203. Treaster, "Cocaine Is Again Surging out of Panama," sec. A, p. 1.

204. American Embassy Panama to Secretary of State Washington, DC, "1994 International Narcotics Control Strategy Report for Panama," Panama 07995 191505Z, December 1994, 17.

205. General Accounting Office, *The War on Drugs*, 2.

The Colombian Cartels Expand Their Reach   **139**

206. US Department of State, *1998 International Narcotics Control Strategy Report Vol. I*, 167.

207. American Embassy Panama, "1994 International Narcotics Control," 15.

208. US Department of State, *1998 International Narcotics Control Strategy Report Vol. I*, 164–167.

209. General Accounting Office, *The War on Drugs*, 3.

210. American Embassy Panama, "Subject: 1994 International Narcotics Control," 3.

211. James S. Henry, "Panama: Dirty Business as Usual; Noriega Is Gone, but the Drug Traffic and Corruption Live On," *Washington Post*, July 28, 1991, sec. C, p. 1.

212. Jim Defede, "Falcon and Magulta," *Miami New Times*, February 12, 1992, www.miaminewtimes.com; Webster Tarpley and Anton Chaitkin, *George Bush: The Unauthorized Biography*, 2nd ed. (Joshua Tree: Tree Life Books, 2004), 499–541. The banks used were Banco General, Banco de Colombia, Banco Alemán, Primer Banco de Ahorros, Sudameris, Banaico, and Banco del Istmo (a bank owned by Panamanian foreign minister Gabriel Lewis Galindo).

213. American Embassy Panama to Secretary of State Washington, DC, "Subject: Panama One Year After," Panama 10665 271539Z, November 1990, 2. The reporter was Dagoberto Franco.

214. Tarpley and Chaitkin, *George Bush: The Unauthorized Biography*, 499–541.

215. General Accounting Office, *Drug Control: Interdiction*, 24.

216. American Embassy Panama to Secretary of State Washington, DC, "Subject: Official-Informal," Panama 07990 042146Z, September 1990, 1.

217. James R. Richards, *Transnational Criminal Organizations, Cybercrime and Money Laundering: A Handbook for Law Enforcement Officers, Auditors, and Financial Investigators* (London: CRC Press, 1999), 253–254; Georgia Tech Panama Logistics Innovation and Research Center, "Colon Free Trade Zone Statistics" (Panama City, Panama: Georgia Tech Panama, December 2019), http://logistics .gatech.pa/en/assets/special-economic-zones/colon-free-zone/statistics.

218. General Accounting Office, *The War on Drugs*, 4–5.

219. General Accounting Office, *Drug Control: Interdiction*, 24.

220. Richards, *Transnational Criminal Organizations*, 58. Although the transactions occurred in the CFTZ, the drug money often stayed in the United States. Because of Panamanian banking secrecy laws, the transactions were untraceable and merely a matter of transferring credit from one account to another through brokerages and accounts within the CFTZ.

221. General Accounting Office, *Drug Control: Interdiction Efforts*, 25; Mark P. Sullivan, *Panama-U.S. Relations: Continuing Policy Concerns* (Washington, DC: Congressional Research Service, August 4, 1994), 12.

222. Bunck and Fowler, *Bribes*, 9.

7

The War on Drugs Spills into Central America

In the 1990s, a lack of resources, a myopic governmental response, and endemic corruption hindered the development of Central American counternarcotics programs. Drained by civil war, the Central American governments possessed neither the resources nor the institutional capability to address new drug trafficking modes.[1] As Colombian and Mexican traffickers started to "Colombianize" Central America, Washington began to phase out military aid to the region.[2] Despite the reduction in aid, the United States believed that proactive measures were necessary to assist Central America.[3] As one 1990 State Department cable put it, "A well-coordinated Central American counternarcotics strategy is desirable and worthy of pursuit." The cable added, "though we must avoid overly ambitious goals which practically cannot be achieved; this does not mean that we should not try." In 1990, the US embassy in Panama observed that "Central American countries need to understand better that they're in it with the rest of us" and "should take the problem seriously."[4] CISEN director Carrillo Olea opined "that it did not take long for drug traffickers to fly over" Central America. For that reason, he made the point that it was extremely important for Central America to "possess the capability to react quickly and to share information on illegal flights in a timely fashion."[5] Despite the concern, the US General Accounting Office reported in 1994 that Central American governments did not have the resources "to purchase sophisticated equipment and to develop well-trained personnel to combat well-financed, creative, and highly adaptable traffickers."[6] The success or failure of Central America's counternarcotics police depended on their reorganization and cooperation.

142 *Narcostates*

Regional Counternarcotics Coordination

Since 1961, Central American governments have belonged to a regime of international narcotics control. In that year, Guatemala, Honduras, El Salvador, Nicaragua, Costa Rica, and Panama all signed the UN Single Convention on Narcotic Drugs (amended in 1972), and later signed the 1971 UN Convention on Psychotropic Substances, which prohibited the production and supply of substances designated as narcotics. All signatory nations were expected to regulate narcotics within their own borders.[7] In 1986, the epidemic of drug trafficking and abuse led the Organization of American States (OAS) to meet in Rio de Janeiro to pass a resolution that led to the formation of the Comisión Interamericana para el Control del Abuso de Drogas (CICAD). The commission developed a Latin American approach to drug control by establishing "illicit drug control, not as a stand-alone issue, but firmly in the context of socioeconomic development, environmental protection, human rights, and respect for the customs of national and regional groups."[8] In 1988, Central American nations acceded to the UN Convention Against Illicit Traffic in Narcotic Drugs and Psychotropic Substances, which set international regulations and criminal penalties against money laundering, precursor chemicals, and the extradition of drug traffickers. In April 1990, all member states of the OAS General Assembly adopted the Ixtapa Declaration and Program of Action. The declaration set CICAD's priorities by establishing collective responsibility among member nations to redouble national and international efforts against drug trafficking, now recognized as a criminal activity.[9]

To coordinate their activities, Central American nations enacted the Sistema de la Integración Centroamericana (SICA) in 1991. As an economic and political organization, SICA represented Central America's first attempt to coordinate counternarcotics activities within the CICAD framework. The 1991 Tegucigalpa Convention, which created the SICA, stemmed from the 1986–1987 Esquipulas I and II peace accords. The accords agreed upon regional economic cooperation and provided the framework to end the wars in Nicaragua in 1990 and El Salvador in 1992, and for the 1993 Oslo Accords, which ended the war in Guatemala in 1996. The 1991 Tegucigalpa Convention also established a regional economic integration system and reaffirmed a commitment to strengthen the Central American Parliament and the Central American Court of Justice.[10] Most importantly, the 1991 SICA agreement called for the development of a new model to eradicate corruption, terrorism, narcotrafficking, and the trafficking of arms.[11]

The culmination of the regional agreements led to an unprecedented 1993 meeting of Central American presidents during which they discussed greater antidrug cooperation and pledged their commitment to develop specific regional counternarcotics programs.[12] The attendees agreed that Central American governments and several drug consuming countries, including the United States, would stop drug trafficking organizations (DTOs) from exploiting the region's ideal geographic location and the imprint of corruption on the region's fragile democracies.[13] Stemming from the 1993 meeting and the 1991 Tegucigalpa SICA agreement, the Constitutive Agreement of the Permanent Central American Commission for the Eradication of the Production, Trafficking, Consumption, and Illicit Use of Narcotics and Psychotropic Substances—Comisión Centroamericana Permanente (CCP)—was formed. The CCP served as a consultative and advisory body to control the production, trafficking, consumption, and illicit use of narcotics and psychotropic substances. Ministers from every Central American government except Belize signed the agreement.[14]

Beyond all these agreements, the inability to develop an effective counternarcotics police force presented the biggest obstacle for every Central American nation in the post–civil war era. All countries in the region, especially the war-torn countries—El Salvador, Guatemala, Nicaragua, and Panama—lacked financial resources, and each questioned how best to reorganize their respective national police forces. Creating new security forces to fight narcotrafficking weighed heavily on the reconstituted Central American governments. Debates centered on governmental power sharing, demilitarization, and the professionalization of the counternarcotics police forces. The possibility that the newly established counternarcotics forces could become politicized and used to undermine democratization through police intimidation lingered in the back of many Central American minds— especially among the revolutionaries who laid down their weapons. In order to understand how the Central American narcocorridor became a permanent feature in the war on drugs, an evaluation of how each country implemented its nascent counternarcotics programs is imperative.

Guatemala:
Is There an Alternative to the Military?

During the country's long civil war (1960–1996), the Guatemalan military limited its participation in counternarcotics efforts. The military's size and inadequate logistical abilities made it difficult to mount simultaneous operations against guerrillas and traffickers.[15] Although the Guatemalan military maintained a presence along the border, the head of the D-2 considered the military's role against narcotrafficking to be auxiliary. Due to civil war prerogatives, Guatemala's D-2 only committed 30 percent of its resources to disrupt and destroy drug trafficking networks, while it directed the remaining 70 percent against the URNG, then an armed guerrilla movement.[16]

144   *Narcostates*

Nonetheless, because the D-2 was in charge of the country's surveillance apparatus, the DEA periodically collaborated with them to coordinate roadblocks and drug interdiction operations.[17]

In 1992, the Guatemalan government implemented La Ley Contra Narcoactividad Decreto Número 48-92, declaring that in "recent years" Guatemala had become a "victim of the criminal activity of narcotrafficking."[18] The law placed overall responsibility for drug matters concerning both demand and supply reduction in the office of the vice president and created the Commission Against the Addictions and the Illicit Traffic of Drugs (Comisión Contra las Adicciónes y el Tráfico Ilícito de Drogas). The vice president and the ministers of government, defense, public health, and social assistance chaired the commission. Despite Guatemala's implementation of a counternarcotics program in 1993, the US government criticized the vice president's office for harboring pro-legalization sentiment and failing to provide overall leadership and strategy in the drug war as mandated by law.[19]

In response to rampant corruption within the Guatemalan police, the government created the Departamento de Operaciones Antinarcóticas (DOAN) in 1994.[20] The DOAN was a specially trained and equipped force within Guatemala's treasury police. It carried out narcotics investigations, interdiction operations, and opium poppy eradication operations. The Ministry of Government developed a plan to train 500 national and treasury police officers with annual counternarcotics courses.[21] The government designed the DOAN to be immune from corruption via the use of handpicked "clean" recruits, who received proper training and wages sufficient to support their families. The DOAN became one of the few units in Latin America that performed regular eradication missions and sought to prosecute growers.[22] The Guatemalan government received significant assistance from the DEA and the State Department's Bureau of International Narcotics and Law Enforcement Affairs to help select, train, and equip DOAN officers.[23] The US government also worked with the DOAN to institutionalize their training capabilities, methods, and programs, such as the DOAN's canine training school.[24] In 1994, treasury police units conducted eradication operations, destroyed marijuana drying sheds, and manually eradicated 200 hectares of opium and another 78 hectares using aerial eradication.

The end of the civil war in 1996 allowed the Guatemalan government to place more emphasis on counternarcotics matters. As a part of the peace accords, the government created the Policía Nacional Civil (PNC) in 1997 and placed it under the direct supervision of the Ministry of Interior. Maintaining internal security became the PNC's main responsibility. The PNC excluded all active military personnel from its command structure.[25] As part of the police reorganization, the PNC incorporated the DOAN into its ranks with the DOAN continuing to act as the lead counternarcotics agency.[26] It

The War on Drugs Spills into Central America   145

concentrated operations on border points with Mexico and El Salvador, conducted highway traffic checks in Zacapa, and ran mobile interdiction operations along the southern coastal highway.[27] It also pursued an aggressive opium and marijuana eradication campaign after the government authorized the creation of separate drug eradication units within the DOAN.[28] Specifically, it reduced the opium poppy crop from its high of 2,500 hectares in 1991 to less than 10 hectares in 1998.[29]

While this transition occurred, the Guatemalan government frequently ordered the army to support the DOAN and the PNC because of the belief that these agencies were ill-equipped and lacked resources.[30] DOAN officers received a poorly maintained .38 caliber revolver in contrast to narcotraffickers who carried .45 caliber or 9 mm semiautomatic weapons loaded with armor-piercing ammunition.[31] After much criticism for its weak counternarcotics commitment, the Guatemalan military created an "army of the jungle," consisting of self-sustaining units with drug interception capabilities that patrolled the Petén jungle for extended periods.[32]

Despite limited successes, Guatemala's counternarcotics forces made little headway. Since Guatemala lacked radar and chase-plane capabilities, the State Department encouraged the Guatemalan air force and navy to develop aerial and maritime interdiction programs.[33] Yet, because Guatemala's resources were stretched thin, and the US government was transferring assets to other areas of importance, particularly Colombia, the program suffered from inertia.[34] A 1996 memo circulated within the DEA argued that as the "gateway to Mexico," trafficking in Guatemala would increase if the United States did not maintain its "capability to interdict that traffic."[35]

Because Guatemala did not have codified laws to deal with extradition, money laundering, and chemical controls, Guatemalan counternarcotics efforts lacked the teeth necessary to disrupt the soft underbelly of narcotrafficking. Although the extent of money laundering in Guatemala remains unknown, the potential for its occurrence remained high because of weak controls over financial transactions and the lack of laws designed to combat it. Traffickers faced few obstacles when moving currency between Guatemalan financial institutions, US banks, and safe-haven offshore banks. In 1996, the discovery of a customs corruption ring that involved Guatemalan civilian and military officials gave impetus to money laundering reform. Although Guatemala's counternarcotics police were not involved in this ring, the case reached deep into the military and the PNC. Both the vice minister of government, Mario René Cifuentes, and the third in command of the treasury police were charged with criminal conspiracy, tax evasion, and extortion. What made this incident significant was the decision by the Arzú government (1996–2000) to dismiss the individuals involved in the scandal. In the past, the government covered up corruption by reassigning—not firing—those involved.[36]

146   Narcostates

Laws to regulate the movement of precursor chemicals through Guatemala did not exist. Traffickers imported ephedrine, the product used to make crystal methamphetamine, into Guatemala from Europe and then transited it into Mexico. Often, the ephedrine was delivered to the Colón Free Trade Zone in Panama, then transported through Guatemala and into the hands of the Mexican cartels. Between 1993 and 1996, the importation of ephedrine into Guatemala went from grams to tons, especially in 1994 when authorities recorded a 300 to 500 percent increase.[37] In 1999, Guatemala passed legislation to monitor the movement of precursor chemicals and promised to provide more funding for narcotics control.[38] That same year, the United States and Guatemala signed letters of agreement on counternarcotics cooperation, and with US help, the DOAN established a new command and control headquarters.[39] Out of that agreement came Operation Mayan Jaguar, a combined effort between the DOAN and the Guatemalan military, aided by the DEA and US Customs, in which 3,000 kilos of cocaine were seized.[40]

In February 2002, President Alfonso Portillo Cabrera (2000–2004) ordered the immediate dismissal of several military officers from positions in the Ministry of Interior and abolished the DOAN. Portillo's decision occurred after sixteen DOAN agents raided the village of Chocón and held its residents hostage for three days. They killed two villagers and tortured another villager, who went missing and was later registered as disappeared. The officers claimed that they were in Chocón because it was a drop-off point for narcotics. Others claimed that the agents went there to steal two tons of cocaine allegedly stashed in the town.[41] US and Guatemalan authorities estimated that in the last year of its existence, DOAN officials stole more than twice the amount of cocaine they legally seized. To weed out corruption within the DOAN, the Guatemalan government fired 80 percent of its officers. By the end of 2002, the DOAN had been replaced by the US-aided Servicio de Análisis y Información Antinarcóticos (SAIA).[42]

El Salvador:
Remaking the Police

El Salvador's counternarcotics program suffered from political divisions between the government and the FMLN. While the two sides worked out a new security framework, the Salvadoran government relied on a demobilized and demoralized National Guard to deter crime.[43] As part of the 1992 Chapultepec Peace Accord, the military demobilized and was halved in size. The government abolished El Salvador's public security force (Policía Nacional, PN) and the Treasury Police (Policía Hacienda, PH) and transformed them into a new professionalized force, the National Civilian Police (Policía Nacional Civil, PNC), which was outside of the Ministry of Defense's control.[44]

During the 1990–1992 ceasefire and transition to democracy, the composition of PNC forces became a contentious issue.[45] At the start of the ceasefire, the PNC grew from 6,000 to 12,000 men. The FMLN considered this expansion a violation of the ceasefire accords and expressed concern about the politicization of the PNC by alleging that the Armed Forces of El Salvador (ESAF) was transferring demobilized military personnel, especially those from a search and destroy battalion—the Batallones de Infantería de Reacción Inmediata (BIRI)—into the new national police force.[46] Guided by the UN, the Salvadoran government forced several members of the military out of the new PNC.[47] Another problem that emerged during the reorganization process was the failure of many FMLN members to meet the education requirements needed to join the PNC.[48] To solve this impasse, the FMLN and the government agreed that the PNC would consist primarily of individuals who had not participated in the conflict, while allowing a minority of ex-FMLN and ex-National Police members (20 percent for each group) to enter the PNC.[49]

During the peace process, the Executive Antinarcotics Unit or Unidad Ejecutiva Antinarcóticos (UEA) became El Salvador's elite counternarcotics unit.[50] Trained by US Customs, UEA agents were installed at Comalapa International Airport and at the Port of Acajutla. The Salvadoran attorney general's office provided legal support by providing six prosecutors to support the UEA and ensure they followed legal norms.[51] Even though the unit had not mastered the basics of law enforcement, US authorities considered the UEA to be a solid antinarcotics force.[52] At the time of the 1992 Chapultepec Peace Accord, the UEA had grown from 200 to 350 agents, staffed primarily by members of the National Guard and the Treasury Police.[53]

The State Department initially considered the UEA a model for the region. It conducted intelligence operations and developed links with its counterparts in Guatemala, Honduras, Nicaragua, and Mexico. The UEA made 70 percent of all arrests in 1992 and claimed that the careful selection of officers made their success possible.[54] In 1992, it netted 280 drug suspects. During one incident in 1993, it intercepted six tons of cocaine worth $205 million and arrested one Colombian and four Mexicans affiliated with El Chapo's Sinaloa cartel who were allegedly involved in the May 1993 assassination of Cardinal Posadas Ocampo.[55]

In 1993, the government transferred the UEA into the PNC. Because of the UEA's military composure, the FMLN raised questions regarding the UEA's autonomy. The FMLN favored keeping it separate from the PNC, arguing that the UEA interfered with police investigations, including the 1993 murders of FMLN leaders Óscar Grimaldi and Francisco Velis. In their view, the PNC should be the "sole armed police force" with "national jurisdiction."[56] The FMLN also raised objections about former National Guard members holding executive positions within the UEA, especially

148   *Narcostates*

Óscar Peña Durán as the deputy director of the PNC. Peña Durán was a former major in the National Guard who had graduated from the School of the Americas—a US training school known for graduating officers who committed human rights abuses. From the FMLN's perspective, the military's dominant presence within the PNC and control over the UEA would undermine them as legitimate police forces.[57]

Peña Durán attempted to do an end run around the FMLN by keeping the UEA stacked with National Guard members. According to the State Department, the UEA became "irredeemably identified with the old security forces. . . . Critics of those units believed that replacing their active service leadership with civilians and retaining the rank and file could 'rehabilitate' those units."[58] Peña Durán further inflamed tensions by charging that the FMLN grew marijuana and opium along the Honduran border. In 1994, President Cristiani ordered Peña Durán not to violate the ceasefire and in May signed Agreement No. 221, which forced Peña Durán and twenty-five other officers within the security forces to resign from their positions.[59]

That same year, the Salvadoran National Assembly passed legislation converting the UEA into a new antinarcotics division within the PNC called the División Anti-Narcóticos (DAN). Like the UEA, the DAN received broad investigative powers but was required to report to the minister of the interior.[60] After the establishment of the Joint Information Coordinating Center (JICC) by the US government in 1992, the DAN received drug trafficking information that supported their investigations.[61] Despite its auspicious inauguration, the DAN struggled through the early stages of its integration into the PNC and did not become fully operational until mid-1995.[62] When ARENA candidate Armando Calderón Sol (1994–1999) was elected president, he spoke in favor of the DAN. Still, the DAN struggled. Disputes between the government, the FMLN, and the UN mission over how best to integrate the DAN within the PNC eroded the DAN's capabilities.

The clearance of officers with suspected ties to traffickers held up the integration of the DAN into the PNC. For example, in 1994, PNC director Rodrigo Ávila expressed his concerns to US ambassador Alan H. Flanigan about drug-related corruption in the DAN, stating that the DAN's chief had "provided credentials for corrupt but well-connected individuals." Ávila went on to say that some DAN officers belonged to death squads and that he knew of one individual connected to the murder of Archbishop Óscar Romero. When Ávila denied credentials to what he perceived to be corrupt members of ARENA, elements within the party accused Ávila of being a communist.[63] Ultimately, in order to root out corruption, the Salvadoran government and the FMLN reached an agreement that required all experienced officers to take the PNC's basic training course. The effort to professionalize the DAN helped allay FMLN concerns about the integration of their former military adversaries into the DAN and PNC. Nevertheless, most officers

The War on Drugs Spills into Central America **149**

who took the course were weeded out of the DAN. Instead, new investigators with little experience became substitutes for experienced officers.[64]

By 1997, the DAN's performance improved, but it still faced many hurdles. That year, increased drug flows through El Salvador and the economic destruction caused by Hurricane Mitch led US President Clinton to designate El Salvador as a "country of concern." An incremental increase in cocaine seizures demonstrated El Salvador's growing importance as a transit country. Seizures made by the DAN went from 67.3 kilos in 1995 up to 100.4 kilos in 1996 and to 230 kilos in 1997. Because traffickers also used El Salvador to move precursor chemicals into Mexico and Colombia, the government ordered the DAN to develop a precursor chemical control program. Despite these advances, the DAN did not possess the resources to pursue major maritime and air-interdiction operations.[65] It used what did exist of its air wing to eradicate local cannabis fields, destroying 3,776 plants in 1997, increasing to 7,338 plants in 1998. A setback for the DAN occurred in 1998 when the legislature passed a new criminal code that prohibited undercover police operations, sowing confusion over operational procedures among law enforcement officers, prosecutors, and judges.[66]

In the late 1990s, El Salvador implemented several improvements to its counternarcotics program. In 1997, the Salvadoran government passed money laundering legislation to target drug deposits in the banking system.[67] The most important improvement came in 1999 when a radar control system was installed at the Comalapa airport. The radar gave El Salvador the ability to detect suspect aircraft transiting Salvadoran airspace and could track up to 2,000 targets simultaneously with a range of eighty nautical miles into the Pacific Ocean. The radar revealed previously unknown clandestine flights crossing over and landing in El Salvador during the night.[68] That same year, El Salvador developed the shiprider agreement, which allowed US or Salvadoran law enforcement officers to participate in counternarcotics operations on board counterpart ships. The agreement also granted permission for US ships to pursue suspect watercraft into Salvadoran waters if evidence warranted an investigation.[69] With US assistance, the technical expertise of the DAN improved. Despite these improvements, El Salvador faced a growing danger—gang activity—whose threat to state security would become as great as the one posed by the guerrillas during its civil war.

Honduras:
Get-Tough Measures

Because Hondurans did not produce or consume significant amounts of drugs, counternarcotics was not a priority for the Honduran government in the early 1990s. Other national security concerns were prioritized and reflected the government's limited political will to detect and interdict

150 *Narcostates*

narcotics traffic. However, the country's location on the isthmus turned it into a major transit hub, and the State Department expressed concern that the interdiction program in Mexico would force traffickers into Honduras.[70] Although its counternarcotics capabilities were basic, the State Department believed that Honduras had an opportunity "to get ahead in the game," as efforts in Mexico and Guatemala "continued to reap success."[71] Seeing the growing threat posed by narcotrafficking, President Rafael Callejas Romero (1990–1994) declared that the 1990s would be "dedicated to the fight against narcotics," whereby Honduras would take the "lead in the region's counternarcotics efforts."[72]

The national police force, the Fuerza de Seguridad Pública (FUSEP), became the most important branch of the military to deal with counternarcotics issues. Within the FUSEP, the Preventative Police conducted counternarcotics investigations. In the view of the US State Department, the FUSEP was "poorly trained, poorly equipped, and poorly motivated." Its efforts were hampered by a "judicial system widely criticized for laxness and corruption."[73] Because of this fact, the State Department considered the Honduran government's statistics for arrests and seizures to be unreliable and incomplete.[74] In 1990, as Honduras moved toward civilian control, the government established a ministry-level National Drug Council Against Narcotics Trafficking headed by the Honduran president. The government designed the council to coordinate civilian and military resources to address the issue of narcotrafficking. In April of that same year, the Honduran Armed Forces (HOAF), which included the FUSEP, collaborated with the US Southern Command (SOUTHCOM) to develop a plan that laid out the strategic objectives necessary to establish a functional military counternarcotics organization.[75]

To prevent traffickers from exploiting the country's porous border, the United States promoted an air interdiction program. To deter air trafficking, in 1991 the United States launched the Caribbean Basin Radar Network, a $143 million initiative that installed radar stations in Honduras.[76] As part of the air interdiction program, the Honduran government showed a willingness to shoot down drug smuggling aircraft. In May 1992, a Honduran F-5S aircraft intercepted a Colombian-registered plane. After warning shots were fired, the plane, which attempted to take evasive measures, was shot down off of Swan Island. The wreckage was later recovered with an unspecified amount of cocaine.[77] Although the shoot-down policy was not official government policy, the threat of F-5S aircraft and the installation of three radar stations served as a warning to traffickers.[78] The State Department maintained that the use of the F-5S squadron provided an "essential and a strong deterrent for narcotraffickers considering violating Honduran airspace."[79]

The United States provided vital assistance to the FUSEP. The JICC acted as a command and control center that provided tactical information on drug trafficking for the Honduran FUSEP. The JICC used international databases and the DEA's El Paso Intelligence Center (EPIC) to help investigate narcotics-related crimes.[80] In 1995, marijuana eradication programs netted 1.43 metric tons, up from 0.36 tons in 1994.[81] In addition, the Honduran government proposed utilizing joint US-Honduran deep-water and navy port facilities with air and sea radar capabilities after it constructed a radar site tied into the US-sponsored Caribbean Basin Radar Network.[82] This proposal led to the creation of a task force to patrol Honduras's Bay Islands and a joint oceanic drug interdiction and training program called Operation Handshake, which established a nucleus of navy personnel capable of conducting boarding operations.

Although the Honduran government willingly initiated proactive measures such as the air interdiction program and the Bay Islands Task Force, as of 1995, it still did not have a counternarcotics master plan. Because the military directed the Honduran National Police until 1994, the line between civilian law enforcement activities and military operations negatively impacted drug enforcement efforts. In 1996, the FUSEP was transferred to civilian control, and the first group of Honduran agents began working independently from the military as part of a new antinarcotics directorate called the Dirección Nacional Antinarcóticos (DNA). However, the strain on the judicial system from corrupt judges and the lack of training and equipment for the DNA led to persistent weaknesses in the Honduran counternarcotics program.[83] Calling for a "new agenda," President-Elect Carlos Flores Facussé (1998–2002) initiated a serious effort to deal with the mounting problem. In 1998, the government began a reorganization of the National Police, which it did not complete until 2001. Within the new National Police, the Dirección Nacional de la Policía Preventiva (DNPP) took over counternarcotics matters.[84] During the reorganization, the Honduran Congress supported legislation that addressed the issue of narcotics control through public education and money laundering. The legislature also ratified regulations pertaining to precursor chemicals in 1998.[85] Unfortunately, 1998's Hurricane Mitch placed the government and the economy under severe strain.[86] Like all of its Central American counterparts, Honduras fell several steps behind the narcotrafficking industry.

Nicaragua:
The Question of Police Politicization

Nicaragua was one of the first Central American nations to develop a counternarcotics initiative.[87] The 1990 Sandinista defeat and the electoral victory of President Violeta Chamorro (1990–1997) improved relations between the US and Nicaraguan governments, allowing for the development of law

152   Narcostates

enforcement and intelligence sharing capabilities to counter narcotrafficking.[88] The need to do something became apparent following the 1990 seizure of 323 kilos of cocaine in the capital city of Managua. According to the Ministry of the Interior, the seizure revealed that narcotrafficking was now an "urgent matter."[89] However, with stubborn economic problems facing the government, the United States considered it unlikely that Nicaragua would make any progress in this direction without assistance from outside sources.[90] The State Department believed that US-led initiatives would bring Nicaragua "closer to the level of other countries in the region" and make it a "more effective force in the counternarcotics effort."[91] US initiatives included bolstering border police and customs enforcement, boosting intelligence sharing, and upgrading the police's organizational structure. Nevertheless, like its neighbors, Nicaragua's counternarcotics programs remained ineffective because the country lacked sufficient resources to sustain its own programs and US aid only went so far.

Chamorro initiated the reorganization of the Policía Nacional.[92] In the aftermath of the civil war, the politicization of the police remained a general concern. Several reorganization plans were offered, including a separate Contra police force to work alongside the Sandinista police in rural areas.[93] The finalized plan, called Decree 64-90: The Organic Law of the Ministry of Government, placed the police under the control of the Dirección General de la Policía Nacional (DGPN), which consisted of uniformed Sandinista police. To prevent the DGPN's politicization and to retain civilian control, the DGPN reported to the Ministry of Governance, which had replaced the Sandinista Ministry of Interior in 1990. The reorganization plan also created an independent antinarcotics unit called the Dirección Antinarcóticos (DAN), within the Ministry of Government but outside of the DGPN's command.[94]

Despite the reorganization, narcocorruption within the police—the average police officer only earned $100 a month—and the intimidation of court authorities remained a perennial concern. In 1991, the DAN discovered a trafficking ring within the local police force patrolling Nicaragua's Pacific coast. The ring transported Colombian cocaine into Nicaragua from Costa Rica by air or land. From Nicaragua, they moved their shipments into Honduras where the cargo was loaded onto ships destined for the United States.[95] Judicial corruption also became more blatant. In 1995, a lower-level court released twelve suspected traffickers despite ample evidence against them. In another case, in April 1996, the court released six suspects caught with 1,401 kilos of cocaine because there was a lack of evidence. In both cases, police suspected that drug money influenced the outcome of the trials. By 1997, the Nicaraguan Supreme Court had placed over 100 judges and magistrates under investigation for corruption.[96]

Another impediment to Chamorro's reforms was the US decision to limit its cooperation with Nicaragua as long as the Ministry of Government staff remained populated by Sandinista personnel, most notably René Vivas Lugo, the Sandinista police commander.[97] The United States requested that Nicaragua depoliticize its Policía Nacional while leaving the structure of the police force intact. The State Department expressed concern that Nicaragua's reforms would fail because of an "intense Sandinista campaign against it."[98] In order to receive $100 million in US aid, the Chamorro government dismissed Vivas Lugo and twelve other officers from the Sandinista-run police in 1992.[99]

In 1993, the United States offered $100,000 to assist Nicaragua with the creation of three counternarcotics units that covered airport activity as well as national and international trafficking. In the arrangement, the Nicaraguan government would establish the counternarcotics units and the United States would provide the training, equipment, and technical assistance for them. Because the new units were under the control of the Nicaraguan military, which remained in the hands of Sandinista General Humberto Ortega, the US government withheld assistance until he was removed. Due to previous allegations that the Sandinistas had trafficked in cocaine, the United States made the case that Nicaragua's counternarcotics operations would lack independence as long as Ortega remained in command of the army.[100]

In 1995, Nicaragua's police and military command structures changed. In February of that year, in accordance with a new military code enacted in 1994, General Cuadra Lacayo replaced Humberto Ortega as the commander of the Sandinista Popular Army. Cuadra Lacayo espoused a policy of greater professionalism in the renamed Army of Nicaragua. In August 1996, the National Assembly ratified Law 228, the National Police Law, which reorganized the police forces.[101] This law codified both civilian control of the police and methods to professionalize them.[102] The State Department positively welcomed these events, stating that the police made great strides toward the "professionalization of their institution as an effective and clearly apolitical entity." Relations improved, and the DEA established a country office at Nicaragua's request in 1997. Moreover, in 1998, the US government provided significant counternarcotics assistance to the National Police, including $75,000 for patrol craft to conduct missions along the Caribbean coast.[103]

Costa Rica:
A Standing Security Force?

As the regional conflict wound down, Costa Rica's northern and southern borders stabilized. Combating the flow of illegal drugs became its newest, if not biggest, challenge. The view of the State Department was that Costa Rica lacked the law enforcement expertise and infrastructure necessary to counter well-financed and sophisticated narcotraffickers. Costa Rica could

154   Narcostates

only provide limited resources for its security and police forces.[104] Many prominent Costa Ricans, such as Óscar Arias, considered it unconstitutional to expand the country's security forces. In their view, narcotics were a US problem foisted on Costa Rica. Given President Óscar Arias's opposition to militarism, US aid programs stressed economic and social development. Security development received little support until the presidencies of Rafael Calderón Fournier (1990–1994) and José Figueres Olsen (1994–1998) reversed this view.

Because of constitutional limitations on the size and role of its security forces, Costa Rica dedicated minimal resources to counternarcotics. Since 1948, the Guardia Civil had served as Costa Rica's primary defense force to maintain order.[105] The Guardia operated within the Ministry of Public Security, which also managed the military police, metropolitan police, a presidential guard, an air section, and a maritime section.[106] Chronic infighting between the Ministry of Public Security, the Ministry of Government, and the judicial police known as the Organismo de Investigación Judicial (OIJ) hindered the implementation of a counternarcotics program.[107] To overcome the bureaucratic morass, Costa Rican ministers of justice drafted Law 7233 in 1991, which created a counternarcotics strategy to coordinate antidrug measures across government institutions such as the Costa Rican Consejo Nacional de Drogas (CONADRO) and the Central American CICAD.[108]

Although it was well aware of the mounting narcotrafficking problem, Costa Rica lacked the resources to do anything about it. Despite the reforms initiated by President Calderón Fournier, the Ministry of Public Security's air and maritime sections could only conduct limited counternarcotics patrols. Costa Rica's large public sector deficit, heavy debt load, and low international reserves placed limitations on its ability to support security programs. According to the US embassy, Costa Rica's "fiscal straits" meant that Calderón Fournier's administration expected to receive the "bulk of its security assistance in the form of economic support" from the United States.[109] The 1994 collapse of the nationally owned Banco Anglo Costarricense added to the problem. Because the bank printed money for the government, its shuttering created an inflationary banking crisis that further eroded Costa Rica's ability to support its counternarcotics programs.[110]

Costa Rica relied heavily on the United States to maintain, train, and equip its counternarcotics forces, but US aid was limited.[111] In the post–civil war era, the US government expected Costa Rica to shoulder a greater share of the burden for its own internal security.[112] In 1993, the State Department's Bureau of International Narcotics Matters (INM) provided an estimated $272,000 in aid. A year later, US aid declined slightly to an estimated $250,000 to be distributed among several enforcement agencies.[113] In 1995, owing to US fiscal constraints and Washington's diminishing interest

The War on Drugs Spills into Central America   155

in Central America, funding declined to $133,000.[114] When Figueres Olsen became president, he reaffirmed Costa Rica's commitment to US counternarcotics objectives, and both nations pledged to renew their efforts. By the end of his presidency, Costa Rica had modified its existing programs through the creation of the Centro Nacional de Prevención Contra Drogas (CENDARO), which emphasized both supply and demand reduction.[115] Figueres Olsen also increased the number of Costa Rican officers participating in counternarcotics operations. In 1999, the INM trained 402 officers, an all-time high. INM funding also surpassed what it had been in 1993; it reached $281,000 in 1999 and then climbed to $833,000 the next year.[116] Nevertheless, by 2000, as was the case in most Central American countries, the renewed commitment by the United States and Costa Rica was too little, too late.

Panama:
The Remilitarization of the Police

After Noriega's ouster in late 1989, the government of Guillermo Endara Galimany (1989–1994) reorganized the Panamanian Defense Forces (PDF) into the Panamanian Public Forces (PPF) in 1990. Endara sought to convert the PPF into a police force while taking steps to reduce the drug flow into Panama. However, the carryover of Noriega loyalists into the PPF led to allegations of corruption, which impeded the Endara government's ability to develop an effective police force. According to the State Department, "The Panamanian government's performance on narcotics" was a "mix of sound accomplishment and exasperating delays."[117]

Three years into Endara's presidency, the US and Panamanian governments attempted to achieve the total demilitarization of the public security forces by eliminating all militarized aspects of the previous twenty years. This ambitious goal encountered the same problem that existed prior to 1989: the military's dominance over Panama's political system. Historically, the Panamanian military protected the interests of Panama's power elite, which included many high-ranking officers. This allegiance became ingrained in the consciousness of all echelons within the PDF.[118] Because the military remained predominant in domestic affairs, the government delayed the implementation of its counternarcotics program to ensure it would not strengthen the military. Opposition to remilitarization went so far as to cause the Panamanian government to refuse to join any regional counternarcotics operation that required military participation because it might become a vehicle by which the Panamanian military could recrudesce.[119] According to the State Department, "Any actions by the embassy now or in the near future with other than a sharp focus on domestic civil police functions would impede or jeopardize the evolution" of the National Police.

156 *Narcostates*

The US goal was to help Panama make an orderly transition from a state of emergency to a normal civil society with a view toward developing a cooperative bilateral relationship and a law enforcement system based on democratic values.[120] With this purpose in mind, the United States and Panama signed the Mutual Legal Assistance Treaty (MLAT) in 1991 to reduce the demand and use of narcotics as well as the illicit production and traffic in narcotics.[121] The destruction of illegal drug processing sites and laboratories, the regulation of precursor chemicals, and the prosecution of money laundering crimes became its main components.[122]

By 1993, Panama had reorganized the PPF into independent units under the direction of the ministers of government and justice. Within the reorganized PPF were the Policía Nacional de Panamá (PNP), the Servicio Maritimo Nacional (SMN), the Servicio Aero Nacional (SAN), the Policía Técnica Judicial (PTJ), all of which accepted counternarcotics duties. The US INM, in association with the DEA, Coast Guard, FBI, and Customs, assisted with the training and equipping of Panama's counternarcotics forces.[123] A year earlier, the United States made $6 million available for technical assistance and training to help professionalize the civilian police force, of which $3 million went to the procurement of vehicles, communication gear, bullet-proof vests, handcuffs, computers, and training. None of the equipment included could be lethal.[124] In 1994, the United States trained 925 police officers. Despite previous Panamanian misgivings about the military's involvement in counternarcotics activities, the State Department concluded that Panama now provided the "biggest bang for the US counternarcotics buck."[125]

Panama's transition from Noriega's dictatorship left it wary of renewed militarism, causing it to drag its feet despite the fact that it was a center of narcotics trafficking and money laundering. The United States considered Endara as "morally committed to drug control efforts," but his "government did not have the political will to implement counternarcotics policies in politically sensitive areas such as money laundering."[126] Exasperated, the United States threatened to decertify Panama's antidrug program in April 1994. Ultimately, though, the United States certified Panama on the basis of national security, which allowed the United States to continue managing the canal while it withdrew its forces from Panama.[127] US pressure persisted into the presidency of Pérez Balladares (1994–1999), who promised to improve Panama's judicial system and prosecutorial efforts against traffickers. Even prior to his election, US pressure convinced Panama to ratify the 1988 UN Convention Against Illicit Traffic in Narcotics Drugs and Psychotropic Substances in January 1994.[128] However, as the United States withdrew from the Canal Zone, US counternarcotics assistance waned. Panama would become a haven for traffickers once again. The Panamanian government was aware of the growing problem. At a regional meeting in Colombia, Panama's foreign minister stated that narcotics trafficking and terrorism were "regional

The War on Drugs Spills into Central America   157

problems that must be confronted." The minister added that Panama needed to professionalize its national police forces, improve capabilities along the Colombian border, and strengthen its money laundering investigations.[129] For Panama, these would be lofty goals.

The New Millennium: The Permanency of Narcotrafficking

Every Central American nation faced similar problems when they implemented their nascent counternarcotics programs. The people were exhausted from civil war. They did not want narcotrafficking to be used as an excuse for giving the military extra powers. Central America's hesitancy to embrace aggressive counternarcotics measures stemmed from decades of misrule by military dictators. The downside was that it left the region vulnerable to the dangers presented by the drug trade. Drained by civil war, most Central American governments possessed neither the resources nor the institutional capability to address drug trafficking.[130] Progress was hampered by political infighting over the composition of the police, while corruption undermined each nation's counternarcotics initiatives.

The lack of US resources available for Central American counternarcotics programs also impeded advancements as the US role in the region declined during the 1990s. The winding down of conflicts, the departure from the Panama Canal Zone, and the pivot of US foreign policy to the Middle East led to changing priorities. Moreover, Central America was not the focal point in the war on drugs—Mexico and the Andean region were. Because the United States did not consider the region to be a major transitory route in the early 1990s, Central America did not receive precedence when it came to counternarcotics assistance. As a result, Central American governments did not have the resources "to purchase sophisticated equipment and to develop well-trained personnel to combat well-financed, creative, and highly adaptable traffickers."[131] Within less than a decade, Central America became a hub for drugs moving north. The weak development of Central America's counternarcotics programs during the 1990s left Central America unprepared to deal with the powerful drug trafficking networks. Within the vacuum, the DTOs secured for themselves a permanent foothold in Central America.

Mexico's War on Drugs Spills over into Central America, 2000–2010

At the start of the new millennium, the escalating war on drugs in Mexico only added to Central America's plight. High unemployment and sluggish economic growth, accompanied by a violent US street gang culture, exacerbated

158 Narcostates

Central America's narcotics problem. The presence of Mexican cartels and Central American gangs greatly diminished regional security. As the gangs grew in strength, they started to provide auxiliary support for the Mexican cartels. Gangs and narcotraffickers alike committed brazen acts of violence, robbery, bribery, and extortion. In response, Central American governments, particularly the Northern Triangle countries of Guatemala, El Salvador, and Honduras, implemented strict antigang laws called the *mano dura* (heavy hand). The mano dura intensified confrontations between the police and gangs, creating an even more violent, seemingly lawless situation in many cities, towns, and villages. The security situation was much worse in the Northern Triangle than it was in Nicaragua, Costa Rica, and Panama, although the DTOs and their gang affiliates made their presence felt everywhere. Threats of *plata o plomo* (money or bullets) and rampant corruption advanced the narcotrafficking agenda. Mexican DTOs, working in conjunction with Colombian producers and Central American middlemen and gangs, created a near-invincible force.

As narcotrafficking organizations lined up against governmental authority, the Central American nations initiated regional efforts to limit their growth. In 2000, Costa Rica held the first regional counternarcotics and anticorruption summit for Central America. The conference focused on developing a demand-reduction program along with a coordinated legal mechanism to terminate the cross-border impunity enjoyed by drug traffickers. Out of the summit came the Declaration of San José, proclaiming that drug trafficking was a crime against humanity. It outlined steps to eliminate narcotrafficking and public corruption, recognizing the threat to Central America as a drug transit zone, and the threat of drug consumption itself.[132] In November 2000, the United Nations passed the Convention Against Transnational Organized Crime, which proposed a legal framework for international cooperation against organized crime. The convention recognized the growing ties between traffickers and terrorist organizations and established international legal norms that defined money laundering. The UN also presented a means for international cooperation over extradition and property seizures.[133] Starting with Nicaragua in 2002, the remaining Central American states ratified the resolution between 2003 and 2004. Gang activity and narcotrafficking became indistinguishable. As the decade drew to a close, leaders in the United States and Central America realized that greater regional efforts were required to rein in the cartels and gangs.

The Origins of the Gang Problem

Central America's gang problem began at the end of the civil war era when displaced and uneducated youth turned to crime as a personal solution to the challenges they faced. Throughout Central America, soldiers and guerrillas were demobilizing, turning in their weapons, and looking for work to rebuild their lives.[134] With few prospects, Central America's unemployed youth were attracted to the opportunities offered by gang membership. Central American gangs (*pandillas*) such as Mara Salvatrucha (MS-13) and Calle 18 (18th Street) initially worked for organized crime as "guns for hire." Soon thereafter, they engaged in other criminal activities, including human trafficking, kidnapping, robbery, extortion, and assassination. By the mid-2000s, Central American gangs were a key part of Mexican DTO operations.

The gang problem was an unintended consequence of the 1994 Clinton administration decision to deport gang members who were illegal immigrants and convicted felons. In 1996, Congress passed the Illegal Immigration Reform and Immigrant Responsibility Act. The law expanded the definition of an aggravated felony. Gang members with legal permanent residence who had been convicted of an aggravated felony were now considered deportable. Deportations could not be suspended on the basis of hardship.[135] The US government considered the gang deportees dangerous and did not want to house them in US prisons. According to the State Department, the deportees were either members of the MS-13 or the Calle 18 with criminal records for murder, car theft, or drugs.[136] Between 1993 and 1997, the Immigration and Naturalization Service (INS) deported some 4,000 gang members to El Salvador.[137] Between 2000 and 2004, deportations accelerated, with an estimated 20,000 people deported.[138] More than 90 percent of those deportees were returned to Guatemala, Honduras, and El Salvador. By 1999, the number of street gangs had swelled into the thousands. In 2006, there were an estimated 8,000–10,000 gang members in Guatemala and another 10,000–15,000 in Honduras.[139] In Honduras, one in every twenty males fifteen to twenty-four years old belonged to a gang.[140]

Acts of violence, assaults, and robberies against innocent civilians became daily occurrences in the Northern Triangle. For example, drunken gang members under the influence of narcotics attacked a suburban San Salvador city bus, broke its windows, stoned the driver, and robbed the passengers.[141] In August 1997, the Jesuit-run Central American University in San Salvador released findings from a survey of the city's residents. The survey indicated that one-fifth were victims of violent crime and a further one-fifth dealt with extortion threats as a result of gang activity.[142] In 2016, a reported 60 percent of Salvadoran schools had been threatened.[143] Gang rivalries heightened the level of violence spilling onto El Salvador's streets. For instance, Calle 18 members launched an intimidation campaign against MS-13 and the government, which they called "Crazy Week." Calle 18 members in the San Salvador neighborhood of Mejicanos set fire to a bus full of passengers and machine-gunned another bus, leaving fourteen people dead and

160   *Narcostates*

dozens more injured.[144] American tourists and residents in El Salvador received weekly written or telephonic extortion threats, which the Salvadoran police could not address because they lacked the training.[145] Tourists were not the only targets; the MS-13 also issued threats against US embassies in El Salvador and Honduras.[146]

High unemployment and limited government resources to assist former civil war combatants led to a further expansion of gang membership.[147] For instance, ex-combatants, many of them campesinos, expected that they would receive land or loans when they laid down their arms. They came from both sides of the conflict and included demobilized regular soldiers, FMLN guerrillas, and members from irregular units of the FMLN and the ESAF. The inability to provide them with economic assistance led to their alienation. In one instance, a mob of machete-wielding former paramilitary units occupied the National Assembly for an entire day to demand land payments.[148] As their means of financial support disappeared, they pursued crime in order to survive.[149] Because of their young age and the failure of the Salvadoran government to address their desperate economic situation, many of the demobilized FMLN guerrillas joined gangs.[150] According to a 1994 State Department cable, a portion of the former combatants who knew "little of life but violence, will opt for a peacetime career in crime." The cable added that there were a number of combatants dissatisfied with the peace process who were unlikely to hand over their weapons. The concern was that former members of the FMLN or URNG would sell their weapons to common criminals. The cable went on to say that unemployed soldiers also provided new recruits to the gangs.[151]

Another factor that contributed to the rise of the gangs in Central America was the breakdown of the family due to the lack of economic opportunities. Many families did not possess a solid economic or social footing. Parents left their children with relatives or a single parent when they migrated to the United States to find work. With no role models, the children turned to gangs for acceptance and a sense of family and community.[152] Symbolic rituals related to Santa Muerte or Satanism (*narcocultura*) were used to supplant the family and strengthen gang cohesion.[153]

Economic liberalization policies that culminated with the 2005 Central American Free Trade Agreement (CAFTA) did not generate enough growth to alleviate social and economic troubles. Industrialization and tariff reductions undermined traditional economies and displaced rural populations that moved into cities, where competition for low-skilled jobs was fierce.[154] Between 1995 and 2005, fifteen- to twenty-four-year-olds represented 21 percent of Central America's total population. Guatemala's youth represented 45 percent of its unemployed. In El Salvador, Nicaragua, and Panama, elevated levels of youth unemployment declined but never fell below 10 percent. In Costa Rica, youth unemployment expanded from 11 to

The War on Drugs Spills into Central America   **161**

15 percent between 1995 and 2005, while in Honduras it increased from 6 percent in 1995 to 10 percent in 2004 and settled at 7 percent in 2005.[155] Urbanization combined with the lack of opportunity increased the appeal of gangs because they provided Central America's disenfranchised youth with a source of employment.[156]

Unlike MS-13 and Calle 18 in the United States, the gangs in El Salvador, Honduras, and Guatemala were well-disciplined and maintained a vertical command structure. According to the US National Drug Intelligence Center, "contrary to popular belief, the gangs were highly structured and modeled" like a "guerrilla organization."[157] Many leaders were former special forces members from both sides of the civil wars who instilled enhanced military discipline. Former soldiers and guerrillas from Honduras, Nicaragua, Guatemala, and El Salvador instructed MS-13 and Calle 18 gang members how to fire weapons, engage in hand-to-hand combat, fabricate explosives, and lead men.[158] Because of their military regimen, the gangs were able to take over urban neighborhoods, which led to the curtailment of law enforcement in those communities.[159] An extra layer of security was added to their organizational structure due to the fact that their leadership ran their operations from prison. Easy access to cell phones and the development of safe houses near the prisons facilitated their operational capabilities.[160] In 2004, to prevent gang riots within the prisons, the Salvadoran government segregated rival gangs and transported them to remote jails. The consequence of this decision was increased gang power, because it turned the prisons into individual strongholds for the simultaneous coordination of *clika* (a semiautonomous cell) activities.[161]

Many MS-13 members reentered the United States after being deported. Their ability to cross borders at will created a "revolving door" phenomenon whereby gang members moved in a circular fashion from north to south and from south to north.[162] In the process of doing so, they employed prison gang networks to operate international contraband routes through the Northern Triangle in association with Mexican coyotes and Mexican DTOs. The gangs soon evolved into a transport network throughout Central America and Mexico, working with established gang-based drug distribution networks in the United States.[163] The Central American diasporas provided an ethnic network between Mexico and the United States that became an important vehicle for moving contraband into the United States.[164]

The Mano Dura

Gang-related crimes, including extortion, hired assassination, and human and narcotics trafficking, stunned Central America's governments. Sensational media coverage of gang violence politicized the issue, prompting

162   *Narcostates*

demands for drastic measures.[165] As a result, El Salvador, Guatemala, and Honduras implemented strict antigang laws—the *mano dura*, or heavy hand.

When the gang crisis emerged in the mid-1990s, the Salvadoran national police (PNC) and the Salvadoran public were taken aback. Security expert Hal Brands argued that the gangs were seeking to intimidate the state into submission to win a free hand to pursue their business dealings.[166] Gang members burned down schools, murdered police, and raped women and young girls with near impunity. The gangs also smuggled immigrants and trafficked in weapons and illegal drugs. Combined with high levels of delinquency, gang activity forced the PNC to carry out foot patrols in the most dangerous sectors of San Salvador, but it was unable to control all street crimes.

Contributing to the violence was the ready availability of non-decommissioned weapons remaining after the civil war.[167] Numerous caches were scattered throughout the country. An estimated 400,000 illegal weapons could be purchased on the streets of El Salvador, including AK-47s and M-16 assault rifles, semiautomatic hand guns, and hand grenades.[168] In 2009, the State Department reported that some members of El Salvador's political parties were acting as intermediaries in arms deals with Colombia's FARC and also in kidnapping and drug smuggling operations.[169] Salvadoran corruption evolved to the point where the political system itself was contributing to the inability of El Salvador's police to maintain order.

In response to the gang threat, the Salvadoran government led by President Francisco Flores Pérez (1999–2004) passed Decree 158 in 2003, known as the La Ley Anti-Mara (antigang law), also referred to as the mano dura. The mano dura granted increased area sweeps and joint police-military patrols. It also included a law that permitted the police to arrest gang members on the basis of their physical appearance, such as their haircuts, tattoos, and clothing.[170]

The gangs responded by toughening their entry requirements, adopting more conventional dress, and using heavier weaponry, which in turn only increased the Salvadoran crackdown. In 2004, El Salvador had Latin America's third highest homicide rate, trailing only Colombia and Honduras.[171] In July of that year, El Salvador's Congress unanimously approved President Tony Saca's (2004–2009) Super Mano Dura package of antigang reforms that also incorporated prevention and rehabilitation into the plan. Over 11,000 arrests were made under these laws.[172] In 2005, El Salvador's legislature tightened gun ownership laws and initiated joint military and police patrols in high-crime areas. Despite those efforts, El Salvador recorded 3,697 murders in 2005, 34 percent more than in 2004. In response, the United States and El Salvador created the Transnational Anti-Gang (TAG) Center in 2007 to bring about collaboration between the FBI and the Salvadoran PNC to track the MS-13 and Calle 18 gangs.[173]

The War on Drugs Spills into Central America 163

Honduras, too, saw higher levels of gang violence and brutality. Hondurans were haunted daily with menacing images in newspapers and on television of heavily tattooed gangsters being arrested and accused of massacring entire families or sending antigovernment messages with severed heads.[174] Under the 2001 Police and Social Order Law, police were allowed to detain gang members and vagrants without a warrant. At the time, 90 percent of the gang members who were arrested and imprisoned were not even charged with a crime.[175] In 2003, Honduran President Ricardo Maduro Joest (2002–2006) helped pass reform legislation, dubbed Ley Antimaras (antigang law), that elevated the penalty for criminal association up to twelve years and imposed fines of $500 to $10,000 (US dollars) for criminal association.[176] The provision included a twelve-year mandatory sentence for gang leaders.[177] The law also gave the police the right to detain young people suspected of being gang members and pull them off the street for suspicious behavior or for having distinctive tattoos.[178]

The Honduran Ministry of Defense labeled youth gangs as national security threats and called for coordinated efforts between the armed forces and government agencies to strengthen the national campaign against gangs. Following the passage of the Ley Antimaras, some 1,500 gang members were imprisoned in 2004.[179] However, as in El Salvador, many gang members were quickly released because of the lack of evidence and an unwillingness to prosecute them. Those who remained incarcerated coordinated gang activity from inside prison. By 2005, the Honduran government estimated that there were more than 30,000 active gang members in the country. To adapt to the mano dura, the gangs eliminated the use of tattoos and pursued clandestine activities, such as infiltrating the police and army.[180]

In Guatemala, gang violence and crime eventually led to aggressive law enforcement, but after its civil war had finally ended, the people were tired of militarization. However, by the late 1990s, Guatemala's 300-plus gangs made the country more violent than during its civil war. The diversion of public money to security initiatives put Guatemala's economy under considerable economic strain. By 1999, Guatemalan businesses lost an average of $5,500 annually to crime.[181] In 2002, Guatemala City police suspected that gangs committed 258 murders of women in what some observers labeled bloody, satanic rituals.[182] That same year, the Guatemalan Congress considered a law to incarcerate gang members for up to twelve years but determined that the law would violate the human rights of Guatemala's citizens. To pass the 2002 antigang law, the Guatemalan Congress demanded prevention and rehabilitation programs for Guatemala's at-risk youth. As a result, Guatemala's antigang law was more watered down compared to the mano dura in El Salvador or Honduras.[183]

Guatemala's policies were toughened in 2004 when its congress approved President Alfonso Portillo's (2000–2004) Plan Escoba (Clean

164   *Narcostates*

Sweep), which attempted to dismantle gang networks by increasing arrests and police presence in areas with high crime levels.[184] The law contained new provisions that treated minors as adults. It also deployed army reserves in Guatemala City's troubled neighborhoods.[185] As in El Salvador, Plan Escoba allowed the police to detain suspected gang members on the basis of their clothing, hair, and tattoos.[186] In 2003, some 2,582 gang members were locked up, but they were often released by the courts. According to police spokesperson Según Sánchez, the leniency of judges allowed gang members to go free, act with impunity, and show little respect for the police.[187]

In December 2005, Guatemalan President Óscar Berger (2004–2008) announced the deployment of joint military and police patrols to contain crime. The joint deployments were necessary after the 2005 dismissal of more than 4,000 police officers for irregular or criminal activities. To assist the police in urban areas, the military's presence along the Mexican border was reduced, giving the gangs unfettered access to Mexico.[188] Critics opposed to Plan Escoba maintained that prison reform should have been included to address the gang problem because jail had become an "appendage of crime and a sanctuary for criminals."[189] With members of the same gang sharing cells, prisons evolved into graduate schools and criminal training camps for gang members. Between 1996 and 2005, Guatemala's prison population increased by almost 25 percent. In Guatemala's forty-one prisons, there were 8,480 inmates, of which 1,357 were MS-13 or Calle 18. The incarceration of gang members overwhelmed the prison system, and gang warfare within the prisons resulted in thirty-five deaths and sixty-four wounded in five prisons between August and September 2005.[190]

The mano dura policies of El Salvador, Guatemala, and Honduras started an exodus of gang members to the Mexico-Guatemala border region, with the goal of gaining access to Mexico and the United States. Gangs along the Chiapas border posed a serious challenge for Mexico, which was taking actions of its own to address the gang phenomena spreading within its own jurisdiction. In 2001, an estimated 200 MS-13 gang affiliates, consisting of roughly 3,000 members, operated in Mexico. Three years later, that number increased to 5,000, concentrated primarily in Chiapas. In November 2004, a gun battle raged in the streets of the Mexican city of Tapachula between the MS-13 and Calle 18 during a commemoration of Mexico's revolution. The municipal police rounded up thirty-four suspects—all Mexican nationals.[191]

Nicaraguan gangs were less violent than their northern counterparts.[192] Nicaragua adopted a national youth crime prevention strategy that actively involved the police while focusing on family, school, and community interventions. MS-13 *clikas* in El Salvador moved into the southern Nicaraguan province of La Unión around the Gulf of Fonseca. Because of La Unión's

The War on Drugs Spills into Central America   165

geographic position joining Honduras and Nicaragua, MS-13 controlled much of the overland movement of drugs north through La Unión.[193]

In July 2004, Panamanian President Mireya Moscoso Rodríguez (1999–2004) declared war against pandillas in Panama with her own mano dura plan. In Panama, there were fifty gangs dedicated to narcotrafficking, robbery, and assassinations. They operated primarily in Panama City and Colón. The Panamanian government's plan was to round up the pandillas in crime zones where they hid out. Curfews were set for minors, while the police conducted searches for criminals and gang leaders. The minister of government and justice, Arnulfo Escalona, said that the mano dura did have an effect on reducing crime, such as the disappearances of women, kidnappings of businessmen, assaults on taxi drivers, and carjackings.[194] With a country still wary of militarization, in 2004 President Martín Torrijos Espino (2004–2009) launched Mano Amiga (Friendly Hand), a crime prevention program supported by domestic and international nongovernmental institutions (NGOs) that provided alternatives to gang membership for at-risk youth. Aimed at children aged fourteen to seventeen, the program provided access to theater and sports activities for 10,000 Panamanian youths.[195]

Extrajudicial Killings of Gang Members

As the regional mano dura strengthened, some gang leaders claimed that they were targeted by death squads. In the case of El Salvador, gang members claimed they were targeted by the Sombra Negra (Black Shadow), an organization of rogue police and military personnel who dealt out vigilante justice.[196] The Sombra Negra first made its presence known in 1994. According to the US Defense Intelligence Agency (DIA), they consisted of current and former PNC officers, ESAF members, and ex–national guard police forces.[197] They mimicked the death squads that participated in El Salvador's civil war. Blindfolded with their hands tied behind their backs, the Sombra Negra's victims were shot execution-style. In one instance, the Sombra Negra, wearing masks and armed with assault weapons, blocked off the streets in the El Tesoro neighborhood of San Miguel for over an hour. Without any concern about the presence of witnesses, they interrogated and executed four gang members.[198]

The Sombra Negra's extrajudicial activities had the potential to undermine El Salvador's fragile peace. The 1997 Santa Elena Report, which had called for a military coup to root out narcocorruption, further illustrated the problem of death squads working on behalf of the government to "target gang members and undesirables."[199] Between 2001 and 2006, an alleged 2,825 extrajudicial killings occurred. In 2009, the DIA reported that the Sombra Negra was completely reactivated and that they had decided to restart their death squad activities because of the Salvadoran government's

166   *Narcostates*

failure to control crime. As the gang menace heated up, the Sombra Negra issued leaflets containing these words:

> Be patriotic, kill a gang member. Use anything available to you, machete, pistol, garrote, poison. Set their home on fire or come up with your own technique, but think of the future of your children or it will be too late. . . . We are close. We will provide you with assistance.

Little had changed since the 1992 peace accord. Even FMLN death squads had been reactivated. They reportedly executed gang members deported from the United States in October 2009, and assassinated gang members from Suchitoto and Tonacatepeque in February 2010.[200]

Guatemalan and Honduran police were also accused of carrying out extrajudicial killings. As early as 2000, the corpses of tattooed young males who appeared to have been tortured were discovered around Guatemala City. The Guatemalan police were accused of conducting an extrajudicial operation sanctioned by the government. According to the Grupo de Apoyo Mutuo (GAM), death squads connected to the security forces executed as many as twenty alleged criminals every week. Vigilante groups operating under names such as the Avenging Angels or the Justice Makers took matters into their own hands. Between 2004 and 2005, there were twenty-five lynchings of gang members in Guatemala and thirty-two in Honduras. The citizens of Guatemala referred to the killings as "social cleansing." For Guatemalan *sicarios* (assassins), combating gangs became a lucrative business. One *sicario* said, "Our contracts are $500 and up, no less. It depends on who the person is. If it's someone powerful, someone who will require more time and more study, it goes up to $2,000. Our clients are bus companies, taxi companies, store owners, lawyers—anyone with money."[201]

By 2005, reports concerning the existence of Honduran death squads surfaced. On March 11, 2005, the Honduran government announced an investigation into the US State Department's February 2005 Human Rights Report, which claimed that "death squads" targeted gang members. According to the report, vigilante activities led to "more than 970 killings in the last 7 years of suspected criminals, as well as gang members, street children, and youth."[202] Extrajudicial killings in Honduras would escalate in the following decade.

Looking Back:
1990–2010

The conflict between the death squads and gang members, many of whom were returning war refugees, was a continuation of Central America's civil wars, which had now become a part of the drug war. By 2010, it was impossible to deny that the gangs and drug traffickers worked together. In

The War on Drugs Spills into Central America   167

the minds of many, the two were synonymous. The gangs had evolved into surrogates for the Mexican cartels, eventually becoming transnational DTOs in their own right.

As the region's civil wars came to an end, the United States attempted to put in place a framework to help Central America formalize its counternarcotics programs. The institutionalization of those programs was met with resistance due to fears of remilitarization or the possibility that the counternarcotics police could become politicized, or both.[203] While the deliberations over police reorganization occurred, violent gangs began to appear. Deportees from the United States imported gang culture to Central America—particularly to the Northern Triangle—sowing mayhem. To crack down on the gangs, several Central American nations enacted proscriptive mano dura laws. Due to limited police resources, the mano dura had a minimal impact on gangs, which quickly learned to adapt to those laws. As the Central American gangs proliferated, they spread into Mexico and formed an alliance with the Mexican Mafia (La eMe). From that point onward, the gangs performed the dirty work for the DTOs while also broadening their transnational reach. Central America's gangs, in conjunction with the Mexican DTOs, became the new security crisis.

Notes

1. General Accounting Office, *Drug Control: Interdiction Efforts in Central America Have Had Little Impact on the Flow of Drugs*, report to the chairman, Subcommittee on Information, Justice, Transportation, and Agriculture, Committee on Government Operations House of Representatives, NSIAD 94-233 (Washington, DC, August 2, 1994), 5–6.

2. American Embassy Mexico, "Subject: Drug Trafficking Through Southeastern Mexico," 13075 032142Z, 3.

3. Mark B. Rosenberg and Luis G. Solis, *The United States and Central America: Geopolitical Realities and Regional Fragility* (New York: Routledge, 2007), 38.

4. American Embassy Panama to Secretary of State Washington, DC, "Subject: Central American Counternarcotics Strategy," Panama 11409 181444Z, December 1990, 2–3.

5. American Embassy Mexico to Secretary of State Washington, DC, "Subject: Narcotics Roundup September 9–October 8, 1992," Mexico 25205 151709Z, October 1992, 3–4.

6. General Accounting Office, *Drug Control: Interdiction Efforts*, 7.

7. United Nations, *Single Convention on Narcotic Drugs, 1961, Amended by the Protocol Amending the Single Convention on Narcotic Drugs, 1961*, Treaty Series No. 976, Chapter VI, Narcotics Drugs and Psychotropic Substances (New York: United Nations, August 8, 1975), 105.

8. Organization of American States, *CICAD History* (Washington, DC: OAS July 18, 2014), http://cicad.oas.org/Main/Template.asp?File=/Main/AboutCICAD/History/History_ENG.asp.

168 Narcostates

9. Organization of American States, Inter-American Drug Abuse Control Commission, *Declaration and Program of Action of Ixtapa* (Ixtapa, Mexico: OAS, April 2, 1990), www.cicad.oas.org/Main/Template.asp?File=/main/aboutcicad/basicdocuments/ixtapa_eng.asp.

10. International Justice Resource Center, *Central American Court of Justice* (San Francisco, CA: International Justice Resource Center, n.d.), https://ijrcenter.org/regional-communities/central-american-court-of-justice; Project on International Courts and Tribunals, "Central American Court of Justice," World Legal Information Institute, November 17, 2003, www.worldlii.org. The Charter of the Organization of Central American States was signed in 1951. The Central American Court of Justice was founded in 1962. The Central American Parliament was established at Esquipulas I in 1986.

11. Sistema de la Integración Centroamericana, *XI Cumbre de Presidentes Centroamericanos: Protocol de Tegucigalpa a la Carta de la Organización de Los Estados Centroamericanos* (Tegucigalpa, Honduras, December 13, 1991), 2.

12. General Accounting Office, *Drug Control: U.S. Counterdrug Activities in Central America*, GAO/T-NSIAD-94-251, Washington, DC, August 2, 1994, 2.

13. American Embassy Mexico, "Drug Trafficking Through Southeastern Mexico," 13075 032150Z, 3.

14. Sistema de la Integración Centroamericana, *Permanent Central American Commission for the Eradication of Production, Trafficking, Consumption and Illicit Use of Narcotic and Psychotropic Substances and Related Crimes* (Tegucigalpa, Honduras: Edificio de Comisiones October 29, 1993), www.sica.int/buscar.

15. American Embassy Guatemala to Secretary of State Washington, DC, "Subject: Guns, Drugs, and Guerrillas," Guatemala 02162 220001Z, December 1993, 3.

16. American Embassy Guatemala, "Subject: The de León Administration," 13761 201650Z, 4.

17. Edgar Celada and Sandra Davila, *Central America: On the Brink of a New War* (Amsterdam, Netherlands: Transnational Institute for Drugs and Democracy, April 1, 1997), www.tni.org; US Department of State, *1993 International Narcotics Control Strategy Report Vol. I*, 154–155.

18. Gobierno de Guatemala, *La Ley Contra la Narcoactividad* (Ciudad de Guatemala: Organismo Legislativo: Congreso de La Republica de Guatemala Decreto Numero 48–92, September 23, 1992), 2.

19. American Embassy Guatemala, "Subject: The De León Administration," 13761 201649Z, 4.

20. Scott Stewart, "Mexico's Plan to Create a Paramilitary Force" (Austin, TX: Stratfor Global Intelligence, April 19, 2012), www.stratfor.com.

21. US Department of State, *1996 International Narcotics Control Strategy Report Vol. I*, 131–132.

22. American Embassy Guatemala to Secretary of State Washington, DC, "Subject: Guatemala Quarterly Narcotics Report, Second and Third Quarter, April–September 1995," Guatemala 00781 121443Z, February 1996, 4.

23. Stewart, "Mexico's Plan."

24. American Embassy Guatemala, "Subject: Guatemala Quarterly Narcotics Report," 00781 121444Z, 4.

25. US Department of State, Bureau of Democracy, Human Rights, and Labor, *2002 Country Reports on Human Rights and Labor: Guatemala* (Washington, DC: US Department of State, March 31, 2003), www.state.gov/j/drl/rls/hrrpt/2002/18333.htm. Until 1997, the security forces were composed of three institutions: the

The War on Drugs Spills into Central America   **169**

National Police, the Treasury Police, and the Prison Guards. The first was responsible for public security, the second combated contraband and narcotrafficking, the third took custody of criminals. See American Embassy Guatemala, "Subject: Guatemala's Quarterly Narcotics Report," 00781 121444Z, 3.

26. US Department of State, *1996 International Narcotics Control Strategy Report Vol. I*, 131–132.

27. American Embassy Guatemala to Secretary of State Washington, DC, "Subject: Guatemala Monthly Narcotics Report," Guatemala 06850 241542Z, December 1997, 3.

28. American Embassy Guatemala to Secretary of State Washington, DC, "Subject: International Narcotics Control Strategy Report for Guatemala—1996/1997," Guatemala 00378 221546Z, January 1997, 3.

29. US Department of State, *1998 International Narcotics Control Strategy Report Vol. I*, 137–138.

30. US Department of State, Bureau of Democracy, Human Rights, and Labor, *2002 Country Reports on Human Rights and Labor: Guatemala* (Washington, DC: US Department of State, March 31, 2003), www.state.gov/j/drl/rls/hrrpt/2002/18333.htm.

31. American Embassy Guatemala, "Subject: Guatemala Quarterly Report," 06850 121445Z, 3.

32. American Embassy Guatemala to Secretary of State Washington, DC, "Subject: Army to Form Forest Protection Unit in Petén," Guatemala 05909 271557Z, October 1997, 2.

33. American Embassy Guatemala, "Subject: International Narcotics Control Strategy Report for Guatemala—1996/1997," 00378 221546Z, 3–4.

34. American Embassy Guatemala to Secretary of State Washington, DC, "Subject: Transfer of INL UH-1H Helicopters," Guatemala 07191 191801Z, December 1996, 2–3.

35. American Embassy Guatemala to DEA Headquarters, Washington, DC, "Subject: Importance of Additional DEA Agents for Guatemala Now," Guatemala 01990 032358Z, April 1996, 2.

36. American Embassy Guatemala to Secretary of State Washington, DC, "Subject: International Narcotics Control Strategy Report for Guatemala—1996/1997," 2–3.

37. American Embassy Guatemala, "Subject: Guatemala Quarterly Narcotics Report," 06850 121447Z, 3.

38. American Embassy Guatemala to Secretary of State Washington, DC, "Subject: International Narcotics Control Strategy Report for Guatemala—1999/2000," Guatemala 04471 081423Z, December 1999, 3.

39. Bureau of International Narcotics and Law Enforcement Affairs, *1999 International Narcotics Control Strategy Report*s (Washington, DC: US Department of State, 2000), www.state.gov/j/inl/rls/nrcrpt/1999/920.htm.

40. American Embassy Guatemala to Secretary of State Washington, DC, "Subject: Operation Mayan Jaguar: A Success in All Respects," Guatemala 001146 261834Z, March 1999, 4.

41. Rob Fischer, "Tracing an Invisible Line: How Guatemalan Security Forces Have Taken Over the Drug Trade," *Mesoamerica* 25, no. 1 (January 2006): 1–2.

42. US Department of State, *2002 Country Reports on Human Rights and Labor: Guatemala*.

43. American Embassy San Salvador, "Subject: GOES Launches National Plan," 01942 250044Z, 4.

170 Narcostates

44. Research Directorate, Immigration and Refugee Board, Canada, "El Salvador: The National Civilian Police" (Ottawa, Canada: Immigration and Refugee Board of Canada, April 1, 1994), www.refworld.org; Fabrice Lehoucq, *The Politics of Modern Central America: Civil War, Democratization, and Underdevelopment* (New York: Cambridge University Press, 2012), 66–86.

45. American Embassy San Salvador to Secretary of State Washington, DC, "Subject: GOES/FLMN Agree to UN 23 October Plan with Annex, Subject to Modifications," San Salvador 11625 091953Z, November 1992, 1; American Embassy San Salvador to Secretary of State Washington, DC, "Subject: [Redaction] FMLN Legalization Contingent on Demobilization," San Salvador 11402 302320Z, October 1992, 1.

46. American Embassy San Salvador to Secretary of State Washington, DC, "Subject: FMLN Accuses ESAF of Engaging in a Shell Game," San Salvador 11285 282121Z, October 1992, 1.

47. American Embassy San Salvador to Secretary of State Washington, DC, "Subject: GOES Anti-Narcotics Unit—Uncertain Institutional Future," San Salvador 11859 140007Z, November 1992, 4.

48. Research Directorate, "El Salvador: The National Civilian Police."

49. American Embassy San Salvador, "Subject: GOES Anti-Narcotics Unit," 11859 140007Z, 4.

50. Ibid., 2.

51. American Embassy San Salvador to Secretary of State Washington, DC, "Subject: INSCR El Salvador's Mid-Year Update," San Salvador 08869 112322Z, July 1991, 2.

52. American Embassy San Salvador, "Subject: GOES Anti-Narcotics Unit," 11859 140007Z, 3.

53. Research Directorate, "El Salvador: The National Civilian Police."

54. Secretary of State Washington, DC, to American Embassy San Salvador, "Subject: A Salvadoran View of Drug Trafficking in Central America," State 337887 160110Z, October 1992, 2.

55. American Embassy San Salvador to Secretary of State Washington, DC, "Subject: Official-Informal," San Salvador 01908 041909Z, March 1994, 4.

56. American Embassy San Salvador, "Subject: GOES Anti-Narcotics Unit," 11859 140007Z, 2. In 1985, the UEA was folded into the PNC through the Comisión de Investigación de Hechos Delictivos, created to investigate cases such as the assassination of Archbishop Óscar Romero.

57. Research Directorate, "El Salvador: The National Civilian Police."

58. American Embassy San Salvador, "Subject: GOES Anti-Narcotics Unit," 11859 140010Z, 2–4.

59. American Embassy San Salvador to Secretary of State Washington, DC, "Subject: Evolving ESAF Views of the PNC," San Salvador 005288 281824Z, June 1994, 2–3.

60. American Embassy San Salvador, "Subject: Official-Informal," 4.

61. US Department of State, *1996 International Narcotics Control Strategy Report Vol. I*, 130; American Embassy San Salvador to Secretary of State Washington, DC, "Subject: Revised San Salvador FY 99 International Letter of Agreement," San Salvador 02778 131528Z, August 1999, 2.

62. American Embassy San Salvador to Secretary of State Washington, DC, "Subject: 1995 International Narcotics Control Strategy Report: El Salvador," San Salvador 09848 131638Z, December 1994, 2.

63. American Embassy San Salvador to Secretary of State Washington, DC, "Subject: Alleged PNC Corruption," San Salvador 00068 051854Z, January 1995, 2–3.

The War on Drugs Spills into Central America 171

64. American Embassy San Salvador, "Subject: 1995 International Narcotics," 4.

65. American Embassy San Salvador to Secretary of State Washington, DC, "Subject: 1997/1998 International Narcotics Control Strategy Report," San Salvador 04990 052114Z, December 1997, 3–4.

66. US Department of State, *1998 International Narcotics Control Strategy Report Vol. I*, 136.

67. Ibid.; American Embassy San Salvador, "Subject: 1997/1998," 2.

68. American Embassy San Salvador to Secretary of State Washington, DC, "Subject: New Salvadoran Air Traffic Control Radar Spotlights Clandestine Flights and Drug Corruption," San Salvador 01103 032002Z, April 1999, 3.

69. Secretary of State Washington, DC, to American Embassy San Salvador, "Subject: Maritime Counternarcotics Cooperation Agreement," San Salvador 030584 182023Z, February 1999, 7–11.

70. American Embassy Tegucigalpa to Secretary of State Washington, DC, "Subject: Request for FY 92 International Narcotics Training for Honduras," Tegucigalpa 05897 010029Z, May 1991, 1–3.

71. American Embassy Tegucigalpa, "Subject: Request for FY 92," 05897 010031Z, 3.

72. American Embassy Tegucigalpa, "Subject: Request for FY 92," 05897 010029Z, 4.

73. American Embassy Tegucigalpa to Secretary of State Washington, DC, "Subject: Draft 1991 International Narcotics Control Strategy Report for Honduras," Tegucigalpa 20876 102254Z, December 1990, 2. The Honduran armed forces absorbed the FUSEP in 1973.

74. American Embassy Tegucigalpa, "Subject: Draft 1991," 20876 102255Z, 2.

75. American Embassy Tegucigalpa, "Subject: Draft 1991," 20876 102254Z, 2; General Accounting Office, *Drug Control: Interdiction Efforts*, 19.

76. Laura Brooks, "US Military Extends War into Central America," *Christian Science Monitor*, June 25, 1991, World sec., p. 1.

77. American Embassy Tegucigalpa to Secretary of State Washington, DC, "Honduran Air-Force Downs Suspected Trafficker Aircraft," Tegucigalpa 06866 071806Z, May 1992, 2.

78. General Accounting Office, *Drug Control: Interdiction Efforts*, 17.

79. American Embassy Tegucigalpa to Secretary of State Washington, DC, "Subject: FY 93 Military Assistance for Honduras," Tegucigalpa 12791 222202Z, September 1992, 3.

80. General Accounting Office, *Drug Control: Interdiction Efforts*, 20; American Embassy Tegucigalpa to American Embassy Rome, "Subject: 1996 Narcotics Workplan for Honduras," Tegucigalpa 02009 262229Z, April 1996, 4. The JICC was not fully operational until 1993.

81. US Department of State, *1998 International Narcotics Control Strategy Report Vol. I*, 147.

82. American Embassy Tegucigalpa, "Subject: Draft 1991," 20876 102254Z, 2.

83. US Department of State, *1999 International Narcotics Control Strategy Report*, 163.

84. La oficina en Washington para asuntos Latinaméricanos, "¿Proteger y servir?: El estado de los procesos de reforma Policíal en Centroamérica" (Washington, DC: La oficina en Washington para asuntos Latinaméricanos, December 2009), 5–6; "Honduras: Public Security Force," *Jane's Intelligence Review* (London), February 1993, 90–93, www.country-data.com/cgi-bin/query /r-5725.html. Decree 229-96 initiated the police transfer over to civilian control.

172 Narcostates

85. US Department of State, *1997 International Narcotics Control Strategy Report Vol. I*, 138.

86. American Embassy Tegucigalpa to Secretary of State Washington, DC, "Subject: International Narcotics Control Strategy Report," Tegucigalpa 04358 221754Z, December 1999, 3.

87. American Embassy Managua to Secretary of State Washington, DC, "Subject: Text of GON Note on Narcotics Cooperation," Managua 05338 202225Z, September 1989, 2.

88. American Embassy Managua to Secretary of State Washington, DC, "Subject: Narcotics Control Strategy: Nicaragua," Managua 02535 041451Z, May 1990, 2.

89. American Embassy Managua to Secretary of State Washington, DC, "Subject: GON Seeks U.S. Assistance on Narcotics Matters," Managua 03617 121417Z, June 1990, 2.

90. American Embassy Managua to Secretary of State Washington, DC, "Subject: FY 92 Narcotics Control Budget," Managua 02388 201417Z, March 1992, 1.

91. Ibid.

92. American Embassy Managua to Secretary of State Washington, DC, "Subject: GON Seeks Support for Its Participation in Narcotics Control Seminar," Managua 03786 161853Z, June 1990, 2.

93. Cynthia Arnson and David Holiday, "Fitful Peace: Human Rights and Reconciliation in Nicaragua Under the Chamorro Government," Human Rights Watch, July 1,1991, 16.

94. American Embassy Managua to Secretary of State Washington, DC, "Subject Official Informal," Managua, 09036 052012Z, November 1991, 1–4; Roberto Cajina, "Security in Nicaragua: Central America's Exception?" (working paper, Inter-American Dialogue, January 2013), 5. The reorganization was called Decree 64-90: The Organic Law of the Ministry of Government. Decree 1-90 created the Ministry of Government.

95. American Embassy Managua to Secretary of State Washington, DC, "Subject: Narcotics Trafficking Developments," Managua 01411 191342Z, February 1991, 2–3. The ring was run by Subcomandante Gilberto Chávez and Captains Isfrajin García and Domingo Gayo.

96. US Department of State, Bureau for International Narcotics and Law Enforcement Affairs, *1996 International Narcotics Control Strategy Report Vol. I* (Washington, DC: US Department of State, March 1997), 152.

97. American Embassy Managua to Secretary of State Washington, DC, "Subject: Anti-Narcotics Program for Nicaragua," Managua 03728 141924Z, June 1990, 1.

98. American Embassy Managua, "Subject: Official Informal," 4.

99. Tim Johnson, "12 Removed from Nicaraguan Police, but New Sandinista Chief Draws Fire," *Baltimore Sun*, September 6, 1992, http://articles.baltimoresun.com.

100. General Accounting Office, *Drug Control: Interdiction Efforts*, 24.

101. La oficina en Washington para asuntos Latinaméricanos, "¿Proteger y servir?," 7.

102. Winslow and Martínez, *Crime and Society*.

103. US Department of State, *1998 International Narcotics Control Strategy Report Vol. I*, 162–163.

104. American Embassy San Jose to Secretary of State, Washington, DC, "Subject: FY 1995 Security Assistance Reporting Requirements (Part 1): FMF ESF and Narcotics AIASA," San Jose 05427 192342Z, July 1993, 3.

The War on Drugs Spills into Central America   **173**

105. American Embassy San José to Secretary of State Washington, DC, "Subject: FY 1992 Annual Integrated Assessment of Programs by Increasing Demands in Eastern Europe for U.S. Economic Assistance, Relaxation of East-West Tensions, per-se, Has Little Further Effect on Costa Rica's Security Situation," San José 06862 072216Z, June 1990, 3.

106. American Embassy San José to Secretary of State Washington, DC, "Subject: FY 1992 Annual Integrated Assessment of Security Assistance (AIASA): Costa Rica," San José 06862 072215Z, June 1990, 3.

107. American Embassy San José to Secretary of State Washington, DC, "Subject: FY 1993 Security Assistance Reporting Requirements (AIASA)," San José 05437 212121Z, May 1991, 2–3.

108. Louis Emmanuel Peréz Bolaños, *El estado costarricense frente al narcotráfico: el caso del Plan Nacional sobre Drogas, 2006–2011* (Universidad de Costa Rica, Facultad de Ciencias Sociales, Escuela de Ciencias Políticas, 2013), 10–11.

109. American Embassy San José, "Subject: FY 1992 Annual Integrated Assessment," 06862 072216Z, 3–4.

110. Luis I. Jácome H., "Central Bank Involvement in Banking Crises in Latin America," (Working Paper 08/135, Washington, DC: International Monetary Fund, May 2008), 43. Following the bank's collapse, the ratio of overdue loans to the net worth of state commercial banks exceeded 100 percent in June 1995, leading to rising inflation. Allegations circulated that Panamanian foreign minister Gabriel Lewis Galindo, the owner of the Banco del Istmo, may have played a role in Banco Anglo's collapse. See American Embassy Panama to Secretary of State Washington, DC, "Subject: Panama: Charge Pushes Noriega Document Destruction, Money Laundering Fight in Farewell Call on President," Panama 03444 222027Z, June 1995, 3.

111. US Department of State, *1993 International Narcotics Control Strategy Report Vol. I*, 147.

112. American Embassy San José to Secretary of State Washington, DC, "Subject: Costa Rican Request for Military Academy Ties," San José 00120 062252Z, January 1995, 2.

113. American Embassy San José, "Subject: FY 1995 Security Assistance Reporting Requirements (Part 1)," 4.

114. American Embassy San José to Secretary of State Washington, DC, "Subject: FY 1996 Request for Promoting Peace," San José 05136 292224Z, July 1994, 2; General Accounting Office, *Drug Control: Interdiction Efforts*, 8.

115. Louis Emmanuel Peréz Bolaños, *El estado costarricense frente al narcotráfico: El caso del Plan Nacional sobre Drogas, 2006–2011* (Universidad de Costa Rica, Facultad de Ciencias Sociales, Escuela de Ciencias Políticas, 2013), 10–11. CONADRO is located within the presidential branch of the government.

116. General Accounting Office, *Drug Control: Interdiction Efforts*, 8.

117. US Department of State, Bureau of Democracy, Human Rights, and Labor, *Panama* (Washington, DC: US Department of State, February 28, 2005), www.state.gov/j/drl/rls/hrrpt/2004/41769.htm.

118. American Embassy Panama to Secretary of State Washington, DC, "Subject: Proposal: Regional Counternarcotics Strategy for Panama, Mexico, and Central America," Panama 05361 082123Z, June 1992, 1.

119. Ibid., 2.

120. Ibid., 2.

121. US Congress, Senate, Committee on Foreign Relations, Senate Executive Report 104-3, *Treaty with Panama on Mutual Assistance in Criminal Matters*, 105th Cong., 1st sess., May 1, 1995.

174   Narcostates

122. American Embassy Panama to Secretary of State Washington, DC, "Subject: Panama Signs Mutual Cooperation Agreement on Narcotics," Panama 00193 102243Z, January 1990, 1; "Narcotic Drugs Mutual Cooperation Agreement Between the United States and Panama," January 10, 1990, *United States Treaties and Other International Acts Series* 12409, Articles I–II, 2–3.

123. American Embassy Panama to Secretary of State Washington, DC, "Subject: FY 95 Panama Budget Submission," Panama 03448 232308Z, April 1993, 2.

124. US Congress, House of Representatives, *Foreign Operations, Export Financing, and Related Programs Appropriations Act, 1994*, Public Law 104-107, H.R. 2295, 103rd Cong., 1st sess., September 30, 1993, 962. American Embassy Panama to Secretary of State Washington, DC, "Subject: FY 95 Panama Budget," 2.

125. US Department of State, *1995 International Narcotics Control Strategy Report Vol. I*, 153.

126. American Embassy Panama to Secretary of State Washington, DC, "Subject: 1994 International Narcotics Control Strategy Report for Panama (INCSR)," Panama 07995 191503Z, December 1994, 2–4; General Accounting Office, *Drug Control: Interdiction Efforts*, 25.

127. General Accounting Office, *Drug Control: Interdiction Efforts*, 25.

128. United Nations, *United Nations Convention Against Illicit Traffic in Narcotic Drugs and Psychotropic Substances*, Treaty Series Vol. 1582, Chapter VI Narcotics and Psychotropic Substances (Vienna: December 20, 1988), https://treaties.un .org/Pages/ViewDetails.aspx?src=IND&mtdsg_no=VI-19&chapter=6&clang=_en.

129. American Embassy Bogotá to Secretary of State Washington, DC, "Subject: Colombia: Regional Security Conference an Important First Step," Bogotá 002481 192233Z, March 2003, 2–3.

130. General Accounting Office, *Drug Control: Interdiction Efforts*, 5–6.

131. Ibid., 7.

132. American Embassy San José to Secretary of State Washington, DC, "Subject: Central America Counternarcotics and Anti-Corruption Policy Summit," San José 000596 032140Z, March 2000, 2.

133. United Nations, *Convention Against Transnational Organized Crime*, Treaty Series Vol. 2225, Resolution Adopted by the General Assembly 55/25, 55th Sess., Session, Item 105 (New York: United Nations, January 8, 2001), 1–51.

134. Hal Brands, *Crime, Violence, and the Crisis in Guatemala: A Case Study in the Erosion of the State* (Carlisle Barracks, PA: Strategic Studies Institute, May 2010), 25.

135. Mary Helen Johnson, "National Policies and the Rise of Transnational Gangs" (Washington, DC: Migration Policy Institute, April 2006), www .migrationinformation.org.

136. American Embassy San Salvador to ACLA Collective, "Subject: More on Salvadoran Gangs," San Salvador 01849 102117Z, March 1995, 2.

137. Immigration and Refugee Board of Canada, "El Salvador: The National Civilian Police"; Patrick J. McDonnell and H. G. Reza, "Salvadorans Fear Deportations: Future Uncertain for Refugees After Federal Decision," *Los Angeles Times*, December 3, 1994, http://articles.latimes.com. The INS was the precursor to the Immigration and Customs Enforcement (ICE).

138. Clare Ribando Seelke, *Gangs in Central America*, Report R-L34112 (Washington, DC: Congressional Research Service, October 17, 2008), 7.

139. Thomas Bruneau, Lucia Dammert, and Elizabeth Skinner, *Maras: Gang Violence and Security in Central America* (Austin: University of Texas Press, 2011), 88–89.

The War on Drugs Spills into Central America   175

140. United Nations, Office on Drugs and Crime, *Crime and Development in Central America*, 60.

141. American Embassy San Salvador to Secretary of State Washington, DC, "Subject: Recent Gang Activity," San Salvador 02510 052218Z, April 1995, 1.

142. Immigration and Refugee Board of Canada, "El Salvador: The National Civilian Police," 15.

143. Jaime López, "Pandillas cerraron por un mes escuela de Izalco," ElSalvador.com (San Salvador), July 19, 2016, www.elsalvador.com.

144. American Embassy San Salvador to Secretary of State Washington, DC, "Gang Rivalries Trigger Spike in Violence," San Salvador 000223 222248Z, June 2010, 1.

145. American Embassy El Salvador to Secretary of State Washington, DC, "Subject: El Salvador—Annual OSAC Crime/Safety Report for CY-2008," San Salvador 000058 222253Z, January 2008, 2.

146. American Embassy Tegucigalpa to Secretary of State Washington, DC, "Subject: Update on Gang Threat to Embassies in El Salvador and Honduras," Tegucigalpa 000866 111863Z, May 2006, 1.

147. Thelma Mejía, "Central America: Soaring Violent Crime Threatens Democracy," Inter Press Service, September 22, 2008, 2.

148. Secretary of State Washington, DC, to American Embassy San Salvador, "Subject: UNGA Meeting Between A/S Watson and El Salvador President Armando Calderón del Sol, September 26," State 267944 032312Z, October 1994, 3.

149. American Embassy Guatemala to Secretary of State Washington, DC, "Subject: Security Challenges in a Post-War Guatemala," Guatemala 08197 072122Z, September 1994, 3–4; Joint Chiefs of Staff Washington, DC, to AIG 11888, "Subject: IRR [Redacted] Comments by Senior Army Officer Concerning Drugs," R 090104Z, June 1990, 6 (National Security Archive, Guatemala Project). The commander was Colonel Luis Ortega Menaldo.

150. American Embassy Tegucigalpa to Secretary of State Washington, DC, "Subject: A Permanent Tattoo: The Systematic Failure to Squelch the Proliferation of Gangs in Honduras," Tegucigalpa 001843 192253Z, August 2004, 1.

151. American Embassy Guatemala, "Subject: Security Challenges in a Post-War," 3–4.

152. American Embassy San Salvador to Secretary of State Washington, DC, "Subject: El Salvador: Gangs Threaten Mission's Goals," San Salvador 002232 041830Z, August 2004, 4.

153. Robert J. Bunker and John P. Sullivan, "Mara Salvatrucha Links to Occult Rituals and Santa Muerte Veneration and Worship," in *Strategic Notes on Third Generation Gangs,* ed. John P. Sullivan and Robert J. Bunker (North Haven, CT: Small Wars Foundation, 2022), 144.

154. Héctor Perla Jr., "The Impact of CAFTA: Drugs, Gangs, and Immigration," *Telesur* (Mexico), March 1, 2016, www.telesurtv.net.

155. International Labor Organization, Regional Office for Latin America and the Caribbean, *2007 Labor Overview, Latin America and the Caribbean* (Geneva: International Labor Organization, January 1, 2008), www.ilo.org.

156. "Part II: Gangs, Deportation, and Violence in Central America," InSight Crime, November 30, 2012, www.insightcrime.org.

157. American Embassy San Salvador, "Subject: El Salvador: Gangs," 1.

158. Organization of American States, *Pandillas Delictivas* (Washington, DC: OAS, January 28, 2012), 11, http://scm.oas.org/pdfs/2010/CP23778S.pdf.

176 Narcostates

159. American Embassy San Salvador, "Subject: El Salvador: Gangs," 12.

160. American Embassy San Salvador, "Gang Rivalries Trigger Spike," 2.

161. Roberto Valencia, "El país que entregó las cárceles a sus pandilleros," *El Faro* (El Salvador), September 1, 2014, www.salanegra.elfaro.net. In 2004, the gangs were transferred between four prisons: Quezaltepeque and Ciudad Barrios for MS-13, and Chalatenago and Cojutepeque for Calle 18.

162. US Agency for International Development, "Central American and Mexican Gang Assessment" (Washington, DC: USAID Bureau for Latin American and Caribbean Affairs Office of Regional Sustainable Development, April 2006), 19.

163. Howard Abadinsky, *Organized Crime* (Belmont, CA: Wadsworth Cengage Learning, 2010), 188–189.

164. United Nations Office on Drugs and Crime, *Crime and Development in Central America: Caught in the Crossfire* (New York: United Nations, May 2007), 45–46.

165. US Congress, House of Representatives, Committee on Foreign Affairs, Western Hemisphere Subcommittee of the House Foreign Affairs Committee, *Hearing on Violence in Central America*, 110th Cong., 1st sess., June 26, 2007, 40.

166. Hal Brands, "Third Generation Gangs and Criminal Insurgency in Latin America," in *Strategic Notes on Third Generation Gangs,* ed. John P. Sullivan and Robert J. Bunker (North Haven, CT: Small Wars Foundation, 2022), 30.

167. American Embassy San Salvador to Secretary of State Washington, DC, "Subject: El Salvador—Annual OSAC Crime/Safety Report January 2008," San Salvador 000058 222253Z, January 2008, 3.

168. American Embassy San Salvador to Secretary of State Washington, DC, "Subject: El Salvador: Gangs Threaten Mission's Goals," San Salvador 002232 041830Z, August 2004, 1.

169. American Embassy San Salvador to Secretary of State Washington, DC, "Deputy Secretary Negroponte Meeting with Salvadoran Attorney General Safie," San Salvador 000722 181792Z, June 2008, 1.

170. Sonja Wolf, "Mano Dura: Gang Suppression in El Salvador" (Oxford Research Group: Sustainable Security, March 2011), 1–2, www.academia.edu.

171. American Embassy San Salvador, "Subject: More on Salvadoran Gangs," 3.

172. American Embassy San Salvador to Secretary of State Washington, DC, "Subject: El Salvador Updated Assessment of Central American Security Requirements," San Salvador 002402 132134Z, December 2007, 5.

173. Federal Bureau of Investigation, "Going Global on Gangs," Washington, DC, October 10, 2007, https://archives.fbi.gov/archives/news/stories/2007/october /ms13tag_101007.

174. American Embassy Tegucigalpa, "Subject: A Permanent Tattoo," 1.

175. United Nations Office on Drugs and Crime, *Crime and Development in Central America*, 64; CICAD, "Institutional Building/National Anti-Drug Strategy: Evaluation of Progress on Drug Control 2001–2002" (Washington, DC: Organization of American States, 2003), 1.

176. American Embassy Tegucigalpa, "Subject: A Permanent Tattoo," 4.

177. Luke Dowdney, ed., "Tratamiento del Problema de Niños y Jóvenes Involucrados en La Violencia Armada Organizada, Parte IV," in *Nem Guerra Nem Paz: Comparaciones Internacionales de niños y jóvenes en violencia armada Organizada* (São Paulo: 7 Letras, 2005), 119–122.

178. American Embassy Tegucigalpa, "Subject: A Permanent Tattoo," 4.

179. Dowdney, *Nem Guerra Nem Paz*, 122.

180. Sebastian Amar, Amy Fairchild Haer, Shaunna Bailey, and Abraham Jacob, *Seeking Asylum from Gang-Based Violence in Central America: A Resource Manual*

(Washington, DC: Central American Immigrants' Rights Coalition, 2007), 34, www.unhcr.org/uk/585a96a34.pdf.

181. Brands, *Crime, Violence, and the Crisis in Guatemala*, 28.

182. "Guatemala violencia capturan a jovenes acusados de asseniar mujeres en rito Satanico," Spanish Newswire Service, August 13, 2003.

183. Organization of American States, *Pandillas Delictivas*, 4.

184. US Agency for International Development, "Central American and Mexican Gang Assessment," 79.

185. Revista Envío, "The Gangs of Central America: Major Players and Scapegoats," *Revista Envío,* no. 317 (Managua: Universidad Centroamericana, December 2007), www.envio.org.

186. Dowdney, *Nem Guerra Nem Paz*, 123.

187. "Guatemala-pandillas Policía ha capturado 2582 pandilleros en lo que va de año 2003," Spanish Newswire Services, August 20, 2003.

188. Organization of American States, *Pandillas Delictivas*, 5.

189. "Divulgan situación de cárceles tras muerte violenta de 35 reos en Guatemala," Agence France-Presse, August 22, 2005.

190. US Agency for International Development, "Central American and Mexican Gang Assessment," 110–113.

191. Ibid., 110; Julio Navarro, "Dispara la 'Mara Salvatrucha' en desfile," *Es Más* (Mexico), November 20, 2004, www.esmas.com.

192. United Nations Office on Drugs and Crime, *Crime and Development in Central America*, 64.

193. Jamie Dettmer, "MS-13 and Calle 18 Developing Strong Relationships with Drug Cartels," *El Dialogo*, December 19, 2011, www.dialogo-americas.com.

194. James Aparicio, "President Moscoso declaro guerra ala delincuencia al fin de su mandato," Agence France-Presse, July 7, 2004, International sec.

195. Seelke, *Gangs in Central America*, 3.

196. US Agency for International Development, "Central American and Mexican Gang Assessment," 20.

197. US Defense Intelligence Agency to US Department of Homeland Security, "Salvadoran Vigilante Organization Known as the Sombra Negra Is Allegedly Reorganizing," Washington, DC, 11254979 251718Z, November 29, 2009, 1.

198. Roberto Valencia, "La Sombra Negra," *Elfaro.net* (El Salvador), April 26, 2014, www.salanegra.elfaro.net.

199. American Embassy San Salvador to Secretary of State Washington, DC, "Subject: Group Argues Military Should Act to End Narco-Corruption; Finding No Resonance, Leader Recants," San Salvador 04328 220305Z, October 1997, 3.

200. US Defense Intelligence Agency, "Salvadoran Vigilante Organization," 1; US Agency for International Development, *Central American and Mexican Gang Assessment*, 96.

201. Immigration and Refugee Board of Canada, Guatemala: Violence by Criminal Gangs and Cases of Popular Justice; Protection Offered by the State (March 2005–February 2007), GTM102404.FE, March 2, 2007, https://www.refworld.org/docid/469cd6a31c.html.

202. US Department of State, Bureau of Democracy, Human Rights, and Labor, *Honduras*, Washington, DC: US Department of State, March 8, 2006, https://2009-2017.state.gov/j/drl/rls/hrrpt/2005/61732.htm.

203. Richard L. Millett and Orlando J. Pérez, "New Threats and Old Dilemmas: Central America's Armed Forces in the 21st Century," *Journal of Political and Military Sociology* 33, no. 1 (2005): 57–59.

8

Mexico's Cartel Wars

Nobel laureate Octavio Paz's *Labyrinth of Solitude* suggested that Mexico's history revolves in a circle perpetuated by death. The new cycle of death that ravaged the country at the beginning of the twenty-first century was reminiscent of the Mexican Revolution. Behind it all was the cult of Santa Muerte—the celebration of death incarnate—justifying everything they did.[1] Through sheer brutality, fear, and violence, the Mexican cartels attempted to dominate Mexico's political system while fighting their rivals for control over the narcotrafficking corridors. To all in their way, revenge, murder, and death became the reality under which they lived and died.

At the dawn of the new millennium, four major cartels dominated Mexico. The Sinaloa, Arellano Félix (Tijuana), Juárez, and Gulf cartels emerged from the 1990s disrupted but intact, and their operations continued to flourish despite the imprisonment and/or murder of their capos. To prove their relative power, the cartels sought to expand their territorial control, leading to increased fighting among themselves and with the authorities. The result was a further decentralization and splintering of the DTOs. Former enforcer groups—the Beltrán Leyva cartel, Los Zetas, La Familia Michoacana, the Cártel de Jalisco Nueva Generación, Los Caballeros Templarios, and other mini-affiliates—branched out on their own to become Mexico's third-generation cartels. To counter these upstarts, the second-generation cartels altered their alliances. Enemies became allies and former allies became enemies. By 2010, Mexico's cartels no longer resembled those that had existed at the turn of the century.

It is not possible to list the daily acts of violence and corruption that occurred during this period in Mexico's history. However, the story of the cartel wars and their impact on Mexico is key to understanding the evolution of the drug war. The Mexican government went to war with a sector of its

180   *Narcostates*

population that depended on the drug trade as a vital source of income. Many of those who were employed by it were landless and jobless campesinos or poor *maquiladora* workers looking for a way to improve their lot in life. For Mexico, the war on drugs became another "dirty war," but this time with horrific public displays of extreme brutality.

The Formation of the
Sinaloa Cartel's Federation

Juan José Esparragoza Moreno ("El Azul") had the dream of creating a supercartel. El Azul joined the Juárez cartel in May 1993, immediately following his release from prison on drug trafficking charges. That same year, his negotiating skills helped form a temporary pact between the Juárez, Sinaloa, and Gulf cartels called "The Peace of the North," which put an end to rivalries in Chihuahua and Tamaulipas.[2] Following the 1997 death of Juárez cartel leader Amado Carrillo Fuentes, he opposed the selection of Vicente Carrillo Fuentes ("El Viceroy") as the new boss. As a result, he left the cartel to join El Chapo's organization and to turn his idea of a supercartel into reality.[3] Through familial ties of marriage and children, he helped forge an alliance between the Beltrán Leyva brothers, El Chapo, and Ismael Zambada ("El Mayo").[4] Reminiscent of alliance formation during the medieval era, this alliance would become known as the Alianza de Sangre—the Alliance of Blood.

El Chapo's January 19, 2001, escape from the Puente Grande maximum security prison finalized El Azul's plan. Immediately after his escape, El Chapo organized a summit of twenty-five cartel bosses in Cuernavaca. It was there that El Chapo completed the creation of the Sinaloa Federation. El Chapo also laid out his plans to take over the states of Nuevo León and Tamaulipas (especially the border cities of Nuevo Laredo and Matamoros) from the Gulf cartel, while driving the Arellano Félix cartel out of Tijuana.[5] By 2002, his ambition led the Sinaloa cartel to assume control over divided factions within the Juárez cartel, which had been severely disrupted by the Mexican government's Maxi-Proceso—a coordinating effort between the Mexican police and the PGR to go after the cartels as organized structures.[6] Territorial disputes between Juárez cartel leader El Viceroy and El Chapo weakened the cohesion of the federation, which led to the Juárez cartel's departure in 2004.[7]

Prior to El Chapo's 2001 prison escape, Arturo, Carlos, Alfredo, and Héctor Beltrán Leyva played a significant role in what would become the federation. Alongside El Chapo, the Beltrán Leyva brothers worked for the Guadalajara cartel as hit men and traffickers.[8] While El Chapo was imprisoned, the brothers brought him bags of cash and worked with El Chapo's brother, Arturo Guzmán, to protect Sinaloa interests in the states of Guerrero, Michoacán, Morelos, and Sonora.[9] Within the Beltrán Leyva cartel Arturo ("El Barbas") became a leader along with his brother Alfredo ("El Mochomo"). During his time with the Guadalajara cartel, El Barbas had been tutored by Amado Carrillo Fuentes. Like Carrillo Fuentes, his ability to corrupt the Mexican government's law enforcement agencies went deep. Enjoying the protection of the Mexican navy, he moved narcotics north out of the Icacos naval base in Acapulco. He later infiltrated the Subprocuraduría Especializada en Investigación de Delincuencia Organizada (SEIDO), an elite anticrime unit within the Mexican PGR. The discovery of corruption within SEIDO was a public relations disaster for Mexico because it had been formed in 2003 following revelations of cartel corruption within the PGR.

As part of the Beltrán Leyva–Sinaloa alliance, El Barbas recruited one of the most notorious criminals in modern Mexican history—Edgar Valdez Villarreal ("La Barbie"). With a history of drug dealing in the United States and Mexico dating back to 1993, La Barbie permanently fled the United States on marijuana trafficking charges in 1998 and joined a gang known as Los Chachos that operated out of Nuevo Laredo.[10] In 2002, the capo of the Gulf cartel, Osiel Cárdenas Guillén, sent Los Zetas to assert the Gulf cartel's control over Nuevo Laredo and to eliminate Los Chachos, killing their leader in May 2002. As a result of the assassination, La Barbie was recruited by El Barbas into the federation and given command over Los Negros, a Sinaloa *sicario* gang fighting the Gulf cartel for control over Nuevo Laredo.[11] La Barbie gained notoriety by employing terrorist tactics to intimidate his enemies, including beheadings, videos of killings, and sending corpses as messages to his enemies. In one self-recorded video, he showed himself wiping the blood of a Gulf cartel *sicario* he had just murdered onto a Santa Muerte figurine.[12] According to the Agencia Federal de Investigación (AFI), La Barbie had an agreement with MS-13 to do his dirty work in Nuevo Laredo. Like his mentor, El Barbas, La Barbie skillfully corrupted Mexican government officials. He bought off González Díaz, the head of the AFI, by paying him $1.5 million to remove the AFI commander in Nuevo Laredo and replace him with one who would help drive Los Zetas out.[13] Reports alleged that González Díaz received another $4 million to find the eight houses where Osiel Cárdenas Guillén hid out in Tamaulipas. That information led to the arrest of Osiel in March 2003. After two informants reported that González Díaz took Sinaloa money, he left his job and went missing.[14]

The Arellano Félix Cartel's War Against All

Meanwhile, at the turn of the millennium, the Arellano Félix cartel found themselves on the defense and became increasingly emboldened to strike

182   *Narcostates*

out at any enemy. In 1996, the deputy attorney general for the state of Baja, Ernesto Ibarra Santes, swore to apprehend the Arellano Félix brothers, but he would not live to see the year out. Despite his professed claims of law and order, he was on the payroll of the Sinaloa cartel, which meant his days were numbered. The narcojuniors finished him off on September 14, 1996.[15] As the Mexican government cracked down on the cartel, El Chapo's 2001 prison escape led to a resumption of the Arellano Félix–Sinaloa cartel war.[16] Although by mid-decade police and Sinaloa pressure would make it appear as though the Arellano Félix cartel was finished, the cartel proved to be resilient.

On March 11, 2000, the PJFM captured the cartel's financier, Jesús Labra Avilés ("El Chuy"), while he was watching his son's soccer game. When police agents swept onto the field, he attempted to flee, but he could not run fast enough. His bodyguards were not present because he had just given them permission to go to the bathroom.[17] Responding to his arrest, the cartel kidnapped and killed Patino Moreno, a deputy attorney general for the PGR, and two aides while walking in Tijuana. Their corpses were almost unrecognizable. A policeman stated that Moreno's body felt like a sack of ice cubes—the killers broke every bone in his body by crushing him in an industrial press.[18]

Following these gruesome killings, the Mexican government intensi-fied its effort against the Arellano Félix cartel. In May 2000, Mexican law enforcement arrested Ismael Higuera Guerrero ("El Mayel"), whose duty was to bring narcotics into Mexico and arrange for their transport to the United States. On the heels of Labra Avilés's incarceration, El Mayel's arrest devastated the cartel. It lost two of its principal lieutenants within a matter of months. The US and Mexican governments declared the Arellano Félix organization dead. On May 11, prosecutors in San Diego unsealed a ten-count indictment accusing brothers Benjamín and Ramón of ordering a string of murders and kidnappings across Mexico. Both brothers faced life in prison and fines of $27 million.[19]

More pressure was heaped on the Arellano Félix cartel when El Chapo escaped from the Puente Grande prison in January 2001 and the war between the two cartels resumed. Previously, between 1999 and 2001, a hit squad called the El Comando de la Muerte led by El Mayo's son, Vicente Zambada Niebla ("El Vicentillo"), assassinated several associates of the Arellano Félix cartel.[20] El Mayo was trying to take over Tijuana by creating as much mayhem as possible. On February 23, 2000, El Mayo's assassins ambushed and killed Tijuana's police chief Alfredo de la Torre Márquez as he drove along the Tijuana River canal.[21] In response to the murder, Mexican President Vicente Fox vowed to eradicate organized crime in Tijuana.[22]

On February 10, 2002, the police stopped Ramón Arellano Félix and several henchmen who were packed into his Volkswagen Beetle on their way to kill Sinaloa leader El Mayo during Mazatlán's Mardi Gras festival. The official story reported that the police stopped Ramón for driving the wrong way down a one-way street. As an officer approached the car, Ramón shot and killed him. Other officers returned fire and killed Ramón. An alternate version of the story claimed that police on the payroll of El Mayo hunted down and killed Ramón. Because Ramón carried papers that identified him as Jorge Pérez López, the police did not realize whom they had killed until Arellano Félix family members, identifying themselves as relatives, retrieved the body from the coroner.[23]

One month later, the PJFM tracked Benjamín Arellano Félix to a house in Puebla using cell phones found at the scene of Ramón's murder. Following a brief surveillance, the police raided the house and arrested Benjamín without a shot fired. Inside, they found an altar with candles lit in memory of Ramón and $100 bills scattered all over the floor. To all observers, the altar confirmed Ramón's death.[24] Rumors floated that El Chapo or El Mayo fed the police the information leading to Benjamín's capture.[25]

The death and capture of the two top leaders of the cartel sent the organization reeling. After the arrest of Benjamín, the PJFM arrested Tijuana's police chief, twenty Tijuana police officers, and twenty Baja state police officers on the cartel's payroll, crippling their trafficking operations.[26] Moreover, in February 2002, between the death of Ramón and the capture of Benjamín, Mexican police discovered an Arellano Félix tunnel that ran from a house in Tierra del Sol into the United States.[27] Despite these losses, the cartel was down but not out. Ramón and Benjamín's younger siblings—Javier, Eduardo, and Enedina—would step up to run the cartel.

Nicknamed "El Tigrillo," Francisco Javier became the cartel's new enforcer, although according to reporter Jesús Blancornelas, "Javier was not an important capo" but rather a "playboy . . . dedicated to partying." To defend Tijuana, he recruited formerly unknown narcojuniors into the cartel, naming these recruits the "New Generation." Although he failed to retake Mexicali, he maintained the Arellano Félixes' control over trafficking in Baja and Tijuana.[28] In the process of doing so, the New Generation drew too much public attention. A $5 million bounty was put on Francisco Javier's head. An informant's tip led to his arrest by the US Coast Guard on August 16, 2006, while he was fishing in international waters off Baja. Upon his arrest, Enedina and Eduardo assumed control over the cartel and reorganized its modus operandi by establishing new front companies to conduct massive smuggling operations. Demonstrating their sophistication and resiliency in the post-Ramón and Benjamín era was the January 2006 discovery of a 2,400-foot-long tunnel that extended from a warehouse near the Tijuana airport to a warehouse in the industrial zone of southern San Diego.[29]

184 *Narcostates*

Juárez Cartel:
The War for Ciudad Juárez

Pressure had been mounting on Juárez cartel leader Amado Carrillo Fuentes following the February 1997 arrest of two government officials on the cartel payroll. To increase his security, on July 3, 1997, Carrillo Fuentes, accompanied by two surgeons from Sinaloa and a third from Colombia, checked into Mexico City's Santa Monica Hospital under a false name to undergo plastic surgery that would radically alter his face. This was not his first facial operation. His willingness to undergo plastic surgery earned him another nickname—"the capo without a face." During the eight-and-a-half-hour operation, three surgeons performed liposuction to remove fourteen kilos of fat, changed the shape of his nose and eyes, broke his lower jaw, and inserted a prosthesis to alter his jaw line.[30] During the postoperation recovery, Carrillo Fuentes died of either a heart attack or respiratory failure; the surgeons were accused of murder and went into hiding.[31]

The Mexican government's launching of the Maxi-Proceso in 1998 further disrupted the Juárez cartel.[32] The Maxi-Proceso issued 110 arrest warrants, 65 of them for members of the Juárez cartel. It also ensnared some officials, such as Villanueva Madrid, governor of Quintana Roo. Mexican authorities accused him of being an accomplice to the Juárez cartel and charged him with cocaine trafficking and money laundering. Villanueva received a six-year sentence for money laundering, but during his imprisonment, the courts convicted him for conspiring to traffic cocaine and sentenced him to another thirty-six years.[33]

In 1997, after the death of his brother, Vicente Carrillo Fuentes won a power struggle to wrest control over the cartel.[34] After assuming power, he partnered with El Azul and formed an alliance with El Mayo and the Beltrán Leyvas. Not all members of the Juárez cartel were happy with him being the replacement for his brother, though. Distaste for Vicente's violent personality caused many Juárez lieutenants to leave. El Azul also defected to the Sinaloa cartel. The Milenio cartel, an independent cartel affiliated with the Juárez cartel, broke away and was later absorbed into the Sinaloa Federation after the arrest of its leader, Armando Valencia Cornelio, on August 16, 2003.[35] According to the State Department a "serious split existed within the Juárez cartel."[36]

Due to territorial disputes between Vicente and El Chapo, the Juárez cartel's participation in the federation did not last long. On September 11, 2004, armed commandos, some of them former policemen, assassinated Vicente's brother Rodolfo and his wife at a cinema complex. The PGR alleged that El Chapo was exacting revenge on Rodolfo for the assassination of several Sinaloa associates who had moved drugs through Juárez territory without Vicente's consent. Reprisals related to the slaying of Rodolfo accounted for eighteen deaths by the end of September. Current and former police officers played roles in many of the killings, either as targets or as triggermen. Two of the murders involved ex–Sinaloa state police officers on Vicente's payroll. Through 2004, cartel assassins killed eleven state and local police in Sinaloa.[37] The revenge killings did not stop with the police. On December 31, 2004, El Chapo's brother, Arturo Guzmán Loera ("El Pollo"), was assassinated on Vicente's orders. Arturo had represented El Chapo in the Sinaloa cartel while El Chapo was imprisoned. In September 2001, nine months after El Chapo's escape, Arturo was captured by the AFI. He was shot while using the Puente Grande prison phone booth.[38]

The assassinations set off a war between the two cartels that lasted until 2010. Because the Sinaloa cartel was preoccupied with the Gulf cartel in Nuevo Laredo, the war did not really heat up until 2006.[39] When the war did escalate, Ciudad Juárez became one of the deadliest cities in Mexico. To subdue the Juárez cartel, the Sinaloa cartel financed an enforcer gang known as the Nueva Gente, which was assisted by the Juárez street gang known as the Los Mexicles.[40] On the opposing side, the Juárez cartel employed its La Linea paramilitary wing, primarily composed of Chihuahua state police officers, and the Los Aztecas street gang. The Mexicles and the Aztecas were long-standing rival Texas prison gangs whose feud spilled over into Juárez.[41] By 2010, the violence in Ciudad Juárez peaked with an average of ten homicides per day.[42] The 2011 arrest of La Linea leader Antonio Acosta Hernández ("El Diego") was a severe blow to the Juárez cartel; he had allegedly ordered more than 1,500 murders, including an employee from the US consulate in Juárez.[43] Although Vicente Carrillo Fuentes remained in control of the Juárez cartel until his capture in 2014, the time of the Juárez cartel had passed. Its fortunes had shifted in favor of the Sinaloa cartel.

Gulf Cartel

Pressure from Mexican authorities also took its toll on the Gulf cartel. Juan García Ábrego lost much of his protection in January 1990, when a bribe of $10 million failed to reach Coello Trejo, the head of the PJFM.[44] Mexican authorities jailed eighteen members of the cartel for firearms, cocaine, and marijuana possession. In October 1990, when Coello Trejo was dismissed from the PJFM for human rights violations, García Ábrego lost his best inside man. Between 1993 and 1995, police arrested more than thirty cartel members. Mexican officials also seized Ábrego's ranches and other property in Matamoros. In 1994, García Ábrego looked for a way out. He realized that his protection within the Salinas administration no longer existed. He attempted to negotiate with the Mexican government for his surrender,

186   Narcostates

because he feared that he would be assassinated in a maximum-security prison by supporters of Carlos Salinas, then president of Mexico, and Salinas's brother Raúl. As part of the negotiations with the Mexican government, he wanted to choose the prison where he would be incarcerated. In exchange, he promised to conceal any ties between the Gulf cartel and the Salinas administration. Rumors of other deals circulated, but if there was a pact, the Mexican government did not uphold it. On March 9, 1995, the US government put García Ábrego on the top ten most wanted list.[45] Ten months later, Mexican authorities arrested him in his driveway without a shot fired. No bodyguards were present. Upon his capture, the police injected him with a large dose of valium, transported him to Mexico City, and extradited him to Houston because he was a US citizen. In January 1997, Ábrego received eleven life sentences and a fine of $128 million.[46] That same year García Ábrego's brother Humberto escaped from jail and attempted to take over the cartel, but his bid for leadership was rejected.[47] Cartel infighting soon began.

Osiel Cárdenas Guillén ("El Loco") took control of the cartel in July 1999 after ordering Guzmán Decena ("Z-1"), the future founder of Los Zetas, to assassinate Salvador Gómez Herrera ("El Chava")—his rival within the cartel. The assassination won Osiel the nickname "El Mata Amigos" or "friend-killer."[48] In 2001, the Gulf cartel split into two factions. Territorial control was fiercely contested. Osiel directed his faction, which controlled Matamoros, Reynosa, and Ciudad Miguel Alemán, to take over Nuevo León and Nuevo Laredo, which were under the control of Baudelio López Falcón ("El Yeyo"). To put an end to the infighting, Osiel had El Yeyo murdered, but by this point, the Gulf cartel's factionalism had opened the door for the Sinaloa Federation to move in on Nuevo León and Nuevo Laredo.[49]

To defend the Gulf cartel's territory, Osiel hired former members of the Mexican army's Grupos Aeromómoviles de Fuerzas Especiales (GAFES) as assassins. The GAFES were an elite group trained in intelligence collection, counterinsurgency, and counternarcotics. They called themselves Los Zetas. Members came from the lower ranks of the GAFES, from lieutenant down. The Gulf cartel first employed Los Zetas to fight against Los Chachos—members of the MS-13 that became affiliated with the Beltrán Leyva cartel and later the Sinaloa Federation. The reduction of Los Chachos gave Osiel control over Nuevo Laredo, but the Sinaloa Federation, now unified by El Azul and El Chapo, responded by forming their own paramilitary unit called Los Negros under the command of La Barbie. The standoff in Nuevo Laredo initiated a bloody war between the Gulf cartel and the Sinaloa Federation.[50]

While Osiel was consolidating his control over the Gulf cartel, the government net closed in on him. From July 2000 through September 2001, the DEA seized more than 2,000 kilos of Gulf cartel cocaine. The June 2001 confiscation of the cartel's drug ledgers in Atlanta revealed that it generated more than $41 million in drug proceeds over a three-and-a-half-month period in the Atlanta area alone.[51] As part of the 1999 US Foreign Narcotics Kingpin Designation Act, the US Treasury Department designated Osiel as a kingpin in June 2001.[52] The arrests of Osiel's personal pilot in 2001 and a top Gulf cartel lieutenant in 2002 provided enough intelligence to capture Osiel. In March 2003, during a morning raid, heavily armed soldiers surrounded his home in Matamoros. When the Mexican government rushed the house, Osiel's hired guns opened fire with automatic weapons, wounding three soldiers, two of whom received critical wounds.[53]

From La Palma prison, Osiel ran the Gulf cartel until his extradition to the United States in 2008.[54] Like Pablo Escobar, he tried to maintain his popular appeal with the poor even after his arrest. On Children's Day in April 2004, Osiel sent truckloads of bicycles, dolls, and other toys to the children of Nuevo Laredo. Mexican authorities considered his toy distribution a ploy to build sympathy among the Mexican people while the charges against him were being made.[55] Despite Osiel's long reach from La Palma, the Gulf cartel lacked leadership on the outside.[56] Osiel's brother Ezequiel Antonio ("Tony Tormenta") became the surrogate cartel leader in 2003, but he proved too incompetent to run the cartel.[57] His mental state was described as "a few bricks short of a load."[58] His addiction to drugs, women, and gambling weakened his authority. His weaknesses and Osiel's incarceration fomented dissent within the cartel and encouraged rivals to dispute Gulf cartel territory.[59]

Over the Barrel of a Gun

In these first years of the new millennium, competition for territory and control of trafficking corridors escalated, heightening the pressure on cartel leaders and creating openings for upstart DTOs. The Gulf cartel and the Sinaloa Federation vied for new territory, while the Arellano Félix cartel fought to retain control over its territory. Mexican states along the US border, such as Baja, Sonora, Chihuahua, Coahuila, Nuevo León, and Tamaulipas, and states that bordered Sinaloa, such as Durango, became extremely important for the cartels. According to the State Department, Durango became a "free fire area where the Sinaloa cartel, the Gulf cartel, and the Juárez cartel competed for highways leading to the U.S. border." Gangs operating in groups of up to sixty men, equipped with automatic weapons and fragmentation grenades, were able to overrun police stations, burn police vehicles, and threaten officers with impunity.[60] In Tijuana, violent shootouts, the mutilation of bodies, *pozoles* (putting people in acid and cooking them in barrels), kidnappings, and the use of psychological tactics such as *narcomantas* (narcobanners) were common.[61] In disputed cities, such as Nuevo Laredo, the cartels increasingly targeted Mexican law

188 *Narcostates*

enforcement officers because they were thoroughly corrupted. According to one source, "Hand in hand with the growing presence of the cartels was the rampant corruption at all levels of the police forces—state, local, and federal."[62] In the struggle for Tijuana, the cartels brazenly attacked military personnel during daylight hours.[63] Since many law enforcement officers were de facto cartel members, the adversarial cartels had little reason to back down when confronted by anyone, including law enforcement.

Los Zetas

A group of thirty-one former lieutenants and lower-ranked soldiers who deserted from the Mexican Army's GAFES joined the Gulf cartel in the late 1990s and created Los Zetas.[64] Trained by the CIA and the Israeli Mossad, the GAFES were initially utilized to provide security for the 1986 World Cup soccer tournament in Mexico. In 1994, they were deployed to Chiapas to help quell the Zapatista rebellion.[65] In 1999, they deserted the army to become "a private army" for Osiel, providing three to five layers of security around him.[66] Beyond that, they also collected debts, protected trafficking routes, kept subordinates in line, and executed opponents for Osiel.[67]

Despite several early assassinations and arrests, such as Arturo Guzmán Decena ("Z-1") in 2002, the Los Zetas survived because they were organized along a more horizontal, decentralized operational structure. The Los Zetas cartel evolved into a three-level hierarchy with the original members, referred to as Zetas Viejos (Old Zetas), brought in by Osiel. These older, better-trained military men each controlled their own plaza of distribution and participated in the overall command of the organization. They directed the second-generation members known as Zetas Nuevos (New Zetas). Made up of Mexican military deserters, former policemen, and family members, the Zetas Nuevos were regional lieutenants who replaced deceased or captured Zetas Viejos. They later included members of the Guatemalan Special Forces, known as Los Kaibiles. Only individuals with a military background attained the rank of Zeta Nuevo. Los Cobras were a third tier that provided security for drug shipments and the Zetas Nuevos. They were commanded by the Cobras Viejos (Old Cobras) who were men of confidence but did not have military training.[68] The lowest tier was known as Los Halcones (Falcons). These members were recruits and apprentices who moved up the ladder according to their skills. They were local civilian followers of the cartel who provided "street" intelligence.[69]

Los Zetas employed extreme measures of violence and attracted much public attention because of it. They combined massive firepower with expertise in infantry tactics and other military techniques, including the use of shoulder-fired missiles, armor-piercing ammunition, fragmen-

Mexico's Cartel Wars   189

tation grenades, heavy machine guns, and improvised explosive devices. Their techniques created a public perception that they were insurgents and a threat to the Mexican state.[70] In carrying out their responsibilities, they were known for their extreme brutality, often committed on behalf of Santa Muerte. They not only beheaded their enemies, but they also used "necklacing" to kill their enemies. Necklacing occurs when a tire is filled with gasoline and placed around a victim's neck and set ablaze.[71] Los Zetas also committed high-profile murders. In September 2010, they killed a US citizen named David Hartley, and in February 2011, they attacked two US Immigration and Customs Enforcement (ICE) agents, leaving one dead. They soon became enemy number one in Mexico and the United States.[72]

After Osiel was extradited to the United States in 2007, the Gulf cartel and Los Zetas agreed that both cartels could work on the same routes independently, defend the territory as if they were a single organization, and maintain their own separate leadership.[73] However, by 2009, the agreement no longer existed. The Gulf cartel began to view Los Zetas as a strategic and territorial rival. Los Zetas had become a full-fledged drug trafficking organization; their membership had grown from 1,000 to 3,000 members.[74] Their area of influence spread from Tamaulipas into plazas belonging to the Gulf cartel, such as Nuevo León and Coahuila. By 2010, Los Zetas had developed a presence in twelve Mexican states.[75]

La Familia Michoacana:
Los Zetas's Sanguine Adversaries

La Familia Michoacana cartel initially emerged as part of the alliance between Los Zetas and the Gulf cartel. La Familia started out as a vigilante group known as La Empresa that persecuted drug traffickers in Michoacán. It established ties with Osiel in the late 1990s and took over the drug trade in Michoacán on his behalf.[76] Around 2003, La Familia became the primary manufacturer and exporter of methamphetamine to the United States.[77] By 2010, they were moving into other areas of crime, including pirating DVDs, kidnapping, human trafficking, and extorting local businesses.

La Familia combined an odd, paradoxical mixture of spirituality and criminality. Torture, murder, extortion, and drug trafficking were common practices. Juxtaposed against their criminal behavior was a bible titled *Pensamientos* written by their founder, Nazario Moreno González ("El Chayo"). As part of their spiritual code, they adopted strict rules of behavior, espoused religious messages, and promoted social welfare. They were also the first cartel to fully embrace Santa Muerte. Cartel members referred to the marijuana and cocaine markets as "God's gifts," because they provided revenue to carry out their social welfare programs in

190   Narcostates

Michoacán.[78] They extorted "taxes" from businesses, paid for community projects, controlled petty crime, and settled local disputes.[79] The cartel also provided assistance to abused women and youth centers which focused on drug use prevention.[80]

La Familia provided a substitute means of employment for those willing to follow its moral code. To the delinquents and the unemployed, La Familia promised, "Enter a rehabilitation center, clean up your life, and we will provide meaningful opportunities." After a person shed his addiction and completed a two-month quasi-monastic program based on vows of silence, Bible study, and La Familia indoctrination, he became eligible for employment and integration into the cartel and its smuggling operations.[81]

From 2003 to 2006, La Familia and Los Zetas participated in a short-lived alliance that turned into war. In 2004, the two cartels developed a plan to free Osiel from prison. However, that plan never came to fruition despite a successful rehearsal attempt at the Michoacán state prison, which freed twenty-five prisoners.[82] As Osiel's power waned, Tony Tormenta's defective leadership caused La Familia to break away from the Gulf cartel in 2006. From Michoacán, they spread into the adjoining states of Guanajuato, Guerrero, and Colima.[83] As Los Zetas began to flex their muscles and assert their independence from the Gulf cartel, they confronted La Familia in Michoacán and Guerrero. In 2006, a series of violent murders and beheadings occurred as these two upstart DTOs fought for control over Michoacán and the port of Lázaro Cárdenas.[84] In September of that same year, La Familia gained notoriety when gunmen barged into a nightclub in Uruapan, Michoacán, shooting their guns and forcing all of the patrons to lie on the floor. They dumped five human heads belonging to members of Los Zetas on the dance floor and placed a calling card on each that read, "La Familia doesn't kill for money, kill women, or kill innocents. Only those who deserve to die will die. Let everyone know that this is divine justice." The rumor was that the slain men had raped a waitress/prostitute who refused to have sex with them. According to the coroner, the assassins used a Bowie knife to sever their heads while they were still alive.[85]

In opposition to Los Zetas, La Familia put aside its territorial disputes and entered into an alliance with the Sinaloa and Gulf cartels called Cárteles Unidos. La Familia agreed to coexist with the Sinaloa cartel in Guerrero and reached an accord with El Azul in Guanajuato to block Los Zetas intrusions. In exchange for knowledge on how to run methamphetamine labs, El Chapo went so far as to allow La Familia to bring cocaine from Guatemala into Michoacán using Sinaloa routes. By 2009, La Familia soldiers were joining the fight against Los Zetas in Tamaulipas and Nuevo León alongside the Sinaloa and Gulf cartels.[86]

Anyone who presented a challenge to La Familia was dealt with harshly, including Mexican authorities. In 2009, the cartel launched a deadly campaign against law enforcement that was unprecedented in scope. Precipitating this campaign was the July 2009 arrest of the cartel's coordinator for drug smuggling operations by the Policía Federal (PF).[87] Within an hour of the arrest, La Familia attacked federal police headquarters in Michoacán with grenades and automatic weapons but failed to obtain his release. Cartel operatives then kidnapped, tortured, and beheaded twelve police officers and left them along the main highway of Michoacán with a banner that read, "Come for us again. We are waiting for you."[88] By the end of 2009, the cartel war in Michoacán was reaching new heights. Human rights organizations denounced the military's response, including collateral killings, arbitrary detention, rape, and robbery, alleging that the federal forces spent more time pursuing La Familia than Los Zetas.[89]

Los Caballeros Templarios:
The Chivalrous Cartel

In 2011, an offshoot of La Familia formed, calling themselves Los Caballeros Templarios. The death of La Familia leader Nazario Moreno González in a shootout with the Mexican Federal Police on December 10, 2010, and the arrest of his successor seven months later led to desertions from La Familia. La Familia spokesman, Servando Gómez Martínez ("La Tuta"), spearheaded the defection, taking cartel members and drug routes with him. Like La Familia, the Knights Templar cartel claimed to have a code of conduct and published a twenty-two-page booklet outlining its ethical code, which emulated La Familia's commitment to "social justice."[90] La Tuta portrayed himself as a man of the people, allowing himself to be photographed sitting in front of a statue of a knight, a sword, a Mexican flag, and framed pictures of Che Guevara and Pancho Villa. Knights Templar recruits were initiated wearing the costumes of medieval warriors, complete with plastic helmets and swords.[91] According to other sources, they forced their initiates to eat children's hearts to prove their loyalty.[92] The cartel developed a local support base, especially among those who opposed federal forces accused of disappearing innocent bystanders. The cartel also administered justice in disputes ranging from disagreements over boundary fences, unpaid debts, to spousal abuse.[93]

The Knights Templar muscled La Familia out of some of its territory in the states of Michoacán, Mexico, Morelos, and Guerrero. With bullet-ridden bodies strewn throughout Michoacán, people fled their villages. Both cartels confiscated land as battles for turf escalated in 2011.[94] The port of Lázaro Cárdenas became a locus for the cartels, because it functioned as a gateway for Colombian cocaine and for Asian chemicals used in the production of methamphetamine.[95] To fatten their coffers, the Knights Templar resorted to kidnapping, large-scale extortion, and intimidation.[96]

192   *Narcostates*

Taking advantage of the divisions, Los Zetas made their move to seize control over Michoacán in 2011. To counter Los Zetas, the Knights Templar joined the Sinaloa and Gulf cartels in the aforementioned alliance known as Cárteles Unidos, to which La Familia also belonged.[97] At a high cost in human lives, they pushed Los Zetas back into Aguascalientes and Jalisco, but once they did so, the alliance fell apart.[98]

Cártel de Jalisco Nueva Generación:
The Upstarts

Although Los Zetas remained powerful into the first decade of the century, internal conflicts among its leadership enabled imitation gangs to challenge its power. One gang of traffickers that rivaled Los Zetas was the Cártel de Jalisco Nueva Generación (CJNG), founded in 2009 by Rubén Oseguera Cervantes ("El Mencho"). El Mencho had been a member of the Milenio cartel—a Juárez cartel offshoot that was absorbed by the Sinaloa Federation in 2003.[99] In 2010, the Milenio cartel fractured after the death of their leader, Ignacio Coronel Villarreal, a close associate of Carrillo Fuentes. After his death, the Milenio cartel broke into two by joining either La Resistencia led by Ramiro Pozos González ("El Molca"), or Los Torcidos led by El Mencho. Once established, El Mencho reformed the Los Torcidos into the CJNG and took over Jalisco.[100] The CJNG initially specialized in methamphetamine and the importation of precursor chemicals from China and India into the state of Jalisco, where Puerto Vallarta and Guadalajara are located. As the CJNG grew, they expanded into the heroin and cocaine trade.[101]

In 2011, the CJNG entered the war for control over Jalisco, Michoacán, and Veracruz, challenging both the Knights Templar and Los Zetas. For pragmatic reasons, the CJNG allied itself with the Sinaloa cartel to confront Los Zetas, forming a death squad known as Los Matazetas (the Zeta Killers). In March 2012, Los Matazetas uploaded a video on the *Blog del Narco* declaring that they planned to "clean up the states of Guerrero and Michoacán."[102] In September 2014, during rush hour, they dumped the bodies of thirty-five Los Zetas members into the streets of Veracruz.[103] Vigilante self-defense groups suspected of being connected to the CJNG started appearing on the streets of Veracruz city.[104]

Fighting between the CJNG and the Knights Templar escalated following a 2012 public communiqué that declared the CJNG planned to start a turf war "against the Knights Templar cartel," who were "abusing innocent people" by conducting "kidnappings, extortion, protection racketeering, property theft, and rape."[105] To counter the CJNG, the Sinaloa cartel formed a paramilitary force called La Corona to challenge the CJNG's control over Jalisco. Up until this point, the Sinaloa cartel did not contest Jalisco because the CJNG and the Sinaloa cartels mutually opposed Los

Zetas. The Sinaloa cartel's support for La Corona and the kidnapping and release of El Chapo's two sons by the CJNG in 2016 signaled that any alliance between the CJNG and the Sinaloa cartel was over. In its war with the Sinaloa cartel, the CJNG became the most powerful cartel in Jalisco and Michoacán.[106]

Shifting Alliances and Cartel Wars, 2007–2014

A major shift in Mexico's cartel alliances occurred between 2007 and 2009. The Sinaloa Federation led by El Chapo, El Mayo, and El Azul attempted to consolidate its control over Mexico's most important plazas of distribution. In 2006, the Sinaloa cartel reignited its conflict with the Juárez cartel. In 2008, it turned on the Beltrán Leyva cartel because the Beltrán Leyvas (especially La Barbie) were drawing too much attention from the authorities. When Alfredo Beltrán Leyva ("El Mochomo") was arrested by the federal police, the Beltrán Leyva bosses blamed El Chapo for orchestrating his arrest. In retaliation, the Beltrán Leyvas were accused of killing El Chapo's son, Édgar Guzmán López, though other reports claimed that Édgar was killed accidentally by El Chapo's own men, who thought they were firing on Arturo Beltrán Leyva's car.[107] Concurrent with the Sinaloa–Beltrán Leyva rupture, Los Zetas broke with the Gulf cartel after Osiel's extradition to the United States.[108] Archrival enemies became allies. The Zetas and the Beltrán Leyvas allied, while the Sinaloa Federation banded together with the Gulf cartel. The shifting alliances also impelled El Chapo to move on Tijuana again. The 2008 arrest of Eduardo Arellano Félix created a power struggle within the cartel, which El Chapo saw as an opportunity to seize Tijuana.[109] Crime and murder in Tijuana spiked, but the Arellano Félixes persevered once again, with Enedina's son, Luis Sánchez Arellano ("El Ingeniero") taking over the cartel.

With the resurgence of cartel warfare, Mexico's third-generation cartels arose. As Los Zetas attempted to take away plazas from the Gulf cartel, La Familia allied itself with the Sinaloa and Gulf cartels to oppose Los Zetas's expansion into Michoacán. During the fight for Central Mexico, the La Familia cartel fractured and gave birth to the Knights Templar, which displaced La Familia in Michoacán. Despite this rupture, the Knights Templar retained the alliance with the Sinaloa cartel against Los Zetas. In Jalisco, the CJNG was formed as part of the resistance to Los Zetas, but by 2012 it was at odds with the Knights Templar and the Sinaloa cartel—its former allies—as the CJNG expanded beyond the borders of Jalisco. Within Los Zetas, violent internal squabbles broke out following the death of Heriberto Lazcano Lazcano ("El Lazca" or "Z-3"), who led the cartel from 2008 to 2012. His successor, Miguel Ángel Treviño Morales ("El 40"), was not an

194   Narcostates

original Zeta and had earned the nickname "El Judas" for allegedly betraying several high-ranking members of Los Zetas, including El Lazca.[110] The arrest and killing of a large portion of Los Zetas's leadership between 2013 and 2015 made it appear as though they were defeated, but this was wishful thinking. Throughout Mexico and Central America, Los Zetas vied for power wherever they could.

The February 2014 arrest of El Chapo by the Mexican navy marked a temporary end to the new millennium cartel wars. It also registered a major victory for the Mexican government, but it did not halt the Sinaloa cartel's operations. Allegations existed that El Mayo, El Chapo's closest partner, had betrayed him. El Mayo allegedly asked El Chapo to step down as head of the Sinaloa cartel to reduce the Mexican government's pressure on the Sinaloa cartel and to let a new generation of leaders take over.[111] For the Sinaloa cartel, El Chapo's arrest was important, but his notoriety had become a liability. El Mayo's son waited in the wings and was already directing the Sinaloa cartel along with his father, El Azul, and El Chapo's sons.[112] The indictment of sixty Sinaloa cartel members in January 2015 by US federal authorities showed that the Sinaloa cartel continued to function without El Chapo in charge.[113]

The shifting alliances and intercartel contests spread fear throughout many of Mexico's cities and villages as the cartels fought three wars: against the government, against other cartels, and within their own organizations. The dynamics of the war on drugs brought a new level of meaning to the adage that politics makes strange bedfellows. Mexican President Felipe Calderón stressed that the escalating violence in Mexico was due to the multiplicity of conflicts. It was no longer "Gulf versus Sinaloa" but rather "Beltrán versus Sinaloa, Sinaloa versus Juárez, Gulf versus Los Zetas, La Familia versus Los Zetas, Beltrán versus La Familia."[114] The shifting alliances, combined with the Mexican government's aggressive counternarcotics operations, led to increased costs for trafficking organizations and unprecedented levels of criminal violence.[115] To escape Mexican pressure, the cartels moved deeper into Central America where it was easier for them to operate. But before looking at how Central America became a focal point in the war on drugs, the effect of US-Mexican counternarcotics efforts against the cartels must be considered.

Notes

1. John Lee Brook, *Blood and Death: The Secret History of Santa Muerte* (London: Headpress Books, 2016), 25.

2. Humberto Padgett, "En La Cabeza de Juan José Esparragoza, 'El Azul,'" *SinEmbargo*, March 9, 2013, www.sinembargo.mx; "Los secretos de El Azul," *Proceso* (Mexico), March 18, 2014, reprint *Borderland Beat*, www.borderlandbeat .com; "The Mystery of El Azul Deepens," *Borderland Beat*, June 30, 2014,

www.borderlandbeat.com. El Azul was incarcerated from 1986 to 1993. He was transferred from Reclusorio Sur to Almoloya de Juárez in 1992.

3. "El Azul, un narco con cuatro décadas en el negocio," Infomador.com.mx, September 9, 2013, www.informador.com. El Azul learned the trafficking business from Juan Quintero Payán and Pedro Avilés Pérez.

4. Christopher Woody, "Mexico Caught the Cartel Boss Who Reportedly Almost Took Out 'El Chapo' Guzmán's Mother and Sons," *Business Insider*, December 13, 2016, www.businessinsider.com; Laura Islas "El Azul, el narco más discreto," *El Unión*, January 18, 2018; "Juan José Esparragoza Moreno, alias El Azul," InSight Crime, March 10, 2017, www.insightcrime.org. El Azul was the godfather to Amado Carrillo Fuentes's son and Ismael Zambada's sons. El Azul married El Chapo's sister-in-law, who was related to Ignacio Coronel Villareal ("El Rey de Cristal"), a member of the Juárez cartel. El Chapo married Emma Coronel, the niece of Coronel Villareal. El Azul's oldest son, Juan José Esparragoza Monzón ("El Negro"), married into the Beltrán Leyvas. Alfredo Beltrán Leyva ("El Mochomo") married El Chapo's niece Patricia Nunez Guzmán, while Laura Beltrán Leyva married El Chapo's brother Arturo.

5. Alberto Nájar, "La guerra del narco por dentro," *Journada* (Mexico), July 10, 2005, www.jornada.com.mx; Kevin Sullivan, "Mexicans Question Escape of Drug Lord; Fox Vows Action on Crime, Prisons," *Washington Post*, January 25, 2001, sec. A, p. 16.

6. James F. Smith, "Mexico Arrests Alleged Cartel Kingpin," *Los Angeles Times*, October 31, 1999, http://articles.latimes.com; American Embassy Mexico to Secretary of State Washington, DC, "Subject: Mexico: Continuing Counter Drug Challenges," Mexico 007087 142304Z, September 2004, 8; Colleen W. Cook, *Mexico's Drug Cartels*, Report R-L32724 (Washington, DC: Congressional Research Service, February 25, 2008), 8. The Maxi-Proceso was based on the Italian government's plan to break up the mafia. It brought long prison sentences, but the appeals process allowed traffickers to avoid extradition to the United States, thus preventing it from becoming a combustible issue as it had been in Colombia.

7. Héctor de Mauleón, "La ruta de sangre de Beltrán Leyva," *Nexos*, February 1, 2010, www.nexos.com.mx.

8. Steven Dudley, "How the Beltrán Leyva Sinaloa Cartel Feud Bloodied Mexico," InSight Crime, February 2, 2011, https://insightcrime.org.

9. José Reveles, *El Cártel Incómodo: El Fin de los Beltrán Leyva y la Hegemonía del Chapo Guzmán* (Mexico City: Random House Mondadori, 2010), 32–40.

10. Otis B. Fly Wheel, "Arturo Beltrán Leyva: The Life and Death of El Barbas Part I," *Borderland Beat*, March 31, 2016, www.borderlandbeat.com. The Los Chachos were run by José Dionisio García Sánchez ("El Chacho").

11. Nájar, "La guerra del narco."

12. Brook, *Blood and Death*, 74–75.

13. Ibid.; James C. McKinley Jr. and Elisabeth Malkin, "U.S. Student Became Mexican Drug Kingpin," *New York Times*, September 8, 2010, www.nytimes.com.

14. Anabel Hernández, "Una historia de corrupción y fracaso," *Por Esto*, August 15, 2014, www.poresto.net; "Sandra Ávila Beltrán: la Reina del Pacífico," lanacion.com (Argentina), September 14, 2008, www.lanacion.com.ar.

15. Tijuano, "The War for Tijuana: Part I," *Borderland Beat*, May 22, 2013, www.borderlandbeat.com. Ibarra Santes was seen as an uncorrupted man, but he went after the Arellano Félixes because, in reality, he had been bought off by El Mayo and Amado Carrillo Fuentes.

16. Tracey Eaton and Alfredo Corchado, "Mexico Intensifies Hunt for Escaped Drug Lord as Turf War Rages," *Dallas Morning News*, April 15, 2005.

196   *Narcostates*

17. Julian Borger and Jo Tuckman, "Blood Brothers," *Guardian*, March 14, 2002, www.theguardian.com.

18. Mark Fineman and Chris Kraul, "Deadly Messages to Mexico," *Los Angeles Times*, May 15, 2000, http://articles.latimes.com. His two aides were Óscar Pompa Plaza and Captain Rafael Torres Bernal.

19. "Arellano Félix Tijuana Cartel: A Family Affair," *Frontline*, www.pbs.org /wgbh/pages/frontline/shows/drugs/business/afo/afosummary.html.

20. Tijuano, "The War for Tijuana: Part 2," *Borderland Beat*, May 31, 2013, www.borderlandbeat.com. Other notable victims included Joaquín Báez Lugo, an attorney for the cartel; Jesús Araiza Sánchez,a smuggler for the cartel; and Pedro Vázquez,a police agent working for the cartel.

21. Ken Ellingwood and Tony Perry, "Tijuana Police Chief Slain in a Hail of Fire," *Los Angeles Times*, February 28, 2000, http://articles.latimes.com.

22. Tijuano, "The War for Tijuana: Part 2."

23. Kevin Sullivan, "Mexico Investigates Reported Killing of Drug Lord," *Washington Post*, February 23, 2002, sec. A, p. 15. Also killed with Ramón was Efrain Quintero.

24. Tim Weiner, "Mexican Drug Lord's Arrest Helps Fox as He Awaits Bush," *New York Times*, March 11, 2002, sec. A, p. 3; African Blog, "Tijuana Cartel," *African Narco News*, January 3, 2013, http://african-business.blogspot.com/2013/01 /tijuana-cartel.html#!/2013/01/tijuana-cartel.html.

25. Tim Weiner, "New Web of Trust Topples a Mighty Mexican Cartel," *New York Times*, April 26, 2002, sec. A, p. 3.

26. Tim Weiner, "Mexico Holds 41, Including Tijuana Police Chief, in Crackdown," *New York Times*, April 12, 2002, sec. A, p. 5.

27. Jo Tuckman, "Police Chief and 40 Officers Held in Mexican Drug Sting," *Guardian*, April 12, 2002, Foreign sec., p. 12.

28. Tijuano, "The War for Tijuana—a 20+ Year Conflict Part III," *Borderland Beat*, August 15, 2013, www.borderlandbeat.com; Jennifer Stienhauer and James C. McKinley Jr., "US Officials Arrest Suspect in Top Mexican Drug Gang," *New York Times*, August 17, 2006, sec. A, p. 21. He also recruited his brother-in-law, Jorge Briseño López ("El Cholo"). One of the "unknown" narcojuniors was Saúl Montés de Oca Morlett ("El Ciego"), who worked for the Baja Policia Estatal Preventiva and provided the Arellano Félixes with intelligence while running a cocaine and kidnapping ring for the cartel.

29. Samuel Logan, "Toppling the Tijuana Cartel Dynasty," International Relations and Security Network, April 9, 2006, www.samuellogan.com/articles /toppling-the-tijuana-cartel-dynasty.html.

30. Phil Gunson, "End of the Line," *Guardian*, July 17, 1997, sec. T, p. 2.

31. Douglas Farah and Molly Moore, "Doctor in Drug Lord's Operation Sheltered in the U.S.," *Washington Post*, April 11, 1998, sec. A, p. 10. The corpses of two surgeons, Dr. Jaime Godoy Singh and Dr. Ricardo Reyes Rincón, were found in concrete-filled barrels beside a Mexico City highway. The third surgeon, Carlos Ávila Meljem, fled to the United States and continued his practice in Beverly Hills.

32. James F. Smith, "Mexico Arrests Alleged Cartel Kingpin," *Los Angeles Times*, October 31, 1999, http://articles.latimes.com.

33. American Embassy Mexico to Secretary of State Washington, DC, "Subject: Mexico: Continuing Counter Drug Challenges," Mexico 007087 142304Z, September 2004, 8.

34. Sam Dillon, "Mexico Drug Trafficker Slain, Major Figure Near U.S. Border," *New York Times*, September 12, 1998, www.nytimes.com. He defeated

Rafael Muñoz Talavera, a former Juárez cartel member who defected to the Tijuana cartel in an attempt to take over the Juárez cartel.

35. Buggs, "Los Zetas Forging an Alliance with La Resistencia in Jalisco," *Borderland Beat*, September 21, 2011, www.borderlandbeat.com. Since the 1970s, the Milenio cartel existed as an independent gang based in Michoacán. They dealt directly with the Medellín cartel but were affiliated with the Juárez cartel.

36. American Embassy Mexico to Secretary of State Washington, DC, "Subject: Mexico Narco Violence Going Strong," Mexico 008345 271958Z, October 2004, 1.

37. American Embassy Mexico, "Subject: Mexico Narco Violence," 2. The assassins finished off Rodolfo execution-style. Two former Sinaloa state police officers acting as Rodolfo's bodyguards were also shot dead.

38. "El Año Nuevo más triste para el Chapo: Un asesinato, una pérdida y una traición," *Infobae* (Mexico), August 6, 2020, www.infobae.com.

39. Buggs, "Juárez Cartel," *Borderland Beat*, May 15, 2009, www.borderlandbeat .com.

40. Alejandro Domínguez, "De cómo El Chapo controló Juárez," *Milenio* (Mexico), February 26, 2014, www.milenio.com. José Torres Marrufo ("El Jaguar") led the Nueva Gente.

41. "The Ultimate Prison Gang Guide: Partido Revolucionario Mexicano (PRM) aka Mexicles," PrisonOffenders.com, www.prisonoffenders.com/prm_gang.html; "The Ultimate Prison Gang Guide: Barrio Azteca," PrisonOffenders.com, www .prisonoffenders.com/barrio_azteca.html.

42. American Embassy Mexico to Secretary of State Washington, DC, "Subject: Mexico's Bloodiest Days," Mexico 000333 161736Z, June 2010, 3.

43. Gari, "José Antonio Acosta Hernández, Also Known as 'El Diego,' Is Presented to the Media," *Borderland Beat*, July 31, 2011, www.borderlandbeat.com.

44. Marjorie Miller, "Mexico's Tough Drug Czar Loses His Job," *Los Angeles Times*, October 16, 1990, www.latimes.com. Coello Trejo was removed as the head of the PJFM in October 1990 for committing human rights violations.

45. Yolanda Figueroa, *El Capo del Golfo: Vida y Captura de Juan García Ábrego* (Mexico City: Editorial Grijalbo, 1996), 273–274. Óscar Malherbe de León (aka Martín Becerra Mireles) assumed control of the cartel until his arrest in 1997. Humberto García Ábrego had been arrested on October 24, 1994.

46. Mark Fineman and Lianne Hart, "Drug Lord Sentenced to 11 Life Terms, Fined $128 Million," *Los Angeles Times*, February 1, 1997.

47. Helen Thorpe, "Anatomy of a Drug Cartel," *Texas Monthly*, January 1998, www.texasmonthly.com.

48. Buggs, "Gulf Cartel."

49. Jorge Fernández Menéndez, "El narcotraficante, el gobernador, la foto," *Milenio* (Mexico), May 8, 2013, http://fredalvarez.blogspot.com/2009/12/edelio -López-falcon-el-yeyo.html; Ramon J. Miro, *Organized Crime and Terrorist Activity in Mexico, 1999–2002* (Washington, DC: Federal Research Division, Library of Congress, February 2003), 18.

50. Luis Astorga, *El Siglo de las Drogas*, 2nd ed. (Mexico City: Random House, 2016), 211–212; Brook, *Blood and Death*, 78.

51. Federal Bureau of Investigation, "Osiel Cárdenas-Guillén, Former Head of the Gulf Cartel, Sentenced to 25 Years' Imprisonment," US Attorney's Office, Southern District of Texas, February 24, 2010, www.fbi.gov/houston/press-releases /2010/ho022410b.htm.

52. Office of Foreign Assets Control, "Designations Pursuant to the Foreign Narcotics Kingpin Designation Act" (Washington, DC: US Department of the Treasury,

198   *Narcostates*

June 1, 2001), www.treasury.gov/resource-center/sanctions/OFAC-Enforcement/Pages /20010601.aspx.

53. Ken Sullivan, "Mexico Seizes Reputed Drug Lord: Arrest Is Latest Blow Against Traffickers by President Fox," *Washington Post*, March 15, 2003, sec. A, p. 20. Alejandro Morales Betancourt ("Z-2") was Osiel's pilot. Adán Medrano Rodríguez ("El Licenciado") was the Gulf cartel lieutenant arrested in 2002.

54. Ricardo Ravelo, *Osiel: Vida y Tragedia de un Capo* (Mexico City: Grijalbo, 2009), 232–233.

55. Kevin Sullivan and Mary Jordan, "The Gifts of a Mexican Drug Lord; Jailed Kingpin Courts the Poor with Alms for Children," *Washington Post*, June 10, 2004, sec. A, p. 1.

56. American Consul Monterrey to Secretary of State Washington, DC, "Subject: Gulf Cartel Drug Violence Returns to Matamoros," Monterrey 001856 1181145Z, December 2003, 1.

57. Aurora Vega, "Another Cardenas Gullien Inherits the Gulf Cartel," *Excelsior* (Mexico), November 7, 2011. www.borderlandbeat.com.

58. Michael Diebert, *In the Shadow of Saint Death: The Gulf Cartel and the Price of America's Drug War in Mexico* (Guilford, CT: Lyons Press, 2014), 34.

59. American Consul Mexico, "Subject: Gulf Cartel Drug Violence," 1.

60. American Consul Monterrey to RUEHC Secretary of State Washington, DC, "Subject: Cartels Wrestle for Control of Durango," Monterrey 000223 162136Z, June 2009, 2.

61. American Consul Tijuana to US Ambassador Mexico City, "Subject: Major Development in Effort to Combat Cartel Violence: Arrest of Kingpin "El Teo" Eduardo Teodoro García Simental," Tijuana 1275 000035, January 12, 2010, Wikileaks, http://wikileaks.org/plusd/cables/10TIJUANA35_a.html.

62. American Consul Monterrey, "Subject: Cartels Wrestle," 3.

63. American Consul Tijuana to RUEHC Secretary of State Washington, DC, "Subject: War Between Cartels Flares with a Vengeance: Surge in Violence and Shooting Incidents in Tijuana," Tijuana 001275 172359Z, December 2009, 1.

64. Cook, *Mexico's Drug Cartels*, 10.

65. George W. Grayson, *The Cartels: The Story of Mexico's Most Dangerous Criminal Organization and Their Impact on U.S. Security* (Santa Barbara, CA: Praeger Books, 2014), 57; Chris Arsenault, "U.S. Trained Cartel Terrorizes Mexico," Al Jazeera, November 3, 2012, www.aljazeera.com.

66. Cook, *Mexico's Drug Cartels*, 10; George W. Grayson and Samuel Logan, *The Executioner's Men: Los Zetas, Rogue Soldiers, Criminal Entrepreneurs, and the Shadow State They Created* (London: Transaction Publishers, 2012), 7.

67. American Consul, Nuevo Laredo to Secretary of State, Washington, DC, "Subject: 2004 Starts with a Flurry in the Desert," Nuevo Laredo 3761AA 292113Z, June 2004, 4.

68. Francisco Gómez, "Los Zetas por dentro," *El Universal* (Mexico), December 31, 2009, www.eluniversal.com.mx.

69. American Consul Nuevo Laredo, "Subject: 2004 Starts," 4; Francisco Gómez, "11 Zetas Originales permanecen en Grande," *Borderland Beat*, February 7, 2011, www.borderlandbeat.com; Hal Brands, "Los Zetas and Mexico's Transnational Drug War," *World Politics Review*, December 25, 2009, www .worldpoliticsreview.com. Los Zetas also had a group of women known as Las Panteras who were used to negotiate with and bribe government officials. See Brook, *Blood and Death*, 95.

70. Brands, "Los Zetas and Mexico's Transnational."

71. American Consul Nuevo Laredo, "Subject: 2004 Starts," 4; Gómez, "11 Zetas Originales."

72. Chivis Martínez, "Thinking Zetas Are Finished?," *Borderland Beat*, October 27, 2013, www.borderlandbeat.com.

73. Chivis Martínez, "Part I Don Alejo: One Man Revolution Against Mexican Cartels," *Borderland Beat*, November 3, 2013, www.borderlandbeat.com.

74. Brands, "Los Zetas and Mexico's Transnational."

75. Buggs, "The Origins of the Los Zetas," *Borderland Beat*, April 15, 2012, www.borderlandbeat.com. Those states were Nayarit, Sonora, Sinaloa (Los Mochis), Puebla, Hidalgo, Zacatecas, Aguascalientes, San Luis Potosi, Durango, Tabasco, Campeche, Guanajuato, Queretaro (San Juan del Rio), Veracruz, Oaxaca, and Tlaxcala.

76. American Embassy Mexico to Secretary of State Washington, DC, "Subject: Mexico: Continuing Drug Challenges," Mexico 007087 142229Z, September 2004, 6; George W. Grayson, *La Familia Cartel: Implications for U.S. Mexican Security* (Carlisle Barracks, PA: Strategic Studies Institute, 2010), viii–15.

77. Buggs, "A Narco-Evangelist Cartel," *Borderland Beat*, November 26, 2009, www.borderlandbeat.com.

78. American Embassy Mexico to Secretary of State Washington, DC, "Subject: La Familia Continues Rampage in Michoacán," Mexico 0022093 171946Z, July 2009, 2–3; Brook, *Blood and Death*, 25–26.

79. "Taking on the Unholy Family," *Economist*, July 23, 2009, www.economist.com.

80. Arturo Cano, "Crea La Familia un sistemaparalelo de justiciaexpedita," *La Jornada* (Mexico), December 19, 2010, www.jornada.unam.mx.

81. Grayson, *La Familia Cartel*, iv.

82. Eliseo Caballero, "Se fugan 25 reos de penal de Michoacán," *Es Más* (Mexico), January 5, 2004, https://web.archive.org/web/20090123215954/http://www.esmas.com/noticierostelevisa/mexico/335078.html. The state prison was in Apatzingán.

83. Grayson, *La Familia Cartel*, 21–30.

84. Un Vato, "The War in Michoacán: Brief Chronology," *Borderland Beat*, January 15, 2014, www.borderlandbeat.com.

85. "Taking On the Unholy Family," *Economist*; James C. McKinley Jr., "With Beheadings and Attacks, Drug Gangs Terrorize Mexico," *New York Times*, October 26, 2006, sec. A, p. 1. The nightclub was called Sol y Sombra.

86. Grayson, *La Familia Cartel*, 21–58; Itzli, "Overview of the Criminal Organizations Operating in Guerrero," *Borderland Beat*, December 3, 2014, www.borderlandbeat.com.

87. American Embassy Mexico to Secretary of State Washington, DC, "Subject: La Familia Cartel Retaliates for Arrest of High Ranking Leader," Mexico 002039 132101Z, July 2009, 1–3, Arnolodo Rueda Medina ("La Minsa").

88. American Embassy Mexico, "Subject: La Familia Continues," 2–3.

89. American Embassy Mexico to Secretary of State Washington, DC, "Subject: Michoacán Faces Trifecta of Economic, Security, and Migration Problems," Mexico 002749 211247Z/38, September 2009, 4.

90. June S. Beittel, *Mexico's Drug Trafficking Organizations: Source and Scope of the Rising Violence*, Report R-41576 (Washington, DC: Congressional Research Service, April 15, 2013), 18; Jo Tuckman, "Mexico: They Call the Shots, How a War on Drugs Gave Cartel Its Own Kingdom," *Guardian*, International sec., p. 34. José de Jesús Méndez Vargas ("El Chango") was Moreno's replacement. He was later killed on June 21, 2011.

200 Narcostates

91. Tuckman, "Mexico: They Call the Shots," 34.

92. "Members of Knights Templar Drug Cartel in Mexico 'Made to Eat Children's Hearts' to Prove Their Loyalty to Leader El Chayo," *Belfast Telegraph*, March 24, 2014.

93. Tuckman, "Mexico: They Call the Shots," 34.

94. "29 Dead, 700 Flee in Mexico," *New Zealand Herald*, May 27, 2011.

95. Joshua Partlow, "Mexican Army Deployed to Sever Port's Drug Ties," *Washington Post*, December 1, 2013, sec. A, p. 3.

96. Howard LaFranchi, "Mexico's Vigilantes: The Aftershocks of Ousting a Cartel," *Christian Science Monitor*, March 9, 2012.

97. Beittel, *Mexico's Drug Trafficking Organizations*, 18; Rosario Castro Mosso and Enrique Mendoza Hernández, "Drug Traffickers Are Restructured into 28 Cartels," trans. Chivis Martínez and *Boderland Beat, Zeta Weekly*, January 3, 2012, www.borderlandbeat.com.

98. Chivis Martínez, "Taking a Look at the 'Zetas-Cross' Theory," *Borderland Beat*, August 25, 2012, www.borderlandbeat.com.

99. American Embassy Mexico to Secretary of State Washington, DC, "Subject: Mexico: Continuing Drug Challenges," Mexico 007087 142229Z, September 2004, 6.

100. American Consul Monterrey to Secretary of State Washington, DC, "Subject: Crime Drops in Nuevo Léon, Heats Up in Coahuila and Zacatecas," Monterrey 000276 101737Z, July 2012, 1; Chivis Martínez, "La Corona Reshapes Alliances in Jalmich," *Borderland Beat*, February 12, 2103, www.borderlandbeat .com. Ignacio Coronel Villarreal defected to the Sinaloa cartel in 2001. He took over the Milenio cartel when it was absorbed by the Sinaloa cartel in 2003. Ignacio Coronel Villarreal's death in 2010 and the arrest of Milenio cartel leader Orlando Nava Valencia and his brother Juan in 2009 led to its fracture. Carteles Unidos was also called La Resistencia, but should not be confused with the renewed La Resistencia that appeared after the Milenio cartel split. See "Ramiro Pozos, el 'Molca': el líder criminal de La Resistencia fue sentenciado a 28 años de prisión," *Infobae*, December 8, 2021, www.infobae.com.

101. Josh Elles, "The Brutal Rise of El Mencho," *Rolling Stone Magazine*, July 11, 2017, www.rollingstone.com.

102. "Cártel de Jalisco Nueva Generación va contra todos," *Blog del Narco*, September 6, 2011, www.blogdelnarco.com.

103. David Argen, "Authorities Find 49 Bodies Dumped on Mexican Highway; Country's Drug War Escalates," *USA Today*, May 14, 2014, sec. A, p. 4.

104. Enrique Krauze, "Mexico's Vigilantes on the March," *New York Times*, February 4, 2014, sec. A, p. 19.

105. "Cártel de Jalisco Nueva Generación," *Blog del Narco*.

106. Martínez, "La Corona Reshapes."

107. Malcom Beith, *The Last Narco: Inside the Hunt for El Chapo, the World's Most Wanted Drug Lord* (New York: Grove Press, 2020), 139–150; Rick Martin, "El Chapo Son's Death: Monument of Édgar Guzmán López Adorned with Giant Flower Wreath," *Latin Post*, November 2, 2022, www.latinpost.com.

108. American Embassy Mexico to Secretary of State Washington, DC, "Subject: Weakening of Gulf, Sinaloa Cartels Generates Mexico's Spike in Violence," Mexico 001766 1612158, June 2008, 1; "Who Is El Mochimito, Narcojunior of the Beltrán Leyva Accused of Kidnapping El Chapo's Children in 2016?" *World News Today*, May 25, 2020, www.world-today-news.com. To protect profits, Arturo Beltrán Leyva made a temporary truce with the Zetas's Heriberto Lazcano ("Z-3") in June 2007 called the Valle Hermoso Truce. Alfredo managed drug and money laundering operations.

Mexico's Cartel Wars 201

109. American Consul Tijuana, "Subject: War Between Cartels," 1.

110. Will Grant, "Heriberto Lazcano: The Fall of a Mexican Drug Lord," British Broadcasting Service, October 13, 2012, www.bbc.com; George W. Grayson, *The Evolution of Los Zetas in Mexico and Central America: Sadism as an Instrument of Cartel Warfare* (Carlisle Barracks, PA: US Army War College Press, January 25, 2015), 5–6. Treviño Morales was allegedly betrayed by Jesús Enrique Rejón Aguilar ("Z-7" or "El Mamito").

111. Marguerite Cawley, "Was Mexico's El Chapo Betrayed by His Sinaloa Partner?," InSight Crime, March 10, 2014, www.insightcrime.org.

112. Jo Tuckman, "Mexico Drug Kingpin Juan José 'El Azul' Esparragoza Believed to Have Died," *Guardian*, June 9, 2014, www.theguardian.com.

113. Victoria Kim, "Sweeping Federal Indictments Issued Against 60 Sinaloa Cartel Members," *Los Angeles Times*, January 16, 2015, www.latimes.com.

114. American Embassy Mexico, "Subject: Mexico's Bloodiest Days," 3.

115. American Embassy Mexico to Secretary of State Washington, DC, "Subject: The Battle Joined: Narco Violence Trends in 2008," Mexico 000193 232312Z, January 2009, 1.

9

The Militarization of the US-Mexican War on Drugs

While Mexico's cartels fought among themselves, bringing murder and mayhem to communities throughout the nation, the Mexican military's involvement in counternarcotics operations grew during the presidency of Vicente Fox (2000–2006). By expanding the military's role, Fox opened the door to corruption within the military and other branches of the Mexican government, such as the Agencia Federal de Investigación (AFI). Although the Mexican military assisted in the arrest of major capos such as Benjamín Arellano Félix and Osiel Cárdenas Guillén, they did not dismantle the cartels. Instead, traffickers continued to act with impunity. Fox's successor, Felipe Calderón (2006–2012), campaigned on a platform of law and order, which led to the implementation of the Mérida Initiative in 2008.

With US assistance, the Mérida Initiative became a massive counternarcotics and anticrime program. The Mérida Initiative aimed to reform the military and police while also boosting their counternarcotics capabilities. As the war on drugs became militarized, Calderón implemented the "kingpin strategy" by going after high-level targets. The kingpin strategy increased cartel resistance to the government and sparked internal and external fighting among the cartels. From that point onward, Mexico's violence skyrocketed. Much of the violence was concentrated in key cities and states along the US-Mexico border in places such as Juárez, Nuevo Laredo, Tijuana, and Durango, but also along Mexico's Pacific and Caribbean coasts. Beheadings and mutilations of individuals cooperating with the police or other rival cartels became everyday news stories, creating the perception that Mexico faced an existential crisis. Since the Los Zetas were considered the primary threat, the United States commenced Operation Fast and Furious to bring them down. Ironically, the urgent need to bring down Los Zetas created an unusual situation where the US government found itself cooperating with

204   *Narcostates*

members of the Sinaloa cartel against Los Zetas. When Fast and Furious became public, it turned into a scandal that helped bring down Eric Holder, the US attorney general. At this point, the violence, corruption, and incessant flow of narcotics through Mexico imbued the war on drugs with a sense of failure. Militarization combined with the myriad of conflicts—the cartels against the government, wars with other cartels, and battles within their own organizations—*Colombianized* Mexico.

The Fox-Calderón Steps Toward Militarization

Cooperation in the war on drugs between the United States and Mexico stalled in the early to mid-1990s as US counternarcotics authorities developed a sense of mistrust for their Mexican counterparts. They were skeptical of the Mexican government's level of cooperation because of Mexico's objections to US drug certification procedures, most notably the partial decertification in 1996, which restricted $2.5 million in aid to Mexico.[1] In 1997, members of both houses of Congress attempted to block President Clinton's certification of Mexico, but the administration provided additional reports on Mexican compliance to obtain certification.[2] Congressional threats of decertification improved Mexico's cooperation. In 1996, Mexico and the United States created the Grupo Contacto de Alto Nivel para el Control de Drogas (GCAN) to coordinate counternarcotics activities at the highest levels of government. They created binational groups to strengthen cooperation in combating drug and arms trafficking, money laundering, and the diversion of precursor chemicals. In November 1996, Mexico passed an organized crime law that authorized law enforcement to employ modern techniques to combat crime. Although an extradition treaty had existed since 1978, the extradition of Mexican nationals to the United States on drug-related offenses did not begin until the United States started pressuring Mexico with decertification in 1996.[3] Mexico's willingness to deal with the issue and the formation of GCAN led to a US-Mexico Bi-National Drug Threat Assessment report in 1997, which created a US-Mexico Declaration of Alliance Against Drugs.[4] Consequently, the two countries signed the Bi-National Drug Control Strategy in February 1998, opening the door for an increase in US counternarcotics assistance to Mexico.[5] State Department aid totaled nearly $170 million from 2000 to 2006, and Defense Department assistance totaled an additional $228 million. Much of that money was spent on equipment to enhance border security and to upgrade Mexican law enforcement entities to develop an interdiction strategy (see Figure 9.1).[6]

After the World Trade Center attack on September 11, 2001, the US government linked terrorism with the war on drugs, which led to an increase in military aid to Mexico. Attorney General John Ashcroft (2001–2005) made claims that linked al-Qaeda, the Mexican cartels, and Central

Figure 9.1 Department of State Counternarcotics Assistance to Mexico, 1997–2006

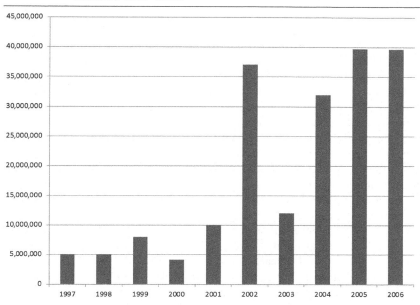

Source: Based on US Department of State 1998–2007 *International Narcotics Control Strategy Reports Vol. I: Budget Allocations for Mexico.*

American gangs (specifically the MS-13) to the trafficking of possible terrorists into the United States.[7] In a 2004 incident, US authorities arrested an Egyptian national named Ashref Ahmed Abdallah at the Miami National Airport for smuggling Middle Eastern illegal aliens through Central America to the United States.[8] Fears also grew that narcotics were being used to finance Islamic terrorism. According to DEA Deputy Administrator for Intelligence Anthony P. Placido, cocaine proceeds deposited into accounts owned by Hezbollah and Hamas (designated by the United States as Islamic terrorist organizations) would be used for terrorist acts.[9] A report by the Naval War College in 2004 revealed that Hezbollah raised close to $10 million a year in the South American tri-border area, with much of the revenue coming from the drug trade. Michael Braun, the DEA chief of operations, remarked, "What concerns me the most is the fact that the cocaine trade brings Hezbollah and Hamas into close contact with Colombian and Mexican drug trafficking cartels."[10]

With the onset of the war on terror and improving binational coordination, the Mexican military stepped up its counternarcotics role. Between

206 *Narcostates*

2000 and 2006, the United States trained roughly 2,500 members of the Mexican military to use aircraft, vessels, and vehicles that expanded interdiction capabilities. The US also maintained twenty-eight Bell VH-1 "Huey" helicopters and refurbished eight other helicopters for the Mexican army. However, US defense officials reported that the Mexican military was slow to use US expertise or intelligence to combat narcotrafficking, despite the increased aid.[11] The decision to have the Mexican military execute law enforcement operations alarmed many Mexicans. Their fear stemmed from the prospect that the military's involvement in the drug war might undermine Mexico's tradition of civilian control over domestic issues.

The administration of President Vicente Fox (2000–2006) took gradual but significant steps against narcotraffickers. The scale of the government's crackdown was impressive: Between 2000 and 2003, the Mexican government made more than 24,000 drug-related arrests.[12] As part of the Maxi-Proceso, the military arrested 8,041 associates of the Juárez cartel between December and June 2004. In the same period, the military arrested 7,367 Arellano Félix, 5,699 Sinaloa, and 4,220 Gulf cartel members. According to the US State Department, "In every case, small-time collaborators and retail dealers" comprise nearly all of these arrest totals.[13] In addition, Mexico increased the number of low-level traffickers extradited to the United States from seventeen in 2001 to sixty-three in 2006.[14]

Despite several high-profile arrests, public discontent with the Fox administration's efforts against crime continued, especially following the 2004 discovery of the "house of death" in Juárez, where Vicente Carrillo Fuentes tortured, murdered, and buried informants in the cellar of the house. Critics said Fox's crackdown on the cartels did not slow the flow of drugs; it "only created tremendous violence."[15] Fox responded to the narcoviolence with surges in the deployment of the Policía Federal Preventiva (PFP), created in 1999 out of the federal highway police, the fiscal police, CISEN, and the Mexican army's Third Military Police Brigade.[16] Public discontent also prompted Fox to restore $90 million in federal law enforcement aid to the Mexican states in 2004.[17]

Notwithstanding the Mexican government's efforts, corruption remained within Mexico's federal agencies. To deal with the problem, Mexican authorities created the AFI within the PGR and disbanded the PJFM in 2001. The AFI enacted stringent standards of conduct, much higher than other federal law enforcement branches such as the PFP, by requiring its employees to undergo polygraph and drug testing. Despite the standards of conduct being laid down, Mexican authorities were forced to dismiss twenty-five midlevel officials from the PGR for narcocorruption in 2002.[18] The Mexican government suffered a public embarrassment in 2005, when the PGR reported that it had placed 1,500 of 7,000 AFI agents under investigation for suspected criminal activity, with 457 facing charges of corruption. At one point, the PGR was investigating nearly one-fifth of the AFI for collaborating with the Sinaloa cartel.[19] In June 2005, DEA Assistant Administrator for Intelligence Anthony Placido told the US Congress that "the single largest impediment impacting the drug trafficking problem in Mexico is corruption." He added that "law enforcement in Mexico is all too often part of the problem rather than part of the solution."[20] In November 2008, the PGR arrested the AFI's no. 2 official for providing information from 2003 to 2005 to the Beltrán Leyva cartel in return for monthly payments.[21] Allegations of corruption within the AFI became so great that in 2009, the Mexican government reformed the AFI into the Policía Federal Ministerial (PFM). According to Anabel Hernández, the author of *Narcoland*, Mexico's drug war strategy safeguarded the Sinaloa cartel because, in the view of Genaro García Luna, the 2006–2012 secretaría de seguridad pública (secretary of public security) and founder of the Policía Federal (PF) in 2009, it was easier to negotiate with just one cartel than five. In the veins of Mexico, corruption ran deep.[22]

Rather than relying on the local and federal police, who were compromised by endemic corruption, the Mexican government increasingly turned to the Mexican military to combat narcotraffickers. Previously, the administration of President Ernesto Zedillo (1994–2000) limited the military solely to eradication and interdiction programs. Due to concerns about corruption within some police units, Zedillo put the army in charge of a number of sensitive operations. In the case of Chihuahua, the severity of corruption forced him to place the state's entire antidrug effort under the army's control.[23] Fox changed the military's role by giving the secretary of defense complete responsibility for counternarcotics operations, including the dismantling of DTOs. Fox also nominated former military officers to direct the PGR. For example, in November 2002, Fox placed 227 officers in the PGR; 20 officers controlled important bureaus, including intelligence, eradication, interdiction, and asset seizures.[24] The second and seventh sections of Mexico's Department of Defense (SEDENA) were put in charge of military intelligence and military operations, respectively. They investigated the cartels' leadership and ran operations to catch kingpins.[25] During Fox's second year as president, fifty-six GAFE groups (from which Los Zetas originated) were reorganized and integrated into three brigades and nine special forces battalions that then designated a GAFE group to conduct operations in each of Mexico's forty-four military zones.[26]

In June 2005, the murder of Nuevo Laredo's public safety director prompted federal authorities to launch México Seguro (Secure Mexico). This operation increased Mexico's federal participation in the war on drugs by using federal resources to bring order to lawless cities along the US-Mexico border.[27] For example, in Nuevo Laredo the government took the police off the streets and replaced them with vetted police from the federal government.

208   *Narcostates*

For the Fox administration and Mexico in general, the federalization of the security situation seemed like the only solution to rein in corruption and stop lawlessness.[28] Still, corruption spilled over into the military. In October 2002, the PGR investigated and dismantled the army's 65th Infantry Battalion, stationed in Guamúchil, Sinaloa, for protecting poppy and marijuana crops for the Sinaloa cartel.[29] The US State Department proffered that Mexican authorities could do little to stop the violence when local and state officials cooperated with traffickers. Moreover, federal law enforcement lacked the wherewithal to reach into the provinces in any comprehensive way.[30]

Fox's decision to federalize the war on drugs did not go without criticism. As the head of an important human rights organization, retired Brigadier General Gallardo Rodríguez criticized the military's role. Previously, the Mexican government imprisoned Gallardo Rodríguez from 1993 to 2002 on "trumped-up charges" because he criticized the military's human rights record. Gallardo Rodríguez's renewed criticism warned that the military's role in counternarcotics could potentially subvert the government. He argued that the Mexican military operated in the shadows as the power broker for the presidential throne. Mexican congressional power did not adequately regulate the military's activities; their participation in counternarcotics operations would become an impediment to democracy. He added that the army was beset with corruption problems for two reasons. The first was that lower-ranking officers received inadequate benefits, which led current and former members of the military to engage in gun-for-hire activities. Second, the routine use of military personnel to conduct police functions set a dangerous precedent for army incursions into civilian affairs. As a result, Gallardo supported the creation of a national guard independent of the army that would intervene in civilian law enforcement affairs only in situations where conventional police forces could not quell domestic unrest.[31]

By the end of Fox's presidency, the GAO reported that despite positive steps toward greater coordination between the United States and Mexico and increasing professionalism within Mexico's judiciary, drug seizures along the US-Mexico border remained relatively small. In 2000, 66 percent of the cocaine in the United States flowed through Mexico. By 2003, this estimate increased to 77 percent, and by 2005, as much as 90 percent (see Figures 9.2 and 9.3).[32] US seizures of marijuana remained constant and averaged less than 2,500 metric tons annually. The GAO also reported the persistence of corruption within the Mexican government, adding that Mexican DTOs operated with "impunity" along the US border and in other parts of Mexico.[33]

In 2006, PAN leader Felipe Calderón Hinojosa (2006–2012) became president of Mexico by a slim margin in a hotly contested election. Although the PRI nominated national leader Roberto Madrazo as their candidate, Calderón's only real challenger was Andrés Manuel López Obrador, the

Figure 9.2 Marijuana Seizures in Metric Tons, 2000–2005

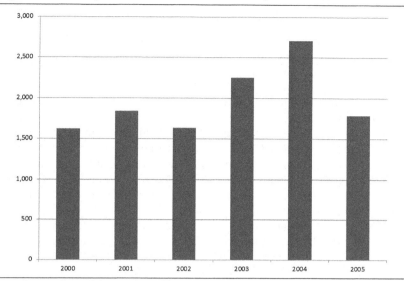

Source: General Accounting Office, *U.S. Assistance Has Helped Mexican Counternarcotics Efforts, but Tons of Drugs Continue to Flow into the United States*, GAO-07-1018, 11.

Figure 9.3 Cocaine Seizures in Metric Tons, 2000–2005

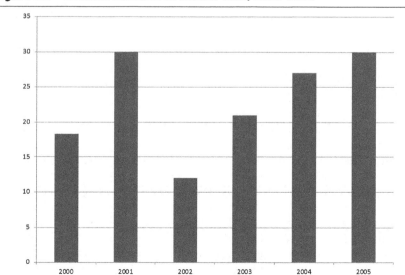

Source: General Accounting Office, *U.S. Assistance Has Helped Mexican Counternarcotics Efforts, but Tons of Drugs Continue to Flow into the United States*, GAO-07-1018, 11.

210   *Narcostates*

leader of the Partido de la Revolución Democrática (PRD) and mayor of Mexico City from 2000 to 2005. Obrador ran against Calderón as a populist candidate, appealing to the poor and the ideals of the Mexican Revolution.[34] Calderón's campaign ran on a law-and-order platform, which was countered by Obrador, who argued that in order to combat organized crime, Mexico needed to address poverty, stop the disintegration of the family, and root out corruption in government.[35] Calderón received 243,000 more votes than Obrador, who quickly challenged the vote tally by claiming voting irregularities and asking for a complete recount of the vote.[36] A partial recount was held confirming Calderón's victory. Obrador held several protests over the election, and, in November 2006, he declared he was the legitimate president and proclaimed the creation of a shadow government to apply pressure on Calderón's government.[37]

As Calderón ascended to the presidency, the cartel war was reaching its zenith. Calderón responded by increasing the military's participation.[38] Calderón declared drug trafficking a threat to Mexico and pledged to expand the fight by deploying troops to "hot spots" around the nation.[39] Within days of taking office, he sent the Mexican military into his home state of Michoacán. In early 2007, he deployed 27,000 military and federal police officers across eight Mexican states. Their mission was to eradicate drug crops, intercept drug shipments, and apprehend wanted criminals.[40]

Calderón made combating DTOs the top priority of his administration and called upon the United States to provide more assistance. Under the Fox administration, US counternarcotics aid totaled $597 million between 2000 and 2006. On October 22, 2007, Presidents George W. Bush and Felipe Calderón announced the Mérida Initiative, a $1.6 billion, three-year counternarcotics and anticrime package for Mexico during fiscal years 2008–2010. In 2008 alone, the first round of funding totaled $400 million.[41]

The Mérida Initiative sought to break the power and impunity of criminal organizations; strengthen border, air, and maritime controls; improve the capacity of judicial systems in the region; curtail gang activity; and diminish local drug demand.[42] The Bush administration's appropriations for Mexico came largely in the form of equipment and training that included helicopters, surveillance aircraft, scanners, training, and information technology for Mexican federal law enforcement and intelligence agencies. The ultimate goal was to create a secure environment in which criminal organizations no longer wielded the power to threaten national and regional security, while also blocking the entry and spread of illicit drugs and transnational threats across Mexico.[43]

Countering money laundering operations was an important aspect of the Mérida Initiative. According to the US government, "Mexican and Colombian drug trafficking organizations annually generate, remove, and launder between $18 billion and $39 billion in wholesale distribution proceeds, a large portion of which is believed to be smuggled in bulk cash out of the United States through the Southwest border." Cash smuggling was the primary means by which DTOs laundered money, but they also used electronic techniques, such as prepaid cards. Mapping the financial structures and tracking money transfers of the Mexican DTOs was critical. To help Mexico achieve this goal, the US Congress required the filing of suspicious activity reports for individual purchases of $2,000 or more on prepaid cards at a single store.[44]

The Mérida Initiative also focused on reforming Mexican institutions, especially the military and the police, to improve Mexico's counterdrug effectiveness. US assistance to Mexico hit its peak between 2008 and 2010, ranging from $405.9 million in 2008, $786.8 million in 2009, and $403.7 million in 2010 (see Figure 9.4).[45] By 2010, the United States delivered eight Bell 412 helicopters to the Mexican army and three Black Hawk helicopters to the Mexican Federal Police. Because the Mérida Initiative did not include measurable targets or outcomes, critics of military aid questioned its efficacy.[46]

Figure 9.4 Total US Assistance for the Mérida Initiative in Millions of Dollars, 2007–2014

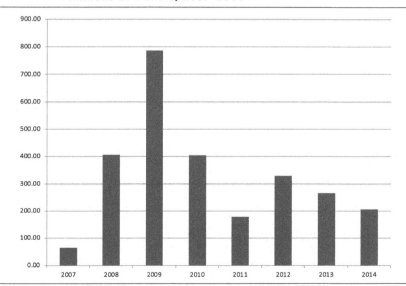

Sources: Based on Clare Ribando Seelke and Kristin Finklea, *US-Mexican Security Cooperation: The Mérida Initiative and Beyond*, Report R-41349 (Washington, DC: Congressional Research Service, April 8, 2014); US Department of State, Bureau of International Narcotics and Law Enforcement Affairs, *2008 International Narcotics Control Strategy Report Vol. I* (Washington, DC: US Department of State, March 2008), 43–44.

212   Narcostates

Throughout his six-year term, Calderón committed an average of 45,000 soldiers annually to the drug war. In 2011, at the height of Calderón's counternarcotics program, 96,000 troops participated in operations.[47] The number of military men who filled traditional law enforcement positions increased from six in February 2009 to thirty-six in April 2012.[48] The problem for Calderón was that the military's presence did not reduce drug-related violence.[49] Its objective was to confront and dismantle drug trafficking organizations by going after high-value targets—the so-called "kingpin strategy." As they implemented this strategy, the drug organizations adapted by decentralizing and democratizing. The cartels were like hydras—the loss of one head was quickly replaced by two others. Following in the footsteps of the Colombian cartels after the collapse of the Medellín and Cali cartels, some cartels, such as the Sinaloa cartel, adopted a more horizontal organizational structure, rather than a vertical structure. They developed an independent cell-like framework that made them harder to dismantle.[50]

The Mexican Department of Defense (SEDENA) recorded the growing number of criminals the military killed: 2007 (22), 2008 (78), 2009 (211), 2010 (734), and through December 2011 (1,246). The majority of these deaths were because of the military's hard-line, "take-no-prisoners" approach. The public security director in the city of Torreón told a reporter that he preferred to kill members of organized crime groups rather than interrogate them. He added, "I have no confidence in the federal police."[51] During the same time period (2007–2011), the military reported its losses as 267 killed in action, 744 wounded, and 196 kidnapped.[52] High-level assassinations and intimidation significantly dampened law enforcement efforts. In February 2008, General Tello Quiñones, the retired director general of SEDENA, had his arms and legs broken until his bones were exposed, and was then shot eleven times. Quiñones was the highest-ranking military man assassinated by the cartels to that date.[53] In November 2009, Los Zetas hit men gunned down Brigadier General Esparza García four days after he took office as the secretary of public security for Nuevo León. And in Escobedo, Nuevo León, the secretary of public security resigned after a few hours in office. That same month, more than half of the fifty-one municipal security secretary positions in Nuevo León remained vacant.[54]

As Calderón's war on drugs heated up, the murder rate in Mexico climbed steadily (see Figure 9.5). From 1968 to 1986, Mexico's murder rate averaged 10–15 murders per 100,000 citizens. The rate climbed to 20 homicides per 100,000 people in 1987. Between 2000 and 2007, the murder rate dropped below 10 homicides per 100,000 people until the election of Calderón as president in 2008. During Calderón's presidency, the homicide rate rose from 12.2 murders in 2008 to 22.8 murders per 100,000 people by 2012.[55] The SEDENA estimated that, between December 2006 and Decem-

The Militarization of the US-Mexican War on Drugs   213

Figure 9.5   Mexican Murder Rate (percentage per 100,000 inhabitants)

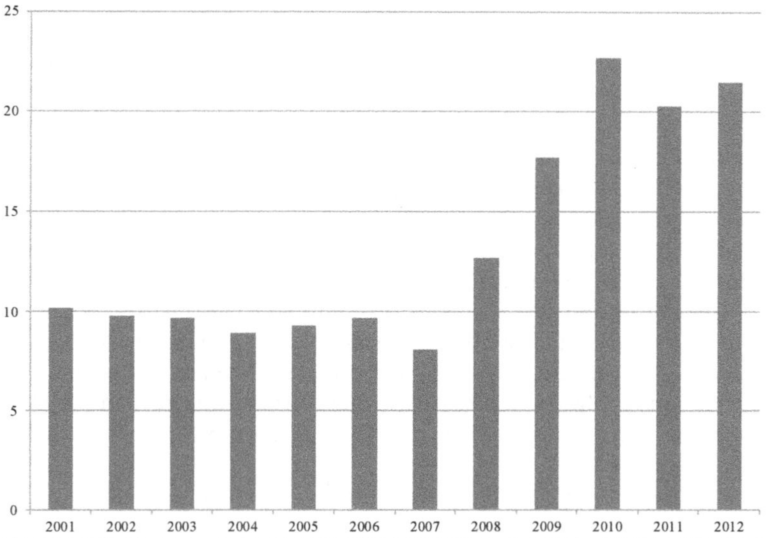

Source: United Nations Office on Drugs and Crime, *2013 Global Study on Homicide* (Vienna: United Nations, March 2014), 126.

ber 2011, it arrested 41,023 suspects and killed 2,321 criminals.[56] The estimated death toll associated with the drug war during Calderón's presidency (2008–2014) was approximately 120,000 lives.[57] This figure was twice the 80,000 homicides that were reported during the presidency of Ernest Zedillo (1994–2000) and the 60,000 homicides that occurred during the presidency of Vicente Fox (2000–2006). The spike in the homicide rate was clearly tied to the war on drugs.[58]

The military-trafficker confrontation increased human rights abuses against civilians. Between 2006 and 2010, the number of civilian killings increased from 2,826 in 2007 to a shocking 15,273 in 2010.[59] The Mexican government estimated that 23,000 people were killed because of drug-related violence.[60] During that same period, Human Rights Watch reported 170 cases of torture (beatings, asphyxiation with plastic bags, water boarding, electric shock, and sexual torture), 39 disappearances, and 24 cases of extrajudicial killings in the states of Baja, Chihuahua, Nuevo León, Guerrero, and Tabasco. In all cases, the victims were accused of being tied to organized crime.[61] In 2010, the US Congress placed human rights conditions on 15 percent of the Mérida Initiative's funds. As a result, the State Department withheld $36 million in funding to force Mexico to pass human rights reforms within its constitution and Military Code of Justice.[62]

214 *Narcostates*

In 2013, Senator Patrick Leahy held up $95 million in Mérida Initiative funds because of human rights abuses committed during the last year of Calderón's presidency.[63] It was not until May 2014 that Mexico changed its Military Code of Justice.[64] Changes in constitutional law also led to other human rights questions. For example, the passage of *arraigo* (precharge detention) allowed authorities to detain a suspect with links to organized crime for forty days, which could be extended to eighty days without the suspect ever being charged.[65]

The Mexican military's involvement in the war on drugs provoked confrontations between the military and the police. General Galván Galván, the head of SEDENA (2006–2012), told US officials that joint operations with the police did not work: "Leaks of planning and information by corrupted officials compromised past efforts." From 2007 to November 2009, the military clashed with local, state, or federal law enforcement agencies at least sixty-five times.[66] In August 2010, the mass firing of more than 3,000 Mexican police officers testified to the level of corruption within Mexico's police forces.[67]

Corruption remained the single most important issue that served to undermine the military's effort in the war on drugs. As early as 2007, the Mexican people's concern was heightened with the discovery of a video hidden with a stash of money found during a raid on a narcohouse in the state of Nuevo León. In the video, an unidentified man claimed that the highest-ranking members of the Mexican government, including General Galván Galván and Mexican President Calderón, were on the narcotraffickers' payroll. The government called the video a fraud. Still, its existence undermined public confidence.[68] According to Calderón's secretary of the navy, criminal gangs were using the "banner of human rights to try to undermine the reputation of [government] institutions," meaning the army and navy.[69] In May 2012, four high-ranking army officers were arrested on drug trafficking and corruption charges.[70] The arrested included retired general Ángeles Dauahare, who had served as deputy secretary of defense under Calderón from 2006 to 2008.

The GAO stated that because the Mérida Initiative lacked any performance criteria to demonstrate progress toward achieving strategic goals, monitoring its funding was challenging because the various bureaus handling Mérida funds used different tracking methodologies. The GAO's analysis stated, "Almost all the performance measures do not provide specific measurable targets with milestones to indicate success in the short-term and long-term."[71] The GAO's criticism carried into the presidency of Enrique Peña Nieto (2012–2018). In 2013, a staffer for Senator Patrick Leahy stated, "We toss them money, but there's never any accounting. We've received less than three pages explaining their strategy. The violence and drug trafficking continue."[72]

Despite the lack of oversight, Mexico did disrupt the cartels during Calderón's presidency. Calderón actively worked with the United States to extradite wanted criminals, which climbed from 63 in 2006 to 107 in 2009. In 2012, the Mexican government arrested twenty-five of thirty-seven criminals it identified as most wanted.[73] Although Mexican victories against organized crime were significant, the State Department reported in 2014 that available supply reduction data "indicate that interdiction remains a major challenge for Mexico. Only a small portion of the cocaine, marijuana, methamphetamine, and heroin originating in or transiting Mexico is interdicted inside the country" (see Figures 9.6 and 9.7).[74]

Los Zetas:
The Existential Threat

Of all the Mexican DTOs, the military prowess of Los Zetas became an ever growing threat to the Mexican government. In order to counter the Los Zetas cartel, the US government collaborated with the Sinaloa cartel to collect intelligence on them. According to allegations made by DEA and CIA insiders, such as DEA director of intelligence Phil Jordan and former CIA

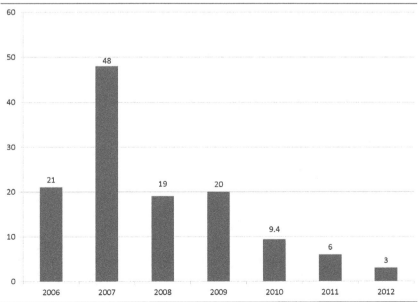

Figure 9.6 Mexican Cocaine Seizures in Metric Tons, 2006–2012

Source: Based on data from US Department of State, *2008–2014 International Narcotics Control Strategy Reports Vol. 1: Supply Reduction Statistics for Mexico.*

216 *Narcostates*

Figure 9.7   Mexican Marijuana Seizures in Metric Tons, 2006–2012

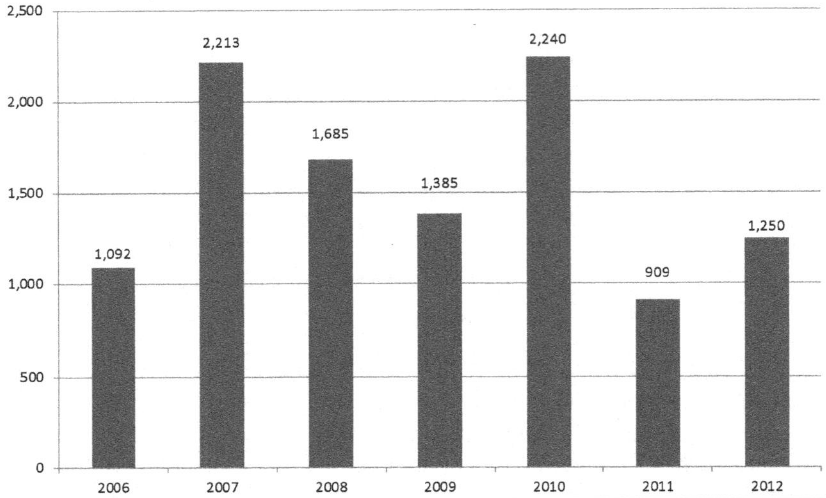

Source: Based on data from US Department of State, *2008–2014 International Narcotics Control Strategy Reports Vol. I: Supply Reduction Statistics for Mexico.*

contract pilot Robert Tosh Plumlee, US officials actively aided organizations such as the Sinaloa cartel with guns and immunity in an effort to dismantle Los Zetas.[75] Former Sinaloa cartel member Vicente Zambada Niebla confirmed the weapons information and further alleged that the FBI assisted the Sinaloa cartel to bring down Los Zetas.[76]

The story of Vicente Zambada Niebla ("El Vicentillo") is essential to fully understand how deeply tied the US government was to the Sinaloa cartel in order to stop Los Zetas. The DEA considered El Vicentillo, the son of El Mayo Zambada, to be the logistical coordinator for the Sinaloa cartel. In 2009, the Mexican military arrested and extradited him to the United States on drug trafficking charges. Upon his extradition, El Vicentillo claimed that he worked for the US government and had an agreement that prevented his prosecution. The US government allegedly negotiated the agreement with Sinaloa cartel lawyer Humberto Loya Castro. Manuel Castanon, a DEA agent present when the agreement was signed, testified that El Vicentillo's agreement did exist. The agent told the Chicago District Court that on "March 17, 2009, I met for approximately 30 minutes in a hotel room in Mexico City with Vicente Zambada Niebla and two other individuals—DEA agent David Herrod and a cooperating source [Sinaloa lawyer Loya Castro] with whom I had worked since 2005. I did all of the talking on behalf of [the] DEA." After the agreement was

The Militarization of the US-Mexican War on Drugs   217

signed, Mexican Marines arrested El Vicentillo. As part of the plea, he was convicted of smuggling cocaine and heroin and agreed to forfeit his assets of $1.37 billion to the US government. In exchange, he was sentenced to ten years in prison.[77]

The Chicago District Court documents demonstrated a long-standing relationship between the US government and the Sinaloa cartel. According to the documents, El Mayo encouraged El Vicentillo to cooperate with the authorities. Moreover, the court documents explained that in 1995, Loya Castro negotiated a deal with US agents, whereby the Sinaloa cartel provided information on rival drug traffickers if the United States minimized its interference in the cartel's trafficking operations.[78] To provide credence to Loya Castro's story, the court documents revealed that DEA agents met with Sinaloa cartel members at least fifty times starting in 2000.[79]

The coordinated DEA-Sinaloa effort against Los Zetas led to violations of US law. According to his court testimony, El Vicentillo alleged that the US government allowed the Sinaloa cartel to fly a Boeing 747 cargo plane packed with cocaine into the United States. Their cooperation also included allowing Loya Castro to sit in on DEA meetings concerning the Sinaloa cartel and promises by the DEA not to share information about the cartel with the Mexican government. When Mexican authorities were conducting investigations into the Sinaloa cartel, the US government warned cartel leaders so that they could take appropriate measures to evade investigators. As time progressed, El Vicentillo personally met with US officials in Mexico City and provided information to the DEA. In exchange, the DEA granted the Sinaloa cartel protection to smuggle drugs into the United States.[80]

Fast and Furious

In order to collect information against the Mexican cartels, particularly Los Zetas, the Department of Justice, the FBI, and the ATF designed the Fast and Furious gun-running operation. The stated concept of Fast and Furious was to trace guns to Mexican drug cartels to obtain intelligence and evidence against them. According to the Department of Justice inspector general's report, the ATF and DOJ believed that they needed to pursue investigations in a more "creative and comprehensive manner by allowing straw purchasers to buy weapons in the U.S. illegally, so agents could learn the traffickers' routes in and out of Mexico." The agents were expected to intervene before the guns reached the cartels, but this was not always the case.[81]

Operation Fast and Furious expanded the ATF's 2009–2011 "gun walking program." The program originated with the Bush administration's Operation Wide Receiver, which made several weapons deliveries

218   *Narcostates*

to Mexico in 2007. Wide Receiver evolved into two other operations known as the Hernández and the Medrano cases, both directed by the Phoenix ATF. Because the ATF considered both operations ineffective, the Obama administration's Attorney General's Office devised Fast and Furious. Previously, in Wide Receiver the ATF controlled the gun dealers and Mexican law enforcement agencies arrested the gun buyers. In Operation Fast and Furious, the ATF did not control the gun dealers who sold weapons to the buyers.

During the operation, US gun stores shipped about 2,000 weapons to Mexican drug cartels. According to the ATF Phoenix Field Division Commander, William Newell, the IRS, DEA, and ICE acted as "full partners" in Fast and Furious. ATF agents knew that the subjects were purchasing weapons for other persons, converting firearms into illegal weapons, and transferring firearms to Mexico. But rather than arresting the buyers of the weapons, Fast and Furious attempted to track the flow of weapons into Mexico. The ATF did not assist the Mexican government in making arrests because the arrest of suspects solely on weapons trafficking charges would damage the attorney general's case against drug trafficking organizations.[82] Instead, the US Attorney General's Office hoped to trace the gun purchases to the cartels, which in turn would provide them with intelligence and the possibility of making arrests.

The exposure of Fast and Furious following the deaths of two government agents and the denial by the US Attorney General's Office of playing a role in the operation amplified the public's perception of US government criminality. FBI ballistic tests proved that one of the weapons used in Fast and Furious led to the death of US border agent Brian Terry on December 14, 2010.[83] Two months later, ICE agent Jaime Zapata became another US agent killed by a weapon provided by a straw gun purchaser under investigation by the ATF. Politics obfuscated any possibility of finding the truth. Attorney General Eric Holder claimed ignorance and accused Republicans in the US Congress of politicizing the matter.[84] President Barack Obama insisted that neither he nor Holder knew that federal ATF agents permitted illegal gun purchases on the Southwest border.[85] Still, allegations of a cover-up persisted. On June 20, 2012, Obama used his executive privilege to withhold 15,000 documents from congressional investigations concerning Fast and Furious.[86] In response, the US House of Representatives voted to place Holder in contempt of Congress.[87] By November 2014, the Obama administration had turned over 64,280 documents related to Fast and Furious. Because many of the documents were heavily redacted and because many of the documents solicited by Congress were not turned over, the House Oversight Committee pressed their case against President Obama and Attorney General Holder for withholding documentation.[88] In 2016, a federal judge ruled that the documents were not protected by executive privilege. However, the Democratic Party's takeover of the House of Representatives in 2019 led to a decision to block the release of further documents, leaving the American people in the dark as to the extent of their government's role in arms trafficking to Mexican cartels.

Officially, the Mexican government considered Fast and Furious an act of betrayal.[89] The head of Mexico's Chamber of Deputies called Fast and Furious a "grave violation of international rights."[90] Former Mexican attorney general Marisela Morales stated, "At no time did we know . . . that there might have been arms trafficking permitted," and "in no way would we have allowed it, because it is an attack on the safety of Mexicans."[91] The Fast and Furious cover-up drew attention to the proliferation of US weapons across the border into Mexico, which had been a point of contention between the two nations for nearly a century. The fact that the United States was covertly delivering weapons to Mexico's cartels heightened tensions between the United States and Mexico, as weapons from Fast and Furious turned up at nearly 200 crime scenes where an estimated 300 people were killed.[92] In the end, Fast and Furious upended US-Mexico diplomatic relations and gave the Mexican government cover to deflect US criticism concerning its counternarcotics efforts.

A Mérida Retrospective:
Mexico on Fire

Peter Watt and Roberto Zepeda argue in *Drug War Mexico* that up until 2000, the PRI regulated and profited from the drug trade, ensuring stability. It was only when the PRI edifice started to crumble that the cartels started to assert themselves more forcefully in an attempt to capture the state.[93] The transfer of power to the PAN under Fox and Calderón, US pressure on Mexico, and the expansion of the Mexican military's counternarcotics role inflamed Mexico's drug war. Fox was the first Mexican president to dedicate the Mexican military to the drug war and to battle corruption inside the PGR by forming professional organizations such as the AFI. The problem for Fox was that increasing the role of the military and federal agencies in the war on drugs opened the door to further corruption. Although several capos were arrested or killed during the Fox administration, the Mexican government did not put an end to cartel operations. Following Felipe Calderón's 2006 election victory, Mexico experienced unprecedented murder rates as the cartel war became militarized. The cartels were not only fighting among themselves; they were also battling the Mexican military. The Mérida Initiative had inadvertently exacerbated the drug war by increasing the Mexican military's role in law enforcement efforts without any benchmarks to measure its success.

Like Hernán Cortés scuttling his ships at Veracruz, Fox and Calderón offered only one way forward. Mexico would meet fire with fire. As long as

220   Narcostates

narcotics remained illegal, Fox and Calderón had few other options. If they did nothing, the cartels' vast wealth would have made it possible for them to capture the state itself. As Mexico's drug war became more militarized, the importance of Central America's narcocorridor grew.

Notes

1. Clare Ribando Seelke, Liana Sun Wyler, June S. Beittel, and Mark. P Sullivan, *Latin American and the Caribbean: Drug Trafficking and U.S. Counterdrug Programs*, Report R-41215 (Washington, DC: Congressional Research Service, March 19, 2012), 14.

2. Name redacted, *Mexican Drug Certification Issues: U.S. Congressional Action 1986–2002*, Report 98-174 F (Washington, DC: Congressional Research Office, October 22, 2002), 1–3, www.everycrsreport.com/reports/98-174.html. Proposed resolutions on decertification in 1998 and 1999 never made it beyond committee hearings.

3. General Accounting Office, *U.S.-Mexican Counternarcotics Efforts Face Difficult Challenges*, NSIAD 98-54 (Washington, DC, June 30, 1998), 11–12; "Treaty Between the United States of America and Mexico," May 4, 1978, *United States Treaties and Other International Acts*, Series 9656, Extradition, Pursuant to Public Law 89-497. The treaty was signed in 1978 but was not ratified until 1980.

4. General Accounting Office, *U.S.-Mexican Counternarcotics Efforts*, 11–25.

5. General Accounting Office, *Update on U.S. Mexican Counternarcotics Efforts*, T-NSIAD 99-86 (Washington, DC, February 24, 1999), 5.

6. General Accounting Office, *U.S. Assistance Has Helped Mexican Counternarcotics Efforts, but Tons of Drugs Continue to Flow into the United States*, GAO-07-1018 (Washington, DC, August 2007), 9.

7. "Al Qaeda Seeks Ties to Local Gangs," *Washington Times*, September 28, 2008, www.washingtontimes.com; Paul L. Williams, *The Al Qaeda Connection: International Terrorism, Organized Crime, and the Coming Apocalypse* (Amherst, NY: Prometheus Books, 2005), 161.

8. Michele Miranda and Mark R. Shulman, "Central America, The Forgotten Frontier; War on Terrorism," *International Herald Tribune*, November 23, 2004, Opinion, p. 6.

9. US Congress, House of Representatives, Subcommittee on National Security and Foreign Affairs Committee on Oversight and Government Reform, *Transnational Drug Enterprises (Part II): Threats to Global Stability and U.S. Policy Responses*, 111th Cong., 2nd sess., March 3, 2010, 7, Testimony of Anthony P. Placido, DEA Assistant Administrator for Intelligence.

10. Edwin Mora, "Hezbollah, Hamas, Raise Money for Terrorist Activities from Drug Trade in South America Congressional Research Service Says," CNSNEWS .com, June 8, 2010, http://cnsnews.com.

11. General Accounting Office, *US Assistance Has Helped*, 30.

12. Kevin Sullivan, "Massacre Still Casts Its Shadow in Mexico; '98 Killings Revisited as Violence Grows," *Washington Post*, February 1, 2004, sec. A, p. 20.

13. American Embassy Mexico, "Subject: Mexico: Continuing Counter Drug," 5.

14. General Accounting Office, *US Assistance Has Helped*, 21.

15. David Rose, "The House of Death," *Observer* (England), December 3, 2006, 38.

The Militarization of the US-Mexican War on Drugs 221

16. American Embassy Mexico to Secretary of State Washington, DC, "Subject: Mexico Narco Violence Going Strong," Mexico 008345 271958Z, October 2004, 1–4; Benjamín Reames, *Encyclopedia of Law Enforcement: Mexico* (Thousand Oaks, CA: Sage Publications, 2004), 9.

17. American Embassy Mexico, "Subject: Mexico Narco Violence," 5.

18. General Accounting Office, *US Assistance Has Helped*, 14.

19. Colleen W. Cook, *Mexico's Drug Cartels*, Report R-L32724 (Washington, DC: Congressional Research Service, February 25, 2008), 9.

20. American Embassy Mexico to Secretary of State Washington, DC, "Mexico—Violence Continues," Mexico 003908 191813Z, June 2005, 5.

21. Gustavo Castillo García, "La libertad absoluta a de la Guardia García revés legal a Marisela Morales," *La Journada* (Mexico), January 10, 2013, www.jornada .unam.mx. The AFI number two man was Rodolfo de la Guardia García. He was never convicted. The federal court ruled there was not enough evidence.

22. Anabel Hernández, *Narcoland: The Mexican Drug Lords and Their Godfathers*, trans. Ian Bruce (New York: Verso Books, 2013), 7.

23. US Department of State, "Vital National Interests: Certification Mexico" (Washington, DC: US Department of State, February 9, 1996), 11–12.

24. Jorge Luis Sierra Guzmán, "Mexico's Military in the War on Drugs," *Drug War Monitor* 2, no. 2 (April 2003): 2.

25. Luis Astorga, *El Siglo de las Drogas*, 2nd ed. (Mexico City: Random House, 2016), 223.

26. Sierra Guzmán, "Mexico's Military in the War on Drugs," 5.

27. Presidencia de La Republica de México, *Ordena Presidente Vicente Fox puesta en marcha del Operativo México Seguro contra el crimen organizada* (Los Pinos: Presidencia de La Republica de México, June 11, 2005), http://fox .presidencia.gob.mx/actividades/orden/?contenido=18872.

28. American Embassy Mexico, "Mexico—Violence Continues," 4.

29. Sierra Guzmán, "Mexico's Military in the War on Drugs," 6. Six hundred members of the battalion were investigated before it was dismantled.

30. American Embassy Mexico, "Subject: Mexico Narco Violence," 5.

31. American Embassy Mexico to Secretary of State Washington, DC, "Subject: Retired Mexican General Critical of SEDENA's Role," Mexico 001618 050524Z, March 2005, 1–3.

32. General Accounting Office, *U.S. Assistance Has Helped*, 12.

33. Ibid., i.

34. David Reiff, "The Populist at the Border," *New York Times*, June 4, 2006, Sunday Magazine, sec. 6, p. 36.

35. Marina Jiménez, "Voodoo Politics," *Globe and Mail* (Canada), June 17, 2006, Focus, p. 1.

36. James C. McKinley Jr., "In Presidential Tone, Calderón Rejects Recount," *New York Times*, July 14, 2006, sec. A, p. 8.

37. Louie Gilot, "Experts Say Border Not on Calderón's Agenda for Now," *El Paso Times*, December 16, 2006, News, p. 1.

38. Laurence Iliff and Alfredo Corchado, "Mexico's Power Vacuum Lets Drug Terror Spread," *Dallas Morning News*, August 26, 2006.

39. Beittel, *Mexico's Drug Trafficking Organizations*, 3.

40. General Accounting Office, *US Assistance Has Helped*, 7.

41. US Congress, Senate, Caucus on International Narcotics Control, *US-Mexican Reponses to Mexican Drug Trafficking Organizations*, 112th Cong., 1st sess., May 25, 2011, 35.

222 *Narcostates*

42. Seelke, Wyler, and Beittel, *Latin American and the Caribbean*, 15.

43. Cook, *Mexico's Drug Cartels*, 16.

44. Senate, Caucus on International Narcotics Control, *US-Mexican Reponses*, 39.

45. Clare Ribando Seelke and Kristin Finklea, *U.S.-Mexican Security Cooperation: The Mérida Initiative and Beyond*, Report R-41349 (Washington, DC: Congressional Research Service, April 8, 2014), 36.

46. Senate, Caucus on International Narcotics Control, *U.S.-Mexican Reponses*, 35–36.

47. Beittel, *Mexico's Drug Trafficking Organizations*, 33.

48. George W. Grayson, *The Impact of President Felipe Calderón's War on Drugs on the Armed Forces: The Prospects for Mexico's Militarization and Bilateral Relations* (Carlisle Barracks, PA: US Army War College Strategic Studies Institute, January 2013), 3.

49. Beittel, *Mexico's Drug Trafficking Organizations*, 3.

50. Grayson, *The Impact of President Felipe Calderón's*, 33.

51. Ibid., 32.

52. Beittel, *Mexico's Drug Trafficking Organizations*, 3.

53. "El clan de los Gori," *Proceso* (Mexico), December 15, 2009, www.proceso.com.mx.

54. American Embassy Mexico to Secretary of State Washington, DC, "Subject: Narcotics Affairs Section Mexico Monthly Report for November 2009," Mexico 003555 152303Z, December 15, 2009, 2; Dallas News Administrator, "Mexico's Zetas Gang Buys Business Along Border in Move to Increase Legitimacy," *Dallas Morning News*, December 7, 2009.

55. United Nations Office on Drugs and Crime, *2013 Global Study on Homicide* (Vienna: United Nations Office on Drugs and Crime, March 2014), 126.

56. Grayson, *The Impact of President Felipe Calderón's*, 3.

57. William Robert Johnston, "Data on Mexican Drug War Violence," *Johnston's Archive*, February 28, 2011, www.johnstonsarchive.net.

58. Brianna Lee, "Mexico's Drug War," Council on Foreign Relations, March 5, 2014, www.cfr.org; Cory Molzahn, Octavio Rodriguez Ferriera, and David A. Shirk, "Drug War Violence in Mexico," Trans-Border Institute, February 2013, 13–14.

59. Human Rights Watch, "Neither Rights nor Security: Killings, Torture, and Disappearances in Mexico's War on Drugs" (Washington, DC: Human Rights Watch, November 4, 2011), 4.

60. Maureen Meyer, "Abused and Afraid in Ciudad Juárez: An Analysis of Human Rights Abused in Mexico" (Washington, DC: Washington Office on Latin America, September 2010), 2.

61. Human Rights Watch, "Neither Rights nor Security," 5–6.

62. Human Rights Watch, "US: Withholds Funds for Mexico Tied to Human Rights Performance" (Washington, DC: Human Rights Watch, September 14, 2010), 1; Witness for Peace, "Fact Sheet: The Mérida Initiative," 2011, 1.

63. "Senator Patrick Leahy Blocks $95 Million in Mérida Initiative Funds," *Mexico Gulf Reporter*, August 15, 2013.

64. Jennifer Johnson, "Mexico Passes Historic Reform to the Military Justice Code" (Washington, DC: Latin America Working Group, April 30, 2014), www.lawg.org.

65. Meyer, *Abused and Afraid in Ciudad Juárez*, 4.

66. Grayson, *The Impact of President Felipe Calderón's*, 25–30.

67. AMCONSUL Monterrey to RUEHC/SECSTATE, "Subject: Drug Cartel Produced Videotape Alleges Corruption at Highest Levels of Mexican Government," Monterrey 00472 1172107, April 27, 2007, 2.

The Militarization of the US-Mexican War on Drugs   223

68. Ibid., 2.

69. Human Rights Watch, "Neither Rights nor Security," 10.

70. Beittel, *Mexico's Drug Trafficking Organizations*, 34.

71. Government Accountability Office, *Mérida Initiative: The United States Has Provided Counternarcotics and Anti-Crime Support, but Needs Better Performance Measures*, GAO-10-837 (Washington, DC: GAO, July 2010), 15.

72. "Senator Patrick Leahy Blocks $95 Million," Mexico Gulf Reporter.

73. Seelke and Finklea, *U.S.-Mexican Security Cooperation*, 3.

74. US Department of State, Bureau of International Narcotics and Law Enforcement Affairs, *2014 International Narcotics Control Strategy Report Vol. I.* (Washington, DC: US Department of State March 2014), 233–237. The State Department stopped providing graphs with their reports that included cultivation, interdiction, seizure, and eradication rates after 2009. To compile this information, each State Department report was consulted to obtain the annual statistics provided.

75. Alex Newman, "Reports: CIA Working with Mexican Cartels," *New American*, August 15, 2011, www.thenewamerican.com; Robert Farago and Ralph Dixon, "Was CIA Behind Operation Fast and Furious?" *Washington Times*, August 11, 2011.

76. Farago and Dixon, "Was CIA Behind."

77. Alex Newman, "Trafficker: US Feds Aided Mexican Drug Cartel," *New American*, August 8, 2011, www.thenewamerican.com; *United States v. Jesús Vicente "El Vicentillo" Zambada Niebla*, Memorandum of Law in Support of Motion for Discovery Regarding Defense of Public Authority, United States District Court Northern District of Illinois Eastern Division, Case Number 09 CRC 383, November 10, 2011, 26–56.

78. Susan Vera, "U.S. Government Struck Deal with Mexican Drug Cartel in Exchange for Information," Reuters, January 14, 2014, http://rt.com/usa/sinaloa-drug-cartel-deal-dea-551.

79. *United States v. Jesús Vicente "El Vicentillo" Zambada Niebla*, Case Number 09 CRC 383, 26–56.

80. Ibid.; Newman, "Trafficker: US Feds."

81. Office of the Inspector General, *The Review of ATF's Operation Fast and Furious and Related Matters* (Washington, DC: US Department of Justice, September 2012), 24–28.

82. Ibid.

83. FBI Laboratory Quantico Virginia to Phoenix Squad C-6/Tucson RA SA Michelle L. Terwilliger, "Report of Examination: Brian Terry (Victim); U.S. Border Patrol Agent; Assault on Federal Officer," Federal Bureau of Investigation Case Number 89B-PX-86010, December 23, 2010.

84. Richard Serrano, "Attorney General Holder Accuses Critics of Politicizing Fast and Furious Case," *Los Angeles Times*, December 8, 2011.

85. Richard A. Serrano, "President Obama Defends Attorney General Regarding ATF Tactics," *Los Angeles Times*, October 6, 2011.

86. Kellan Howell, "Over 15,000 Fast and Furious Records Withheld Under Obama Executive Privilege," *Washington Times*, October 23, 2014.

87. Ed O'Keefe and Sari Horowitz, "House Votes to Hold Attorney General Holder in Contempt," *Washington Post*, June 28, 2012.

88. Katie Pavlich, "Breaking: DOJ Turns Over 64,000 Fast and Furious Documents Held Under Obama's Executive Privilege," November 4, 2014, TownHall.com, http://townhall.com.

89. US Congress, House of Representatives, Committee on Oversight and Government Reform, *Operation Fast and Furious: The Other Side of the Border*, 112th Cong., 1st sess., July 26, 2011, 1.

90. Nacha Cattan, "Mexico Law Makers Livid over Fast and Furious," *Christian Science Monitor*, March 9, 2011.

91. Ken Ellingwood, Richard A. Serrano, and Tracy Wilkinson, "Mexico Still Waiting for Answers on Fast and Furious Gun Program," *Los Angeles Times*, March 19, 2014.

92. Ibid.

93. Peter Watt and Roberto Zepeda, *Drug War Mexico: Politics, Neoliberalism, and Violence in the New Narcoeconomy* (London: Zed Books, 2012), 8.

10

The Mexican Cartels and Youth Gangs in Central America

The combination of drug trafficking and gangs wreaked havoc on the Northern Triangle countries of Guatemala, El Salvador, and Honduras in the first decade of the new millennium. With the Mexican cartel war heating up, Mexican drug trafficking organizations (DTOs) redirected their operations through the Central American narcocorridor. As they moved into Central America, the Mexican DTOs strengthened alliances with the region's gang networks, which were active along Mexico's southern and northern border areas, as well as in the United States. While the conditions in Nicaragua, Costa Rica, and Panama were not as bad as they were in the Northern Triangle, each country's security situation deteriorated during this time period. Gangs and narcotraffickers seemed omnipresent, undermining Central America's institutions. As governments faltered, insecurity burgeoned. The problem was not confined to a single state, but rather to a region plagued by Mexican DTOs and their Central American gang affiliates.

The Central American Gang–Mexican Cartel Connection

The imprisonment and deportation of Central American gang members following the 1992 Los Angeles riots transformed Central America's gangs into transnational criminal networks. Salvadoran and Guatemalan illegal immigrants were not readily accepted by Hispanic communities in places like Los Angeles.[1] Mexican street gangs in the United States, such as the Mexican Mafia (La eMe), reacted to any threat by engaging in turf wars with Central American gangs in order to defend their territory.[2] While the gangland wars were being fought, the United States stepped up deportations of Central American illegal immigrants who often worked their way back to

226   *Narcostates*

the United States. As a result, the Central American gang networks began to proliferate along international contraband routes throughout Central America and Mexico.[3] Rather than continuing to engage in a constant turf war with the Central Americans, La eMe proposed that the MS-13 and Calle 18 gangs could have their own drug and weapons territory, but in exchange they would provide La eMe with taxes and muscle.[4] MS-13 and Calle 18 agreed to this proposal and became *sureños* (subordinates) to La eMe in the *tregua de sur* (truce of the south).[5] The alliance solidified La eMe's control over a major portion of the US-Mexico cross-border drug trade because of its close association with Mexican DTOs.[6] For example, the Knights Templar would pay the Mexican Mafia to use its MS-13 *sureños* dispersed throughout California to protect and sell their shipments of methamphetamine.[7] By 2009, the National Gang Intelligence Center estimated that there were 125,000 *sureños* living in the United States, many of them trafficking in drugs and committing other crimes on behalf of La eMe.[8]

Not all researchers agree on the extent of relations between the Mexican cartels and Central American gangs. One argument postulates that gang members and DTOs represented different interests because a distinction existed between *pandilleros* (street gang members), *banderos* (members of organized crime groups), and *transeros* (drug traffickers). According to the UN, relations between these groupings varied. They could be fully integrated, purely commercial, or even hostile toward each other.[9] Despite these arguments, the gangs undoubtedly assisted Mexican cartels in smuggling drugs, weapons, and humans across Mexico's southern border. On the northern border, multiple cross-border criminal enterprises attracted the Central American gangs who were employed by the cartels to assist with narcotics distribution and assassinations.[10] Initially, the MS-13 and Calle 18 trafficked immigrants northward using freight trains as the means of transportation between the United States, Mexico, and Central America. According to USAID, the gang presence along the US-Mexico border was the result of several factors: the cartels; the trafficking of drugs, people, weapons, and other illegal substances; the *maquiladora* industry; the lack of educational opportunities; substance abuse among youths; dysfunctional families; and familial traditions to join gangs.[11] Lucrative criminal opportunities and a flourishing drug trade brought the cartels and gangs together.

Acting as contract workers and middlemen for the various Mexican DTOs, the Central American gangs morphed into transnational crime networks.[12] According to FBI agent Robert Hart, MS-13 became a closely knit, structured entity, with national leaders asserting control, collecting dues, and presiding over activities resembling those of organized crime. Hart added that *ranfleros* (senior gang leaders) from El Salvador and Southern California imposed tight discipline and coordination over street-level activities. Furthermore, members of *clikas* in El Salvador and California were

The Mexican Cartels and Youth Gangs in Central America   227

directed to organize *clikas* on the East Coast of the United States.[13] In 2012, the US Treasury placed MS-13 on a list that made it illegal to conduct business with them because of their "transnational criminal activities."[14] According to Brian Trucheon, director of the FBI's MS-13 National Gang Task Force, MS-13 became "a gang that operates across borders." Trucheon added that "it's common to see members of the L.A. clika in El Salvador, or Salvadoran members in New York, recruiting or sharing tactics. The scary thing for us is how quickly they can evolve to move around obstacles that law enforcement throws up."[15]

Because of their former FMLN connections, ties with Mexican coyotes, and connections to Mexican cartels, the El Salvadoran and Guatemalan gangs ran contraband routes established during their civil wars to move guns south and humans and narcotics north.[16] By 2004, the MS-13 in Honduras was trafficking marijuana, cocaine, weapons, and humans across the border into Mexico. In 2005, the Mexican government reported that MS-13 had established 200 cells in Mexico, 90 percent of which were active in the drug trade in Chiapas. In Nuevo Laredo, MS-13 members from El Salvador, Dallas, and North Carolina coordinated closely with Los Zetas.[17] Los Zetas also provided military training and weapons to MS-13 *clikas*.[18] The Mexican government expressed growing concern that MS-13 was capable of running large-scale drug trafficking and human smuggling operations.[19] In the case of human trafficking, MS-13 charged 500 to 2,000 pesos to deliver an illegal immigrant to Virginia, North Carolina, or New York. Migrants who could not afford passage paid their debts by committing various crimes for the MS-13.[20] One MS-13 leader stated that he collected fees from the immigrants to support fellow gang members in jail, pay attorney fees, and provide money for food and laundry.[21] Remittances also provided a means to launder money and pay these fees. As the gang network evolved, they developed connections in Spain, the largest point of entry for cocaine into Europe.[22]

The vertical integration of the Central American and US gangs cemented the transnational nature of the MS-13 by establishing links between Central America and factions in Virginia, Maryland, New York, California, and Texas.[23] By 2014, MS-13 attempted to coordinate its activities throughout the United States as part of a national program. Called the "unification of the barrio," MS-13 sought to organize all US *clikas* under a single leadership structure. According to the FBI, the unification plan sought to increase the collection of extortion proceeds, known as "rent," which would be used to establish drug distribution channels that supplied cheap methamphetamine and other narcotics to MS-13 members across the country.[24] Alliances with La eMe, and Mexican DTOs such as La Familia Michoacana, would facilitate their plan.[25] Unquestionably, the MS-13's far-reaching network began to resemble a transnational DTO.

228 *Narcostates*

Guatemala:
Losing Control

Control over the Central American routes became increasingly important to Mexican DTOs with the capacity to project themselves into the region. Los Zetas became the most prominent DTO to move into Central America, and by 2010 it had a well-cemented pipeline running through Guatemala. In order to establish its foothold, Los Zetas gunmen engaged in bloody shootouts with Guatemalan traffickers. From Guatemala, Los Zetas moved Colombian cocaine into southern Mexico. There, the cocaine made its way to Nuevo Laredo, where Los Zetas transported the product north. Black market economics and the strength of their organization as a criminal brand name held the loosely networked cells together all the way from Guatemala to Zacatecas in central Mexico to the borders of Tamaulipas and Nuevo León.[26] Even as the Mexican government arrested or killed Los Zetas's leaders, its disciplined command structure ensured the cohesion of its operations in Central America.

To add a layer of protection for its cocaine shipments moving through Guatemala, Los Zetas recruited members of Guatemala's special operations unit, Los Kaibiles. The State Department mentioned the connection in 2005 when it reported that the Mexican government was investigating the group for links to Los Zetas. The State Department expressed concern that the Guatemala-Mexico border could see an increase in narcoviolence similar to the US-Mexico border.[27] Los Kaibiles provided military training for Los Zetas recruits, some of whom were members of MS-13 and Calle 18.[28] Their training was to prepare them to act as security along the Guatemalan and Honduran borders with Mexico.[29] As Los Zetas and the gangs grew closer, the gangs prohibited the consumption of drugs by members and required them to remove or cover up their tattoos because their markings made it easy for authorities to identify them.

A lack of resources constrained the Guatemalan government's response. Weak Guatemalan counternarcotics programs were set back after the US government briefly decertified Guatemala in 2003 because the United States considered President Alfonso Portillo's (2000–2004) counternarcotics efforts insufficient.[30] Despite receiving $61 million in US foreign aid between 1997 and 2004 to improve its judicial system, Guatemala lacked transportation and equipment for the police to challenge narcotraffickers.[31] Moreover, as part of the 1996 peace accords, Guatemala's military intelligence was curtailed, resulting in a decrease in its interdiction capabilities. In an attempt to stop traffickers from transiting through Guatemala, President Óscar Berger (2004–2008) sent a task force to establish control over the Petén border. However, the State Department considered Berger's strategy problematic, because the "blurred national border

The Mexican Cartels and Youth Gangs in Central America   229

[with Mexico] prevented host country forces from pursuing traffickers across the frontier."[32]

Guatemala's vast and porous border with Mexico and Honduras made it vulnerable to illegal trafficking. In 1999, the State Department reported that "drug running, arms trafficking, and immigrant smuggling" were flourishing along the Mexico-Guatemala border. They added that a "large business in the sale and distribution of clandestine arms from ex-Guatemalan and Salvadoran guerrillas to the Mexican cartels" was occurring along the Guatemalan border with Chiapas. The human trafficking of people primarily from Guatemala, El Salvador, and Honduras grew along with the drug trade. Human and narcotics traffickers corrupted key officials at Guatemala's La Aurora Airport and at the border with Mexico.[33] Between 1996 and 1999, more than 500 homicides occurred as a result of human trafficking along the Mexican border.[34] Hurricane Stan in 2005 aggravated the border issue even further. The destruction of 30,000 homes, combined with flooding that destroyed much of the infrastructure within Chiapas and Petén, drew resources away from counternarcotics programs. The hurricane also broadened the presence of trafficking networks by enabling the MS-13 and Calle 18 gangs to push into central Mexico due to the lack of law enforcement along the border.[35]

Drug trafficking and violent crime skyrocketed in Guatemala. By 2003, the US and Guatemalan governments reported dramatic increases in gang activity, corresponding with a rise in crime. The dramatic growth of theft, carjackings, armored car heists, and bus robberies was directly attributable to the cross-border migration of street gangs. Often those crimes ended with fatalities of police officers and civilians.[36] Most criminals operated in groups greater than four and were confrontational.[37] Guatemalan criminals were exceptionally well-armed and adept at procuring powerful weapons and explosives, committing most crimes using AK-47s.[38] In one incident, gangs fired AK-47s at each other during a drug-related shootout nine blocks from the American Embassy in Guatemala City. In another instance, a fragmentation grenade was thrown into a police substation in San José Pinula injuring two pedestrians. Twenty-five minutes after this attack, a call to the same police substation threatened to continue attacks against all officers if the police did not immediately cease their antigang activities.[39]

Guatemalan *transportistas* (contraband smugglers) were drawn into the cartel wars as they deepened their ties to the Mexican DTOs. For example, the Mendozas in Petén and the Leónes in Zacapa were among the most important Guatemalan *transportistas* that became minicartels. They acted as subcontractors for the Mexican and Colombian cartels operating in Guatemala. Sophisticated weapons combined with a willingness to use force led to numerous battles with law enforcement and heavy losses on both sides.[40] In 2001 and 2002, Guatemala's homicide rate was

230   Narcostates

27 per 100,000 inhabitants.[41] By 2006, the homicide rate reached 47 per 100,000 inhabitants. The problems of drugs and homicide were not unrelated. For example, Petén, a 70 percent rural province, maintained the second highest murder rate in the country (116 per 100,000), largely attributable to trafficking operations.[42] According to another estimate, approximately 40 percent of the total number of murders were directly connected to drug trafficking in Guatemala.[43] The murders often involved an element of sadism, and in some cases, women were mutilated.[44] Following the arrival of Los Zetas in Guatemala around 2007, Guatemala's *transportistas* were eliminated.[45] After this point, most trafficking operations through Guatemala fell under the purview of Los Zetas and their Los Kaibiles allies.

Guatemala's drug war intensified in February 2007, when the charred bodies of three Salvadoran congressmen and their chauffeur were found on a Guatemalan farm near the town of El Jocotillo just off of the Inter-American Highway.[46] One of the bodies was that of Congressman Eduardo D'Aubuisson, the son of ARENA party founder Roberto D'Aubuisson. At first, the killings were believed to be politically motivated, but the crime scene indicated that the legislators were tortured and had their car torn apart in a search for drugs and money. FBI agents sent to investigate the murders were stonewalled by the Guatemalan government.[47] In the months that followed, several high-ranking Guatemalan officials and at least twelve civilians and police officers were prosecuted in connection with the murders. The mayor of Jutiapa and a Salvadoran congressman were accused of conspiring with drug traffickers, although observers speculated that they were not at the top of the chain.[48] The editor of the newspaper *La Hora* summed up the situation succinctly: "When the war stopped, the state apparatus kept operating the same way, [but now] it protects organized crime."[49]

Government corruption was rampant. Suspicions about a clique within military intelligence known as the Cofirada became widespread. A UN-backed anti-impunity commission called the Comisión Internacional contra la Impunidad en Guatemala (CICIG) reinforced the perception of corruption within the government when it named Guatemalan judges as conspirators with organized crime. In August 2007, the CICIG gave Guatemalan authorities the ability to conduct covert eavesdropping operations to obtain information on organized crime and institutional corruption.[50] The investigations led to indictments against former president Alfonso Portillo in 2011 for embezzlement; PNC chief Erwin Sperisen in 2010 for extrajudicial murder, drug trafficking, and money laundering; and Byron Lima Oliva, a D-2 intelligence officer jailed in 2001 for the 1998 murder of human rights advocate Bishop Juan Gerardi Conedera.[51] In a November 2012 report, eighteen judges were accused of offering impunity to organized crime syndicates and members of the security

The Mexican Cartels and Youth Gangs in Central America   231

forces engaged in drug trafficking. The majority of those indicted by the report did not face formal charges.[52]

Guatemala began to spin out of control. In 2009, the US State Department reported that the government of Guatemala lost control over "large swaths of national territory—primarily the border regions—to narcotraffickers."[53] In 2010, an estimated 250 metric tons of cocaine were smuggled through Guatemala, doubling the amount from 2008. At the same time, law enforcement budgets were cut back because of the lack of revenue.[54] For example, a detail of only 250 soldiers patrolled the 5,000 square miles of Petén. More importantly, law enforcement officials were susceptible to *plata o plomo* (bribery or bullets).[55] In ten years, Guatemala's murder rate had doubled and was four times higher than Mexico's rate. Murders reached 52 homicides per 100,000 citizens. The impunity rate for murder stood at 96.5 percent in 2010.

Coordinating their operations from prison, gang leaders in cooperation with Mexican DTOs started to replace the state. By providing employment and charity, the gangs gained influence over local municipalities in order to control the flow of narcotics. In one case, the local population in the town of San Marcos near the Mexican border demonstrated against the government following the arrest of a trafficker named Mauro Ramírez Barrios, because he was so important to the local economy. As the police mounted counternarcotics raids, they came under heavy fire in places like San Marcos, where campesinos cultivated marijuana and opium poppy fields.[56] The border was completely lost. The government declared a state of siege in the departments of Alta Verapaz in December 2010 and Petén in May 2011.[57] According to Francisco Dall'Anese, the head of the CICIG, "Fighting organized crime posed a double challenge. The first is to win the battle against organized crime, the second is to win it [while] maintaining the rule of law."[58] Dall'Anese's recommendation was quixotic.

El Salvador:
No End in Sight

Violence in El Salvador reached all-time highs as the murder rate rose from 2,346 in 2002 to 3,182 in 2005.[59] The crisis became apparent when the Policía Nacional Civil (PNC) estimated that from January through July of 2005, 2,040 homicides were committed in El Salvador, compared to 1,501 during the same time period in 2004; about 55 out of every 100,000 Salvadorans fell victim to murder in 2005. The majority of homicide victims were men between the ages of nineteen and fifty-nine living in urban areas.[60] An estimated 400,000 illegal weapons, including AK-47s and M-16s, were on the streets. It was unknown how many of these were non-decommissioned weapons from the civil war.[61] The government of El

232 Narcostates

Salvador attributed most of the killings to gang activity but also to narco-traffickers. Because of the increase in homicides, the people of El Salvador remained supportive of the government's mano dura policies.[62]

In 2006, the Salvadoran government began referring to the violence as a criminal epidemic. At more than 10,000 members, the Salvadoran gangs were allegedly concentrating on narcotics, arms trafficking, murder for hire, and carjackings. The gangs roamed freely day and night and were quick to engage in violence if resistance was offered.[63] PNC director Rodrigo Ávila's first act was to remove corrupt PNC members and traffic-control officers who took bribes from petty street dealers in San Salvador.[64] Despite Ávila's efforts, he lacked the resources necessary to confront institutional corruption and the gang problem. The cost of dealing with the gangs had already consumed more than 11 percent of El Salvador's GDP.

According to the US State Department, the biggest problem for El Salvador was the US deportation of gang members. A catch-22 situation existed; US deportations exacerbated crime in El Salvador, but US taxpayer money was needed to fight crime in El Salvador or the problem would return to the United States. The US State Department considered the deportations money well spent and that they had a positive impact on US national security, especially with the gang issue in the United States. Unfortunately, deportations simultaneously drained El Salvador's national treasury while exacerbating the frequency of gang-related crime.[65]

The gangs contributed to El Salvador's transformation into a transnational drug conduit. The Pacific maritime route through El Salvador became a frequent route used by narcotraffickers. In 2007, the US State Department reported that there was evidence of a growing collusion between gangs and transnational drug smuggling rings. The Salvadoran government mobilized to curtail some of this trade, with limited success. In 2008, the Salvadoran government seized 9 kilos of heroin, 300 kilos of marijuana, 1,350 kilos of cocaine, and more than $2 million in hard cash from drug dealers.[66] A year later, the Salvadoran government seized 5 kilos of heroin, 323 kilos of marijuana, and 1,769 kilos of cocaine. That same year, the joint US-Salvadoran Transnational Anti-Gang (TAG) unit reported links between transnational gangs, street-level drug distribution, and related violence.[67]

By June 2009, when ex-journalist and FMLN leader Mauricio Funes Cartagena (2009–2014) became president, the gang problem had become intractable. MS-13 and Calle 18 spread into marginalized urban communities, committing a variety of crimes with increasing brutality. In November 2009, Funes deployed 3,500 soldiers to occupy twenty-eight of the most violent areas of the country for 180 days. These forces were sent to supplement the 2,000 PNC officers already mobilizing against

The Mexican Cartels and Youth Gangs in Central America   **233**

gangs. According to the US State Department, more than half of the Salvadoran military's 10,000 troops were engaged in domestic law enforcement.[68] The Funes government also announced a comprehensive crime policy, including institutional and legal reforms, prevention, rehabilitation, victim support, and law enforcement.[69] A community policing program to bring the police into closer contact with the populations they served was a part of this policy. To control the prisons, the Salvadoran government introduced a body orifice scanning system and cell phone detection monitors to reduce the number of cell phones, chips, and chargers smuggled into the system.[70] The US State Department thought Funes's goals were ambitious because "Funes inherited an economy in a recession" with a fiscal deficit that "severely limited his ability to provide immediate relief."[71]

Although the mano dura and super mano dura increased arrests, they also inadvertently allowed the gangs to expand their territory.[72] In September 2010, threats of gang violence caused a forced three-day shutdown of transportation networks. The gangs issued a communiqué calling for a dialogue with the government; apparently they felt "oppressed" by the mano dura laws. The military deployed 2,000 troops to help the police restore order. According to the US State Department, the deployment stretched "the military's financial and personnel resources to the breaking point." When interviewed on national television, Salvadoran gang members claimed the antigang laws were repressive and discriminatory. They said that violence begets more violence and blamed the increase on the security services. The gang's press release contained phrases used by a student revolutionary group called the Brigadas Revolucionarias de El Salvador (BRES), which was linked to the FMLN. Funes declared that the government "would not allow itself to be blackmailed."[73]

As El Salvador moved into the next decade, its importance as a transit location for gangs and DTOs was critical. Reports of FARC drugs and guns operations being run through El Salvador surfaced. In 2008, a former member of the FMLN arranged arms purchases on behalf of the FARC through El Salvador. In another instance, a Salvadoran trafficking organization in the Department of San Miguel bordering Honduras transshipped cocaine and heroin for the FARC to Honduras, Guatemala, Mexico, and the United States.[74] In 2012, the Salvadoran antinarcotics police (DAN) seized $2 million worth of South American cocaine being transported by MS-13 through the province of Sonsonate along the Pacific coast into Guatemala.[75] The problem for El Salvador was that its limited resources were being squandered on counternarcotics programs run by the military. Rather than acting as an external security force (designated as its role in the 1992 peace accords), the military was conducting internal security operations once again. For El Salvador, it seemed like there was no way out.

234   *Narcostates*

Honduras:
Plata o Plomo

The importance of Honduras as a waypoint between Andean source countries, Mexico, and the United States grew. By 2002, 90 percent of all narcotics moving through Honduras were going to the United States.[76] The lack of law enforcement in rural areas, especially along the Honduran coastline, facilitated narcotrafficking. The Policía Nacional (PN) forces were few in number, and their limited resources were directed primarily toward urban crime and murder. Violent crime reached 46 murders per 100,000 inhabitants in 2002, equaling 8 murders every day. The regions with the highest murder rates were the narcotrafficking corridors along the north coast and the border with Guatemala.

In 2002, the US and Honduran governments improved counternarcotics operations, signing a letter of agreement to strengthen the Honduran version of the DEA—La Dirección de Lucha Contra el Narcotráfico (DLCN). This increased the professionalization of the PN. In 2005, the US State Department noted that President Ricardo Maduro (2002–2006) made a significant commitment to improve Honduran counternarcotics operations, including making gang membership a crime.[77] That same year, the Honduran government passed a money laundering law that allowed the police to launch investigations for crimes not directly linked to narcotics. The definition of money laundering now included the transfer of assets that proceeded directly or indirectly from the trafficking of drugs, weapons, human organs or people, auto theft, kidnapping, financial fraud, terrorism, or the movement of assets that lacked any economic justification. The law also required all persons entering or leaving Honduras to declare and present money and convertible securities if the amount exceeded $10,000. The penalty for money laundering was a prison sentence of fifteen to twenty years.[78] Between 2002 and 2004, the value of asset seizures jumped from $2 million in cash and $584,000 in goods to $4.1 million in cash and $2 million in goods. The US State Department considered the money laundering laws a step in the right direction, but even then it still considered the law weak and wanted greater international coordination.[79] While Honduras showed a willingness to cooperate with the United States, no specific written agreement existed to establish a mechanism for exchanging records related to narcotics, terrorism, terrorist financing, or other crime investigations.[80]

Although Maduro willingly confronted narcotraffickers, a major problem for his government was the extent and depth of corruption. The US State Department maintained that "the penetration of law enforcement agencies by narcotraffickers and other criminals" continued to mount. To deal with corruption, the Honduran government created the Council Nacional Anticorrupción (CNA) in 2001, and in 2002, the Tribunal Supe-

The Mexican Cartels and Youth Gangs in Central America   235

rior de Cuentas (TSC), but the US State Department received reports that "neither institution lived up to [its] potential."[81] In 2001, Honduras's minister of security fired 2,500 officers, representing 30 percent of the PN, but the Honduran Supreme Court ruled that the dismissals were unconstitutional.[82] In 2003, President Maduro passed a constitutional amendment that eliminated immunity for all legislative, judicial, and government officials, leading to the arrest of three members of the National Congress on drug trafficking charges in 2003.[83]

Corruption scandals within the Honduran military and police attracted public attention. The inability of the pension system to meet its promises to military officers opened the door to corruption. The military denied the charges, but evidence of corruption burgeoned.[84] In one case, the Honduran immigration director, Ramon Romero, was arrested for allowing the illegal entry of Colombians into Honduras and for drug trafficking. The US government considered his release on bail the result of corruption within the Honduran judiciary.[85] Polls showed that the majority of people felt that the Honduran government did not take corruption seriously and that 75 percent of the police were in the pay of drug traffickers and gangs.[86]

The US State Department believed that DTOs were leveraging violence and corruption to render Honduran law enforcement incapable of disrupting drug trafficking. The US State Department did not believe that Honduran gangs directed large-scale shipments of cocaine, but they did believe the gangs worked for the cartels to secure shipments.[87] Further adding to the gang-trafficker nexus was the fact that Honduran laws did not stop the use of remittances to launder money. Traffickers transferred an estimated $1 billion in remittances back to Honduras, further extending their influence.[88] According to the US State Department, "The growing narcotics problem deterred foreign investment under the Central American Free Trade Agreement (CAFTA), led Honduran youth to seek illegal entry into the U.S. at the rate of 200 persons daily, and resulted in a largely unhindered drug flow into the U.S."[89]

In 2009, President Manuel Zelaya (2006–2009) was ousted in a constitutional crisis. As early as 2007, the US State Department conjectured that Zelaya's failure to take effective measures against trafficking and its related violence would turn the public against him.[90] An unfortunate effect of the constitutional crisis was increased narcotrafficking in Honduras. With corruption rampant at the highest levels of the Honduran government, narcotics trafficking exploded. Zelaya placed narcotics interdiction on the back burner of his national priorities and was accused of using the military and police for political purposes. With Zelaya's ouster and the subsequent breakdown of the Honduran political system, counternarcotics operations became nonexistent. The US government added to the failure when it suspended counternarcotics cooperation with the Honduran government to

236   *Narcostates*

protest the "coup." Illegal flights through Honduran airspace substantially increased. The State Department reported that the Joint Interagency Task Force South (JIATF-S) recorded 75 suspect air flights into Honduras during 2010, compared with 54 in 2009, and 31 in 2008.[91] The tonnage of cocaine passing through Honduras increased from 182 metric tons in 2008 to 200 metric tons in 2009.[92] At least one to two narcotics shipments passed through Honduran airspace daily. It was not until 2010 that the United States began to work with Honduran officials again. US support was precipitated by President Porfirio Lobo's (2010–2014) deployment of 2,000 soldiers along the Atlantic coast and the passage of a law in 2013 that created the Policía Militar del Orden Público (PMOP), which gave the military a greater role in domestic security to combat organized crime and gangs such as the MS-13 and Barrio-18.[93]

As the power of the Sinaloa cartel grew, the threat of *plata o plomo* ruled the day. According to Honduran intelligence, El Chapo established a school for assassins in Honduras. Between 2007 and 2008, El Chapo's assassins executed various heads of criminal organizations in Honduras.[94] To roll back Honduran counternarcotics forces, El Chapo also coordinated the assassination of General Julián González Irías, the Honduran director of the DLCN, on December 8, 2009. Assassins riding motorcycles fired nine bullets into his utility vehicle.[95] Just before his murder, General González alleged that both the Sinaloa cartel and the Venezuelan government assisted the FARC in smuggling narcotics into Honduras in exchange for guns. He also claimed that Manuel Zelaya was under investigation for his possible involvement in the smuggling of cocaine.[96] Even prior to the assassination, the government alleged there was a large FARC presence in Honduras. In 2005, the Honduran minister of public security Óscar Álvarez alleged that members of the FARC 14th Front were involved in drugs-for-arms deals between Colombia and Honduras and that FARC assassination plots existed against President Maduro. Álvarez may have overstated the allegations to drum up political support. The US State Department claimed that no substantive evidence of FARC attempts to conduct subversive activity beyond drug trafficking existed.[97] To deflect political opposition following Zelaya's removal, interim president Roberto Micheletti (2009–2010) alleged that Zelaya's administration facilitated narcotrafficking, and Micheletti also filed an international complaint against Venezuela.[98]

On April 4, 2016, the Honduran newspaper *El Heraldo* published a set of documents that implicated the PN in the assassination plot of General González.[99] According to *El Heraldo*, "Winter Blanco," a Honduran narcotrafficker allied to the Colombian Cártel del Atlántico ordered the police on his payroll to murder González when he refused to look the other way.[100] The newspaper also alleged that in December 2011, the same assassins murdered the minister of the Secretaría de Seguridad (Secretariat of Security).[101] The PN director denied the accusations and claimed that they were part of a program to undermine the Honduran government's anticorruption program—Misión de Apoyo contra la Corrupción y la Impunidad (MAC-CIH).[102] Today, the public remains uncertain as to who murdered General González, but his assassination certainly revealed the power of narcotraffickers in Honduras. The 2011 discovery of a cocaine processing lab spoke for itself. According to US ambassador Hugo Llorens, the presence of a lab in Honduras was a "worrisome signal that trafficking groups feel that they can operate here relatively easily."[103]

Nicaragua:
The Central American Model Succumbs

In the first decade of the twenty-first century, Nicaragua appeared to be the most stable country in Central America. As a result of the Esquipulas Accords, Nicaragua's transition from civil war left it with a stable police force able to control crime to a greater extent than its neighbors. The police became professionalized by reducing the size of the force and by developing a promotion system to depoliticize the police. Still, progress against narcotrafficking was slow. It was not until 2007 that Nicaragua revised its money laundering laws by making it an autonomous offense, meaning no evidence of a previous crime was needed. Until that point, Nicaraguan law required a predicate criminal offense to be committed (i.e., drug trafficking) before it would press money laundering charges. Yet, the greatest problem for Nicaragua was the cost of maintaining order. In 2006, the CICAD warned that there was no specific allocation made within the general budget for the implementation of a national strategy and that there was no common interagency database to share information.[104] By the end of the decade, 10 percent of Nicaragua's GDP went to crime prevention and related services to reduce crime.[105]

Since only a minor gang problem existed in Nicaragua, the government adopted an antigang approach geared toward prevention and intervention. In 2006, there were an estimated 2,200 gang members in Nicaragua. They committed petty crime and fought for territory in Managua, but they did not pose the same threat as organized gangs in the Northern Triangle.[106] A major reason why the Nicaraguan gangs did not evolve in the same way as the Northern Triangle gangs did was because they had long resisted foreign gangs attempting to move into their barrios. The police also lived in the areas they patrolled, which created a sense of community that helped prevent the proliferation of foreign gangs. The continuation of the neighborhood watch program implemented by the Sandinistas to keep tabs on potential political enemies during the civil war era also put a damper on foreign gang intrusions.[107] Despite Nicaragua's successes, gangs started to smuggle and distribute narcotics along Nicaragua's

238 *Narcostates*

Caribbean coast, and by 2011 the number of gang members had increased to 4,500.[108]

The situation with narcotrafficking and DTOs became worse as the new decade wore on. Between 2006 and 2011, the army seized more than thirty-five tons of cocaine, more than half the amount seized by the police between 2002 and 2005.[109] During this time, the Nicaraguan police concentrated on dismantling the cartels' logistical networks. A 2011 study showed that eight DTOs with ties to Colombian traffickers operated along Nicaragua's Caribbean (Miskito) coast, while the Mexican DTOs based themselves in Managua and operated on the Pacific coast from the southern city of Rivas. The DTOs were utilizing Nicaragua as a service station and used drugs to pay for logistical support, thereby fueling the growth of the domestic market for drugs and of local criminal rings.[110] According to a Nicaraguan rear admiral, drug traffickers were "corrupting Nicaragua's institutions" and setting up "logistical bases" to run their illicit businesses.[111]

The most dangerous area was Nicaragua's Miskito Coast. Unemployment stood at nearly 80 percent in the Bluefields, a city on the Miskito Coast where mining and small-scale fishing were the major industries.[112] Trafficking in the Bluefields sprang up because of government corruption and inattention to the region. Nicaragua's murder rate increased from 9.3 per 100,000 people in 2000 to 14.0 per 100,000 in 2009, and the rate in the Bluefields reached 42.1 murders per 100,000 inhabitants in 2012.[113] Half of those arrested for homicide were between the ages of fifteen and twenty-five.[114] People living along the Miskito Coast referred to bundles of cocaine thrown overboard by traffickers as "white lobsters." Colombian traffickers and Nicaraguan middlemen offered financial rewards to those who found cocaine bales along the coastline. A landowner and shipbuilder named Frank Zeldon and a hotel owner named Archibald Clayburn coordinated the majority of shipments running through the Bluefields. The Mendoza syndicate—once affiliated with the Cali cartel—also moved cocaine through the Miskito Coast.[115] To deal with the increase in trafficking, Nicaragua developed a retaining wall strategy that incorporated land, air, and maritime patrols in key locations. The problem was that Nicaragua's resources were stretched thin against DTOs that employed the latest military technology to move narcotics. In 2011, Nicaragua deployed 250 officers to the region, but that only equaled one officer for every 38.2 square miles.[116]

Drug trafficking through Nicaragua created problems with its neighbors, especially Costa Rica. Along the Pan-American Highway at the Costa Rica–Nicaragua border, traffickers moved drugs and money concealed in cars and tractor trailers with hidden compartments. For example, in August 2005, Nicaragua seized $1.2 million in US currency from a vehicle at the Peñas Blancas checkpoint. Further investigation revealed that the driver

The Mexican Cartels and Youth Gangs in Central America   239

carried out at least twelve additional currency smuggling transactions in only three months.[117] Along Costa Rica's border, the Sinaloa cartel transported cocaine by foot or horseback to the San Juan River and from there to Lake Nicaragua.[118] On more than one occasion, Nicaraguan authorities pursued traffickers over to the Costa Rican side of the San Juan River. Because of an ongoing border dispute dating to the early twentieth century, Costa Rica accused Nicaragua of using its counternarcotics operations as a pretext to extend its control over the river.[119]

Costa Rica:
Pura Vida Forever?

From 1995 to 1999, Costa Rica did not have a significant counternarcotics program. Costa Rica's efforts primarily focused on reducing demand. In 1999, Costa Rica signed the Agreement Between the Government of the Republic of Costa Rica and the Government of the United States of America for Cooperation in Suppressing Illicit Trafficking. Known as the Joint Patrol Agreement, it was designed to prevent traffickers from using Costa Rican territorial waters and airspace. Following its implementation, 72 percent of Costa Rica's cocaine seizures came from maritime shipments between 2000 and 2002.[120] Because Costa Rica did not produce narcotics, it received limited funding for supply-reduction programs. Nevertheless, the budget for supply reduction increased from $545,997 in 2002 to $973,918 in 2006.[121] However, Costa Rica considered demand reduction more important, and its budget reflected that view. Between 2001 and 2002, Costa Rica increased this budget from $2.8 million to $4.9 million. As part of the program, they developed youth programs for children and young adults to resist drug use. In January 2002, Costa Rica enacted Law 8024 to strengthen money laundering laws to regulate, among other crimes, financial transactions associated with trafficking in drugs, firearms, and human beings.

While Costa Rica's programs showed success, they did not prevent it from becoming a transit country. Between 1997 and 2002, Costa Rican authorities seized 25,700 kilos of cocaine.[122] The number of seizures remained steady between 2000 and 2004, with six metric tons seized in 2000 and five metric tons in 2004.[123] Costa Rica's seizure rate reached its apex in 2006 with 32,435 kilos seized.[124] Costa Rica was slowly becoming an ideal place to store Colombian cocaine on its way to Mexico, the United States, or Europe. By 2010, drug traffickers were storing nearly fifteen metric tons of cocaine in the country. Small-time smugglers no longer operated independently. Instead, transnational DTOs—the Sinaloa cartel, La Familia Michoacana, the Gulf cartel, and Los Zetas—took charge over Costa Rican trafficking operations.[125] The DTOs were quick to reroute their operations across Central America to take advantage of regions with the least resistance, and

240   *Narcostates*

this meant Costa Rica.[126] An estimated 85 percent of the cocaine transiting through Costa Rica was carried over land during 2009–2010.[127]

Associated with the rise in narcotrafficking was an increase in gang activity. In 2006, an estimated 2,660 gang members, some of whom came from Nicaragua and El Salvador, were present in Costa Rica.[128] That number equaled 62 gang members per 100,000 people.[129] Although Costa Rica was economically better off than its neighbors, its shadow economy represented roughly 28 percent of its GDP in 2006. While this number was smaller than in Guatemala, where the shadow economy represented 52 percent of its GDP, and Panama, where it represented 65 percent, narcotics were playing a substantial role in Costa Rica's economy.[130]

Corresponding with the rise in trafficking and the appearance of gangs was an increase in murder—a rare crime in a country whose reputation rested on tranquility. From 1999 to 2001, the number increased from 5 to 7 murders per 100,000 citizens. By 2008, that figure escalated to 11 murders per 100,000 people.[131] Between 2007 and 2010, the crime rate climbed 20 to 25 percent annually. What prompted an escalation in crime was the fact that criminals faced few threats from law enforcement and the legal system.[132]

Costa Rican authorities also became increasingly worried about the criminal activities of Colombian guerrillas operating in the country. In 2006, they arrested a former member of the M-19 on money laundering and narcotics trafficking charges. That same year, a FARC guerrilla living as a small-scale fisherman in Costa Rica was arrested for trafficking narcotics through Puntarenas in order to buy weapons for the FARC.[133] The 2009 discovery of two FARC operatives led to increased cooperation between Colombia and Costa Rica. Because of the spike in narcotrafficking, growing economic ties, and the disappearance of other allies in the hemisphere, Colombia became Costa Rica's second closest partner in Latin America after Panama. The Costa Rican government came to believe that its deteriorating domestic security situation was linked to an increase in narcotrafficking-related crime, which coincided with the FARC or narco-related Colombians seeking refuge in Costa Rica due to its soft-on-crime reputation.[134] As a result, Costa Rica moved away from viewing narcotics solely as a domestic matter that required treatment, but rather as an international and national security issue.

Costa Rica tried to do everything right to stop the contagion of narcotrafficking, but it still fell behind. Despite government controls, money laundering thrived. An annual $4.47 billion slipped through Costa Rica via tax evasion, crime, and corruption. The chief public prosecutor stated, "It's now impossible to distinguish what part of the economy is illicit money and what part is legitimate. They're so mixed up it's impossible to distinguish."[135] Incidents of corruption became more common. While Costa Rica's problems

The Mexican Cartels and Youth Gangs in Central America   241

paled in comparison to its neighbors, Costa Ricans feared that this might not be the case in the future.[136] The problem for Costa Rica was perpetual: Costa Rican authorities were underequipped, undermanned, undertrained, underfunded, and lacking in coordination. The State Department demurred that money alone would not change the trajectory for Costa Rica or Central America; instead, Central America needed to carry out strategic planning at the regional level.[137]

Panama:
The Wild West

Ten years after Noriega, a shadow of uncertainty hovered over Panama. The withdrawal of 30,000 US military personnel from the Canal Zone deeply affected Panama's economy. In addition, speculation stemming from artificial interest rates created a recession when the dot-com bubble in US stocks imploded between 2000 and 2002. Poverty, economic disparity, and unemployment became Panama's biggest problems.[138] Crime went on the upswing. A rise in kidnappings and carjackings was reflective of Panama's economic malaise.[139] As US forces departed Panama, Panamanian President Mireya Moscoso (1999–2004) expressed her concern that Colombian drug traffickers, guerrillas, and paramilitaries were being drawn into Panama and that they were using the Colón Free Trade Zone for logistical and financial support.[140]

During Moscoso's presidency, narcotics and weapons trafficking exploded. In 2001, the US State Department reported a 60 percent increase in black market arms deals over the previous two years. Many of the weapons were left over from Central America's civil wars (primarily Nicaragua) bound for South America, particularly Colombia. The Pan-American Highway was the main route for transporting weaponry into Panama, where it was transferred to Colombian guerrillas by boat.[141] Frequently, authorities seized cocaine along with weapons, showing a distinct link between the arms and drugs trade.[142] Nicaraguan arms were also exchanged for drugs in the port of Colón. The Panamanian seizure of the ship *Otterloo* in 2001, carrying 3,000 automatic firearms through Panama from Nicaragua to the AUC in Colombia, demonstrated the importance of Panama in arms-for-drugs transactions.[143] At the time, the US embassy noted that Colombian gangs were colonizing Panama's slums to provide logistical bases for the movement of drugs, people, and cash. Specifically, Colón had become increasingly dangerous because of the arms-for-drugs trafficking.[144]

By 2008, the US State Department reported that Colombian and Mexican cartels, as well as other organizations, including the FARC and the AUC (both designated as terrorist organizations by the United States), used Panama for drug trafficking and money laundering. In addition to the

242   *Narcostates*

Atlantic and Pacific coasts, smugglers employed Panama's four major container seaports, Tocumen Airport, and its uncontrolled airfields.[145] Large ships originating in Venezuela and Ecuador were often the main conduits of cocaine through the port of Colón.[146] While the United States provided financial support to the Panamanian government to increase river and ocean patrols, smuggling continued along Panama's unguarded coastline in the Darién region.[147] Traffickers simply waited for a break in the security patrols before making the trip to pick up their cargo.[148] Because the Panamanian government maintained no standing army after 1989, it faced serious difficulties confronting the well-armed traffickers, who used Darién for rest and relaxation and as a location to organize drug shipments.[149] In Darién, firefights between the Policía Nacional and the FARC occurred as the FARC increasingly pushed into Panama.[150] Colombian guerrillas and DTOs turned Panama into a sieve for narcotics trafficking.

The number of seizures reported by the Panamanian government served as evidence that Panama was a major transitory route, although there was no way to know what escaped detection and exactly how much moved through Panama. Between 2003 and 2007, seizures spiked. In 2003, the Panamanian government seized 9,487 kilos of cocaine, 1,478 kilos of marijuana, and 210 kilos of heroin.[151] In 2007, the rate increased significantly with the seizure of 60,000 kilos of cocaine, 3,900 kilos of marijuana, and 96 kilos of heroin.[152] The seizure rate remained close to that level until 2011, when Panama saw a decrease to 34,000 kilos of cocaine and 4,900 kilos of marijuana seized. However, heroin confiscation increased to 194 kilos. The US government estimated that the drop in seizures was attributable to the disruption of established trafficking organizations and a shift away from trafficking multiton shipments.[153]

Narcotics contributed to gang violence, with revenge killings making up the majority of murders.[154] In 2007, there were an estimated ninety-four different gangs with an estimated 1,385 gang members throughout Panama.[155] While the gangs could not be held responsible for all of the violent crime, the public perception was that they were responsible. By the end of the decade, it was evident that Panama's gangs were assisting the DTOs with drug trafficking and money laundering.[156] Between 2007 and 2010, authorities attributed many murders in Panama City to fighting among *tumbadores*—thieves who robbed drug shipments. Throughout Panama, the murder rate steadily climbed between 2000 and 2009. In 2000, the murder rate stood at 9.8 per 100,000 citizens; it rose to 22.6 murders per 100,000 by 2009. Analysts argued that Panama's murder rate was a contagion from its northern neighbors. On the other hand, the thesis that Panama's violence came from the Northern Triangle ignored the proximity of Panama to Colombia. According to the US State Department, drug trafficking caused the upsurge in violent crime.[157] Cocaine moved north, not south, and the

The Mexican Cartels and Youth Gangs in Central America   243

presence of the FARC, AUC, and BACRIM, all of which trafficked narcotics, made bloodshed inevitable.[158]

Money laundering remained the primary attraction for traffickers in Panama, even though Panama's Unidad de Análisis Financiero (UAF) tracked potential money laundering operations. Traffickers laundered more than $400 million through Panama's Tocumen International Airport. The estimated amount of drug money transported through Tocumen totaled roughly $5 million per month, originating from Colombia and $4 million per month from Mexico.[159] The DEA maintained that the Colón Free Trade Zone (CFTZ) attracted the majority of the drug cash. Because there were more than 100 international banks located in the CFTZ and because the US dollar served as the primary means of exchange, the CFTZ provided traffickers with multiple opportunities to launder drug money using layering, transfers, fronts, and couriers. Once the currency entered the free trade zone, brokers converted US dollars into Panamanian pesos by purchasing the dollars at a discount and then reselling them to other buyers.[160] The situation in the CFTZ provided ample room to conceal smuggling and financial crimes that supported international criminal or subversive organizations.[161]

The proliferation of narcotics and money through Panama opened it up to corruption. Several scandals occurred during the Moscoso (1999–2004) and Torrijos (2004–2009) presidencies. In the words of the US State Department, during the Moscoso regime, the list of scandals involving corruption by Panamanian officials was "long and growing." Allegations existed that government officials took part in arms trafficking operations with former Peruvian intelligence chief Vladimiro Montesinos and with Argentina's Menem government. Most importantly, money laundering allegations were leveled against high-ranking people such as Attorney General José Antonio Sossa.[162] Large money laundering cases continued throughout Moscoso's presidency. Within the CFTZ, HSBC Bank enabled the formation of more than 2,300 shell companies, while other large banks, such as UBS and Credit Suisse Group AG helped create more than 1,100 shell companies each.[163]

Corruption and money laundering scandals continued throughout the decade, despite President Torrijos's concerted efforts. In 2005, an independent audit of six narcotrafficking cases led to a criminal complaint against eight Supreme Court justices. In 2006, the Panamanian government dismissed Major Óscar Herazo, the chief of police in the Santa Fe de Veraguas region of Panama, because of his involvement in a *tumbadores* network that stole drugs from traffickers. Lastly, in 2007, the director of Panama's national maritime service and four of his subordinates were arrested on charges of narcotics-related corruption and illicit enrichment from the sale of more than 1,000 kilos of cocaine that he had confiscated from a hidden compartment on a ship named *Perseus V*.[164]

244 *Narcostates*

In May 2010, President Ricardo Martinelli Berrocal (2009–2014) called for a war against crime without mercy. He refused to pardon any police involved in robbery, corruption, or narcotrafficking. Despite his get-tough rhetoric, the December 2010 Narcoavioneta scandal rocked the country when a drug prosecutor in Los Santos y Herrera released four Colombian traffickers who had been arrested after landing a plane with fake Red Cross markings. As the investigation unfolded, allegations arose that the secretary general for the attorney general's office knew about the plan to release the Colombians. The public relations disaster ultimately forced the attorney general to resign.[165] President Martinelli Berrocal was fighting an uphill battle: Panama was too close to the Andean drug producing countries and it was too attractive for narcotraffickers not to do business there. As long as weapons and drug trafficking, corruption, gang violence, and money laundering propagated, Panama had to deal with the consequences.

The Central American Regional Security Initiative (CARSI)

Throughout Central America, murder, the proliferation of gangs, and narcotics trafficking went hand in hand. In every country, homicide rates increased. In 2005, the murder rate in Central America was greater than that of New York City. Per 100,000 citizens, the murder rate stood at 56 in El Salvador, 41 in Honduras, and 38 in Guatemala. Murder rates doubled in drug trafficking hotspots, leading to a general perception that gangs were primarily responsible for drug trafficking and the high murder rates.[166]

In 2006, an estimated 62,700 gang members existed in Central America. Conservative estimates recorded approximately 19,000 members of the MS-13 and Calle 18 operating along Mexico's borders.[167] The gangs had become deeply involved in drug, human, and weapons trafficking, as well as assassination, prostitution, auto theft, and kidnapping. They had adapted to the mano dura by developing countersurveillance techniques and by infiltrating law enforcement.[168] More importantly, the gangs began to accept payment in kind rather than cash from the Mexican DTOs, fueling higher crime rates as they began to fight over market distribution.[169]

Throughout the decade, Central American leaders sought ways to coordinate security and information about gang activity by engaging in unprecedented forms of cooperation. A September 2003 regional summit declared gangs to be "a destabilizing menace, more immediate than any conventional or guerrilla war."[170] In January 2004, El Salvador, Guatemala, Honduras, and Nicaragua agreed to lift legal barriers to the cross-country prosecution of gang members, whatever their nationality. This arrangement was followed by another agreement between Presidents Tony Saca of El Salvador and Óscar Berger of Guatemala in March 2005 to set up a joint security force to patrol their common border.[171]

The Mexican Cartels and Youth Gangs in Central America 245

A reduction in US assistance following the start of the 2003 Iraq War forced Central Americans to take the initiative on their own. By 2005, the US government had scaled back institution building and interdiction programs in Central America because of "budget priorities elsewhere over the last several years"—meaning the Iraq War.[172] As a result of the decline in US assistance, the OAS passed a June 2005 resolution urging member states to develop their own solutions to the gang problem. The conferences that followed led to the biometric fingerprinting of gang members, so it would be impossible for applicants and detainees to hide their criminal records or gang affiliations.[173] As part of a regional security plan, proposals to control crime and narcotrafficking included the development of a Central American red alert system to effect arrest warrants, assign police attachés to regional embassies, and create a Transnational Anti-Gang Center using Interpol to track down criminals in Central America.[174] Despite these steps, USAID's April 2006 assessment found that the regional efforts to address gangs were "fragmented (and) disjointed," underscoring the need for "coordinated action."[175]

Unfortunately, Central American states had not developed their democratic and legal institutions to defend against the corrupting onslaught of drug trafficking in the post–civil war period. By 2008, five Central American countries—Guatemala, Honduras, Nicaragua, Costa Rica, and Panama—were on the US government's list of twenty major illicit drug transit or major illicit drug producing countries.[176] In 2011, a kilo of cocaine in Colombia was worth approximately $1,000. As that kilo made its way to the United States, its value inflated to $100,000.[177] The Mexican cartels earned an estimated $15–30 billion annually from the drug trade. Compared to the regional GDP of $106.6 billion for Central America as a whole in 2006, the cartels could easily buy off poorly paid police and judges. With an inefficient legal system, "get tough" tactics could not solve the problem. The money that DTOs spent on public works projects for outlying rural communities gained favor with those populations, who then abetted the traffickers.[178] With corruption at the highest levels of government and overcrowded prison populations, the cycle of violence and narcotrafficking became self-perpetuating. A decline in national and international investment followed suit, meaning that Central America lost desperately needed revenue. Central American coffers were too thin to comprehensively fight crime. Governments found themselves attempting to extinguish a "root fire"—law enforcement would snuff out the fire in one area, only to have it flare up in another.

The United States, Mexico, and Central America responded to the crime wave by launching a regional counternarcotics program. When the United States launched the Mérida Initiative, it sought to assist not only Mexico but also Central America.[179] Planned to run between 2007 and 2010, the stated goal of the Mérida Initiative for Central America was to

246 Narcostates

"increase regional capabilities to prosecute criminals, interdict contraband, reform criminal justice systems, and restore public confidence in law enforcement institutions."[180] During the 2008 fiscal year, Central America received $65 million. In that budget, the United States allotted $16.6 million for counternarcotics and border issues, $21 million for police training, $5 million for youth violence prevention, and $8 million for strengthening judicial systems. During the 2009 fiscal year, the Mérida Initiative contributed $110 million to Central America.[181] Two years later, the United States sent $361 million.

The implementation of the Mérida Initiative in Mexico and the renewal of Plan Colombia in 2008 (which maintained Colombian pressure along Panama's southern border) affected Central American security. Because Central America received much less assistance, the Mérida Initiative and Plan Colombia had the effect of pushing narcotrafficking deeper into Central America. By 2009, Central American leaders were calling for a Central American Mérida Initiative. The US State Department agreed, and believed that institution building would take more time and money than what had been previously dedicated to the region. Because of successes with institution building in Colombia, the US government believed it needed to replicate similar programs in Central America.[182] In 2010, President Funes of El Salvador called for an emergency meeting of SICA following the murder of over a dozen civilians by MS-13 when they torched a bus in San Salvador. During that meeting, Costa Rican President Laura Chinchilla called on the United States to fund a Central American counternarcotics strategy.[183]

The proliferation of drug trafficking and drug-related violence forced the United States to recognize that a counternarcotics program designed solely for Central America was needed. In 2010, the United States renamed the Central American portion of the Mérida Initiative and called it the Central America Regional Security Initiative (CARSI).[184] CARSI continued to carry out Mérida Initiative objectives while integrating security efforts throughout the region, including the littoral waters of the Caribbean.[185] The stated objective of CARSI was "to maximize the effectiveness [of joint] efforts to fight criminal organizations so as to disrupt drug-trafficking (including precursor chemicals), weapons trafficking, illicit financial activities, currency smuggling, and human trafficking."[186] According to Honduran President Porfirio Lobo, CARSI represented more than just funding; it was an opportunity for a coordinated strategy with countries like Guatemala and El Salvador to combat the shared security threat from transnational DTOs.[187]

CARSI began with a meeting of Central American leaders in July 2007 to discuss security issues within the SICA framework.[188] Founded in 1993, the SICA served as a governing body that focused on regional coordination and economic integration, such as the implementation of CAFTA in August 2005. At the 2007 SICA meeting, the governments of the region identified gangs, narcotics, and weapons trafficking as their most pressing concerns. Salvadoran President Tony Saca declared that the gang problem showed the importance of coordinated anticrime efforts, while adding that an important element of those efforts was prevention. The SICA dialogue estimated that the cost to implement its regional security plan could exceed $953 million.[189] Through SICA and under the umbrella of Plan Puebla, a regional integration program for Central America, Mexico, and Colombia, was developed. Mexican and Guatemalan police worked together to control the flow of people and contraband across their border, while El Salvador, Guatemala, Honduras, and Mexico provided the FBI with fingerprints for a shared database. To implement their security agenda, Plan Puebla nations also agreed to coordinate their militaries.[190]

CARSI sought to reaffirm the US commitment to coordinate with Central America. To integrate various efforts, the initiative harmonized regional security operations, facilitated the exchange of information among various regional agencies, strengthened the institutional capabilities of Central American governments to prevent corruption within law enforcement agencies, and identified training requirements for overseeing security. Prior to CARSI, the Mérida Initiative was a collaborative effort to halt the Mexican cartels and their use of the MS-13 and Calle 18 gangs to smuggle drugs and weapons along the US border.[191] According to the US assistant secretary of state for international narcotics matters, William R. Brownfield, CARSI's two principal targets were the violence and drugs tied to gang activity. Brownfield added that "while not all gangs are drug traffickers, and not all drug trafficking is done by gangs," they were connected.[192] Through CARSI, the United States renewed its commitment to help Central America focus on gangs while implementing initiatives to disrupt criminal DTOs.[193] The State Department outlined the goals of CARSI in five points: (1) to create safe streets for the citizens; (2) to disrupt the movement of criminals and contraband within and between the nations of Central America; (3) to support the development of strong, capable, and accountable Central American governments; (4) to reestablish effective state presence and security in communities at risk; and (5) to foster enhanced levels of security and rule-of-law cooperation between the nations of the region.[194] CARSI prioritized its efforts in the Northern Triangle—El Salvador, Guatemala, and Honduras—where crime and violence were most severe.[195]

CARSI was divided into three pillars: (1) counternarcotics, counterterrorism, and border security; (2) public security and law enforcement; and (3) institution building and the rule of law. Pillar one included funding for aviation, port, and document security; pillar two provided support-capacity and community-prevention activities to combat gangs; and pillar three

248 Narcostates

focused on professionalizing police and judicial systems.[196] Between 2011 and 2014, as part of CARSI, the United States committed $544.2 million. As the regional situation deteriorated, the US government delivered $270 million to Central America in 2015 alone.[197]

Financing for pillar one of CARSI went to enhance Central American law enforcement training and equipment capacity. This financing included the Central American Fingerprinting Exploitation (CAFE), which shared information about gang members. Other financing assisted with technical operations, such as firearms tracing and port, airport, and border security.[198] DEA, ICE, and the State Department's Bureau of International Narcotics and Law Enforcement Affairs (INL) vetted counternarcotics unit programs that conducted investigations into money laundering, bulk cash smuggling, and the trafficking of narcotics, firearms, and people.[199] Regional interagency coordination was essential. Standardizing equipment for partner organizations across the region became a primary goal to enhance law enforcement capabilities.[200] For instance, CARSI provided communications, border inspection, and security force equipment, such as radios, computers, X-ray scanners, narcotics identification kits, weapons, ballistic vests, and night-vision goggles.[201] The maritime component of pillar one was linked to Operation Enduring Friendship, a naval program started in 2006 by the US SOUTHCOM that provided equipment to "detect, deter, disrupt, and defeat" illicit activity.[202]

Pillar two of CARSI went toward gang prevention and antigang programs. The aid improved the capabilities of the Transnational Anti-Gang units that the FBI had established in El Salvador and later in Guatemala and Honduras.[203] The initiative changed the general focus on gangs by making them not just a criminal problem but also a social problem. The gang issue was related to family structures and economic issues, and the goal was to provide a way for gang members to leave the gangs and reintegrate into society.[204] From 2011 to 2013, the Gang Resistance Education and Training (GREAT) program provided job training to over 12,000 students as part of a larger community development program that included the use of church and community centers. Addressing unemployment and rehabilitation for those leaving a gang was essential. However, the process of rehabilitation often started in prison, where there was an opportunity to engage gang members.[205] Every country was committed to this approach, although most funds for these programs were ad hoc and insufficient.[206]

With pillar three, financing went to court management, reforming prison management, supporting community-policing programs, and providing asset forfeiture training.[207] The Villa Nueva program in Guatemala was an example of this type of community policing. It sought to create a public image of the police as protectors. Simultaneously, antigang and antinarcotics programs like DARE (Drug Abuse Resistance Education) reached out to the

The Mexican Cartels and Youth Gangs in Central America   249

local youth while the police established greater ties with community leaders. Twenty-four-hour courts were also founded to provide protection to victims and witnesses, as well as prosecutors, clerks, and judges associated with sensitive cases. To broaden the community-policing aspect of the Villa Nueva program, the State Department funded on-the-job training for local police forces, which taught them to work closely with community leaders. The program achieved a high level of success by eliminating gang activity in seventy-eight schools throughout Villa Nueva.[208] Guatemala's success with the program led to further CARSI funding for similar programs in Central America.[209] In addition to community policing, the development of Sensitive Investigation Units (SIUs) in Guatemala and Panama and DEA-vetted units in El Salvador and Honduras was a major part of pillar three. SIUs investigated financial transactions and were seen as a way to prevent corruption, attack DTO assets, and thwart drug and human trafficking operations.[210]

The enforcement aspect of CARSI did not come without criticism. World leaders, including the presidents of Brazil, Colombia, and Mexico, concluded that US counternarcotics policies "failed to effectively curtail supply or consumption." They stated that "supply reduction and incarceration strategies were futile" and that demand reduction would be a more effective use of resources.[211] In his 2011 remarks to the press, Mario Funes stated that "narco-activity [was] not only a problem for El Salvador and Nicaragua, [or for] Colombia or Mexico alone." Narcotrafficking was "a problem that attacks the region." According to Funes, CARSI should "not only be approached through the prosecution of crime by our armies and police," but it also had "to stress prevention policies," which included investments in social policies.[212] Former Costa Rican minister of justice and president Laura Chinchilla recognized that "violent crime in the region was due to the strong presence of organized crime, drug trafficking, and transnational crime." However, Chinchilla added that instead of opting for public security policies that focused on prevention and rehabilitation, Central America had decided to take a mano dura, or "every man for himself approach: hire private security, buy guns, etc."[213] Chinchilla's cynical view came from the perspective that US help always arrived late and that it only "gives significant aid after countries have been invaded by organized crime."[214]

Another criticism of CARSI was that even though Central America had become more violent than either Mexico or Colombia, it received less aid. Honduran security minister Óscar Álvarez called US aid "a drop in a bucket."[215] Following the inclusion of Honduras as a major transit country in September 2011, newspapers throughout the country reported that CARSI was inadequate in comparison to US projects in Mexico and Colombia, leading President Porfirio Lobo to declare before the UN that the United States needed to do more to reduce demand.[216]

250   *Narcostates*

With the implementation of CARSI, human rights became a concern. Because the Colombian government defeated the major Colombian cartels with Washington's help, some policymakers advocated that Washington should follow a similar solution for Mexico and Central America.[217] However, the implementation of a Plan Colombia–style initiative raised human rights concerns. The State Department considered human rights an integral part of CARSI. All funding was expected to go through rigorous human rights vetting. To receive CARSI funding, governments had to create police complaint commissions, reform judiciaries, and prosecute officials for human rights violations. In 2010, the Obama administration required the secretary of state to submit a report detailing human rights problems that needed to be addressed. For instance, in 2012, the US State Department withheld 20 percent of the funds allocated for the Honduran military and police until it could verify that Honduras allowed for the freedom of expression and association, the due process of law, and the prosecution of personnel who committed human rights abuses.[218]

Drawing similarities to Plan Colombia, the US State Department argued that Central American governments were "increasingly recognizing the need to invest in their own security and are passing new laws on taxes to support investments in citizen security programs, judicially authorized wiretapping programs, extradition, and asset forfeiture," even though those changes were "slow to take hold as corruption and impunity remains widespread."[219] Still, the US State Department recognized that replicating Plan Colombia for the Mexican–Central American corridor could have a "balloon effect."[220] A Plan Colombia–type program for Mexico and Central America held the potential to force traffickers to move deeper into Caribbean nations, such as Haiti and the Dominican Republic, where little funding existed to deal with narcotrafficking.[221]

Despite the ever-shifting nature of narcotrafficking, US seizure rates in the Caribbean and littoral waters of Central America did increase. The January 2012 launch of Operation Martillo led to the seizure of 693 metric tons of cocaine and $25 million in cash, the detention of 581 vessels and aircraft, and the arrest of 1,863 suspects.[222] William Brownfield countered the criticism of CARSI, stating in 2013 that after four years "less than one-third of the $496 million ($160 million) that had been made available under CARSI . . . goes to drug programs at all." The remainder goes to "model precinct programs in vulnerable communities; to anti-gang youth programs; to community policing and community development programs; and it goes to police, prosecutor, and corrections reform throughout the Central American region." Brownfield further added that CARSI was "designed to build institutions," and it was "those institutions that will eventually deliver." He added that at the "end of the day," CARSI's success would be measured "through a variety of factors," including rates of homicide, prosecution, poverty, education, air and maritime tracking, and gang activity in places

The Mexican Cartels and Youth Gangs in Central America   251

like El Salvador. The totality of those "factors and the statistical story" would eventually tell "if CARSI is or is not a success," but those statistics would not "tell us that in days, weeks, or months [but in] years."[223]

Notes

1. Tom Diaz, *No Boundaries: Transnational Latino Gangs and American Law Enforcement* (Ann Arbor: University of Michigan Press, 2009), 29.

2. American Embassy Tegucigalpa, "Subject: A Permanent Tattoo," 1.

3. US Agency for International Development, "Central American and Mexican Gang Assessment" (Washington, DC: USAID Bureau for Latin American and Caribbean Affairs Office of Regional Sustainable Development, April 2006), 19.

4. "MS-13 Seen as a Growing Threat," *Dallas Morning News*, October 29, 2006, www.securityinfowatch.com/press_release/10552964/ms-13-gang-seen-as-growing-threat?print=true.

5. US Agency for International Development, "Central American and Mexican Gang Assessment," 109.

6. Thomas Bruneau, Lucia Dammert, and Elizabeth Skinner, *Maras: Gang Violence and Security in Central America* (Austin: University of Texas Press, 2011), 3.

7. Carlos García, "How the MS-13 Got Its Foothold in International Drug Trafficking," InSight Crime, November 30, 2016, www.insightcrime.org.

8. Al Valdez and Rene Enriquez, *Urban Street Terrorism: The Mexican Mafia and the Sureños* (Santa Ana, CA: Police and Fire Publishing, 2011), 24–39.

9. United Nations Office on Drugs and Crime, *Crime and Development in Central America: Caught in the Crossfire* (New York: United Nations, May 2007), 64.

10. US Agency for International Development, "Central American and Mexican Gang Assessment," 16–19; American Embassy Mexico to Secretary of State Washington, DC, "Subject: Evaluation of the Second International Forum of Citizen Participation and Crime, Drugs and Gang Prevention Tracker # 20697," Mexico 005489 152025Z, July 2004, 2.

11. US Agency for International Development, "Central American and Mexican Gang Assessment," 112–113.

12. "Part II: Gangs, Deportation, and Violence in Central America," InSight Crime, November 30, 2012, www.insightcrime.org.

13. Cynthia L. Sarita, *The Mounting Threat of Domestic Terrorism: Al Qaeda and the Salvadorian Gang MS-13* (El Paso: LFB Scholarly Publishing, 2009), 93.

14. Hannah Stone, "U.S. Ranks MS-13 Alongside Zetas in Gang List," InSight Crime, October 12, 2012, www.insightcrime.org.

15. "MS-13 Seen as a Growing Threat," *Dallas Morning News*.

16. Sarita, *The Mounting Threat of Domestic Terrorism*, 50; Paul L. Williams, *The Al Qaeda Connection: International Terrorism, Organized Crime and the Coming Apocalypse* (Amherst, NY: Prometheus Books, 2005), 156.

17. American Consul Nuevo Laredo to Secretary of State Washington, DC, "Subject: 2004 Starts with a Flurry in the Desert," Nuevo Laredo 3761AA 292113Z, June 2004, 5.

18. Hannah Stone, "Street Gang No More, MS-13 Moves into Organized Crime," InSight Crime, March 9, 2011, www.insightcrime.org.

19. American Embassy Mexico to Secretary of State Washington, DC, "Mexico's Southern Border: Border Security Equals National Security—Sound Familiar?" Mexico 007191 302111Z, November 2005, 5.

20. American Embassy Tegucigalpa, "Subject: A Permanent Tattoo," 4.

252   *Narcostates*

21. US Agency for International Development, "Central American and Mexican Gang Assessment," 116.

22. United Nations Office on Drugs and Crime, *Crime and Development*, 45–46.

23. Sam Logan and Ashley Morse, "MS-13 Organization and Response," February 2007, 2, www.samuellogan.com.

24. US Attorney's Office, Newark, New Jersey, "National and International Leadership of MS-13 Indicted in New Jersey for Racketeering Conspiracy," US Department of Justice, July 17, 2014, www.fbi.gov. California MS-13 leader, José Rodríguez Juárez, drove the national program.

25. "Leasing a Narco-Plaza with Signs of Alliance," *El Diario* (translated and reprinted by Borderland Beat Reporter Buggs) March 20, 2011, www.borderlandbeat .com. La Familia formed ties with the Tijuana cartel in 2011 after Luis Fernando Sánchez Arellano gave La Familia the right to operate in Tijuana as long as they paid tribute.

26. American Embassy Guatemala to Secretary of State Washington, DC, "Subject: Embassy Guatemala: Mérida Central America 2.0," Guatemala 001126 212214Z, October 2009, 3; Douglas Farah and Pamela Phillips Lum, *Central American Gangs and Transnational Criminal Organizations* (Washington, DC: Woodrow Wilson International Center for Scholars, International Assessment and Strategy Center, February 2013), 14.

27. American Embassy Mexico, "Subject: Mexico's Southern Border," 3.

28. Tim Johnson, "Drug Gangs Muscle into New Territory: Central America," *McClatchy News*, April 21, 2011.

29. Douglas Farah, "Transnational Criminal Threats in El Salvador: New Trends and Lessons from Colombia" (Miami: Florida International University, Western Security Hemisphere Center, August 2011), 21–22.

30. Ivan Briscoe and Marlies Stappers, "Breaking the Wave: Critical Steps in the Fight Against Crime in Guatemala," Clingendael Institute, January 2012, 12–13. Portillo was convicted in 2010 for laundering $70 million.

31. Ibid., 32.

32. American Embassy Guatemala to Secretary of State Washington, DC, "Subject: Security Environment Profile Questionnaire, Guatemala," Guatemala 001721 311930Z, August 2006, 2.

33. American Embassy Guatemala to USINS Washington, DC, "Subject: Arzú Government Gears Up on Immigration Issues," Guatemala 01990 012304Z, April 1996, 2.

34. American Embassy Mexico to Secretary of State Washington, DC, "Subject: Down South Trafficking in Drugs, Arms, and Immigrants," Mexico 006908 291521Z, July 1999, 1–3.

35. American Embassy Mexico, "Mexico's Southern Border: Border," 5.

36. American Embassy Guatemala to Secretary of State Washington, DC, "Subject: Guatemala Quarterly Status Report, October–December 2002," Guatemala 000039 081424Z, January 2003, 2–3.

37. Ibid.

38. American Embassy Guatemala, "Subject: Security Environment," 1; American Embassy Guatemala, "Subject: Guatemala Quarterly," 2–3.

39. SvcSMARTMFI to SMARTCore, "Subject: Guatemala: Escalating Violence," Guatemala 000147 171738Z, February 19, 2009, 1–3.

40. American Embassy Guatemala to Secretary of State Washington, DC, "Subject: Security Environment Profile Questionnaire, Spring 2009," Guatemala 000384 221850Z, April 2009, 1.

41. American Embassy Guatemala, "Subject: Guatemala Quarterly," 2–3.

The Mexican Cartels and Youth Gangs in Central America   253

42. United Nations Office on Drugs and Crime, *Crime and Development in Central America*, 45–55.

43. Kevin Casas-Zamora, "Paying Attention to Central America's Drug Trafficking Crisis" (Washington, DC: Brookings Institution, October 27, 2010), www.brookings.edu.

44. United Nations Office on Drugs and Crime, *Crime and Development in Central America*, 56.

45. Karen Hooper, "The Mexican Drug Cartel Threat in Central America" (Austin, TX: Stratfor Global Intelligence, November 17, 2011), www.stratfor.com; International Crisis Group, "Guatemala Drug Trafficking and Violence," Latin America Report no. 39, International Crisis Group, October 11, 2011, 4. In March 2008, the Zetas killed the León family leader, his brother, and nine other associates. The Zetas then took over the states of Morales, Izabal, and Petén. The Zetas finished off the León family in 2011 and then pressured the Mendozas, who fled to Belize.

46. Héctor Tobar and Alex Renderos, "3 Salvadoran Politicians Slain on Trip to Guatemala," *Los Angeles Times*, February 21, 2007.

47. James C. McKinley Jr., "Lawlessness in Guatemala Touches Neighbor: Role of Police Drawing Scrutiny," *New York Times*, March 6, 2007, sec. A, p. 2.

48. Ricardo Quinto, "Sin detalles de crimen Manolito Castillo," *El Periodico* (Guatemala), December 16, 2019, https://elperiodico.com.gt; Juan Francisco Solórzano Foppa, "Los Riveritas, la ejecuciones extrajudiciales y el Cacif," *Plaza Publica*, December 9, 2018, www.plazapublica.com.gt.

49. McKinley, "Lawlessness in Guatemala," sec. A, p. 2.

50. United States Congress, House of Representatives, *Violence in Central America*, 7.

51. Cameron McKibben, "Corruption, Impunity and the International Commission Against Impunity in Guatemala," Council on Hemispheric Affairs, April 30, 2015, www.coha.org.

52. Geoffrey Ramsey, "CICIG Names 18 Judges of Impunity in Guatemala," InSight Crime, December 4, 2012, www.insightcrime.org. The report referred to the military members as Cuerpos Ilegales y Aparatos Clandestinos de Seguridad (CIACS).

53. American Embassy Guatemala, "Subject: Embassy Guatemala: Mérida Central America 2.0," 1.

54. American Embassy Guatemala to Secretary of State Washington, DC, "Subject: Embassy Guatemala: CARSI Review and Assessment," Guatemala 001848 222043Z, October 22, 2010, 1.

55. Julian Migilierini, "Guatemala Fears Mexican Drug Gangs Advancing," BBC News, December 20, 2010.

56. American Embassy Guatemala, "Subject: Embassy Guatemala: CARSI Review," 1–2.

57. Nicholas Casey, "Guatemala Declares a State of Siege: Government Claims Northern Province Has Become Overrun by Mexican Trafficking Organization," *Wall Street Journal*, December 20, 2010.

58. Migilierini, "Guatemala Fears Mexican Drug."

59. American Embassy San Salvador to Secretary of State Washington, DC, "Subject: Violence Spirals in El Salvador/Government Grasps for Solutions," San Salvador 000418 171734Z, February 2006, 1–2.

60. American Embassy San Salvador to Secretary of State Washington, DC, "Subject: El Salvador Crime Rate Rises to Wartime Levels," San Salvador 002374 251808Z, August 2005, 1–2.

254   Narcostates

61. American Embassy San Salvador to Secretary of State Washington, DC, "El Salvador—Annual OSAC Crime/Safety Report January 2009," San Salvador 000075 271418Z, January 2009, 2.

62. American Embassy San Salvador, "Subject: El Salvador Crime Rate," 2.

63. American Embassy San Salvador, "El Salvador—Annual OSAC," 2. In 2006, the Salvadoran government created a special unit within the PNC to identify and capture gang members who killed public transportation workers.

64. American Embassy San Salvador, "Subject: Violence Spirals," 3.

65. Ibid.

66. American Embassy San Salvador to Secretary of State Washington, DC, "Subject: El Salvador Update on Regional Security Plan," San Salvador 001006 241528Z, May 2007, 1–2.

67. US Department of State, Bureau of International Narcotics and Law Enforcement Affairs, *2010 International Narcotics Control Strategy Report Vol. I* (Washington, DC: US Department of State, March 2010), 265–266.

68. Joseph P. Taves to svcSMARTHBTSPOP9, "Subject: Your Visits to El Salvador," San Salvador 1099 072241Z, December 7, 2009, 4.

69. Sonja Wolf, "Mano Dura: Gang Suppression in El Salvador," Oxford Research Group, Sustainable Security, March 2011, http://sustainablesecurity.org.

70. American Embassy El Salvador to Secretary of State Washington, DC, "Subject: El Salvador December Mérida Initiative Implementation Report," San Salvador 0005 0061427, January 6, 2010, Wiki Leaks, https://wikileaks.org/plusd /cables/10SANSALVADOR5_a.html.

71. Jami Thompson to svcSMARTHBTSPOP4, "Subject: Your Visit to El Salvador," San Salvador 1069 172010Z, November 17, 2009, 4.

72. Farah and Phillips Lum, *Central American Gangs*, 23.

73. American Embassy San Salvador to Secretary of State Washington, DC, "Subject: Gangs Paralyze Transportation, Businesses," San Salvador 000303 102247Z, September 2010, 1–4.

74. American Embassy El Salvador to Secretary of State Washington, DC, "Subject: El Salvador: 2008 Country Reports on Terrorism," San Salvador 001372 162303Z, December 16, 2008, Wiki Leaks, https://wikileaks.org/plusd/cables /08SANSALVADOR1372_a.html.

75. Claire O'Neill McCleskey, "Salvador Police Link MS-13 to International Cocaine Shipment," InSight Crime, November 9, 2013, www.insightcrime.org.

76. American Embassy Tegucigalpa to Secretary of State Washington, DC, "Subject: International Narcotics Control Strategy Report—INSCR Honduras," Tegucigalpa 000383 051812Z, February 2002, 2.

77. American Embassy Tegucigalpa to Secretary of State Washington, DC, "Subject: Honduran President Maduro Meets with Charge on Corruption and Other Issues," Tegucigalpa 001790 302055Z, August 2005, 5.

78. American Embassy Tegucigalpa to Secretary of State Washington, DC, "Subject: Honduras 2004–2005 INCSR Part II, Money Laundering and Financial Crime," Tegucigalpa 002816 211214Z, December 2004, 2.

79. US Department of State, Bureau of International Narcotics and Law Enforcement Affairs, *2005 International Narcotics Control Strategy Report Vol. I* (Washington, DC: US Department of State March 2005), 185.

80. American Embassy Tegucigalpa, "Subject: Honduras 2004–2005," 7.

81. American Embassy Tegucigalpa, "Subject: International Narcotics Control Strategy Report," 2.

82. David R. Dye, "Police Reform in Honduras: The Role of the Special Purge and Transformation Commission" (Washington, DC: Woodrow Wilson Center, 2017), 5.

83. American Embassy Tegucigalpa, "Subject: International Narcotics Control Strategy Report," 7.

84. American Embassy Tegucigalpa to Secretary of State Washington, DC, "Subject: Drugs for Arms Part Three: Stolen Narco Weapons Part of Alleged FARC Cache," Tegucigalpa 001155 312105Z, May 2005, 1–3.

85. American Embassy Tegucigalpa to Secretary of State Washington, DC, "Subject: Honduran Immigration Director Ramon Romero Released on Bail," Tegucigalpa 001726 192214Z, August 2005, 1–2.

86. American Embassy Tegucigalpa to Secretary of State Washington, DC, "Subject: Drifting Towards a Narco-State," Tegucigalpa 000949 301530Z, May 2007, 5.

87. American Embassy San Salvador, "Subject: Gangs Paralyze," 1–2.

88. American Embassy Tegucigalpa, "Subject: Drifting Towards," 1.

89. American Embassy Tegucigalpa to Secretary of State Washington, DC, "Subject: (SBU) U.S. Anti-Narcotics Program Diminishes as Narco-Threat Increases in Honduras," Tegucigalpa 002198 21236Z, November 2006, 2.

90. American Embassy Tegucigalpa, "Subject: Drifting Towards," 1.

91. US Department of State, Bureau of International Narcotics and Law Enforcement Affairs, *2011 International Narcotics Control Strategy Report Vol. I* (Washington, DC: US Department of State, March 2011), 292–295. A majority of the flights were concentrated in La Mosquitia.

92. US Department of State, *2010 International Narcotics Control Strategy Report Vol. I*, 330.

93. James Bosworth, "Honduras: Organized Crime Gaining amid Political Crisis" (Working Paper Series on Crime in Central America, Washington, DC, Woodrow Wilson International Center for Scholars, Latin American Program, December 2010), 22–25; American Embassy Tegucigalpa to Secretary of State Washington, DC, "Subject: Honduran Military Police (PMOP): Recent High-Profile Successes, but Also Significant Concerns," Tegucigalpa 13526 061603Z, October 6, 2014, 1.

94. "'La Barbie' formó escuela de sicarios en Honduras," *La Prensa*, September 1, 2010, www.laprensa.hn; "Cártel de Sinaloa ordenó muerte de zar antidrogas," *El Siglo*, June 16, 2010, www.elsiglodetorreon.com.mx.

95. Mariano Castillo, "Anti-Drug Chief Killed in Honduras" CNN, December 8, 2009, www.cnn.com.

96. Ioan Grillo, "Behind the Murder of Honduras's Drug Czar," *Time Magazine*, December 17, 2009, www.time.com.

97. American Embassy Tegucigalpa to Secretary of State Washington, DC, "Subject: Drugs for Arms: FARC Caught Red Handed; Threat to Honduras Overstated," Tegucigalpa 000787 132314Z, April 2005, 1.

98. Bosworth, "Honduras: Organized Crime," 22.

99. "Policías tambíen mataron a Alfredo Lanverde," *El Heraldo* (Honduras), April 4, 2016, www.elheraldo.hn.

100. "Winter Blanco quiso sobornar al zar antidrogas," *La Tribuna* (Honduras), April 19, 2016, www.latribuna.hn. His full name was Winter Blanco Ruiz.

101. "Cobarde cimen contra Alfredo Lanverde," *El Heraldo* (Honduras), April 7, 2014, www.elheraldo.hn. The minister's name was Gustavo Alfredo Landaverde Hernández. He was also the founder of the Partido Demócrata Cristiano (PDC).

102. Dan Alder, "Denials Follow Revelations in Honduras Drug Czar's Assassination," InSight Crime, April 19, 2016, www.insightcrime.org. The PN director was Ricardo Ramírez del Cid.

103. Tim Johnson, "Cocaine Lab Found in Honduras Signals Big Shift in Drug Business," *McClatchy News*, April 8, 2011, www.mcclatchydc.com.

256 *Narcostates*

104. Organization of American States, Inter-American Drug Abuse Control Commission (CICAD), Multilateral Evaluation Mechanism, "Evaluation of Progress in Drug Control 2005–2006: Nicaragua" (Washington, DC: Organization of American States, 2008), 1–23.

105. World Bank, Sustainable Development Department in Poverty Reduction and Economic Management Unit, Latin American and the Caribbean Region, "Crime and Violence in Central America: A Developmental Challenge" (Washington, DC: World Bank, 2011), 7.

106. Ibid., 15–17.

107. US Agency for International Development, "Central American and Mexican Gang Assessment," 38.

108. Ibid., 125.

109. Roberto Cajina, "Security in Nicaragua: Central America's Exception?" (Working Paper, Inter-American Dialogue, January 2013), 6.

110. José Adán Silva, "Nicaragua Stands Out in War on Drugs in Central America," Inter Press Service, September 15, 2012, www.ipsnews.net.

111. Jen Skotach, "Organized Crime Working to Corrupt Nicaragua's Military: Admiral," InSight Crime, July 19, 2011, www.insightcrime.org. The naval officer was Rear Admiral Roger González.

112. Cajina, "Security in Nicaragua: Central America's Exception?," 13.

113. United Nations Office on Drugs and Crime, *2013 Study on Global Homicide*, 126.

114. World Bank, "Crime and Violence in Central America," 15.

115. Jeremy McDermott, "Bluefields: Nicaragua's Cocaine Hub," InSight Crime, July 8, 2012, www.insightcrime.org. The Mendozas were led by Donly Mendoza and Amauri Camarona Morelos (aka Alberto Ruiz Cano).

116. Cajina, "Security in Nicaragua: Central America's Exception?," 13.

117. United Nations Office on Drugs and Crime, "Crime and Development," 21. The money was seized as part of a border control operation called Operation All Inclusive.

118. "Nicaraguan Official Says Sinaloa Drug Cartel Using New Drug Trafficking Route," BBC Latin America, August 16, 2008. Melvin Gómez was the head of the Judicial Investigation Agency.

119. American Embassy San José to Secretary of State Washington, DC, "Subject: Embassy San José October 2010 CARSI Implementation Report," 10 San José 1578 261930Z, November 26, 2010, 1.

120. Organization of American States, Inter-American Drug Abuse Control Commission (CICAD), Multilateral Evaluation Mechanism, "Evaluation of Progress in Drug Control 2001–2002: Costa Rica" (Washington, DC: Organization of American States, 2003): 5–12; Agreement Between the United States and Costa Rica, San Jose 2 July 1999, Treaties and Other International Acts Series 13005, Pursuant to Public Law 89-497 (80 Stat. 271; 1 U.S.C. 113), 1–28.

121. Organization of American States, Inter-American Drug Abuse Control Commission (CICAD), Multilateral Evaluation Mechanism, "Evaluation of Progress in Drug Control 2007–2009: Costa Rica" (Washington, DC: Organization of American States, January 2011), 6.

122. Organization of American States, "Evaluation of Progress in Drug Control 2001–2002: Costa Rica," 5.

123. United Nations Office on Drugs and Crime, "Crime and Development," 47.

124. Organization of American States, "Evaluation of Progress in Drug Control 2007–2009: Costa Rica," 6.

The Mexican Cartels and Youth Gangs in Central America   257

125. José Meléndez, "Carteles usan como un bodega a Costa Rica," *El Diario* (Mexico), January 2, 2012, http://archivo.eluniversal.com.mx/nacion/203000.html.

126. American Embassy San José to Secretary of State Washington, DC, "Subject: Central America Regional Security Initiative: What Works," San José 000179 230150Z, October 2010, 3.

127. US Department of State, *2011 International Narcotics Control Strategy Report Vol. I*, 206.

128. United Nations Office on Drugs and Crime, "Crime and Development," 17; US Agency for International Development, *Central America and Mexico Gang Assessment* (Washington, DC: USAID Bureau for Latin American and Caribbean Affairs, April 2006), 124.

129. United Nations Office on Drugs and Crime, "Crime and Development," 60.

130. Ibid., 21.

131. United Nations Office on Drugs and Crime, "2013 Study on Global Homicide," 126.

132. American Embassy San José, "Subject: Central America Regional Security Initiative: What Works," 2.

133. American Embassy San José to Secretary of State Washington, DC, "Subject: The Colombian Connection: Former Guerrillas Turned Criminals in Costa Rica," San José 000069 122243Z, January 2007, 1. The M-19 guerrilla was named Libardo Parra Vargas. Para participated in the M-19's 1985 assault on the Palace of Justice and lived in Costa Rica on false Nicaraguan and Guatemalan identities while operating a liquor import front company. The FARC guerrilla was named Héctor Martínez Quinto. Panamanian authorities considered him to be the head of the José María Córdoba bloc of the FARC operating out of Ciudad Colón. He was alleged to have directed the May 2, 2002, "Bojayá Massacre" in Colombia, where 110 civilians were killed.

134. American Embassy San José to Secretary of State Washington, DC, "Subject: Costa Rica's Close Relations with Colombia," San José 000812 241802Z, September 2009, 1–3.

135. Alex Leff, "Fear and Money Laundering in Costa Rica," *Global Post*, December 27, 2011, www.pri.org. The chief public prosecutor was Jorge Chavarría Guzmán, who was equivalent to the US attorney general.

136. Nick Miroff, "For Costa Rica's Pura Vida, a Drug War Test," *Washington Post*, December 29, 2011, www.washingtonpost.com.

137. American Embassy San José, "Subject: Central America Regional Security Initiative: What Works," 3.

138. American Embassy Panama to Secretary of State Washington, DC, "Subject: Scene Setter: The Secretary's Visit to Panama's Centennial Celebrations, November 3," Panama 002773 172127Z, October 2003, 2.

139. American Embassy Panama to Secretary of State Washington, DC, "Subject: Transnational Crime in Panama—Why the U.S. Should Care," Panama 002034 202326Z, June 2001, 2.

140. American Embassy Panama to Secretary of State Washington, DC, "Subject: Panama Facing Colombian Spill-Over Troubles," Panama 004324 271955Z, October 1999, 1–2.

141. American Embassy Panama to Secretary of State Washington, DC, "Subject: Panama Seeks Solutions to Arms-for-Drugs Trade Crossing Isthmus," Panama 002923 032108Z, December 2004, 1.

142. American Embassy Panama, "Subject: Transnational Crime in Panama," 2.

143. American Embassy Panama, "Subject: Panama Seeks," 2.

258 Narcostates

144. American Embassy Panama to Secretary of State Washington, DC, "Subject: Colombian Narcoguerrillas," Panama 002849 212152Z, July 2000, 3.

145. American Embassy Panama to Secretary of State Washington, DC, "Subject: Draft for 2008–2009 International Narcotics Control Strategy Report for Panama: Part I, Drugs and Chemical Diversion Control," Panama 137250 212102Z, November 2008, 1–2.

146. United Nations Office on Drugs and Crime, "Transnational Organized Crime in Central America and the Caribbean: A Threat Assessment" (Vienna: United Nations Office on Drugs and Crime, September 2012), 33.

147. American Embassy Panama, "Subject: Draft for 2008–2009," 1–2.

148. United Nations Office on Drugs and Crime, "Transnational Organized Crime in Central America," 32.

149. American Embassy Panama to Secretary of State Washington, DC, "Subject: Scene Setter for CODEL Boehner," Panama 000894 031417Z, December 2009, 3.

150. American Embassy Panama to Secretary of State Washington, DC, "Subject: Panama: July Visit of Minister of Government and Justice," Panama 000545 041403Z, July 2008, 1–2; American Embassy Panama to Secretary of State Washington, DC, "Subject: Scene Setter: Panamanian President Torrijos September Visit to Washington," Panama 000726 051957Z, September 2008, 2–3.

151. US Department of State, Bureau of International Narcotics and Law Enforcement Affairs, *2003 International Narcotics Control Strategy Report Vol. I* (Washington, DC: US Department of State, March 2004), 173.

152. US Department of State, Bureau of International Narcotics and Law Enforcement Affairs, *2008 International Narcotics Control Strategy Report Vol. I* (Washington, DC: US Department of State, March 2008), 185–186.

153. US Department of State, Bureau of International Narcotics and Law Enforcement Affairs, *2012 International Narcotics Control Strategy Report Vol. I* (Washington, DC: US Department of State, March 2012), 355.

154. American Embassy Panama, "Subject: Draft for 2008–2009," 1–2.

155. World Bank, "Crime and Violence in Central America," 15.

156. "Pandilleros operan como transnacionales de crimen," *Panama América*, September 19, 2014, www.panamaamerica.com.pa.

157. American Embassy Panama, "Subject: Scene Setter for CODEL," 2.

158. World Bank, "Crime and Violence in Central America," 12.

159. American Embassy Panama to Secretary of State Washington, DC, "Subject: Understanding Panama's Colón Free Trade Zone," Panama 002524 121814Z, October 2004, 2.

160. United Nations Office on Drugs and Crime, "Crime and Development," 22.

161. American Embassy Panama to Secretary of State Washington, DC, "Subject: Panama Facing Colombian Spill-Over Troubles," Panama 004324 271955Z, October 1999, 2.

162. American Embassy Panama to Secretary of State Washington, DC, "Subject: Corruption in Panama: How Bad Is It? Who's Involved? Is the Government Cracking Down, and Does It Really Matter to the USG?," Panama 001941 121834Z, June 2001, 2; American Embassy Panama to American Embassy San José, "Subject: The Politicization of Money Laundering: Two Current Case Studies," Panama 000800 252223Z, February 2000, 1.

163. Greg Farrell and David Kocieniewski, "UBS, HSBC Offshore Dealings Thrust into Panama Papers Spotlight," *Bloomberg News*, April 5, 2016.

164. "Capturan ex-jefe naval de Panamá por narcotráfico," *Crónica* (Mexico), May 28, 2007, www.cronica.com.mx; American Embassy Panama to Secretary of State Washington, DC, "Subject: Likely Arrest of Former National Maritime Service

The Mexican Cartels and Youth Gangs in Central America   259

Director," Panama 000868 252117Z, May 2007, 1–2. Another 1,000 kilos were hidden in separate compartment of the *Perseus V*.

165. American Embassy Panama to Secretary of State Washington, DC, "Subject: Narco-Corruption Scandal Forces Resignation of Interim Attorney General," Panama 000533 291952Z, December 2010, 1–3. The attorney general was Giuseppe Bonissi. Milagros Valdés, the Los Santos y Herrera prosecutor, was jailed. No charges were filed against the secretary general for the Attorney General's Office.

166. US Congress, House of Representatives, *Hearing on Violence in Central America*, 16–21.

167. US Agency for International Development, Central American and Mexican Gang Assessment, 17.

168. Ibid., 19; Bosworth, "Honduras: Organized Crime," 9.

169. Farah and Phillips Lum, *Central American Gangs,* 14.

170. Clare M. Ribando Seelke, *Gangs in Central America,* Report R-L34112 (Washington, DC: Congressional Research Service, October 17, 2008), 3.

171. "The Gangs of Central America: Major Players and Scapegoats," *Revista Envío* (Nicaragua), December 2007, www.envio.org.ni/articulo/3704.

172. US Congress, House of Representatives, Committee on International Relations, Subcommittee on the Western Hemisphere, *Illicit Drug Transit Zone in Central America*, 109th Cong., 1st sess., November 9, 2005, 12, Statement of Jonathan D. Farrar, Deputy Assistant Secretary, International Narcotics and Law Enforcement Affairs.

173. American Embassy San Salvador to Secretary of State Washington, DC, "Subject: Securing U.S. Borders Against Salvadoran Gangs: The Initial Success of INA," San Salvador 003283 222234Z, November 2005, 3.

174. American Embassy San Salvador to Secretary of State Washington, DC, "Subject: El Salvador's Regional Security Plan," San Salvador 000837 032018Z, May 2007, 1–2.

175. Seelke, *Gangs in Central America*, 2.

176. Randall C. Archibald and Damien Cave, "In Central America, the Curse of Location; Drug Cartels to the North and South Drive into Their Weaker Neighbors," *International Herald Tribune*, March 25, 2011.

177. World Bank, "Crime and Violence in Central America," 12.

178. US Department of State, *2010 International Narcotics Control Strategy Report Vol. I*, 437–443; and US Department of State, US Bilateral Relations Fact Sheets, 2009–2017, archived content.

179. US Department of State, Bureau of Public Affairs, *The Central America Regional Security Initiative: A Shared Partnership* (Washington, DC: US Department of State, August 5, 2010), http://www.state.gov/r/pa/scp/fs/2010/145747.htm; US Congress, House of Representatives, Committee on Foreign Affairs, Subcommittee on the Western Hemisphere, *Central America and the Mérida Initiative*, 110th Cong., 2nd sess., May 8, 2008, 9.

180. American Embassy Guatemala to Secretary of State Washington, DC, "Subject: Embassy Guatemala: Mérida Central America 2.0," Guatemala 001126 212214Z, October 2009, 4.

181. US Congress, House of Representatives, *Central America and the Mérida Initiative*, 34.

182. American Embassy Guatemala, "Subject: Embassy Guatemala: Mérida," 1.

183. Bosworth, "Honduras: Organized Crime," 27.

184. Secretary of State Washington, DC, to American Embassy Guatemala (SMARt Core to svcSMARTHBTSPOP#2state.sgove.gov), "Subject: Central America Regional Security Initiative (CARSI)—The New Names for Mérida–Central America," State

260 *Narcostates*

28360 231801Z, March 2010, 1; US Congress, House of Representatives, *Central America and the Mérida Initiative*, 9; William R. Brownfield, "Remarks at the Council of Americas," Washington, DC: Carnegie Endowment, March 22, 2013, https://2009-2017.state.gov/j/inl/rls/rm/2013/207231.htm.

185. US Department of State, Bureau of Public Affairs, *The Central America Regional Security Initiative*, www.state.gov/r/pa/scp/fs/2010/145747.htm.

186. US Congress, House of Representatives, *Central America and the Mérida Initiative*, 34.

187. American Embassy Tegucigalpa to Secretary of State Washington, DC, "Subject: Honduras: President Lobo and Ambassador Preside over Mérida/CARSI TF Meeting," Tegucigalpa 000507 151432Z, June 2010, 1.

188. US Congress, House of Representatives, Committee on Homeland Security, Subcommittee on Border, Maritime, and Global Counterterrorism, *The Mérida Initiative: Examining United States Efforts to Combat Transnational Criminal Organizations*, 110th Cong., 2nd sess., June 5, 2008, 8.

189. Meyer and Seelke, *Central American Regional Security Initiative*, Report 41731, May 7, 2013, 14–18.

190. US Congress, House of Representatives, *Central America and the Mérida Initiative*, 9.

191. US Congress, House of Representatives, *The Mérida Initiative*, 1–2.

192. William R. Brownfield, "Remarks at the Institute of the Americas, Gangs, Youth, and Drugs—Breaking the Cycle of Violence and Crime," San Diego, CA, October 1, 2012, https://2009–2017.state.gov/j/inl/rls/rm /199133.htm.

193. US Department of State, Bureau of International Narcotics and Law Enforcement Affairs, *2015 International Narcotics Control Strategy Report Vol. I* (Washington, DC: US Department of State, March 2015), 10.

194. US Department of State, Bureau of Public Affairs, *The Central America Regional Security Initiative*, www.state.gov/r/pa/scp/fs/2010/145747.htm.

195. US Congress, House of Representatives, House Appropriations Committee, Subcommittee on State Foreign Operations and Related Programs, *Security Challenges to Latin America*, 112th Cong., 2nd sess., March 29, 2012, https://2009-2017.state.gov/j/inl/rls/rm/187097.htm; US Congress, House of Representatives, Committee on Foreign Relations, *Emerging Threats and Security in the Western Hemisphere: The Next Steps for U.S. Policy*, Serial No. 112-75, 112th Cong., 2nd sess., October 13, 2011, 14–18.

196. Cook, *Mexico's Drug Cartels*, 16.

197. Consolidated Appropriations Act 2016, Public Law No: 114-113, Stat. 2796, 114th Cong., 1st sess., December 18, 2015, 554–556; Peter J. Meyer and Claire Ribando Seelke, *Central American Regional Security Initiative: Background and Policy Issues for Congress*, Report 41731 (Washington, DC: Congressional Research Service, December 17, 2015), 17.

198. Clare Ribando Seelke, *Mérida Initiative: U.S. Anticrime and U.S. Counterdrug Assistance for Mexico and Central America*, Report S22837 (Washington, DC: Congressional Research Service, July 7, 2008), 1–5.

199. Meyer and Seelke, *Central American Regional Security Initiative*, 26.

200. Thomas Harrigan, "Statement Before the Senate Caucus on International Narcotics Control, Hearing Entitled US–Central America Security Cooperation" (Washington, DC: US Department of Justice, May 25, 2011), 6.

201. Meyer and Seelke, *Central American Regional Security Initiative*, 26.

202. US Congress, House of Representatives, *Central America and the Mérida Initiative*, 18; US Southern Command, "News: Operation Enduring Freedom"

(Doral, FL: US Southern Command), www.southcom.mil/newsroom/Pages/Enduring-Friendship-program.aspx.

203. Meyer and Seelke, *Central American Regional Security Initiative*, 26.

204. US Congress, House of Representatives, *Central America and the Mérida Initiative*, 23–26.

205. Brownfield, "Remarks at the Institute of the Americas."

206. Meyer and Seelke, *Central America Regional Security Initiative*, 13–14.

207. Stephen Hendrix, "The Mérida Initiative for Mexico and Central America: The New Paradigm for Security Cooperation, Attacking Organized Crime, Corruption and Violence," *Loyola University Chicago International Law Review* 5, no. 2 (2008): 121-122.

208. David T. Johnson, "Efforts to Combat Organized Crime in Guatemala: Address to the Council of the Americas" (Washington, DC: US Department of State, October 5, 2010), www.state.gov/j/inl/rls/rm /149055.htm. Johnson served as assistant secretary of the INLE from 2007 to 2011.

209. Meyer and Seelke, *Central American Regional Security Initiative*, 27.

210. Thomas Harrigan, Statement Before the Senate Caucus on International Narcotics Control, 6–7.

211. Meyer and Seelke, *Central American Regional Security Initiative*, 19.

212. White House Office of the Press Secretary, Remarks by President Obama and President Funes of El Salvador in Joint Press Conference, National Palace San Salvador El Salvador, March 22, 2011, www.whitehouse.gov/the-press-office/2011 /03/22/remarks-president-obama-and-president-funes-el-salvador-joint-press-conf.

213. Thelma Mejía, "Central America: Soaring Violent Crime Threatens Democracy," Inter Press Service, Tegucigalpa, September 22, 2008, 2.

214. "Central America: The Tortured Isthmus," *Economist*, April 14, 2011.

215. Ibid.

216. American Embassy Tegucigalpa to Secretary of State Washington, DC, "Subject: Honduras Takes Its Inclusion on the Narcotrafficking 'Majors List' in Stride," Tegucigalpa 000603 232359Z, September 2011, 2.

217. R. C. Bonner, "The New Cocaine Cowboys: How to Defeat Mexico's Drug Cartels," *Foreign Affairs* 89 no. 4 (August 2010): 35.

218. Meyer and Seelke, *Central American Regional Security Initiative*, 24–25.

219. US Congress, House of Representatives, *Security Challenges to Latin America*.

220. William R. Brownfield, "Remarks at the Council of Americas."

221. US Congress, House of Representatives, *Central America and the Mérida Initiative*, 9.

222. United States Southern Command, "Operation Martillo" (Doral, FL: US Southern Command Headquarters, August 22, 2016), www.southcom.mil/newsroom /Pages/Operation-Martillo.aspx.

223. Brownfield, "Remarks at the Council of Americas."

11

Narcotrafficking and the Immigration Crisis

For Mexico and Central America, the more things changed, the more they remained the same. In Mexico, President Enrique Peña Nieto (2012–2018) continued to cooperate with US interdiction goals while trying to abate Felipe Calderón's hard-line policies. Corruption ran rampant through Mexico's institutions while the third-generation cartels persisted in their quest to achieve the upper hand over the Sinaloa and Gulf cartels, especially in Juárez and Central Mexico. In Central America, the implementation of CARSI led to increased seizure rates, but gangs and DTOs persevered as corruption continued to fester inside the region's political institutions. In Northern Triangle countries, unceasing lawlessness, grinding poverty, and economic malaise became intolerable to the point where masses of refugees fled their homes for the United States. By 2020, 74 percent of all US cocaine was moving through the Pacific corridor of Central America and Mexico. Another 16 percent moved along the western Caribbean corridor.[1] Throughout the decade, Andean coca production rose steadily (see Figure 11.1) to compensate for increased Mexican and Central American seizure rates. Access to the Mexico–Central America narcocorridor remained vital for the cartels.

Peña Nieto's Balancing Act

In 2012, Enrique Peña Nieto was the PRI's choice for the presidency. After a twelve-year absence from Mexico's National Palace, his campaign restored the PRI to power when he defeated PRD candidate Andrés Manuel López Obrador and PAN candidate Josefina Vázquez Mota. Upon his inauguration, Peña Nieto altered Mexico's counternarcotics policies by promoting violence prevention programs and avoiding direct confrontation with Mexico's cartels. In 2016, he stated that "Mexicans know all too well the

264   *Narcostates*

Figure 11.1   Andean Coca Production, 2010–2020, in Hectares

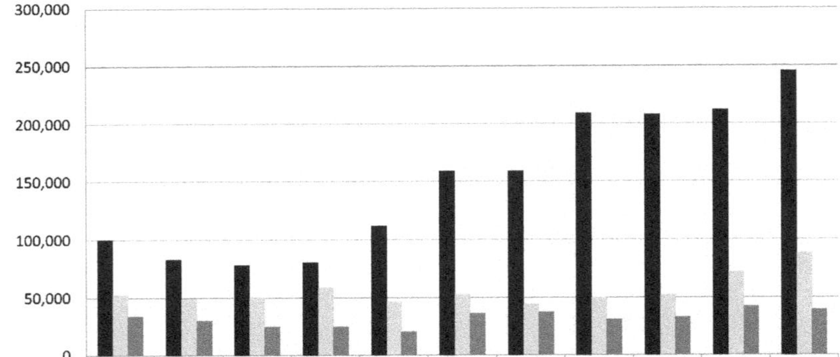

	2010	2011	2012	2013	2014	2015	2016	2017	2018	2019	2020
■ Colombia	100,000	83,000	78,000	80,500	112,000	159,000	159,000	209,000	208,000	212,000	245,000
Peru	53,000	49,500	50,500	59,000	46,500	53,000	44,000	49,800	52,100	72,000	88,200
■ Bolivia	34,000	30,000	25,000	25,000	20,400	36,500	37,500	31,000	32,900	42,180	39,400

Source: Based on data from US Department of State, "Coca Production Statistics for Bolivia, Colombia, and Peru," *International Narcotics Control Strategy Report* (Washington, DC: US Department of State, 2011–2021).

range and the defects of prohibitionist and punitive policies of the so-called war on drugs that has prevailed for 40 years."[2] As part of his promise to de-escalate the war on drugs, he made medical marijuana legal in 2017. In October 2018, the Mexican Supreme Court followed suit by ruling that the federal law prohibiting recreational marijuana use was unconstitutional.[3] In order to curtail the cartels' allure among Mexico's disenfranchised youth, Peña Nieto's administration committed $9.2 billion to establish the Interagency Commission for the Prevention of Violence and Criminality. The agency coordinated with nine federal agencies to oversee programs designed to prevent Mexico's youth from joining criminal organizations. According to Peña Nieto, Mexico needed to emphasize crime prevention, because it could not keep employing more "sophisticated weapons, better equipment, more police, and a higher presence of the armed forces . . . [as the] only form of combating organized crime." Critics claimed that Peña Nieto's program was a veiled offer to ease up on the cartels and bring Mexico back to the days when it maintained a more laissez-faire attitude toward drug smuggling.[4]

Despite the change in rhetoric, Mexico continued to accept US narcotics reduction goals. For example, in 2016, Mexico expanded its budget for public security by 3.6 percent to $15.4 billion to combat organized crime, expand crime prevention programs, improve interagency coordination, consolidate police forces, and support judicial reforms. In addition, Peña Nieto announced an eight-point anticorruption plan in February 2015. Notwithstanding the increase in funding, the greatest challenge for Mexico continued to be the Central American maritime and land corridors used to smuggle narcotics into the country. Moreover, between 2014 and 2016, Mexican cartels increased their domestic production of heroin, marijuana, and methamphetamine. Cocaine seizure rates also continued to rise (see Figure 11.2; note that the INCSR only reported six months of data for 2018). According to the State Department, the problem was that "only a small portion of the cocaine, marijuana, methamphetamine, and heroin originating in or transiting Mexico . . . [was] interdicted inside the country."[5]

Mexico: Continuing Corruption

Corruption cast a constant shadow over Peña Nieto's administration. In the 2016 Monexgate scandal, investigative reporter Carmen Aristegui alleged that the PRI received illegal campaign contributions from the Juárez cartel. Peña Nieto was personally tied to the scandal by a man named Rodolfo Dávila Córdova, who had been arrested in 2005 as a money launderer and a coordinator between the Juárez cartel and the Colombian BACRIM. Following Dávila Córdova's release from prison in 2010, he became indirectly involved in Peña Nieto's 2012 election campaign. During the campaign, the PRI handed out cash cards to pay for PRI expenses in the different states.

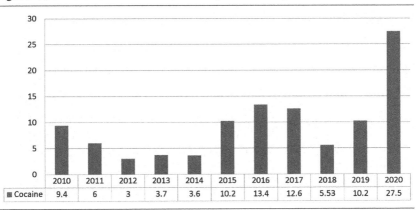

Figure 11.2 Mexican Cocaine Seizures, 2010–2020, in Metric Tons

Source: Based on data from US Department of State, Supply Reduction Statistics for Mexico, *International Narcotics Control Strategy Report Vol. I* (Washington, DC: US Department of State, 2011–2021).

266   *Narcostates*

When the PAN accused the PRI of vote buying, an accounting of the cards revealed that Dávila Córdova had been involved in the financial scheme and that 2,073 cash cards were unaccounted for. Despite the irregularity, the Instituto Federal Electoral (IFE) blocked further investigations into the matter, claiming it would not open a frivolous investigation based on one independent journalist's report.[6]

The most damaging allegations against Peña Nieto came during El Chapo's 2018–2019 trial in New York City. The evidence came from El Chapo's personal secretary and a Colombian trafficker named Hildebrando Cifuentes Villa.[7] Cifuentes Villa worked for the Sinaloa cartel by providing security and logistics support for El Chapo in the Sierra Maestra Occidental Mountains. In 2014, he was arrested at one of El Chapo's hideouts in Culiacán and extradited to the United States, where he provided evidence against the Sinaloa cartel in exchange for lenient sentencing. During the trial, he revealed that in 2012, Peña Nieto had demanded a $250 million bribe from El Chapo to call off the government's manhunt. He further testified that El Chapo paid a $100 million bribe to Peña Nieto with the understanding that the manhunt would be called off as long as El Chapo remained in hiding.[8]

Corruption in Mexico remained rampant, especially at the state level. The case of Javier Duarte de Ochoa, the PRI governor of Veracruz, gained great notoriety in 2011. The 2011 discovery of thirty-five bodies in a mass grave and the 2012 Policía Federal seizure of 25 million pesos in political advertising money being transported on a Veracruz state plane cast suspicion over Duarte de Ochoa. Following these public relations disasters, a series of journalist assassinations forced Duarte de Ochoa to resign on October 12, 2016. The next day, he disappeared. An investigation into his disappearance revealed that he had hired out the Veracruz state police on behalf of the cartels. Duarte de Ochoa hid out in Guatemala until his April 2017 arrest and extradition to Mexico on money laundering charges.[9] In addition to Duarte de Ochoa, a dozen PRI governors throughout Mexico were under investigation for narcocorruption during Peña Nieto's presidency.[10] The DEA's October 2020 detention of Peña Nieto's former secretary of national defense, Salvador Cienfuegos Zepeda, in Los Angeles on narcotrafficking charges added to the growing list of scandals surrounding Peña Nieto's presidency.[11] In November 2020, the United States dropped the charges against Cienfuegos Zepeda and released him from custody, fearing that his continued detention would stifle cooperation between the two nations.[12]

Mexico's embarrassment grew as more instances of high-level corruption surfaced. Iván Reyes Arzate, the commander of the Mexican Federal Police's Sensitive Investigative Units (SIU), was indicted by the United States for aiding the Sinaloa cartel and the Beltrán Leyva organization. Reyes Arzate allegedly offered protection to the cartels in exchange for

Narcotrafficking and the Immigration Crisis   267

hundreds of thousands of dollars. In one instance, he was accused of accepting a $290,000 bribe in return for information on a DEA investigation into El Seguimiento 39, a Mexican cartel associated with the Sinaloa cartel. In February 2022, Reyes Arzate was given a ten-year prison term in a US federal facility.[13] Reyes Arzate worked directly with Felipe Calderón's secretary of public security, Genaro García Luna. In 2019, García Luna was arrested in the United States for accepting millions of dollars in bribes from the Sinaloa cartel. During El Chapo's 2018 trial, it was revealed that García Luna twice met with a Sinaloa representative, who gave him a briefcase with at least $3 million inside each time.[14]

The Continuing Evolution of Mexico's Cartels

Although Mexico's cartels remained splintered and in dispute over Mexico's plazas of distribution, the cartel war paused between 2012 and 2016. The most powerful cartels were the Sinaloa and Los Zetas cartels. Of the other second-generation cartels, the Gulf, Juárez, and Tijuana cartels remained shadows of their former stature, while third-generation cartels, especially the Cártel de Jalisco Nueva Generación (CJNG), became major players in Mexico's drug war.

The Sinaloa cartel remained the most important of all Mexican cartels. It maintained a presence in seventeen Mexican states and within multiple major US cities. In 2012, the cartel was dominated by El Mayo and El Chapo and employed more than 100,000 operatives.[15] By 2016, the Sinaloa cartel had pacified the Tijuana cartel, dominated Juárez cartel territory, and continued its alliance with the Gulf cartel against Los Zetas and the Beltrán Leyva cartel.

The Juárez cartel's defeat by the Sinaloa cartel did not mean that it was defunct.[16] In 2013, the Juárez cartel renamed itself the Nuevo Cartel de Juárez (NCJ). Sources reported that Vicente Carrillo Fuentes was in semiretirement and had handed the cartel over to his brother Alberto. Although Alberto was arrested that same year, the NCJ formed an alliance with Los Zetas and the Beltrán Leyva cartel to fight off the Sinaloa cartel.[17] On October 9, 2014, Vicente was arrested by the army and federal police and sentenced to twenty-eight years in a Puente Grande prison. The imprisonment of the Juárez cartel's leaders forced it to change its methods of operation. Like its Colombian predecessors, the Juárez cartel democratized its operations and, through various affiliates, maintained a presence in twenty-one states. Juárez cartel enforcer gangs, especially La Línea, became involved in the buying, trafficking, and distribution of narcotics. In 2015, La Línea increasingly controlled NCJ operations and was cooperating with cross-border gangs.[18]

In 2012, it appeared as though Los Zetas were on the decline. Only eleven of the thirty-four Zetas Viejos remained at large. Contrary to popular

268   *Narcostates*

belief, Los Zetas remained intact owing to their decentralized military structure and their ability to recruit Mexican police and soldiers.[19] Los Zetas's war against the Sinaloa-Gulf cartel alliance led to their expansion northward. From Tamaulipas and Coahuila, they moved into Gulf cartel territory, including Nuevo León, Veracruz, and Zacatecas. They also maintained an operational presence on the Yucatán Peninsula, the Chiapas-Guatemala border, and the central Pacific states of Guerrero and Michoacán.[20] Divisions over leadership roles split the cartel into the Zetas Viejos and the Cartel del Noreste (CDN), which left the cartel somewhat rudderless, but it did not disrupt its operations. Many leaders ran decentralized factions from the wings.[21]

Like Los Zetas, the Gulf cartel appeared to be a shadow of its former self. The war with Los Zetas and the death of Antonio Cárdenas Guillén ("Tony Tormenta") in 2010 split the cartel. Aspiring to lead the cartel were Mario Cárdenas Guillén ("El Gordo") and Jorge Costilla Sánchez ("El Coss"). As the two men vied for leadership, the Gulf cartel's enforcer gangs—Los Rojos from Reynosa and Los Metros from Matamoros—went to war with each other. As divisions within the Gulf cartel grew, members of the cartel defected to Los Zetas. El Gordo's capture and El Coss's death in September 2012 left the Gulf cartel without a leader.[22] In the fallout, Mario Ramírez Treviño ("X-20"), a former Los Zetas hitman and Tamaulipas police officer, took control of the cartel. To consolidate power, he eliminated all opposition and forged an alliance with the Sinaloa cartel. In August 2013 he was arrested, and the Gulf cartel found itself leaderless once again.[23] Because of the decision to ally with the Sinaloa cartel and because of the sudden loss of its leadership, the Gulf cartel became subordinate to the Sinaloa cartel.

The 2014 arrest of Héctor Beltrán Leyva broke up the Beltrán Leyva cartel. Former members established their own third-generation cartels. For example, the Mazatlecos in Mazatlán were an offshoot of the Beltrán Leyva cartel. They allied with Los Zetas to engage in a war with the Sinaloa cartel for control over Sinaloa and Durango.[24] Another Beltrán Leyva splinter group, La Barredora, allied themselves with the Sinaloa cartel and successfully defeated the Cártel Independiente de Acapulco (CIDA) to gain a permanent foothold in Acapulco.

Sangre and Self-Defense

The states of Guerrero, Michoacán, Morelos, and Jalisco remained hotly contested. They were important to the cartels because they had become conduits for the delivery of precursor chemicals from Asia and cocaine shipments from Central America. Guerrero erupted into a bloody turf war in 2014 as several cartels, including the Guerreros Unidos (GU), La Familia

Michoacana, Los Rojos, and the CJNG, vied for control of Guerrero. The Mexican navy considered many of these new cartels to be more like "street gangs or *superpandillas*."[25]

The September 2014 kidnapping and massacre of forty-three students from Ayotzinapa Rural Teachers' College in Iguala and the discovery of twenty-nine of bodies incinerated and dumped in a mass grave outside Iguala ten days later sent Guerrero into a tailspin. The PGR investigation concluded that the GU and the mayor of Iguala were coconspirators in the murders.[26] According to the PGR, because of Iguala's historic role in the Mexican War of Independence from Spain (the Plan of Iguala), the college was noted for its revolutionary sympathies and encouraged the students to demonstrate against the government of Iguala. While heading to a demonstration, the municipal police detained a bus full of Ayotzinapa students. Based on the testimonies from ninety-seven witnesses, including thirty-six municipal police officers and officials, Iguala Mayor Abarca ordered the bus halted after the GU plaza head informed him that members of the Gulf cartel's Los Rojos were also on board. After a brief interrogation, the authorities turned the students over to the GU. In the aftermath of the murders, the Mexican government launched a relentless war against the GU. Taking advantage of the GU's vulnerability, Los Rojos established a presence throughout Guerrero, including Acapulco, although they were not alone in their effort. The CJNG, Los Zetas, and Knights Templar were also contesting control over Guerrero, Michoacán, and Morelos.[27]

As the conflict along the Pacific coast and in Central Mexico escalated, vigilante groups known as the Autodefensas Comunitaria (Community Self-Defense Groups) or Policía Comunitaria (Community Police) took law enforcement into their own hands.[28] Indigenous campesinos formed vigilante groups in thirteen states, including Michoacán, Morelos, Oaxaca, and Guerrero.[29] The vigilantes armed themselves with AK-47s, M-16s, and M-60s and wore bulletproof vests. They even created makeshift armored vehicles out of their SUVs and trucks. The Mexican government grew concerned because it was unable to control the heavily armed vigilantes and it feared that they might evolve into cartels with similar origins to La Familia. By 2014, roughly 7,000 people belonged to various autodefensas.[30] To gain control over them, the Mexican government ordered the autodefensas to join the Cuerpo de Defensa Rural (Rural Defense Corps) also known as the Rurales. Few did. The government responded by arresting their leaders.[31] The decision to force the autodefensas into the Rurales enabled the government to control the vigilante groups through the SEDENA.[32] By 2015, the vigilante groups were no longer autonomous. Within the vacuum created by the absorption of the autodefensas into the military, Mexico's DTOs renewed their struggle for Central Mexico.

270 Narcostates

El Chapo's Last Hurrah

El Chapo's arrest in Mazatlán and his incarceration between 2014 and 2015 led to realignments within the Sinaloa cartel. During this time, management of the cartel passed over to El Mayo, who went into semiretirement and delegated much of the Sinaloa cartel's operations to Germán Magaña Pasos. No public pictures of him existed, all of his communications were handled by his sublieutenants, and he hid behind an alias—Germán Olivares.[33] Then, on July 11, 2015, El Chapo made his stunning escape from the Altiplano maximum-security prison. His associates bored a thirty-three-foot-deep, one-mile-long tunnel underneath the prison, which surfaced in El Chapo's shower. Within the tunnel was a motorcycle attached to a rail line that was used to hasten El Chapo's getaway.[34] El Chapo was back.

For half a year, Mexico conducted a massive manhunt, beginning with the Mexican navy's raid on El Chapo's safehouse in Los Mochis, Sinaloa. A massive gun battle occurred. El Chapo and a lieutenant escaped through a hidden tunnel. El Chapo then stole two cars and drove twelve miles outside of town, where he was detained by the federal police. El Chapo attempted to bribe and then threatened to kill the officers if they did not release him. With Sinaloa assassins coming to El Chapo's rescue, the officers hid El Chapo in a hotel room until the Mexican Marines arrived with reinforcements and took El Chapo into permanent custody on January 8, 2016.[35] Following El Chapo's second escape, the Mexican government extradited La Barbie and El Coss to the United States in 2015, recognizing that imprisoning high-level traffickers was too difficult for Mexico to handle on its own.[36] With El Chapo once again in custody, the Mexican government came to the realization that it could not incarcerate him in Mexico. Two days after his arrest, Mexico agreed to extradite El Chapo to the United States. Although he initially fought extradition, El Chapo ultimately agreed to it by making a deal that would allow him to avoid a death sentence. On January 19, 2017, he was extradited to the United States.[37]

El Chapo's third incarceration initiated a new struggle within the Sinaloa cartel. El Mayo was El Chapo's successor, but Dámaso López Nuñez challenged his authority. López Nuñez worked for the Sinaloa attorney general's office from 1991 to 1999, and then for Puente Grande prison from 1999 to 2001. While at Puente Grande, he befriended El Chapo and assisted in El Chapo's 2001 escape. After El Chapo's 2016 arrest, López Nuñez quarreled with El Chapo's sons Iván and Jesús Alfredo and then allied with the CJNG until his capture in May 2017. Control over his faction passed down to his son—El Chapo's godson—Dámaso López Serrano ("El Mini Lic"), a playboy trafficker who could not continue the struggle. His surrender to US authorities in July 2018 left El Chapo's sons and El Mayo in firm control of the cartel.[38]

The continuity of the Sinaloa cartel's leadership remained steady until January 2023, when the Mexican army captured El Chapo's son, Ovidio Guzmán López ("El Raton"). His arrest triggered a massive shootout in Culiacán. Cars and buses were torched. Sinaloa cartel members set up barricades in an attempt to obstruct the military from bringing Ovidio to the airport, where they flew him to Mexico City. Ten military personnel and nineteen Sinaloa cartel members were killed.[39] Ovidio and his brothers, Iván Archivaldo Guzmán Salazar and Jesús Alfredo Guzmán Salazar, were known as Los Chapitos. After their father's arrest, they became major producers and traffickers of fentanyl and methamphetamine. However, they were at odds with El Mayo and their uncle, Aureliano Guzmán Loera ("El Guano"), over their role in the cartel. After Dámaso López surrendered, Los Chapitos and El Mayo's factions occasionally clashed. Ovidio's arrest dealt Los Chapitos and their influence within the cartel a devastating blow.[40] On April 14, 2023, the US Justice Department indicted the remaining Los Chapitos, including Iván Archivaldo and Jesús Alfredo as well as Ovidio and twenty-five other members of the Sinaloa cartel. The indictment accused the defendants of fentanyl importation, drug trafficking, money laundering, and homicide.[41] Among the more visceral details of the indictment was the allegation that Los Chapitos used "corkscrews, electrocution, and hot chilies to torture their rivals," while some of their victims were "fed dead or alive to tigers." [42] When the indictments were handed down, only seven of the defendants had been arrested; Iván Archivaldo and Jesús Alfredo remained at large.

The CJNG on the Rise

Following El Chapo's extradition, the CJNG, led by Nemesio Oseguera Cervantes ("El Mencho"), emerged as the up-and-coming cartel. According to an unnamed DEA source, the CJNG possessed more money than the Sinaloa cartel, having an estimated net worth of $20 billion in 2017. An all-out war with the Mexican government broke out when CJNG assassins ambushed and killed five federal policemen in March 2015. A member of Jalisco's state police posted a video claiming that the killings were the result of a "broken pact" between the state government and the CJNG. By July, the CJNG had assassinated forty-seven state officials in Jalisco.[43] The government retaliated with Operation Jalisco, but the CJNG's "Special Forces High Command" repulsed heavily armed paratroopers and federal police backed by two EC-725 helicopters. From that point forward, the CJNG launched a wave of terror and intimidation that forced the Mexican government into a stalemate in Jalisco. Despite its war with the government, the CJNG expanded into the states of Baja California and Sonora, which were largely under Sinaloa control.[44]

272   *Narcostates*

In January 2016, the country's homicide rate increased by more than 20 percent.[45] The splintering of the cartels between 2010 and 2014 and a reassertion of their influence over Mexico's plazas of distribution following El Chapo's rearrest were the primary causes of the renewed violence.[46] Authorities blamed the CJNG for many of the killings as they pushed into new territory. There were more than 20,000 murders in 2016 alone. In the first five months of 2017, the homicide rate increased another 30 percent. Tijuana's murder rate also reached new highs. In the first three months of 2017, 400 murders were committed, representing nearly half the murder rate of 2016.[47] The March 2017 discovery of a secret cemetery containing 249 bodies in Veracruz stunned Mexico.[48] Once considered safe, cities like Acapulco and states like Guanajuato no longer escaped the violence of the cartels. *Plata o plomo* ruled over Mexico.[49]

The AMLO Alternative

In 2012, Andrés Manuel López Obrador left the PRD and joined the Movimiento Regeneración Nacional (MORENA) party, eventually winning the presidency in 2018. López Obrador campaigned as the anti-elite candidate, vowing to take on the narcocorruption that had infiltrated Mexico's political class. One of his first acts was to establish an independent prosecutor's office within the PGR to investigate corruption. He also emphasized human rights initiatives, particularly drug-related disappearances, making the case of the forty-three Ayotzinapa college students a priority.[50] As part of López Obrador's human rights campaign, the Federal Police—which was considered beyond repair—was disbanded in 2019. All of its assets were transferred to the National Guard, which assumed responsibility for internal security operations, particularly combating criminal organizations. As part of the arrangement, the National Guard was transferred to the SEDENA, making it a branch of the military. Although the National Guard and military continued to commit human rights abuses, in 2022, López Obrador received congressional approval to extend the military's law enforcement authority until 2028.[51]

López Obrador sought to de-escalate the drug war with the cartels. He declared, "We will battle them with intelligence and not force. . . . We will not declare war."[52] López Obrador viewed narcotics usage as a US demand problem, and he sought to limit US hegemony over Mexico by restricting the operational capabilities of US law enforcement entities in Mexico. In 2020, he removed diplomatic immunity for US agents in Mexico. In 2022, he disbanded the Special Investigative Unit, Mexico's elite DEA-vetted counternarcotics unit. The SIU had been a part of the Federal Police and was absorbed by the National Guard. As López Obrador reoriented Mexico's drug strategy, the National Guard prioritized deterrence over cartel

Narcotrafficking and the Immigration Crisis   **273**

investigations, resulting in a diminution of the SIU's role. López Obrador also dismantled the SIU because his relationship with the DEA had soured over the DEA's alleged use of false evidence to detain former defense minister Salvador Cienfuegos. The DEA's former chief of international operations, Mike Vigil, stated that López Obrador's decisions meant "more drugs going to the United States and more violence in Mexico."[53]

While the verdict on López Obrador's record is still out, the results have been mixed. Despite his vow to use the National Guard to reduce homicide rates, the National Guard mainly patrolled the US-Mexico border in order to comply with the Trump administration's demands that Mexico minimize the flow of immigrants attempting to enter the United States.[54] López Obrador was also criticized for backsliding on his campaign promises. In 2019, the Washington Office on Latin America reported that twenty-three human rights defenders and twelve journalists were murdered, while the Committee to Protect Journalists named Mexico the world's deadliest country for journalists.[55] That same year, 34 percent of Mexican households had at least one member who was the victim of crime.[56] Amid tremendous security challenges, López Obrador remained dedicated to fighting narcocorruption. In 2023, his administration persuaded the United States to turn over Alejandro Tenescalco, a police supervisor accused of being a major perpetrator in the disappearance of the Ayotzinapa college students. Furthermore, he unsuccessfully lobbied the United States to release Genaro García Luna so that he might face corruption charges in Mexico.[57]

Notwithstanding López Obrador's change in strategy, Mexico's DTOs have remained relentless. As more of their income came from activities other than drug trafficking, Mexico's DTOs sought to further their control by killing uncooperative officials. Mexico's 2021 midterm elections were widely regarded as one of the bloodiest in the country's history. From February to April, Mexico's DTOs were accused of assassinating forty-six elected officials and forcing sixty mayoral candidates to withdraw their candidacies due to death threats.[58] By 2022, outbursts of violence spread across Mexico. Homicides in Mexican border cities such as Tijuana, Mexicali, and Ciudad Juárez, as well as states such as Guanajuato and Jalisco, reached near-all-time highs. It appeared as though López Obrador's self-proclaimed "hugs, not bullets" strategy was failing. López Obrador retorted that his public security policy was working and that his opponents were attempting to create an "atmosphere of uncertainty and fear."[59] To reassure the United States that Mexico was taking action against the cartels, López Obrador authorized the arrest of Ovidio Guzmán López just before his meeting with US President Joe Biden on January 9, 2023. During their meeting, both presidents agreed to continue bilateral efforts to prosecute drug traffickers, dismantle criminal networks, and disrupt the supply of illicit precursor chemicals.[60]

The upsurge in Mexican fentanyl production following López Obrador's election as president was an alarming trend. The Sinaloa and CJNG cartels became the dominant players in the fentanyl trade. Chinese and Indian precursor chemicals used to make fentanyl were smuggled into Mexico inside food and authorized chemical shipments. The chemicals came straight from China or were channeled through third-party countries, such as Guatemala, Germany, and the United States.[61] China's 2019 implementation of a regulatory regime to control domestic fentanyl production prompted Mexico's cartels to produce their own versions of the drug. Fentanyl was less expensive to produce than heroin, which cost approximately $6,000 per kilo. Fentanyl, on the other hand, cost only $200 per kilo to produce.[62] When the cartels took over the fentanyl business, they developed industrial capabilities to manufacture it clandestinely, frequently in pill form. According to the DEA, fentanyl was smuggled across the border in low-concentration, high-volume loads, with kilogram seizures containing less than a 10 percent fentanyl concentration.[63]

Fentanyl powder was occasionally mixed into heroin and cocaine supplies, resulting in overdoses. In March 2015, the DEA issued a nationwide alert identifying fentanyl as a public health threat. By 2019, the DEA was reporting that the flow of fentanyl into the United States was "more diverse than when the fentanyl crisis began in 2014" as new source countries such as Mexico came online.[64] The overall rate of overdoses from narcotics had been on the rise since 1999. In 2018, there was a slight decline in the overdose rate, but in 2019, it accelerated dramatically. Between 2019 and 2020, the number of fentanyl overdose deaths increased by more than 56 percent, from 33,725 to 53,480.[65] In 2020, more than 68 percent of overdose deaths involving heroin also involved fentanyl.[66] In 2021, the number of synthetic opioid deaths related to fentanyl reached 71,238.[67] That same year, 15 percent of the fentanyl-related overdoses were cases where fentanyl was mixed with stimulants such as cocaine. Another 27 percent of overdose deaths were caused by fentanyl alone, with no other opioids or stimulants present.[68] In December 2022, the DEA seized 50.6 million fentanyl-laced counterfeit prescription pills and 10,000 pounds of fentanyl powder. The DEA estimated that the amount seized was equivalent to one lethal dose per US citizen.[69] Future drug trends suggest that fentanyl production will continue to rise as Mexican DTOs seek alternative sources of revenue.

Central America and CARSI, 2014–2020

By 2017, Central America was in worse shape than it had been in 2000. The US State Department considered CARSI a growing success, although US officials acknowledged that it would not substantially alter Central Amer-

Narcotrafficking and the Immigration Crisis   275

ica's security situation. Even with increased narcotic seizure rates, obstacles persisted (see Figure 11.3). Those obstacles included a lack of funding and equipment for security forces, an inability to sustain programs without US assistance, limited political support, and massive corruption. US officials complained about congressional restrictions on aid to the region, including human rights requirements, which delayed the release of funds. According to DEA and State Department officials, legislative restrictions hindered security cooperation by limiting the ability of the United States to fully engage with its regional partners.[70]

In 2013, Central American governments showed varied "degrees of willingness to collaborate with the United States." In Costa Rica, Honduras, and Panama, spending on the security sector increased while other countries in the region spent less. Kidnappings and extortion continued. Critics argued that negotiations with gangs gave them legitimacy and time to consolidate their positions. To deal with the problem of corruption, the State Department believed Central America needed an entire generation to cleanse its institutions. In the short term, vetted units were developed to do

Figure 11.3   Central American Cocaine Seizures, 2010–2020, in Metric Tons

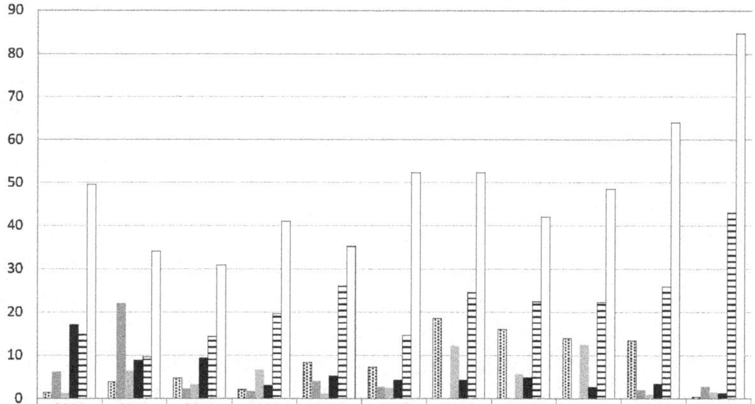

	2010	2011	2012	2013	2014	2015	2016	2017	2018	2019	2020
Guatemala	1.4	3.9	4.7	2.1	8.38	7.25	18.5	16	13.96	13.32	0.425
Honduras	6.134	22	2.25	1.7	4	2.7	0	0	0	2	2.8
El Salvador	1.26	6.49	3.27	6.64	1.066	2.401	12.2	5.67	12.45	0.97	1.5
Nicaragua	17	8.8	9.3	3	5.11	4.25	4.17	4.8	2.58	3.34	1.18
Costa Rica	14.8	9.609	14.3	19.67	26	14.59	24.5	22.4	22.3	25.9	43
Panama	49.5	34	30.8	41	35.1	52.3	52.3	42	48.5	64	84.8

Source: Based on data from US Department of State, "Supply Reduction Statistics for Central America," *International Narcotics Control Strategy Reports Vol. I* (Washington, DC: US Department of State, 2011–2021).

276 *Narcostates*

basic law enforcement duties to buy time for the larger institutions to improve.[71] According to the State Department's assistant secretary of the Bureau of Western Hemisphere Affairs, Thomas Shannon, because of the "political" morass or the "degree of money" that flowed through these countries from organized crime and drug trafficking, Central America and the United States had to be vigilant against "cooperation breaking down, either for ideological predilections or because people are suborned and corrupted."[72]

Guatemala:
A State of Emergency

In 2012, President Pérez Molina attracted international attention by proposing drug decriminalization as a way to limit the violence associated with narcotics trafficking and to reduce the burden on transit zone countries. In September 2014, a special session of the OAS dedicated to regional drug policies was hosted in Guatemala City. The most pressing issues for Guatemala were the high levels of violence fueled by drug trafficking. Corruption and gang warfare also remained omnipresent threats.[73]

Between 2015 and 2019, Guatemala was rocked by high-level corruption scandals. The La Línea customs scandal started an investigation into the Guatemalan political system when investigators discovered that members of Guatemala's customs agency, the Superintendencia de Administración Tributaria, lowered taxes on importers in exchange for financial kickbacks totaling nearly $2.3 billion.[74] Arrests of high-level officials followed, including the 2015 arrests of President Pérez Molina and Vice President Baldetti Elías.[75] Two years later, Baldetti Elías and Interior Minister Mauricio López Bonilla were separately indicted by the US federal court in Washington, DC, for conspiring to import cocaine into the United States. Baldetti Elías was accused of working for Los Zetas, while López Bonilla was accused of aiding the Chacón ring operating out of Guatemala, Honduras, and Panama to supply Mexican DTOs.[76] Neither politician was extradited to the United States. Instead, they were tried in Guatemala and received prison sentences for fraud.[77] Scandals continued to rock Guatemala after former presidential candidate Mario Estrada Orellana was arrested in 2019 for offering protection to the Sinaloa cartel in exchange for $10–$12 million to finance his campaign.[78] As early as 2011, the US State Department opined that Orellana's Unión del Cambio Nacional (UCN) was a narcoparty.[79]

As Guatemala's scandals unfolded, many areas of Guatemala, especially along the Mexican border, fell under the direct influence of Mexican DTOs. Guatemala became more violent than it had been during its civil war. According to Guatemalan estimates, the drug trade caused 40 percent of the violence.[80] Adding to the unrest, traffickers smuggled weapons into

Guatemala via the northern border of Petén and along its Pacific coast. The weapons followed narcotics smuggling routes and went primarily to Guatemala's criminal organizations.[81]

Inside Guatemala's prisons, gangs were largely in control and directed a considerable amount of illegal activity. In November 2016, secret cameras filmed the director of Guatemala's prison system, Nicolás García, negotiating with Barrio 18 gang members over the terms and conditions of their incarceration.[82] In 2017, the gang murdered the Escuintla prison director because he had attempted to restrict their access to the outside world.[83] In 2019, MS-13 took complete control of the El Pavón prison located outside of Guatemala City.[84]

After 2016, coca growing returned to Guatemala. In May 2018, Guatemala's PNC discovered one hectare of coca growing among coffee plants in the state of Alta Verapaz. In 2019, following the slaying of several police officers by narcotraffickers in the state of Izabal, President Jimmy Morales (2016–2020) placed twenty-two municipalities in Izabal under a state of siege. The Guatemalan army then seized 1.5 million coca plants, 223,000 marijuana plants, and four cocaine processing laboratories.[85] In 2022, Guatemala eliminated approximately 4 million coca plants, doubling the amount eradicated in 2021, with Mexican gangs controlling the bulk of production. Guatemala also captured and destroyed a record number of precursor chemicals that year, demonstrating how crucial Guatemala had become as a transit point for precursor chemicals entering Mexico to refine coca paste and produce fentanyl.[86] The escalation of gang and cartel activity, combined with the increase in narcotics production and numerous states of emergency, raised serious questions about the efficacy of CARSI in Guatemala.

El Salvador:
Negotiations with Criminal Gangs?

In March 2012, Salvadoran President Mauricio Funes Cartagena (2009–2014) radically changed El Salvador's antigang approach by negotiating a truce with the MS-13 and Calle 18 gangs. Nearly 40 percent of El Salvador's incarcerated inmates across nineteen major prisons and approximately seventy prison cell blocks were connected to gangs.[87] To facilitate negotiations, El Salvador transferred gang leaders to less secure prisons, and prison authorities eased restrictions on inmates in exchange for good behavior.[88] The gang leaders pledged not to forcibly recruit children into their ranks and surrendered their weapons, although this had little effect on assassinations.[89]

The truce was tenuous from the beginning. The Salvadoran government reluctantly entered into negotiations because they believed the gangs would

278   *Narcostates*

use the truce to increase their political legitimacy. Between March 2012 and May 2013, homicides in El Salvador did decline from an average of twelve to five per day.[90] Residents of communities where the USAID implemented crime prevention programs reported 19 percent fewer robberies, 51 percent fewer extortion attempts, and 51 percent fewer murders than would be expected. Security analysts attributed the reduction in violent crime to the truce negotiated with the major gangs.[91] However, as the truce continued, Salvadoran gang leaders claimed that death squads such as the Sombra Negra still targeted them.[92] Moreover, the Funes administration financed the creation of an MS-13 splinter cell called MS-503 (El Salvador's international phone code) to create divisions within the gang during their negotiations with the government.[93] The November 2013 discovery of a mass grave with forty-four victims murdered by MS-13 and an uptick in the murder rate to an average of 9.48 murders per day in 2013 and 2014 threw cold water on the truce. In 2014, President Funes declared the truce a failure.[94] Because it was negotiated in secret, charges of a conspiracy to coordinate with El Salvador's gangs were brought against the penitentiary system director, eighteen members of the penitentiary system, and the PNC. When the case went to trial, all were acquitted because they were following the orders of the Funes administration.[95] The administration's attempt to develop an alternative to heavy-handed tactics provoked the opposite effect—criminal enfranchisement and death squads.

A major setback for El Salvador was the 2011 investigation into the Salvadoran Texis cartel, which exposed high levels of narcocorruption within the government. The Texis cartel moved cocaine from El Salvador into Honduras and Guatemala. Leaders of the gang were politically well-connected. For this reason, the authorities did not file charges against them. The Salvadoran PNC's investigation into the cartel eventually led to the arrest of cattle rancher Herrera Hernández ("El Burro") in February 2011. The FBI wanted to extradite him on drug trafficking charges, but the PNC released him on the basis that he had been detained using a faulty warrant.[96] By this time, the Salvadoran police had launched an investigation into another Texis cartel member nicknamed Repollo. They followed him to meetings at a car shop where he met with government officials, including Wilber Rivera, a former Salvadoran congressman, Ricardo Menesses, a former PNC director, and Calle 18 leader Carlos Rivas Barahona.[97] The 2013 arrest of Repollo in Guatemala exposed the Texis cartel and the political protection that it received. On April 4, 2017, the attorney general's office arrested hotelier and president of El Salvador's soccer federation, José Salazar Umaña, on money laundering charges. Salazar Umaña was another well-connected member of the Texis cartel who co-owned a property development company with FMLN vice president Óscar Ortiz. The investigation

Narcotrafficking and the Immigration Crisis 279

into Salazar Umaña did not pursue his business dealings with Ortiz, and the charges against him were dropped in 2021.[98]

In 2015, Salvadoran President Salvador Sánchez Cerén (2014–2019) declared a war against the gangs. Sánchez Cerén proclaimed that negotiations with the gangs were outside of the law and that the gangs must be prosecuted.[99] He then launched a security initiative called Plan El Salvador Seguro (PESS) and Operación Jaque, which investigated MS-13 front companies and financial interests used to launder money for the gang. Sánchez Cerén's decision to end the truce led to an increase in the extrajudicial killings of gang members by police and death squads. Several killings were attributed to an elite antigang unit within the PNC. Nearly 700 gang members were killed between January 2015 and August 2016. Responding to Sánchez Cerén's offensive, the MS-13 and Barrio 18 gangs stepped up their attacks against the PNC.[100] Following the breakdown of the truce, MS-13 leader Edwin Mancía Flores attempted to expand his capabilities. He directed US *clikas* on the East Coast to coordinate their criminal activities to assist MS-13 in El Salvador.[101] In response, the Salvadoran Comisión de Seguridad Pública y Combate a la Narcoactividad pushed forward extraordinary regulations that increased restrictions on gang members in prison. Prison directors denied family visits, reduced prison transfers, and jammed communications.[102] The Salvadoran government declared victory, citing declining homicide rates, although critics considered the government's figures faulty.[103] Homicides did decrease between 2015 and 2016, but then increased after 2016. Thirty people were killed in a single day in March 2017. In September 2017 alone, 435 homicides were recorded, equaling about 15 homicides per day.[104]

Murder rates declined after the 2019 election of center-right President Nayib Bukele Ortez (2019–present) of the Gran Alianza por la Unidad Nacional (GANA) party. That year, Bukele Ortez initiated the Territorial Control Plan to put pressure on Salvadoran gangs. Between 2019 and 2020, El Salvador's total number of homicides dropped from 2,398 to 1,341.[105] Bukele Ortez was accused of negotiating with the MS-13 to reduce the number of murders, which he denied. Following several intermittent spikes in violence between 2020 and 2021, Bukele Ortez directed the Salvadoran government to conduct a sweep that netted 10,000 gang members in April 2021.[106] In March 2022, Bukele Ortez issued the State of Exception Plan, a 30-day renewable security measure that suspended constitutional guarantees in order to go after the MS-13 and Barrio 18 gangs. By February 2023, the State of Exception Plan resulted in the seizure of 2,326 firearms and the arrest of 64,000 gang members.[107] More importantly, the Salvadoran government reported only 495 homicides in 2022, a decrease of 56.8 percent from 2021.[108] According to polls conducted by the University Institute of

280 *Narcostates*

Public Opinion and Gallop, Salvadorans supported Bukele Ortez's efforts, 82 percent and 92 percent, respectively.[109]

Despite Bukele Ortez's crackdown, rumors circulated that the government was still negotiating with and even assisting the gangs. In November 2021, Elmer Canales Rivera ("Crook"), a high-ranking member of the MS-13, was aided by Carlos Marroquín, Bukele Ortez's minister who allegedly coordinated talks between the government and the gangs. Marroquín was accused of personally escorting Canales Rivera from prison to Guatemala, where he then journeyed to Mexico to avoid law enforcement.[110] In another case, allegations were leveled against Rodolfo Delgado after he was appointed attorney general in May 2021. Delgado was accused of dismantling the prosecution of Jorge Vega Knight, an associate of the MS-13 who allowed his hotel properties to be used for drug transactions, meetings between gang cells, and as a hideout. Delgado was Vega Knight's defense counsel prior to his appointment as attorney general.[111] Although Marroquín faced an indictment in the United States on the charge of negotiating with MS-13 and Barrio 18 gangs, no official charges were filed by the Salvadoran government against Marroquín or Delgado. Bukele Ortez continued to deny that any deal with the gangs had been made, but both cases indicated that El Salvador's government maintained links to high-ranking members of MS-13.

El Salvador's decision in 2021 to adopt Bitcoin as a national currency in order to manage its sovereign debt (denominated in US dollars) generated concerns that El Salvador was becoming vulnerable to money laundering and terrorist financing. According to Fitch's rating agency, the use of Bitcoin "for all obligations, including bank loans," might route Bitcoin traffic through El Salvador and "increase the risk that proceeds from illicit activities will pass through the Salvadoran financial system." Bukele Ortez disagreed, arguing that the use of Bitcoin for international transfers was crucial because remittances accounted for one-fifth of El Salvador's GDP.[112] Despite assurances that anti-money laundering procedures were in place, critics claimed that El Salvador lacked sufficient anti-money laundering regulations and that its banks failed to meet Basel II or Basel III international banking standards. Even though Bitcoin transactions were electronically traceable, criminals still used Bitcoin either to acquire hard currency or to conduct money laundering transactions involving luxury goods and real estate. Moreover, because the Salvadoran Chivo Wallet (a Bitcoin debit card distributed to all citizens) was widely rejected in favor of alternative Bitcoin wallets, the circulation of multiple Bitcoin wallets made it possible for drug money to be laundered in amounts below the reporting threshold through a process known as "smurfing."[113] At the start of 2023, the impact of Bitcoin on the drug trade in El Salvador was still yet to be determined.

Honduras:
The Forgotten Route—
Reform and Narcocorruption

In 2014, Honduran President Juan Orlando Hernández Alvarado (2014–2022) took office, inheriting one of the world's most violent nations with a murder rate of 80 per 100,000 inhabitants.[114] After his inauguration, Hernández initiated a series of reforms within the Honduran police to grapple with corruption. At the time of his election, police corruption was a public scandal; the Honduran Dirección Nacional de Asuntos Internos (National Directorate of Internal Affairs) reported 5,000 allegations of corruption within the Honduran police forces between 1999 and 2011. Of these cases, 2,868 allegations were against members of the investigative division of the national police Dirección Nacional de Investigación Criminal (DNIC).[115] In 2014, the DNIC's rampant corruption forced the government to suspend 1,400 of its officers and employees and begin an upgrade of the police to handle crimes involving narcotics, homicides, gangs, and human smuggling.[116] Despite a ballooning budget deficit that consumed 7.9 percent of Honduras's GDP in 2013, the Honduran government committed $30 million of its own funds and a $50 million loan from the Inter-American Development Bank to renovate police stations, hire 3,000 new officers, purchase vehicles, and establish crime labs. In 2014, Hernández put the military in charge of the fight against organized crime and ordered the creation of the Fuerza Nacional Interinstitucional de Seguridad, an interagency task force made up of military and police personnel including the PMOP.[117] By 2017, the Honduran police forces doubled in size to 23,000 officers. As part of the reforms, the Honduran government also created the Dirección Policial de Investigaciónes to investigate crimes within six of its eighteen police departments.[118] In 2017, the Policía Nacional de Honduras (PNH) conducted further reforms by expanding the number of police in its other narcotics investigative agencies, including the Agencia Técnica de Investigación Criminal (ATIC).

The police reforms brought about mixed results. In 2014, the PNH captured Sinaloa-affiliated drug trafficker Carlos Lobo ("El Negro"), who was labeled by the US Treasury as a kingpin and became the first Honduran extradited to the United States on drug trafficking charges.[119] Between 2016 and 2018, the US State Department's narcotics control report did not provide complete seizure statistics for Honduras, but stated that Honduras remained a "primary destination country in Central America for cocaine-laden aircraft departing from South America." The US State Department added that street gangs, such as MS-13 and Calle 18, committed the majority of homicides (primarily in Tegucigalpa), although the number of homicides in 2017 "declined to 45 per 100,000 people from

282 *Narcostates*

the peak of 86 per 100,000 in 2011." The State Department also noted that gangs continued to facilitate trafficking through Honduras.[120] The traffickers' resiliency was apparent in 2017 when authorities discovered 84,000 square meters of coca growing on separate plantations in the Olancho department.[121] In April 2019, the ATIC arrested four Colombian traffickers and seized 110 kilos of cocaine along the Atlantic coastline, showing that Honduras remained an important transit zone in the narcocorridor.[122] In 2021, the Honduran government announced that it had seized 14.2 metric tons of cocaine, four times the amount intercepted in 2020. As in Guatemala, coca production soared. In 2022, Honduras eradicated 6.5 million coca bushes, outstripping its 2021 total of 531,000 bushes. Increasingly, Honduran authorities discovered processing laboratories among the coca fields.[123] Also in 2022, the Salvadoran crackdown on the maras spilled over into Honduras. That year, President Xiomara Castro de Zelaya (2022–present), the wife of Manuel Zelaya, declared a national emergency to prevent the entry of drug traffickers and to recover the lawless territories after more than 400 truckers were murdered by the maras for not paying them a "war tax."[124]

Like its neighbors, Honduras was not immune to high-profile narcotics-related corruption scandals. In January 2015, the DEA negotiated a deal with the leaders of the Honduran Cachiros gang to surrender themselves. In exchange for clemency, the gang agreed to be extradited to the United States and to provide evidence against high-ranking members of the police and government, including Congressman Antonio Hernández Alvarado, the president's brother. On November 23, 2018, the DEA arrested Antonio Hernández in Miami on drug trafficking charges. During his two-week trial, US prosecutors provided ledgers that detailed Antonio Hernández's business relationship with a Honduran narcotrafficker. US prosecutors also provided evidence that El Chapo hand-delivered $1 million to Antonio Hernández to give to his brother, the president. Victor Díaz Morales ("El Rojo"), another Honduran trafficker, testified that he gave Hernández $100,000 for Hernández's congressional race in 2009. Antonio Hernández promised Díaz Morales that his contribution would "provide better information concerning police and military investigations."[125] President Orlando Hernández denied all accusations and won reelection in November 2017 despite alleged voting irregularities.[126] On October 18, 2019, a US federal court convicted Antonio Hernández on drug trafficking charges and sentenced him to life in prison. At the end of his administration in April 2022, President Hernández was extradited to the United States on charges of drugs and weapons trafficking. Any Honduran successes made through CARSI had been badly besmirched by narcocorruption.[127]

Nicaragua:
The Return of Daniel Ortega

Daniel Ortega's reelection as president in 2007 led to concerns that Nicaragua might limit its counternarcotics cooperation with the United States because of past allegations against the Sandinista government and because of Ortega's support for Latin American revolutionary movements accused of involvement in drug trafficking.[128] Ortega's return was also sullied by rumors of a corrupt deal with former president Arnoldo Alemán Lacayo (1997–2002). In 2003, Alemán had been sentenced to twenty years in prison on money laundering and embezzlement charges and had been unofficially accused of narcocorruption when police discovered that he traveled on a stolen Lear jet linked to cocaine smuggling. In exchange for his release, Alemán allegedly agreed to use his Partido Liberal Constitucionalista (PLC) to back Ortega's political campaign.[129] The prognosis for the United States and Nicaragua looked bleak.

Ortega's antidrug cooperation with the United States started off poorly following the Colombian military's 2008 cross-border raid on a FARC camp in Ecuador. Ortega accused the Colombian government of conducting state-sponsored terrorism and offered asylum to three FARC guerrillas.[130] Ortega's support for the FARC—an internationally recognized DTO—bode poorly for Nicaragua's drug fighting credentials. Those credentials were called into further question due to Ortega's unwavering support for Venezuela, which had been accused of protecting narcotraffickers along the Venezuela-Colombia border.[131] In 2016, reporter Douglas Farah testified before the US Congress that Albanisa, a subsidiary of Venezuela's state-owned oil company operating in Nicaragua, facilitated money laundering for the FARC. Farah further explained that Daniel Ortega and the inner circle of the FSLN siphoned off $4 billion from Albanisa to support their political campaigns and to line their pockets.[132]

General corruption remained a concern for Nicaragua. When asked who the mafia in Nicaragua were, Roberto Orozco, a Nicaraguan security expert, claimed, "When I say that Nicaragua manages organized crime, I mean that the business deals are made with representatives from the state."[133] In 2010, WikiLeaks released a 2006 US State Department cable stating that the FSLN used drug money to finance their electoral campaigns. The cable stated, "Daniel Ortega and the Sandinistas regularly received money to finance FSLN electoral campaigns from international drug traffickers, usually in return for ordering Sandinista judges to allow traffickers caught by the police and military to go free."[134] Between 2010 and 2013, the Nicaraguan judiciary reduced sentences for more than 1,000 convicted traffickers, including affiliates of the Sinaloa cartel.[135] More

284   *Narcostates*

recent allegations of corruption occurred in 2019, when the Nicaraguan attorney general alleged that the FSLN representative to the Central American Parliament ran a trafficking network through Costa Rica, Nicaragua, and Honduras.[136]

According to the US State Department, Nicaragua's capacity to conduct successful interdiction operations was challenged by its limited law enforcement and intelligence gathering capabilities, compounded by sparsely populated regions that were difficult to police. Between 2014 and 2016, the volume of cocaine seized by Nicaragua declined.[137] Moreover, the decreasing trend in seizures was attributed to Nicaragua's decision to disband its DEA-trained naval antidrug unit in 2013, a reduction in US counternarcotics assets in Nicaragua's coastal waters, and the need for the Nicaraguan navy to patrol an additional 30,000 square miles in the Caribbean awarded to it by the International Court of Justice in 2012.[138] In 2016, Nicaragua initiated a Strategic Plan for 2016–2022 by proposing a retaining wall strategy to prevent traffickers from entering the country entirely. Nevertheless, traffickers continued to utilize clandestine airstrips in the interior and shifted their operations between the Atlantic and Pacific corridors as needed.[139] By 2020, the same problems remained. Despite the government's claim that the retaining wall was working, large seizures were being made, including a 1.5-ton cocaine haul in 2020, prompting US President Donald Trump to label Nicaragua a major transit country. Daniel Ortega disputed this claim, but according to Nicaragua national security expert Elvira Cuadra, it was "impossible to think that organized crime groups avoid passing through the country."[140] Simply put, Nicaragua did not have the capability to cover its entire air, land, and sea borders.

Costa Rica:
Tico Mexicanization

President Laura Chinchilla's (2010–2014) government made a concerted effort to strengthen its institutions in order to meet certain security goals, including an expansion of the police force by 880 officers, constructing a Caribbean coast guard outpost, and spending $1 million to improve security along the Peñas Blancas Inter-American Highway border crossing.[141] Costa Rica also worked to coordinate with regional governments, especially Nicaragua. By 2017, both Costa Rica and Nicaragua agreed to tighten security on their common border. They also agreed to share intelligence for the purpose of intercepting drug smuggling vessels and fishing boats.[142]

Despite Costa Rica's efforts, several obstacles remained. According to the State Department, those obstacles included a lack of funding for security forces engaged in interdiction efforts and an inability to sustain programs started with US assistance. Police hiring did not keep up with the rate of attrition. The OIJ (judicial police) remained understaffed. Fiscal problems forced the Costa Rican government to reduce the 2016 budget for the Ministerio de Seguridad Pública (MSP) by 27 percent.[143] Despite those obstacles, in October 2015, Costa Rica made headlines when authorities arrested one Cuban and several Costa Rican citizens working with members of the Italian mafia to transport forty kilos of cocaine to the United States.[144] Events like this helped the MSP justify an increase its counternarcotics budget by 5 percent in 2018 on top of an 11 percent increase in 2017.[145]

Costa Rican domestic crime syndicates increasingly provided logistical support for Colombian and Mexican traffickers.[146] The 2019 arrest of several Costa Rican traffickers affiliated with Mexican and Colombian cartels illustrated just how much Costa Rica had transformed from being a bridge for drug trafficking to being a warehouse and trading center for drug cartels.[147] The highest-profile case came with the August 2019 arrest of José López Mendoza (M-1), the leader of the Costa Rican DTO Movimiento Revolucionario de Crimen Organizado (MORECO). López Mendoza maintained ties to El Mayo of the Sinaloa cartel and used MORECO to transport Colombian cocaine through Costa Rica toward Guatemala, Mexico, and the United States.[148] Other high-profile arrests of Costa Rican *transportistas* moving cocaine for Colombian and Mexican cartels included the 2019 arrests of leaders from the El Gringo and El Pellejo DTOs.[149]

Although Costa Rica had a low homicide rate compared to other countries in the region, homicides increased by 14 percent between 2013 and 2014 and were on pace to increase further. In 2017, homicides had increased by 20 percent, reaching a record high.[150] Costa Rican authorities rightfully placed the blame on the drug trade. Attorney General Jorge Chavarría blamed the homicide rate on the "Mexicanization" of Costa Rica's criminal groups.[151] Many homicides occurred in Puntarenas, with an increasing number of tourists becoming victims. Puerto Limón on Costa Rica's Atlantic coast soon surpassed Puntarenas as the homicide capital, accounting for nearly a quarter of all killings in the country. Many of the homicides were attributed to a 2016–2021 turf war between two drug trafficking gangs, led by narcotraffickers known as Diablo and Pechuga. According to the OIJ, 90 percent of the killings in Limón were due to clashes between organized crime groups moving cocaine through the container port of Moín.[152] In 2022, Costa Rica set a national record with 657 homicides. Eighty percent of the cases were drug-related. The majority occurred in Limón, where the battle for control of the port grew to include four well-organized Tico criminal factions. In his remarks to the Costa Rican Legislative Assembly, Security Minister Jorge Torres criticized the justice system for being too lenient toward drug-related

286 *Narcostates*

offenses and advocated for a larger police presence on the streets.[153] According to former Costa Rican Security Minister Gustavo Mata Vega, "Criminality in the country" revolved "increasingly around the drug trade, whereas previously it largely consisted of bank robbery, vehicular theft, and kidnapping."[154]

The growing drug trade also exposed Costa Rica's renowned democratic institutions to corruption. In 2013, President Laura Chinchilla became embroiled in a scandal when it became public that she twice flew on a private jet owned by Colombian traffickers. The jet was owned by THX Energy, a Colombian oil company whose owner was associated with Norte de Valle cartel leader Juan Ramírez Abadía ("Chupeta"). Although Chinchilla claimed no knowledge of the connection, the circumstantial evidence created a scandal. Chinchilla responded by dismissing Costa Rica's DIS chief and the minister of communications.[155] In another high-profile case, the former director of Costa Rica's national police was arrested in June 2017 while guarding 237 kilos of cocaine.[156] Several incidents of judges and police officers being imprisoned for assisting international drug trafficking gangs were recorded between 2020 and 2021. According to Fernando Cruz, president of the Supreme Court of Justice, organized crime has "people within [the court] who offer them information."[157] Newly elected President Rodrigo Chaves Robles's (2022–present) reform agenda faced many challenges ahead.

Panama:
The Cocaine and Money Laundering Deluge

Panama's importance as a narcotics transshipment point never diminished.[158] In 2013, the Sinaloa, Gulf, Beltrán Leyva, Los Zetas, and Juárez cartels were all active in Panama. Out of the 2,500 foreign prisoners in Panamanian jails, 90 to 100 were Mexican nationals incarcerated on drug trafficking charges. Sinaloa and Los Zetas *sicarios* took their war to Panama, and they were accused of being involved in the disappearances of those who had betrayed them in money laundering activities.[159] On a daily basis, drug traffickers utilized Panama's transportation infrastructure, including the CFTZ, airports, four major container seaports, and the Pan-American Highway.[160] Traffickers also exploited Panama's remote southern Darién province to transport coca paste and refined cocaine from the Andes. Local Panamanian DTOs provided logistical support to traffickers smuggling cocaine through Panama. Based along Panama's Caribbean coast, these DTOs coordinated "go-fast" vessels from Colombia into Darién. Once in Darién, the boats were rapidly refueled in secluded locations in order to move shipments further up the coastline.[161] Although the FARC disbanded in 2017, Colombia and Panama both

Despite the implementation of tighter legislation by the Panamanian government, Panamanian banks remained a hub for money laundering. Bulk cash flowed unabated into the CFTZ with no verification process to confirm its lawful use.[164] In April 2016, Bastian Obermayer, working for the Munich newspaper *Süddeutsche Zeitung*, made public a series of documents known as the "Panama Papers" that uncovered how wealthy elites used Panama as a tax haven. The papers also exposed the use of the Panamanian banking system to launder drug money. The papers revealed that the Panamanian law firm Mossack Fonseca bought real estate in Uruguay to launder money for the CJNG and that it also laundered money for Rafael Caro Quintero through real estate transactions in Costa Rica.[165] The Panama Papers further disclosed that Mossack Fonseca helped the Sinaloa cartel launder $4 million through a front company known as Broadway Commerce, and an undisclosed amount through a Colombian real estate company called Lindley Services Incorporated.[166] After its exposure, Mossack Fonseca destroyed many documents, leaving questions as to who else used its services. To prevent future financial scandals, Panama passed Executive Decree 122 in 2018, requiring its banks to share financial information with thirty-three nations.[167]

Areas of concentrated gang and drug activity also brought high rates of murder and crime, especially in the urban provinces of Colón and Panamá where the canal is located. By 2016, there were 204 gangs operating in Panama.[168] In response, Panama adopted a US-styled intelligence-led policing model in 2017.[169] Still, by 2018, two rival gangs—known as Bagdad and Calor Calor—dominated Panama's gang networks. They established collection agencies to work directly with Colombian and Mexican DTOs.[170] The gangs infiltrated Panama's port facilities to load cocaine onto cargo ships passing through Colón. They also manipulated compromised employees known as *cuadrillas* to look the other way while they loaded cocaine onto European-bound container ships.[171] Despite the February 2022 arrest of Bagdad gang leader Jorge Rubén Camargo Clarke, both gangs continued to operate as normal without engaging in a power struggle.[172]

Panama witnessed a sizable increase in drug seizures between 2014 and 2020. According to the United Nations 2019 *World Drug Report*, after the United States, Panama accounted for the largest quantity of cocaine seized in the Americas.[173] While the statistics showed that the capabilities

288 *Narcostates*

of Panama's police had improved, they also showed an expansion of trafficking through Panama between 2014 and 2020. Corruption also played a large role in the expansion of trafficking. For example, an eighteen-month investigation resulted in the arrest of twenty-seven Panamanian officials on corruption charges in 2021, including members of Panama's air force and navy, a captain in the presidential guard, and airport security personnel.[174] In 2021, Panama seized 128 metric tons of cocaine; in 2022, it set a new record by seizing 145 metric tons of cocaine.[175] In November 2022, Panama's attorney general, Javier Caraballo, reported that Panamanian traffickers assisted a super cartel in transporting one-third of all cocaine to Europe, providing further evidence of Panama's importance to the drug trade.[176] According to the State Department, the "increased volume of drugs from Colombia and the spillover of criminality from neighboring countries exceeded the capabilities of Panama's security services to manage these challenges alone."[177]

The Central American Refugee Crisis, 2014–Present

An unprecedented number of Central American refugees flooded the US-Mexico border in 2014. Their appearance raised questions about the success of CARSI. To address this issue, the US government provided $130 million above the budget request for a Central American Migration Prevention and Response program.[178] In September 2014, the Obama administration proposed the Plan of the Alliance for Prosperity in the Northern Triangle. The five-year, $22 billion plan sought to stimulate the productive sector, improve public safety, and strengthen institutions. The US government held that its Alliance for Prosperity would stem the flow of refugees. At the time, the State Department asserted that community policing programs had reduced homicide rates by more than 60 percent in certain areas of El Salvador, although a separate NGO report blamed gangs for 84 percent of El Salvador's displaced population.[179]

The Central American response to the Alliance for Prosperity plan was positive, but many believed its success depended on the private sector. Guatemalan President Otto Pérez Molina called the plan necessary to spur economic growth despite the country's insecurity and out-migration crisis. Salvadoran Vice President Óscar Ortiz underscored that the business community was the driving force behind the plan's success. Honduran President Juan Orlando Hernández emphasized the link between social conditions and economic growth, warning that the private sector would not be able to grow if communities were allowed to fail. According to one Honduran businessman, the problem was that foreign investors were still staying away because "they think we are at war, but we are not." Conditions were indeed difficult, and any gains made could easily be reversed.[180]

Despite the economic assistance and policing programs, the migrant crisis continued unabated. Following a temporary respite between 2015 and 2016, an increasing number of migrants traveled north after 2016. According to various sources, 250,000 to 500,000 Central American migrants entered the United States annually between 2016 and 2019.[181] Running on a campaign promise to halt illegal immigration, US President Donald Trump took aggressive actions to curb the influx. In 2017 and 2018, the Trump administration ended the Temporary Protected Status for Central American migrants, who had previously claimed protected status because of natural disasters.

The passage of several Central American migrant caravans moving through Mexico toward the United States in 2018 attracted significant news attention. Concerns grew after Guatemalan President Jimmy Morales reported in 2018 that 100 members of the Islamic State in Iraq and Syria (ISIS) and 1,000 members of MS-13 were detained as the caravans passed through Guatemala. Previously, Mexico's CISEN claimed that ISIS had established a training camp near Juárez and intended to exploit the railways and airport facilities to infiltrate the United States.[182] Calling the caravans "an invasion," the Trump administration threatened to impose tariffs on Mexico to force it to control the passage of migrants across its southern border. In June 2019, Mexico agreed to use its national guard to curb irregular migration and take stronger measures to disrupt human smuggling and trafficking organizations. The agreement with Mexico also expanded the Migrant Protection Protocols, which meant that migrants seeking asylum in the United States would have to wait in Mexico while their claims were adjudicated.[183] Those asylum seekers faced many dangers from criminal gangs along the border, including extortion, kidnapping, and torture. Migrants who could not pay for their passage were sometimes brutally tortured and murdered; others ended up working for their kidnappers as drug couriers or prostitutes as a way to secure their release or passage. The US Department of State reported the existence of evidence suggesting that Mexican migration authorities and local police often turned a blind eye to or colluded in these criminal activities.[184] Following its agreement with Mexico, the Trump administration reached a deal with Guatemala in July 2019 requiring Central American migrants to make their asylum requests in Guatemala before seeking asylum in the United States. In September 2019, similar deals were signed with El Salvador and Honduras.[185]

As a result of the new asylum requirements, Central American asylum applications in Mexico increased from 2,000 to more than 14,000 between 2014 and 2018.[186] The number of Central American deportations from Mexico also increased from 141,828 in 2017 to 196,061 in 2018.[187] In June 2019, the US Customs and Border Protection Agency apprehended more than 363,000 illegal migrants from the Northern Triangle during the first nine months of the fiscal year.[188] Still, Central American migrants would

290 *Narcostates*

not be deterred. In January 2020, a caravan of 2,000 to 4,000 Honduran migrants attempted to make the journey to the United States.[189] However, following the onset of the Covid-19 pandemic, new limitations known as Title 42 were placed on migrants in March 2020, when the US Centers for Disease Control ordered the expulsion of undocumented immigrants and asylum seekers based on health concerns.[190]

In 2022, US Customs recorded approximately 2.2 million arrests of migrants attempting to cross the US border illegally. Many of those migrants came from "nontraditional" countries such as Venezuela and Haiti. Despite this change in migration trends, Central America continued to account for more than half of those individuals crossing the border in 2022.[191] At the beginning of 2023, Andean political instability caused a spike in the number of Andean migrants, who overtook the number of Central American migrants attempting to reach the United States.[192] Panama documented 49,291 migrants crossing the Darién Gap into Central America between January and February 2023, a fivefold increase over the 8,964 migrants recorded during the same period in 2022.[193] The Department of Homeland Security estimated that between 2018 and 2022, the revenue earned from illegal immigration skyrocketed from $500 million to $13 billion. Much of that money went into the coffers of the cartels and their gang affiliates.[194] The bustling business for coyotes and cartels did not remove the dangers for migrants. In 2022, 890 migrant bodies were recovered along the border—another record.[195]

It is unknown what effect the May 2023 lifting of the Covid-19 emergency status and the consequent end of Title 42 expulsions will have on illegal migration into the United States. More quantitative and qualitative data are necessary to thoroughly analyze the cause and impact of the refugee crisis. It is evident, though, that the refugee caravans are a consequence of endemic crime in Latin America, driven by the war on drugs and decades-long economic despair. In many ways, the refugee crisis of 2014–2022 mirrors the refugee crisis of the 1980s that occurred at the height of the Central American conflict. The difference now is that narcotrafficking has replaced revolutionary insurgency as a major propellant upending the lives of millions of people. Mexican and Central American institutions simply cannot withstand the unrelenting economic power and terroristic force wielded by the cartels.

Notes

1. Drug Enforcement Administration, 2020 *National Drug Threat Assessment* DEA-DCT-DIR-008-21 (Washington, DC: US Department of Justice, March 2021), 35.

2. British Broadcasting Service, "Mexico's President Peña Nieto Proposes Relaxing Marijuana Laws," BBC News, April 22, 2016, www.bbc.com.

Narcotrafficking and the Immigration Crisis 291

3. Samuel Osborne, "Mexico Legalizes Medical Marijuana," *Independent*, June 21, 2017, www.independent.co.uk.

4. Associated Press, "Mexico Unveils New Strategy in War on Drugs and for Preventing Crime," *Guardian*, February 13, 2013, www.theguardian.com.

5. US Department of State, Bureau of International Narcotics and Law Enforcement Affairs, 2016 *International Narcotics Control Strategy Report Vol. I* (Washington, DC: US Department of State, March 2016), 225.

6. Carmen Aristegui, "Cártel de Juaréz, proveedor del PRI y financiador de en la campaña de Peña Nieto," *Aristegui Noticias*, March 16, 2016, http://aristeguinoticias.com; Ildefonso Ortiz, "Report: Juárez Cartel Used Shell Companies to Finance Mexican President's Election," *Brietbart News*, March 18, 2016, www.breitbart.com. Dávila Córdova was a Bank of Mexico manager who laundered money through exchange houses. He was connected to the Juárez cartel after he was arrested in October 2005 with $750,000 in cash.

7. Christopher Woody, "How One Colombian Family Allegedly Helped 'El Chapo' Dominate Global Drug Trafficking," *Business Insider*, February 5, 2016, www.businessinsider.com. The Cifuentes Villa clan was associated with the Medellín cartel and started working for the Sinaloa cartel in 2007 after they lost the protection of the Autodefensas Unidas de Colombia (AUC). The Cifuentes influence in Colombia declined following the 2011 arrest of Dolly Cifuentes Villa, the mistress of Colombian President Álvaro Uribe's brother. The 2012 arrest of the cartel's leader, Jorge Cifuentes Villa, ended their role as traffickers in Colombia.

8. Ryan Saavedra, "Drug Lord El Chapo Paid $100 Million Bribe to Mexican President Enrique Pena Nieto, Witness Says," *Daily Wire*, January 16, 2019, www.dailywire.com. Cifuentes revealed that El Chapo paid the Mexican military $10–$12 million to conduct operations against his enemies.

9. Juan Pablo Reyes, "Dejan sin efecto proceso contra Javier Duarte por tráfico de influencias," *Excelsior* (Mexico) November 5, 2019, www.excelsior.com.mx; Kirk Semple, "Javier Duarte, Mexican Ex-Governor Accused of Diverting Money, Is Captured," *New York Times*, April 16, 2017, www.nytimes.com.

10. Elisabeth Malkin, "Corruption at a Level of Audacity Never Seen in Mexico," *New York Times*, April 19, 2017, www.nytimes.com.

11. Jorge Monroy, "AMLO reveló que Salvador Cienfuegos no es investigado en México," *El Economista* (Mexico), October 16, 2020, www.eleconomista.com.mx.

12. José de Córdoba and Santiago Pérez, "Mexico Law to Rein in U.S. Agents," *Wall Street Journal*, December 16, 2020, sec. A, p. 9; José de Córdoba, "Mexico Accuses U.S. of Concocting Drug Charges," *Wall Street Journal*, January 16, 2021, sec. A, p. 9.

13. US Attorney's Office, Eastern District of New York, "Former Mexican Federal Police Commander Arrested for Drug Trafficking Conspiracy," US Department of Justice, January 24, 2020, www.justice.gov/usao-edny/pr/former-mexican-federal -police-commander-arrested-drug-trafficking-conspiracy.

14. Haleema Shah, "Mexico's Top Cop Is on Trial Along with the War on Drugs," *Vox*, January 27, 2023, www.vox.com; US Attorney's Office, Eastern District of New York, "Former Mexican Secretary of Public Security Genaro García Luna Charged with Engaging in a Continuing Criminal Enterprise, US Department of Justice, July 30, 2020, www.justice.gov/usao-edny/pr/former-mexican-secretary -public-security-genaro-garcia-luna-charged-engaging-continuing.

15. Malcolm Beith, "The Current State of Mexico's Many Drug Cartels," InSight Crime, September 25, 2013, www.insightcrime.org; Héctor Becerra and Richard A. Serrano, "Mexico Cartel Kingpin Reported Dead of a Heart Attack," *Los Angeles*

292 Narcostates

Times, June 9, 2014, www.latimes.com. In June 2014, rumors floated that El Azul had died of a heart attack. El Azul's son confirmed his death in August 2014.

16. Buggs, "Sinaloa Cartel Takes Ciudad Juárez," *Borderland Beat*, April 9, 2010, www.borderlandbeat.com; Lucio R., "Part One: The Miracle of Juárez—Sinaloa vs. Juárez Cartel," *Borderland Beat*, May 23, 2015, www.borderlandbeat.com.

17. Tijuano, "New Juárez Cartel Leader Identified: Ugly Betty," *Borderland Beat*, June 2, 2013, www.borderlandbeat.com.

18. Tristan Reed, "Mexico's Drug War: Stability Ahead of the Fourth Quarter" (Austin, TX: Stratfor Global Intelligence, October 10, 2013), https://worldview .stratfor.com; Froilán Meza Rivera Vivito y Coleando, "el Cártel de Juárez tiene aún una estructura operativa," *La Crónica de Chihuahua* (Mexico), May 1, 2015, www.cronicadechihuahua.com; Mike Gallagher, "The Cartels Next Door: Far from Dead, Juárez Cartel Flexes Its Muscles," Albuquerque Journal, February 13, 2017, www.abqjournal.com. The NCJ cartel was run by Julio Olivas Torres ("El Sexto") until his arrest in 2018. As of January 2022, La Línea/Juárez hitman, Juan Pablo Ledezma ("El JL") ran the NCJ. Gonzalo García García ("El Chalo") ran La Línea until his death in 2015. His son, Ignacio García ("El Nacho"), ran La Línea until his arrest in 2018.

19. Chivis Martínez, "Despite a Major Government Crackdown, Zetas Keep Expanding Their Reach," *Borderland Beat*, January 16, 2012, www.borderlandbeat.com.

20. Proceso, "Contraofensiva zeta en el noreste," *Proceso* (Mexico), October 30, 2013, www.proceso.com.mx. Following the arrest of Miguel Treviño Morales ("Z-40"), his brother Óscar Omar Treviño Morales ("Z-42") took over the Zetas. Opposition to Omar Treviño Morales came from the Z-Renegades. In 2015, Z-42 was arrested, causing the cartel to split.

21. Chivis Martínez, "Z-40: The Aftermath of Miguel Treviño's Arrest and Looking at the Contenders," *Borderland Beat*, July 17, 2017, www.borderlandbeat .com. Two such leaders were Maxiley Barahona Nadales ("El Contador"), who controlled Tabasco and Chiapas, and Sergio Basurto Peña ("El Grande"), who managed the city of Veracruz.

22. "Gulf Cartel Leader Presumed Dead by Mexican Authorities," Borderland Beat, September 2, 2011, www.borderlandbeat.com; Tracy Wilkinson, "A Reputed Leader of the Gulf Cartel Is Captured in Mexico" *Los Angeles Times*, September 4, 2012, http://latimesblogs.latimes.com; Sivera Otero and Doris Gomora, "Presenta Marina a Hermana de Osiel Cárdenas," *El Universal* (Mexico), September 4, 2012, http://archivo.eluniversal.com.mx/notas/868308.html.

23. Edward Fox, "Gulf Cartel Leader Assassinated in Northern Mexico," InSight Crime, January 17, 2013, www.insightcrime.org; Steven Dudley, "X-20 Capture Leaves Another Power Vacuum in Gulf Cartel," InSight Crime, August 18, 2013, www.insightcrime.org.

24. ACI, "The Gang That Took on El Chapo: Los Mazatlecos," *Borderland Beat*, July 28, 2012, www.borderlandbeat.com.

25. Melissa Galván, "Diez cárteles se pelean Guerrero con más brutalidad y violencia, mientras la pobreza se acentúa," *Sin Embargo* (Mexico), March 19, 2017, www.sinembargo.mx.

26. Joe Tuckman, "Former Mayor Charged in Kidnapping of Missing 43 Students," *Guardian* (England), January 14, 2015, www.theguardian.com; Lucio R., "G.U. Turncoats Sierra Unida Cleans Up Iguala Plaza for Los Rojos," *Borderland Beat*, March 11, 2015, www.borderlandbeat.com.

27. Lucio R., "Los Rojos, Los Ardillos, and CIDA Are Now Dominant in Guerrero," *Borderland Beat*, May 4, 2016, www.borderlandbeat.com. In the 1960s, the uni-

versity graduated Lucio Cabañas Barrientos, a leader of the Partido de los Pobres, and Genaro Vázquez Rojas, the founder of the Asociación Cívica Nacional Revolucionaria.

28. Rosario Castro Mosso and Enrique Mendoza Hernández, "Drug Traffickers Are Restructured into 28 Cartels," trans. Chivis Martínez and Borderland Beat, *Zeta Weekly*, January 3, 2012, www.borderlandbeat.com.

29. James Bargent, "Vigilante Standoff Highlights Mexico Security Dilemma," InSight Crime, March 22, 2013, www.insightcrime.org. In Michoacán, the autodefensas were organized by Hipólito Mora Chávez and Dr. José Mireles Valverde.

30. Jan-Albert Hoosten, "Mexico's Last Vigilantes," *Newsweek*, August 28, 2015, www.newsweek.com; José Gil Olmos, "Policías comunitarios y grupos de autodefensa," *Proceso* (Mexico), November 12, 2013, www.proceso.com.mx.

31. Kyra Gurney, "Mexico Senators Propose Amnesty for Self-Defense Forces," InSight Crime, September 23, 2014, www.insightcrime.org.

32. Marguerite Cawley and James Bargent, "Following Arrests, Mexico Vigilantes Take Soldiers Hostage," InSight Crime, March 12, 2013, www.insightcrime.org.

33. "El Paisa lidera el cártel de Sinaloa," *La Silla Rota* (Mexico), October 13, 2014, https://lasillarota.com.

34. Larry Buchanan, Josh Keller, and Derek Watkins, "How Mexico's Most Wanted Drug Lord Escaped from Prison Again," *New York Times*, January 8, 2016, www.nytimes.com; "El Chapo Guzmán Escape, Mexican Prison Officials Charged," BBC News, September 8, 2015, www.bbc.com. Four jail employees were charged with failing to alert their superiors of the escape. Two monitored security screens and two were members of the CISEN.

35. José de Córdoba and Dudley Althaus, "El Chapo Felled by Quest for Fame," *Wall Street Journal*, January 11, 2016, sec. A, p. 10. El Chapo's interview with actor Sean Penn enabled the Mexican government to trace him, nearly leading to his arrest in October 2015. From that point on, El Chapo's ability to evade detection deteriorated. The effort to capture El Chapo was called Operation Black Swan. Orso Iván Gastelum Cruz ("El Cholo Iván") was El Chapo's lieutenant.

36. American Embassy Mexico to Secretary of State Washington, DC, "Subject: Mexican Media Suggest That El Chapo's Prison Break Leads Mexico to Cooperate on Extradition," Mexico 13526 022123Z, October 2, 2015, 1.

37. José de Córdoba, "Mexico's Drug Lord's Extradition Fuels Bloody Turf War," *Wall Street Journal*, July 18, 2017, sec. A, p. 2.

38. "Capturan a Dámaso López 'El Licenciado,' sucesor de El Chapo Guzmán," *El Heraldo de Saltillo* (Mexico), May 2, 2017, http://elheraldodesaltillo.mx; Christopher Woody, "A Major Player in the Struggle for Control over the Sinaloa Cartel Just Surrendered in the U.S.," *Business Insider*, July 28, 2017,www.businessinsider.com.

39. Anthony Harrup, "Mexico Tightens Security After Drug Arrest," *Wall Street Journal,* January 7, 2023, sec. A. p. 9.

40. "Chapitos," InSight Crime, January 9, 2023, https://insightcrime.org.

41. Office of Public Affairs, "Justice Department Announces Charges Against Sinaloa Cartel's Global Operation," US Department of Justice, April 14, 2023, https://www.justice.gov/opa/pr/justice-department-announces-charges-against -sinaloa-cartel-s-global-operation; United States v. Ovidio Guzmán López, Sealed Indictment 21 U.S.C. §§ 846, 848, 963 and 18 U.S.C. 924, US Attorney's Office Southern District of New York, January, 25 2023; United States v. Iván Archivaldo Guzmán Salazar, Jesús Alfredo Guzmán Salazar, and Ovidio Guzmán López, 21 U.S.C. 841, 846, 848(a), (b) and (e)(1)(A), 952, 959, 963, and Title 18 United States Code, Sections 924(c)(1)(A), (c)(1)(B) and 1956(h), United States District Court Northern District Of Illinois Eastern Division, April 5, 2023.

294 Narcostates

42. Stephen Smith, "Sons of El Chapo used corkscrews, hot chiles and electrocution for torture and victims were fed to tigers, Justice Department says," CBS News, 20 April, 2023.

43. American Consulate Guadalajara to Secretary of State Washington, DC, "Jalisco: 47 Public Officials Killed Thus Far in 2015," Guadalajara 13526 201503Z, July 20, 2015, 3.

44. Josh Elles, "The Brutal Rise of El Mencho," *Rolling Stone Magazine*, July 11, 2017, www.rollingstone.com. In the May 2015 operation, the CJNG destroyed one helicopter and killed eight soldiers as well as one police officer.

45. Hanaa' Tameez, "Mexico Grapples with a Rise in Killings," *Wall Street Journal*, September 26, 2016, sec. A, p. 16.

46. Robbie Whelan, "Mexico's Violent Drug War Is Back," *Wall Street Journal*, June 6, 2017, sec. A, p. 1.

47. "Tijuana Homicides Soar to 411 in 2017," *Mexico News Daily*, April 22, 2017, http://mexiconewsdaily.com.

48. José de Córdoba, "Mexican Mothers Unearth a Mass Grave," *Wall Street Journal*, March 16, 2016, sec. A, p. 16.

49. Kevin Sieff, "36 Candidates Have Been Assassinated in Mexico," *Buffalo News*, May 21, 2018, sec. A, p. 8.

50. American Embassy Mexico to Secretary of State Washington, DC, "Subject: President López Obrador Going Strong After 100 Days," Mexico 13526 191853Z, March 19, 2019, 1.

51. US Department of State, Country Reports on Human Rights Practices: Mexico 2022 Human Rights Report, Washington, DC, 2021, 1–2; Human Rights Watch, "Mexico: Extending Military Policing Threatens Rights," August 26, 2022, https://www.hrw.org/news/2022/08/26/mexico-extending-military-policing-threatens-rights.

52. Carrie Kahn, "As Mexico's Dominant Cartel Gains Power, the President Vows Hugs, Not Bullets," NPR, July 23, 2020, www.npr.org.

53. Mark Moore, "Mexico Reportedly Disbands Elite Anti-Drug Unit That Worked with DEA," *New York Post*, April 19, 2022, https://nypost.com; Ginger Thompson, "Justice Department Inspector General to Investigate DEA Program Linked to Massacres in Mexico," ProPublica, September 19, 2018, www.propublica.org.

54. Anthony Esposito, "Mexico's New National Guard Was Created to Fight Crime, but Now It's in a Face-Off with Immigrants," Reuters, July 7, 2019, www.reuters.com.

55. American Embassy Mexico to Secretary of State Washington, DC, "Subject: López Obrador Administration Has Mixed Results on Human Rights," Mexico 13526 052045Z, February 5, 2020, 4.

56. American Embassy Mexico to Secretary of State Washington, DC, "Subject: One Year in President López Obrador's Approval Ratings Break Records Despite Challenges," Mexico 13526 092159Z, December 9, 2019, 5.

57. Associated Press, "U.S. Hands Over Suspect in Missing Students Case," *Buffalo News*, January 20, 2023, sec. A, p. 10.

58. Juan Montes and José de Córdoba, "Mexican Election Season Turns Deadly," *Wall Street Journal*, May 26, 2021, sec. A, p. 20.

59. Juan Montes, "Cartel-Led Violence Tests Mexican President," *Wall Street Journal*, August 18, 2022, sec. A, p. 16.

60. White House Briefing Room, "Readout of President Joe Biden's Meeting with President López Obrador of Mexico," White House, January 9, 2023, www.whitehouse.gov/briefing-room/statements-releases/2023/01/09/readout-of-president-joe-bidens-meeting-with-president-lopez-obrador-of-mexico.

Narcotrafficking and the Immigration Crisis 295

61. Steven Dudley, "Five Takeaways From US Indictments of Chapitos, Associates," InSight Crime, April 17, 2023, https://insightcrime.org/news/five-takeaways-us-indictments-chapitos/.

62. Jon Kamp, José de Córdoba, and Julie Wernau, "Inside the Mexican Cartels That Rule Fentanyl Smuggling," *Wall Street Journal*, August 8, 2022, sec. A, p. 1.

63. Strategic Intelligence Section, *Fentanyl Flow to the United States*, DEA-DCT-DIR-008-20 (Washington, DC: Drug Enforcement Agency, January 2020), 3.

64. Ibid.; Drug Enforcement Agency, "DEA Issues Nationwide Alert on Fentanyl as a Threat to Health and Public Safety," March 8, 2015, www.dea.gov/press-releases/2015/03/18/dea-issues-nationwide-alert-fentanyl-threat-health-and-public-safety.

65. National Center for Injury Prevention and Control, "Death Rate Maps and Graphs" (Washington, DC: Centers for Disease Control and Prevention, June 2, 2022), www.cdc.gov/drugoverdose/deaths/index.html; National Safety Council, "Drug Overdoses" (Itasca, IL: National Safety Council, 2022), https://injuryfacts.nsc.org/home-and-community/safety-topics/drugoverdoses/data-details.

66. National Institute on Drug Control, "Overdose Death Rates: Trends and Statistics" (Washington, DC: US Department of Health and Human Services, January 20, 2022), https://nida.nih.gov/research-topics/trends-statistics/overdose-death-rates.

67. Kamp "Inside the Mexican Cartels," sec. A, p. 1. National Center for Health Statistics "US Overdose Deaths Increased Half as Much in 2021 as in 2002—But Are Still Up 15%," (Washington, DC: Centers for Disease Control and Prevention, May 11, 2022), https://www.cdc.gov/nchs/pressroom/nchs_press_releases/2022/202205.htm.

68. National Center for Injury Prevention, "Death Rate."

69. Drug Enforcement Agency, "Drug Enforcement Administration Announces the Seizure of Over 379 Million Deadly Doses of Fentanyl in 2022" (Washington, DC: DEA Headquarters, December 20, 2022), https://www.dea.gov/press-releases/2015/03/18/dea-issues-nationwide-alert-fentanyl-threat-health-and-public-safety.

70. Meyer and Seelke, *Central America Regional Security Initiative*, Report 41731, December 17, 2015, 23–26.

71. Meyer and Seelke, *Central America Regional Security Initiative*, Report 41731, May 6, 2014, 14.

72. US Congress, House of Representatives, *Central America and the Mérida Initiative,* 17–21.

73. US Department of State, 2015 *International Narcotics Control Strategy Report* Vol. I, 176.

74. James Bargent, "Fraud, Contraband Equivalent to 3.5% of Guatemala GDP: Report," InSight Crime, January 20, 2017, www.insightcrime.org.

75. Michael Lohmuller, "Guatemala's Government Corruption Scandal Explained," InSight Crime, June 21, 2016, www.insightcrime.org.

76. US Embassy Guatemala, "Press Release: Roxana Baldetti and Mauricio López Bonilla Indicted in US Court," US Department of State, February 24, 2017, https://gt.usembassy.gov/roxana-baldetti-mauricio-lopez-bonilla-indicted-us-court; "Treasury Targets Top Guatemalan Drug Trafficker," US Department of the Treasury, January 19, 2012, www.treasury.gov/press-center/press-releases/Pages/tg1395.aspx.

77. "Guatemala: Ex-President Otto Pérez Molina Sent Back to Prison," *Telesur* (Venezuela), August 2, 2018, www.telesurenglish.net. Baldetti received a sentence of sixteen years, and Bonilla received nine years. Health issues delayed Molina's trial until January 2022.

78. US Attorney's Office Southern District of New York, "Guatemalan Presidential Candidate Charged with Conspiring to Import Cocaine into the United States and

296   *Narcostates*

Related Firearms Offense" (Washington, DC: US Department of Justice, April 17, 2019), www.justice.gov/usao-sdny/pr/guatemalan-presidential-candidate-charged -conspiring-import-cocaine-united-states-and.

79. Parker Asmann, "Guatemalan Presidential Candidate Solicited Sinaloa Cartel for Campaign Cash," InSight Crime, April 18, 2019, www.insightcrime.org; American Embassy Guatemala to Secretary of State Washington, DC, "Congress Elects New Executive Board; Pre-Election Jockeying Under Way," Guatemala 1573 000969, November 9, 2009, 1–3, https://wikileaks.org/plusd/cables /09GUATEMALA969 _a.html.

80. US Department of State, 2016 *International Narcotics Control Strategy Report* Vol. I, 168–169.

81. Evelyn Boche, "Incautación de armas se concentra en ruta al Atlántico y sur del país," *El Periódico* (Guatemala), October 2, 2017, https://elperiodico.com.gt. Narcotics entered Guatemala through the state of Escuintla.

82. Tristan Clavel, "Top Guatemalan Prison Official Filmed Negotiating with Gangs," InSight Crime, May 5, 2017, www.insightcrime.org.

83. Parker Asmann and Mike LaSusa, "Gang Members, Guards Accused in Guatemala Prison Director's Murder," InSight Crime, December 5, 2017, www.insightcrime.org. The director was José Pérez Corado.

84. "Cómo Howard Wilfredo Barillas Morales alias el matazetas se convirtió en 'el rey' de Pavoncito," *Prensa Libre* (Guatemala), March 26, 2019, www.prensalibre.com. Barillas Morales ran MS-13 in the prison.

85. Lucía Contreras, "Estado de sitio: 'Estamos evitando que Guatemala sea un país productor de cocaína,' afirma ministro de la Defensa," *Agencia Guatemalteca de Noticias*, September 30, 2019, www.agn.com.gt.

86. US Department of State, Bureau of International Narcotics and Law Enforcement Affairs, 2022 *International Narcotics Control Strategy Report Vol. I* (Washington, DC: US Department of State, March 2022), 130-132; Alex Papadovassilakis and Gavin Voss, "Guatemala Sees Record Coca, But No Cocaine," InSight Crime, February 10, 2023, https://insightcrime.org.

87. US Department of State, 2015 *International Narcotics Control Strategy Report Vol. I*, 176–177.

88. Meyer and Seelke, *Central American Regional Security Initiative*, Report 41731, May 6, 2014, 14.

89. James Bargent, "MS-13 Use of Guns in Guatemala Shows Modus Operandi," InSight Crime, May 8, 2013, www.insightcrime.org. For instance, only thirty-two weapons were used for 238 homicides in El Salvador. See Hugo Alvarado and Sandra Valdez, "Pandilla usó 32 armas de fuego en homicidios," *La Prensa Libre* (San Salvador), May 8, 2013, www.prensalibre.com.

90. Meyer and Seelke, "Central American Regional Security Initiative," Report 41731, May 6, 2014, 14.

91. Meyer and Seelke, "Central American Regional Security Initiative," Report 41731, December 17, 2015, 22.

92. US Agency for International Development, *Central American and Mexican Gang Assessment,* 20; Roberto Valencia, "La Sombra Negra," *El Faro* (San Salvador), April 26, 2014, www.salanegra.elfaro.net; Marguerite Cawley, "El Salvador's Gangs Call on New Government to Revive Truce," InSight Crime, June 6, 2014, www.insightcrime.org.

93. Carlos Martínez, "Gobierno conspiró para crear facción disidente de la Mara Salvatrucha: la 503," *El Faro* (El Salvador), December 30, 2019, https://elfaro.net.

94. Carlos Martínez and José Luis Sanz, "Gobierno dismantela la treuga y los homicido alcanzan 30 en un día," *El Faro* (El Salvador), May 24, 2014, www.salanegra.elfaro.net.

95. María Cidón Kiernan, "La Fiscalía se equivocó de pruebas y testigos en el juicio por la Tregua," *Factum* (SA de CV), August 30, 2017, www.revistafactum.com. The director was Nelson Rauda Portillo.

96. "Imponen pena de 35 años en prisón al Burro Herra," *El Diario de Hoy* (El Salvador), September 21, 2015, https://historico.elsalvador.com. In 2015, El Burro was sentenced to thirty-five years in prison for auto theft.

97. Héctor Silva Avalos, "Timing in Arrest of Salvadoran Drug Trafficker Raises Questions," InSight Crime, March 20, 2013, www.insightcrime.org.

98. Héctor Silva Ávalos and Súchit Chávez, "El Salvador Vice President Started Company with Chepe Diablo," InSight Crime, April 5, 2016, www.insightcrime.org.

99. Roberto Valencia, "Sánchez Cerén: Nosotros no podemos volver al esquema de negociar con las pandillas," *El Faro* (El Salvador), January 5, 2015, https://elfaro.net.

100. David Gagne, "El Salvador Authorities Blame MS-13 for Surge in Killings of Police," InSight Crime, November 17, 2017, www.insightcrime.org. The unit was called the Fuerza Especializada de Reacción (FERES).

101. *United States v. Edwin Manica Flores*, Indictment 18 U.S.C. § 1962(d)—Conspiracy to Conduct Enterprise Affairs Through a Pattern of Racketeering Activity, United States District Court, District of Massachusetts, September 20, 2017, https://ia800808.us.archive.org/8/items/gov.uscourts.mad.192204/gov.uscourts.mad.192204.1.0.pdf. José Martínez Castro ("Chucky") was the US East Coast leader.

102. Carta de Mauricio Ernesto Ramírez Landaverde a Señores Secretaríos de la Honorable Asamblea Legislativa, "Disposiciones Especiales Transitorías y Extraordinarías en los Centros Penitenciarias, Centros Intermedios y Centros Temporales de Reclusíon," March 30, 2016, www.insightcrime.org/images/2016/April-2016/El_Salvador_Prison_Proposals.pdf; Michael Lohmuller, "El Salvador Moves to Clamp Down on Prisons," Gangs, InSight Crime, April 1, 2016, www.insightcrime.org.

103. Parker Asmann, "El Salvador Citizen Security Plan Struggling to Reduce Insecurity," InSight Crime, July 16, 2018, www.insightcrime.org.

104. Tristan Clavel, "Murderous Day: A Reality Check for El Salvador Government," InSight Crime, March 17, 2017, www.insightcrime.org; Héctor Silva Ávalos, "El Salvador Violence Rising Despite 'Extraordinary' Anti-Gang Measures," InSight Crime, October 3, 2017, www.insightcrime.org.

105. Eddie Galdamez, "El Salvador Homicide Rate (2010-2023): The Daily Murder Rate for 2023 is 0.4," *El Salvador INFO*, May 14, 2023, https://elsalvadorinfo.net/homicide-rate-in-el-salvador/.

106. Anna-Catherine Brigida and Mary Beth Sheridan, "El Salvador's Leader Wins Control of Legislature in Midterm Vote; Critics Fear Rising Authoritarianism," *Washington Post*, March 1, 2020, www.washingtonpost.com; El Salvador Investigative Unit, "El Salvador Shifts Mano Dura Security Policies into Overdrive," InSight Crime, April 12, 2022, https://insightcrime.org.

107. "Salvadoran Congress Extends State of Exception Plan For 11th Time," *teleSUR*, February 15, 2023, https://www.telesurenglish.net/news/Salvadoran-Congress-Extends-State-Of-Exception-For-11th-Time-20230215-0010.html.

108. Galdamez, "El Salvador Homicide," https://elsalvadorinfo.net/homicide-rate-in-el-salvador/.

109. Eddie Galdamez, "El Salvador State of Exception, A Security Measure Implemented to Fight Gangs," *El Salvador INFO*, March 29, 2023, https://elsalvadorinfo.net/el-salvador-state-of-exception/.

110. Parker Asmann, "Political Connections in El Salvador Help MS-13 Leaders Escape Abroad," InSight Crime, July 19, 2022, https://insightcrime.org; Office of Foreign Assets Control, "Treasury Targets Corruption Networks Linked to Transnational Organized Crime" (Washington, DC: US Department of the Treasury, December 8, 2021), https://home.treasury.gov/news/press-releases/jy0519. Marroquín was the director for the reconstruction of social fabric.

111. Juan Martínez D'Aubuisson and Efren Lemus, "El Salvador's Attorney General Worked for Top MS-13 Ally," InSight Crime, October 31, 2022, https://insightcrime.org.

112. "El Salvador Bitcoin Move Opens Banks to Money Laundering, Terrorism Financing Risks – Fitch," *Reuters*, June 25, 2021.

113. Nick Henderson, "El Salvador's Crypto-Bro President Is Flirting With AML Disaster," *Corporate Compliance Insights,* January 25, 2022, https://www.corporatecomplianceinsights.com.

114. American Embassy Tegucigalpa to Secretary of State Washington, DC, "Subject: The Hernández Administration at One Year," Tegucigalpa 13526 291914Z, January 29, 2015, 3.

115. Immigration and Refugee Board of Canada, Research Directorate, *Honduras: Police Corruption, Police Participation in Criminal Activities and Measures Taken by the Government,* HND103832.FE, Government of Canada, November 3, 2011, www.justice.gov/sites/default/files/eoir/legacy/2014/02/04/HND103832.FE.pdf.

116. Ricardo Swire, "Honduras: The Rogue Cop," *Tuck Magazine*, September 18, 2018, http://tuckmagazine.com.

117. "Honduran Armed Forces in the Fight Against Crime," *Diálogo*, July 26, 2021, https://dialogo-americas.com; Evan Ellis, "Honduras—Innovation in the Fight Against Gangs and Narcotrafficking," *Global Americans*, September 24, 2015, https://theglobalamericans.org.

118. La Dirección Policial de Investigaciones, "Acerca de la Dirección Policial de Investigaciones" (El Ocotal: Academia de Policía, Policía Nacional, n.d.), www.policianacional.gob.hn/dpiipd. Marilyn Méndez Montenegro, "Policía inicia nueva etapa en la investigación criminal con la DPI," *La Prensa* (Honduras), August 30, 2015, www.laprensa.hn.

119. Office of Foreign Assets Control, "Carlos Arnaldo Lobo: Honduran Maritime Kingpin," US Department of the Treasury, April 2014, https://home.treasury.gov/system/files/126/20140409_Lobo.pdf.

120. US Department of State, Bureau of International Narcotics and Law Enforcement Affairs, 2018 *International Narcotics Control Strategy Report Vol. I* (Washington, DC: US Department of State, March 2018), 184–185. Lobo received a sentence of twenty years in December 2015.

121. Leonardo Goi, "Coca Plantation 'Experiment' in Honduras Raises Eyebrows," InSight Crime, May 26, 2017, www.insightcrime.org.

122. Valentina Posada, "Cocaine Haul Shows Sophisticated Trafficking Route Through Honduras's La Mosquitia," InSight Crime, April 15, 2019.

123. US Department of State, 2022 *International Narcotics Control Strategy Report Vol. I*, 139; Gavin Voss, Coca May Have Permanently Taken Root in Central America, InSight Crime, March 15, 2023, https://insightcrime.org/news/coca-permanently-taken-root-central-america/.

124. "Honduras envía cientos de policías militares a fronteras para combatir pandilleros," *El Díario* (El Salvador), November 27, 2022, https://diarioelsalvador.com/honduras-envia-cientos-de-policias-militares-a-fronteras-para-combatir-pandilleros/300379.

125. Claudia Torrens, "Narco Testifies He Gave $100,000 to Honduran Candidates in 2009," Associated Press, October 4, 2019, https://apnews.com; Parker Asmann, "Alleged El Chapo Bribe to Honduras President Sets Stage in U.S. Drug Trial," InSight Crime, October 3, 2019, www.insightcrime.org.

126. Gustavo Palencia, "OAS May Request New Honduras Election to Correct Irregularities," Reuters, December 6, 2017, www.reuters.com. Early tallies gave the presidency to Salvador Alejandro César Nasralla Salum, the Alianza de Oposición Contra la Dictadura candidate.

127. US Attorney's Office Southern District of New York, "Juan Orlando Hernandez, Former President of Honduras, Extradited to the United States on Drug-Trafficking and Firearms Charges" (Washington, DC: US Department of Justice, April 21, 2022), www.justice.gov/usao-sdny/pr/juan-orlando-hernandez-former-president -honduras-extradited-united-states-drug.

128. US Congress, House of Representatives, *Central America and the Mérida Initiative*, 17–21.

129. US Department of State, Bureau for International Narcotics and Law Enforcement Affairs, 1999 *International Narcotics Control Strategy Report* (Washington, DC: US Department of State, March 2000), 179.

130. Fred Burton and Scott Stewart, "Nicaragua: The Inherent Dangers of Being a Militant Mecca" (Austin, TX: Stratfor Global Intelligence, June 25, 2008), www .stratfor.com.

131. "Pick Your Poison: Drug Gangs Now Dominate Where Guerrillas Once Reigned," *Economist*, April 28, 2012, www.economist.com.

132. US Congress, Senate, Caucus on International Narcotics Control, A*dapting US Counternarcotics Efforts in Colombia*, 115 Cong., 1st sess., September 12, 2017, 7–11, Testimony of Douglas Farah.

133. "Nicaraguan Security Expert Says Government Manages Organized Crime," BBC News, November 5, 2014.

134. American Embassy Nicaragua to Central Intelligence Agency Washington, DC, "Subject: Nicaragua's Most Wanted, Part II: The Crimes of the Sandinistas (FSLN)," Managua 001003 051717Z, May 5, 2006, WikiLeaks, https://wikileaks .org/plusd/cables /06MANAGUA1003_a.html. The cable added, "These schemes are orchestrated by Lenin Cerna, the former director of state security," and judges "Rafael Solis and Roger Camillo Arguello."

135. "The Unsuspected Dimensions of Drug Trafficking in Nicaragua," InSight Crime, April 15, 2013, www.insightcrime.org.

136. Parker Asmann, "Nicaragua Government's Alleged Drug Trade Ties Deepen with Arrest," InSight Crime, October 18, 2019, www.insightcrime.org. The FSLN representative was named Francisco Sarria García.

137. Meyer and Seelke, "Central American Regional Security Initiative," Report 41731, May 6, 2014, 17.

138. US Department of State, *2015 International Narcotics Control Strategy Report Vol. I*, 246–248.

139. US Department of State, *2018 International Narcotics Control Strategy Report Vol. I*, 228.

140. "Nicaragua Not Spared as Cocaine Flows Through Central America," InSight Crime, October 29, 2020, https://insightcrime.org.

141. Marguerite Cawley, "Costa Rica Losing Its Fight Against Drug Trafficking," InSight Crime, March 14, 2013, www.insightcrime.org.

142. Tristan Clavel, "Costa Rica, Nicaragua Join Efforts to Combat Organized Crime," InSight Crime, March 1, 2017, www.insightcrime.org.

300   Narcostates

143. US Department of State, 2016 *International Narcotics Control Strategy Report Vol. I*, 138–140.

144. Álvaro Sánchez, "Costa Rica Takes Down More Suspects in Cocaine Trafficking Network Rub by Italian Mafia," Tico Times, October 14, 2015, https://ticotimes.net.

145. US Department of State, Bureau of International Narcotics and Law Enforcement Affairs, 2019 *International Narcotics Control Strategy Report Vol. I* (Washington, DC: US Department of State, March 2019), 142.

146. Katrine Thompson, "Transportista Groups Expand Operations in Costa Rica," InSight Crime, December 3, 2019, www.insightcrime.org.

147. Carol Vaughn, "Costa Rican Drug Kingpin Captured in Panama," Costa Rican Star, September 13, 2019, https://news.co.cr.

148. Yuri Neves, "Arrest Uncovers Costa Rica's Drug Boss' Sinaloa Links," InSight Crime, August 16, 2019, www.insightcrime.org.

149. Carol Vaughn, "Violent Gang Leader 'Queen of the South' Wanted by Interpol Captured in Costa Rica," *Costa Rican Star*, August 21, 2019, https://news.co.cr; Carol Vaughn, "Costa Rican Drug Kingpin Captured," https://news.co.cr.

150. US Department of State, *2016 International Narcotics Control Strategy Report Vol. I*, 138–141; Alejandro Zúñiga, "Costa Rica Registers Decrease in Homicides for the Second Straight Year," *Tico Times*, January 3, 2020, https://ticotimes.net. Costa Rica recorded 405 homicides in 2013, 471 in 2014, 566 in 2015, 577 in 2016, and 603 in 2017. Homicides decreased slightly to 587 in 2018 and 560 in 2019.

151. Claire Dennis, "Costa Rican Local Drug Consumption Fueling Rising Murder Rate," InSight Crime, July 20, 2017, www.insightcrime.org.

152. Alessandro Ford, "Costa Rica's Limón Province Becomes Murder and Drug Trafficking Center," InSight Crime, May 23, 2022, https://insightcrime.org; Chris Dalby, "Costa Rica's Devil—Bloody Drug Feud Catches Authorities off Guard," InSight Crime, November 24, 2021, https://insightcrime.org; Marycruz Brenes Mejía, "Guerra a muerte entre diablo y pechuga," *Diario Extra* (Costa Rica), November 27, 2021, https://www.diarioextra.com. Alejandro Arias Monge was known as "Diablo" and Moreno Borbón was known as "Pechuga."

153. Javier Cordoba, "Drug Trafficking Blamed as Homicides Soar in Costa Rica," *Buffalo News*, April 2, 2023, sec. A, p. 15.

154. Carol Vaughn, "Drug Cartels Spike Murder Rate in Costa Rica," *Costa Rican Star*, September 17, 2019, https://news.co.cr.

155. Daniel Hopsicker, "Narco-Jet in Costa Rica Scandal Tied to Iran-Contra Figure," *Mad Cow Press*, August 12, 2013, www.madcowprod.com; L. Arias, "Costa Rica's Communications Minister Resigns After Presidential Flight Tied to Businessman with Suspected Links to Drug Cartels," *Tico Times*, May 15, 2013, https://ticotimes.net. THX Energy was a subsidiary of Birch Island Capital, which was owned by Toronto nightclub owner Andy Defrancesco, who also owned Montco Energy. Montco Energy was run by David Scott Weekly, an alleged CIA asset who took part in the Contra cocaine ring directed by FDN Comandante Oscar Danilo Blandón.

156. Parker Asmann, "Are Crime Groups Increasingly Corrupting Costa Rican Police?," InSight Crime, June 23, 2017, www.insightcrime.org. José Fabio Pizarro was director of the FP from 2007 to 2008.

157. Sharon Cascante Lizano, "No me soprende que narco penetre la Corte," *Diario Extra* (Costa Rica), December 16, 2020, www.diarioextra.com; Katie Jones, "Why Courtroom Corruption Has Costa Rica Concerned," InSight Crime, January 6, 2021, https://insightcrime.org.

158. Marguerite Cawley, "Four of México's Cartels Operate in Panama," InSight Crime, September 17, 2013, www.insightcrime.org.

159. Anonymous, "Mexican Cartel's Pandemonium in Panama," *Borderland Beat*, September 19, 2013, www.borderlandbeat.com.

160. US Department of State, Bureau of International Narcotics Matters, *2017 International Narcotics Control Strategy Report Vol. I* (Washington, DC: US Department of State, March 2017), 234–235.

161. US Department of State, *2015 International Narcotics Control Strategy Report Vol. I*, 262.

162. "FARC 57th Front in Panama," InSight Crime, November 4, 2016, www.insightcrime.org.

163. "FARC, nuevo peligro para los migrantes en la ruta del Darién," Radio Televisón Martí, September 13, 2019, www.radiotelevisionmarti.com. Radio Televisón Martí is directed by the US Agency for Global Media (USAGM).

164. US Department of State, Bureau of International Narcotics Matters, *2017 International Narcotics Control Strategy Report Vol. II* (Washington, DC: US Department of State, March 2017), 140.

165. Martha M. Hamilton, "Cartel Linked Suspects Arrested After Panama Papers Revelations," International Consortium of Investigative Journalists, April 25, 2016, https://www.icij.org; Martha M. Hamilton, "Panama Papers Figure Added to FBI Most Wanted List," International Consortium of Investigative Journalists, May 1, 2018, https://www.icij.org. As of 2022, Quintero remains in hiding and on the FBI's most wanted list since his release in August 2013.

166. Tim Johnson, "For Cartels, Offshore Companies Are a Good Fix," *McClatchy News*, April 5, 2016, www.mcclatchydc.com; Christopher Woody, "The World's Most Powerful Drug Lord Has Been Linked to the Panama Papers," *Business Insider*, April 7, 2016, www.businessinsider.com.

167. El Presidente de República de Panamá, "Decreto Ejecutivo No. 122," República de Panamá Ministerio de Economía y Finanzas, June 11, 2018.

168. Mimi Yagoub, "Mapped: Where Panama's Gangs Are Strongest, Homicides Are Highest," InSight Crime, October 19, 2016, www.insightcrime.org.

169. US Department of State, *2017 International Narcotics Control Strategy Report Vol. I*, 234–235.

170. "Panama Profile," InSight Crime, April 24, 2018, www.insightcrime.org.

171. Maria Alejandra Navarrete Forero, "Drug Gangs Corrupt Panama's Shipping Industry," InSight Crime, April 9, 2019, www.insightcrime.org.

172. Peter Appleby, Chris Dalby, Sean Dorherty, Scott Mistler Ferguson, and Henry Shuldiner, "InSight Crime's 2022 Homicide Roundup," InSight Crime, February 8, 2023, https://insightcrime.org.

173. United Nations, Policy Analysis and Public Affairs, *UNODC 2019 World Drug Report Book 4: Stimulants* (Vienna: UN Office on Drugs and Crime, June 2019), 19–22.

174. Anastasia Austin, "Panama Unveils Extent of Official Participation in Drug Trafficking," InSight Crime, September 9, 2021, https://insightcrime.org.

175. US Department of State, Bureau of International Narcotics Matters, *2023 International Narcotics Control Strategy Report Vol. I* (Washington, DC: US Department of State, March 2023), 186–187.

176. Raquel Ballestín, "Panama Became Logistics Hub For Drug Trafficking Super Cartel," InSight Crime, December 9, 2022, https://insightcrime.org.

177. US Department of State, *2019 International Narcotics Control Strategy Report Vol. I*, 234–236.

302 Narcostates

178. US Department of State, Division J, Foreign Operations and Related Programs Appropriations Act, 2015, Report No. 114-79, 114th Cong., 1st sess., July 9, 2015, 46–47.

179. Meyer and Seelke, "Central America Regional Security Initiative," Report 41731, December 17, 2015, 15–22; Parker Asmann, "El Salvador Gangs Responsible for 84% of Forced Displacement: Report," InSight Crime, January 30, 2017, www.insightcrime.org. The NGO report was created by the Observatorio de la Mesa de Sociedad Civil contra el Desplazamiento Forzado por Violencia y Crimen Organizado en El Salvador.

180. American Embassy Tegucigalpa to Secretary of State Washington, DC, "Northern Triangle Leaders Engage Private Sector on Alliance Plan," Tegucigalpa 13526 041815Z, March 4, 2015, 1–3.

181. Stephanie Leutert and Sarah Spalding, "How Many Central Americans Are Travelling North?," Lawfare Institute, August 12, 2019, https://www.lawfareblog.com.

182. "100 ISIS Terrorists Caught in Guatemala as Central American Caravan Heads to US," Judicial Watch, October 18, 2018, www.judicialwatch.org; "ISIS Camp a Few Miles from Texas, Mexican Authorities Confirm," Judicial Watch, April 14, 2015, www.judicialwatch.org.

183. US Department of State, Office of the Spokesperson, "U.S.-Mexico Joint Declaration" (Washington, DC: US Department of State, June 7, 2019), 1.

184. American Embassy Mexico to Secretary of State Washington, DC, "A Perilous Road Through Mexico for Migrants," Mexico 13526 312243Z, January 31, 2011, 1–3.

185. Molly O'Toole and Eli Stokols, "Trump Administration Guatemala Sign Pact Barring Migrants from Claiming Asylum in the U.S.," *Los Angeles Times*, July 26, 2019, www.latimes.com; Michelle Hackman and Juan Montes, "U.S. Honduras Sign Asylum-Seekers Pact," *Wall Street Journal*, September 26, 2019, sec. A, p. 6.

186. Ioan Grillo, "'There Is No Way We Can Turn Back': Why Thousands of Refugees Will Keep Coming to America Despite Trump's Crackdown," *Time*, June 21, 2018, https://time.com.

187. Jason Peña, "Mexico Deports Record Number of Central Americans," Center for Immigration Studies, August 16, 2019, https://cis.org.

188. Allison O'Connor, Jeanne Batalova, and Jessica Bolte, "Central American Immigrants in the United States," Migration Policy Institute, August 15, 2019, www.migrationpolicy.org.

189. Montes and Corobá, "Hondurans Restart Efforts to Reach U.S.," sec. A, p. 8.

190. Santiago Pérez and Alicia A. Caldwell, "Record Number of Migrants Dying at US-Mexico Border," *Wall Street Journal*, March 18, 2023.

191. Alicia A. Caldwell, "Migration Wave Fuels Record Arrests at the Border," *Wall Street Journal*, October 24, 2022, sec. A, p. 3.

192. Ryan Dube, "Andes Turmoil Rattles Officials, Spurs Migration," *Wall Street Journal*, April 21, 2023, sec. A, p. 10. From October 2022 to March 2023, there were 233,700 people from Colombia, Ecuador, Venezuela, and Peru who were detained, compared to 172,000 people from El Salvador, Honduras, Guatemala.

193. Ryan Dube and Shen Lu, "US-Bound Migrants Surge at Darién Gap," *Wall Street Journal*, March 17, 2023.

194. Miriam Jordan, "Smuggling Migrants at the Border Is Now a Billion-Dollar Business Controlled by the Cartels," *Buffalo News*, July 26, 2022, sec. A, p.4.

195. Pérez, "Record Number."

12

Closing the Corridor?

The destabilizing effects of Central America's civil wars, combined with the rise of Mexico's drug trafficking organizations (DTOs) and their takeover of the drug trade from the Colombians, created an uncontrollable narcocorridor running through Central America and Mexico into the United States. Following the chaos caused by civil war, peace, combined with the exhaustion of regional security forces, limited government resources, and porous borders, turned the region into a storage and transshipment point for land, sea, and air operations moving narcotics across the US-Mexico border. Central America's geographic location in relation to the Andes and Mexico, as well as rampant corruption, exposed the region to unprecedented levels of narcotrafficking. Containing, not stopping, narcotrafficking was all that Mexico and Central America could expect to achieve.

The Mexican DTOs' use of violence, intimidation, and corruption became an existential threat to the Mexican state. Mexico found itself torn between its international legal obligation to combat narcotrafficking and the dangers posed by cartel power. Mexico's willingness to collaborate with the United States on counternarcotics initiatives led to the militarization of its drug war, which carried its own set of problems. The Mexican military's participation in domestic law enforcement efforts resulted in clashes with traffickers and corrupt cops alike, while also exposing it to internal corruption. Militarization unintentionally increased criminal violence as well. It resulted in a three-way war being waged in Mexico: a war among cartels for control over the plazas of distribution, internecine wars within the cartels, and a cartel war against the Mexican state. As the drug war became more militarized, the ruthless nature of the drug war became amplified, leading to human rights violations. Mexico's drug war made the cycle of death, which has symbolized much of the country's history, all too visible.

304   *Narcostates*

The United States did not take decisive action against the growing danger until the crisis for which it was partially culpable began to escalate out of control. As drugs, corruption, and violence engulfed Mexico and Central America, the United States provided counternarcotics assistance through Mexico's Mérida Initiative and the Central American Regional Security Initiative, but these were open-ended programs that produced uncertain outcomes at best. Regrettably, Central America received the least amount of aid in comparison to Mexico or Colombia. As a result, US policy inadvertently drove traffickers deeper into the region while igniting a "root fire" in its effort to stop the flow of narcotics. As governments in one country responded aggressively to curb DTOs, traffickers shifted operations to another, where enforcement efforts were not as rigorous.

As cartel operations expanded, a lethal combination of Mexican DTOs and Central American street gangs emerged as a direct consequence of Central America's civil wars morphing into Mexico's drug war. The ongoing conflict is rooted in the political and economic crises that took place during the second half of the twentieth century. With elevated crime rates, a constant flow of refugees, and a ubiquitous flow of narcotics moving northward, the Central American gang–Mexican DTO nexus has become the region's most pressing concern. The question is whether Mexico and Central America have the willpower to resist their subversive influence or whether they will succumb to it.

The Colombianization of Mexico and Central America

The drug war has Colombianized Mexico. In 2007, George W. Grayson, a prolific writer on Mexico's drug war, stated that the conditions in Mexico and Colombia were too distinct to draw comparisons.[1] While there are many differences between Mexico and Colombia, they do share experiences which illustrate Mexico's Colombianization. The Medellín and Cali cartels waged war against their government over the issue of extradition, but lost because they failed to usurp Colombia's military and police, which had received large amounts of financing and training from the United States. While it has willingly accepted US aid, Mexico, unlike Colombia, has historically sought to preserve its sovereignty by restricting US interference in its domestic and military affairs. Although the Mexican cartels employed equal amounts of force as the Colombians, they did not use high-profile terrorist tactics that attracted international attention like the Medellín and Cali cartels did with the attack on the Palace of Justice on November 6, 1985, the bombing of Avianca Flight 203 on November 27, 1989, and the destruction of Colombia's Departamento Administrativo de Seguridad building on December 6, 1989. This is not to say that Mexican cartels did not also employ terrorist tactics, but unlike their Colombian counterparts, they did not declare all-out war on the government over extradition. In addition, unlike the political killings in Colombia, which were clearly linked to the cartels, the PRI cast a shadow over Mexico's political homicides, shifting the blame away from Mexico's cartels. Like the Colombians, the Mexican cartels were fighting not only the government but also rival cartels. The major difference between the Colombians and the Mexicans was that in Mexico, the ever-changing nature of the drug war and questions of territorial control led to savage, internecine battles within each cartel. Tragically, citizens of both nations were caught in the crossfire.

As in Colombia, a significant factor in Mexico's cartel war was the ability of its DTOs to corrupt the Mexican political system.[2] However, the Mexicans understood the importance of subverting the government from within to a much larger degree than the Medellín and Cali cartels ever envisioned. In Colombia, the government's alliance with the cartels and their paramilitaries was mainly political and directed against Colombia's FARC guerrillas, who were also involved in narcotrafficking. In Mexico, the cartels' ties to the government were purely financial and directed toward corrupting officials, controlling it from within so that the cartels could conduct business and thwart their rivals. Furthermore, like Colombia, Mexico's economic malaise facilitated the power of its narcotraffickers, who were creating a multibillion-dollar alternative economy. As the Mexican state expanded its role in the war on drugs, traffickers penetrated all levels of government, the military, and the police to protect and advance their interests. The scandals within the AFI, CISEN, and army exposed to the world just how vulnerable Mexican institutions were. Mexican DTOs continue to corrupt elements within Mexico's political and military establishments with great success. The arrests of Genaro García Luna in 2019 and Iván Reyes Arzate in 2022 highlight this point, while also raising concerns about whether the United States can ever fully trust Mexico. Because Colombia was successful in rooting out much of the corruption in its armed forces, it may be possible to say that Mexico has become more Colombianized than Colombia ever was.

Using its military, Mexico moved aggressively to root out narcotrafficking. And like Colombia, Mexico's confrontation with the narcotraffickers reached a crescendo as the conflict became militarized. Since that point, the Mexican government's ability to enforce its monopoly over law and order has proved elusive. Along the US-Mexico border, drug trafficking, accompanied by the refugee crisis, allowed lawlessness to persist. Several prominent cities, including popular tourist destinations such as Acapulco, Cancún, and Puerto Vallarta, became Colombianized drug war zones. Violence such as the cold-blooded murders of the Le Barón and Langford families in November 2019, the CJNG's bold attempt to assassinate Mexico

306 *Narcostates*

City's police chief in 2020, the senseless murder of two Jesuit priests inside a Chihuahua church by a Sinaloa cartel boss in 2022, the all-out gun battle in Culiacán after the arrest of El Chapo's son Ovidio in January 2023, and the March 2023 kidnapping and murder of two medical tourists in Matamoros raise serious questions about whether Mexico will ever be able to de-escalate its drug war.

Trapped by geography, Central America was also vulnerable to Colombianization. Mexican and Colombian DTOs exploited Central America's institutional weaknesses, infiltrating the highest levels of government in each country and taking advantage of poorly trained and equipped law enforcement institutions. Stretching their already thin budgets, governments were forced to divert valuable resources to combat the DTOs. The presence of DTOs combined with the arrival of US gang culture heightened Central America's preexisting levels of economic instability, corruption, and violence. Modeled off of Mexico's and Colombia's efforts to rein in their DTOs, Central American counternarcotics operations began to resemble the internal security policies that they employed during the civil war era. The legacy of civil war combined with the drug war and limited economic opportunities directly resulted in a refugee crisis, the end of which is nowhere in sight. Institutional weaknesses, corruption, violence, and aggressive counterdrug and anti-mara operations have only served to Colombianize Central America.

US Policy Considerations

Is it possible to close the narcocorridor? As long as narcotics remain illegal and in high demand, the answer is no. To imagine that it can be done without fundamental changes in policy and societal behavior is a Sisyphean task. The United States needs to ask itself if it wants to legalize highly addictive narcotics like cocaine, heroin, and methamphetamine. The war against drugs makes them more valuable, and US proscriptive policies have not worked. With that said, Say's law presents the caveat that legalization might increase demand as supplies become readily available and legal. If legalization were to occur, how should the United States handle individuals who become addicted to these drugs? Another question to consider is whether legalized narcotics would become cartelized and bureaucratized as a consequence of regulations and licenses issued to well-connected corporations. Moreover, legalization will bring an array of new legislation governing employment, safety, and health.

Regardless of these questions, ending the idea of a "war" on drugs is essential. Decriminalization and/or legalization would end the US government's mass incarceration of nonviolent drug offenders. It could also normalize relations with Mexico and Central America, allowing them to focus on job creation and institution building. Even though black markets will continue to exist in order to circumvent taxes and regulations, legalization or decriminalization has the potential to reduce the price of narcotics and the criminality associated with them, thereby diminishing the power of the DTOs. Furthermore, stringent money laundering regulations, tighter precursor chemical controls, effective border-control countermeasures, police professionalization, treatment programs, and political lobbying regulations would hit cartel syndicates where it hurts the most, limiting their ability to project power both nationally and internationally. A coordinated international strategy that focuses on geographical lines of distribution would severely disrupt the cartels' supply chains and finances. The cartels may continue to compete for contraband routes, but as their influence over the government, police, and society fades, so will the low-intensity conflict that has come to symbolize the drug war.

The militarization of the war on drugs has raised many questions. The pouring of foreign aid into counternarcotics efforts and the security apparatuses of Mexico and Central America has not worked. The current proscriptive policies accompanied by the kingpin strategy have only served to foment a low-intensity conflict that has wreaked havoc on civil society in the region. Leaders who reject the militarization of the war on drugs want to develop an alternative response to the problem, just as Central Americans did in the 1990s when they ended their armed conflicts. Both Mexico's and Central America's governments recognize that reform needs to start from within. Beyond security reforms, however, Mexico and Central America need political and economic reforms that serve the general public, not just corrupt officials or the oligarchies alone. It is clear that the cartels, gangs, and the refugee crisis are a regional problem for both Mexico and Central America, stemming from the desperation and hopelessness of its poor citizens, and the failure of institution building. Restoring political stability and implementing responsible fiscal policies would pave the way for investment and employment, which are the only real means to upend the crisis presented by narcotrafficking.

Notes

1. George W. Grayson, "Mexico and the Drug Cartels," Foreign Policy Research Institute, August 2017, https://web.archive.org/web/20120309155416/http://www.fpri.org/enotes/200708.grayson.mexicodrugcartels.html.

2. Héctor Aguilar Camín, "La captura criminal del Estado," *Nexos* (Mexico), January 1, 2015, www.nexos.com.mx/?p=23798.

Appendix
Narcotraffickers by Name and by Cartel Affiliation

Beltrán Leyva Cartel

Beltrán Leyva, Alfredo ("El Mochomo")
Beltrán Leyva, Carlos
Beltrán Leyva, Hector ("El H")
Beltrán Leyva, Marcos Arturo ("El Barbas" or "Jefe de Jefes")
Beltrán Leyva, Mario Alberto
Montemayor González, Carlos ("El Charro")
Valdez Villarreal, Edgar ("La Barbie")

Cali Cartel

Castrillón Henao, José
Herrera Buitrago, Francisco Hélmer ("Pacho")
Herrera Zuelta, Benjamin ("La Papa Negro de la Cocaína")
Rodríguez Orejuela, Gilberto ("El Ajedrecista")
Rodríguez Orejuela, Miguel ("El Señor")
Santacruz Londoño, José ("Chepe")

Cártel de Jalisco Nueva Generación

Mendoza Gaytán, Gonzalo ("El Sapo")
Orozco Rodríguez, Sergio Armando ("Chocho")
Oseguera Cervantes, Rubén ("El Mencho")

La Familia Cartel

Moreno González, Nazario ("El Chayo" or "El Más Loco"). Founder of the cartel.

310   *Appendix*

Gómez Martínez, Servando ("La Tuta"). Founded Knights Templar offshoot.
Méndez Vargas, José de Jesús ("El Chango")
Rosales Mendoza, Carlos Alberto ("El Carlitos")
Rueda Medina, Arnolodo ("La Minsa")

Guadalajara Cartel

Félix Gallardo, Miguel ("El Padrino"). Head of the cartel.
Caro Quintero, Rafael ("El Narco de Narcos")
Esparragoza Moreno, Juan José ("El Azul"). Helped unify the Sinaloa Federation in 1993.
Fonseca Carrillo, Ernesto ("Don Neto")
Salcido Uzeta, Manuel ("El Cochi Loco")

Gulf Cartel

Nepomuceno Guerra, Juan. Founder of the cartel.
García Ábrego, Juan ("El Mayor"). Head of the cartel.
Cárdenas Guillén, Antonio Ezequiel ("Tony Tormenta"). Directed Gulf cartel with El Coss from 2003 to 2010.
Costilla Sánchez, Jorge Eduardo ("El Coss"). Directed Gulf cartel with "Tony Tormenta."
Ramírez Treviño, Mario Amando ("X-20"). Head of the cartel from 2011 to 2013.
Cárdenas Guillén, Osiel ("El Loco"; "El Mata Amigos"). Successor to García Ábrego.
Cárdenas Guillén, Homero ("El Majadero")
Cárdenas Guillén, Mario Alberto ("M-1"; "El Gordo")
Delgado Santiago, Héctor ("El Metro 4")
Espinosa Campos, Casmiro ("El Cacho")
Flores Borrego, Samuel ("El Metro 3")
García Ábrego, Humberto ("El Chichí")
García Mena, Gilberto ("El June")
Gómez Herrera, Salvador ("El Chava")
Gómez, Sergio ("El Checko")
López Falcón, Baudelio ("El Yeyo")
Lopez Olivares, Oscar ("El Profe")
Malherbe de León, Oscar ("El Licenciado")
Medrano Rodríguez, Adán Javier ("El Licenciado")
Pérez de la Rosa, José ("El Amable")
Sauceda Gamboa, Héctor Manuel ("El Karis")

Juárez Cartel

Aguilar Guajardo, Rafael ("El Profesor")

Carrillo Fuentes, Alberto ("Betty la Fea")
Carrillo Fuentes, Amado ("El Señor de los Cielos")
Carrillo Fuentes, Rodolfo ("El Niño de Oro")
Carrillo Fuentes, Vicente ("El Viceroy"; "El General")
Carvajal Paternina, Frank
Muñoz Talavera, Eduardo
Muñoz Talavera, Rafael
Ontiveros Lucero, Gilberto ("El Grenas")
Pacheco Abraham, Luis Amado ("Barbaschocas")
Quintero Payán, Juan José ("Don Juanjo")
Quintero Meraz, Jesús Albino ("El Beto")
Colonel Villareal, Ignacio ("El Rey de Cristal"). Later joined Sinaloa.

Knights Templar Cartel

Loya Plancarte, Dionisio ("El Tío")
Gómez Martínez, Servando ("La Tuta")
Plancarte Solís, Enrique ("La Chiva")

Medellín Cartel

Bermudez Suaza, Pedro Antonio ("El Arquitecto")
Bernal Madrigal, Alejandro ("El Juvenal")
Catania Ponsiglione, Giuseppe
Escobar Gaviria, Pablo Emilio ("El Patrón")
Gaviria Rivero, Gustavo de Jesús
Matta-Ballesteros, Juan. Middleman for Medellín cartel and Guadalajara
   cartel.
Ochoa Vásquez, Fabio
Ochoa Vásquez, Jorge Luis
Rodríguez Gacha, Gonzalo ("El Mejicano")

Milenio Cartel

Valencia Cornelio, Armando ("El Maradona")
Valencia Valencia, Luis ("El Juanito")
Nava Valencia, Óscar ("El Lobo")

Norte de Valle del Cauca Cartel

Gomez Bustamante, Luis Hernando ("Rasguno")
Henao Montoya, Archangel Jesús ("El Mocho")
Henao Montoya, Orlando ("El Hombre del Overol")
López López, Andrés ("Florecita")

312 *Appendix*

Montoya Sánchez, Diego León ("Don Diego")
Rentería Mantilla, Carlos Alberto ("Beto")
Ramírez Abadia, Juan Carlos ("Chupeta")
Varela Fajardo, Wilber Alirio ("Jabon")
Ortiz Escobar, Juan Carlos ("Cuchilla"). Nephew of Pablo Escobar who
   joined the Cali cartel.

Nuevo Cartel de Juárez

Carrillo Fuentes, Alberto ("Betty la Fea")
Carrillo Leyva, César ("Cesarin")
Carrillo Leyva, Juan
Carrillo Leyva, Vicente ("El Ingeniero")

Pre–Guadalajara Cartel

Acosta Villarreal, Pablo ("El Zorro de Ojinaga")
Avilés Pérez, Pedro ("El Leon del Norte")
Sicilia Falcón, Alberto

Sinaloa Cartel/Federation

Guzmán Loera, Arturo ("El Pollo")
Guzmán Loera, Aureliano ("El Guano")
Guzmán Loera, Joaquín Archivaldo ("El Chapo")
Guzmán Salazar, Iván Archivaldo ("El Chapito")
Guzmán Salazar, Jesús Alfredo
Guzmán Salazar, Ovidio ("El Raton")
López, Armando ("El Rayo")
López Nuñez, Dámaso ("El Licenciado")
Palma Salazar, Héctor Luis ("El Güero")
Colonel Villareal, Ignacio ("El Rey de Cristal"; "Nacho")
Zambada García, Ismael ("El Mayo")
Zambada Niebla, Jesús Vicente ("El Vicentillo")
Zambada Sicairos, Ismael ("El Mayito Flaco")

Sonora Cartel

Caro Quintero, Miguel Ángel. Absorbed by Sinaloa cartel through El Azul
   between 1993 and 2003.

Tijuana Cartel, Arellano Félix Organization

Arellano Félix, Benjamín ("Min")

Arellano Félix, Eduardo ("El Doctor")
Arellano Félix, Francisco Javier ("El Tigrillo")
Arellano Félix, Francisco Rafael ("Pancho"; "El Pelón")
Arellano Félix, Ramón ("Món")
Briseño López, Jorge ("El Cholo")
Caro Payán, Javier ("El Doctor")
García Simental, Teodoro ("El Teo")
Higuera Guerrero, Gilberto ("El Gilillo")
Higuera Guerrero, Ismael ("El Mayel")
Labra Avilés, Jesús ("El Chuy"; "Don Chuy")
Sánchez Arellano, Luis Fernando ("El Ingeniero")
Rodríguez Bañuelos, Humberto ("La Rana")

Los Zetas Cartel

Almanza Morales, Ricardo ("El Gori I")
Almanza Morales, Eduardo ("El Gori II")
Almanza Morales, Raymundo ("El Gori III")
Almanza Morales, Octavio ("El Gori IV")
González Durán, Jaíme ("El Hummer")
González Pizaña, Rogelio ("El Kelín")
Guízar Valencia, José María ("Z-43")
Guzmán Decena, Arturo ("Z-1")
Lazcano Lazcano, Heriberto ("Z-3"; "El Lazca")
Peña Mendoza, Victor ("Concord 3")
Martínez Escobedo, Salvador Alfonso ("La Ardilla")
Morales Betancourt, Alejandro Lucio ("Z-2")
Oliva Castillo, Carlos Alberto (La Rana)
Pérez Moreno, Ramiro ("El Rana")
Rejón Aguilar, Jesús Enrique ("Z-7"; "El Mamito")
Treviño Morales, Miguel Ángel ("El 40")
Treviño Morales, Omar ("Z-42")
Velazquez Caballero, Ivan ("El Taliban"; "Z-50")

Acronyms

ACNR	Asociación Cívica Nacional Revolucionaria (Revolutionary National Civic Association, Mexico)
AFI	Agencia Federal de Investigación (Federal Bureau of Investigation, Mexico)
AFILD	American Institute for Free Labor Development, USA
ALBA	Alianza Bolivariana para los Pueblos de Nuestra América (Bolivarian Alliance for the Peoples of Our America)
ALPROMISU	Alanzia por el Progreso del Miskitos and Sumos (Alliance for the Progress of Miskitos and Sumos, Nicaragua)
APRE	Alianza por la República (Alliance for the Republic, Nicaragua)
ARDE	Alianza Revolucionaria Democrática (Democratic Revolutionary Alliance, Nicaragua)
ARENA	Alianza Republicana Nacionalista (Nationalist Republican Alliance, El Salvador)
ATF	Bureau of Alcohol, Tobacco, and Firearms, USA
ATIC	Agencia Técnica de Investigación Criminal (Criminal Investigative Technical Agency, Honduras)
AUC	Autodefensas Unidas de Colombia (United Self-Defense Forces of Colombia)
BACRIM	Bandas Emergentes y Bandas Criminales (Emerging Gangs and Criminal Gangs, Colombia)
BCCI	Bank of Commerce and Credit International
BNDD	Bureau of Narcotics and Dangerous Drugs, USA
CAFTA	Central American Free Trade Agreement
CANADOR	Operación Combate Contra el Narcotráfico (Operation Fight Against Narcotrafficking, Mexico)

315

316   *Acronyms*

CARSI	Central American Regional Security Initiative
CAS	Corporate Air Services, USA
CCP	Comisión Centroamericana Permanente
CDN	Coordinadora Democrática Nicaragüense (Nicaraguan Democratic Coordination)
CENDARO	Centro Nacional de Prevención Contra Drogas (National Center for Drug Prevention, Costa Rica)
CENTAC	DEA Central Tactical Program, USA
CIA	Central Intelligence Agency, USA
CICA	Centro Inteligencia Conjunto Antidrogas (Joint Anti-Drugs Intelligence Center)
CICAD	Comisión Interamericana para el Control del Abuso de Drogas (Inter American Drug Abuse Control Commission)
CICIG	Comisión Internacional Contra la Impunidad en Guatemala (International Commission Against Impunity in Guatemala)
CISEN	Centro de Investigación y Seguridad Nacional (Center for Investigation and National Security, Mexico)
CJNG	Cártel de Jalisco Nuevo Generación
CONADRO	Consejo Nacional de Drogas (National Drug Council, Costa Rica)
COSEP	Consejo Superior de la Empresa Privada (Superior Council of Private Initiative, Nicaragua)
CST	Central Sandinista de Trabajadores (Sandinista Labor Federation, Nicaragua)
DAN	Dirección Antinarcóticos (Anti-Narcotics Directorate, Nicaragua)
DAN	División Antinarcóticos (Anti-Narcotics Division, El Salvador)
DCG	Democracia Cristiana Guatemalteca (Christian Democrat Party, Guatemala)
DEA	Drug Enforcement Administration, USA
DFS	Dirección Federal de Seguridad (Federal Security Directorate, Mexico)
DGI	Dirección General de Inteligencia (General Intelligence Directorate, Cuba)
DGIM	Dirección General de Inteligencia Militar (General Military Intelligence Directorate, Cuba)
DGISN	Dirección General de Investigación y Seguridad Nacional (Directorate General of Investigation and National Security, Mexico)
DGPN	Dirección General de la Policía Nacional (General Directorate of the National Police, Nicaragua)

DGSE	Dirección General de Seguridad del Estado (Directorate General for State Security, Nicaragua)
DIA	Defense Intelligence Agency, USA
DLCN	La Dirección de Lucha Contra el Narcotráfico (Directorate in the Fight Against Drug Trafficking, Honduras)
DNI	Directorio Nacional de Investigación (National Board of Investigations, Honduras)
DNIC	Dirección National de Investigación Criminal (National Department of Criminal Investigation, Honduras)
DNPP	Dirección Nacional de la Policía Preventiva (National Directorate of Preventive Police, Honduras)
DNU-MRH	Directorio Nacional Unificado Movimiento de Unidad Revolucionario (United Revolutionary Board of the National Unified Movement, Honduras)
DOAN	Departamento de Operaciones Antinarcóticas (Department of Anti-Narcotics Operations, Guatemala)
DOJ	Department of Justice, USA
DPI	Dirección Policial de Investigación (Directorate of Police Investigations, Honduras)
DRU	Dirección Revolucionaria Unificada (Unified Revolutionary Directorate, El Salvador)
DTO	drug trafficking organization
EGP	Ejército Guerrillero de los Pobres (Guerrilla Army of the Poor, Guatemala)
ELN	Ejército de Liberación Nacional (National Liberation Army, Colombia)
ENABAS	Empresa Nicaragüensede Alimentos Básicos (Nicaraguan Basic Food Company)
EPIC	El Paso Intelligence Center, USA
EPS	Ejército Popular Sandinista (Sandinista Popular Army, Nicaragua)
ESAF	Armed Forces of El Salvador
EZLN	Ejército Zapatista de Liberación Nacional (Zapatista National Liberation Army, Mexico)
FAA	Federal Aviation Administration, USA
FAH	Fuerza Aérea Hondureña (Honduran Air Force)
FAO	Frente Amplio Opositor (Broad Opposition Front, Nicaragua)
FAR	Fuerzas Armadas Rebeldes (Rebel Armed Forces, Guatemala)
FARC	Fuerzas Armadas Revolucionarias de Colombia (Revolutionary Armed Forces of Colombia)
FBI	Federal Bureau of Investigation, USA
FDN	Fuerza Democrática Nicaragüense (Nicaraguan Democratic Force)

318   *Acronyms*

FDR	Frente Democrático Revolucionario (Revolutionary Democratic Front, El Salvador)
FEADS	Fiscalía Especializada en Atención de Delitos contra la Salud (Specialized Prosecutor's Office in Crime Against Health, Mexico)
FER	Frente de Estudiantes Revolucionarios (Revolutionary Student Front, Mexico)
FMLN	Frente Farabundo Martí para la Liberación Nacional (Farabundo Marti National Liberation Front, El Salvador)
FROC	Frente Revolucionario de Obreros y Campesinos (Revolutionary Front of Workers and Peasants, Nicaragua)
FSLN	Frente Sandinista de Liberación Nacional (Sandinista National Liberation Front, Nicaragua)
FUSEP	Fuerza de Seguridad Pública (Public Security Force, Honduras)
FUSINA	Fuerza Nacional Interinstitucional de Seguridad (National Inter-Institutional Security Force, Honduras)
GAFES	Grupos Aeromómoviles de Fuerzas Especiales (Special Forces Aeromobile Groups, Mexico)
GAO	Government Accountability Office, USA
GCAN	Grupo Contacto de Alto Nivel para el Control de Drogas (High Level Contact Group for Drug Control)
GOPES	Grupo de Operaciones Especiales (Special Operations Group, Mexico)
ICA	Instituto Costarricense Antidrogas (Costa Rican Anti-Drug Institute)
ICE	Immigration and Customs Enforcement, USA
IMF	International Monetary Fund
INCD	Instituto Nacional para el Combate a las Drogas (National Institute for the Combat of Drugs, Mexico)
INL	Bureau of International Narcotics and Law Enforcement Affairs (US Department of State)
INM	International Narcotics Matters, USA (1979–1995)
INS	Immigration and Naturalization Service, USA
IRS	Internal Revenue Service, USA
JCS	Joint Chiefs of Staff, USA
JICC	Joint Information and Coordination Center, Honduras
JRG	Junta Revolucionaria de Gobierno (Revolutionary Government Junta, El Salvador)
M-19	Movimiento Abril 19 (April 19 Movement, Colombia)
MAAG	Military Assistance Advisory Group, USA
MAR	Movimiento de Acción Revolucionaria (Revolutionary Action Movement, Mexico)

Acronyms 319

MAS	Muerte a Secuestradores (Death to Kidnappers, Colombia)
MDN	Movimiento Democrático Nicaragüense (Nicaraguan Democratic Movement)
MH	Marina de Honduras (Honduran Navy)
MINFAR	Ministerio de las Fuerzas Armadas (Armed Forces Ministry, Cuba)
MININT	Ministerio del Interior de la República de Cuba (Ministry of the Interior, Cuba)
MLN	Movimiento de Liberación Nacional (National Liberation Movement, Guatemala)
MLP	Movimiento Popular de Liberación "Cinchoneros" (Popular Liberation Movement, Honduras)
MNR	Movimiento Nacionalista Revolucionario (Revolutionary Nationalist Movement, El Salvador)
MRA	Movimiento Revolucionario Auténtico (Authentic Revolutionary Movement, Costa Rica)
MRFM	Movimiento Revolucionario Francisco Morazán (Francisco Morazán Revolutionary Movement, Honduras)
MRP	Movimiento Revolucionario del Pueblo (People's Revolutionary Movement, Costa Rica)
NAFTA	North American Free Trade Agreement
NHAO	Nicaraguan Humanitarian Assistance Office (US State Department)
NSC	National Security Council, USA
OAS	Organización de los Estados Americanos (Organization of American States)
ODECA	La Carta de la Organización de Estados Centroamericanos (The Charter of the Organization of Central American States)
OEN	Organización de Emergencia Nacional (National Emergency Organization, Costa Rica)
OPBAT	Operation Bahamas, Turks, and Caicos
ORPA	Organización Revolucionario del Pueblo en Armas (People's Revolutionary Organization in Arms, Guatemala)
PAN	Partido Acción Nacional (National Action Party, Mexico)
PASO	Partido Acción Socialista Obrera (Socialist Workers Action Party, Costa Rica)
PCD	Partido Conservador Demócrata (Democratic Conservative Party, Nicaragua)
PCN	Partido de Concertación Nacional (National Coalition Party, El Salvador)
PCS	Partido Comunista de El Salvador (Communist Party of El Salvador)

320 *Acronyms*

PDC	Partido Demócrata Cristiano (Christian Democratic Party, El Salvador)
PDF	Fuerzas de Defensa de Panamá (Panama Defense Forces)
PEMEX	Petroleos Mexicanos (Mexican Petroleum)
PFM	Policía Federal Ministerial (Federal Ministerial Police, Mexico)
PFP	Policía Federal Preventiva (Federal Preventative Police, renamed the Policía Federal [PF] in 2009, Mexico)
PGR	Procuraduría General de la República (Attorney General of the Republic, Mexico)
PH	Policía Hacienda (Treasury Police, El Salvador)
PJFM	Policía Judicial Federal de México (Mexican Federal Judicial Police)
PLC	Partido Liberal Constitucionalista (Liberal Constitutional Party, Nicaragua)
PLH	Partido Liberal de Honduras (Liberal Party of Honduras)
PLN	Partido Liberación Nacional (National Liberation Party, Costa Rica)
PLN	Partido Liberal Nacionalista (Nationalist Liberal Party, Nicaragua)
PMOP	Policía Militar del Orden Público (Military Police for Public Order, Honduras)
PMT	Partido Mexicano de los Trabajadores (Mexican Workers' Party)
PN	Policía Nacional de Honduras (Honduran National Police)
PNC	Policia Nacional Civil (National Civil Police, Guatemala and El Salvador)
PNG	Guardia Nacional de Panamá (Panama National Guard)
PNH	Partido Nacional de Honduras (National Party of Honduras)
PNP	Policía Nacional de Panamá (Panama National Police)
PPA	Partido Panaméñista Auténtico–Arnulfistas (Authentic Panamanian Party)
PPF	Fuerza Pública de la República de Panamá (Panama Public Forces)
PPSC	Partido Popular Social Cristian (Social Christian Popular Party, Nicaragua)
PRD	Partido de la Revolución Democrática (Revolutionary Democratic Party, Mexico)
PRD	Partido Revolucionario Democrático (Revolutionary Democratic Party, Panama)
PRI	Partido Revolucionario Institucional (Institutional Revolutionary Party, Mexico)
PRN	Partido Republicano Nacional (National Republican Party, Costa Rica)

PRTC	Partido Revolucionario de los Trabajadores Centroamericanos (Revolutionary Central American Workers Party, Costa Rica)
PRUD	Partido Revolucionario de Unificación Democrática (Revolutionary Party of Democratic Unification, El Salvador)
PSD	Partido Social Demócrata (Social Democratic Party, Nicaragua)
PTJ	Policía Técnica Judicial (Technical Judicial Police, Panama)
PTRC	Partido Revolucionario de los Trabajadores Centroamericanistas de Honduras (Revolutionary Party of Honduran Central American Workers)
PUN	Partido Unión Nacional (National Union Party, Costa Rica)
PVP	Partido Vanguardia Popular (Popular Vanguard Party, Costa Rica)
SAIA	Servicio de Análisis e Información Antinarcóticos (Anti-Narcotics Analysis and Information Service, Guatemala)
SAN	Servicio Aero Nacional (National Air Service, Panama)
SAT	Southern Air Transport, USA
SEBIN	Servicio Bolivariano de Inteligencia Nacional (Bolivarian National Intelligence Service)
SEDENA	Secretaría de la Defensa Nacional (Secretariat of National Defense, Mexico)
SEGOB	Secretaría de Gobernación (Secretariat of the Interior, Mexico)
SEIDO	Subprocuraduría Especializada en Investigación de Delincuencia Organizada (Special Investigative Attorney in Organized Crime, Mexico)
SICA	Sistema de la Integración Centroamericana (Central American Integration System)
SMN	Servicio Maritimo Nacional (National Maritime Service, Panama)
SOUTHCOM	US Southern Command
SPI	Servicio Protectivo Institucional (Institutional Protective Service, Panama)
SSP	Secretaría de Seguridad Pública (Secretariat of Public Security, Mexico)
TAG	Centro Antipandillas Transnacional (Transnational Anti-Gang Center, El Salvador)
UAF	Unidad de Análisis Financiero (Financial Analysis Unit, Panama)
UDEL	Unión Democrática de Liberación (Democratic Union of Liberation, Nicaragua)

322 Acronyms

UDN	Unión Democrática Nicaragüense (Nicaraguan Democratic Union)
UEA	Unidad Ejecutiva Antinarcóticos (Executive Anti-Narcotics Unit, El Salvador)
UEDO	Unidad Especializada en Delincuencia Organizada (Special Unit in Organized Crime, Mexico)
UIF	Unidad de Investigaciones Financieras (Financial Investigations Unit, Panama)
UNO	Unidad Nicaragüense Opositora (United Nicaraguan Opposition)
UP	Unión Patriótica (Patriotic Union, Colombia)
URNG	Unidad Revolucionaria Nacional Guatemalteca (Guatemalan National Revolutionary Union)
USAID	US Agency for International Development

Bibliography

Abadinsky, Howard. *Organized Crime*. Belmont, CA: Wadsworth Cengage Learning, 2010.

Agreement Between the United States and Costa Rica, San Jose, July 2, 1999. Treaties and Other International Acts Series 13005, Pursuant to Public Law 89-497. 80 Stat. 271; 1 U.S.C. 113.

Aguilar Camín, Héctor. "Narcos Historias Extraordinarias." *Nexos*, May 2007. www.nexos.com.mx/?p=12886.

"Alberto Sicilia Falcón, el narcostar bisexual." *Nuestra Aparente Rendición*, February 10, 2012. http://nuestraaparenterendicion.com.

Alegría, Claribel, and D. J. Flakoll. *Nicaragua: la revolución sandinista*. Mexico City: Ediciones, 1982.

Alexander, Robert J. "Latin American Communism." In *U.S. Policy in Latin America*, edited by Grant S. McClellan. New York: H. W. Wilson Company, 1963.

Amar, Sebastian, Amy Fairchild Haer, Shaunna Bailey, and Abraham Jacob. *Seeking Asylum from Gang-Based Violence in Central America: A Resource Manual*. Washington, DC: Central American Immigrants' Rights Coalition, 2007. www.unhcr.org/uk/585a96a34.pdf.

Andrade Borges, José Alfredo. *La Historia Secreta del Narco: Desde Navolato Vengo*. Mexico City: Editorial Oceano de México, 1999.

Ardón, Sergio Erick. "Communicado: La Situacion in Costa Rica." Centro de Documentación de los Movimientos Armados. August 8, 1971. www.cedema.org/uploads/MRA_1971-08.pdf.

Armstrong, Karen. *The Great Transformation: The Beginning of Our Religious Traditions*. New York: Random House Digital, 2007.

Arnold, Guy. *The International Drugs Trade*. New York: Routledge, 2005.

Arnson, Cynthia. *Crossroads: Congress, the President, and Central America, 1976–1993*. University Park: Pennsylvania State University Press, 1993.

Arnson, Cynthia, and David Holiday. "Fitful Peace: Human Rights and Reconciliation in Nicaragua Under the Chamorro Government." Human Rights Watch, July 1991.

Arnson, Cynthia, and Eric L. Olson, eds. *Organized Crime in Central America: The Northern Triangle*. Woodrow Wilson Institute Reports on the Americas No. 29. Washington, DC: Woodrow Wilson Institute, November 2011.

324 Bibliography

Ashby, Timothy. *The Bear in the Back Yard.* New York: Prentice Hall, 1987.
Astorga, Luis. "Drug Trafficking in Mexico: A First General Assessment." Discussion Paper No. 36. Management of Social Transition Project. United Nations Educational, Scientific, and Cultural Organization. www.unesco.org/most/astorga.htm.
———. *El Siglo de las Drogas.* 2nd ed. Mexico City: Random House, 2016.
Barber, Walter F., and C. Neale Ronning. *Internal Security and Military Power: Counterinsurgency and Civic Action in Latin America.* Cincinnati: Ohio State University Press, 1966.
Barrett, Claudia. "The Breakdown of Cartel Culture." Council of Hemispheric Affairs, June 14, 2014. www.coha.org.
Barry, Tom, and Deb Preusch. *The Central America Fact Book.* New York: Grove Press, 1986.
Beckhusen, Robert. "As Colombian Gangs Collapse, Mexican Cartels Get Tons of Cheap Coke." *Wired*, April 11, 2013. www.wired.com.
Beith, Malcolm. *The Last Narco: Inside the Hunt for El Chapo, the World's Most Wanted Drug Lord.* New York: Grove Press, 2011.
Beittel, June S. *Mexico's Drug Trafficking Organizations: Source and Scope of the Rising Violence.* Report R-41576. Washington, DC: Congressional Research Service, April 15, 2013.
Bernath-Plaisted, Shandra, and Max Rennebohm. "Mexican Students Protest for Greater Democracy, 1968." Swarthmore College Global Non-Violent Action Database, October 20, 2008. https://nvdatabase.swarthmore.edu/content/mexican-students-protest-greater-democracy-1968.
Blancornelas, Jesús. *El Cartel: Los Arellanos Félix: La mafia más poderosa en la historia de América Latina.* Mexico City: Random House Mondadori, 2002.
Bolaños Geyer, Alejandro. *La Gran Piñata.* Managua: Copi-Zás, October 21, 2001.
Bonner, R. C. "The New Cocaine Cowboys: How to Defeat Mexico's Drug Cartels." *Foreign Affairs* 89 no. 4 (August 2010): 35–47.
Bosworth, Barry, Susan M. Collins, and Nora Claudia Lustig, eds. *Coming Together? Mexico–United States Relations.* Washington, DC: Brookings Institution Press, 1997.
Bosworth, James. "Honduras: Organized Crime Gaining amid Political Crisis: Working Paper Series on Crime in Central America." Washington, DC: Woodrow Wilson International Center for Scholars, Latin American Program, December 2010.
Brands, Hal. "Los Zetas and Mexico's Transnational Drug War." *World Politics Review*, December 25, 2009. www.worldpoliticsreview.com.
———. *Crime, Violence, and the Crisis in Guatemala: A Case Study in the Erosion of the State.* Carlisle Barracks, PA: Strategic Studies Institute, May 2010.
Briscoe, Ivan, and Marlies Stappers. "Breaking the Wave: Critical Steps in the Fight Against Crime in Guatemala." The Hague, Netherlands: Clingendael Institute, January 2012.
Brook, John Lee. *Blood and Death: The Secret History of Santa Muerte and the Mexican Drug Cartels.* London: Headpress Publishing, 2016.
Brownfield, William R. "Remarks at the Council of Americas." Washington, DC: Carnegie Endowment, March 22, 2013. https://2009-2017.state.gov/j/inl/rls/rm/2013/207231.htm.
———. "Remarks at the Institute of the Americas, Gangs, Youth, and Drugs—Breaking the Cycle of Violence and Crime." San Diego, CA, October 1, 2012. https://2009–2017.state.gov/j/inl/rls/rm /199133.htm.
Bruneau, Thomas, Lucia Dammert, and Elizabeth Skinner. *Maras: Gang Violence and Security in Central America.* Austin: University of Texas Press, 2011.

Bibliography 325

Bunck, Marie, and Michael Ross Fowler. *Bribes, Bullets, and Intimidation.* University Park: Pennsylvania State University Press, 2012.

Burton, Fred, and Scott Stewart. "Nicaragua: The Inherent Dangers of Being a Militant Mecca." Austin, TX: Stratfor Global Intelligence, June 25, 2008. www.stratfor.com.

Cajina, Roberto. "Security in Nicaragua: Central America's Exception?" Working Paper, Inter-American Dialogue, January 2013.

Caprio, Gerard, and D. Klingebiel. "Episodes of Systemic and Borderline Financial Crises." Washington, DC: World Bank, October 1999.

Carter, Jimmy. *Keeping Faith: Memoirs of a President.* London: William Collins Sons, 1982.

Casas-Zamora, Kevin. "Paying Attention to Central America's Drug Trafficking Crisis." Washington, DC: Brookings Institution, October 27, 2010. www.brookings.edu.

Castillo, Fabio. *La Coca Nostra.* Bogotá: Editorial Documentos Periodísticos, 1991.

———. *Los Jinetes de la Cocaína.* Bogotá: Editorial Documentos Periodísticos, 1987.

Celada, Edgar, and Sandra Davila. "Central America: On the Brink of a New War." Transnational Institute for Drugs and Democracy. Amsterdam, Netherlands. April 1, 1997. www.tni.org.

Central Intelligence Agency. "Appendices: The Contra Story—Jack Terrell." CIA Library: General Reports, Cocaine, The Contra Story. www.cia.gov/library/reports/general-reports-1/cocaine/contra-story/append.html.

———. "Memorandum for Deputy Director of Central Intelligence. Subject: PFIAB." Washington, DC: Central Intelligence Agency, CIA-RDP88G01117R001003990002-7, September 9, 1986.

———. "Other Individuals Involved in Trafficking: John Floyd Hull." CIA Library: General Reports, Cocaine, The Contra Story. www.cia.gov/library/reports/general-reports-1/cocaine/contra-story/other.html.

———. "Pilots, Companies and Other Individuals Working for Companies Used to Support the Contra Program." CIA Library: General Reports, Cocaine, The Contra Story. www.cia.gov/library/reports/general-reports-1/cocaine/contra-story/pilots.html.

———. "Report of Investigation: Allegations of Connections Between CIA and the Contras in Cocaine Trafficking to the United States, Line 896." Washington, DC: Central Intelligence Agency, October 8, 1998. http://ciadrugs.homestead.com/files/index-cia-ig-rpt.html.

———. "Report of Investigation: Guatemala Volume I." Central Intelligence Agency Inspector General 95-0024-IG, ESDN (CREST): 0000690161. July 15, 1995.

———. Special National Intelligence Estimate. "Nicaragua: Soviet Bloc and Radical Support for the Sandinista Regime." Washington, DC: Central Intelligence Agency, March 1985.

Chaparro, Luis, and J. Jesús Esquivel. "A Camarena lo ejecutó la CIA, no Caro Quintero." *Proceso.* December 12, 2013. www.proceso.com.mx.

Chepesiuk, Ron. *Drug Lords: The Rise and Fall of the Cali Cartel.* London: Milo Books, 2005.

Chomsky, Noam. *Turning the Tide: U.S. Interventions in Central America and the Struggle for Peace.* Boston: South End Press, 1999.

Christian, Shirley. *Nicaragua: Revolution in the Family.* New York: Vintage Books, 1986.

Cockburn, Alexander, and Jeffery St. Clair. *Whiteout: The CIA, Drugs, and the Press.* New York: Verso Books, 1998.

Congressional Quarterly. *U.S. Foreign Policy: The Reagan Imprint.* Washington, DC: Congressional Quarterly Incorporated, 1986.

326 Bibliography

Cook, Colleen W. *Mexico's Drug Cartels*. Report R-L32724. Washington, DC: Congressional Research Service, February 25, 2008.

Cordero, Carlos G. "Panama Update: New Regime on Bearer Shares Effective in 2015." International Institute for the Study of Cross-Border Investment and M&A. March 5, 2014. http://xbma.org/forum/panama-update-new-regime-on -bearer-shares-effective-in-2015.

Cottam, Martha. "The Carter Administration's Policy Toward Nicaragua: Images, Goals, and Tactics." *Political Science Quarterly* 107, no. 1 (April 1992): 123–146.

Council on Hemispheric Affairs. "Violence in Mexico and Latin America." February 21, 2014. www.coha.org/violence-in-mexico-and-latin-america.

Craig, Richard B. "La Campaña Permanente: Mexico's Antidrug Campaign." *Journal of Interamerican Studies and World Affairs* 20, no. 2 (May 1978): 107–131.

Crane, Stephen. "#1 Mexican Cartel Was Created by US Government: A Milieu of CIA, Mafia and Ultra-Right Cubans." *My Left Wing*, March 25, 2009. www .myleftwing.com/diary/24575.

Cruz, Arturo. "Anatomy of an Execution." *Commentary*, November 1989.

De la Puente, Luis. "The Revolutionary Path." In *Revolution and Revolutionaries: Guerrilla Movements in Latin America*, edited by Daniel Castro. Wilmington, DE: Scholarly Resources Incorporated, 1999.

Debray, Régis. "To Free the Present from the Past." In *Revolution and Revolutionaries: Guerrilla Movements in Latin America*, edited by Daniel Castro. Wilmington, DE: Scholarly Resources Incorporated, 1999.

Diaz, Tom. *No Boundaries: Transnational Latino Gangs and American Law Enforcement*. Ann Arbor: University of Michigan Press, 2009.

Diebert, Michael. *In the Shadow of Saint Death: The Gulf Cartel and the Price of America's Drug War in Mexico*. Guilford, CT: Lyons Press, 2014.

Dillon, Samuel, and Julia Preston. *Opening Mexico: The Making of a Democracy*. New York: Farrar, Strauss and Giroux, 2004.

———. *Our Man in Panama*. New York: Random House, 1990.

———. *The Condor Years: How Pinochet and His Allies Brought Terrorism to Three Continents*. New York: The New Press, 2004.

Diskin, Martin. *Trouble in Our Backyard*. New York: Pantheon Books, 1983.

Douglas, Joseph D. *Red Cocaine: The Drugging of America and the West*. 2nd ed. London: Edward Harle, 1999.

Dowdney, Luke, ed. "Tratamiento Del Problema De Niños y Jóvenes Involucrados En La Violencia Armada Organizada, Parte IV." In *Nem Guerra Nem Paz: Comparaciones Internacionales de niños y jóvenes en violencia armada Organizada*. São Paulo: 7 Letras, 2005.

Drug Enforcement Agency. Strategic Intelligence Section. *Fentanyl Flow to the United States*. DEA-DCT-DIR-008-20. Washington, January 2020.

———. "Confidential DEA Summary Guillermo González Calderóni Family Tree." *Frontline* no. 1510: *Murder, Money, and Mexico*. April 8, 1997. www.pbs.org /wgbh/pages/frontline/shows/mexico/family/secretdea.html.

———. "Tosh Plumlee DEA Files." RUEHFB # 0152 2900600 162150Z. October 17, 1989. www.scribd.com/doc/180778600/Tosh-Plumlee-DEA-files.

———. "DEA Issues Nationwide Alert on Fentanyl as a Threat to Health and Public Safety." Washington, DC: DEA Headquarters, March 8, 2015. www.dea.gov /press-releases/2015/03/18/dea-issues-nationwide-alert-fentanyl-threat-health -and-public-safety.

———. "Drug Enforcement Administration Announces the Seizure of Over 379 Million Deadly Doses of Fentanyl in 2022." Washington, DC: DEA Headquar-

ters, December 20, 2022. www.dea.gov/press-releases/2015/03/18/dea-issues
-nationwide-alert-fentanyl-threat-health-and-public-safety.

Durango, Hernán. "Ojalá el Estado deje de perseguir a los luchadores del pueblo: Iván Arenas, exconcejal de Turbo, Antioquia." *Colarebo*, September 25, 2017. https://colarebo.wordpress.com.

Dye, David R. "Police Reform in Honduras: The Role of the Special Purge and Transformation Commission." Washington, DC: Woodrow Wilson Center, 2017.

Ehrenfeld, Rachel. *Narco-Terrorism*. New York: Basic Books, 1990.

El Presidente de República de Panamá. "Decreto Ejecutivo No. 122." República de Panamá Ministerio de Economía y Finanzas, June 11, 2018.

Elles, Josh. "The Brutal Rise of El Mencho." *Rolling Stone Magazine*, July 11, 2017. www.rollingstone.com.

Enciso, Froylan. *Drogas, narcotráfico y política en México protocolo de hipocresía 1969–2000*. Mexico City: Editorial Oceano, 2004.

Enders, Thomas O. *Nicaragua: Threat to Peace in Central America*. Washington, DC: US Department of State, Bureau of Public Affairs, April 12, 1973.

Executive Intelligence Review Special Correspondent. "Medellín Cartel Loses Top Agent in Mexico." *Executive Intelligence Review* 16, no. 9 (May 5, 1989): 46–47.

"EZLN Terrorists: A Foreign Invasion of Mexico." *Executive Intelligence Review*, November 10, 1995. www.larouchepub.com/other/1995/2245_ezln.html.

Fagen, Richard R. *The Future of Central America*. Stanford, CA: Stanford University Press, 1983.

Farah, Douglas. "Organized Crime in Central America: The Homegrown and Transnational Dimensions." Washington, DC: Woodrow Wilson International Center for Scholars, February 2011.

———. "Transnational Criminal Threats in El Salvador: New Trends and Lessons from Colombia." Florida International University, Western Security Hemisphere Center, August 2011.

Farah, Douglas, and Pamela Phillips Lum. *Central American Gangs and Transnational Criminal Organizations*. Washington, DC: Woodrow Wilson International Center for Scholars, International Assessment and Strategy Center, February 2013.

Federal Bureau of Investigation. "Osiel Cárdenas-Guillén, Former Head of the Gulf Cartel, Sentenced to 25 Years' Imprisonment." US Attorney's Office Southern District of Texas, February 24, 2010.

———. "Going Global on Gangs." Washington, DC: Federal Bureau of Investigation, October 10, 2007. https://archives.fbi.gov/archives/news/stories/2007/october/ms13tag_101007.

Felton, John. "Rebuffing Democrats Attack, Senate Approves 'Contra' Aid." *Congressional Quarterly* 44 (August 16, 1986): 1876–1881.

Fernández Menédez, Jorge, and Víctor Ronquillo. *De los maras a los zetas: Los secretos del narcotráfico, de Colombia a Chicago*. Mexico City: Debosillio, 2007.

Figueroa, Yolanda. *El Capo del Golfo: Vida y Captura de Juan García Ábrego*. Mexico City: Editorial Grijalbo, 1996.

Fischer, Rob. "Tracing an Invisible Line: How Guatemalan Security Forces Have Taken Over the Drug Trade." *Mesoamerica* 25, no. 1 (January 2006): 1–2.

Frente Sandinista de Liberacion Nacional. *The 72-Hour Document: The Sandinista Blueprint for Constructing Communism in Central America*. Washington, DC: Department of State, Coordinator of Public Diplomacy for Latin America and the Caribbean, 1986.

328 Bibliography

Frontline. "Arellano Félix Tijuana Cartel: A Family Affair." Drug Wars Episodes 379–380. WGBH Educational Foundation of the Public Broadcasting Service, October 9–10, 2000. www.pbs.org/wgbh/pages/frontline/shows/drugs /business/afo/afosummary.html.

———. "Cuba and Cocaine." Episode 910. WGBH Educational Foundation of the Public Broadcasting Service. February 5, 1991.

General Accounting Office. *Drug Control in South America, Having Limited Success—Some Progress but Problems Are Formidable.* GAO 78-45. Washington, DC. March 28, 1978.

———. *Drug Control: Interdiction Efforts in Central America Have Had Little Impact on the Flow of Drugs.* Report to the Chairman, Subcommittee on Information, Justice, Transportation, and Agriculture, Committee on Government Operations House of Representatives. NSIAD 94-233. Washington, DC. August 2, 1994.

———. *Drug Control: U.S. Counterdrug Activities in Central America.* GAO/T-NSIAD-94-251. Washington, DC. August 2, 1994.

———. *Efforts to Stop Narcotics and Dangerous Drugs Coming from and Through Mexico and Central America.* GAO B-175425. Washington, DC. December 31, 1974.

———. *Gains Made in Controlling Illegal Drugs, yet the Drug Trade Flourishes.* GAO 80-4. Washington, DC. October 25, 1979.

———. *Opium Eradication Efforts in Mexico: Cautious Optimism Advised.* GAO 77-6. Washington, DC. February 18, 1977.

———. *Report to the Congress: Difficulties in Immobilizing Major Narcotics Traffickers.* GAO-B175424. Washington, DC. December 21, 1973.

———. *The War on Drugs: Narcotics Control in Panama.* GAO/NSIAD-91-233. Washington, DC. July 1991.

———. *U.S. Assistance Has Helped Mexican Counternarcotics Efforts, but Tons of Drugs Continue to Flow into the United States.* GAO-07-1018. Washington, DC. August 2007.

———. *U.S.-Mexican Counternarcotics Efforts Face Difficult Challenges.* NSIAD 98-54. Washington, DC. June 30, 1998.

———. *Update on U.S. Mexican Counternarcotics Efforts.* T-NSIAD 99-86. Washington, DC. February 24, 1999.

Georgia Tech Panama Logistics Innovation and Research Center. "Colon Free Trade Zone Statistics." Panama City, Panama: Georgia Tech Panama, December 2019. http://logistics.gatech.pa/en/assets/special-economic-zones/colon-free -zone/statistics.

Gobierno de Guatemala. *La Ley Contra la Narcoactividad.* Ciudad de Guatemala: Organismo Legislativo, Congreso de La Republica de Guatemala Decreto Numero 48-92, September 23, 1992.

González, Hector. "Los Prófugos del Salinato." Agencia Mexicana de Información, edición no. 781. February 21, 2007. www.red-ami.com/cgi-bin/ed_seccion.cgi ?dt=21/02/2007&ref=20070221/090/20070220-132332.txt.

González, Saúl. "Orlando Henao Montoya." Colombia: Narcos Famosos.

Gooberman, Lawrence A. *Operation Intercept: The Multiple Consequences of Public Policy.* New York: Pergamon Press, 1974.

Grayson, George W. "Mexico and the Drug Cartels." Foreign Policy Research Institute, August 2017. https://web.archive.org/web/20120309155416/http://www .fpri.org/enotes/200708.grayson.mexicodrugcartels.html.

———. "NAFTA and the War on Drugs." *Journal of Commerce*, July 7, 1993, sec. A, p. 8.

———. *La Familia Cartel: Implications for U.S. Mexican Security.* Carlisle Barracks, PA: Strategic Studies Institute, 2010.

———. *Mexico: Narco Violence and a Failed State?* New York: Taylor and Francis, 2009.

———. *The Cartels: The Story of Mexico's Most Dangerous Criminal Organization and Their Impact on U.S. Security.* Santa Barbara, CA: Praeger Books, 2014.

———. *The Evolution of Los Zetas in Mexico and Central America: Sadism as an Instrument of Cartel Warfare.* Carlisle Barracks, PA: US Army War College Press, January 25, 2015.

———. *The Impact of President Felipe Calderón's War on Drugs on the Armed Forces: The Prospects for Mexico's Militarization and Bilateral Relations.* Carlisle Barracks, PA: US Army War College Strategic Studies Institute, January 2013.

Grayson, George W., and Samuel Logan. *The Executioner's Men: Los Zetas, Rogue Soldiers, Criminal Entrepreneurs, and the Shadow State They Created.* London: Transaction Publishers, 2012.

Greco, Emily Schwartz, and Geoff Thale. "Behind the Honduran Coup." Institute of Policy Studies, Foreign Policy in Focus. Washington, DC. July 1, 2009. http://fpif.org/behind_the_honduran_coup.

Grillo, Ioan. "Behind the Murder of Honduran Drug Czar." *Time*, December 17, 2009. http://content.time.com/time/world/article/0,8599,1948258,00.html.

———. *El Narco: Inside Mexico's Criminal Insurgency.* New York: Bloomsbury Press, 2012.

Grossman, Karl. *Nicaragua: America's New Vietnam?* Sag Harbor, NY: The Permanent Press, 1984.

———. "There Is No Way We Can Turn Back: Why Thousands of Refugees Will Keep Coming to America Despite Trump's Crackdown." *Time*, June 21, 2018. https://time.com/5318718/central-american-refugees-crisis.

Guevara, Che. *Guerrilla Warfare.* 3rd ed. Wilmington, DE: Scholarly Resources Incorporated, 1997.

Hager, Richard P. "Soviet Bloc Involvement in the Salvadorian Civil War." *Communist and Post-Communist Studies* (December 28, 1995): 437–468.

Hahn, Walter F. *Central America and the Reagan Doctrine.* New York: University Press of America, 1987.

Haig, Alexander M. *Caveat: Realism, Reagan, and Foreign Policy.* New York: MacMillan, 1984.

Hamilton, Martha M. "Panama Papers Figure Added to FBI Most Wanted List." International Consortium of Investigative Journalists, May 1, 2018. www.icij.org.

Harrigan, Thomas. "Statement Before the Senate Caucus on International Narcotics Control, Hearing Entitled U.S.–Central America Security Cooperation." Washington, DC: US Department of Justice, May 25, 2011.

Hart, Gary, to Senator John F. Kerry. "William Robert Tosh Plumlee." February 14, 1991. https://web.archive.org/web/20120210160349/http://toshplumlee.info.

Heritage Foundation. "Backgrounder: Honduras's Role in U.S. Policy for Central America." The Heritage Foundation, February 28, 1985. www.heritage.org.

Hernández, Anabel. *Narcoland: The Mexican Drug Lords and Their Godfathers.* Translated by Ian Bruce. New York: Verso Books, 2013.

Hesterman, Jennifer L. *The Terrorist Criminal Nexus: An Alliance of International Drug Cartels, Organized Crime and Terrorist Groups.* Boca Raton, FL: CRC Press, 2013.

Hooper, Karen. "The Mexican Drug Cartel Threat in Central America." Austin, TX: Stratfor Global Intelligence, November 17, 2011. www.stratfor.com.

330   Bibliography

Hopsicker, Daniel. *Barry and the Boys: The CIA, the Mob, and America's Secret History*. Venice, FL: Madcow Press, 2006.

———. "Narco Jet in Costa Rica Scandal Tied to Iran Contra Figure." *Mad Cow News*, August 12, 2013. www.madcowprod.com.

Horowitz, Irving Louis. "Norm of Illegitimacy: The Political Sociology of Latin America." In *Latin American Radicalism: A Documentary Report on Left and Nationalist Movements*, edited by Irving Louis Horowitz, Josué de Castro, and John Gerassi. New York: Vintage Books, 1969.

Huizer, Gerrit. *The Revolutionary Potential of Peasants in Latin America*. Lexington, MA: Lexington Books, 1972.

Human Rights Watch. "World Report 1992: Americas Watch Overview—Guatemala." 1992. www.hrw.org/reports/1992/WR92/AMW-09.htm.

———. "Guatemala: Return to Violence, Refugees, Civil Patrollers, and Violence." *Human Rights Watch* 8, no. 1 (January 1996): 1–32.

———. "Neither Rights nor Security: Killings, Torture, and Disappearances in Mexico's War on Drugs." November 4, 2011.

Hunter, Jane. "Cocaine and Cutouts: Israel's Unseen Diplomacy." *Americans for Middle Eastern Understanding* 22, no. 1 (January–March 1989): 2–3.

Imerman, Vicky. "Notorious Salvadoran School of the Americas Graduates." www.derechos.org/soa/elsal-not.html.

Immigration and Refugee Board of Canada, Research Directorate. *El Salvador: The National Civilian Police*. Government of Canada. April 1, 1998. www.refworld.org/docid/3ae6a800e.html.

———. *Guatemala: Violence by Criminal Gangs and Cases of Popular Justice; Protection Offered by the State (Mar. 2005–Feb. 2007)*. GTM102404.FE. March 2, 2007. www.refworld.org/docid/469cd6a31c.html.

———. *Honduras: Police Corruption, Police Participation in Criminal Activities and Measures Taken by the Government*. HND103832.FE. Government of Canada. November 3, 2011. www.justice.gov/sites/default/files/eoir/legacy/2014/02/04/HND103832.FE.pdf.

Inspector General of the Central Intelligence Agency. "Report of Investigation: Allegations of Connections Between CIA and the Contras in Cocaine Trafficking to the United States, Lines 905–908." Washington, DC: Central Intelligence Agency, October 8, 1998.

International Crisis Group. "Guatemala Drug Trafficking and Violence." Latin America Report No. 39. International Crisis Group, October 11, 2011.

International Justice Resource Center. *Central American Court of Justice*. San Francisco, CA: International Justice Resource Center. https://ijrcenter.org/regional-communities/central-american-court-of-justice.

International Labour Organization, Regional Office for Latin America and the Caribbean. *2007 Labor Overview, Latin America and the Caribbean*. Geneva: ILO, January 1, 2008. www.ilo.org.

Jácome H., Luis I. "Central Bank Involvement in Banking Crises in Latin America." Working Paper 08/135. International Monetary Fund. Washington, DC, May 2008.

Jane's Intelligence Review [London]. "Honduras: Public Security Force." February 1993. www.country-data.com/cgi-bin/query/r-5725.html.

John F. Kennedy Library. The Papers of Arthur M. Schlesinger Jr., Writings: Alliance for Progress/General Speeches, box W-2.

———. The Papers of President John F. Kennedy, President's Office Files, Countries: Cuba 1961, box 115.

Bibliography 331

Johnson, David T. "Efforts to Combat Organized Crime in Guatemala: Address to the Council of the Americas." Washington, DC: US Department of State, October 5, 2010. www.state.gov/j/inl/rls/rm /149055.htm.

Johnson, Mary Helen. "National Policies and the Rise of Transnational Gangs." Washington, DC: Migration Policy Institute, April 2006. www.migrationinformation.org.

Jones, Gareth A. "Drugs, Violence, and Insecurity in Mexico." In *South America, Central America, and the Caribbean 2012.* 20th ed. London: Europa Editions, 2011.

Kobrak, Paul. "The Illusion of Democracy." In *Organizing and Repression in the University of San Carlos, Guatemala: 1944–1996.* New York: Science and Human Rights Program, American Association for the Advancement of Science, 1999.

Kornbluth, Peter. *Nicaragua: The Price of Intervention.* Washington, DC: Institute for Policy Studies, 1987.

Kwitny, Jonathan. *The Crimes of Patriots: A True Tale of Dope, Dirty Money, and the CIA.* New York: W. W. Norton, 1987.

La Dirección Policial de Investigaciones. "Acerca de la Dirección Policial de Investigaciones." El Ocotal: Academia de Policía, Policía Nacional. www.policianacional.gob.hn/dpiipd.

"La Nueva Generación de Narcotraficantes." *Dossier Politico* (Hermosillo, Mexico), June 12, 2005. www.dossierpolitico.com.

La oficina en Washington para asuntos Latinaméricanos. "¿Proteger y servir? El estado de los procesos de reforma policial en Centroamérica." Washington, DC: La oficina en Washington para asuntos Latinaméricanos, December 2009.

"La Verdadera Historia de los Arellano Félix." *Narcotrafico,* October 27, 2009. http://lamafiamexicana.blogspot.com/2009/10/la-verdadera-historia-de-los-arellano.html.

Lana, Sara Miller. "The Central American Peace Accord Celebrates 25 Years, but Has It Brought Peace?" *Christian Science Monitor,* August 7, 2012.

Lasso Guevara, Dr. Ricardo. *U.S.A. vs. Noriega: Enemigos o Amigos.* Panamá City: Litho Impresora Panamá, 1994.

Layne, Mary, Scott Decker, Meg Townsend, and Caben Chester. "Measuring the Deterrent Effect of Enforcement Operations on Drug Smuggling 1991–1999." *Trends in Organized Crime* 7 (March 2002): 66–87. https://doi.org/10.1007/s12117-002-1013-2.

Lee, Brianna. "Mexico's Drug War." Council on Foreign Relations, March 5, 2014. www.cfr.org.

Lehoucq, Fabrice. *The Politics of Modern Central America: Civil War, Democratization, and Underdevelopment.* New York: Cambridge University Press, 2012.

Leiken, Robert S., ed. *Central America: Anatomy of a Conflict.* New York: Pergamon Press, 1984.

———. *Soviet Strategy in Central America.* New York: Praeger Publishers, 1982.

Leo Grande, William. "The Revolution in Nicaragua: Another Cuba." *Foreign Affairs* 58, no. 1 (Fall 1979): 28–50.

Leutert, Stephanie, and Sarah Spalding. "How Many Central Americans Are Travelling North?" Washington, DC: Lawfare Institute, April 12, 2019. www.lawfareblog.com.

Levinson, Jerome, and Juan de Onís. *The Alliance That Lost Its Way.* Chicago: Quadrangle Books, 1970.

332   Bibliography

Lifson, Thomas. "High Ranking Defector from Venezuela Accuses Regime of Narcotics Trafficking." *American Thinker,* January 28, 2015. www.americanthinker.com/blog/2015/01/highranking_defector_from_venezuela_accuses_regime_of_narcotics_trafficking_.html.

Linares, Adriana. "La Leyenda Negra." *Drogas México,* November 22, 2005. www.drogasmexico.org.

Logan, Samuel. "Inside Los Zetas." *Security in Latin America,* January 14, 2009. http://samuellogan.blogspot.com/2009/01/inside-los-zetas.html.

———. "The Future of Los Zetas After the Death of Herbierto Lazcano." Combating Terrorism Center, October 29, 2012. www.ctc.usma.edu.

———. "The Reality of Mexican Mega Cartel: How Mexican Crime Could Become a U.S. National Security Threat on the Border." 2006. www.files.ethz.ch/isn/46400/The-Reality-of-a-Mega-Cartel.pdf.

———. "Toppling the Tijuana Cartel 'Dynasty.'" International Relations and Security Network. April 9, 2006. www.samuellogan.com.

López, Julie. "Otto Roberto Herrera García 'El Pipa." Persona de Intres, Organized Crime and Corruption Reporting Project (OCCRP). 2014. https://aleph.occrp.org.

López López, Andrés. *El Cártel de los Sapos.* Bogotá: Editorial Planeta Colombiana, 2008.

Loría Quirós, Carlos Roberto. *De Caro Quintero a Ricardo Alem.* San José, Costa Rica: Editorial Magenta, 2001.

Marcy, William L. *The Politics of Cocaine.* Chicago: Lawrence Hill Books, 2010.

Marentes, Alex (Buggs). *Borderland Beat: Reporting on the Mexican Drug War.* 11th ed. Morrisville, NC: Lulu Publishing, September 29, 2019.

Mario Ruiz Massieu v. Janet Reno. United States Court of Appeals for the Third Circuit. US District Court for the District of New Jersey. 915 F. Supp. 681. February 28, 1996. https://law.justia.com/cases/federal/district-courts/FSupp/915/681/1618129.

McGuiness, Colleen, and Patricia M. Russotto. *U.S. Foreign Policy: The Reagan Imprint.* Washington, DC: Congressional Quarterly Incorporated, 1986.

McKibben, Cameron. "Corruption, Impunity, and the International Commission Against Impunity in Guatemala." Council on Hemispheric Affairs, April 30, 2015. www.coha.org.

McRae, Patricia B. "Reconceptualizing the Illegal Narcotics Trade: Its Effect on the Colombian and Mexican State." Southeastern Conference on Latin American Studies. Savannah, GA, April 12, 1998. http://historicaltextarchive.com/sections.php?action=read&artid=456.

"Medellín Cartel Loses Top Agent in México." *Executive Intelligence Review* 16, no. 19 (May 15, 1989).

Meiners, Stephen. "Central America: An Emerging Role in the Drug Trade." Austin, TX: Stratfor, March 25, 2009. www.stratfor.com.

Mejía, Thelma. "Central America: Soaring Violent Crime Threatens Democracy." Inter Press Service (Tegucigalpa), September 22, 2008.

———. "Unfinished Business: The Military and Drugs in Honduras." Transnational Institute, Drugs and Democracy Program, December 1, 1997. www.tni.org.

Merrill, Tim, ed. *Honduras: A Country Study.* Washington: GPO for the Library of Congress, 1995. http://countrystudies.us/honduras.

Mexico Institute. "The Félix Gallardo Organization." Washington, DC: Woodrow Wilson Institute, January 14, 2000. www.wilsoncenter.org.

Meyer, Maureen. *Abused and Afraid in Ciudad Juárez: An Analysis of Human Rights Abused in Mexico.* Washington, DC: Washington Office on Latin America, September 2010.

Meyer, Peter J., and Clare Ribando Seelke. *Central America Regional Security Initiative: Background and Policy Issues for Congress.* Report R-41731. Washington, DC: Congressional Research Service, May 6, 2013.

Millett, Richard L., and Orlando J. Pérez. "New Threats and Old Dilemmas: Central America's Armed Forces in the 21st Century." *Journal of Political and Military Sociology* 33, no. 1 (2005): 57–59.

Mills, James. *The Underground Empire: Where Crime and Governments Embrace.* New York: Dell, 1986.

Miro, Ramon J. *Organized Crime and Terrorist Activity in Mexico, 1999–2002.* Washington, DC: Federal Research Division, Library of Congress, February 2003.

Molzahn, Cory, Octavio Rodriguez Ferriera, and David A. Shirk. "Drug War Violence in Mexico." Trans-Border Institute, February 2013.

Morley, Morris H. *Washington, Somoza and the Sandinistas.* Cambridge: Cambridge University Press, 1994.

Narcos Famosos. Mexico City: Aimee SBP, 2009.

National Archives (College Park, MD). General Records of the Department of State: Central Foreign Policy Files, Bureau of Inter-American Affairs, Records Relating to Mexico, boxes 49–59.

————. General Records of the Department of State: Central Foreign Policy Files, Political and Defense, Records Relating to Mexico, 1967–1969, box 2343, boxes 2475–2476.

————. Nixon Presidential Materials Project, Nixon Presidential Materials Staff, National Security Council Files, 1969–1973, boxes 357 and 359.

————. Nixon Presidential Materials Project, Nixon Presidential Materials Staff, Staff Member and Office Files, Egil Krogh, 1969–1973, boxes 30–32.

————. Records of the Drug Enforcement Administration, Subject Files of the Bureau of Narcotics and Dangerous Drugs, Cuba, box 154.

————. Records of the Drug Enforcement Administration, Subject Files of the Bureau of Narcotics and Dangerous Drugs, 1916–1970, box 151.

National Archives and Records Administration. *Public Papers of the Presidents of the United States, Ronald Reagan* (1981–1988). Washington, DC: Office of the Federal Register.

————. *Public Papers of the Presidents of the United States, Richard Nixon* (1969–1974). Washington, DC: Office of the Federal Register.

National Center for Injury Prevention and Control. "Death Rate Maps and Graphs." Washington, DC: Centers for Disease Control and Prevention, June 2, 2022. www.cdc.gov/drugoverdose/deaths/index.html.

National Institute on Drug Control. "Overdose Death Rates: Trends and Statistics." Washington, DC: US Department of Health and Human Services, January 20, 2022. https://nida.nih.gov/research-topics/trends-statistics/overdose-death-rates.

National Safety Council. *Drug Overdoses.* Itasca, IL: National Safety Council, 2022. https://injuryfacts.nsc.org/home-and-community/safety-topics/drugoverdoses/data-details.

National Security Archive (George Washington University, Washington, DC). Mexico Project. The Tlatelolco Massacre: U.S. Documents of Mexico and the Events of 1968. http://nsarchive.gwu.edu/NSAEBB/NSAEBB99.

————. Negroponte File. https://nsarchive2.gwu.edu/NSAEBB151/index.htm.

————. The Iran-Contra Affair: The Making of a Scandal, 1983–1988. https://proquest.libguides.com/dnsa/irancontra.

————. The Oliver North File: His Diaries, E-Mail, and Memos on the Kerry Report, Contras, and Drugs.

————. Narcotics Collection, Carter FOIA, box 39.

334 Bibliography

―――. Narcotics Collection, Drug Documents from U.S. Policy/Military, box 23.
―――. Narcotics Collection, Drug Documents from Presidential Libraries, boxes 46 and 54.
―――. Narcotics Collection, Drug Documents, box 51.
―――. Narcotics Collection, Drug Documents from GAO Reports, box 54.
―――. Narcotics Collection, FOIA Releases, box 39.
Nixon, Richard M. "Remarks at Opening Session of the Governors' Conference at the Department of State (December 3, 1969)." *Public Papers of the Presidents of the United States*. Washington, DC: Office of the Federal Register, National Archives and Records Service, 1971.
Noriega, Manuel, and Peter Eisner. *America's Prisoner: The Memoirs of Manuel Noriega*. New York: Random House, 1997.
Norland, Rod. "Is There a Contra Drug Connection?" *Newsweek*, January 26, 1987.
O'Connor, Allison, Jeanne Batalova, and Jessica Bolte, "Central American Immigrants in the United States." Washington, DC: Migration Policy Institute, August 15, 2019. www.migrationpolicy.org.
Organization of American States. *CICAD History*. Washington, DC: Organization of American States, July 18, 2014. http://cicad.oas.org/Main/Template.asp?File=/Main/AboutCICAD/History/History_ENG.asp.
―――. Inter American Drug Abuse Control Commission (CICAD). Multilateral Evaluation Mechanism. *Evaluation of Progress in Drug Control 2007–2009: Nicaragua*. Washington, DC: Organization of American States, 2010.
―――. Inter-American Drug Abuse Control Commission (CICAD). *Declaration and Program of Action of Ixtapa*. Ixtapa, Mexico: Organization of American States, April 2, 1990. www.cicad.oas.org/Main/Template.asp?File=/main/aboutcicad/basicdocuments/ixtapa_eng.asp.
―――. Inter-American Drug Abuse Control Commission (CICAD). Multilateral Evaluation Mechanism. *Evaluation of Progress in Drug Control 2001–2002: Costa Rica*. Washington, DC: Organization of American States, 2003.
―――. Inter-American Drug Abuse Control Commission (CICAD). Multilateral Evaluation Mechanism. *Evaluation of Progress in Drug Control 2007–2009: Costa Rica*. Washington, DC: Organization of American States, January 2011.
―――. *Pandillas Delictivas*. Washington, DC: Organization of American States, January 28, 2012.
―――. *Report on Drug Use in the Americas 2011*. Washington, DC: Inter-American Observatory on Drugs, March 21, 2012.
Pardo-Maurer, R. *The Contras, 1980–1989: A Special Kind of Politics*. New York: Center for Strategic and International Studies, 1990.
Paterno, Susan. "The Sad Saga of Gary Webb." *American Journalism Review* (June/July 2005). http://ajrarchive.org/Article.asp?id=3874.
"Pedro Avilés Pérez." *Todo Sobre Narcotráfico en Mexico*, January 15, 2010. http://todosobrenarcotraficoenmexico.blogspot.com.
Peréz Bolaños, Louis Emmanuel. *El estado costarricense frente al narcotráfico: El caso del Plan Nacional sobre Drogas, 2006–2011*. Universidad de Costa Rica, Facultad de Ciencias Sociales, Escuela de Ciencias Políticas, 2013.
Petras, James F., and Robert La Porte Jr. *Cultivating Revolution: The United States and Agrarian Reform in Latin America*. New York: Random House, 1971.
Plumlee, Tosh. "Robert Tosh Plumlee Declaration." *JFK Murder Solved*, November 21, 2004. www.jfkmurdersolved.com.
Poppa, Terrence E. *Drug Lord: The Life and Death of a Mexican Kingpin*. 3rd ed. El Paso, TX: Cinco Puntos Press, 2010.

Presedencia de La Republica de México. *Ordena Presidente Vicente Fox puesta en marcha del Operativo México Seguro contra el crimen Organizada.* Los Pinos: Presedencia de La Republica de México, June 11, 2005. http://fox.presidencia.gob.mx/actividades/orden/?contenido=18872.

Presidente de República de Panamá. Decreto Ejecutivo No. 122. República de Panamá Ministerio de Economía y Finanzas, June 11, 2018.

Pyes, Craig, and Laurie Becklund. "Inside Dope in El Salvador." *New Republic* (April 15, 1985): 15–19.

Ravelo, Ricardo. *Osiel: Vida y Tragedia de un Capo.* Mexico City: Grijalbo, 2009.

Reames, Benjamín. *Encyclopedia of Law Enforcement: Mexico.* Thousand Oaks, CA: Sage Publications, 2004.

Reed, Terry. *Compromised: Clinton, Bush, and the CIA.* New York: SPI Books, 1994.

Reed, Tristan. "Mexico's Drug War: Stability Ahead of the Fourth Quarter." Austin, TX: Stratfor Global Intelligence, October 10, 2013. https://worldview.stratfor.com.

"Reportaje Especial: Investigaciones vinculan a Oscar Arias con el Dictador Manuel Antonio Noriega y con redes del narcotráfico." *El Jojoto* (Venezuela), June 21, 2016. www.eljojoto.net.

Reveles, José. *El Cártel Incómodo: El Fin de los Beltrán Levya y la Hegemonía del Chapo Guzmán.* Mexico City: Random House Mondadori, 2010.

Revista Envío. "The Gangs of Central America: Major Players and Scapegoats." December 2007. www.envio.org.ni.

Richards, James R. *Transnational Criminal Organizations, Cybercrime and Money Laundering: A Handbook for Law Enforcement Officers, Auditors, and Financial Investigators.* London: CRC Press, 1999.

"The Rise and Fall of the Juárez Cartel." U.S. Open Borders, March 5, 2012. http://usopenborders.com/2012/03/the-rise-fall-of-the-juarez-cartel.

Roback, Patrick. "AML 101: Trade Based Money Laundering." New York: Roback Consulting, August 28, 2017. www.robakconsulting.com/blog/2017/8/28/trade-based-money-laundering.

Robbins, David. *Heavy Traffic: 30 Years of Headlines and Major Ops from the Case Files of the DEA.* New York: Chamberlain Brothers, 2005.

Rodríguez Mega, Emiliano. "Cocaine Trafficking Is Destroying Central America's Forests." *Science,* June 16, 2017. www.sciencemag.org.

Rogers, William D. *The Twilight Struggle: The Alliance for Progress and the Politics of Development in Latin America.* New York: Random House, 1967.

Roncken, Theo. "Narco Jets and Police Protection in Bolivia." Transnational Institute, December 1, 1997. www.tni.org/es/node/11387#1b.

Ropp, Steve C., and James A. Morris, eds. *Central America: Crisis and Adaptation.* Albuquerque: University of New Mexico Press, 1983.

Rosenberg, Mark B., and Luis G. Solis. *The United States and Central America: Geopolitical Realities and Regional Fragility.* New York: Routledge, 2007.

Rush, Valerie, and Gretchen Small. "The Crimes of the Medellín Cartel." *Executive Intelligence Review* 14, no. 8 (February 20, 1987): 40–42.

Salama, Pierre. "Homicidios, ¿es ineluctable la violencia en América Latina?" *Frontera norte* 25, no. 49 (January–June 2013): 10.

Sarita, Cynthia L. *The Mounting Threat of Domestic Terrorism: Al Qaeda and the Salvadorian Gang MS-13.* El Paso: LFB Scholarly Publishing, 2009.

Schmidt, Wayne. "Report of Investigation." Washington, DC: Drug Enforcement Agency, February 13, 1990. https://web.archive.org/web/20120217172856/http://toshplumlee.info/pdf/DEAfiles.pdf.

336 Bibliography

Schmitz, David F. *Thank God They're on Our Side: The United States and Right Wing Dictatorships 1921–1965.* Chapel Hill: University of North Carolina Press, 1999.

Schneider, Ronald M. *Communism in Guatemala.* New York: Praeger Publishers, 1958.

Scott, James M. "Interbranch Rivalry and the Reagan Doctrine in Nicaragua." *Political Science Quarterly* 112, no. 2 (Summer, 1997): 237–260.

Scott, Peter Dale, and Jonathan Marshall. *Cocaine Politics: Drugs, Armies, and the CIA in Central America.* Berkeley: University of California Press, 1991.

Seelke, Clare M. Ribando. *Gangs in Central America.* Report R-L34112. Washington, DC: Congressional Research Service, October 17, 2008.

———. *Mérida Initiative: U.S. Anticrime and U.S. Counterdrug Assistance for Mexico and Central America.* Report S22387. Washington, DC: Congressional Research Service, July 7, 2008.

Seelke, Clare Ribando, and Kristin Finklea. *U.S.-Mexican Security Cooperation: The Mérida Initiative and Beyond.* Report R-41349. Washington, DC: Congressional Research Service, April 8, 2014.

Seelke, Clare Ribando, Liana Sun Wyler, June S. Beittel, and Mark P. Sullivan. *Latin American and the Caribbean: Drug Trafficking and U.S. Counterdrug Programs.* Report R-41215. Washington, DC: Congressional Research Service, March 19, 2012.

Shultz, George P. "The Struggle for Democracy in Central America." Draft speech. US Department of State, Dallas, TX, April 1, 1983.

Sierra Guzmán, Jorge Luis. "Mexico's Military in the War Drugs." *Washington Office on Latin America* 2, no. 2 (April 2003): 1–20.

Sistema de la Integración Centroamericana. *XI Cumbre de Presidentes Centroamericanos: Protocol de Tegucigalpa a la Carta de la Organización de Los Estados Centroamericanos.* Tegucigalpa, Honduras, December 13, 1991.

———. Permanent Central American Commission for the Eradication of Production, Trafficking, Consumption, and Illicit Use of Narcotic and Psychotropic Substances and Related Crimes. Tegucigalpa, Honduras: Edificio de Comisiones October 29, 1993. www.sica.int.

Skidmore, Thomas E. *Modern Latin America.* New York: Oxford University Press, 1992.

Skocpol, Theda. "France, Russia, and China: A Structural Analysis of Social Revolutions." *Comparative Studies in Society and History*, April 18, 1976.

Smith, James. "Economic Migrants Replace Political Refugees." The Migration Institute, April 1, 2006. www.migrationpolicy.org.

Stavenhagen, Rodolfo. "Seven Erroneous Theses About Latin America." In *Latin American Radicalism: A Documentary Report on Left and Nationalist Movements*, edited by Irving Louis Horowitz, Josué de Castro, and John Gerassi. New York: Vintage Books, 1969.

Stewart, Scott. "Mexico's Plan to Create a Paramilitary Force." Stratfor Global Intelligence, April 19, 2012. www.stratfor.com.

———. "The Real El Chapo." Stratfor Global Intelligence, November 1, 2012. www.stratfor.com.

Stewart, Scott, and Tristan Reed. "Mexico's Zetas Are Not Finished Yet." Stratfor Global Intelligence, August 24, 2013. www.stratfor.com.

Stich, Rodney. *Defrauding America: Encyclopedia of Secret Operations by the CIA, DEA, and Other Government Offices.* 4th ed. Alamo, CA: Silverpeak Enterprises, 2008.

Suchlicki, Jaime. "Cuba's Continuous Support for Terrorism." *Institute for Cuban and Cuban-American Studies*, no. 238 (March 4, 2015). http://ctp.iccas.miami.edu/FOCUS_Web /Issue238.htm.

Bibliography 337

Sullivan, John P., and Robert J. Bunker, eds. *Strategic Notes on Third Generation Gangs.* North Haven, CT: Small Wars Foundation, 2022.

Sullivan, John P., and Adam Ekus. "State of Siege: Mexico's Criminal Insurgency." In *Mexico's Criminal Insurgency*, edited by John P. Sullivan and Robert J. Bunker. Bloomington, IN: IUniverse Inc., 2012.

Sullivan, Mark P. *Panama-U.S. Relations: Continuing Policy Concerns.* Washington, DC: Congressional Research Service, August 4, 1994.

Sutton, James. "U.S. Counternarcotics Strategy in Latin America: Good Intentions and Poor Results." *The Americas* 4, no. 1 (October–November 1991).

Tarpley, Webster, and Anton Chaitkin. *George Bush: The Unauthorized Biography.* 2nd ed. Joshua Tree: Tree Life Books, 2004.

Thoumi, Francisco E. *Illegal Drugs, Economy, and Society.* Baltimore: Johns Hopkins University Press, 2003.

Trueba Lara, José Luis. *García Ábrego.* Mexico City: Editorial Posada, 1996.

Turner, Robert F. *Nicaragua v. United States: A Look at the Facts.* Washington, DC: Pergamon-Brassey's International Defense Publishers Incorporated, 1987.

22 U.S. Code, 2291 (c), Foreign Relations and Intercourse Act, amended as Public Law 94–329, title V, §504(b), June 30, 1976, 90 Statute. Drug Enforcement Administration—Functions and Guidelines Relating to Operations in Foreign Countries, June 30, 1976.

United Nations Office on Drugs and Crime. *2013 Global Study on Homicide.* Vienna: United Nations, March 2014.

———. "Development in Central America Stymied by Crime and Drugs, UN Warns." New York: United Nations News Service, May 23, 2007.

———. *Convention Against Transnational Organized Crime.* Treaty Series Volume 2225. Resolution Adopted by the General Assembly 55/25. 55th Sess., Item 105. New York: United Nations, January 8, 2001.

———. *Crime and Development in Central America: Caught in the Crossfire.* New York: United Nations, May 2007.

———. Policy Analysis and Public Affairs. *UNODC 2019 World Drug Report Book 4: Stimulants.* Vienna: United Nations Office on Drugs and Crime, June 2019.

———. *Single Convention on Narcotic Drugs, 1961, Amended by the Protocol Amending the Single Convention on Narcotic Drugs, 1961.* Treaty Series Vol. 976, Chapter VI, Narcotics Drugs and Psychotropic Substances. New York: United Nations, August 8, 1975.

———. *Single Convention on Narcotic Drugs 1961: Treaty Obligations of the United States Relating to Marihuana.* New York: United Nations, 1961. From the Files of Geoffrey C. Shepard, Washington, DC: National Archives, Nixon Presidential Materials Project, White House Special Files, Staff and Member Files, 1969–1973.

———. *Tegucigalpa Protocol to the Charter of Organization of Central American States* (OCAS). Treaty Series No. 8048. Tegucigalpa: December 13, 1991.

———. *United Nations Convention on Illicit Traffic in Narcotics Drugs and Psychotropic Substances*, Article 12, Vienna, Austria: United Nations Commission on Narcotics Drugs, December 20, 1988.

———. *United Nations Convention Against Illicit Traffic in Narcotic Drugs and Psychotropic Substances, Treaty Series.* Vol. 1582, Chapter VI: Narcotics Drugs and Psychotropic Substances. Vienna: United Nations Commission on Narcotics Drugs, December 20, 1988.

United States. "Narcotic Drugs Mutual Cooperation Agreement Between the United States and Panama." January 10, 1990. *United States Treaties and Other International Acts* Series 12409, Articles I–II.

338   *Bibliography*

———. "Treaty Between the United States of America and Mexico." May 4, 1978. *United States Treaties and Other International Acts* Series 9656, Extradition, Pursuant to Public Law 89-497.

United States–Mexico Joint Working Group. "Narcotics, Marihuana, and Dangerous Drugs: Report of the United States Mexico Joint Working Group." December 12, 1969.

United States v. Edwin Manica Flores. Indictment 18 U.S.C. § 1962(d)—Conspiracy to Conduct Enterprise Affairs Through a Pattern of Racketeering Activity. United States District Court, District of Massachusetts. September 20, 2017.

United States v. Fabio Porfirio Lobo, 15 CR 0174, United States Southern District of New York. March 6, 2017.

United States v. Jaime Guillot Lara, Fernando Ravelo Renedo, Gonzalo Bassols Suarez, Aldo Santamaría. United States District Court Southern District of Florida, No. 82-643 Cr-Je, November 6, 1982. www.latinamericanstudies.org /drugs/indictment-82.htm.

United States v. Jesús Vicente "El Vicentillo" Zambada Niebla. Memorandum of Law in Support of Motion for Discovery Regarding Defense of Public Authority, United States District Court Northern District of Illinois Eastern Division, Case Number 09 CRC 383, November 10, 2011.

United States v. Juan García Ábrego. United States Court of Appeals, Fifth Circuit, No. 97-20130, May 5, 1996. http://caselaw.findlaw.com/us-5th-circuit/1396381 .html.

United States v. Juan Ramon Matta Ballesteros. "Order Denying Motion to Dismiss Indictment." No. PCR 86-00511-RV. 700 F. Supp 528. United States District Court, N.D. Florida, Pensacola Division, August 4, 1988.

United States v. Marciano Millan Vasquez. US District Court Western Division of Texas, San Antonio Division, Case Number: 5:13-CR-00655-XR, May 6, 2016.

United States v. Oumar Issa, Harouna Toure and Idriss Abelrahman. United States District Court, Southern District of New York. Docket Number 09MAG, Case Number 2719, United States Code Title 21 Section 960a, and Title 18 Section 2339B, December 15, 2009.

United States v. Rafael Caro Quintero. T.18, U.S.C.,§§ 924(c)(l)(A)(i),924(c)(l)(A) (ii),924(c)(l) (A)(iii). United States District Court Eastern District of New York, January 20, 2017.

Universidad de Costa Rica. "Narcotráfico, Democracia y Soberanía Nacional en Costa Rica." *Anuario de Estudios Centroamericanos* 25, no. 2 (1999): 33–47.

US Agency for International Development. *Central American and Mexican Gang Assessment.* Washington, DC: USAID Bureau for Latin American and Caribbean Affairs Office of Regional Sustainable Development, April 2006.

US Attorney's Office, Eastern District of New York. "Colombian Trafficker with Links to Mexican and Colombian Cartels Extradited from Mexico to the United States." Washington, DC: United States Department of Justice, June 10, 2010. www.justice.gov/usao/nye/pr/2010/2010jun17.html.

US Attorney's Office, Newark, New Jersey. "National and International Leadership of MS-13 Indicted in New Jersey for Racketeering Conspiracy." US Department of Justice, July 17, 2014. www.fbi.gov/contact-us/field-offices/newark /news/press-releases/national-and-international-leadership-of-ms-13-indicted -in-new-jersey-for-racketeering-conspiracy.

US Attorney's Office, Southern District of New York. "Guatemalan Presidential Candidate Charged with Conspiring to Import Cocaine into the United States and Related Firearms Offense." US Department of Justice, April 17, 2019.

www.justice.gov/usao-sdny/pr/guatemalan-presidential-candidate-charged-conspiring-import-cocaine-united-states-and.

US Congress, House of Representatives and Senate. House Select Committee to Investigate Covert Arms Transactions with Iran and Senate Select Committee to Investigate Military Assistance to Iran and the Nicaraguan Opposition. Daniel Inouye and Lee H. Hamilton, Report of the Congressional Committees Investigating the Iran Contra Affair. S. Rept. no. 100-216 and H. Rept. no. 100-433.100th Cong., 1st sess., November 17, 1987.

US Congress, House of Representatives. Appropriations Committee. Subcommittee on State Foreign Operations and Related Programs. *Security Challenges to Latin America.* 112th Cong., 2nd sess., March 29, 2012. www.state.gov/j/inl/rls/rm/187097.htm.

———. Committee on Foreign Affairs. *Developments in Latin American Narcotics Control, November 1985.* 99th Cong., 1st sess., November 12, 1985.

———. Committee on Foreign Affairs. *Emerging Threats and Security in the Western Hemisphere: The Next Steps for U.S. Policy.* Serial No. 112-75, 112th Cong., 2nd sess., October 13, 2011.

———. Committee on Foreign Affairs. Subcommittee on the Western Hemisphere. *Hearing on Violence in Central America.* 110th Cong., 1st sess., June 26, 2007.

———. Committee on Foreign Affairs. Subcommittee on the Western Hemisphere. *Central America and the Mérida Initiative.* 110th Cong., 2nd sess., May 8, 2008.

———. Committee on Foreign Affairs. *The World Narcotics Problem: The Latin American Perspective: Report of Special Study Mission to Latin America and the Federal Republic of Germany.* 93rd Cong., 1st sess., March 21, 1973.

———. Committee on Foreign Relations. Senate Executive Report 104-3. *Treaty with Panama on Mutual Assistance in Criminal Matters.* 105th Cong., 1st sess., May 1, 1995.

———. Committee on Government Operations. *Law Enforcement on the Southwest Border: Hearings Before the Subcommittee of the Committee on Government Operations.* 93rd Cong., 2nd sess., August 10–14, 1974.

———. Committee on Homeland Security. Subcommittee on Border, Maritime, and Global Counterterrorism. *The Mérida Initiative: Examining United States Efforts to Combat Transnational Criminal Organizations.* 110th Cong., 2nd sess., June 5, 2008.

———. Committee on International Relations. Subcommittee on the Western Hemisphere of the Committee on International Relations. *Illicit Drug Transit Zone in Central America,* 109th Cong., 1st sess., November 9, 2005.

———. Committee on International Relations. *The Shifting Pattern of Narcotics Trafficking: Report of a Study Mission to Mexico, Costa Rica, Panama, and Colombia.* 94th Cong., 2nd sess., January 6–18, 1976.

———. Committee on Oversight and Government Reform. *Operation Fast and Furious: The Other Side of the Border.* 112th Cong., 1st Sess. July 26, 2011. www.govinfo.gov/content/pkg/CHRG-112hhrg72802/html/CHRG-112hhrg72802.htm.

———. House Report 105-780. *Intelligence Authorization Act for Fiscal Year 1999, Comments by Reps. Millinder-McDonald, A Tangled Web: A History of CIA Complicity in Drug International Trafficking.* 105 Cong. 2nd sess., May 7, 1998.

———. Select Committee on Narcotics Abuse and Control. *Investigation of Narcotics and Money Laundering in Chicago Report of the Select Committee on Narcotics Abuse and Control.* 95th Cong., 1st sess., February 1978.

340 Bibliography

———. Subcommittee on National Security and Foreign Affairs Committee on Oversight and Government Reform. *Transnational Drug Enterprises (Part II): Threats to Global Stability and U.S. Policy Responses.* 111th Cong., 2nd Sess., March 3, 2010.

———. Subcommittee on Security and Terrorism of the Committee on the Judiciary, the Subcommittee on Western Hemisphere Affairs of the Foreign Relations Committee, and the Senate Drug Enforcement Caucus. *The Cuban Government's Involvement in Facilitating International Drug Traffic.* 98th Cong., 1st sess., April 30, 1983.

———. Subcommittee on Western Hemisphere Affairs of the Committee on International Relations. *The Illicit Drug Transit Zone in Central America.* 109th Cong., 1st sess., November 9, 2005.

———. *Foreign Operations, Export Financing, and Related Programs Appropriations Act, 1994.* Public Law 104-107, HR 2295, 103rd Cong., 1st sess., September 30, 1993.

US Congress. Senate. Caucus on International Narcotics Control. *Adapting U.S. Counternarcotics Efforts in Colombia,* 115 Cong., 1st sess., September 12, 2017.

———. Caucus on International Narcotics Control. *U.S.-Mexican Reponses to Mexican Drug Trafficking Organizations.* 112th Cong., 1st sess., May 25, 2011.

———. Committee on Foreign Relations. *Central America: Hearing Before the Committee on Foreign Relations.* 98th Cong., 1st sess., August 4, 1983.

———. Committee on Foreign Relations. *International Traffic in Narcotics: Hearing Before the Committee on Foreign Relations.* 92nd Cong., 1st sess., July 1, 1971.

———. Committee on Foreign Relations. Subcommittee on the Western Hemisphere, Peace Corps, Narcotics, and Terrorism. *International Organized Crime Syndicates and Their Impact on the United States.* 105th Cong., 2nd sess., February 26, 1998.

———. Committee on Foreign Relations. *U.S. Policy Options with Respect to Nicaragua and Aid to the Contras: Hearing Before the Committee on Foreign Relations.* 100th Cong., 1st sess., January 28, 1987.

———. Committee on Government Operations. *Federal Drug Enforcement Part 5: Hearings Before the Permanent Subcommittees on Investigations.* 94th Cong., 2nd sess., August 23–26, 1976.

———. Committee on Government Operations. *Illicit Traffic in Weapons and Drugs Across the United States Mexican Border.* 95th Cong., 1st sess., January 12, 1977.

———. Committee on Governmental Affairs, Permanent Subcommittee on Investigations. *Structure of International Trafficking Organizations.* 101st Cong., 1st sess., September 12–13, 1989.

———. Committee on the Judiciary. *Federal Efforts to Stem the Flow of Drugs Across the U.S.-Mexican Border.* 95th Cong., 1st sess., April 18, 1978.

———. Committee on the Judiciary of the United States Senate. *World Drug Traffic and Its Impact on U.S. Security, Hearings Before the Subcommittee to Investigate the Administration of the Internal Security Act and Other Internal Security Laws.* 92nd Cong., 2nd sess., August 14, 1972.

———. Subcommittee on Alcoholism and Drug Abuse of the Committee on Labor and Human Resources. *Drugs and Terrorism, 1984.* 98th Cong., 2nd sess., August 2, 1984.

———. Subcommittee on Alcoholism and Drug Abuse of the Committee on Labor and Human Resources. *Nicaraguan Government Involvement in Narcotics Trafficking.* 99th Cong., 2nd sess., March 11, 1986.

Bibliography 341

———. Subcommittee on Alcoholism and Drug Abuse of the Committee on Labor and Human Resources. *Role of Nicaragua in Drug Trafficking.* 99th Cong., 1st sess., April 19, 1985.

———. Subcommittee on Terrorism, Narcotics, and International Operation of the Committee on Foreign Relations. *Drugs, Law Enforcement, and Foreign Policy.* 100th Cong., 2nd sess., December 1988.

———. Subcommittee on Terrorism, Narcotics, and International Communications. *Drugs, Law Enforcement, and Foreign Policy: Panama.* 100th Cong., 2nd sess., February 8–11, 1988.

US Department of Justice, Office of the Inspector General. *The Review of ATF's Operation Fast and Furious and Related Matters.* Washington, DC: US Department of Justice, September 2012.

———. "United States Announces RICO Charges Against Leadership of Colombia's Most Powerful Cocaine Cartel." Washington, DC: US Department of Justice, May 6, 2004.

US Department of State, Bureau of Democracy, Human Rights, and Labor. *2002 Country Reports on Human Rights and Labor: Guatemala.* Washington, DC: US Department of State, March 31, 2003. www.state.gov/j/drl/rls/hrrpt/2002/18333.htm.

———. Marcy, William L. Personal Archive. US State Department Declassification Process (2009–2016).

———. "Economic Sanctions Against Nicaragua." *U.S. Department of State Bulletin* 85, July 1985.

———. "Narcotics Rewards Program: Rafael Caro Quintero." www.state.gov/j/inl/narc/rewards/215334.htm.

———. "Nicaragua: The Stolen Revolution." *U.S. Department of State Bulletin* 85, June 1985.

———. "Review of Nicaragua's Commitments to the OAS." *U.S. Department of State Bulletin* 84, September 1984.

———. "Statement by Deputy Secretary of State Warren Christopher Before the Subcommittee of Foreign Operations, U.S. House of Representatives." Washington, DC: US Department of State, September 11, 1979.

———. "Vital National Interests: Certification Mexico." Washington, DC: US Department of State, February 9, 1996.

———. *Background Paper: Central America.* Washington, DC Department of State, May 27, 1983.

———. *Background Paper: Nicaragua's Military Build-up and Support for Central American Subversion.* Washington, DC: US Department of State, July 18, 1984.

———. Bureau of Democracy, Human Rights, and Labor. *Honduras Human Rights Practices, 1995.* Washington, DC: US Department of State, January 31, 1994. www.refworld.org.

———. Bureau of Democracy, Human Rights, and Labor. *Panama.* Washington, DC: US Department of State, February 28, 2005. www.state.gov/j/drl/rls/hrrpt/2004/41769.htm.

———. Bureau of Intelligence and Research. "Mexico: Outlook for the López Portillo Administration." US Department of State report number 675, January 6, 1977.

———. Bureau of International Narcotics and Law Enforcement Affairs. "Fact Sheet: Counternarcotics and Law Enforcement Country Program: Costa Rica." Washington, DC: US Department of State, May 13, 2010. www.state.gov/j/inl/rls/fs/141844.htm.

———. Bureau of International Narcotics and Law Enforcement Affairs. "Narcotics Rewards Program: Jorge Mario Paredes-Cordova." Washington, DC:

342   *Bibliography*

US Department of State, May 1, 2008. www.state.gov/j/inl/narc/rewards/115398
.htm.

———. Bureau of International Narcotics and Law Enforcement Affairs. *1995 International Narcotics Control Strategy Report.* Washington, DC: US Department of State, March 1995. In 1995 the INM was renamed the Bureau of International Narcotics and Law Enforcement Affairs.

———. Bureau of International Narcotics and Law Enforcement Affairs. *1996 International Narcotics Control Strategy Report.* Washington, DC: US Department of State, March 1997.

———. Bureau of International Narcotics and Law Enforcement Affairs. *1997 International Narcotics Control Strategy Report.* Washington, DC: US Department of State, March 1998.

———. Bureau of International Narcotics and Law Enforcement Affairs. *1998 International Narcotics Control Strategy Report.* Washington, DC: US Department of State, March 1999.

———. Bureau of International Narcotics and Law Enforcement Affairs. *1999 International Narcotics Control Strategy Report.* Washington, DC: US Department of State, March 2000.

———. Bureau of International Narcotics and Law Enforcement Affairs. *2003 International Narcotics Control Strategy Report Vol. I.* Washington, DC: US Department of State, March 2004.

———. Bureau of International Narcotics and Law Enforcement Affairs. *2005 International Narcotics Control Strategy Report Vol. I.* Washington, DC: US Department of State, March 2005.

———. Bureau of International Narcotics and Law Enforcement Affairs. *2006 International Narcotics Control Strategy Report Vol. I.* Washington, DC: US Department of State, March 2006.

———. Bureau of International Narcotics and Law Enforcement Affairs. *2007 International Narcotics Control Strategy Report Vol. I.* Washington, DC: US Department of State, March 2007.

———. Bureau of International Narcotics and Law Enforcement Affairs. *2008 International Narcotics Control Strategy Report Vol. I.* Washington, DC: US Department of State, March 2008.

———. Bureau of International Narcotics and Law Enforcement Affairs. *2009 International Narcotics Control Strategy Report Vol. I.* Washington, DC: US Department of State, March 2009.

———. Bureau of International Narcotics and Law Enforcement Affairs. *2010 International Narcotics Control Strategy Report Vol. I.* Washington, DC: US Department of State, March 2010.

———. Bureau of International Narcotics and Law Enforcement Affairs. *2011 International Narcotics Control Strategy Report Vol. I.* Washington, DC: US Department of State, March 2011.

———. Bureau of International Narcotics and Law Enforcement Affairs. *2012 International Narcotics Control Strategy Report Vol. I.* Washington, DC: US Department of State, March 2012.

———. Bureau of International Narcotics and Law Enforcement Affairs. *2015 International Narcotics Control Strategy Report Vol. I.* Washington, DC: US Department of State, March 2015.

———. Bureau of International Narcotics and Law Enforcement Affairs. *2016 International Narcotics Control Strategy Report Vol. I.* Washington, DC: US Department of State, March 2016.

Bibliography 343

———. Bureau of International Narcotics and Law Enforcement Affairs. *2018 International Narcotics Control Strategy Report Vol. I*. Washington, DC: US Department of State, March 2018.

———. Bureau of International Narcotics and Law Enforcement Affairs. *2019 International Narcotics Control Strategy Report Vol. I*. Washington, DC: US Department of State, March 28, 2019.

———. Bureau of International Narcotics Matters. *1985 International Narcotics Control Strategy Report to the Committee on Foreign Relations and the Committee on Foreign Affairs*. Washington, DC: US Department of State, February 1985.

———. Bureau of International Narcotics Matters. *1988 International Narcotics Control Strategy Report*. Washington, DC: US Department of State, March 1989.

———. Bureau of International Narcotics Matters. *1989 International Narcotics Control Strategy Report*. Washington, DC: US Department of State, March 1990.

———. Bureau of International Narcotics Matters. *1991 International Narcotics Control Strategy Report*. Washington, DC: US Department of State, March 1992.

———. Bureau of International Narcotics Matters. *1993 International Narcotics Control Strategy Report*. Washington, DC: US Department of State, March 1994.

———. *Central America Briefing Paper*. Washington, DC: US Department of State, January 5, 1985.

———. *Communist Interference in El Salvador*. Washington, DC: US Department of State, 1981.

———. Division J. Foreign Operations and Related Programs Appropriations Act, 2015. Report No. 114–79. 114th Cong., 1st sess., July 9, 2015.

———. *El Salvador: The Search for Peace*. Washington, DC: US Department of State, September 1981.

———. Office of the Spokesperson. *U.S.-Mexico Joint Declaration*. Washington, DC: US Department of State, June 7, 2019.

———. Overseas Security Advisory Council. "Panama 2019: Crime and Safety Report." US Department of State, Bureau of Diplomatic Security, March 27, 2019. www.osac.gov/Country/Panama/Content/Detail/Report/c101bd67-03d9 -41b2-91ac-15f4aebd03de.

———. *Revolution Beyond Our Borders*. Washington, DC: US Department of State, September 1985.

———. *The Soviet-Cuban Connection in Central America and the Caribbean*. Washington, DC: US Department of State, 1985.

———. *Central America*. Washington, DC: November 20, 1987.

US Drug Enforcement Agency. *The DEA Years: DEA History Book 1970–1975*. Washington, DC. www.dea.gov/sites/default/files/2018-07/1970-1975%20p %2030-39.pdf.

US Federal Bureau of Investigation. FBI Laboratory Quantico Virginia to Phoenix Squad C-6/Tucson RA SA Michelle L. Terwilliger. "Report of Examination: Brian Terry (Victim); U.S. Border Patrol Agent; Assault on Federal Officer." Federal Bureau of Investigation Case Number 89B-PX-86010. December 23, 2010.

US Southern Command. "Operation Martillo." Doral, FL. August 22, 2016. www .southcom.mil/newsroom/Pages/Operation-Martillo.aspx.

———. "News: Operation Enduring Freedom." Doral, FL. www.southcom.mil /newsroom/Pages/Enduring-Friendship-program.aspx.

US Treasury. "Press Release: Treasury Targets Drug Trafficking Networks in Colombia and Mexico." Washington, DC. July 15, 2010. www.treasury.gov /press-center/press-releases/Pages/tg775.aspx.

344 Bibliography

———. Office of Foreign Assets Control. "Designations Pursuant to the Foreign Narcotics Kingpin Designation Act." Washington, DC. June 1, 2001. www.treasury.gov/resource-center/sanctions/OFAC-Enforcement/Pages/20010601.aspx.

Valdez, Al, and René Enríquez. *Urban Street Terrorism: The Mexican Mafia and the Sureños*. Santa Ana, CA: Police and Fire Publishing, 2011.

Véliz, Rodrigo. "El Caso SAT: el legado de la inteligencia militar." *Centro de Medios Independientes de Guatemala*, April 17, 2015. https://cmiguate.org/el-caso-sat-el-legado-de-la-inteligencia-militar.

Veloza, Gustavo. *La Guerra Entre los Carteles del Narcotráfico*. Bogotá: G. S. Editores, 1988.

Wagner, Stephen J., and Donald Schulz. *The Awakening: The Zapatista Revolt and Its Implications for Civil-Military Relations and the Future of Mexico*. Carlisle Barracks, PA: Strategic Studies Institute, US Army War College, December 30, 2004.

Waller, Michael J. *Financing Terrorism in El Salvador: The Secret Support Network for the FMLN*. Washington, DC: Council for Interamerican Security, June 4, 1987.

Walsh, Lawrence E. *Final Report of the Independent Counsel for Iran/Contra Matters*. Washington, DC: US Court of Appeals for the District of Colombia Circuit, August 1983.

Watt, Peter, and Roberto Zepeda. *Drug War Mexico: Politics, Neoliberalism, and Violence in the New Narcoeconomy*. London: Zed Books, 2012.

Weathers, Bynum E. *Guerrilla Warfare in Nicaragua: 1975–1979*. Maxwell Air Force Base, AL: Documentary Research Division Center for Aerospace Design, Research and Education, November 1983.

Webb, Gary. *Dark Alliance: The CIA, Contras, and the Crack Cocaine Explosion*. Toronto: Hudson House, 1998.

Whelan, James Robert, and Franklin A. Jaeckle. *The Soviet Assault on America's Southern Flank*. Washington, DC: Regnery Gateway, 1988.

White House Office of the Press Secretary. Remarks by President Obama and President Funes of El Salvador in Joint Press Conference. National Palace San Salvador, El Salvador, March 22, 2011. www.whitehouse.gov/the-press-office/2011/03/22/remarks-president-obama-and-president-funes-el-salvador-joint-press-conf.

Wickham-Crowley, Timothy P. *Guerrillas and Revolution in Latin America*. Princeton: Princeton University Press, 1992.

WikiLeaks. Public Library of US Diplomacy. https://wikileaks.org.

Williams, Paul L. *The Al Qaeda Connection: International Terrorism, Organized Crime, and the Coming Apocalypse*. Amherst, NY: Prometheus Books, 2005.

Winslow, Robert, and Emmanuel Martínez. *Crime and Society: A Comparative Criminology Tour of the World–Nicaragua*. San Diego: San Diego State University. www.rohan.sdsu.edu/faculty/rwinslow/namerica.html.

Wolf, Sonja. "Mano Dura: Gang Suppression in El Salvador." Oxford Research Group, Sustainable Security, March 2011. www.academia.edu/503075/Mano_Dura_Gang_Suppression_in_El_Salvador.

World Bank. *World Economic Development Indicators*. Washington, DC. 2020. https://data.worldbank.org/indicator.

Index

Acapulco, 20, 75, 272, 305; Cártel Independiente de Acapulco (CIDA), 268; cartel war over, 269; Icacos naval base, 181
Acosta Villareal, Pablo, 2, 66–67, 74–75, 103
aerial counternarcotics operations: eradication and interdiction in Mexico, 25; ten-ton cocaine seizure in Mexico, 110; US-Mexican bilateral programs, 18
aerial photographic detection system, 25
Agencia Federal de Investigación (AFI; Federal Bureau of Investigation, Mexico), 206–207, 219
Aguilar Guajardo, Rafael, 75; formation of the Juárez cartel, 75
aid: Central American Regional Security Initiative (CARSI), 246–250; Contra leaders diverting US aid, 53; Mérida Initiative, 245–246; total US assistance for the Mérida Initiative, 211(fig.); US aid to Costa Rica's counternarcotics units, 154–155; US aid to Honduras, 39, 57(n16); US aid to Nicaragua's counternarcotics program, 153; US military aid to Mexico, 204–206, 211–212; US phasing out aid to Central America, 141. *See also* Mérida Initiative
air trafficking, 66; air-interdiction programs, 119; Cali cartel establishing routes, 104–105, 107–108; CARSI action pillars, 247–248; Colombian-Mexican corridor, 102–103; El Salvador's counternarcotics program, 149; guerrilla groups protecting shipments, 113; Honduras's counternarcotics programs, 150–151; Nicaragua's maritime and air drug corridors, 120–121; Panama's Narcoavioneta scandal, 244; smuggling through El Salvador, 117–118

Alem León, Ricardo, 123–124
Alemán Lacayo, Arnoldo, 283
Alianza Republicana Nacionalista (ARENA; El Salvador), 38, 57(n13), 148; allegations of drug trafficking, 117, 135(n113), 230
Alianza Revolucionaria Democrática (ARDE; Democratic Revolutionary Alliance, Nicaragua), 51–52, 55, 58–59(n34), 58(n33)
al-Qaeda, 204–205
Arellano Félix cartel, 73–74, 76, 82(n59), 195(n15); cartel wars and expansion of, 89; gang involvement, 7; manhunt for cartel members, 87; war against the other cartels, 181–183. *See also* cartel wars; Juárez cartel
Arias, Oscar, 42, 123, 154
arms trafficking, 28; ARDE's drugs-for-guns enterprise, 51–52; Central American operations, 112; Costa Rica, 44, 121–124; Cuban provision of weapons for M-19 guerrillas, 49–50; El Salvador's increase in violent crime, 231–233; on the Guatemalan-Mexican border, 229–230; Guatemala's drug trade and, 276–277; Medellín cartel's Mexican connection, 103; Noriega's provisions for the Movimeinto Abril 19, 45; US Fast and Furious gun-running operation, 217–219; violence and crime following the Chapultepec Peace Accord, 116
Aronson, Bernard, 94
assassinations, 5; Aguilar Guajardo, 75; assassination plot against General González, 236–237; attempts on El Cacho, 77; Buendía's murder, 69–70; Cardinal Posadas Ocampo, 74, 86–90; cartel wars, 85, 192; CJNG war with the Mexican government, 271–272; Donaldo

345

346   Index

Colosio, 5, 11, 90, 96; El Chava, 186; Falcón's CIA involvement, 66; Guatemalan justice, 114–115; Guatemala's drug war, 230; journalists and human rights defenders, 266, 273; mano dura approach to gang violence, 161–165; Nicaragua's Chamorro, 40; Pastora, 44; Rodolfo Carrillo Fuentes, 184–185; Ruiz Massieu, 93–94; Salcido Uzeta, 105; school for assassins in Honduras, 236; Somoza, 58(n29); torture and murder of Kiki Camarena, 3, 68–72, 74–75, 80(n29). *See also* homicides
authoritarian governance: the shift from political to criminal violence, 3–8
autodefensas, 268–269
Autodefensas Unidas de Colombia (AUC), 109–110, 119, 241, 243, 268–268, 291(n7)
auto-golpe (self-coup), Guatemala's, 37
Avianca Flight 203, bombing of, 304–305
aviation, trafficking by. *See* air trafficking
Avilés Pérez, Pedro, 2, 66–68, 72, 185(n3)
Ayotzinapa Rural Teachers' College, kidnappings from, 269

Baja California, 20, 66, 67, 74, 183, 271; drug smuggling in 105, 108, 187; extrajudicial killings in 213
balance of payments crisis: Costa Rica, 43; Mexico, 90–91
Banco Internacional, 75–76
Bandas Emergentes y Bandas Criminales (BACRIM; Colombia), 110, 243, 265
banderos (members of organized crime groups), 226
Bank of Commerce and Credit International (BCCI), 45
banking, money laundering and, 67–68, 75–76, 106, 125, 173(n110), 287
Barrio 18 gang, 277, 279, 280. *See also* Calle 18
Bay Islands, 119, 151
beheadings, 190, 203–204
Beltrán Leyva cartel, 179–181, 184, 207, 267, 286
Berger, Óscar, 164, 228, 244
bilateral relations (US and Central American countries): Honduras's counternarcotics programs, 150–151; Nicaragua's counternarcotics program, 151–152; regional counternarcotics programs, 143; security sector spending, 275–276
bilateral relations (US and Mexico): effect of López Obrador's presidency on, 273; Mexico's political and military corruption, 23, 27–29, 266–267, 305–306; Operation Intercept straining, 17–18; US policy considerations, 306–307; US-Mexican counternarcotics programs under Nixon,

16–17. *See also* war on drugs (Mexico and the US)
Bi-National Drug Control Strategy (1998), 204
Bitcoin, 280
Bluefields, 6, 121, 238
border activities: human trafficking along the Guatemalan-Mexican border, 229–230; narcotrafficking along the Guatemala-Mexico border, 112–113; Sandinistas' disruptions on the Nicaraguan-Honduran border, 39–40; smuggling economy, 23
border control, 16; failing to control trafficking from 1974-1978, 24; keeping Guatemala's borders insecure, 115; Nicaragua's border security with Costa Rica, 284–285; Operation Intercept and Operation Cooperation, 15, 17–18
Borge, Tomás, 48–49
Brownfield, William R., 247, 250
Bukele Ortez, Nayib, 279–280
Bureau of Alcohol, Tobacco, and Firearms (ATF; US): Fast and Furious gun-running operation, 217–219
Bureau of Narcotics and Dangerous Drugs (BNDD), 16, 18

Calderón Fournier, Rafael, 154
Calderón Hinojosa, Felipe, 208–210, 212–213, 215, 219–220, 263
Cali cartel (Colombia), 45, 72; the collapse facilitating Mexico DTO dominance, 108–110; Colombia's BACRIM syndicate, 110; controlling Mexican traffic routes, 104–106; creation of minicartels, 101–102; money laundering, 106; smuggling through El Salvador, 117–118
Calle 18 (18th Street) gang, 5, 159–160, 226, 232–233, 277–280
Camarena Salazar, Enrique "Kiki": torture and murder, 3, 68–72, 74–75, 80(n29)
campaign contributions: corruption in Costa Rica, 124; Mexican scandal over, 265–266
campesino population: allegations of Caro Quintero's crimes against, 68; Costa Rica's economic crisis, 43; crop substitution programs, 26–27; dirty war, 21–22; El Chapo's employees, 73; El Salvador's abortive land reforms, 38; rebellion against the PRI government, 85; resistance to crop eradication programs, 19–22; vigilante groups during the cartel war, 268–269; Zapatista rebellion, 92–93, 96
Cancún, 20, 75–76, 105, 305
Cárdenas Guillén, Osiel, 181, 186, 203
Caro Quintero, Rafael, 287; escape, 81(nn38, 44); the Guadalajara cartel, 67–68; marijuana trafficking, 66; sentencing,

Index 347

81(n45); torture and murder of Kiki Camarena, 68–71

Carrillo Fuentes, Amado "El Señor de los Cielos," 67, 74–75, 89–90, 96, 106, 180–181, 184, 195(n15); Acosta Villareal's death, 74–75; agreement with the Cali cartel, 105–106; Cali cartel operations in Mexico, 106; collapse of the Cali cartel, 108–109; Colombian-Mexican narcotrafficking route, 102. *See also* Juárez cartel

Carrillo Fuentes, Vicente "El Viceroy," 180, 184, 185, 206, 267

Cártel de Jalisco Nuevo Generación (CJNG), 3, 179, 192–193, 271–272, 274, 287, 294(n44)

Cartel del Noreste (CDN), 268

cartel networks: Mexico's first-generation *narcotraficantes*, 66–67

cartel wars (Mexico), 305; Arellano Félix cartel's war, 181–183; Beltrán Leyva, 186, 193, 267–268; cartel evolution resulting from, 267–268; CJNG, 192–193; El Chapo, 76, 85, 182–186, 193–194; Guatemalan smugglers' involvement in, 229–230; Gulf cartel, 185–187; Juárez cartel, 184–185; La Familia Michoacana, 189–191; Los Zetas, 188–189; murder of Cardinal Posadas Ocampo, 86–90; redirecting activity to Central America, 225; rise of new cartels, 187–188; shifting alliances from 2007-2014, 193–194; Sinaloa cartel federation, 180–181; third wave, 8–9

Carteles Unidos, 200(n100)

cartels, Colombian: the legacy of Central America's civil wars, 56; Mexican cartels replacing, 96; moving into Central America, 111–112; narcotraffic through Nicaragua, 120–121; opening operations in Guatemala, 112–115. *See also* Cali cartel; Medellín cartel

cartels, Mexican: Central America's Mexican cartels-youth gangs connection, 225–227; Colombians building a narcotrafficking route, 101–102; evolution of, 2–3; moving into Central America, 111–112; narcotraffic through Nicaragua, 120–121; opening operations in Guatemala, 112–115; shifting operations into Central America, 110–111; street gangs and, 225–227; US Fast and Furious gun-running operation, 217–219. *See also* Arellano Félix cartel; Guadalajara cartel; Gulf cartel; Juárez cartel; Sinaloa cartel

Castro, Fidel, 46, 51, 66

Catholic Church, 42; Jesuits, 306; the murder of Cardinal Posadas Ocampo, 74, 86–90; Papal Nunciature and Noriega, 47

Central America: cocaine seizures, 2010–2020, 275(fig.); Colombian and Mexican cartels moving into, 110–112; Colombianization of, 304–306; effect of CARSI on the security situation, 274–276; extrajudicial killings of gang members, 165–166; inability to address the growth of narcotrafficking, 141; Iran-Contra scandal, 63(n100); mano dura approach to gang violence, 161–165; Mérida Initiative, 245–246; Mexico's war on drugs spilling over into, 157–158; Noriega and Contra operations in Panama, 46–47; origins of the gang problem, 158–161; refugee crisis, 288–290. *See also* civil wars; *specific countries*

Central American Free Trade Agreement (CAFTA), 160–161

Central American Regional Security Initiative (CARSI), 8, 11, 244–251, 274–276, 282, 304; Central American refugee crisis, 288–289; militarization of the war on drugs, 5; pillars, 247–248. *See also* civil wars

Central Intelligence Agency (CIA): Central American drug trade and counternarcotics operations, 111; Falcón's ties, 66; Honduran narcotrafficking, 118–119; Iran-Contra scandal, 45–46; Los Brasiles sting operation, 48; Nicaragua's Contra war, 42; torture and murder of Kiki Camarena, 69–70, 80(n29); US-Contra connection and drug trafficking, 51–554

Centro de Investigación y Seguridad Nacional (CISEN), 65, 71–72, 81(n52), 206; Colosio assassination, 90; Carrillo Olea, 141; El Chapo's second escape, 293(n34); ISIS in Mexico, 289

certification procedures, 94–95, 204, 228–229

Chamorro, Violeta, 43, 151–153

Chapultepec Peace Accord (1992), 115–116

Chaves Robles, Rodrigo, 286

Chiapas, 1, 20; drug trafficking, 93, 96, 107; MS-13, 164, 227, 229; Los Zetas, 189, 268, 292(n21); Zapatistas (EZLN), 85, 92–93

Chinchilla, Laura, 246, 249, 284–286

civil wars (Central America), 1–2, 4; Costa Rica, 43–44; creation of the Mexican narcocorridor, 303–304; El Salvador, 38–39; El Salvador's military narcotrafficking, 116–117; Guatemala, 36–37; Honduras's secret war, 39–40; keeping Guatemala's borders insecure, 115; legacy of violence, 5–6; the legacy of violence and drugs, 54–56; narcotrafficking after the civil wars, 111–112; Nicaragua, 40–41; origins of the gang problem, 158–159; Oslo Accords, 142

clikas (semiautonomous cells), 161, 164, 226–227, 279

348   Index

Clinton, Bill: El Salvador as a country of concern, 149; Mexico's decertification, 95, 204

coca production: Andean growth in, 263–264, 264(fig.); Guatemala, 277; Honduras, 282; Panama, 125

cocaine trafficking, 74, 263; Central American seizures, 2010–2020, 275(fig.); during Central America's civil wars and guerrilla insurgencies, 35–36; coca growing in Guatemala, 277; Colombian-Mexican corridor, 102–104; connection to terrorist organizations, 205; Costa Rica as transshipment point, 122–123; Cuban involvement in, 50–51; facilitating the Colombia-Mexico connection, 101–102; financing Contra operations, 42–43; formation of the Juárez cartel, 75; Guadalajara cartel monopoly, 65, 67–68; Guatemala's trafficking and corruption, 115, 231; Gulf cartel cocaine seizure, 186–187; Gulf cartel transformation, 77–78; Honduran traffickers, 118–120, 282; increasing violence surrounding, 7–8; Mexican seizures, 2000–2005, 209(fig.); Mexican seizures, 2006–2012, 215(fig.); mixing fentanyl with, 274; Nicaragua's interdiction operations, 152, 284; Noriega and the Medellín cartel, 45–47; by Panamanian officials, 125; Panama's trafficking, 242, 286–288; Sandinistas' involvement in, 48–49; seizure figures, 1989–1995, 89(fig.); seizure figures, 2010–2020, 265(fig.); ten-ton seizure in Mexico, 110; through El Salvador, 115–118; US investigation of the Contras, 51–54. *See also* Cali cartel; interdiction; Medellín cartel

Coello Trejo, Javier, 83(n72), 95, 101–102, 185–186

Cold War: US support for Central American oligarchies, 35; US-Soviet assistance to revolutionary and counterrevolutionary forces, 4

Colombia: Castro's mediation between Noriega and the Medellín cartel, 46; Matta-Ballesteros's incarceration, 63(n103); Plan Colombia, 246; shifting narcotrafficking to Mexico from, 1–2, 5. *See also* Cali cartel; cartels, Colombian; Medellín cartel

"Colombian necktie," 73–74

Colombianization, 13(n15), 141, 304–306

Colón Free Trade Zone (CFTZ), 124–126, 139(n220), 146, 243, 286–287

Colosio Murrieta, Luis Donaldo, 11, 85, 90–93, 96

Comisión Centroamericana Permanente (CCP), 143

Comisión Interamericana para el Control del Abuso de Drogas (CICAD), 142

community policing initiative, 248–249

conflict. *See* war and conflict

Congress, US: decertification of Mexico, 94–95; Fast and Furious operation and investigation, 218; human rights conditions on Mérida Initiative's assistance, 213–214; Iran-Contra scandal, 47, 60(n57); tracking Mexico's money laundering, 211

constitutional crisis, Honduras, 235–236

consumer demand for narcotics: CARSI initiative failures, 249; Costa Rica's counternarcotics initiative, 155, 158, 239–240; DARE program implementation, 248–249; DEA eradication programs, 25; Guatemala's counternarcotics initiative, 144; López Obrador's view of the drug war, 272–273; Mérida Initiative goals, 210; Panama's counternarcotics initiative, 156; reducing demand for narcotrafficked products, 28–29, 95–96; US policy considerations, 306–307

Contadora peace process, 42–43

Contras, Nicaraguan: downing of a C-123, 59(n38); drug trafficking, 35–36; Honduran support for, 39–40; Iran-Contra scandal, 40, 45–46, 60(n57), 63(n100); murder of Kiki Camarena, 69; Nicaragua's Contra War, 42–43; Noriega and the Harari Network, 45–46; US investigation of narcotrafficking, 51–54

Coronel Villarreal, Ignacio, 192, 195(n4), 200(n100)

corruption, 245; Acosta Villareal's network, 67; Caro Quintero's payoffs, 68; Carrillo Fuentes's commercial success, 75–76; cartel control of military, politicians and police, 2–3; cartel wars and the struggle for Tijuana, 187–188; Central America and CARSI efforts, 275–276; Costa Rica, 123–124, 240–241, 285–286; Cuban drug trafficking case, 51; El Salvador's counternarcotics programs, 148–149; El Salvador's political elites, 117; the escape of Caro Quintero, 70; facilitating the Colombia-Mexico connection, 101–102; Fox's counternarcotics operations increasing Mexico's, 203–204; Gallardo and the Guadalajara cartel, 67–68; García Abrego bribing Mexican officials, 78; government involvement in the Massieu assassination, 93–94; Guatemalan human and narcotics trafficking, 229–231; Guatemala's high-level corruption scandals, 276–277; Guatemala's law enforcement, military, and political institutions, 114–115, 276–277;

Index   349

Guatemala's money laundering reform, 145; Gulf-Cali cartel connections, 105; Honduran reform and narcocorrruption, 234–235, 281–282; INCD protection of the cartels, 76; La Barbie's skill, 181; limiting Mexico's counternarcotics capabilities, 95–96; López Obrador campaign against, 272; luxurious incarceration of Caro Quintero, 70–71; Mexico's attempts to curtail institutional corruption, 206–207; Mexico's cartel war, 305; Mexico's Fox targeting, 219; Mexico's military, 207–208, 214; Mexico's movement towards state failure, 94–96; Mexico's persistent corruption and bilateral disputes, 27–29; Mexico's police, 15, 65–66, 106–107; NAFTA connection to drug trafficking, 92; Nicaragua under Ortega, 283–284; Nicaragua's police, 152–153; Nicaragua's Somoza, 40, 58(n22); Panama, 125, 243; Peña Nieto's policies and strategies, 265; police involvement in the Guadalajara cartel and Camarena's murder, 72; political involvement in drug trafficking, 22–23; Salvadoran officials' gang involvement, 280; shadows over Peña Nieto's administration, 265–267; stemming from Operation Intercept, 10; Texis cartel control in El Salvador, 278–279; widespread corruption of Mexico's public officials, 65–66
Costa Rica: ARDE's drugs-for-guns enterprise, 52; becoming a transit conduit, 239–241; cocaine seizures, 2010–2020, 275(fig.); counternarcotics efforts, 153–155, 284–286; drug trafficking through Nicaragua, 238–239; drugs and arms smuggling, 121–124; Nicaragua's Contra war, 42–43; Sandinistas' subversive activities, 59(n46); Vesco's flight, 61(n78); youth unemployment and the rise of gangs, 160–161
Council Nacional Anticorrupción (CNA; Honduras), 234–235
counterinsurgency operations, 5; Guatemala under Arévalo, 37; Sandinistas' activities in Honduras, 40
counternarcotics programs (Central America), 141; Costa Rica, 153–155; El Salvador, 146–149; Honduras, 149–151; military role in Guatemala, 143–146; Nicaragua, 151–153; Panama, 155–157; the permanency of narcotrafficking, 157; regional collaboration, 158; regional coordination, 142–143
counternarcotics strategies: Central America's programs, 11; history of US-Mexican cooperation, 16–17; López Obrador's declaration of de-escalation, 272–273; narcotics taking hold in

Mexico, 1974-1978, 24; Peña Nieto's policies, 263–264; US efforts in Mexico, 15–21. *See also* bilateral relations; Central American Regional Security Initiative; war on drugs (US)
coups d'état: coup against Manuel Zelaya, 235; Honduras, 118; Noriega, 60 (n53); Santa Elena Report (El Salvador), 117, 165; Serrano's *auto-golpe* in Guatemala, 37; Torrijos, 59(n50)
Coverdell-Feinstein Amendment (1997), 95
Cristiani, Alfredo, 117, 148
crop eradication programs, 15; eradication and interdiction efforts in Mexico, 18–22, 24–26; Guatemala's coca production, 277; Honduras's coca eradication, 282; marijuana eradication 1989–1995, 88(fig.); straining US-Mexican relations, 23
crop substitution programs, 26–27
Cuba: allegations of Sandinista-Cuban drug trafficking, 47–51; Castro's mediation between Noriega and the Medellín cartel, 46; Contra narcotrafficking, 55; Guatemalan revolutionaries, 36–37; Noriega's civilian paramilitary forces, 47; Operation Mongoose assassination program, 66; supporting Nicaragua's Sandinistas, 40–41; supporting Salvadoran guerrillas, 38
Culiacán, 20, 266; Félix Gallardo 67–68; police, 72; Ovidio Guzmán López, 271, 306
currency smuggling: Costa Rica-Nicaragua conduit, 238–239
Customs Service, US, 18, 53, 91, 117, 146, 147, 289, 290; El Chapo's tunnels, 73

Darién, 6, 125, 242, 286–287, 290
D'Aubuisson Arrieta, Roberto, 38, 117, 230
Death Command, Costa Rican Supreme Court kidnapping, 122–123
decapitations, 190, 203–204
Declaration of Alliance Against Drugs, 204
decriminalization of narcotics, 276, 306–307
Departamento de Operaciones Antinarcóticos (DOAN; Guatemala), 144–146
Department of Defense (SEDENA; Mexico), 26, 207, 212–213, 269, 272
Dignity Battalions (paramilitary force), 47
Dirección Federal de Seguridad (DFS; Mexico), 22, 53, 68–70, 72, 74–75, 77, 81–82(n52), 90, 98(n23), 106
dirty war (Mexico), 4, 10, 20–22
disappeared persons, 146, 165, 191, 272; El Salvador's civil war 38–39; Honduras 58(n21); Javier Duarte de Ochoa, 266; Jehovah's Witnesses 80(n35); Manuel Muñoz Rocha, 93; Mexico, 213; Panamanian money launderers, 286. *See*

also Ayotzinapa Rural Teachers' College; Sombra Negra

Drug Abuse Resistance Education (DARE) program, 248–249

Drug Enforcement Administration (DEA): Acosta Villareal's death, 74–75; air-interdiction programs, 119; the case of El Vicentillo, 216–217; Colombian-Mexican connection, 104; criminal violence by Mexico's cartels, 3; El Salvador's military narcotrafficking, 116–117; fentanyl threat, 274; Gulf cartel cocaine seizure, 186–187; high-level police corruption under Peña Nieto, 266–267; Honduran corruption scandals, 282; Mexico's decertification, 95; Nicaragua's maritime drug corridors, 120–121; souring of López Obrador's relationship with, 273; torture and murder of Kiki Camarena, 69–71. *See also* Camarena Salazar, Enrique "Kiki"

drugs-for-guns enterprises, 52–55, 103, 121

Echeverría, Luis, 19–21, 26, 66, 75

El Salvador: antigang efforts, 277–280; arms trafficking, 44; civil war, 4, 38–39, 54–55; cocaine seizures, 2010–2020, 275(fig.); Colombian and Mexican cocaine trafficking through, 115–118; Contras' drugs-for-guns enterprise, 52; counternarcotics programs, 146–149; creation of transnational criminal networks, 225–226; gang violence, 162; Honduran coca processing, 282; increasing gang violence, 231–233; targeting gang violence, 254(n63)

elections, 299(n126); Honduras, 118–119; Juárez cartel's campaign contributions to the PRI, 265–266; López Obrador campaign, 272; Nicaragua, 58–59(n34), 283–284

Endara Galimany, Guillermo, 125–126, 155–156

Escobar, Pablo, 45, 47–48, 51

Esparragoza Moreno, Juan José "El Azul," 180–181, 184, 194–195(n2), 195(n3), 291–292(n15)

Esquipulas I and II plans, 42–43, 142

Esquipulas Peace Agreement (1987), 120

Federal Bureau of Investigation (FBI), 25, 54, 63(n102), 74, 81(n44), 156, 227, 247, 248, 278; Fast and Furious gun-running operation, 217–219; Guatemala's drug war, 230; Transnational Anti-Gang Center, 162–163

Félix Gallardo, Miguel Ángel, 103; Avilés Pérez's connections to, 66–67; cartel evolution, 3; cartel wars, 85; Colombian-Mexican trafficking route, 102; drug

trafficking from prison, 72; Juárez-Sinaloa cartel alliance challenging, 76; Palma Salazar and, 72; partnership with El Chapo, 72–73; scope and reach of the Guadalajara cartel, 67–68; second-generation cartels, 65; torture and murder of Kiki Camarena, 71

fentanyl production, 274, 277

Ferrari, Mary and Mario, 118

Figueres Ferrer, José, 44, 59(n41)

Figueres Olsen, José, 154–155

financial sector. *See* money laundering

Fonseca Carrillo, Ernesto, 66–67; Carrillo Fuentes's entry into the drug trade, 74; the Guadalajara cartel, 67–68; torture and murder of Kiki Camarena, 70–71

Fox, Vicente, 5, 203, 206–208, 219–220

French Connection, 16, 103–104

Frente de Estudiantes Revolucionarios (FER), 21

Frente Farabundo Martí para la Liberación Nacional (FMLN; El Salvador), 38, 47, 113, 115–116, 146–149

Frente Sandinista de Liberación Nacional (FSLN), 40–41

Fuerzas Armadas Revolucionarias de Colombia (FARC), 7, 233–234, 236, 242–243, 257(n133), 283–284, 286–287

Fuerzas de Defensa de Panamá (PDF), 46–47, 60(n58), 155 (as Panama Defense Forces)

Funes Cartagena, Mauricio, 232–233, 246, 249, 277–278

Gallardo Rodríguez, José, 208

gang activity and culture, 254(n63); CARSI pillars for antigang programs, 248; cartels' turf wars, 268–269; Colombianization of Central America, 306; control of Guatemala's prison system, 277; El Salvador's increase in violent crime, 231–233; extrajudicial killings of gang members, 165–166; gang leaders replacing Guatemala's state, 231; Gulf cartel's internecine war, 268; Honduras's corruption scandals, 282; Honduras's criminalization of gang membership, 234; Honduras's homicide rate, 281–282; increasing crime in Central America, 244; mano dura approach to gang violence, 161–165; Mexican gang movement into Guatemala, 228–231; militarization of the war on drugs, 5; Nicaragua's post-war shift towards, 237–239; origins of, 158–161; Panama's networks and activities, 242–243, 287; role in Mexico's drug war, 304; Salvadoran antigang approach through negotiations, 277–280; Salvadoran underworld, 39; US linking terrorism to the war on drugs, 204–205. *See also* Central American Regional Security Initiative

García Ábrego, Juan, 3, 65, 77–78, 95–96, 105–106, 185–186

García Luna, Genaro, 267, 273, 291(n14), 305

Grupo Contacto de Alto Nivel para el Control de Drogas (GCAN), 204

Grupos Aeromómoviles de Fuerzas Especiales (GAFES), 186–188

Guadalajara cartel: Cali cartel's control of Mexican routes, 104–105; cartel evolution, 3; collapse of, 65; Colombian cartels expanding into Central America, 101–102; Colombian-Mexican connection, 104; El Güero and El Chapo, 72–73; formation of the Juárez cartel, 75; Gallardo's management of, 67–68; Matta-Ballesteros uniting the Medellín cartel with, 53; murder of Kiki Camarena, 68–72

Guardia Civil (Costa Rica), 154

Guatemala, 1; alternatives to the Colombian-Mexican route, 102, 110–111; Cali cartel operations across Mexico, 107; civil war and guerrilla insurgencies, 4, 36–37, 54–55; cocaine seizures, 2010–2020, 275(fig.); Colombian and Mexican cartels moving into, 111–115; creation of transnational criminal networks, 225–226; Duarte de Ochoa's refuge in, 266; extrajudicial killings of gang members, 166; gang violence, 163–164; military intelligence, 57; military role in counternarcotics efforts, 143–146; Oslo Accords ending the war, 142; Somoza's exile, 58(n29); state of emergency, 276–277; success of the CARSI program, 249

guerrilla organizations and insurgencies, 109–110, 257(n133); challenging Guatemala's military rule, 36–37; Cuban provision of weapons for M-19 guerrillas, 49–50; El Salvador, 38–39; Guatemala-Mexico border region, 113; militarization of the war on drugs, 5; military suppression, 35–36; Noriega's arms provisions for, 45; Panama's black market arms trafficking, 241; questioning Nicaragua's counternarcotics efforts, 283; resistance to crop eradication programs, 19–20; Sandinistas' activities in Honduras, 40; shifting from political to criminal violence, 3–4; US crop eradication programs in Mexico, 15. *See also* Frente Farabundo Martí para la Liberación Nacional

Gulf cartel, 65, 76–78; cartel wars, 185–187; Colombian cartels expanding into Central America, 101–102; evolution after the cartel war, 268; moving cocaine with the Cali cartel, 105; Panama operations, 286; trafficking through Costa Rica, 239–240. *See also* cartel wars; Juan García Ábrego; Osiel Cárdenas Guillén

Gulf of Fonseca, 6, 164

gunrunning. *See* arms trafficking

guns-for-drugs operations, 52–55, 66, 103, 121

Gutiérrez Rebollo, Jesús, 76

Guzmán Loera, Joaquín "El Chapo," 195(n4), 293(n35), 294(n42); arrest and incarceration, 89, 270–271; assassination of Rodolfo Carrillo Fuentes, 184–185; Avilés Perez and, 66; cartel wars, 85, 192–193; Honduran corruption scandal, 282; Juárez-Sinaloa cartel alliance, 76; manhunt for cartel members, 87–88; prison escape, 3, 293(n34); school for assassins in Honduras, 236; Sinaloa cartel, El Güero and, 72–73; Sinaloa cartel federation, 180–181; testimony about Mexico's corruption, 266; trial of, 267

Hernández Alvarado, Orlando, 281–282, 288

heroin production and trafficking, 16; CJNG expansion, 192; Colombia's minicartels, 109; eradication and interdiction, 24–25; FARC involvement, 233; Mexico's cartels controlling, 78, 265; mixing fentanyl with, 274; Panama's trafficking, 242; Salvadoran interdiction, 232; shipment routes through Central America, 111–112, 116, 122; taking hold in Mexico, 24. *See also* opium cultivation and trafficking

homicides, 1; Calle 18 gang violence, 159–160; Colombian cartels' kingpin strategy, 109; "Colombian necktie," 73–74; Costa Rica, 285–286; drug-related murders and violence, 7; extrajudicial killings of gang members, 165–166; Guatemala, 231; human trafficking along the Guatemalan-Mexican border, 229–230; increase after the cartel war, 272; increase in Central America, 244; increase in Costa Rica, 240; mano dura approach to gang violence, 161–165; Mexico's, 212–213, 213(fig.); during Mexico's 2021 midterm elections, 273; Mexico's cycle of death, 179; Panama, 242–243; police killings during cartel wars, 182–183; results of Fast and Furious, 218; Salvadoran antigang offensive, 279–280; using the National Guard to reduce, 273. *See also* assassinations

Honduras: cocaine seizures, 2010-2020, 275(fig.); cocaine transit route, 118–120; counternarcotics programs, 149–151; disappeared persons, 58(n21); extrajudicial killings of gang members, 166; gang violence, 163; Guatemala's cross-border trafficking, 229; guerrilla

352 Index

movements, 57(n20); migrant crisis, 290; Nicaragua's Contra war, 42–43; *plata o plomo* (bribery or bullets) operation, 231, 234–237; political reform and narcocorruption, 281–282; secret war, 39–40; US aid, 57(n16)

human rights abuses: CARSI implementation, 250; Guatemala, 37; Mexico's drug wars, 213–214, 303–304; Mexico's National Guard, 272

Human Rights Watch, 213–214

human trafficking, 205, 227, 229

Hurricane Mitch, 149, 151

Hurricane Stan, 229

Ilopango air base, 6, 52, 116

immigration: Central America's refugee crisis, 288–290; creation of Central American transnational criminal networks, 225–226

institution building: CARSI action pillars, 247–248

institutional reform: Mérida Initiative, 211

Instituto Nacional para el Combate a las Drogas (INCD), 76

Interagency Commission for the Prevention of Violence and Criminality (Mexico), 264

interdiction, 18; allegations of Sandinista-Cuban drug trafficking, 47–51; cocaine seizure figures, 2010–2020, 265(fig.); Costa Rica's cocaine traffic, 239–241; DTOs altering trafficking methods to avoid, 114; Guatemala's coca production, 277; Guatemala's counternarcotics programs, 145; Guatemala's decertification, 228–229; Honduran cocaine, 282; Honduras's counternarcotics programs, 150–151; Mexican cocaine seizures, 2006–2012, 215(fig.); Mexican marijuana and cocaine seizures, 2000–2005, 209(fig.); Mexican marijuana seizures, 2006–2012, 216(fig.); Nicaragua's cocaine seizures, 152, 238; Nicaragua's lack of capacity, 284; Panama, 242, 287–288; Salvadoran cocaine seizure, 117–118; Salvadoran drug trade, 232–233; straining US-Mexican relations, 23

internecine battles within the cartels, 85, 268, 303–307

Iran-Contra scandal, 40, 45–46, 60(n57), 63(n100)

Joint Declaration of the United States and Mexican Delegations, 17–18

Joint United States–Mexico Narcotic Commission, 16–17

journalists: assassinations of, 222, 273; exposure of Panama's tax haven, 287

Juárez cartel, 2–3; buying law enforcement protection, 96; Cali cartel's move into Mexico, 105–106; cartel wars, 184–185, 267–268; collapse of the Cali cartel, 108–109; formation of, 75; Milenio cartel, 197(n35); money laundering, 106; origins of, 65; Sinaloa supercartel, 180–181. *See also* Carrillo Fuentes, Amado; Carrillo Fuentes, Vicente

Junta Revolucionaria de Gobierno (JRG; Guatemala), 38

kidnappings, 45, 269; cartel wars, 192; Costa Rican Supreme Court justices, 122–123; Knights Templar, 191–192

kingpin strategy, 95–96, 109–110, 203–204, 307

Knights Templar, 179, 191–193, 226

Labra Avilés, Jesús "El Chuy," 73, 182. *See also* Arellano Félix cartel

La Dirección de Lucha Contra el Narcotráfico (DLCN; Honduras), 234

La Familia Michoacana, 179, 227, 252(n25); cartel evolution, 3; cartel wars, 189–193; formation of Los Caballeros Templarios, 191; trafficking through Costa Rica, 239–240

Lake Izabal, 6, 114

Lake Nicaragua, 6, 239

La Ley Anti-Mara (antigang law; El Salvador), 162

La Ley Contra Narcoactividad Decreto Número 48-92 (Guatemala), 144

La Línea (Juárez cartel), 185, 267, 292(n19)

Lázaro Cárdenas, port of, 20, 190–191

Lazcano Lazcano, Heriberto "El Lazca," 193–194, 200(n108)

legalization of narcotics, 264, 276, 306–307

legitimacy, political: El Salvador's gangs, 277–278

Lehder, Carlos, 45, 49–50

Levitsky, Melvyn, 109, 115, 124

Limón, 6, 122, 285

Lobo, Porfirio, 236, 246, 250

López Obrador, Andrés Manuel (AMLO), 208–209, 263–264, 272–274

López Portillo, José, 25, 67

"Lord of the Skies." *See* Carrillo Fuentes, Amado

Los Angeles riots (1992), 225

Los Caballeros Templarios (Knights Templar), 179, 191–193, 226

Los Chapitos, 271

Los Kaibiles (Guatemala's special operations unit), 228

Los Zetas, 179, 267–268, 292(n20); alliance with La Familia, 190; cartel evolution, 3;

Index 353

cartel wars, 188–189; controlling Guatemala's trafficking operations, 230; countering the threat to the Mexico state, 215–217; defeating the León family, 254(n45); establishing a foothold in Guatemala, 228–231; Guatemala's Baldetti Elías's relationship with, 276; Knights Templar and, 191–192; Las Panteras women's group, 198(n69); MS-13 *clikas* and, 227; Panama operations, 286; shifting alliances from 2007-2014, 193–194; trafficking through Costa Rica, 239–240; US Fast and Furious gun-running operation, 203–204, 217–219; violence and murder, 7

M-19 guerrillas, 45, 49–50, 122–123, 257(n133)
Maduro Joest, Ricardo, 163, 234–236
mano dura (heavy-handed) policies, 8, 158, 161, 162, 163, 164, 165, 167, 232, 233, 244, 249
maquiladoras, 91, 96
Mara Salvatrucha (MS-13), 1, 252(n24), 277–280; Beltrán Leyva cartel, 186; expanding networks, 5; increase in Salvadoran gang violence, 232–233; origins of the gang problem, 159–160; refugee caravans, 289; transnational operations, 226–227, 229; turf wars with La eMe, 226; work for La Barbie, 181
marijuana cultivation and trafficking, 4; Caro Quintero's payoffs for protection, 68; Colombian-Mexican corridor, 102–105; Cuban government involvement in, 50; eradication and interdiction efforts in Mexico, 24–26, 88(fig.); during Guatemala's civil war, 37; legalization under Peña Nieto, 264; Mexican seizures, 2000–2005, 209(fig.); Mexican seizures, 2006–2012, 216(fig.); Mexico's first generation *narcotraficantes,* 66; Nixon's redirection of, 16; Panama's trafficking, 242; US crop eradication programs, 18–19
maritime drug movement and smuggling, 107, 265; CARSI initiatives, 248; Costa Rica as transshipment point, 122–123; Honduran narcotrafficking, 119–120; mini submarines, 109; Nicaragua, 120–121; Panama, 125, 241–242
Martinelli Berrocal, Ricardo, 244
Matamoros, 20; El Chapo, 180; Gulf cartel 65, 76, 77, 78, 185–187, 268, 306
Matamoros cartel. *See* Gulf cartel
Matta-Ballesteros, Juan Ramon, 52–53, 63(n103), 67; Colombian-Mexican trafficking route, 102; Honduran narcotrafficking, 118–119; torture and murder of Kiki Camarena, 69, 71–72, 80(n29)

Maxi-Proceso (Mexico), 184, 195(n6), 206
Medellín cartel: Colombianization of Mexico and Central America, 304–306; Colombia's BACRIM syndicate, 110; creation of minicartels, 101–102; establishing a Mexican cocaine connection, 102–104; expansion into Nicaragua, 48; Guadalajara cartel connection, 67–68; Gulf and Cali cartels' cooperation, 105; Matta-Ballesteros uniting the Guadalajara cartel with, 53; Matta-Ballesteros's incarceration, 63(n103); Noriega's work for, 44–47; torture and murder of Kiki Camarena, 69–70
Mérida Initiative, 2–3, 245–246, 304; CARSI and, 247; GAO criticism, 214–215; goals of, 210–211; human rights conditions on funding, 213–214; increasing violence and corruption in Mexico, 203–204; total US assistance, 211(fig.)
methamphetamine trafficking, 146, 189, 190–192, 215, 226–227, 265, 271
Mexican government: cartels replacing government institutions, 219–220; Central American refugee crisis, 289; CJNG war with, 271–272; Colombianization of Mexico, 304–306; crop substitution programs, 26–27; demise and shift of the Medellín cartel, 104; DTO tactics threatening, 303–304; early US counternarcotics efforts, 15–21; eradication and interdiction efforts, 24–26; instability following Colosio's assassination, 90–93; Mérida Initiative, 246; the murder of Cardinal Posadas Ocampo, 87–90; torture and murder of Kiki Camarena, 70–72. *See also* militarization of the drug war; Policía Judicial Federal de México
Mexican Mafia (La eMe), 5, 225–226
Mexico: becoming a narco state, 94–96; cartel evolution, 2–3, 10–11; Central American gang migration to, 164–165; Guatemalan insurgency, 36–37; Guatemala's cross-border trafficking, 229; marijuana and cocaine seizures, 209(fig.); Matta-Ballesteros's arrest and imprisonment, 63(n103); Medellín cartel operations in, 102–104; NAFTA and economic collapse, 11; narcotics taking hold in 1974–1978, 24; persistent corruption and bilateral disputes, 27–29; porous borders with Guatemala, 112–113; regional map, 20(fig.); shifting narcotrafficking from Colombia to, 1–2, 5; US Fast and Furious gun-running operation, 217–219. *See also* bilateral relations (US and Mexico); cartel wars; cartels, Mexican; *specific cartels*

354 Index

Mexico City (México D.F.), 20, 26, 89, 129(n18), 186, 271; AMLO, 210; Cali cartel, 104; Carrillo Fuentes's doctors 196(n31); CIA, 90; DEA, 27, 216–217; drug trafficking, 107; URNG 133(n107)

México Seguro (Secure Mexico) operation, 207–208

Michoacán, 20; territorial control, 268–269

Milenio cartel, 192, 197(n35), 200(n100)

militarization of the drug war, 303–304; cartels replacing Mexico's government institution, 219–220; countering the Los Zetas threat, 215–217; effect on the credibility of Mexico's countertrafficking efforts, 305–306; Fox and Calderón's path towards, 204–215; of Los Zetas recruits in Guatemala, 228; Mexico militarizing the war on drugs, 5; Mexico's counternarcotics programs under Calderón, 210–212; Panama's militarization of the police, 155–157; through US policies, 2

military forces and actions: absorption of vigilante groups, 268–269; corruption in Guatemala's military, 114–115; crop eradication, 19; DTO tactics threatening the Mexican state, 303–304; elite assassination force, 186–187; human rights abuses, 272; Los Zetas tactics and violence, 188–189; Mexican cartel violence and territorial disputes, 3; Mexico's crop eradication through herbicide use, 25; military role in Guatemala's counternarcotics programs, 143–146; origins of Central America's gang problem, 158–159; professionalization of Nicaragua's military, 153; suppressing guerrilla movements, 35; US diplomatic pressure on Mexico, 16; US training after 9/11, 205–206. *See also* militarization of the drug war

military juntas: El Salvador, 38, 57(n9); Guatemala, 36–37

minicartels, 109–110, 179

Miskito Coast, 6, 121, 238; Miskito Indians, 42, 120

Monexgate scandal, 265–266

money laundering, 28; accusations of Duarte de Ochoa, 266; Cali and Juárez cartels' operations, 106; Caro Quintero's escape, 81(n38); Carrillo Fuentes's commercial success, 75–76; corruption of Panamanian officials, 243; Costa Rica, 123–124, 240–241; El Salvador's counternarcotics program, 149; Gallardo's control in Jalisco, 67–68; Guatemala's counternarcotics programs, 145; Gulf cartel under García Abrego, 77; Gulf-Cali

cartel connections, 105; Honduran anti-laundering law, 234; investigation of Raúl Salinas, 94; Mérida Initiative, 210–211; Muñoz Talavera brothers, 104; Noriega's work for the Medellín cartel, 45–47; North's transfers for the Contras, 54; Panama, 125–126, 173(n110), 241–242, 286–288; Salvadoran adoption of Bitcoin, 280; Salvadoran gang activities, 279; starting operations in Central America, 112; Vesco case, 48–49, 61(n78)

Monge Álvarez, Luis Alberto, 43, 122

Monterrey, 20; Cali cartel, 107; Gulf cartel 77

moral code: La Familia Michoacana, 189–190

mordida system (bribery), 23, 92

Moscoso, Mireya, 241, 165

Movimiento Abril 19. *See* M-19 guerrillas

Movimiento Popular de Liberación (MLP; Honduras), 40

Movimiento Regeneración Nacional (MORENA) party, 272

Movimiento Revolucionario de Crimen Organizado (MORECO), 285

MS-13. *See* Mara Salvatrucha

MS-503 gang (El Salvador), 278

Muerte a Secuestradores (MAS), 45

multinational counternarcotics program, 101–102

murder. *See* assassinations; homicides

Mutual Legal Assistance Treaty (MLAT), 156

NAFTA, 11, 85, 90–91, 96, 112

narco-guerrilla nexus, 47–48

National Guard (El Salvador), 117, 146–148, 165

National Guard (Mexico), 272–273, 289

National Guard (Nicaragua), 41

National Guard (Panama), 45, 60(n58)

Negroponte, John, 92, 119

Nepomuceno Guerra, Juan, 76–77

Nicaragua: addressing gang violence, 164–165; border security with Costa Rica, 284–285; civil war, 4, 40–41, 55; cocaine seizures, 2010–2020, 275(fig.); counternarcotics programs, 151–153; elections, 58–59(n34); guerrilla groups, 58(n33); Honduran support for the Contras, 39–40; Noriega's civilian paramilitary forces, 47; Ortega's reelection, 283–284; post-civil war shift towards gang violence, 237–239; post-war narcotrafficking, 120–121; revolution and counterrevolution, 35; supporting Salvadoran guerrillas, 38; tying contra narcotrafficking to, 55; the Vesco money laundering case, 48–49, 61(n78). *See also* Contras, Nicaraguan; Sandinistas

Nixon administration, 15–18, 61(n78)

Noriega, Manuel, 44–47, 50, 59(n50), 60(nn53, 66), 124–126, 156
Norte de Valle cartel (Colombia), 109, 119, 286
North, Oliver, 42, 45, 52–53. *See also* Iran-Contra
Northern Triangle. *See* El Salvador; Guatemala; Honduras
Nuevo Cartel de Juárez, 267–268. *See also* Juárez cartel
Nuevo Laredo, 20, 203, 207, 228; Beltrán Leyva, 181; El Chapo, 180; Gulf cartel, 185–187; MS-13, 227

Obama administration: Fast and Furious operation, 218
Ochoa Vásquez, Fabio and Jorge, 45, 46, 47, 48, 49, 61(n76)
Ojinaga, 20, 74, 103
Operación Jaque, 279
Operation Alliance, 91
Operation Bahamas, Turks, and Caicos (OPBAT), 101
Operation Black Swan, 293(n35)
Operation Cadence, 106
Operation CANADOR, 19, 30(n24), 66, 68
Operation Condor, 30(n24)
Operation Cooperation, 15, 17–19, 23
Operation End-Run, 25
Operation Enduring Friendship, 248
Operation Fast and Furious, 203–204, 217–219
Operation Green Ice, 123
Operation Handshake, 151
Operation Intercept, 10, 15, 17–18
Operation Jalisco, 271
Operation Just Cause, 124
Operation Martillo, 250
Operation Mayan Jaguar, 146
Operation Mongoose (assassination program), 66
Operation SEA/M (Special Enforcement Activity in Mexico), 25
Operation Trident, 25–26
Operation Wide Receiver, 217–218
opium cultivation and trafficking, 4; El Chapo's family connections, 72–73; El Salvador, 148; eradication and interdiction efforts in Mexico, 24–26; eradication efforts in Guatemala, 144–145; during Guatemala's civil war, 37; Guatemala's organized crime, 231; guerrilla protection along the Guatemala-Mexico border, 113–115; redirecting French and Turkish sources, 16; US crop eradication programs, 18–19. *See also* heroin production and trafficking
Ordaz, Díaz, 18, 20–21,
Organización de Emergencia Nacional (OEN), 44

Organization of American States (OAS), 142
Ortega, Daniel, 43, 283–284
Ortega, Humberto, 153
Ortiz Ascencio, Óscar, 278, 288
Oseguera Cervantes, Nemesio "El Mencho," 192, 271–272, 294(n44)
Oslo Accords (1993), 142

Palma Salazar, Héctor "El Güero," 72, 76, 89–90
Panama: cocaine and money laundering, 286–288; cocaine seizures, 2010-2020, 275(fig.); counternarcotics program, 155–157; economic and political downturn, 241–244; money laundering, 173(n110), 286–288; Noriega's connections to and work for the Medellín cartel, 44–47; post-Noriega political instability, 124–126; US invasion, 4
Panama Papers, 259(n163), 287
Pan-American Highway, 112, 238, 241, 286
pandilleros (street gang members), 226
paramilitary groups, 109–110
Partido Acción Nacional (PAN; Mexico), 208–209, 219
Partido Revolucionario Institucional (PRI; Mexico), 3; cartels' involvement in state capture, 219–220; Colosio assassination, 85; Juárez cartel's campaign contributions, 265–266; Mexico's political and economic instability, 90; Peña Nieto's presidency, 263–265; political homicides, 305; political involvement in drug trafficking, 22–23; the threat of state failure, 94–96
Pastora, Edén, "Comandante Cero," 41, 44
Paz García, Policarpo, 52, 118–119. *See also* Matta-Ballesteros
peacebuilding after Central America's civil wars, 55–56
Peña Durán, Óscar, 148
Peña Nieto, Enrique, 214–215, 263–267
Pérez Molina, Otto, 276, 288
Petén, 7, 145; drug trafficking, 114, 228–231, 253(n45); URNG operations, 113
Placido, Anthony, 206–207
Plan Colombia, 246, 250
Plan El Salvador Seguro (PESS), 279
Plan Escoba (Clean Sweep; Guatemala), 163–164
Plan Puebla, 247
plata o plomo (bribery or bullets), 231, 234–237
police: Central American regional counternarcotics programs, 143; CJNG war with the Mexican government, 271–272; confrontation with Mexico's military, 214; corruption and drug trafficking, 23;

356 Index

corruption of Guatemala's law enforcement institutions, 114; corruption of Panamanian police, 243; Costa Rica's understaffing problems, 284–285; El Chapo's arrest and incarceration, 270–271; El Güero's co-optation of, 89; El Salvador's counternarcotics program, 146–149; extrajudicial killings of gang members, 166; Guatemala's counternarcotics programs, 143–146; high-level corruption under Peña Nieto, 266–267; Honduran reforms targeting police corruption, 281–282; Honduras's counternarcotics programs, 149–151; kidnapping and mass murders of students, 269; La Familia's campaign against, 190–191; manhunt for cartel members, 87–88; Mexico's corruption within, 15, 27; Mexico's PFP, 206; militarization of Panama's, 155–157; Nicaragua's counternarcotics programs, 152–153; politicization of Nicaragua's counternarcotics programs, 151–152; protecting the Guadalajara cartel, 72; Tlatelolco Massacre, 20–21; training and equipment funding through CARSI, 248. *See also* Policía Judicial Federal de México

Policia Federal Preventiva (PFP; Mexico), 206

Policía Judicial Federal de México (PJFM; Mexican Federal Judicial Police), 66, 68; Acosta Villareal's death, 74–75; Cali cartel operations in Mexico, 106–107; Caro Quintero's payment for protection, 68; cartel wars, 182–183; Medellín cartel's Mexican connection, 103; protection of García Abrego, 78; torture and murder of Kiki Camarena, 69–70

Policía Nacional Civil (El Salvador), 146–148, 162, 165, 170(n56), 232, 254(n63), 278

Policía Nacional Civil (Guatemala), 144–145, 230, 277

political dissent, war on drugs as pretext for controlling, 22

Portillo Cabrera, Alfonso, 146, 163, 228–229, 252(n30)

PRI. *See* Partido Revolucionario Institucional

prisons: CARSI pillars for prison reform and support, 248–249; gang control of Guatemala's, 277; Salvadoran antigang initiative, 278–279

Procuraduría General de la República (PGR; Attorney General of the Republic, Mexico), 65, 72, 78, 87, 90, 93, 104, 106–107, 180–182, 184, 206–208, 219, 269, 272

protection: Coello Trejo, 75, 78, 83(n72), 185; García Luna, 267, 273, 305; González Calderóni, 78, 83(n72); the Gulf cartel, 78;

high-level police corruption under Peña Nieto, 266–267; INCD protection of the cartels, 76; Pavón Reyes, 70; Reyes Arzate, 266–267

Puente Grande prison (Mexico), 185, 267, 271; El Chapo, 89, 180, 182

Puntarenas, 6, 121, 240, 285

Reagan administration: Contras' move into narcotrafficking, 51–54; Nicaragua's Contra war, 42–43; Sandinistas' activities in Honduras, 40; Sandinistas' involvement in drug trafficking, 48

real estate market: Gallardo's money laundering connections, 67–68

Reclusorio Norte prison (Mexico), 70–71

Reclusorio Sur prison (Mexico), 72, 75, 195(n2)

refugees, 263; the Central American crisis, 288–290

regional coordination for Central American counternarcotics initiatives, 142–143, 158

regional security, 11. *See also* Central American Regional Security Initiative

religion, La Familia Michoacana juxtaposing violence with, 189–190

revolutionary movements: Costa Rica's democratization, 43–44; Guatemalan challenge to military rule, 36–37. *See also* guerrilla organizations and insurgencies

Rodríguez Orejuela, Gilberto, 46, 49

Rurales (Cuerpo de Defensa Rural), 269

Salinas de Gortari, Carlos, 77; cartel access from within Mexico's government, 65; cartel wars, 186; murder of Cardinal Posadas Ocampo, 87–88; NAFTA connection to drug trafficking, 92; public mistrust of the government, 96; ties to narcotraffickers, 85; Zapatista rebellion, 90–93

Salinas de Gortari, Raúl, 78; linked to Massieu assassination, 93–94; bribed by García Ábrego, 106, 186

San Andrés Island, 121–122

Sánchez Cerén, Salvador, 279

Sandinistas, 39–43, 121; allegations of Sandinista-Cuban drug trafficking, 47–51; arms trafficking, 44; drugs as a political weapon, 61(n68); Nicaragua's guerrillas and factions, 58(n33); subversive activities in Costa Rica, 59(n46)

San Juan River, 6, 239

San Pedro Sula, 6, 119, 57(n20)

Santa Muerte, 160, 179, 182, 189

SAVAK, 60(nn56, 57)

School of the Americas, 148

Seal, Barry, 61(n73), 61(n76); Los Brasiles, 4

secret war: Honduras, 39–40

security. *See* Central American Regional Security Initiative

September 11, 2001, 204–205

SETCO airline, 52–53, 119

Sinaloa cartel, 2–3, 8–9; AFI collaboration with, 206–207; assassination of Rodolfo Carrillo Fuentes, 184–185; CJNG war with the Mexican government, 271–272; control of Jalisco, 192–193; drug cultivation in the Triángulo Dorado, 24; El Chapo's arrest and incarceration, 270–271; El Chapo's violence, 73; eradication and interdiction, 25; fentanyl trade, 274; formation of the federation, 180–181; growing presence in Honduras, 236; Guatemala's corruption connections, 276; Gulf cartel's subordination to, 268; Gulf-Cali cartels' cooperation, 105; high-level police corruption under Peña Nieto, 266–267; intelligence gathering on Los Zetas, 215–216; Juárez cartel alliance, 76; legacy of the cartel war, 267–268; manhunt for cartel members, 87–88; Operation Fast and Furious, 203–204, 217–219; origins of, 65; Panama operations, 286; primary *narcotraficantes,* 72–73; Salvadoran cocaine seizure, 117–118; trafficking through Costa Rica, 239–240. *See also* cartel wars

Sinaloa Federation, 180, 184, 186–187, 192–193

Sinaloa-Gulf cartel alliance, 268

Sistema de la Integración Centroamericana (SICA), 142–143, 246–247

slavery: El Chapo's employees, 73

social justice, La Familia's commitment to, 189–191

Sombra Negra (Black Shadow) vigilantes, 165–166

Somoza, Anastasio, 35, 40–41, 52, 58(n22), 58(n29)

Soviet Union: Sandinistas' ties to, 41

Spain, 269; Mario Massieu, 94; Matta-Ballesteros, 119; MS-13, 227; Ochoa and Orejuela, 49

Special Investigative Unit (SIU; Mexico), 272–273

state capture: the cartels replacing Mexico's PRI, 219–220

State Department, US: Cali cartel assuming control in Mexico, 105; Central American counternarcotics strategies, 141; corruption of Panamanian officials, 243; Costa Rica's counternarcotics program, 153–154; Honduran constitutional crisis, 234–235; Honduran narcotrafficking, 118–120; Medellín cartel's Mexican connection, 103; Mexico's Maxi-Proceso arrests, 206; militarization of Panama's

police, 155–156; Nicaragua's counternarcotics programs, 152; Nicaragua's drugs-for-guns enterprises, 121; Panama's black market arms trafficking, 241; Sandinista-Cuban drug trafficking, 47–48; violence and crime following the Chapultepec Peace Accord, 116. *See also* United States

state failure: Honduran constitutional crisis, 235–236; Mexico, 94–96

street gangs. *See* gang activity and culture

student radicals: resistance to crop eradication programs, 19–22

supercartels, 102

sureños (subordinates), 226

Tegucigalpa Convention (1991), 142

Tequila Crisis (Mexico), 90–95

territorial wars: Mexican and Central American gang wars, 225–226. *See also* cartel wars

terrorism: Central American cartels, 304–305; CJNG war with the Mexican government, 271–272; drug trafficking and money laundering in Panama, 241–242; Guatemalan challenge to military rule, 36–37; linking with the war on drugs, 204–206

Texis cartel (El Salvador), 278–279

Tijuana cartel, 2–3, 187–188; Arellano Félix family, 74; La Familia connections, 252(n25); manhunt for cartel members, 87–88; origins of, 65

Tlatelolco Massacre (1968), 20–21

Torrijos Espino, Martín, 165, 243

Torrijos Herrera, Omar, 45, 59(n50)

torture, 206, 213–214, 271, 294(n42); carne asada, 74; "Colombian necktie," 73–74; el guiso, 7; Los Zetas tactics and violence, 188–189; necklacing, 7–8, 189; *pozoles,* 187; torture and murder of Kiki Camarena, 3, 68–72, 74–75, 80(n29)

trafficking routes, 6(fig.)

transeros (drug traffickers), 226

Transnational Anti-Gang (TAG) Center, 162–163

transnational crime networks, 225–227

treason: Cuban drug trafficking case, 51

Treviño Morales, Miguel, 193–194, 201(n110), 292(n20)

Tribunal Superior de Cuentas (TSC; Honduras), 234–235

Trump, Donald: immigration policy, 273, 289; Nicaragua, 284

UN Convention Against Drug Traffic and Dependency on Psychotropic Substances, 87, 142

358 *Index*

UN Convention Against Transnational Organized Crime, 158
UN Single Convention on Narcotic Drugs (1961), 15, 23, 142
unemployment: Central America's gang problem, 160–161
Unidad Ejecutiva Antinarcóticos (UEA; El Salvador), 147–148
Unidad Revolucionaria Nacional Guatemalteca (URNG), 113–114, 143–144
United States: capture of Noriega, 47; the case of El Vicentillo, 216–217; Central American refugee crisis, 289; Central American Security Initiative, 245; collapse of the Cali cartel and the rise of the Juárez cartel, 108–109; Colombian and Mexican cartels moving into Guatemala, 112–113; Colombian-Mexican narcotrafficking corridor, 102–103; Contras' move into narcotrafficking, 51–54; Cuban government involvement in marijuana smuggling, 50; deportation of Central American gang members, 232; deportation of Central American immigrants, 225–226; El Salvador's civil war, 38–39; Fast and Furious gun-running operation, 217–219; Honduran aid, 39; Honduran narcotics traffic, 234; investigation of Raúl Salinas, 94; Iran-Contra scandal, 40; legacy of counternarcotics assistance, 304; Mexico's financial crisis, 90–92; Mexico's potential state failure, 94–95; Nicaragua's Contra War, 42–43; Noriega's incarceration and death, 60(n66); origins of Central America's gang problem, 159–160; Sandinistas' overthrow of Nicaragua's Somoza, 41–42; student-campesino unity against, 21; supporting Guatemala's oligarchy, 37; training El Salvador's counternarcotics unit, 147; US and Central American gang integration, 227. *See also* bilateral relations (US and Mexico); Central American Regional Security Initiative; Central Intelligence Agency; Drug Enforcement Administration; Federal Bureau of Investigation; Mérida Initiative; militarization of the drug war; State Department, US
US Foreign Relations and Intercourse Act (1976), 28

Valdez Villareal, Edgar "La Barbie," 181, 186, 193, 270
Varadero, air base, 51
Veracruz, city of, 20, 53, 192, 292(n21)

Vesco, Robert, 124; Nicaragua cocaine operations, 48–49; criminal enterprises, 61(n78); Jitze Kooistra, 62(n79
vigilante groups, 165–166, 189, 192, 268–269. *See also* Sombra Negra; Rurales
Villa Nueva program (Guatemala), 248–249
violence, 1; Arellano Félix family members, 73–74; arrest of El Chapo's son, 271; criminal, 3–8; El Chapo's treatment of employees, 73; El Salvador's gang negotiations, 278; increase in Guatemala's, 276–277; political, 3–8; student-campesino unity movement, 22; Tlatelolco Massacre, 20–21

war and conflict, 35–36; the Contra war, 42–43; Costa Rica's civil war, 43–44; drug smuggling during Nicaragua's civil war, 4; evolution of the cartel war, 8–11; internecine battles within the cartels, 85, 268, 303–307; Medellín cartel and M-19, 45; Mexico's three-way war, 303–304; Mexico's Zapatista rebellion, 92–93. *See also* cartel wars; civil wars
war on drugs (Mexico and the US), 76; evolution of Mexico's cartels, 2–3; linking to terrorism after 9/11, 204–206; López Obrador's attempt to de-escalate, 272; Mexico's decertification, 95; Mexico's narcotics reduction goals, 264–265; militarization, 5, 204–215, 303–304; origins of the Mérida Initiative, 8; Peña Nieto's de-escalation policies, 263–265; policy considerations regarding decriminalization, 306–307; spilling over into Central America, 157–158. *See also* militarization of the drug war
weapons trafficking. *See* arms trafficking
Webb, Gary: Contra-CIA drug smuggling, 54–55
Wrobleski, Ann B., 111

Zacapa, 115, 134(n117), 145, 229
Zambada García, Ismael "El Mayo," 8–9, 182–184, 270–271
Zambada Niebla, Vicente "El Vicentillo," 182, US government informant, 216–217
Zapatista rebellion, 92–93, 96
Zedillo, Ernesto, 207, 213; Colosio assassination, 90; Massieu assassination, 93–94; US cooperation, 94–95
Zelaya, Manuel, 7; allegations against, 236; constitutional crisis, 235; Xiomara Castro de Zelaya, wife of, 282
Zetas. *See* Los Zetas

About the Book

How did Mexico and Central America become a lawless corridor for conveying narcotics into the United States? How did the drug cartels rise to power, succeeding in institutionalizing the narco-industry? Why have the police and military failed to rein the cartels in? What have been the consequences of the US-led "war on drugs?" William Marcy's *Narcostates* provides answers to these questions and more.

Tracing the evolution of narcotrafficking across the region, and drawing on newly declassified documents, Marcy unravels the tangled web of violence, corruption, and political instability that has empowered drug trafficking organizations since the 1970s.

William L. Marcy is lecturer at Buffalo State University.